Environmental Interiors

Mary Jo Weale
Ph. D., ASID, IDEC, NHFL
Professor and Chairman
Department of Interior Design
The Florida State University

James W. Croake
Ph. D.
Professor of Psychiatry and Behavioral Sciences
School of Medicine
The University of Washington

W. Bruce Weale
Ed. D.
Professor Emeritus
Department of Marketing
College of Business
The Florida State University

environmental

INTERIORS

Macmillan Publishing Co., Inc.
New York

Collier Macmillan Publishers
London

Macmillan Publishing Co., Inc.
866 Third Avenue, New York, New York 10022

Collier Macmillan Canada, Inc.

Library of Congress Cataloging in Publications Data

Weale, Mary Jo.
  Environmental interiors.

  Includes bibliographies and index.
  1. Interior decoration.   2. Interior architecture.
I. Croake, James W., joint author.   II. Weale, W. Bruce,
joint author.   III. Title.
NK2110.W38   729   80-28605
ISBN 0-02-424850-9

Printing: 1 2 3 4 5 6 7 8   Year: 2 3 4 5 6 7 8 9

To Our Mothers

Mary Whitehouse Lindley,
Ruth Croake,
and
Gertrude Bell Weale

They created the ideal interior environments
within which we grew and developed.

Foreword

The last few years has seen the publications or revision of a number of books intended as introductory materials in the field of interior design. Although the profession of interior design has drastically changed in the last decade, many of these works seem barely to touch on these changes. *Environmental Interiors* confronts them directly. Some of the now recognized antecedents of contemporary interior design have been clearly perceived and presented.

Early in their discussion Weale, Croake, and Weale present the family and the family needs as they change with time. An underlying and connecting aspect of the text is that of the functional and psychological or behavioral needs of the individual and the family. To quote the authors:

> Humans are holistic: a change in one aspect of a person's life or his environment will affect his behavior and his total being. A change in one member of a family or in his life space will affect all other members of the family. The interior designer must realize that his work will influence entire families when the house—or even one room—is redesigned. When the interior is designed, it must serve the needs of the entire person and those of the entire family.

The authors have discussed the way the environment is perceived. Too often texts of this nature discuss the effect without the cause—the how of achievement without the why. Even in the obligatory discussion of the design elements and principles, the authors have made reference to behavioral factors: those factors that directly affect the way one uses and enjoys the environment.

Among other topics seldom adequately dealt with the authors have chosen to discuss in detail: lighting; the sound and energy environment; and the "green environment" or indoor plantscaping.

A major portion of the text reviews historical influences upon interior design. In this section, as well as others, the use of summary tables should aid the student in understanding the material. The numerous line drawings of both historical and contemporary furniture and American architecture are another plus. Where most available interior design texts concentrate on pre-mid-nineteenth century periods, *Environmental Interiors* discuss in detail influential nineteenth and early twentieth-century designers. All of the generally recognized influences such as the Shakers, Morris, Wright, Le Corbusier are discussed, but equal emphasis is given to such individuals as Pugin, Ruskin, Godwin, Gimson, Stickley, Bradley and Hubbard. The authors also have devoted a section to important contemporary furniture designers who are making valuable contributions.

Weale, Croake and Weale also have recognized the importance of the role of the interior designer in the area of historic restoration and preservation. Their chapter on this subject introduces the topic, discusses its importance to society and to the designer, and defines the multiplicity of terms used in describing the work done in this area (the pronunciation of foreign terms is also included).

For each chapter of the book, the authors have included a comprehensive glossary and a bibliography important in understanding the subject at hand. The appendix includes a number of business terms in common use. *Environmental Interiors* is a valuable addition to the published material available to both the beginning interior design student and the practicing professional who needs a current reference. This book will also be of value to the interested layperson. With their concern for the behavioral aspects of the practice of interior design, the authors have provided readers with new and valuable insights.

Curt Sherman, IDEC
Associate Professor of Interior Design,
San Diego State University,
President of the Interior Design
    Educators Council 1977–81,
Chairman of the Board, 1981–83

Preface

We speak, as designers, of "total design" and "environmental design." But what do we mean by these terms? How important are these concepts? The concept of total design is based on the assumption that design affects the physical comfort and the emotional and mental well-being of individuals. The designer, therefore, must consider not only appearance and materials, but also the elements that combine to make up the interior of a space. Most important, the designer must consider the people who live, work, and play within that space.

The designer's goal must be to achieve the best possible environment for the fulfillment of specific needs in the home: the need for rest and renewal, personal hygiene, and food preparation; the need for entertainment and group activities; the need for storage of possessions. The designer must perceive the functional components of the total house before he or she can sensitively utilize the space available in the interior. He or she must understand the elements and principles of design before they can be applied to the organization of interior space. And the designer must understand the properties and characteristics of color before these can be manipulated to achieve the desired effects. Such knowledge provides the necessary foundation upon which may be constructed designs for the utilization of space.

Although the modern American family often finds its work, its food, and its entertainment outside the home, the home is still a focus of family life. The home environment still helps to shape the social grouping of the family, whether nuclear or extended, and still provides a place in which children grow and mature. So important is the concept of the home that ownership of one's home remains a primary goal of the modern American family.

An appropriately designed living environment, both at work and at home, can contribute substantially to achieving desired modes of behavior. It can set the stage for work and social interaction, and can influence decision-making and response patterns. In the future, designers, psychologists, and behaviorists must integrate their knowledge, as have the authors of this book, to find new ways of controlling the forces that influence such behavioral patterns in positive directions. It is the client—the home owner or office occupant—and not the designer who must choose the direction. The role of the interior designer is to assist the client in determining and articulating his thoughts and feelings about the planned living and/or working space, and in ascertaining the activities to be carried on in those spaces. The task of the designer is a challenging one: to create a design that will accord with the client's aspirations. This book's purpose is to help the designer meet that challenge successfully. The authors have integrated various specialties and different perspectives. In addition, specialists in specific areas have furnished materials for various chapters. The four parts of this book can be studied in any desired sequence.

Part One deals with the designed environment. There are elements and principles of design which we have come to think of as timeless; this section deals with those aspects of design, with the psychology of color, and with the characteristics of light. The evolution of the family, and the development of interior spaces to fit family needs, is also discussed.

Part Two is concerned with the interior environment. Inner space should determine exterior space, whether for work or for living. This section deals with the sound and energy environment, the background environment (which includes walls, floors, and windows), the selection and arrangement of furniture for best utilization of space, the use of plants in the interior, and the selection and use of accessories.

Part Three describes the historical development of exterior and interior design in France, England, and America, and the evolution of architecture in the United States. This section also discusses the growing interest in the preservation of classic structures, and suggests elements to be considered in the design of living and work spaces planned for the future.

Our book concludes with a chapter on the fundamentals of drawing. This chapter provides instructions and directions for preparing visual representations of interior designs and floor plans. Moreover, a list of business terms unique to the field of interior design is provided in the Appendix.

We are indebted to many people who have helped to make this book possible: Tim Bookout, Professor of Interior Design, Georgia State University (Chapters 3, 16, 17, and most of the architectural drawings in Chapters 16 and 17); Peggy Carlson, ASID, interior designer and part-time instructor in the Department of Interior Design, Florida State University (Chapter 21); Jean Freeman, ASID,

Assistant Professor, Mount Vernon College, Washington, D.C., and formerly on the faculty of Florida State University (Chapter 4); Peter Koenig, IDEC, Associate Professor, Department of Interior Design, Florida State University (the solar energy drawings in Chapter 10); and Dinah Lazor, ASID, interior designer, Vicksburg, Mississippi (Chapter 19).

We are also grateful for the inspiration provided by graduate students of interior design at Florida State University for the study of the work of interior designers, past and present (Chapter 10). We are grateful as well to Kenan Fishburne, who edited much of the material in its early stages and who offered us excellent advice; to Max Zurko for many of the furniture drawings; to the thoughtful and helpful reviews from Curt Sherman, Associate Professor, San Diego State University and Paul Lougeay, Professor, Southern Illinois University; to Dorothy Rachline, Managing Editor of I.D.E.A.S.; to Les Rachline, Photographic Editor of I.D.E.A.S., Coral Gables, Florida, who allowed us to select photographs from his files (sections of this book originally appeared in I.D.E.A.S.); to Dave Novack, Production Supervisor, Patrick Turner, Designer, and Dora Rizzuto, for their exemplary work; and most especially to John Beck, Senior Editor, Macmillan Publishing Co., Inc., who nursed this book along for several years.

Labeled slides and transparencies of the furniture drawings and architecture, scripts of the units as well as multiple choice questions for Part Three may be purchased directly from Mary Jo Weale.

M. J. W.
J. W. C.
W. B. W.

Contents

The French Periods and the Biedermeier Period 225

The English Periods 251

American Architecture and Interior Styles 303

Twentieth-Century American Homes 333

Contemporary Developments in Furniture Design 345

Historic Preservation   387

The Development of the Modern Interior Designer   393

PART FOUR IMPLEMENTATION TECHNIQUES

21 Drafting of the Environmental Interior Plan 405

Appendix 413

Index 415

List of Tables

THE DESIGNED ENVIRONMENT

ONE

Conceptualized Space

Humans have always been concerned with the ornamentation of their interior living and working spaces. Although the profession of interior design is relatively new, interior decoration is as ancient as the oldest dwelling spaces. Drawings made by cave dwellers over thirty thousand years ago are evidence of this human desire for immortality; to leave some record of their existence. It has always been a human tendency to project in anthromorphic terms ideas of the future and hope for the hereafter. These drawings are served to tie an agrarian society to its nomadic past, thus reducing the stress associated with cultural evolution.

In studying the development of interior design, we are studying the manner in which people loved, worked, valued, thought, felt, and related to the environment. We will develop a framework around which the designer, through perceptive observation of his clients and a good grasp of the design process itself, can structure a plan to accommodate their functional and psychological needs. The major thrust of this book is residential; however, most of the areas discussed apply equally to commercial spaces.

Human Needs

Functional Needs

The functional needs of the clients must be considered first. This is perhaps the easiest part of the design process because the clients have often identified their functional needs and, with the aid of the designer, can express them. The specific functional needs of clients will vary widely but the following general checklist is offered as an aid to the clients and to the designer:

1. Accommodate all of the essential physical requirements in residential and/or commercial spaces.
2. Meet the clients' financial constraints.
3. Satisfy the clients' operational expense limits in upkeep, maintenance, and/or repairs.
4. Provide safety and security.
5. Allow flexibility when the life cycle of the family changes (births, empty-nest stage, widowhood, and so on).
6. Supply the physical focal point, the "home," within which the emerging family can grow and its members adapt to their

social, moral, and human goals and aspirations.

A more specific checklist could be made by the designer to note each activity or need important to the particular client. Here is an example for residential needs:

1. Receiving guests
2. Partying
3. Reading books
4. Conversing
5. Relaxing
6. Playing bridge
7. Fireplace
8. Television
9. Sound system
10. Dancing
11. Playing family games
12. Thinking in solitude or quiet
13. Writing and corresponding
14. Studying
15. Reading newspapers and magazines
16. Sleeping
17. Cat-napping
18. Rocking
19. Eating meals
20. Snacking
21. Cooking meals
22. Ironing
23. Washing dishes
24. Engaging in sexual activity
25. Bathing
26. Smoking
27. Painting as a hobby
28. Vacuuming
29. Dusting
30. Applying cosmetics
31. Mixing drinks
32. Exercising
33. Caring for the ill (or the handicapped)
34. Caring for infants
35. Sewing
36. Gardening (exterior potting area)
37. Window-viewing
38. Storage
39. Automobile storage
40. Gourmet cooking
41. Audio-visual needs
42. Air-conditioning and heating
43. Business and occupational activities
44. Toy storage
45. Caring for potted plants
46. Telephoning
47. Sound and acoustical needs
48. Accommodating guests
49. Placing pictures and art objects

50. Caring for household pet
51. Shaving
52. Hair-care
53. Mirror needs, space expansion
54. Electrical wiring and outlets
55. Entrances and exits
56. Cooking-utensil storage
57. Food storage
58. Safety and protection
59. Mildew and dampness control
60. Filing household documents
61. Outdoor cooking
62. Sun-bathing
63. Swimming
64. Inclement-weather buffer (indoor porch, mud area, potting shed)
65. Physical height needs (stoop clearances)
66. Skylight needs
67. Therapy needs (special stair/split-level constraints)
68. Fire safety needs
69. Left-handed people needs
70. Collections
71. Expansion needs (dining table—additional child)
72. Food service
73. Partition needs
74. Music center: piano, organ
75. Repair needs (accessibility)
76. Seating needs
77. Boating or fishing needs
78. Dating needs
79. Porch and patio needs
80. Time-information needs
81. Wig-storage needs
82. Children's discipline problem needs
83. Family argument or differences needs
84. General and specific lighting needs

This checklist is offered not as an exhaustive list of functional residential needs, but as a method of making sure that all needs have been assessed. The client and designer, after checking all selected requirements, can then develop a profile of these specifications to make sure nothing is overlooked in the space requirements. Commercial needs vary widely according to use, but similar profiles can be developed by client and designer.

Within the limitations of rising building costs and on-site labor expenses, most prospective builders find that their original plans have to be scaled down to fit cost realities. This is the upper limit within which functional needs and aesthetic tastes have to be balanced. Yet, within this framework, great lati-

tude is possible if the architect, the interior designer, and/or the purchaser cooperate to make the home an expression of the occupant's personality and living style; or the commercial space fit the client's image and needs.

Psychological Needs

If it makes sense for one to buy and wear only those items of apparel that enhance or complement the wearer's best features, so it follows that one's home should be an extension of one's pattern of living, personality needs, and aspirations.

Homes have personalities and the image they reflect is usually a conscious or unconscious extension of the personalities of their inhabitants. Even an unplanned house, eclectically furnished and decorated, reveals something about its inhabitants. As the concept of the home evolved from a basic shelter to functionality to aesthetic expressions of the owner, the home now seeks to fulfill more social, psychological, physiological, and cognitive needs.

In a time-pressured age, with functionality all-important in the working world, the home is becoming a last place of refuge—a place where by design and/or decor, a person can be himself without needing to conform to others in the expression of his personal desires. Less latitude is permitted in public spaces because they are used by large groups of people, but a private office can be personalized to suit the occupant.

Free to experiment with style, color, and material, each family needs to analyze its psychological needs and requirements. Among these might be listed the following:

1. A place where a distinct contrast from the work environment is provided.
2. A place where rest and relaxation needs are met.
3. A home environment where self-actualizing needs can be met.
4. A place where flexibility of layout allows experimentation with changes of decor, furniture, and color to satisfy changing moods and needs.
5. A place adaptable to the social needs of the upwardly mobile family.
6. And last but not least, a place where the dollars spent to satisfy needs will be likely to be recovered if the resident is forced to sell.

Human beings are unique in their ability to adapt to their environment and in their capacity to alter their environment to suit their wants. With this capability, the threats of pollution or overpopulation do not spell the doom of a way of life.

In very early times, people migrated when the pressure of overpopulation overwhelmed them; later, they moved from country to city for jobs. Today the members of the middle and upper classes look to beach cottages or mountain retreats to "recharge their batteries." The members of the lower classes will continue to be undesirably constricted in their daily lives unless architects and builders of housing complexes take into consideration the totality of personal and family functional and psychosocial wants and desires. There is some evidence of growing awareness of these needs and desires on the part of builders of newer apartment units, condominiums, and model towns.

As we move into an era of higher population density, rising land values, and increased borrowing costs, the architect, the interior designer, the contractor, and the buyer must cooperate in rethinking space needs, rejecting the frivolous, and justifying essential functional and aesthetic features.

Any realistic approach to successful interior design must consider the client the focus of the total process. Unless the interior designer understands the behavioral aspects of his[1] clients and the image constraints under which he must work, unless he has mastered the artful interviewing techniques that must be employed, he will decrease his chances of successfully conceiving and executing a project that is functionally and psychologically satisfying both to his clients and to himself. The suggestions in this book are not meant as strict formulae but, rather, as aids to understanding the nature of the client's decision-making process.

To meet his clients' functional and psychological desires, the interior designer must realize that the human being is a complex of innate and learned drives, motives, and aspirations, and an emerging self. The human being tends to perceive reality selectively, adjusting it to his own mind-set or distorting it whenever it is inconsistent with his self-concept.

To satisfy the clients' perceived needs, the designer must study them not only in terms of

their physical or functional charcteristics (e.g., ages, family size, level of education and income, race, sex), but also in terms of their psychological characteristics: e.g., their perceived status in society, their occupational goals, their self-concepts, their sexual roles. It is important to the interior designer to know some of the following facts:

1. Are the clients satisfied with their chronological ages, or do they want to seem younger (or older)?
2. Are they happy with their occupational or educational level, or are they aspiring to a higher (or lower) level?
3. Do the clients accept stereotyped sex roles, or do they seem to want to modify or change them?

The designer's observations of clients' attitudes on these points can provide meaningful clues to their psychological wants, which are as important as the functional needs they have perhaps more readily described.

Ideally, if the designer wanted to know how he can best satisfy the client's wants, he would find useful the results of accepted personality tests (e.g., the Minnesota Multiphasic Personality Inventory, the California Psychological Inventory, the Thematic Apperception Test, and so on) administered by a reputable psychologist. Obviously, this is impractical and few clients would submit to this inconvenience. However, the designer could do the next best thing and discover the real needs of clients by studying their behavior patterns:

1. How do their clients dress on different occasions? This may tell the designer how they wish to appear to others.
2. How do the clients project themselves? Their degree of insecurity or security, their aggressiveness or timidity are factors that can be ascertained by observation.
3. How mobile are the clients? Twenty per cent of the population move each year. If the clients are highly mobile, they have certain characteristics:
   a. They travel more and move more rapidly through the occupational structure.
   b. They move upward in economic and social status.
   c. They are well educated and have a wide variety of friends.
   d. They have selective and discriminating tastes.

Mobile clients may be more receptive to innovations in furniture and decor. How-

[1] The use of *he* refers to a nongendered person and is not intended to be sexist.

ever, high income is not synonymous with mobility; there can be mobile people at every income level.

4. How resistant to change are the clients? Do they seem to want to preserve the past (traditional furniture and decor), or do they anticipate the future (contemporary settings and decor)? This is not an either/or decision, for a contemporary feeling can be achieved in a basically traditional setting or vice versa, as in the eclectic look.

5. What are the clients' goals in undertaking the project? Is the undertaking an economic necessity, basically? Is it meant to impress their peer group, or to create a new internal environment for increased psychological satisfaction? Is it meant to reject past style and design patterns forced on them by family inheritances or life patterns? Or is it a combination of these factors that impels them to want to change?

6. Does the designer perceive himself as a decision-maker, as a specifier of product characteristics and designs, as an authority figure helping insecure clients make correct choices of furniture and decor, or as a combination of these? If in the beginning the designer can determine the role the clients want him to assume, he can better meet the client's expectations of satisfactory performance.

7. Are the clients more concerned with prestigious brand names or company product images than with the intrinsic values of the total design? To ignore clients' preferences may result in their dissatisfaction with the completed design. Since only about 30 per cent of clients know brand names, prestigious brand names may be less familiar to them than highly advertised names.

8. How do the clients perceive risk? Do they evaluate bad decisions—wrong choices, delivery delays, out-of-production items, inconvenience, breakdown—largely in terms of dollars, or subjectively in terms of loss of face among family or peer group? Clients of high income and status perceive risk differently from members of the middle or lower classes. Middle-class clients are more apt than lower-class clients to regard big price-ticket decisions as an investment in career, reputation, and status.

Status and Roles

The status (or perceived status) of the clients is an important factor to consider. Status is determined by the values placed by the particular society and culture in which the client lives on such factors as income, occupation, education, race, ethnic origin, and so on.

Certain roles are expected by society of members of a given status. The pattern of behavior expected from those who occupy a particular status can largely determine the criteria by which the clients may be measuring their adequacy or success. The designer must determine what roles the clients are playing.

Are they identifying largely with an occupational status and the roles consistent with it? The banker's role can be markedly different from that of the professor or that of the newly successful businessman. The clients' home decor must be consistent with their status because their peers and friends expect a certain kind of decor as an expression of their perceptions of that status and those roles. It is important to consider the many variables which can determine status and roles. More important, in what mix of roles do the clients see themselves?

1. As high-status persons needing to express this status in home decor?
2. As persons who are striving for a higher status and who want an interior consistent with the expressive values that this projects to others?
3. As persons who are trying to "keep up (or down) with the Joneses"?
4. As persons who are not quite sure of their role and who desperately want the advice and assurance of the interior designer?

For those clients who express uncertainty, the interior designer can be of even greater help. He can subtly lead such clients to appropriate and correct design choices. By giving reasons for all the choices, often the designer can remove some of the doubt and uncertainty that attends client's dollar commitment at this point. Usually the decision to expend a significant sum of money causes wavering or trepidation unless the decision-maker has logical reasons to justify his actions. The designer should supply these reasons so clients can make them theirs. Later clients can use the same reasons to explain the choices to friends and peers.

One researcher suggests that the consumer market for goods can be divided into six categories:

1. A habit-determined group of brand-loyal customers, who tend to be satisfied with

Figure 1.1
A luxurious bath with light-colored carpeting can be added after the children have left home. (Courtesy of American Standard)

the last purchased product or brand.

2. A cognitive group of consumers sensitive to rational claims and only conditionally brand-loyal.
3. An impulsive group of consumers who buy on the basis of physical appeal and who are relatively insensitive to brand names.
4. An "emotional" group of consumers who tend to be responsive to what products symbolize and who are heavily swayed by images.
5. A group of new consumers who have not yet stabilized their consumer behavior.[2]

These groups are not mutually exclusive and the categories are very broad descriptions of consumer reaction to purchase decisions. The designer should be aware of his clients' consumer expectations in order to anticipate any problems which may arise when choosing furniture and decor.

Young Couples

Newlyweds and young couples are to be found in Group 5: they have yet to determine the meaning and status of their home possessions. They may have definite likes and dislikes, but are not as familiar as older clients with brand or trade names. Sensitive guidance and reassurance from the interior designer will help them find the styles and brands of furniture which best fulfill their needs.

Younger couples do not usually seek the help of an interior designer, because of financial constraints and the do-it-yourself syndrome. The 1980 census revealed the median age of Americans to be 30.0 years (i.e., one half were above and one half were below that

age); it had been 27.5 in 1970 and 29.5 years in 1960. There is a growing percentage of those over sixty-five. It is estimated that by the year 2000, one in five people will be a senior citizen. Many of these people will be moving to smaller homes and will have money to spend from the sale of larger houses.

The interior designer will find more and more clients in their twenties who are receptive to change and who want to start out on a better level than their parents did at a comparable age. They also are more reluctant to accumulate their furniture and accessories slowly, as their parents did, only to discover later that nothing adds up to the kind of interior they always wanted. Easy (albeit expensive) credit and the hope of instant prosperity intensify this reluctance to postpone, making this a more viable consumer group than ever before. It would obviously be advisable for the designer to encourage participation by younger clients to satisfy their creative, do-it-yourself urges, and yet give them the direction and help they need.

People sixty-five years old and older made up only 11 percent of the population in 1980 but will constitute an increasingly major target market for the interior designer. Depending on their affluence, education, mobility, and life style, this can be a profitable market. Among the senior citizens are people who have second homes in Florida, Arizona, or California, in the mountains or at the beach. In this group are some who now find it possible to satisfy their desire to start over with a new interior. These empty-nesters have new options open to them in the way of furniture and design now that their children have grown up (Fig. 1.1). As it-is-later-than-you-think and be-good-to-yourself attitudes become more prevalent, members of this group

[2] Walter H. Woods, "Psychological Dimensions and Consumer Decisions," *Journal of Marketing* (Jan. 1960), 17.

Figure 1.2
A solid walnut storage piece, such as this one designed by Art Carpenter, will last forever. (Courtesy of Art Carpenter)

become a better market, for less of their disposable income is committed.

Rites of Passage

Social scientists, particularly anthropologists (van Gennep) have explored the rites of passage by which primitive societies mark significant changes in the social status of individuals as they move up the age level, entering adulthood, becoming engaged, getting married, dying, and so on. Different societies evolve rituals and customs befitting these occasions. Literature is replete with the ways different societies have structured these events, but all the rituals are marked by great drama and significance.

This may seem to have little to do with interior design but closer examination reveals an analogy between the rite of passage and the situation in which the client finds himself when deciding to furnish a new home or apartment or to redesign an interior. This can be a traumatic experience characterized by many emotional feelings.

1. It can signify a new beginning, a modified living pattern, or a rejection of an old environment.
2. It can be accompanied by great stress and uncertainty, by reluctance to break ties with the past, and by timidity in accepting the new and uncertain.
3. It has been noted that the transition can be so traumatic as to result in mental breakdown, divorce, and so on.
4. The degree of emotional involvement or intensity of feeling depends, of course, on the client. Some react to changes by agonizing over each decision that must be made, and even the secure seldom accept changes in their environment without introspection or internalization.
5. Women tend to become more involved in this emotional dilemma than men, although there are some men to whom the transition can represent a great emotional readjustment. Usually, however, joint decisions prevail.

Strategy for Handling This Transition Period

The interior designer must develop techniques for helping clients through this transition Period. Some of these are:

1. Recognize, understand, and tolerate this emotional event when it occurs in clients.
2. Give logical reasons for choosing furniture and decor. This helps clients through the time of uncertainty. The designer must realize that it takes secure people (the clients) to work out their own wants and resist the opinions of their neighbors.
3. Be sure to explore the desires and attitudes of all the members of the family. Opposition to the design and negative influence on the client can result if the opinions and attitudes of the spouse or children are ignored.
4. Where appropriate, present the total design through quick sketches to help the undecided client and family over this time of change.
5. Remember, some clients have greater difficulty than others in coping with change. The salvaging of a favorite chair or sofa by reupholstering can help the client accept the total change with less shock and uncertainty.

Sign Expectancies

A principle of behavioral science that is relevant to the interior designer is the concept of sign-expectancies. Briefly, this is the tendency for consumers (clients) to look for signs in a product which will lead them to expect a certain quality or performance. Sometimes these expectations are false or incorrect, but if they are held by the client they may prove difficult if not impossible to change. Some examples are: "Soft fabrics are not as durable as hard fabrics," or "Solid woods (Fig. 1.2), are more lasting than veneers." Product characteristics have an impact on how the clients may evaluate its appropriateness or acceptability.

Value and its relationship to price are judged by sense receptors. Often the heavier of two objects is assumed to be more valuable; a lesser value may be ascribed to the harsher of two finishes; even smell has a role in this process, since many people prefer the smell of natural fabrics over synthethics. Whatever the client's associations are, the designer should be aware of them and either dispel or justify them, depending on the desires of the client and his expectations of the product's performance.

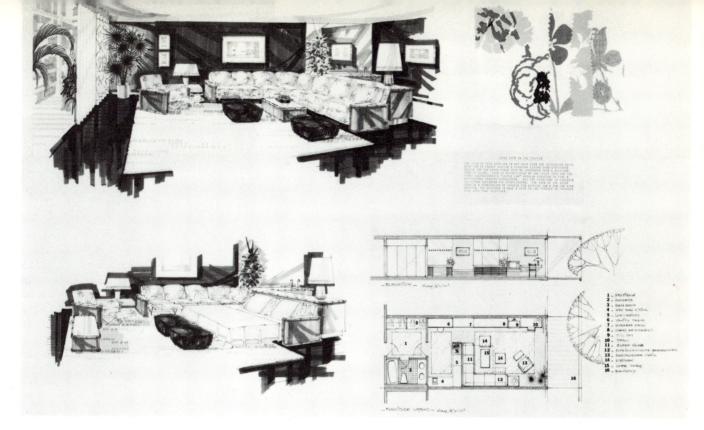

Figure 1.3
Floor plans and perspective sketches help the client to visualize the completed interior. Leon Barmache, interior designer. (Courtesy of Barcalounger)

For example, fabrics with long floats on the surface (satin weave) may prove inadvisable for most upholstery even if color and design are appropriate. Glass-fabric draperies may break at points of contact with sofa backs, or cause allergies. Using Scotchguard or Zepel finishes on upholstery furniture where they will receive heavy use by children can lead to dissatisfaction because of a lack of knowledge of what this finish can be expected to do or how to care for it. Whatever the characteristics, strengths, or weaknesses are, the designer's knowledge should be current and consistent with its use demands.

Price is a sign-expectancy that is generally correlated with quality. The higher the price, the better the quality is believed to be. This belief is not always valid, but when it is, the interior designer should be able to justify the higher-priced line. By pointing out the dowelling in chairs, the backing in carpeting, the precision of veneering in furniture, and so on, the designer can help clients to equate price with their sign-expectancies.

Gestalt Applications

The Gestalt[3] school of psychology views perception as a dynamic process in which the whole is greater than the sum of its parts. The configuration of an object is perceived first; the details, later. This concept is of significance to the interior designer.

Realistically, the client has great difficulty conceptualizing the plan of a room until he sees the total layout or configuration. For this reason, the interior designer should present floor plans or quick sketches of the design whenever possible. Decorative accessories can be added later for accent and to tie together the overall structure or layout. People accept the overall visualization before they perceive the decorative details that are consistent with it. Whether buying a car, a house, or an appliance, or spending a night in a hotel, people tend to evaluate the general structure or impression first (Fig. 1.3).

Anything the interior designer can do to make the total planned design clear to clients will help them earlier to evaluate and to react to the complete design. The interior designer builds the total impression of the room in a step-by-step fashion; when he has finished, has committed and generally allocated design, color, and furnishings to that end. It may then be too late or too costly to redesign or scrap the concept. The client then has pro-

[3] The German word *gestalt* and the psychological term *holism* are similar to the term *organic*. As used throughout this text, the term *organic* refers to that which is conceptualized as a whole. It means that the whole is greater than the sum of its parts. The parts are so interrelated that separation and individual analysis would destroy the total design concept. Just as the individual notes in a musical composition have little meaning unless they are heard in relation to each other and the total composition, the separate elements of design are without meaning until they are considered in connection with the other elements and the interior as a whole. Furthermore, *organic* usually connotes harmony not only within the interior but also between the total house and the surrounding environment. Lastly, *organic* means *living*. An organic design connotes life: flowing and dynamic, not static or mechanical.

Figure 1.4
A quick sketch, such as this one, in opaque watercolor by Tim Bookout, Professor of Interior Design at Georgia State University, will give the client a clear idea of what the completed design will look like.

gressed too far to back away, but if he accepts the design with many reservations and under duress, he will be unhappy with the results.

Whenever possible, the designer should get the whole visualization across first, then get acceptances of related choice options to attain the goal as the plan develops (Fig. 1.4). This will make acceptance more satisfying and final in the mind of the client.

Satisficing

The interior designer is often faced with the problem of selecting furniture, materials, and accessories that are just right for the total concept. The search for these products is often difficult and time-consuming. The program is seldom completed exactly as planned because changes and compromises have to be made.

Psychologists describe this process of substitution as *satisficing*. Shopping for the exact object is a form of search behavior. The time spent at it depends on the strength of the searcher's commitment to find the particular color or shape or texture.

The buying behavior of women who shop for dresses has been analyzed by behaviorists, and it is somewhat analogous to that of the interior designer. After comparison shopping in several stores and examining the dress offerings, a woman often has to abandon the prototype of the dress she had in her mind's eye. If she cannot find what she is seeking, she is very disappointed and discouraged. She must either abandon the quest or adapt her aspiration to the realities of the offerings in terms of price, color, patterns, and so on. She may have to go back to the second-best choice or substitute one of the dresses at first rejected or discarded. This lowering of aspirational level or goal is called *satisficing*.

This process is experienced both by the interior designer and by the client in the complex problem of matching existing product characteristics to preconceived ideas of what is to be achieved. Several strategies or techniques may be used to handle this dilemma:

1. The interior designer could leave unspecified the finer details of the plan when it is first presented to clients, so as to leave options open for substitution.
2. Clients could be forewarned about the pos-

sibility of discontinued items, delivery lags, and so on, to better prepare them for possible disappointment.
3. The interior designer could verify choice options and availability by telephoning vendors, thereby reducing the need for substitutions. This, of course, can be a costly process and is not foolproof. However, keeping up-to-date samples and current price lists could prevent many errors in this regard.
4. Alternate options or planned substitutions should not be presented to client until later or they will have more apprehension and fear of settling for second best.

Cognitive Dissonance

Behavioral scientists have a theory of cognitive dissonance which was advanced by the social psychologist, L. Festinger:

> This theory centers around the idea that if a person knows various things that are not psychologically consistent with one another, he will in a variety of ways try to make them more consistent. Two items of information that psychologically do not fit together are said to be in dissonant relationship to each other. The items of information may be about behavior, feelings, opinions, things in the environment, etc.[4]

The assumption is that the individual strives for internal consistency. Approaching a decision that involves a major commitment of money and/or change in status quo can cause clients to develop this dissonance. Dissonance occurs when clients consider the cost of the decision, the alternate uses to which they could put the money involved, the risk of making a mistake, and so on.

If they can get over the hurdle of decision-making or commit themselves to the proposition, then they feel great relief from the dissonance causing the tension. They are glad to get beyond this task. But at this point, post-purchase dissonance sets in and they wonder if they made the right decision. They then seek various ways of reducing dissonance:

1. They may rescind their decision or void the contract, often the morning after. A wife may say, "My husband doesn't want to spend the money right now."

---

[4] L. Festinger, "Cognitive Dissonance," *Scientific American*, **207**:27 (Oct. 1962), 93.

2. They may seek confirmation that they made the right choice. They look for other people who have used the same brand names or notice, as never before, others who own similar items. They even notice the manufacturer's national advertising of their new possessions.
3. They may avoid dissonance-producing information or advertisements about the rejected options.
4. They may distort such dissonance-producing information to conform with their decision (distortion to produce self-deception).
5. They may change their attitudes about the importance of the purchase decision ("It's really not that crucial," or "The world won't come to an end," or "I'll get used to it," and so on).
6. They may rationalize the decision ("It's lucky we redesigned the interior when we did because inflation is going to make prices rise!" or "We're fortunate to be able to accomplish this," and so on).

The clients may attempt all these techniques or combinations of them to reduce the post-purchase tension or dissonance that they may feel. The perceptive interior designer should take steps to help the client:

1. The designer might assure clients that their decisions were good ones and that they will be happy with their choices.
2. The designer can produce evidence of the quality, style, correctness, or appropriateness of the new appearance.
3. Clients can be supplied with answers for those of their peers who will ask why the design was planned as it was.
4. The designer can request permission to show prospective clients the new interior, either in person or through photographs.
5. The designer can follow up the details of a properly executed job, which will make the clients feel that his interest in the program was not just for a fee.
6. The designer may present a special gift to clients—a plant or an accessory—to help keep the designer-client relationship unique and personal.

Glossary

Aspirational Level. That social goal or level to which a person aspires; this goal level is determined by multi-dimensional influences of family, education, heredity, peer group, and so on.

Cognitive Dissonance. A disturbed state of mind rising out of the inability to make a decision or (having made a decision) to believe that it is the correct one.

Gestalt. A school of psychology that maintains the whole is greater than the sum of its parts, and that we selectively preceive the configuration before we flesh out the image with supporting details.

Rites of Passage. Traumatic events that mark transitions or emotional changes in one's life.

Satisficing. The need to substitute or compromise when an item originally chosen is too costly or unavailable.

Sign Expectancies. Certain cues, hints or bits of information (i.e., color, weight, size, construction, taste, and so on) that the client uses to ascertain the value, quality, or suitability of the product.

Bibliography

Ajzen, Icek, and Martin Fishbein. *Understanding Attitudes and Predicting Social Behavior.* Englewood Cliffs, N.J.: Prentice-Hall, Inc., 1980.

Arnheim, R. *Art and Visual Perception.* Berkeley, Calif.: University of California Press, 1960.

Berelson, B., and G. A. Steiner. *Human Behavior: An Inventory of Scientific Findings.* New York: Harcourt Brace Jovanovich, 1964.

Festinger, L. "Cognitive Dissonance." *Scientific American,* **207,** Vol. IV., New York University Press, 1961.

Foote, N. N. *Consumer Behavior: Household Decision-Making.* Vol. **4.** New York: New York University Press, 1961.

Van Gennep, Arnold. *The Rites of Passage.* Translated by Monika B. Vizedom and Gabrielle L. Caffee. Chicago, Ill.: University of Chicago Press, 1960. Originally published 1908.

Glock, C. Y., and F. M. Nicosia. "Uses of Sociology in Studying 'Consumption' Behavior." *Journal of Marketing,* **28** (July 1974), 51–54.

Goffman, E. *The Presentation of Self in Everyday Life.* New York: Doubleday & Company, Inc., 1959.

Hollaway, J., and R. S. Hancock. *The Environment of Marketing Behavior.* New York: John Wiley & Sons, Inc., 1964.

Howard, J. A. *Marketing: Executive and Buyer Behavior.* New York: Columbia University Press, 1963.

Kelly, G. A. "Man's Construction of His Alternatives." *Assessment of Human Motives.* Ed. by G. Lindzey. New York: Holt, Rinehart and Winston, 1964.

Koffka, K. *Principles of Gestalt Psychology.* New York: Harcourt, Brace Jovanovich, 1935.

Krugman, H. E., and E. L. Hartley. "The Learning of Tastes." *Public Opinion Quarterly,* (Winter 1960), 621–31.

Levy, S. J. "Symbols by Which We Buy." *Advancing Marketing Efficiency.* Ed. by L. H. Stockman. Chicago, Ill.: American Marketing, Association, 1959. Pp. 409–16.

Lewin, K. *A Dynamic Theory of Personality.* New York: McGraw-Hill Book Company, 1936.

Loudon, David L., and Albert J. Della Bitta. *Consumer Behavior: Concepts and Applications.* New York: McGraw-Hill Book Company, 1979.

Martineau, P. "Social Classes and Spending Behavior." *Journal of Marketing,* **23** (October 1958), 121–30.

Maslow, A. H. "A Theory of Human Motivation." *Psychological Review,* (July 1943), 370–96.

Miller, R. L. "Dr. Weber and the Consumer." *Journal of Marketing,* (January 1962), 57–61.

Rainwater, L., R. P. Coleman, and G. Handel. *Workingman's Wife.* New York: Oceana, 1959.

Riesman, D., with N. Glazer and R. Denney. *The Lonely Crowd* New Haven, Conn.: Yale University Press, 1950.

Sommers, M. S. "Product Symbolism and the Perception of Social Strata," in Stephen A. Greyser, ed., *Toward Scientific Marketing,* American Marketing Assn., 1964, pp. 200–216.

Weale, M. J., and J. W. Croake. "The Client as the Focus of the Interior Design Process." *I.D.E.A.S.* (Winter 1977).

———, J. W. Croake, and W. B. Weale. "Client-Centered Design." *The Designer,* (Sept. 1975).

———, J. W. Croake, and W. B. Weale. "Client-Centered Interior Design. *Interior Design,* **48**:3 (March 1977).

———, A. W. Danford, and A. Whiteside. "Evaluating User Satisfaction of Interiors with an Environmental Description Scale." *Summaries of Workshops and Research Sessions.* Papers of the Interior Design Education Council International Meeting, April 1976.

———, A. Whiteside, and A. W. Danford. "User Evaluation Studies in the Design Process." *Journal of Interior Design Education Research,* **3** (Spring 1977).

———, S. Day, A. W. Danford, and A. Whiteside. "Should Users Have Rights?" *I.D.E.A.S.,* **1**:3 (July 1977).

Wolgast, E. H. "Do Husbands or Wives Make the Purchasing Decisions?" *Journal of Marketing,* **23** (Oct. 1958), 151–58.

Woods, W. A. "Psychological Dimensions of Consumer Behavior." *Journal of Marketing* (Jan. 1960), 15–19.

The Family Environment

In keeping with the purpose of this text, the present chapter will describe the historical context of the family as well as its present requirements in interior design. The following historical sketch will provide a firm basis for understanding the current functioning of the family and make clear the reasons for behavior that is accepted as daily practice but little understood in origin.

The Evolution of the Family

Three phases in the history of the family are reasonably clear. Humans, modern archaeologists suggest, have been on earth for two million years. The first phase of the family, the longest, lasted until 3,000 B.C. Written records have existed for five thousand years and describe in detail the second phase of the family. But because we must guess about the conditions that existed before the emergence of written records, our conclusions about the first phase of the family are necessarily more speculative.

The First Phase

The design of the home during the first phase of the family emphasized function first; aesthetics, if considered at all, were a distant second. Because the family was nomadic, the home was likely to be a very temporary haven. When food supplies ran low, the family would merely move on to another area to hunt and gather. A cave provided excellent shelter, and the few implements could be used for preparing meals and for hunting, rather than for constructing dwelling units. Even portable shelters had to be simple in design for ease of erection and for maximum utility.

The family's activities were largely confined to the daylight hours, which were spent securing and preparing food, finding water, and tending to the other basic necessities of life. Procreation was the second most important family activity. Large families helped to insure continuation of the species in an era in which the complete lack of medical care or proper sanitation, the continual threats to life from animals, nature, and other humans, and the often poor nutrition made attrition rates high. Because the design of the home did not allow for privacy, it is likely that copulation was more open and less susceptible to social sanction than it is today. Indeed, the bedroom did not come into existence until thousands of years later.

Socialization, another family function, occurred in conjunction with the work tasks which consumed most of the waking hours, and did not therefore require a living room, a parlor, or a family room. Because there wasn't any food storage or elaborate meal preparation, there was also no need for a kitchen. The home needed to provide only shelter.

The Second Phase

The second phase of the family lasted for some five thousand years, or until the beginning of the Industrial Revolution at the turn of the nineteenth century. Aspects of this phase are still carried forward in the values and traditions of today's family, and a knowledge of this phase is necessary for an understanding of our present society. In this phase, the home evolved from a temporary and simple structure to a permanent and complex one, reflecting both function and aesthetics as well as the family life style (Fig. 2.1).

The Stem Family

Today's family has its heritage in the stem family. Found throughout Europe, the stem family was an excellent model for an agrarian society. The stem family was extended, and patriarchal. The eldest son, after marriage, stayed in the home with his family and inherited the land upon his father's death. The other sons had to find places elsewhere in the world. They might go to the city and find employment. At that time the cities were not large, because there was no industry, and their primary function was to provide administrative and other support to the farmer. If they did not seek employment in the city, younger sons were welcomed by the Church as priests. This meant that there were many women who would not be able to find husbands, and they too could serve the Church as nuns.

The House as Focal Point

By now the family had learned to cultivate the land, to store the harvest, and to domesticate animals. This made the home the focal point of the day's activity and the center of family life. Since the land was the source of wealth, it was imperative that the land not pass from the family. Families tended to remain on the same land; therefore, the family home could be in existence for hundreds of years. For this reason, it was important that the home be sturdy. Stone and mortar, durable materials, were often used, and those an-

Figure 2.1
Montezuma's Castle,
Arizona. A prehistoric
apartment house built into
the side of the cliff.
(Photograph by M. J.
Weale)

cient structures can still be seen in the Old World where they remain functional even today.

Large Homes

It was necessary for the house to be large as well as sturdy. Several generations would occupy the dwelling unit at one time, and the household might also include servants or slaves. Although the house in this phase was simple in design because supplies, tools, and decorative materials were limited, it was the showcase of family wealth, and considerable time and attention were devoted to it.

Special Areas

The family in this second phase was also very concerned with social status. Men were deemed superior to women, the elderly to the young. Those born into the family took precedence over the females who married into it. The men, and in particular the eldest male, had special places at the table. They also occupied a special room in the evening (which later become known as the living room). While the women cleaned up after the evening meal, began preparations for the next day's meals, and tended to their mending in the kitchen, the men discussed agriculture, politics, and religion. Because the males' skill in farm production determined whether the family could maintain its independent existence, their conversation was considered to be more important than women's talk. Because the man inherited the land and was its legal owner, his wealth gave him power as well as superiority over the woman.

The Design

Even though the male occupied a special place, it was the female who determined much of the house design. She was in the home most of the day, and it was her duty to care for the home and make it comfortable for the men. The men considered house activities less important than farming and allowed the women

to control those activities and the interior appearance of the home.

The House as Symbol

The land was not only the source of the family's wealth, it was also sacred because it contained the graves of earlier generations of the family. Therefore, the house, in addition to being the hub of family activity, also symbolized the immortality, the continuity, of the family.

Limited Travel

Families in this agrarian society seldom left the land. On occasion, the men would go into town to barter; later in this period, women accompanied their husbands in order to purchase the few goods that were not produced in the home. Many people lived their entire lives without traveling more than one mile of their houses. At no time in history has the house occupied a more central and important place in the lives of family members.

The Third Phase

The third phase in the evolution of the family began about two hundred years ago, with the onset of industrialization. As a predominantly rural society changed to one with an urban focus, alterations in family roles took place which shook, and are still shaking, the structure of the family. For the first time in history, a woman could exist without male support. She could go to the city and find a factory job which required no previous training or family connections. With this option, she no longer had to accept as law whatever her mate or her father commanded. A woman in an agrarian society had no options. If she disobeyed her husband or her father, she could be ruthlessly suppressed, or even worse, cast out from the family. If she were without a family, no other man would wish to claim her because he could never be sure of her background and, hence, of the "blood" of his children. As soon as women gained freedom, so did children. They too would come to question the authority of the elders and of the men, and they too could, if necessary, go to the city to seek employment.

Concern with Appearance

This new option of work in the city, improvements in transportation, and the greater efficiency in running the home that resulted from the advent of household appliances,

Figure 2.2
This multi-purpose room is enjoyed by all members of the family. The chaise longue on the left was designed by Le Corbusier. George Cianciamino, interior designer. (Courtesy of Solid Fuel Advisory Service)

made the female role in the home less crucial. Improved tools and advances in housing construction made it possible to add ornamentation which might once have been prohibitive in cost when all work was done by hand rather than by machine. With the rising interest in decoration, there was a corresponding decrease in the concern for function in the home.

Education Beyond the Home

During the third phase of the family, formal education became commonplace. In rural society, women had provided all the education for their daughters: the skills necessary for running the home and caring for the family members. The men had educated their sons in agriculture and bartering, and had passed on their political and religious knowledge. With the advent of industry, entirely new skills were necessary. Education was needed to understand the purposes and functions of business and industry, urban planning, city management, and political and social structures. The home lost its central position in the education of the young.

More Privacy

In an underdeveloped agrarian society, children are deemed an economic asset. The larger the family, the greater the number of workers for the fields. When the family left agriculture, it ceased being a producer and assumed the role of consumer. Children came to be, and are, viewed as an economic liability. At one time, one bedroom served all the family members. Then with increasing wealth, fewer births, and a growing desire for privacy, the children came to sleep in a room separate from that of the adults. Later, children of different sexes slept in separate bedrooms. Then, as the economic reality of many children became arduous, fewer children were desired and the house could be smaller.

Loss of Status

Grandparents have disappeared from most homes. In a rural society, in which changes in knowledge or methods tend to be few and slow, the accumulated lifetime knowledge of the elderly was respected and sought. Today, scientific and technological knowledge doubles every ten years, and a human "encyclopedia" of past information may be of little help in solving present problems. With increasing age, Altzheimer's and other diseases which in-

hibit (not forbid, but inhibit) new learning are often present. In the past, respect for one's elders was based on their practical value for daily living. Today, respect is a courtesy. Because grandparents no longer contribute to family functioning in the traditional manner, they, like children, have become an economic liability. This change is reflected in today's home, which makes no space provision for older relatives.

As women moved increasingly into occupations outside the home, their power grew and their status rose. Decline in male dominance has resulted in changes in house design. The special room for male after-dinner discussions has given way to the family room, in which no one has special privileges. Children are heard as well as seen, and they control family activities, such as which television program will be viewed, as effectively as the parents do (Fig. 2.2).

Increased Socialization

The family in an agrarian society tended to be very distrustful of outsiders, who might constitute a threat to the family's property or blood line. When the family moved to the city, there was no further need to protect the land; moreover, increased association with neighbors and fellow workers became necessary. Changes in house design met this need: first a parlor appeared, and later a living room, a recreation room, a patio, and a deck.

Increased Mobility

Once the family moved to the city, it was less important—and less possible—to remain in the same home for generations. The family felt free to move, especially when seeking an improvement in its economic status. If people today moved only as the result of divorce,

Figure 2.3
Construction of Paolo Soleri's home at Arcosanti. The tube at the left rear admits light and heat in the winter, while keeping heat out in summer. (Photograph by M. J. Weale)

millions would change residence each year. On an average, each of us will move fifteen times during our lives. This increased mobility has made apartments and mobile homes more popular, particularly after costs in housing soared beyond the reach of many.

Design Needs of Today's Family

As the family evolves further into the third phase of its existence, change and instability will be intensified. The family, in order to survive, must be flexible and continually able to adapt to constant technological flux. Effective house design can help to provide insulation and respite from the stresses of modern life.

Design for Family Needs

In the middle of the nineteenth century, when four fifths of all families were located in the country, over one half of the families lived in simple houses of one or two rooms. As a result of that heritage and of our concern with efficiency, house design is typically little more than consideration of the number of square feet required for the size of a particular family. The unique needs of the family have been submerged in considerations of efficiency and architecture: usually, the outside of the house is designed first, then the interior. Too much emphasis has been placed on building design and too little on determining the requirements of a particular family.

Individual Space Needs

One of the most commonly mentioned requisites in house design is privacy. This may or may not be the highest priority of every family. There are still some cultures in which large families of several generations live in one room, and seem quite content. In the United States when large numbers of people lived in one- and two-room log houses, family mental health was excellent and far superior to that typically found today. The reason for this was that the family was still in transition from the rural agrarian society to an urban industrialized one, they still had a feeling of belonging in that society that is missing today. In general, however, the individual needs of family members ideally should determine house design.

The kitchen is an example of a room which might vary considerably according to those needs. Most kitchens today are not designed with sufficient space for socialization. Some women (and men too) prefer not to have others about when they are preparing meals or doing dishes, but others are just the opposite and would enjoy more space. The mother with young children may appreciate extra room in the kitchen where the children can play as she works so that she can watch her children and still complete other tasks. A small, though efficiently designed, kitchen may result in children being underfoot much of the time.

All factors considered, today's family will desire more space for individual members than was once deemed necessary. However, housing costs are still rising dramatically and it is predicted that mortgage interest will rise to over twenty per cent. Hence the desire for more space will be increasingly frustrated. The house of 1,000 to 1,200 square feet will become more common, and the division of that space into smaller rooms will only partially satisfy the desire for privacy. Eventually there may be a return to the open plan, which visually seems to provide more space, although it actually does not.

Paolo Soleri's alternative solution to population growth is Arcosanti (Fig. 2.3), located in the desert of central Arizona. When completed the Arcosanti will house about 5,000 people in apartments of about 2,000 square feet on fourteen acres, and could create a wholly new urban civilization.

In the rural phase homes were run autocratically. Every one was assigned a place and specific tasks. Individuality was not a consideration. Now, because males and older family members are rapidly losing the assigned superiority they once enjoyed, house design must now reflect democratic roles. Freedom of operation within the house is one expression of democracy and with that freedom comes the need for increased flexible space that will adapt to the changing needs of the family and its individual members. Permanently planned rooms with fixed design cannot meet these changing needs. Attempts at permanency will frequently result in irritation, friction, and rebellion within the family.

Evolving Family Functions

In the rural society family functioning was simple. The family's task was to produce and to survive. The day was devoted to work. The family today has much more leisure (Fig. 2.4). Recreation is now an important consideration

Figure 2.4
*(Right) Time for social activities has increased
in the home today. George Ciancimino, interior
designer. (Courtesy of Solid Fuel Advisory Service)*
Figure 2.5
*(Bottom) Well planned storage increases satisfaction
and reduces frustration within the home. (Courtesy of
Armstrong Cork Co.)*

in house design. Today, family rooms, game rooms, basements, and TV rooms are important areas in any home.

The typical school-age child, for example, views six hours of television daily, spending more time in front of the television set than he will in school. At eighteen, he will have spent more than 22,000 hours watching television (Croake, 1972). Not all the family members will wish to hear the sound of the television for many hours each day, especially when they are not interested in the particular programs. A sound-contained room may prove to be necessary, especially in smaller homes.

Sound in general must be given specific attention. In a crowded house, turning on the stereo to a high volume will give one a sense of privacy, but it will have the opposite effect on the other family members. Constant noise, even though not consciously noticed, affects the central nervous system. Residents in areas where there is regular overhead air traffic have been found to manifest higher incidence of depression and suicide. The constant loud sounds of rock music produce anxiety and tension, but teenagers probably have no idea that their parents' quick temper and impatience with other family members is associated with the music. Even lower levels of sound—when the sound consists of words—can interfere with concentration, but soft music without lyrics is soothing and not distracting. Sound systems and sound barriers are crucial to design.

Developmental Stages of the Family

Design must take into account the ages of family members. Young children, the mothers of young children and the elderly spend the most time in the house. It is easier to recognize the needs of infants and children in house design because of their obvious dependence. Young mothers often sacrifice their desires to allow more space or particular design for their children. Such a sacrifice is not wise because it results in lessened satisfaction and needless inconvenience. It has been found, for example, that insufficient storage space results in poor temperament and inconsistent discipline by mothers (Lemkau, 1974; Fig. 2.5).

The elderly spend even more time in the house. As their age increases, they reduce the scope of their environment. It is not as easy for them to get around. They are no longer going out to work and transportation may be difficult. Yet, the elderly probably give less at-

Figure 2.6
This combined music-family room has easily maintained durable surfaces, which are ideal for children. (Courtesy of Armstrong Cork Co.)

tention than any other adult age group to the design of their homes. Many elderly people cannot afford to remodel or to change their residences. A goodly number still live in the large homes with many bedrooms in which they raised their families, but the proper maintenance of which is now beyond their strength or their means. The home which may have been practical in past years now consists of a series of stairs too steep to climb, cupboards too difficult to reach, important areas too distant from one another, and unused space too expensive to maintain. Except in retirement homes and housing developments, house design for older citizens is lacking.

Shift in Task Emphasis

The family in an agrarian society had to work long hours just to provide food and shelter. Whether one worked inside the home or out, sufficient exercise was a side benefit of the occupation. Today's family members need to make provision for exercise each day because many occupations are sedentary. House design is now more convenient for the homemaker, obviously, but it is also convenient in less obvious ways. One no longer has to climb to the second floor to use the bathroom or go to the basement for items that are best stored in cool areas. At one time, even those who owned cars would probably have to walk from the distant garage or the street into the house. Today's garage with its automatic door is built into the house. The smaller efficient home reduces expenditure of physical energy. Although excess weight is a problem for most

adults, few would be willing to go without the conveniences and labor-saving devices now considered standard in most homes. Montgomery (1974) has suggested that it might be more reasonable for people to keep physically fit by doing household chores rather than by going to health spas. His suggestion is particularly timely in light of the energy crisis and the tremendous increase in energy consumption as a result of labor-saving devices in the home.

A Sense of Contribution

The household equipment that reduces the time necessary for daily management of the home has another drawback. To be mentally healthy, all of us need to enhance the welfare of others and to have a sense of belonging. The agrarian society easily met this need: every available hand was needed to run the farm and maintain the home, and even the young child knew that he was making a contribution to the welfare of the family. There is much less opportunity in today's home for such contributions. Even in the modern home, however, children as well as parents can contribute to the benefit of others.

The typical twelve-year-old, for example, should be able to perform routine cleaning, tasks, prepare simple meals, and undertake minor repairs. House design can either prohibit or enhance this training for the child. The dwelling that resembles a museum exhibit or department-store showroom will not allow for children's mistakes and accidents (Fig. 2.6). Parents who are more concerned

Figure 2.7
Many activities can take place in this well-planned family room. Storage space is ample for games, sewing equipment, and books. (Courtesy of Armstrong Cork Co.)

with the appearance of their home than with their children's emotional health will deny themselves an opportunity for child training. House design must reflect comfort without perfection if it is to provide a healthy environment (Fig. 2.6).

A Sense of Belonging

In the rural home of centuries past, the feeling of being a part of the natural cycle was more easily achieved. The home had been occupied by one's ancestors, and one knew that his descendants would take over his space and role within the house. Location, family, friends, religion, vocation, and home—even the house implements, which had been used by past generations—were constant touchstones of one's identity. Urban society—with its high mobility, divorces, nuclear family, changing friends, uncertain religion, evolving vocations and frequent abandonment of houses and materials—works against the human need to feel a sense of belonging.

With house construction costs having tripled over the past twenty years, anything but mass-produced, standard design is out of reach for most families. The uniquely designed home that would allow the family to express its individuality is, for many, an economic impossibility (Plate 1). Individuality and the sense of belonging are much more likely to be fostered by interior design than by house design. The designer must increasingly add to his creative inventory so that he can offset the lack of variety in dwelling unit construction.

The Challenge to the Designer

Humans are holistic: a change in one aspect of a person's life or his environment will affect his behavior and his total being. A change in one member of a family or in his life space will affect all other members of the family. The interior designer must realize that his work will influence entire families when the house—or even one room—is redesigned. When the interior is designed, it must serve the needs of the entire person and those of the entire family. If too much attention, for example, is placed on the living room, social and recreational needs may be neglected.

Understanding the Family

Effective interior design is based on a knowledge of the behavior patterns of the family members who will live in the home. The family that always dines out and is rarely home except to sleep may have little use for major investment in the kitchen, but the bedrooms must be conducive to rest. Appealing design can change living patterns, but these changes must be appropriate for the family. A warm inviting family room, for example, can result in more time being spent at home (Fig. 2.7). A designer who has rigid perceptions will see all families as having the same requirements and his styling will reflect a mythical family that exists only in his imagination. If his ideas are rigid, his design could lead to disruption in the family. It has been shown, for example, that when family members do not fulfill their expected roles in the family, they are ostracized (Nye, 1974). Interior design that does not facilitate the performance of each family member's assumed functions can have a devastating effect.

House construction usually has planned adequately the square footage needed for a given family size. This is an important consideration in design: one of the major reasons for changes in residence is improper house size (Morris, Crull, and Winter, 1976). But the size of the house, though important, cannot override attention to specific family patterns. It would behoove the designer, therefore, to observe family movement in and out of the home for several days in order to determine family routines and space utilization. The designer would then have concrete data on which to base his design.

Summary

The family has evolved through three phases and changes in house design have accompanied that evolution. Because technology induces daily changes in our lives, design that was appropriate ten years ago may have less value today. The designer's task is to come to know the family members and to design an interior that will enhance their lives (Plate 2). His planning should not be an extension of his own ego or a reflection of a stereotyped family, but an application of functional and aesthetic principles well grounded in careful study of specific behavior.

Glossary

Agrarian Society. A social network based upon the extended family.
Altzheimer's Disease. A disease in which the brain shrinks away from the cranium, causing irreversible senility.
Holistic. The whole is greater than the sum of its parts.
Stem Family. A family in which the eldest son inherits the property.

Bibliography

AJZEN, ICEK, and MARTIN FISHEIN. *Understanding Attitudes and Predicting Social Behavior.* Englewood Cliff, N.J.: Prentice-Hall, Inc., 1980.

CROAKE, J. W. "Television and the Development of the Getting Personality." *The Minnesota Adlerian* (Nov. 1972).

MONTGOMERY, JAMES E. "The Importance of the House." *Forum* (Fall/Winter 1974).

MORRIS, EARL, SUE R. CRULL, and MARY WINTER. "Housing Norms, Housing Satisfaction, and the Propensity to Move." *Journal of Marriage and the Family* **38**:2 (May 1976).

NYE, F. IVAN. "Emerging and Declining Family Roles." *Journal of Marriage and the Family* **36**:2 (May 1974).

VINOKUR-KAPLAN, D. "To Have or NOT to Have Another Child: Family Planning Attitudes, Intentions, and Behavior." *Journal of Applied Social Psychology* (1978), **8**, 29–46.

WEALE, M. J., J. W. CROAKE, and W. B. WEALE. "The Family as a Basis for Residential Design." *Ideas,* **11**:1 (Winter 1979).

The Designed Environment

Perceiving Environment

Human beings experience their environment in five basic ways:

1. Through the senses—sight, touch, taste, hearing, and smell.
2. Through time and by movement through space.
3. Through reasoning or thought, memory or imagination.
4. Through emotions, both pleasant and unpleasant.
5. Through anticipation or expectation.

The difference between what is actually experienced in a specific environment and what has been anticipated determines the pleasure or discomfort a person will feel in that environment. If the experience meets or exceeds expectation, his reaction is pleasure; on the other hand, if the experience falls short of expectation, his reaction is discomfort. Expectations vary among individuals as well as within a given individual on different occasions. Because the total being reacts to the environment at any time, any alteration in one's senses, feelings, movement, or thoughts will alter his expectations. The designer must understand these anticipations and attempt to create an environment that will not only fit the client's specific personality but also meet his varying anticipations.

It is important to understand the kinds of perceptions an environment can evoke. Each of our senses and feelings affects our perception of the environment. The sight of a soft wool fabric may evoke the memory of its texture. We may feel impelled to run our fingers over it. This is particularly true of artistic individuals who seem to have a compulsion to experience an object with as many different senses as possible.

In today's environment, people are often disappointed when they touch a surface. The texture is visually a simulation of the real thing. Smooth-surfaced plastics appear to be wood or tile (Fig. 3.35). These simulated materials may serve a purpose (Fig. 3.38), but in many cases the integrity of the material may be preserved. Plastics which look like plastics may be admired for the beauty of the material itself (Fig. 3.23). This is what the Pre-Raphaelites in the Victorian Period longed for—a return to the Gothic Period when materials were not simulated and joinery was admired for the

beauty inherent in its honest construction (Fig. 3.35).

Our sense of movement through space is often controlled by the floor plan of the space or by the layout of each room, and it is impossible to isolate each of the many ways we respond to it. At a party in a crowded room, the crush of people is exciting and there is enjoyment in moving slowly through the space. If we are waiting in line in a crowded restaurant, however, we may have very negative feelings. If passage through a room is made difficult by furniture placement, we may feel uncomfortable and yet not understand why.

Our environment also evokes responses from the imagination. A room filled with pleasantly comfortable antiques may remind us of visits to a beloved grandmother and make us feel happy and young. A room full of formal antiques, however, may remind us of a museum and decrease our enjoyment of the space.

Some people respond visually to their surroundings. Others respond to varying textures and surfaces—shiny and dull, rough and smooth. Many people who are sensitive to sound find rooms with many hard (sound-reflective) surfaces distinctly unpleasant and feel more comfortable in rooms furnished with sound-absorbing materials. Others are sensitive to smell, and find pleasing the smell of natural materials such as leather, wool, and wood.

On the other hand, there are people who are not sensitive to color or sound or texture. They may be affected in many ways yet be unable to identify what pleases or displeases them about the space. The role of the interior designer is to assist clients so that they will find the interior pleasing and will be able to develop to their fullest within it. The designer must help clients to verbalize their likes and dislikes. Designers have perhaps a heightened sensory acuity. They may even be conscious of a phenomena of which others are unaware, like some people in primitive cultures, who can intuit impending changes in the environment. These acuities are undeveloped in most people today and the art of responding to nature's cues has largely been lost.

Design Elements

To create an environment, the designer must combine line, a two-dimensional element, with the three-dimensional elements of form, volume, and space. Other elements, such as color, value, texture, emotions, and thought, make up the interior.[1]

Design elements are the fundamental components of a complex visual whole. In the creation of a design, the elements of space, mass, volume, line, texture, surface, movement, and time are all important. The organization of these elements is controlled by basic principles: balance, rhythm, harmony, unity, variety, emphasis, proportion, and scale.

All natural forms have an ordered and regular structure. The human body, for example, is a structure composed of soft, curvilinear forms and hard, angular forms. Skin, lips, eyes, and hair add color, while texture is determined primarily by hair and skin. Some natural forms, such as the amoeba, are simple one-celled changeable forms. Man-made forms are basically rectangular and may be simple or very complex.

People desire and seek order in their environment. The art and crafts of primitive people and young children show that they too seem to have an innate sense of order: shapes and forms are arranged symmetrically in space; masses, lines, and movement are balanced. Unfortunately, as people become civilized and children grow older, this innate sense of order is lost.

People also enjoy contrast in their environment. For example, the Tudor England, well-ordered gardens with geometric mazes served as a contrast to the wilderness areas surrounding the great houses. By the Victorian period, however, life was so structured by the growth of manufacturing centers that gardens imitating the vanishing woodlands became popular. These contrasts provided variety and balance.

To be successful, a design requires not only contrast, but unity as well. Interior details

---

[1] Color is never perceived in isolation, but in association with the total environment and will be discussed in a separate chapter.

must complement exterior form, and form must harmonize with ornamentation. Aesthetic appeal is a vital component of design. By investigating and understanding design elements and principles the designer can set up certain criteria to assist in evaluating good design.

Shape of Space

Space is the most important element in residential design. Enclosed by exterior walls and divided by intersecting planes (the walls) into separate areas, the space may be rectangular or occasionally curvilinear (Fig. 3.1).

Time is another element that must be considered in relation to space. A space can seldom be seen in its entirety unless one moves through it. The Cubists were the first to conceptualize space-time. They portrayed objects simultaneously from all angles, inside and out. An interior should be conceptualized by considering both the inside and outside; however, space must be penetrated—or entered—if it is to be understood.

Space is a negative concept; the forms filling it are positive. The shape of the space is determined by the floor, the intersecting walls, and the ceiling. People have been conditioned for years to spaces enclosed by straight-sided planes that meet at right angles. Today, there are some houses in which space has been enclosed by spherical or curved lines. Such spaces can be exciting and appear larger than they really are since the curve, having no end, seems to extend the space it encloses. Curved spaces are also defined by vertical planes that separate them into rooms. Furniture groupings, plants, and even light may be used to further define interior spaces.

Form

Every object, natural or man-made, has a form or shape—a contour or outline. Form literally pushes space aside so that space surrounds the form. Our awareness of form extends to the internal structure of a form or the physical volume inside the form. Every form has three dimensions: height, width, and depth.

In the infant, auditory receptors first begin to differentiate sound but as the infant's visual acuity sharpens, he begins to differentiate forms and shapes. The development of the perception of contour depends upon the sharp gradient in brightness between the surface of the object and its background. Thus the Ges-

Figure 3.1
*An unusual curvilinear space, as in this vacation
retreat with a circular hearth and seating unit, can be
very exciting. (Courtesy of Tile Council of America)*

talt, or general configuration, is formed by
contrasting shades of gray. This is why many
painters visualize shapes of objects by outlin-
ing them in pencil sketches, thus introducing a
sharp gradient.

As infants develop perceptual ability, they
learn to differentiate between form and background. Later, sensory association, confirmation, and verification of the objects take place
through experimentation with the other
senses of touch, hearing and taste. Psychologists have verified this theory by observing
that people congenitally blind who recover
their sight through surgery learn to "see" in
this same manner. The patient's first perception is that certain parts of the field of vision
differ in brightness from their background
and take on contour or form. This occurs before the patient is able to identify the parts as
objects. After the patient identifies the form or
shape, he fits the decorative details into the
Gestalt or pattern to make a whole or identifi-
able object. In much the same manner, we
perceive mass and form very early in life and
only gradually become aware of details. As we
grow older, we lose this ability to see form
first; by the time we are adults, we first perceive ornamental details or color (if it is intense), and only finally become aware of form.
This can be a distinct disadvantage when evaluating design, because the form may be entirely concealed by ornamentation and color.

Basic Forms

All forms can be reduced to four basic
shapes: cube, sphere, cylinder, and cone. Natural forms, organic in shape, are composed of
spheres, cylinders, and cones. For example, a
spruce tree is conical, its trunk and branches
are cylindrical, and its acorns are spherical.
Cubes are the most frequently seen man-made
forms. Cubes are easy to work with, to make
with machinery, to assemble, and to trans-
port. The cube is a stable form (Fig. 3.2a), but
when used to excess it can be monotonous.
Different shapes may introduce variety and
serve to balance the cubes (Fig. 3.2b).

Rectangular forms are used for floor plans,
doors and windows, and furniture. Seating
pieces, case pieces, tables, and beds are generally straight-sided for each in manufacturing, assembling, and shipping. Rectangular
forms, which have one dimension longer than
the rest, convey a sense of movement which
increases in proportion to their length. Tall
rectangular forms are reminiscent of tradi-

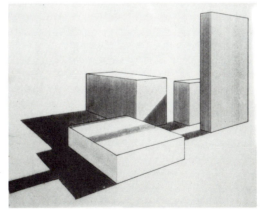

Figure 3.2a
*The four basic forms are the
cube, the sphere, the
cylinder, and the cone.
Cube forms are typical of
man-made objects.
(Courtesy of Jeff Ashworth,
Professor of Interior Design,
Georgia State University)*

tional interiors and create a sense of formality
(Fig. 3.3). If the longer side is horizontal, the
movement carries the eye around the space;
this type of rectangular form is more frequently seen in contemporary interiors (Fig.
3.4).

Even though curves are most often found in
nature, they are also used in the interior: curv-

forms are usually combined with the box-like shapes. The ceiling may be angled (a cathedral ceiling, for example), the staircase may be curved or spiral, and spherical, conical, and cylindrical shapes may make up many of the furnishings and accessories. Shapes should harmonize with and complement one another so that the space around them is as pleasing as the forms themselves.

Line

Line is the result of forms or shapes in space. It may be the perimeter of a form or ornamentation on a form. Some lines are the result of patterns in a room; others are the result of its furnishings; still others are architectural. Lines can direct the eye inward, to emphasize the center of an interior, or outward, toward its perimeter. They may appear thick or thin, and their direction affects our emotions. Dominant and subordinate lines should be combined in the interior to provide a sense of balance as well as variety.

Types of Lines and Their Meanings

Vertical lines have stability and lend dignity and formality to an interior. High ceilings, doors, windows, and tall furniture give a room a traditional, formal feeling (Fig. 3.3). Tall windows and high-backed chairs create a formal, traditional atmosphere even when the furniture is contemporary (Fig. 3.7).

Horizontal lines are calm, quiet, and peaceful, adding a sense of contemporary informality to an interior. Long, low furniture, low ceilings, picture windows are informal and restful, and a horizontal row of paintings creates a sense of peace and relaxation (Fig. 3.8). A more formal feeling may be created with horizontal lines (Fig. 3.9), and horizontal

ing staircases are found in Georgian homes; domed ceilings, in the buildings of ancient Rome and in Renaissance churches. The curve extends space since it has no end, and it is a self-contained, economical form with all points on the surface the same distance from the center. Floral fabrics, plates, and bowls are other examples of the curve used in the interiors (Fig. 3.5). Conical forms may be seen in lamp shades and vases, even though they may not actually terminate in a point. Furniture legs, candles, chair arms, lamp bases, and waste baskets are examples of cylindrical shapes commonly found in interiors (Fig. 3.6). Fireplaces, vases, and lamps may be cylindrical forms.

Interior spaces are usually boxes with many rectangles within them, However, other

Figure 3.4
Horizontal forms convey a contemporary feeling, as in this seating pit with a raised hearth. (Courtesy of Tile Council of America)

Figure 3.5
Curves are repeated in the wallpaper, the furniture, the accessories, and the decanters. (Courtesy of Wallcovering Industry Bureau)

and vertical lines may also be combined (Fig. 3.10).

Diagonal lines produce contrast and create excitement, although too many such lines produce an over-active interior. Diagonal lines created by paneling can produce a quiet tension (Fig. 3.11). Zigzag lines are more electrifying, however, and can create feelings of unease if used carelessly. Diagonal lines used in sloping ceilings, paneling, or in the bases of tables and of chairs produce an effect of dynamic movement. Diagonal lines can enliven

Figure 3.6
Numerous cylindrical shapes are found in this interior—in the fireplace, the vases, the lamps, the candles, and the candleholders. (Courtesy of Kirsch Co.)

Figure 3.7
Vertical stripes create a formal feeling in this room with its glass-topped table and Mies van der Rohe chairs. (Photograph by Yuichi Idaka; courtesy of Jack Denst Designs, Inc.)

Figure 3.8
The long, low lines of the furniture designed by Milo Baughman create a quiet interior. (Courtesy of Thayer Coggin, Inc.)

Figure 3.9
This room is more formal than the one in Fig. 3.8, although horizontal lines predominate here too, because of the materials used; the French Provincial chairs, and the Oriental accessories. (Photograph by Yuichi Idaka; courtesy of Jack Denst Designs, Inc.)

Figure 3.10
*The horizontal and vertical
lines in this room are
emphasized by the diagonal
lines formed at their
juncture. (Courtesy of
Georgia-Pacific)*

Figure 3.11
*The diagonal wood slats
provide an interesting
contrast in this small
conversation area. Carolyn
Goodrich, interior designer.
(Courtesy of Carolyn C.
Goodrich and Assoc., Inc.)*

Radiating curves create a happy, bright, and
hopeful effect. They are often used in combination with horizontal lines and vertical lines
(Fig. 3.18).

Soft, gentle curves are graceful, rhythmical,
and pleasant, often creating a feeling of movement. Gentle curves may be used to complement other curves in furniture and wall coverings (Fig. 3.19), or to contrast with horizontal
shapes and lines (Fig. 3.20).

Petite curves are playful, even frivolous,
and are frequently chosen for patterned fabrics
and wall coverings (Fig. 3.21). Very active
curved lines, as used by Art Nouveau designers, may induce restless, agitated feelings. Ascending curves are uplifting (Fig. 3.22), but
descending curves may be depressing and sad
and are seldom seen in interiors.

Table 3.2
Connotation of Lines

1. Vertical lines: stable, dignified, formal
2. Horizontal lines: calm, quiet, peaceful, contemporary
3. Diagonal lines: tense, exciting, over-active
   (pyramid: stable, dramatic, attention-getting)
4. Zigzag lines: electrifying, frenzied
5. Radiating curved lines: happy, hopeful
6. Soft, gentle curved lines: graceful, rhythmic,
   pleasant, intimate
7. Petite curved lines: playful, frivolous
8. Active curved lines: restless, agitated
9. Ascending curved lines: uplifting
10. Descending curved lines: depressing, sad

an otherwise quiet interior (Fig. 3.12), or define a special space (Fig. 3.13). Diagonal forms
are very stable (Fig. 3.14) and yet can attract
attention and create drama (Fig. 3.15). Diagonal forms are also used in the design of seating
pieces (Fig. 3.16). Triangular forms, also very
stable, are popular motifs for floor tiles, ceiling tiles, wall coverings, and textiles (Fig.
3.17).

Figure 3.12
The diagonal line created by the juncture of the ceiling and the wall is emphasized by the vertical lines of the panels and the dark horizontal band. (Courtesy of Georgia-Pacific)

Textures and Surfaces

The environment is experienced through all the senses; texture through two of them: sight and touch. Very young children explore their world through their mouths and fingers; as they grow older, they no longer have to touch an object to know how it feels, but they may continue to enjoy the pure pleasure that touch can bring. Texture adds immeasurable richness to our lives. In the remodeled Pennsylvania farmhouse shown in Plate 3, the rough textures of stone and wood add visual pleasure as well: we can sense the great age of the wooden French table even before we touch it.

The effectiveness of texture in design depends upon its relationship to forms, surfaces, and colors. Texture may range from rough to smooth from coarse weaves (Fig. 3.18) to soft velvet (Fig. 3.19). Surfaces may be hard, as those of floors and walls, wood and plastic (Fig. 3.23), or they may be soft, as those of fabrics or shag rugs (Fig. 3.24). Surfaces may be shiny—of sparkling glass (Fig. 3.16), polished chrome (Fig. 3.7), or satin-finished wood (Fig. 3.13)—or totally nonreflective (like the fabrics and stucco in Fig. 3.24). Surfaces may also be transparent (Plate 4), translucent (Fig. 3.25), or opaque (Plate 5). The more transparent a surface is, the lighter it will appear. In small spaces, glass or plexiglas furniture visually seem to occupy less space and the area will seem larger.

Value

Our perception of texture is controlled by value. Dark surfaces have fewer shadows and their texture is not as noticeable as that of light surfaces (Figs. 3.8 and 3.10). Light and the direction from which it falls on a surface, also affects perception of texture. Strong light emphasizes texture; diffused light softens it. Strong light falling at an angle creates dramatic lights and shadows and serves to emphasize texture (Fig. 3.26). Light falling from directly overhead minimizes details (Fig. 3.27). Rough textures absorb light (Fig. 3.24) while shiny surfaces reflect it (Fig. 3.28).

Contrast

Our perception of texture is heightened by contrast. For example, the effect of many smooth, light-reflective surfaces, such as metal and glass in a contemporary interior, is heightened by contrast with velvet, leather, and rough tweed upholstery (Fig. 3.29). Forms may be emphasized against back-

Figure 3.13
The diagonal ceiling line serves to enclose the sleeping area. (Courtesy of Georgia-Pacific)

Figure 3.14
The pyramid-shaped solar collectors on the roof of this pool house in San Mateo, California, lend stability to the building. Hood Chatham, AIA, architect. (Photograph by Karl Rick; courtesy of California Redwood Association)

Figure 3.15
The stable pyramid forms in the wallpaper dramatize the dining area. (Courtesy of Wallcovering Industry Bureau)

Figure 3.16
Pyramid forms were used by Paul Evans as the motif on his metal-frame furniture. (Courtesy of Directional)

Figure 3.17
Diagonal lines meet in an inverted pyramid above the sofa and are repeated in the diamond-shaped forms of the ceiling tiles. (Courtesy of Armstrong Cork Co.)

ground through textural contrast (Fig. 3.30). To camouflage forms, textures similar to those of their background should be used, which is one way unimportant architectural details and forms can be effectively hidden (Figs. 3.25, 3.26).

Acoustical Control

Another textural quality is acoustical control. Rough, soft surfaces tend to absorb sound (Fig. 3.18, 3.24, and Plate 35), while smooth, hard surfaces reflect and magnify sound (Plate 3, Figs. 3.23, 3.31, 3.32). The use of texture for the control of sound is an important consideration in planning an interior.

Maintenance

A factor that must be considered when selecting textures is maintenance. Soft, rough surfaces, deep carving, and long carpet pile may appear very luxurious but require extra maintenance (Fig. 3.31). Shag rugs, for example, conceal soil, but are more difficult to clean than short-pile carpets. In the Victorian period, interiors had many dust-collecting accessories and furniture was deeply carved. The daily cleaning required an army of maids, with brooms, dustmops, and feather dusters. With the growing shortage of servants after World War I, women began to demand simpler interiors that were easier to clean. Shiny surfaces appeared and smooth wood, chrome, and glass were used; these showed soil more readily but were easy to clean (Fig. 3.32).

Repeated Forms

Another kind of texture is produced by repeated forms. Plant leaves, fireplace bricks or stones, floor tiles, wood flooring, and woven patterns are examples of this repetition. It is not the individual brick, tile, leaf, or yarn that is perceived but the over-all texture created by the repeated forms (Fig. 3.33).

Flat, two-dimensional patterns on surfaces may simulate the visual effect of a three-dimensional texture. Examples include patterns woven into fabrics and carpets (Fig. 3.34), simulated-brick wallpaper, and marblized glass. These surfaces are easier to maintain than those they simulate (Fig. 3.35).

Structural and Applied Ornament

Texture may be added to forms by structural and applied ornamentation. Structural ornament might include unconcealed joints in

Figure 3.20
The curves of the stairway and the hanging lamp are emphasized by their contrast with the many horizontal lines in the room. Lester Koeser, ASID, interior designer. (Courtesy of Tile Council of America)

Figure 3.22
The ascending curves in the floral wallpaper, repeated in the curve of the lamp, are indicative of happiness. (Courtesy of Sanderson & Sons, Ltd.)

Figure 3.23
The many hard plastic surfaces of the chairs designed by Joe Colombo in this patio area are balanced by the softness of the growing plants. (Courtesy of Beylerian, Ltd.)

Figure 3.24
All the textures in this interior are soft or rough, from the carpet and upholstery to the rough fireplace with its textile hanging. (Courtesy of Wool Bureau, Inc.)

Figure 3.26
The textures of the tablecloth and chairs in this English dining room are emphasized by the strong light from the window at the left, which also emphasizes the details of the mirror and the accessories on the mantle. (Courtesy of Sanderson & Sons, Ltd.)

Figure 3.25
Translucent glass curtains create a feeling of lightness. (Courtesy of Wallcovering Industry Bureau)

Figure 3.27
The diffused light from above minimizes textures and creates interesting shadows. (Photograph by Yuichi Idaka; courtesy of Jack Denst Designs, Inc.)

Figure 3.28
Polished brass is a very reflective metal. (Courtesy of João Isabele, Inc.)

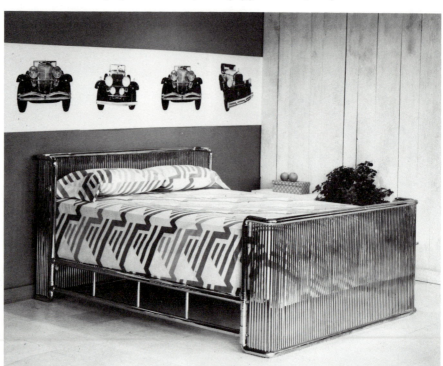

Figure 3.29
There are many textural contrasts in this interior: velvet contrasts with chrome on the chair in the foreground; the opaque Parsons tables contrast with the transparent plexiglas cube table; the metallic-thread draperies contrast with the fur pillow. (Courtesy of Kirsch Co.)

Figure 3.30
The sofa and chair are emphasized by the dark background. The light molding and woodwork emphasize the architectural details in the interior. Furniture designed by Angelo Donghia. (Courtesy of Kroehler)

Figure 3.31
Interior designer Virginia Phillips has combined a Victorian lounge, a 1720 desk, a carved chair from Sumatra, and an old English desk to create a charming room, but one that requires more maintenance than that in Fig. 3.32. (Photograph by Yuichi Idaka; courtesy of Jack Denst Designs, Inc.)

Figure 3.32
Smooth, plastic surfaces do not collect dust and are easy to maintain. (Courtesy of Kirsch Co.)

Figure 3.34
The patchwork pattern on the floor is smooth but appears three-dimensional. (Courtesy of Armstrong Cork Co.)

Figure 3.33
The repeated forms of the bricks, the woven-wood Roman shades with a valance, and the patterns on the upholstery create textures of their own in this Florida room. (Courtesy of Kirsch Co.)

Figure 3.35
This vinyl floor, which appears to be slate, is more comfortable to walk on and easier to clean than slate would be. (Courtesy of Mannington Mills, Inc.)

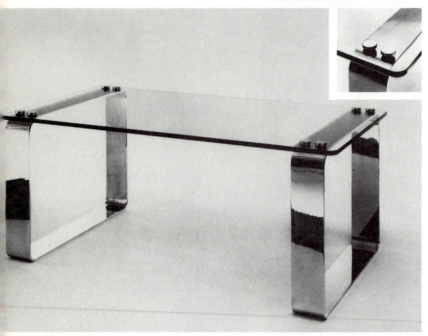

Figure 3.36
The joinery is made part of the design by designer James A. Howell. (Photograph by Bert Hillebrand; courtesy of The Corey Planning + Design Group, Inc.)

furniture, such as those of the early Arts and Crafts designers in England who believed that the inner construction of a design should be revealed if the design was to have integrity (Figs. 3.36, 3.37). Structural ornament also includes wood grain and the woven patterns formed in textiles by the warp and filling. Applied ornament is added to an object after it is completed. This includes printed patterns (Fig. 3.38), etched or painted designs, and molded plaster or gesso trim. Applied ornament is not a part of the structure, but it should be related to the design of the object and appropriate to the material. Applied design should enhance the form and harmonize with it in scale and size and texture.

Design Principles

The organization of the elements of design is controlled by certain basic principles—balance, rhythm, and emphasis—which render the orderly arrangement of elements pleasing to the eye. Other factors in the designed environment—harmony, unity, variety, proportion and scale—must also be considered. Each design, of course, must be assessed within the framework of its culture and time.

Some designers have been able to violate the principles of design successfully, but that is the exception rather than the rule.

Balance

Balance is the arrangement of objects so that they seem to be in a state of equilibrium. The baby animal's first struggles to get up on its feet, the human baby's attempts to stand alone, are natural efforts to achieve mechanical or physical balance. Optical balance, perceived through the eyes, is the kind of balance that is important in design.

Optical balance has four dimensions: length, height, width, and time. Interiors are designed for people and until people move through them the design is incomplete. This movement, together with the actual physical presence of people and their clothing, constantly changes the perceived equilibrium in a room. Another aspect of the dimension of time is the inevitable changes that take place with the replacement of worn or damaged pieces. A well-designed interior does not lose its equilibrium in any of its dimensions.

Both natural and artificial light affect balance. Bright, natural light can be controlled by window coverings to some extent, but on dull days artificial illumination may be needed. Details clear in strong, angled light become indistinct in diffused, low, or bright overhead light.

The following are basic guidelines for creating balance:

1. Bright, small objects can balance large grayed areas of color. Bright upholstery and pillows can balance walls, carpet, and draperies (Plate 29).
2. Opaque, warm areas appear larger than transparent, cool ones (Plate 9: Charlotte Finn has created a one-room studio apartment in cool blues balanced by touches of warm red and pink which appear larger than they actually are).
3. Objects appear heavier when placed above eye level rather than below. This is why paintings should be hung at normal viewing level (seated or standing), or they may appear too heavy (Figs. 3.16, 3.39).
4. Unique or unusual objects balance larger plainer ones (Fig. 3.40).
5. Elaborately ornamented objects create a center of interest and can balance larger, plainer ones (Fig. 3.41).
6. Matching materials, such as wallpaper, draperies, and upholstery conceal architec-

Figure 3.37
The dovetail joints are part of the design of this solid wood easy chair by Robin Day. The chair has down-filled leather cushions. (Courtesy of Hille)

Figure 3.38
Wicker furniture is contrasted with a printed wicker pattern on the wall covering and window curtains. (Courtesy of Wallcovering Industry Bureau)

Figure 3.39
The wall hanging at the left appears heavier at the top because it is above eye level. If it were reversed, it would appear heavier at the floor level. (Courtesy of Kirsch Co.)

tural details and furniture (Fig. 3.42); contrasting colors emphasize details and furniture.

7. Materials known to be heavy (such as iron and granite) appear heavy as well (Fig. 3.43).

Visual balance can best be compared to the mechanical balance of a seesaw: by moving the center support or by changing the weight on either end, objects can be brought into visual balance.

Symmetrical Balance

Symmetrical or formal balance results when each side of an object or space mirrors the other and there is a natural focal point in the center (Fig. 3.44). The center of interest is emphatic, but the total effect is static, quiet, and passive. Symmetrical forms are found in nature and in the bodies of animals and people, but wind or movement can change this symmetry very quickly. Clothing, furnishings, and architectural details such as fireplaces and windows are also symmetrical. People have

Figure 3.40
The dramatically lighted head on the right wall effectively balances the larger étagère on the right. (Photograph by Yuichi Idaka; courtesy of Jack Denst Designs, Inc.)

Figure 3.41
The Coromandel screen, with its lacquered surface and low-relief pattern, balances the elaborate objects in this traditional room. (Courtesy of Kirsch Co.)

Figure 3.43
Marble and stone look heavy because they are known to be heavy materials. Carolyn Goodrich, interior designer. (Courtesy of Carolyn Goodrich and Assoc., Inc.)

Figure 3.44
The furniture is arranged in symmetrical or formal balance. The chair at the left and the plants add informality. Furniture designed by Angelo Donghia. (Courtesy of Kroehler)

built symmetrical buildings since the ancient pyramids were built in Egypt and the classical temples in Greece. In the Federal period, symmetry was so important that, because windows were taxed, false windows were added to the exterior of dwellings.

Humans desire some symmetry in their environment, but too much formal symmetry results in a dull, static interior. Strong areas of contrast on either side of a symmetrical space weaken the formal balance and lead the eye away from the center of the interior.

Asymmetrical Balance

Asymmetrical or informal balance is fluid and flexible and, having movement, can direct attention around a space, making it appear larger than it is. Most interiors are designed

asymmetrically with some symmetrical components.

Asymmetrical balance was very popular in the Louis XV or Rococo Period and was used widely by the Art Nouveau designers. These designers balanced different parts of the design informally or copied the forms of wind-blown growth. In Oriental design, small, detailed areas are balanced by larger, less ornamental parts. Asymmetrical balance is in harmony with nature since wind and movement cause even the most symmetrical of natural forms to become asymmetrical (Fig. 3.45).

Radial Balance

Radial balance is formed when all parts of the whole radiate from a central focal point (Fig. 3.46). The spider web is an example of radial balance in nature. The rose windows of Gothic churches, decorative patterns on dinnerware and textiles, lighting fixtures and the wire sculptures of the late Harry Bertoia are all examples of radial balance. Radial balance, although encountered less frequently than symmetrical or asymmetrical balance, adds an extra dimension to interior space.

Rhythm and Variety

People are conditioned to rhythm before birth by the regularity of a mother's heartbeat perceived in the womb. After birth, the rhythmic sounds of nature surround us: the song of birds, the wind, even the drip of a water tap. Rhythm exists in repeated forms, colors, motifs, and lines which lead the eye around both interior and exterior spaces. Mountains, trees, clouds, and even man-made forms give exterior spaces a sense of movement and harmony.

As a design principle, rhythm is the movement or flow of forms through space at fairly regular intervals. It is the means by which the eye is directed through space to a focal point or goal. It may be a quiet flow, an orderly movement, or an energetic rush. Rhythm can be seen in all periods of design: in the columns of a Greek temple, in the flying buttresses of a Gothic church, or in the delicate mosaics of a Byzantine cathedral. Rhythm may be found in the pattern of a single form in a textile or tile, or in the repeated forms of brick, stone, or wood paneling. It may be found in the progression in size of a single plant's leaves, or in the variety of leaves of several kinds of plants. Oranges have a common spherical shape, but sea shells of different varieties can create rhythm since they are also related (Figs. 3.47, 3.48). Although chairs are all made for the purpose of seating and have a common seat height, each chair in a group may be different.

Rhythm is the repetition of one or more forms in an organized, structured manner that gives design its fluid quality. The designer must consider rhythm not merely as an aesthetic principle but also as a requisite to emotional and physical well-being. In the design of interior space, rhythm also creates a sense of movement to carry the eye around a space, increasing enjoyment and response. Repeated forms provide the simplest type of rhythm (Figs. 3.49, 3.50). Identical shapes of the same size may be monotonous, but varying size or shape avoids monotony. An imaginative use of rhythm directs attention to the dominant areas in a space.

Progression, a forward movement, is achieved by changing the size of the forms or their value or color. A single motif can be used in different ways and sizes and in different combinations (Fig. 3.21). Progression can also be seen in large repeated shapes, such as windows. Forward movement can also be achieved by directional lines and shapes. Gradations of color, tone, and intensity (which will be discussed in Chapter 5) can also be used to achieve progression.

Along with rhythm, variety is a necessary component of design. Though one kind of line or shape must predominate, the eye tires of identical forms and lines. The effect of too many straight forms and lines may be softened by some curved shapes, while the use of secondary rectilinear shapes will prevent monotony in a room composed of soft forms (Fig. 3.51). The de Stijl designers made their interiors appear stiff and uncomfortable by using only straight lines. The end of the Rococo Period in France was marked by an excessive use of curved lines, and some Art Nouveau interiors have too many curves for visual comfort.

Forms, colors, textures, and patterns should be varied yet unified. A room with too many patterns, forms, or textures, has no unity and is over-stimulating. In many Victorian rooms, wallpaper, carpet, and fabrics were all patterned. Many different materials and fabrics were used and there was not enough contrast. The Victorians left no space empty and, as a result, their interiors were confusing. On the

Figure 3.48
The identity of the shells is almost lost in this rhythmic shell-pattern wallpaper. (Courtesy of Wallcovering Information Bureau)

Figure 3.49
Rhythm is created by the repetition of pattern in the quarry tile floor of this atrium in a New York solar house. (Courtesy of Tile Council of America)

Figure 3.50
The repeated patterns in this wallcovering designed by Jack Denst create a rhythm. (Photograph by Yuichi Idaka; courtesy of Jack Denst Designs, Inc.)

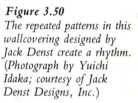

Figure 3.51
The chrome and glass tables and the statue of Selket contrast with the many soft forms in this interior and create variety. (Courtesy of Belgian Linen Association)

when the real cause of such problems may be an overly stimulating, albeit attractive, interior. Often the effect of a room on one's personality is subliminal. One may actually seek out a given room because of its appeal to the eye, and end up experiencing emotional distress.

There are, of course, some individuals who are helped by an over-stimulating interior that would be the undoing of others. But if one is not a psychologist, it is wiser not to guess who might profit from too varied a design. Also, unless the client lives alone and rarely entertains, others would be affected. Care must be exercised in the use of patterns, diagonals, curves, multiple textures, very bright colors, and decorative objects.

In working with rhythm and variety, the prime consideration is the form and its relation to background. Textures should be considered in relationship to each other so that there is contrast as well as unity, and surfaces should be selected according to intended use and ease of maintenance. Careful consideration of light is a factor in the selection of color, pattern, and texture, since matte textures, dark colors and patterns tend to disappear in low or diffused light.

Emphasis

Emphasis is an important component of all design elements. By accenting certain elements, the designer can lead the eye through space and create unity in the design. The eye, quite naturally, returns repeatedly to dominant or emphasized forms.

The many gradations of visual accent and subordination can be divided into three major categories: dominant, subdominant, and subordinate. Dominant forms have the greatest visual impact; subdominant forms support the most important or dominant areas; subordinate areas are relatively unimportant in assessing the total design, yet should be visually interesting and exciting in themselves. Dominance may be achieved in several ways:

1. **Size.** A large piece of furniture is more important than a smaller piece (Fig. 3.52).
2. **Color.** A bright color, a color surrounded by its complement, or a large area of color is more important than a pastel color, a color surrounded by similar colors, or small areas of color. Gradations of color, tone and intensity (see Chapter 5) can also create emphasis (Plate 6).

Figure 3.52
The large rattan chair is the center of interest, yet it is balanced by the small heavily decorated Oriental table at the left. (Courtesy of Kirsch Co.)

other hand, too many shiny surfaces (polished tile floor, chrome and glass furniture, shiny vinyl upholstery), are uninteresting.

When seeking to create variety, the designer must avoid creating a confusing or over-stimulating interior. An area may appear attractive and yet induce emotional discomfort. A client may attribute growing irritability, anxiety, or depression to poor communication within the family, to attempts to adjust to a new environment, or to changes on the job

3. **Texture.** A shiny texture surrounded by rough textures, or the reverse, stands out (Fig. 3.53).
4. **Shape.** Curved shapes in a room of predominantly rectilinear shapes, or the reverse, makes the contrasting shape more important (Fig. 3.54).
5. **Location.** The location of an object will affect its importance (Fig. 3.55).
6. **Ornamentation.** A heavily decorated object will increase in importance, just as an extremely simple one will (Fig. 3.52, Fig. 3.56).
7. **Convergence of lines.** Directional lines can lead the eye naturally to a focal point, making it the center of interest (Fig. 3.57).
8. **Variety.** Contrast is probably the most important element in achieving visual impact and making the dominant forms stand out from the mass of space. Subordinant forms, however, can usually be moved about or changed without disturbing the over-all effect. Too much variety is over-stimulating; too little is boring (Fig. 3.58).

Harmony and Unity

Elements related to each other are said to be in harmony. When the structural lines of an interior are repeated in its furnishings, there is harmony and unity. Forms, colors, lines, textures, patterns, and even light may be harmonious. The principles that apply to harmony also apply to unity. For example, subordinate elements in a room complement the dominant elements. The theme or mood of an interior can be destroyed when discordant textures or patterns are used. Traditional fabrics in a contemporary room may have that effect, just as brocades and damasks may look out of place in a casual interior.

Unity is the result of balance, the use of space, the placement of elements in that space, and their resulting rhythmic relationship. Harmony is the result of that unity.

Proportion and Scale

Human scale is the measure used for interior spaces and their furnishings. Frank Lloyd Wright designed homes and furnishings using a somewhat small module, because he himself was not tall. Mies van der Rohe, on the other hand, designed his furniture and buildings for his own rather large frame. His Barcelona chair, for example, is almost large enough for two people of Wright's size (Fig. 18.23b). Interior space is judged by its relationship to

Figure 3.54
The curve of the bed contrasts with, and is emphasized by, the horizontal and vertical shapes in the room. Furniture designed by Milo Baughman. (Courtesy of Thayer Coggin)

Figure 3.55
The placement of the chairs and table in front of the wall mural increases their importance. (Courtesy of Wallcovering Industry Bureau)

human scale. The interiors of the great houses in England, with their high ceilings and large rooms, reduce people to a smaller scale than do the early homes of the American colonists. Today, interior scale is even *more* important because economic conditions, decreasing

amounts of energy, and a shortage of land, particularly in urban areas, require that homes be much smaller.

Proportion and Forms

Proportion may be defined as a constant ratio between corresponding aspects of a space—of one part to another or of each part to the whole. It involves the estimation and judgment of a creative designer because all of the objects and the space must relate to human scale as well. Proportion is controlled not only by the form and size of objects, but also by their colors, their textures, and the spaces between them. One suggested formula for the determination of scale is to divide a rectangular space so that there is a 2:5 ratio between the parts.

Scale may refer to two things; both are measurements. For example, there is the scaled drawing, in which a measurement on the paper equals a larger measurement in the depicted object. The scale we are referring to, however, is the relationship of one space to another, or of one piece of furniture to another or to human scale. Adult height normally range from about 5'2" to 6'2", and furniture must be of a related size. This is the reason many men dislike the light, delicate furniture of earlier periods: it seems not sturdy enough for modern males.

Figure 3.58
There is a contrast of forms in this child's room: triangular and rectangular forms dominate, but curved forms add variety. The tent form is repeated in the window treatment. Curved shapes—the rocks, stools and stuffed animal—are a foil for the rectangular shapes. (Courtesy of Belgian Linen Association)

Figure 3.59
This furniture, designed by Stephan Gip, is made to fit a child's body, rather than an adult's. (Courtesy of Stephan Gip)

Humans have always desired spaces which fit the body. The early cliff dwellers of Bandelier, New Mexico, carved out sleeping spaces in the volcanic tuff so that they could have an area they could relate to, in relationship to their bodies. In today's interior, doors, windows, the height of stair risers, and furniture must be related to human scale. The space between these objects must also be related to both the objects and human scale. An example of this relationship is children's furniture, which is scaled down to fit a smaller human scale (Fig. 3.59). There is less space between furniture pieces in children's rooms, so that they are comfortable in them. Some furniture designers have even developed environments for children which are made to be placed in a room, leaving space for adults to relate to as well.

The study of design principles and elements which designers have evolved through the ages may serve to develop an awareness and appreciation of design as well as an understanding and a means of evaluating the designs of any particular period. However, design must be judged in the framework of the time in which it was evolved. The customs and styles of that period must be evaluated. It would be inappropriate to evaluate designs of a past period according to contemporary standards.

Glossary

Auditory Receptors. The ears
Perceptual Ability. The ability to sense or observe, which varies among individuals.
Sensory Acuity. The degree of keenness of the organs sight, taste, touch, smell, and hearing.

Bibliography

ANDERSON, DONALD M. *Elements of Design.* New York: Holt, Rinehart and Winston, 1961.

BALLINGER, LOUISE, and T. VROMAN. *Design: Sources and Resources.* New York: Van Nostrand Reinhold Company, 1965.

BEVLIN, MARJORIE E. *Design Through Discovery.* 2nd ed. New York: Holt, Rinehart and Winston, 1970.

CHRISTENSEN, ERWIN O. *The Index of American Design.* New York: Macmillan Publishing Co., Inc., 1950.

DREYFUSS, HENRY. *The Measure of Man: Human Factors in Design.* New York: Watson-Guptill, 1967.

FAULKNER, RAY, and EDWIN ZIEGFELD. *Art Today.* New York: Holt, Rinehart and Winston, 1974.

GRAVES, MAITLAND. *The Art of Color and Design.* 2nd ed. New York: McGraw-Hill Book Co., Inc., 1951.

KEPES, GYORGY. *Man-made Object.* New York: George Braziller, Inc., 1966.

KNOBLER, NATHAN. *The Visual Dialogue.* New York: Holt, Rinehart and Winston, 1971.

PILE JOHN F. *Design: Purpose Form and Meaning,* New York: W. W. Newton and Co. 1979.

DE SAUSMAREZ, MAURICE. *Basic Design: The Dynamics of Visual Form.* New York: Van Nostrand Reinhold Company, 1964.

The Lighting Environment[1]

Man once had only firelight or candlelight to replace the light of the sun and was forced to cease from labor when the sun set. But since the discovery of incandescent light in the late nineteenth century, we have learned to add light to our interior and exterior environment as we need it.

In the winter, leaves fall and more light and heat reach the earth, even though the light and heat are weaker than they are in summer. In the summer, leaves serve to control the intensity of light and heat, affording protection by lowering the temperature as well as add shade. Nature has reflectors and diffusers of light which add interest to the environment. Some of these are unmistakable, such as rain, clouds, atmospheric pollution, and the position of the sun in the sky. At dawn, the light has many reds and oranges in it; as the day progresses light becomes cooler and the sky seems blue; at dusk, the reds and oranges become dominant again. Ripples in water create highlights and serve as reflectors while sandy beaches diffuse light.

The perceived brightness of a given object or area within a space is determined by its position within the total space and by its relation to other perceived objects and spaces. Even the reflected light of a white napkin may appear to glow against the very dark background of a black table. An alabaster vase on the other hand, may appear pale compared to a nearby fluorescent light. A dark room after a time no longer appears dark to its occupants, while other normally lit rooms may appear too bright in comparison. The designer must continually relate light, objects and spaces to one another to judge their effect on each other.

The strength of light can change the color of a given area. Shades of red will appear much brighter under strong light, while weak light will cause blues and greens to stand out. The designer must be aware that plans may need to be adjusted to accommodate desired lighting effects.

The complexities of natural and artificial lighting must be fully understood by the interior designer if he is to make optimum use of his functional and aesthetic values. The use of lighting in interior space is limited only by the imagination of the designer.

Natural Light

Today, it is particularly important to conserve energy by using natural light as much as possible. White walls in a room can reflect up to 90 per cent of the available light (Fig. 3.29). This may be why the colonists' homes on Cape Cod had white interior walls: the sun was weak in the winter and it was necessary to retain as much natural light as possible. Dark colors may reflect as little as 20 per cent of the natural light (Fig. 3.30). If reflection potential were the only aspect of lighting to be taken into account, all interior walls would be painted glossy white. This intense illumination would be physically uncomfortable in most interiors, however, for extreme brightness is fatiguing to the eyes. Occasionally, where intense, close eye involvement is necessary, white walls may be required. But if paints are selected which have a high light reflectance (this is usually indicated on the back of the paint chip), energy can certainly be conserved. This is particularly important for the walls opposite windows.

Other methods of employing natural light are by the use of clerestory windows (windows above an adjoining roof) and by the use of skylights (Fig. 4.1). On the other hand, very dark walls are undesirable. Because it is difficult to see in rooms with dark walls, they require the use of more artificial light, which is expensive and wastes energy. Except where necessary as in museums and rooms used for audio-visual purposes, very dark colors should be avoided.

The designer must keep in mind that natural light evokes cognitive, physical, and emotional responses. We react to light in a variety of ways, depending upon the time, the circumstances, and the location. For example, low levels of light at night can create a sense of intimacy and romance or (when one is alone) a sense of fear. Bright light, stimulating on a sun-drenched beach, can produce tension and strain when one is trying to read or work.

Moderate levels of natural light are most comfortable because they create an enjoyable and harmonious atmosphere. A walk through the woods can reveal many different levels of natural light: the sun filtered through the leaves creates areas of light shade that contrast with areas of deep shadow and sparkling sunlight. This kind of excitement can be reproduced in the interior by creative manipulation of artificial light.

---

[1] Some of the technical material in this chapter was provided by Jean P. Freeman, ASID, Washington, D.C.

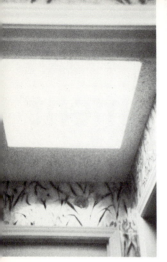

Figure 4.1
The home of Mr. and Mrs. Bruce Weale in Dallas, Texas, has skylights in the kitchen and bath areas, decreasing the need for artificial light. (Courtesy of Bruce Weale)

Artificial Light

Artificial light that simulates natural light is most pleasing. It can transform space with the ease of a switch and at little expense. It can affect perceptions of size, shape, texture, or color. Bright lights can be stimulating and make us feel energetic. In high-traffic cafeterias and fast-food restaurants, where people are moved through rapidly, high levels of light are employed. In restaurants in which it is desirable for people to linger over a cocktail or a meal, light levels are kept low. Poorly lit buildings, however, induce fear rather than intimacy.

Light affects mood to such an extent that low light levels can bring on depression and strain. Unfortunately, residential lighting has not been carefully studied or creatively utilized to any degree, although lighting studies for commercial use are widely published (the Illuminating Engineering Society [IES] has set up minimum standards for lighting specific areas and tasks). Lighting can define space (Fig. 4.2). It can also add to the visual appre-

Figure 4.2
Track lights, here focused on the couch at the right and on the painting at the left, may be moved as desired. J. Neil Stevens, interior designer. (Courtesy of Celanese Fibers)

ciation of one's possessions, such as paintings and sculpture (Figs. 3.40 and 4.2).

Dramatic effects can be produced by spotlighting (Figs. 3.1, 3.4, and 4.2), highlighting (Fig. 3.27), uplighting (Figs. 3.9 and Plate 1), downlighting (Plate 7), backlighting (Fig. 3.10), reflected or bounced lighting (Fig. 3.16), and the use of theatrical lighting techniques. Lights may be recessed (Fig. 4.3), hidden (Fig. 3.10), or highly visible (Figs. 3.24, 3.44, and 4.2). They may be placed on the floor, in a pot, behind a plant (Fig. 3.10 and Plate 1), or under a surface such as a bed or table (Fig. 3.18). They may be placed in or on the ceiling (Figs. 3.16 and 3.18), or on tracks (Figs. 3.18 and 4.2, Plates 8 and 31). Attention can be focused upon an object by the amount of light it receives and by the sharpness (Fig. 3.19) or diffusion of that light (Fig. 3.25).

Areas can also be de-emphasized by an absence of light (Fig. 3.13). If particularly pleasant colors are to be emphasized, direct lighting (such as spotlighting) can be used (Plate 8). In fact light is an all-important element in the total environmental design, but one which is often neglected until after the design concept is completed. Then lighting is selected on the basis of the decorative qualities of its housing, without regard for its potential as a design tool.

Definitions

Before artificial lighting is discussed, the terms to be used must be defined. The word *lamp* refers to the artificial light source, which also includes the bulb and base. The word *bulb* refers to the glass enclosure only, although it is commonly used to refer to the lamp. The *filament* (Fig. 4.4a), normally made of tungsten wire, is the light source in an incandescent lamp. Its heat produces light: the hotter the wire, the brighter the light. Eighty per cent of the energy generated is heat, while only 20 per cent is light. *Electric-discharge lamps* contain a gas (sodium, mercury, neon) or a mixture of gasses and come in two types: *fluorescent lamps* are *low-intensity discharge lamps* that contain mercury and have a coating of fluorescing phosphors which transform ultra-violet energy into visible light (Fig. 4.4b); *high-intensity discharge lamps* (HID) come in shapes similar to that of incandescent lamps and contain a gas (such as sodium, mercury, neon) or a mixture of gases. Both kinds of electric-discharge lamps require a *ballast* which regulates the amount of electricity they receive, and they

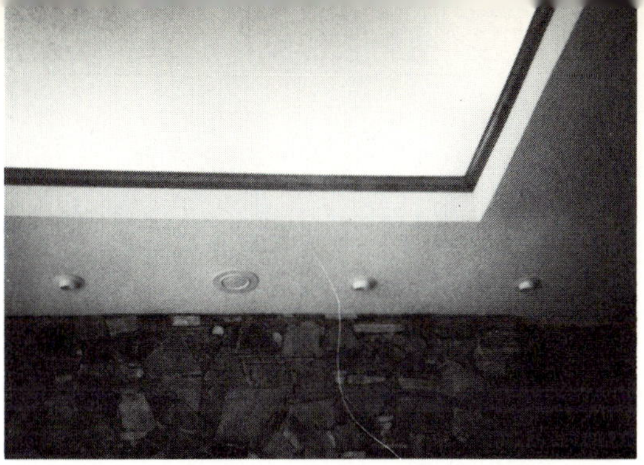

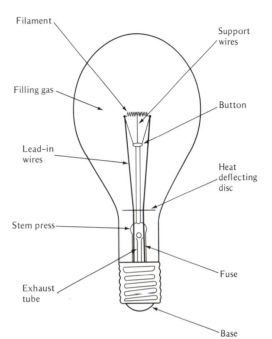

Figure 4.3
Fluorescent tubes, concealed in the recessed ceiling, softly light the living area. Eyeball spots highlight the massive stone fireplace. (Courtesy of Bruce Weale)

Figure 4.4a
The parts of an incandescent lamp. (Courtesy of General Electric)

Filament
Support wires
Filling gas
Button
Lead-in wires
Heat deflecting disc
Stem press
Fuse
Exhaust tube
Base

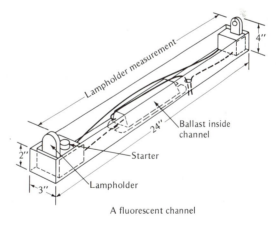

Figure 4.4b
A fluorescent tube. (Courtesy of General Electric)

Lampholder measurement
4"
Ballast inside channel
24"
2"
Starter
3"
Lampholder

A fluorescent channel

cannot be used in household sockets without it (Fig. 4.4b). The name of the lamp comes from its method of producing light. The *luminaire* is another name for the lighting fixture and includes the housing for the light source, the wires, and electrical connections. *Diffusers* (opaque or translucent shields over the light source or a surface treatment of the bulb) are used to disperse the light. *Reflectors* direct the light after it leaves the light source while a *baffle* shields the light source (Figs. 4.4c and 4.4d).

Figure 4.4c
Shades, shields, and louvers are used in lighting equipment to absorb and to redirect light into useful directions. (Courtesy of General Electric)

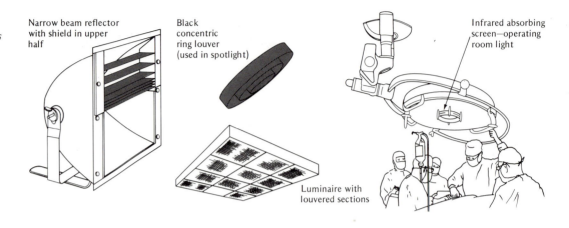

Narrow beam reflector with shield in upper half

Black concentric ring louver (used in spotlight)

Infrared absorbing screen—operating room light

Luminaire with louvered sections

Figure 4.4d
Reflection, diffusion, transmission, refraction, absorption, and polarization are the six common methods of controlling light. (Courtesy of General Electric)

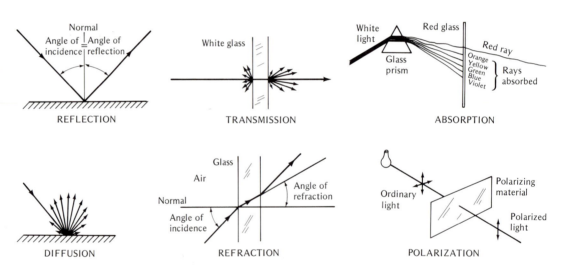

Normal
Angle of incidence | Angle of reflection

REFLECTION

White glass

TRANSMISSION

White light
Glass prism
Red glass
Red ray
Orange
Yellow
Green
Blue
Violet
Rays absorbed

ABSORPTION

DIFFUSION

Glass
Air
Normal
Angle of incidence
Angle of refraction

REFRACTION

Ordinary light
Polarizing material
Polarized light

POLARIZATION

Figure 4.4e
Measurement of light. (Courtesy of General Electric)

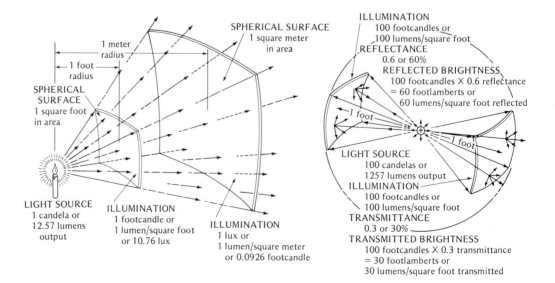

1 meter radius
1 foot radius
SPHERICAL SURFACE 1 square meter in area
SPHERICAL SURFACE 1 square foot in area
LIGHT SOURCE 1 candela or 12.57 lumens output
ILLUMINATION 1 footcandle or 1 lumen/square foot or 10.76 lux
ILLUMINATION 1 lux or 1 lumen/square meter or 0.0926 footcandle

ILLUMINATION 100 footcandles or 100 lumens/square foot
REFLECTANCE 0.6 or 60%
REFLECTED BRIGHTNESS 100 footcandles × 0.6 reflectance = 60 footlamberts or 60 lumens/square foot reflected
1 foot
LIGHT SOURCE 100 candelas or 1257 lumens output
ILLUMINATION 100 footcandles or 100 lumens/square foot
TRANSMITTANCE 0.3 or 30%
TRANSMITTED BRIGHTNESS 100 footcandles × 0.3 transmittance = 30 footlamberts or 30 lumens/square foot transmitted
1 foot

Light is energy, but it does not exist until it strikes an object; objects define and are defined by light (Fig. 3.18). Light can influence the observer's perception a space and is a basic element in the design of interiors (Fig. 4.2). It can define space and functions, so special consideration must be given to centers of interest, the ceiling zone, the perimeter zone, and the occupied zone.

Centers of Interest

Lighting should identify the primary and secondary centers of interest in the interior, whether these are a display or paintings or plants, a fireplace wall, or some other attraction (Fig. 4.5).

Ceiling Zone

The ceiling is usually of secondary importance and the appropriate influence of form, pattern, and brightness should be a consideration in this zone.

Perimeter Zone

Simplicity is desirable in the perimeter zone, where brightness should be greater than in the ceiling zone. Visual clutter may impede spatial comprehension and orientation and may prevent identification of a meaningful center of interest. A sense of relaxation may be created by proper lighting of the perimeter zone (Fig. 4.5).

Occupied Zone

Task lighting is required in the occupied zone, for it is the activity area (Figs. 3.17 and 3.47). Illumination objectives for occupied zones are generally those listed in the Illuminating Engineering Society standards. Other standards are listed in the publications of the American Home Lighting Institute.

A delicate balance must be maintained among ceiling, perimeter, and occupied zones if over-all effectiveness is to be achieved. When the luminance ratio between the perimeter, ceiling, and occupied zones is approximately 2–3:1 or less, visual change tends to be minimal. But when change rather than continuity is desired, the luminance differences should substantially exceed this ratio. The result will be a clearly noticeable transition. For example, task lighting is most comfortable and satisfactory if it is a pool of slightly stronger light in an area of diffused light. A single light for reading in an otherwise dark room can cause tension and eye strain. A spot-

Table 4.1
Considerations in Lighting Design

1. Visibility or general illumination needed (ambient light)
2. Amount and type of light required for specific activities (task light, and so on)
3. Structure of the space, its size, shape, number of windows, textures, surfaces, and colors
4. Decorative characteristics of the space, including shadow patterns, color appearances, and so on
5. Mechanical characteristics of the space:
   a. The method of producing, controlling, and distributing the light (number and placement of outlets, switches, luminaries, and so on)
   b. Whether existing structure or new (recessed lighting is more difficult to use in an existing structure)
   c. Energy efficiency and electrical load
   d. Budget
6. The age of the people using the space (older people require more light for seeing)
7. The number of people using the space
8. The balance of light and shadow, the amount of available natural light
9. The mood or atmosphere desired

light on a piece of sculpture, however, should be substantially brighter than its surroundings if it is to highlight the sculpture.

Footcandle

The level of illumination in a room is measured by footcandles. This is an international calculation of light intensity based on the amount of light falling upon a surface (Fig. 4.4e). The Illuminating Engineering Society publishes a list of the minimum footcandles required for adequate vision. A standard light meter, or a camera with a built-in light meter, can be used to measure footcandles.

Lumen

The quantity of light given off in all directions by a lamp is measured in lumens. This data is included by manufacturers in their lamp information. It is possible to determine the economy of various lamps by comparing the wattage and lumens. For example, if a 75-watt incandescent lamp gives off 1190 lumens, a 40-watt fluorescent lamp gives off 3150 lumens and a long-life 55-watt incandescent lamp gives off 775 lumens, the 40-watt fluo-

Table 4.2
**Method of Determing Footcandles
from Camera Light Meter**

1. Set ASA at 100, and aim the meter at the area to be measured. The shutter-speed reading, taken as a whole number that appears opposite F/4, will correspond to the approximate number of footcandles. For example, an exposure reading of 1/250 second at F/4 will be 125 footcandles (fc).
2. Set ASA at 25 and the shutter speed to 1/60 second. Place an opaque white paper in the area to be measured and frame the paper within the view-finder. Adjust the F stop until the meter indicates the correct exposure. The footcandles are as follows:

F stop	Footcandles
2	40
2.8	75
4	150
5.6	300
8	600
11	1200
16	2400

rescent lamp gives most light for least money and the 55-watt long-life incandescent least. Other qualities must also be considered, however: in some cases, a ceiling luminaire might warrant use of a long-life lamp to avoid frequent replacement (in all long-life lamps, output is sacrificed), in others, a fluorescent luminaire might not have the qualities desired.

Light Control

Natural reflectors and diffusers of light add interest to the environment. Reflectors and diffusers are also used in designing artificial lighting. Too many bright spots in a room are both confusing and wasteful of energy, yet too much diffusion results in a lack of contrast and a flat effect. Diffusers add a soft light to the interior. Shiny silver reflectors can be used to direct light or to focus it on a plant, sculpture, or painting. Some lamps have a built-in reflector.

A diffuser may consist of a lens over a light source, a surface treatment (such as acid etching or sand blasting), or a glass or plastic shield. Wall washers are a kind of diffuser. Some diffusers are bowl-shaped, and others are disc-shaped.

Glare

Glare is prevented by luminaries with louvers, lenses, or some kind of optical chamber around the lamp, which distribute the light more evenly and prevent its concentration in one area on the ceiling. These devices can also direct light so that it will not shine into the

Table 4.3
Planning Lighting for Specific Areas

Before selecting lamps, consider the following factors:
1. The size and location of the light source, the areas, and the tasks to be accomplished in the space
2. The color of the light and its effect on the colors in the space.
3. The reflectance value of flooring, walls, and ceiling. A paint chip may be matched to the colors to be used in a room, and color reflectance determined from the chip. Paints always darken with age, which decreases reflectance.

eyes of the person performing a task, which would reduce visibility and cause discomfort. Glare also occurs when light bounces off a surface into the eyes (Fig. 4.4f). This concept of determining the amount of glare and its effect on visibility has come about because of open-plan offices and the need for flexibility in them, the need for conservation of energy, and the characteristics of furniture-mounted lighting.

Dimmers

Most people enjoy change in their familiar settings and the manipulation of lighting is probably the easiest way to achieve variety. Dimmer switches, one of the easiest and least expensive ways to create variety with the same light source, have been used for many years in dining areas and are now being placed throughout the house to add drama, intimacy, or atmosphere. Easily installed and relatively inexpensive, dimmers conserve energy by reducing voltage requirements and extending the life of the lamp. If the voltage is reduced by half for a dinner party, the subdued light reduces electrical consumption and also encourages a more leisurely meal. Dimmers are more practical when used with incandescent lamps for those designed for fluorescent lamps are still too expensive to be economically feasible.

Light Sources

The major source of light for the home is incandescent but fluorescent and electric-discharge lamps are being increasingly used because they cost less to operate. Each type has its advantages and disadvantages, but each is a vast improvement over candles or firelight.

Incandescent Light

Incandescent light has remained essentially the same since Thomas Edison's day: a filament between two mental supports heats up in a gas atmosphere or in a vacuum and gives off light. Most incandescent lamps screw into a socket, which is the electrical source, al-

Figure 4.4f
Glare zone. (Courtesy of
General Electric)

Veiling reflection
offending zone

60–80% Reflectance

Potential glare
sources

40–60%
Reflectance

Direct
glare zone

25–45%
Reflectance

20–35%
Reflectance

Figure 4.5
Ceiling lights illuminate the
pingpong table and separate
that space from the rest of
the room. Abbe Darer,
interior designer. (Courtesy
of Tile Council of America)

Figure 4.6
Lamp designation.
(Courtesy of General
Electric)

though some are held in place by a spring clip. The changes that have occurred in incandescent light sources are the additions of glass enclosures, diffusers, reflectors, baffles, lens, filters, and housings to control the light. Some lamps are made in an imitation flame form for chandeliers (Fig. 4.6, Plates 3 and 16). In this fashion, incandescent light has become more adaptable and dramatic as well as functional.

Incandescent lamps are made with many finishes and coatings. Some are clear; others are frosted by sand blasting or acid etching; still others have a silica-powder coating inside the bulb, which softens the light. Color coatings are also applied to lamps. Ceramic enamel coatings produce a translucent, colored effect; plastic coatings render a lamp weather-resistant; and transparent coatings, paint or sprayed lacquer and dichroic filters (for high-intensity lamps), give a sparkling effect. Another kind of incandescent lamp — the quartz or iodine lamp, which is a tungsten-halogen light — comes in small-size, long-life lamps.

With incandescent lamps available in so many different shapes and wattages, they do not have to be a hidden light source. Lamp bases are here to stay and light sources may be exposed or not.

There are many shapes, wattages, and sizes available in incandescent lighting, which is probably why it remains the primary light source for homes (Fig. 4.5). Variations in bulb shape are indicated by a standard two-part code: a letter to indicate the shape of the bulb, and a number to indicate its diameter (the maximum measurement of the bulb in eighths of an inch). For example, a G–40 lamp is a globe with a maximum diameter of five inches.

The two bulbs with built-in reflectors are the R and the PAR lamps (Fig. 4.6). R lamps are less expensive and lighter in weight than PAR lamps, and have less accurate beam con-

trol. They are suitable for interior use only. PAR lamps have excellent beam control, for a lens directs the light; although expensive and heavy, they are durable enough for outside use. Both types of reflector lamps are used for spotlight and floodlight effects because the inner coating reflects light basically in one direction.

Specifying Incandescent Lamps. When ordering incandescent lamps, the designer must specify wattage, the shape and size of the bulb, and the size, finish, and color of the base. Many designers specify the life expectancy (in hours), which may vary from one brand to another, the voltage of the wiring system, and the light output in lumens.

Electric-Discharge Lamps

The most recently developed lighting is the electric-discharge lamp. These are generally named for the gas and the pressure used in the bulb. This includes low-pressure lamps (fluorescents), and high-pressure lamps which contain mercury vapor, sodium vapor, or a mixture of gases (high-intensity discharge lamps). None of these lamps can be installed into a household socket without a ballast (an adapter) which regulates the amount of electricity used. These lamps produce light when electricity is conducted through heated metal terminals to form an arc between the terminals.

Fluorescent Lamps. The fluorescent lamp was introduced at the Chicago World's Fair in 1939. It is a low-pressure mercury electric-discharge lamp. Inside the tube is a phosphor coating which transforms ultraviolet energy into visible light. Fluorescent tubes come in a variety of lengths and wattages and shapes. Most installations use the 20-watt (two-foot) or 40-watt (four-foot) tubes. Fluorescent lights are usually concealed when used in a residence except in service areas (Fig. 4.7).

Basically there are several types of fluorescents. The most important are cool white (CW), warm white (WW), delux cool white (CWX), deluxe warm white (WWX), and grow lights. Color variations are controlled by the type of phosphor coating used in the tube. The color of WWX is closest to that of incandescent light. The delux tube emits more red.

Fluorescent tubes produce high-level diffused light. They last about ten to fifteen times

Table 4.4
Incandescent Lamps

Advantages

1. They are a relatively small light source
2. They are inexpensive
3. Most light housings are manufactured for incandescent lamps (including portable fixtures, ceiling and wall fixtures, and concealed fixtures).
4. They are versatile and come in a variety of colors
5. They can be aimed, scattered, diffused and/or dimmed
6. They can be used to give a three-dimensional quality to objects
7. Their typically warm color is flattering to complexions
8. Their yellow color is closest in color to sunlight

Disadvantages

1. Their warm, yellowish light may be undersirable
2. They have a low lumen output for the amount of electrical input they require
3. Their life is relatively short (1000 hours)
4. They generate more heat (80 per cent) than light (20 per cent).

Table 4.5
Bulb Shapes

Code	Type of Bulb
Most Common	
A	Arbitrary shape
PS	Pear-shaped
Decorative	
G	Globe-shaped
GT	Globe-tubular or chimney-shaped
C	Conical
T	Tubular
F	Flame-shaped
B	Flame-shaped with smooth exterior (does not follow code)
S	Straight-sided
Reflector	
R	Reflector
PAR	Parabolic aluminized reflector (mushroom-shaped)

Figure 4.7
Concealed fluorescent lamps and a pendant light over the eating counter make this area very functional. (Courtesy of Poggenpohl)

slight rise in summer air-conditioning costs. However, some buildings are using the heat generated from lamps to heat the interior, so this might be an offsetting consideration. The economic considerations of selecting a light source depend more on its operating costs or energy consumption than on its initial cost. Fluorescent tubes, longer lasting than incandescent lamps and less costly to operate, are more economical at present for general illumination.

Fluorescent tubes commonly come in three types: *rapid-start, preheat,* and *instant-start.* These all start with a mechanism known as the hot cathode. The rapid-start and the preheat tubes emit light shortly after the lamp is switched on. The instant-start tube emits light immediately, but uses slightly more energy. Since the life of a fluorescent tube is directly related to the frequency with which it is started, the instant-start tube is the most expensive in the long run. The rapid-start tube seems to be the most economical in its use of energy.

Fluorescent tubes are available in deluxe lamps and regular lamps. Deluxe lamps are superior in color perception (they emit more red) but about one third of the light is lost, so they are more expensive in the long run. Their superior color rendition makes them worthwhile, however, particularly in the home.

Neon Lamps. Neon electric-discharge lamps are being used for avant-garde lighting or luminal art in the home. They can be made into sculptural designs, mounted on walls or

longer than incandescent lamps, and give about four times as much light per watt. For this reason, they not only conserve energy but also cut down on replacement costs.

Fluorescent lamps have a 20 per cent efficiency while incandescent lamps have a 5 per cent efficiency. In other words, fluorescent tubes use one fourth of the energy for the same amount of light. Incandescent lamps create more waste heat, possibly resulting in a

Table 4.6
Fluorescent Lamps

Advantages

1. Higher lumen output in relation to electrical input (about four times that of incandescent lamps)
2. Longer-lasting than incandescent lamps, especially if not turned off and on continuously
3. Can be color corrected
4. Available in many colors
5. Produce little heat
6. Larger light source and more evenly dispersed light

Disadvantages

1. Tubes gradually lose light (10–per cent during life of tube)
2. Few housings are suitable for residential use
3. Flickering tends to occur when tube nears end of useful life (which varies from three to six years)
4. Light diffusion results in a flat appearance
5. Color correction is difficult and at times not accurate
6. Dimmers are very expensive
7. Special ballasts are required and these generate heat

Table 4.7
Neon Lamps

Advantages

1. Decorative; can be used to execute a wide variety of designs
2. Long life (up to twenty-five times as long as that of incandescent lamps)
3. Low energy consumption
4. Little heat is generated

Disadvantages

1. Special wiring is required
2. Ballast is large and generally must be concealed
3. Mountings must be placed at least 24 inches apart
4. Designs must be custom made and few artisans specialize in executing neon designs
5. The light is primarily for decorative use and not suitable for task or general lighting

ceiling, or used to delineate rooms, ceilings, stairs, fireplaces, or beds. Neon has long been used for commercial signs, but only recently has been seen in the home. The tubing that holds the neon and other gases is rather thin and fragile and must be braced or mounted in some manner, but it can be bent to form interesting designs. It is available in widths from one half to one inch, although occasionally

Table 4.8
High-Intensity Discharge Lamps

Advantages

1. Long-lasting (up to 50 per cent longer than fluorescents and about twenty-five times as long as incandescents)
2. Bulb shapes are similar to those of incandescent bulbs, but are slightly larger
3. Use small amounts of energy
4. Produce large amounts of light
5. Generate little heat

Disadvantages

1. Require a ballast
2. Colors are limited; mercury is cold and sodium is yellowish
3. Effect on complexions ranges from pale gray or green to yellow

artists have made tubes a foot wide. The length of the tubing is determined by the design requirements and by functionality.

The color changes found in neon lamps are caused by the phosphors coating the tube and the various mixtures of gases used to fill the tube. Not all neon tubes have neon vapor; argon and mercury are also used. Neon lamps, like all electric-discharge lamps, must have a ballast, and the brightness of the light depends upon the amount of electric current or voltage the ballast can handle. Neon lamps are fairly expensive, but long lasting.

High-Intensity Discharge Lamps. High-intensity discharge lamps have until recently been used for street lighting and for industrial applications. These compact lights are similar to incandescent lamps in shape, but somewhat larger. They have a screw mount, and are filled with mercury vapor, high-pressure sodium, or a mixture of vapors. They can be color corrected to a certain extent with chemical mixtures or phosphor coatings on the inside of the tube.

Mercury lamps, cool and tending toward the blue end of the spectrum, have been used as street lights in the United States for some time. Sodium lights are yellowish and have been used in England, particularly in London. Multi-vapor lights, cool and greenish in color, are now being used more frequently in architectural installations. HID lamps require a ballast, but are the most economical because they produce large amounts of light and very little heat, and last about 50 per cent longer than fluorescent lamps (some last 24,000 hours).

Spatial Categories of Interior Lighting

Interior lighting can be divided into spatial catagories, such as ceiling, mid-area, and floor. Lighting may be recessed, mounted on surfaces, or portable; concealed or decorative;

Table 4.9
Types of Ceiling Lighting

Incandescent

1. Recessed (flush with surface of the ceiling), includes spotlights, downlights, can lights, and other recessed luminaires
2. Surface-mounted (includes spotlights, downlights, can lights, and other surface-mounted luminaires
3. Track (consists of recessed or surface-mounted electrified wireway to which lamp holders are attached)
4. Bracket lights (includes spotlights, downlights, can lights)
5. Pendant, suspended by a cord or stem from the ceiling (includes chandelier, adjustable luminaries, and so on)

Fluorescent

1. Recessed panel (trans-illuminated surface, commonly called a luminous ceiling)
2. Surface-mounted
3. Pendant
4. Bracket

High-Intensity Discharge

1. Recessed
2. Surface-mounted

Table 4.10
Types of Mid-Area Lighting

1. Wall sconces (luminaires bracketed to the wall; may be highly decorative)
2. Concealed (not recessed)
   a. Soffit: local illumination, usually enclosed, with light directed downward
   b. Cove: light directed toward ceiling, enclosure projects from wall (diffusing glass may be at bottom)
   c. Valance: light source hidden by face board (provides both up- and downlight; may be used for general illumination or accent)
   d. Cornice: behind cornice board; lights walls and directs light downward
3. Recessed (similar to luminous ceiling but attached to wall)
4. Portable (includes self-contained lamps in a decorative housing fitted with a cord and plug; table lamps—top of shade should be approximately 60 inches from floor—are the most common.
5. Wall washers

and used for general illumination or for task lighting.

The mid-area of the interior is generally where task lighting is required as well as general illumination. Usually, portable lamps serve for task lighting (Fig. 4.2), and incandescent lamps for general illumination (Fig. 4.8).

Table 4.11
Floor Lights

1. Usually incandescent
2. Portable (include self-contained lamps in decorative housings, fitted with a cord and plug, which should have the top of the shade about 60 inches from the floor)
3. Portable, decorative lamps for general illumination
4. Baselights (may be incandescent or fluorescent and are frequently a safety measure)
5. Uplights (usually concealed, but may be can lights, spotlights, and so on.)
6. Lighting under surfaces

Floor lighting is often neglected in the design of the interior, with the exception of portable lamps. Uplighting in a plant grouping, lighting behind furniture, and baselights for general illumination and safety can create dramatic effects and contribute to the beauty of the interior (Fig. 3.8). Lighting under a surface—for example, a bed—make it appear to be floating.

Generally the most efficient incandescent lamps are those of higher wattage; they give off more light per watt. For example, a 75-watt lamp gives off 1190 lumens, but a 150-watt lamp produces 2880 lumens—considerably more lumens per watt. Three-way lamps (50/100/150 or 50/200/250) produce more light at three different levels and are flexible as well as economical. Specific tasks, such as reading, sewing, or studying, require a lamp of 150 watts or more.

Task Lighting

Task light is that which is required for a specific function or activity (Figs. 4.5, 4.9). Properly balanced, it increases efficiency, helps to eliminate fatigue and strain, provides a more stimulating atmosphere for work, and helps to prevent monotony. Harsh shadows

can be eliminated by ambient light, which may be dimmed to achieve a better balance between light and shadow and to conserve energy. Some areas, such as the kitchen-dining area, require both general illumination and task lighting. Light is necessary for safety, convenience, and efficiency. General illumination can be provided by luminous ceilings or large fluorescent luminaires, but supplementary lighting is essential for work areas. This may consist of under-cabinet lighting or downlights and pendants (over sinks and areas where under-cabinet lighting is not practical).

Pendant lights are excellent over an eating area. They should be about 30 inches above the table surface and centered over the table to prevent glare from the luminaire (Figs. 3.4, 4.7).

Track Lighting

Track lighting, which consists of a recessed or surface-mounted electrified wireway to which lamp holders are attached, is a flexible system (Figs. 3.8, 4.2, Plates 8 and 29). Tracks can be cut and joined to form different configurations. Most bases and lamps swivel for greater flexibility. They can be used to pick up or flatten textures, to eliminate reflections, or to strengthen or mute color, depending upon where they are placed. They can expand space or differentiate space, and can be used to light walls, draperies, fireplaces, and art objects. Dimmers add further flexibility and make possible the balancing of other room light since track lighting can create glare or overly

bright areas. Track lights can be used as spotlights and wall washers or for wall glazing. Spotlights need not be described; wall washers result in an even, diffused wash of light on draperies or walls, softening texture and shadows. They are usually placed 18 inches or more from the wall to give a greater spread to the light. Wall glazing is accomplished by placing a light six or eight inches from the wall. This creates a visual focus and enhances texture.

Physical and Psychological Effects of Artificial Lighting

The effects of different wavelengths of artificial light have been studied in recent years. We spend a great deal of time indoors, in cars with tinted-glass windshields, and behind sunglasses. Tinted glasses are frequently worn indoors as well as outdoors, distorting the light our eyes receive. Recently it has been discovered that the human eye requires ultra-violet rays for optimum health; the consequence of artifical light or the wearing of sunglasses is that natural sunlight does not reach the eyes.

It was once thought that light enabled people to see. Many early scientific studies dealt with glare, color values, and eye comfort. The findings from these studies now seem superficial compared with those of current experiments. Of course, it was known that exposure to strong sunlight would burn the skin and perhaps predispose one to skin cancer, but its more subtle effects went unrecognized. It is now known that light affects cell reproduction, hormone production, gland secretions, and such biological rhythms as body temperature, physical activity, and food consumption.

Environmental lighting affects us both directly and indirectly. Direct effects are produced by photochemical responses of molecules on the skin and in the underlying tissue, while direct effects are produced by the light that enters the eyes. Recent studies reveal that fluorescent lights used in the classroom over extended periods of time can be a cause nervousness in those children who are not also exposed intermittently to natural light. In many elementary schools as many as 20 per cent of the children are given drugs to control hyperactivity. Early research findings suggest that a decrease in fluorescent lighting may be accompanied by a decrease in the amount of medication necessary to control hyperactivity. On the other hand, the use of fluorescent lighting may be effective in motivating behav-

ior when one is normally sluggish, as is the case after lunch. Fluorescent lights may help one "get going" in the morning. Depressed or low-energy people may benefit from an increased exposure to fluorescent lighting.

The designer needs to keep in mind the general effects of lighting. Brightly lit rooms are more stimulating than dark ones, but such stimulation must be appropriate to the use made of that space (Fig. 4.7). Kitchens need bright light for efficient work, but that light affects social interaction. People well known to each other, such as family members, will collect in the kitchen because the bright light is conducive to social intercourse. People who do not know each other well will feel more comfortable in dimly lit areas (Fig. 4.10).

Parties at which liquor is served will generate movement toward increased light as people come to feel more comfortable with each other and as the alcohol depresses the central nervous system. The depressed nervous system can endure much brighter lights than would be comfortable for a sober indi-

Figure 4.10
A softly lighted room is excellent for relaxing and conversation. (Courtesy of Armstrong Cork Co.)

vidual. In a closely related way, individuals whose mood is generally depressed can profit from more brightly lit areas. These same areas could be too simulating for a normal individual, possibly causing agitation, irritability, headaches, and anxiety. Often individuals living alone, particularly the elderly, can profit from bright lights and color.

The designer must always consider lighting in terms of the desired emotional goals for that space. This may be as simple as darkening a room to quiet the senses or to aid digestion, or it may become quite complex in terms of the symbolic associations which light lends a space (Fig. 4.11).

Glossary

Ambient Light. General room light.
Bulb. The glass enclosure of the light source.
Back Lighting. Lighting of an object from the rear.
Baffle. A structure used to regulate light.
Ballast. Regulates the amount of electricity received by a electric-discharge lamp.
Bracket Light. A luminaire fixed to a surface such as a wall (Fig. 6.2).
Ceiling Zone. The ceiling area of an interior.
Cornice Lighting. Light concealed behind a cornice and directed downward.
Cove Lighting. Lighting concealed behind a structural element near the ceiling and directed upward.

Diffuser. Opaque or translucent shield that disperses light.
Down Lights. Lighting which is directed downward, frequently concealed in the ceiling, or attached to it.
Electric Discharge Lamp. Low-intensity or high-intensity lamp containing a gas or mixture of gases.
Filament. The light source (usually of tungsten wire) in an incandescent lamp.
Fluorescent Lamp. Low-intensity discharge lamp containing mercury and coated with fluorescing phosphors which transform ultra-violet energy into visible light.
Footcandle. Unit of measurement of levels of illumination: the amount of light from one candle falling upon a surface a foot away.
Highlight. Light directed at a specific object.
High-Intensity Discharge Lamp (HID). Lamp containing a gas such as sodium, mercury, neon, or a mixture of gases that generates light by an electric arc.
Incandescent Light. Light produced by means of a filament (usually tungsten wire).
Instant-Start Lamp. A fluorescent lamp that goes on at once (sometimes called trigger-start)
Iodine Lamp. A long-life incandescent lamp.
Lamp. Artificial light source, including bulb and base.
Light Reflectance. Amount of light reflected from a surface.
Lumen. Quantity of light given off in all directions by a lamp.
Luminaire. Light fixture, including housing, wires and electrical connection.
Light Source. Origin of artificial light.
Occupied Zone. Area in an interior where task lighting is required.
PAR Lamp. Reflectorized lamp molded of heavy, heat-resistant glass that can be used outside.
Pendant Lamp. Lamp that hangs from the ceiling.
Perimeter Zone. Area where ambient lighting more than in the ceiling zone but less than in the occupied zone, is required.
Phosphors. Coatings in fluorescent lamps.
Preheat. Fluorescent tubes that must preheat before lighting.
Quartz Lamp. Tungsten-halogen lamp.
R Lamp. Small reflector lamp that focuses a stream of light in a small area.
Rapid-Start. Fluorescent lamp that starts after a short delay.
Recessed Light. Lighting units which are

placed in the ceiling and covered with louvers or with transparent or translucent panes.

Reflected Light. Light reflected from a surface.

Soffit. Lighting, concealed and directed downward, for local illumination.

Spotlight. Light directed at a precise spot to call attention to a center of interest.

Task Light. Light required for a specific activity.

Track Light. Recessed or surface-mounted electrified wireway to which adjustable lamp holders are attached.

Troffer. Light placed in the ceiling with a flush translucent covering.

Tungsten-halogen Light. A long-lasting incandescent source.

Uplight. Light source directed upward.

Valance Lighting. Light concealed at the top of the window opening and providing up- and downlight.

Volt. The tendency of electricity to flow.

Wall Washer. Lights focused on a wall for general lighting.

Wattage. Rate at which electrical energy is converted into energy.

Bibliography

Cox, James A. *A Century of Light.* New York: The Benjamin Co. Inc., 1979.

General Electric Company. *Bulb Selection Guide for Home Lighting.* Cleveland, Ohio, 1974.

———. *Incandescent Lamps.* Cleveland, Ohio, 1977.

———. *The Light Book.* Cleveland, Ohio, 1977.

———. *Light Measurement and Control.* Cleveland, Ohio, 1971.

———. *Office Lighting.* Cleveland, Ohio, 1976.

Kaufman, John E., and Jack F. Christensen, eds. *I.E.S. Lighting Handbook,* 5th ed. New York: Illuminating Engineering Society, 1972.

Lam, William M. C. *Perception and Lighting as Form-givers for Architecture.* New York: McGraw-Hill Book Company, 1977.

Nuckolls, James L. *Interior Lighting.* New York: John Wiley & Sons, 1976.

The Color Environment

Color Sources

Ancient people were surrounded by the colors of nature and they also used natural ingredients for their paints and dyes. These natural colors had a softness not found in many chemical dyes. Natural dyes came from many sources: plants (berries and roots), insects, fish, clays, and minerals. Ivory black was obtained from the charred bones and horns of animals, and lamp black from soot. Sepia was obtained from the ink bag of the cuttlefish. One of the earliest sources of ultramarine blue, lapis lazuli, was very expensive and difficult to procure. Another valuable color was purple, the symbol of royalty: hundreds of Murex snails were required to make enough pigment for a king's robe. The last Tsarina of Russia, Alexandra, had an all mauve bedroom. The cochineal insect was the source for carmine red. Naples yellow (lead antimoniate) has been discovered in ancient Babyonian tiles. White lead (lead carbonate), a very poisonous compound, was used not only as a pigment, but also in cosmetics, where—unknown to them—it slowly poisoned their users. Today, gathering natural materials for dyes is a hobby for some people, for natural dyes are again fashionable.

In 1856, William Henry Perkin, an Englishman, discovered aniline dyes, which made possible more strident, garish colors than had been previously known. The Victorian Period has been called the Mauve Decades by some historians, because of the overuse of the color mauve (a pale lavender, which Perkin's discovery had made possible). English chemists did not pursue the chemistry of colors, however, but left that to the Germans who built their great chemical industry on Perkin's early discoveries.

Today thousands of color variations are possible. The names of colors change yearly: what is called moss green one year may be olive another and avocado the next. These names are meaningless. The matching of colors does not require a name, but an understanding of their different aspects and dimensions.

Color and Light

Light and color are integral parts of our environment. In fact, color is such a natural part of the environment that it is often taken for granted. But without light, there would be no color. Light, which is electromagnetic energy, hits an object or surface, which absorbs or reflects its rays. The color we see is determined by the particular light rays absorbed or reflected by the object or surface. Every object has color. Some objects are the colors of nature while others have been colored by man. There are thousands of variations in any one color. Although light, balanced in all visible wavelengths, appears to be white, it is actually a combination of all colors. White light, passed through a prism, can be separated into its component colors, as Newton discovered in 1667. The spectrum ranges from the shortest rays (infrared) to the longest waves (ultraviolet), both of which are invisible to the human eye.

Much of the information on how we see color is somewhat incorrect in the light of experiments by Edwin Land, the inventor of the Polaroid. Newton's three-color theory, which was revised by T. Young and Hermann van Helmholtz (1821–1894), is responsible for this misconception. It was believed that differential rod and cone responses within the eye, as the eye reacts to light intensity, caused reds to appear much brighter under strong light and blues and greens to stand out in dim light. It was believed that the rods were responsible for determining the brightness or darkness and the shape of objects and the cones were responsible for registration of color and details.

It is now known from Land's experiments, that color receptors in the eye are *not* really specific for red, green, and blue. They respond to a range of wavelengths, each one of them responds more strongly to one wavelength—red, green, or blue—but with diminishing strength to the wavelengths on either side of red, green, or blue. This means that each receptor is responding to all three colors, but in differing proportions. Any number of wavelength combinations will evoke a given subjective color impression. This is exemplified in the confusion interior designers often have when they find objects with different wavelength absorbing qualities that appear to be the same color. As Land said:

> We are forced to the astonishing conclusion that the rays are not in themselves colour-making. Rather they are the bearers of information that the eye uses to assign appropriate colors to the various objects in an image.[1]

[1] Gordon Rattray Taylor, *The Natural History of the Mind* (New York: Elsevier-Dutton Publishing Co., 1979), p. 206.

The eye obviously does not make absolute color decisions. It makes relative judgments and then treats them as absolutely correct. Taylor interprets this to mean that "the subjective experience of colour is thus derived from a synthesis in the brain of three distinct sets of information."[2] These are blue, green, and red. The main concern of the mind is a comparison of warm and cool colors, not the wavelengths.

Scientific studies have revealed many color phenomena, and a number of color systems have been developed for color classification, including the Ostwald, Munsell, Brewster and C.I.E (Commission Internationale de l'Éclairage) color systems. Although a study of these systems is essential to understanding and utilizing color in industrial and printing processes, it is not particularly useful in arriving at an understanding of the effects of color in the environment and of the emotional and psychological connotations of color.

Interiors are normally viewed in both natural and artificial light. Color changes constantly under different conditions. Light can dull or intensify or even alter color. Draperies, curtains, and lamp shades act as filters, changing the color of light falling on an object. Texture also affects color: matte or flat finishes diffuse light; shiny surfaces appear darker in shadowy areas; and highlighted areas appear almost colorless. Diffused light flattens colors and creates soft shadows. Spotlighting, on the other hand, intensifies the color of an object and makes it appear more three-dimensional, with strong, hard-edged shadows. Reflected light alters color because it takes on the color of the surface from which it is reflected. Low, medium, and high levels of light can all change color.

Artificial light adds another dimension to color. Sunlight is white light, a mixture of all colors; but white light is rarely seen outside the laboratory. Natural light is affected by pollution, by clouds, and by the atmosphere. Interior light sources are not perfectly balanced so they rarely approximate a continuous spectrum distribution (all the colors on the color wheel). Incandescent light comes closest to reproducing the color of sunlight, although it has more red and slightly dulls blue colors. The cool white fluorescent tube, the most popular although not the most satisfactory in color delineation, suppresses red rays so that

² *Ibid.*, p. 205.

reds are grayed. For this reason it is less flattering to pink skin tones (see Table 5.1).

Modifying Light Colors

There are two methods of modifying the color of light. The *subtractive* method uses a filter to screen out all wavelengths except those the color of the filter. A red filter, for example, screens out all light rays except red. A dichroic subtractive filter allows only the rays of a particular color to pass through it. For example, the heat-producing wavelengths of incandescent light can be filtered out to produce a cooler light.

The *additive* method requires the use of colored lights which are mixed. For example, if yellow and green lights are focused upon a particular spot, the blue light will predominate because yellow is a component of both yellow and green.

Psychological Effects of Color

Color can relax or excite, calm or cheer, and even raise or lower the perceived temperature of a space. A recent study revealed that people in a red and orange space actually felt warmer than they did in a green and blue space although the temperatures were constant. Colors are associated with emotional states: we speak of a "blue mood," a "sunny disposition," a "purple funk," the "black death." Colored lights create different effects. For example, blue lights in a dining area make food appear unappetizing while incandescent lights stimulate the appetite. Red increases enjoyment of food and drink, particularly under low-light conditions, and for this reason cocktail lounges and many restaurants use reds and oranges in fabrics and carpets and a light high in red tones. Reds and pinks, however, are seldom used in hospitals for they are reminiscent of blood. Green is used in operating theaters, since it is the complement of red, and intensifies skin color as well as the operating field. It is also used to prevent the after-image of green, which will be discussed later.

Color is affected by geographical locations. Strong, vivid colors seem appropriate in Latin countries, where the colors of nature are strong and vivid; rich greens and blues, in northern countries, particularly in Scandinavia, where there are vast expanses of forest, trees, and water. The ancient Egyptians believed red was the color of life and modern

Table 5.1
Artificial Light Sources and Color

Type of Tube	Neutral	Complexion	Red	Orange	Yellow	Green	Blue
Incandescent	Warm, rich	Warm, healthy	Enriches	Intensifies	Warms	Darkens, somewhat brown	Dulls
Cool white fluorescent	Cools	Greys, darkens (pink)	Greys, darkens	Strengthens	Slight greying	Greys, darkens	Clears and cools
Deluxe cool white fluorescent	Rich, clear	Neutral	Clear, warm	True color	Enriches	Clear and bright	Enriches
Warm white fluorescent	Yellowish	Sallow	Brightens	Strengthens	Brightens	Deep and clear	Greys and darkens
Deluxe warm white fluorescent	Somewhat pinkish	Reddish	Rich	Strengthens	Brightens	Enriches	Greys and darkens
High-intensity-discharge mercury	Greenish or bluish	Pale and greenish	Greys	Greys	Strengthens	Intensifies	Intensifies
High-intensity-discharge sodium	Yellowish	Yellows	Greys	Strengthens	Intensifies	Strengthens	Dulls

studies indicate that red can raise the blood pressure of susceptible individuals. Too much red can also over-stimulate children over the age of three.

Color is used to sell products. When Braniff Airlines painted its planes bright colors in 1967, sales tripled the first year. The inside of the plane was not painted a bright color, however, but in earth colors and soft greens, which have a calming effect. Airport lounges, on the other hand, are often painted in blues and greens to suggest the idea that flying is "up and away." Detergent packages are also carefully planned to affect the emotions: yellow boxes are deemed too harsh; blue boxes may suggest that the detergent will not clean well enough; but a combination of yellow and blue is considered just right.

Color is one area in which psychology, medicine, and even superstition unite. Tests indicate the human beings perceive color even when their eyes are closed and that they can determine whether the color is warm or cool. Some sensitive individuals apparently react to colored areas even when blindfolded. People are affected by color in many ways not yet clearly understood. Nevertheless, people are often unaware of its emotional effects.

Personality as a Factor in Color Selection

Color affects the personality and, conversely, personality is a determinant of the individual's receptivity to color. For example, children are attracted to bright colors: a vibrant color will immediately draw the child's attention from other stimuli. Bright objects in infants' rooms help to stimulate intellectual and emotional development. The walls and ceiling do not have to be brightly colored, but objects and designs in the room should be. Babies who have brightly colored and contrasting objects hanging over their cribs, for example, demonstrate higher I.Q.'s and more outgoing personalities than babies who have not been exposed to such stimuli.

The same bright colors so beneficial to the infant can be deleterious to children over two. Bright colors contribute to hyperactivity, and even in the normal child interfere with settling down to sleep. The under-active child, however, can profit from bright colors because they will stimulate increased motor activity.

The kitchen is another area which should not be bright and exciting when there are over-active or even normal children and adolescents in the home. Because children react so strongly to color, too much bright color can result in increased irritability, digestive upsets, arguments, and complaints.

The effect of color on the child is often difficult for adults to understand because adults react very differently to color. Rich, intense, exciting colors are stimulating to the adult, and in general, the older one becomes the greater the benefit to be derived from the very color combinations which are over-stimulating to the child.

Adults are not easily distracted or controlled by color, as young children are. The capacity for abstract thinking increases markedly even into early adulthood. This means that one is increasingly less controlled by immediate stimuli. In addition, the aging adult loses sensory acuity. Bright, intense colors are

Figure 5.1a
Color wheel with the hues
or color names. Warm colors
are on the right; cool colors,
on the left.

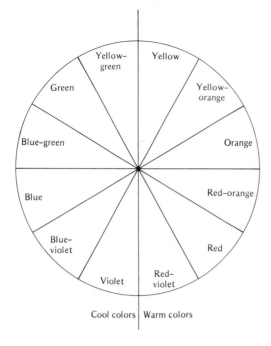

The design for a den is typically darker in color and features wood grains, leather, and heavy furnishings. The interior of a sewing room is brighter in color and features more contrasts of hue, value, and intensity in fabrics and wallpaper, and lighter furnishings. Men and women are usually more comfortable in these traditionally designed interiors, which reinforce their sex-role identity. A strong reversal of these usual choices may result in internal upset and conflict in many people.

Cultural anthropology suggests that particular role functions for males and females is unimportant as long as there is a clear separation between male and female activities and behaviors. The only essential to good emotional adjustment is that clear separation exists. In our culture sex roles are becoming less clearly defined. The effects of this change on children will not be known for some time, so it is safer for the designer to construct interiors with some regard for traditional guidelines. To do otherwise could result in considerable inner turmoil and possible maladjustment in the future.

Color Vocabulary

In 1866, van Helmholtz (1821–94), a German scientist, discovered that every color had three dimensions: *hue, value,* and *intensity.* Helmholz, however, was not interested in the use of color, so his discovery did not have much impact until about the turn of the century, when Albert Munsell developed a system for the analysis and organization of color. That system is still in use today.

Hue

Hue is the color name (Fig. 5.1a); it does not indicate whether the color is dark or light, strong or weak; it classifies the color as red, blue, or yellow (primary colors) or green, orange, or purple (secondary colors made from mixing two primaries), and so on. Hue is the name of the color as it appears on the color wheel (Fig. 5.1a). The closer the color is to another on the color wheel, the more closely related it is to that color. Distant hues, such as those directly opposite one another on the color wheel, have nothing in common (for example, blue-violet and yellow-orange). They contrast strongly and have a neutralizing effect on each other when mixed. When placed next to each other, however, both are intensified.

perceived more dimly, which means that not only is one less stimulated by color as one ages, but also that one is less able to see color. The elderly and the depressed need color in their surroundings. Brightly colored rooms appear cheerful and refreshing to them. Color-rich environments have made a significant contribution to the emotional well being of this group.

In general, outgoing, extroverted individuals are more responsive to color and less responsive to design shapes. Introverted people react more to shape and less to color. A brightly colored interior may stimulate the extrovert but have no noticeable effect on the introvert. In fact, the extrovert may become disorganized and anxious in too color-rich an environment, and may require subdued color to be productive, calmer, and happier.

Sex Role Identity and Color

Masculinity and feminity are delineated by color. Subdued colors have been traditionally associated with males; bright, intense colors, with females. The stereotyped image of the strong, silent male is not associated with rich colors; the "colorful" male, on the other hand, may be strong, but not silent. Prior to World War II, male infants were dressed in blue and girl babies in pink. If one asks a person born before 1941 what his favorite color is, a high percentage of males will reply, "Blue," and females will respond, "Pink." The unconscious association between color and dress in these formative years stays with the individual for the remainder of his life. Now that babies are no longer dressed exclusively in blues and pinks and males are wearing more colorful clothing, future color choices may be modified.

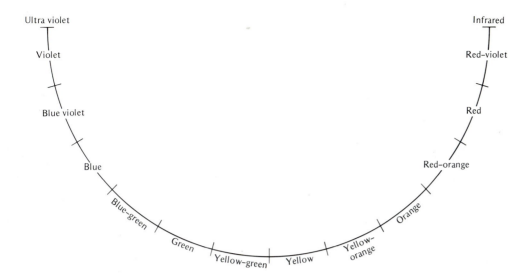

Figure 5.1b
The color bow. Yellow and yellow-green are advancing colors. The colors recede to infra-red and ultra-violet.

Warm and Cool Colors

Colors can be warm or cool. If the color wheel is divided between yellow and yellow-green at the top and between red and red-violet at the bottom (Fig. 5.1a), those colors falling on the yellow side are warmer than those on the yellow-green side of the color wheel. Fire and the sun are associated with heat and are perceived to be warm-colored. Snow, ice, and water are usually perceived to be cool in color. The warmest colors are those centering around orange while the coolest ones center around blue. Yellow-green and red-violet are fairly neutral and have neither warmth or coolness.

Warmth and coolness of colors can be very subtle. For example, yellowish green appears warmer than a bluish green; thus one is called a warm green and the other a cool green. A cool color may be made to appear warmer if some of the color lying next to it on the warm side of the color wheel is added. A green can lean toward the yellow and appear warmer but not appear yellow-green. This is one reason color matching is difficult.

Colors *advance* and *recede* depending upon their warmth or coolness. Warmer colors advance and cooler colors recede. Colors in the distance become cooler, lighter, and grayer (Fig. 5.1b). This is called *aerial perspective* when used to create the illusion of distance. As illustrated on the *color bow* (Fig. 5.1b), the colors that recede most are red (fading into infrared, which is invisible) and violet (fading into the invisible rays of ultraviolet). The colors that advance most are yellow and yellow-green.

Value

Value is the lightness or darkness of a color (Fig. 5.2), and is probably its most important dimension. If there are no contrasting values in an interior, the space will feel uncomfort-able. The values in an interior are more important than the colors. It is not only the value of a single object that is important, however, but the values of all the objects surrounding it. Two objects of similar value seem to blend into each other (Fig. 5.3), but if the objects are of contrasting values, the light one will appear lighter and the dark one will appear darker (Fig. 5.4). If a small, light object is placed against a dark background, even its size will appear to change.

The value of a color is determined by *tint* and *shade*. Tint is varied by the addition of white to a color, which lightens it but does not change the hue; shade is varied by the addition of black to the color, which darkens it but does not change the hue. To determine the value of a color quickly, look at it while squinting the eyes until the color almost disappears and only lightness or darkness is apparent. The value can then be determined when compared with a gray scale.

To handle the colors in an interior correctly, the designer must be able to recognize values and their effect. Light values can make a space appear larger (Figs. 3.19, 5.5), while dark values can make a space appear smaller and more cozy (Fig. 3.18). A ceiling will appear higher when it is lighter than the walls (Fig. 5.2, left), and lower when it is darker than the walls (Fig. 5.2, right). Even a fairly high ceiling (Fig. 5.6) does not appear so when it is dark. Close values obscure architectural details (Fig. 5.3), while strongly contrasting values emphasize these details (Fig. 3.3).

Intensity

Intensity or *chroma,* as it is termed by Munsell, seems to be the most difficult concept in the study of color. Intensity simply refers to the amount of pigment in, or the saturation of, a color. For example, a very intense green has more green pigment in it than one which is

Figure 5.2
The light ceiling at the left appears to be higher than the dark ceiling on the right in this multi-purpose room. (Courtesty of GTR Wall Coverings)

Figure 5.3
The close values in this bedroom, with its matching fabric and wallpaper, conceal the architectural details, including the marble fireplace. (Courtesy of GTR Wall Coverings)

Figure 5.4
The many contrasts in value in this interior call attention to the stairs, the lion, and the Parsons table. (Courtesy of GTR Wall Coverings)

Figure 5.5
An interior with very light values appears larger than it actually is. (Courtesy of American-Standard)

Figure 5.6
The high ceiling in this live-in attic appears lower because of its dark color. Patricia Plaxico, interior designer. (Courtesy of Barcalounger)

less intense, and it is a stronger, purer, and brighter green. Colors can change in value as they change in intensity. The colors of paint become less intense as they age.

Fog and haze and, of course, distance can make colors appear less intense. If two objects of complementary colors are placed close to each other, the colors will appear more intense. If two objects of close values are placed in proximity to each other, however, the colors will appear less intense. Spotlights can increase the apparent intensity of a color while diffused light can decrease it. Intensity can also be decreased or increased by filters, such as draperies or curtains, which alter the brightness of the light falling on an object.

It is almost impossible to alter the intensity of a color without altering another of its dimensions. Grays, blacks, and even whites are either warm or cool and slightly lower or higher in intensity than the color to be altered.

The Munsell System

The system developed by Munsell is the most practical one for the interior designer. Based upon a theoretical solid global form, it divides the spectrum into five principal hues: red, yellow, green, blue, and purple. Halfway between these hues are five intermediate hues (yellow-red, green-yellow, blue-green, purple-blue, and red-purple) and ten secondary intermediate hues (red-yellow-red, yellow-red-yellow, and so on). Hue is indicated by the letter or letters of a color; for example, yellow-red is YR.

The vertical axis of the Munsell solid is divided into nine gray shades ranging from 0 (black) to 10 (white). The colors are also arranged according to intensity or chroma, as termed by Munsell, with the pure intensities on the outside of the wheel being neutralized as they approach the center of the wheel, where they become a pure gray. Any color can be specified as follows:

$$\text{Hue} = \frac{\text{Value}}{\text{Chroma}}.$$

A light grayish blue would be written *B 6/2* and a darker grayish blue would be written *B 3/6*. This means that the hue is the same (blue), but the value and chroma are different. A blue of the same hue and value as *B 6/2* but different chroma would be written *B 6/4*. All colors do not have the same chroma. For example some hues extend further from the cen-

ter. Red extends to /10 as its maximum chroma, but green extends only to /7; yellow-green extends to /7, but blue-green only to /5.

Ostwald System

The Ostwald Color System, an arrangement of colors developed by a German physical chemist and psychologist, Wilhelm Ostwald, about the time of World War I, describes colors in terms of purity, whiteness, and blackness. There are twenty-four basic numbered hues, each with twenty-eight variations of lightness and darkness. The pure colors are arranged clockwise from yellow to red, purple, blue, and green. Today, there are thirty basic numbered hues, rather than the original twenty-four. Complementary hues are twelve numerals apart and basically there are three pairs of complementary light wavelengths opposite each other: black and white, red and green, blue and yellow. If the Ostwald double-cone solid were sliced through any pure hue, there would be a triangle with white at the top, full color at the apex, and black at the bottom. Because the hues are neutralized with white or black, there is no distinction between value and intensity. The color is named with the hue; the white content is represented by the second letter; the black content is represented by the third letter.

There are many other color systems which may be of use to the interior designer, but more important is an understanding of the color wheel and the location of a hue on the wheel, and an understanding of value and intensity.

Metamerism, Simultaneous Contrast, and Visual After-image

Samples of paint, fabrics, and carpets may differ in hue, value, and/or intensity when placed in different surroundings or under different light conditions. They may match closely under one kind of light, but not under another. This is called *metamerism.* Only if two hues have identical reflection distribution curves will they match under any kind of light. This can be determined by the use of a *spectrophotometer,* which gives the radiant energy at each unit wavelength, or measures the reflectance curve. This is more accurate than the *colorimeter,* which is also used for color matching, but which gives only the sum of the radiant energy for each primary color and does not measure minor color variations.

Simultaneous contrast was first noticed by

Michael Eugene Chevreul, the director of dyes in the Gobelins tapestry works in France. He noticed that hue, value, and intensity affect the area adjacent to them. Each hue projects its complement on the color surrounding it so that surrounding a color with its complement makes it appear much brighter. A related phenomenon, *visual after-image,* refers to the projection of the complement on a white surface. If green, for example, were not used for walls, gowns, and linens in an operating room, a green after-image would disturb the doctors and nurses after viewing the red operative area. A visual after-image occurs because of a reaction in the eye. Some after-images persist for weeks or months, and a relationship appears to exist between after-images and hallucinations.[3]

Color Properties

Color is relative: it may appear beautiful or unattractive depending upon the color surrounding it. Color is affected not only by light, but also by texture, finish, pattern, and contrast. Velvet and satin of the same color appear different. Fur fabrics appear even darker due to the deep pile and the number of shadows. Metal, painted, or smooth surfaces all reflect light differently. Some are matte, and others range from semigloss to very shiny. Finishes and textures should be varied in the interior, although too much variety can be confusing.

Surfaces in an interior are not flat, as in a painting; they project into space and receive differing amounts of light. Thus, a surface or pattern that appears one way in a swatch will often appear different when used in a room. Wallpapers, for example, appear one way in a sample book, but quite different on four walls of a room.[4] The ability to evaluate surfaces, textures, and patterns comes with experience but using small color charts and swatches is only moderately helpful in developing color plans.

The primary purpose of a color plan is to provide a background for people. Color can improve the quality of life and meet the nonverbalized needs of the client. It should en-

hance the total design concept and be well balanced in hue, value, and intensity.

Generally, the more intense a color is, the more pleasant is its appearance. High-intensity colors are usually more arousing, especially when combined with strong tints. Reds and oranges are usually more arousing than blues and greens, with yellows falling somewhere between. Reds and oranges stimulate activity, excitement, and desire, and are useful in areas in which one wishes to promote competition, high-energy output, and sexual activity. Blues and greens, which have a calming effect, are useful in areas in which affection, tenderness, sensitivity, and concentration are desired. Yellow, which has been found to stimulate creativity and to energize, is especially useful in areas in which originality and inspiring activities are directed towards lofty goals. The more intense the color, the more likely it is to produce these effects. Colored lights can effectively change the familiar to the novel by modifying the hues of a given space.

One other consideration in planning with color is the presence of mirrors in a space. A mirror reflects the wall opposite it: if the wall is extremely plain, the effect will be a doubled lack of excitement; conversely, if the wall is very rich in color, a reflection may be too exciting. A more appealing balance is the reflection of warmth, moderately stimulating in color and shape.

Color Distribution

One general rule of color distribution is to use a darker value for the floor coverings (representative of the earth), a medium color for the walls and furnishings (representative of trees, rocks, hills, and so on), and the lightest color for the ceiling (representative of the sky). This is the kind of separation of values to which people have become accustomed. In a given setting, however, one sees the dominant color as almost colorless. It seems to be the natural color in relationship to all the other colors in the room and those colors take their cue from the dominant or natural color. For example, a gray object may appear green if it is darker than the predominant color in the room. If the gray is to appear gray, the surrounding area must be darker in contrast to the gray.

All the hues on the color wheel are available for use in the interior, but most successful interiors are built around three hues, varied in

---

[3] *Ibid,* pp. 209–210.
[4] Part of this difference is due to the fact that sample books are hand printed and the actual product is mass produced.

Figure 5.7
Developing a color scheme:
Step 1: Select three hues,
equal amounts of each.
Step 2: Change the values.
Step 3: Adjust intensities.
Step 4: Change the areas.

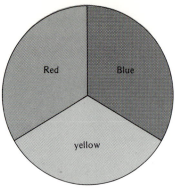

Step 1: Select 3 hues—equal amounts of each.

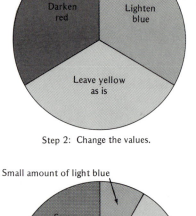

Step 2: Change the values.

Step 3: Adjust intensities.

Step 4: Change of areas.

value and intensity. Bright, warm, advancing colors are generally used in small areas, as accents, to attract attention, while neutral, grayed colors are planned for walls and floors. Too many equally intense colors will compete with each other and cancel the effectiveness of all.

There are many ways to develop a color environment. One method is to build an interior around an important painting or fabric. Another is to select a bouquet of flowers and develop the colors from them. A third way (Fig. 5.7), is to select three hues, to vary the values and the intensities of two of them, and to vary the areas to which they are applied, for an even distribution of color is boring and a common mistake. A good rule of thumb is to have 65–80 per cent shades or tints of one color, 20–35 per cent of another, and about 5–10 per cent of the third. Off-white walls should be treated as part of the floor color.

Color Wheel Schemes

There are many different types of color schemes, including: monochromatic, complementary, split complementary, double complementary, analogous, triad, tetrad, and neutral. These schemes should be creatively developed from a background knowledge of color.

Development of Interior Color Environments

Before a color environment can be developed, several decisions must be made. These are based on the personal taste of the clients, the character of the interior (size, architectural details, light orientation), the climate, and an awareness of the psychological effects of color.

Table 5.2
Development of the Color Environment

1. Personal taste of the client
2. Use of the space; commercial or residential; public or private
3. Character of the interior (use of neutrals, rich, or bright colors)
   a. Historic or contemporary
   b. Formal or casual
4. Backgrounds (accentuation or minimization of architectural details)
5. Orientation (color values required by light conditions—e.g., light walls conserve energy by requiring less artificial light)
6. Climate (warm colors may require more air conditioning for comfort just as cool colors may require more heat)
7. Psychological effects of color

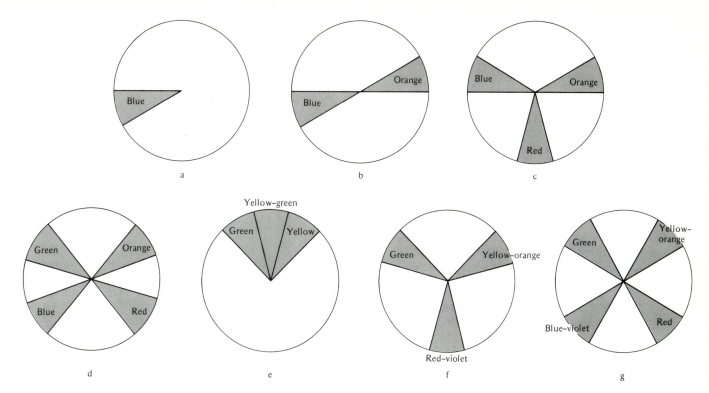

a   b   c

d   e   f   g

A Monochromatic Environmental Color Plan

A monochromatic plan is composed of one hue in many values and intensities (Fig. 5.8a). It is simple and works well with either traditional or contemporary interiors (Plate 12). This plan can be sophisticated, elegant, unified, and relaxing—or it can be dull and monotonous. If the values in a monochromatic plan are kept high, the space seems to expand (Plate 10), but if they are kept low or very warm, the space will be dramatic but appear smaller (Plate 11).

All color environments are most successful when developed with irregularity, so that the intervals between the values are definite and apparent and there are no equal areas of color (Plate 12).

A Complementary Environmental Color Plan

A complementary plan is composed of two colors directly opposite each other on the color wheel, although in reality many plans are developed with colors which are only almost directly opposite each other (Fig. 5.8b). Instead of using blue and orange, a blue of middle value and a yellow-orange of high value might be selected (Plate 13). A complementary color plan can be subdued as well, with the use of soft, dulled tones.

A Split Complementary Environmental Color Plan

A split complementary plan is a variation of the complementary plan. It utilizes one hue

and the two hues on either side of its complement (Fig. 5.8c). Again one of the hues may be further away from the complement for interest. The multi-purpose room in Plate 14 is a split complementary plan. The red and the orange of the wood are opposite blue on the color wheel. This is slightly varied from a true split complementary plan which would have required the use of red-orange and yellow-orange with the use of blue. The variation makes for interest and allows a more creative use of color. Split complementary color plans are less intense than complementary ones.

A Double Complementary Environmental Color Plan

A double complementary plan is simply the use of two pairs of complements (Fig. 5.8d). Sometimes the colors are close on the color wheel and sometimes widely separated. For example blue-green and red-orange combined with yellow-green and red-violet are one double complementary plan, while blue and orange and red and green are another (Plate 15).

An Analagous Environmental Color Plan

An analogous plan is one in which the hues used each contain some of one hue (Fig. 5.8e and Plate 16).

A Triadic Environmental Color Plan

A triadic plan can be intense or subdued depending upon the intensity and values used. These are plans which are composed of colors which are equidistant from each other on the color wheel (Fig. 5.8f, Plates 32 and 17).

Figure 5.8
5.8a. Monochromatic environmental color plan in shades and tints of blue.
5.8b. Complementary environmental color plan in blue and orange.
5.8c. Split complementary environmental color plan in blue, orange, and red.
5.8d. Double complementary environmental color plan in green and red, blue and orange.
5.8e. Analagous environmental color plan in green, yellow-green, and yellow.
5.8f. Triadic environmental color plan in green, yellow-orange, and red-violet.
5.8g. Tetradic environmental color plan in green and red, blue-violet and yellow-orange.

A Tetradic Environmental Color Plan

A tetradic plan is one in which four colors equidistant on the color wheel are used (Fig. 5.8g). It is somewhat similar to the split contemporary plan, except that four colors are used instead of three (Plate 18).

A Neutral Environmental Color Plan

A neutral plan is one in which neutral or grayed colors are used. These interiors usually rely on art or accessories for interest. Neutral color plans are tranquil in feeling (Plate 8).

Selection of an Environmental Color Plan

Color studies have shown that if individuals like a hue, they will generally like adjacent hues. Analogous color plans, therefore, are an obvious safe choice. Other recent studies have shown that in spite of the fact that people believe that colors in a room advance or recede, they perceive only red walls to be closer than blue walls. Apparently people cannot detect differences in other colors. Light values and low intensities will make a room appear larger and dark values and intensities will make it appear smaller, but the color does not appear to matter.

In selecting a color plan, the designer should work carefully with the clients, determining what they like, what they want and what will work best for them. The clients may not always be able to verbalize these desires, but the designer must determine them if the interior color plan is to be successful.

In designing a color plan for an entire house, the designer must relate colors from one room to another, although they need not be the same colors. For example, the living room may be gold, burnt orange and soft green, changing to bright orange and yellow in the next room and citrus green and lemon yellow in the next, and so on. Each room has an element of color from the previous one so that all are related to one another. It should be obvious that all rooms that can be seen belong together and are not totally isolated from each other. There is also an economic factor involved since furniture from one room can be moved into another without appearing out of place. Carefully planned color which flows from one room to another is not monotonous, but unified.

Glossary

Additive. Mixture of colored lights to produce colors.
Advancing Colors. Colors closest to yellow and yellow-green.
Aniline Dyes. Colors made from coal-tar derivitives.
Chroma. Amount of pigment in or saturation of a color.
Color Wheel. Placement of colors on a wheel or circle.
Colorimeter. Device that gives the sum of the radiant energy for a primary color.
Cool Colors. Colors on the blue and violet side of the color wheel.
Dichroic Substractive Filter. Device that allows the wavelengths of a particular color to pass through.
Hue. Name of a color.
Intensity. See Chroma.
Metamerism. Changes in color when viewed under different kinds of light.
Munsell System. Color system developed by Albert Munsell based upon a theoretical solid global form.
Ostwald System. Arrangement of colors developed by Wilhelm Ostwald describing colors in terms of purity, whiteness, and blackness.
Receding Color. Colors nearer to infrared and ultraviolet.
Shade. Determined by addition of black to a color, darkening it.
Simultaneous Contrast. Influences of a color's hue, value, and intensity on those surrounding it.
Spectrophotometer. Device that measures the reflectance curve of a color.
Subtractive Method of Color Production. A filtering out of all wavelengths except those of a certain color.
Tint. Determined by addition of white to a color, lightening it.
Value. Lightness or darkness of a color.
Visual After-image. Projection of a complement of a viewed color onto a white surface.
Warm Colors. Colors on the red, orange, and yellow side of the color wheel.

Bibliography

ALBERS, JOSEF. *Interaction of Color*. New Haven: Yale University Press, 1971.
BIRREN, FABER. *Color Primer: A Basic Treatise on the*

Color System of Wilhelm Ostwald. New York: Van Nostrand Reinhold Company, 1969.

BIRREN, FABER. *Color for Interiors.* New York: Whitney Library of Design, 1963.

———. *Creative Color.* New York: Van Nostrand Reinhold Company, 1961.

———. *Light, Color, and Environment.* New York: Van Nostrand Reinhold Company, 1969.

———. *Principles of Color.* New York: Van Nostrand Reinhold Company, 1969.

GRAVES, MAITLAND. *Color Fundamentals.* New York: McGraw-Hill Book Company, 1952.

———. *The Art of Color and Design,* 2nd ed. New York: McGraw-Hill Book Company, 1951.

General Electric Light and Color. Cleveland, Ohio, 1977.

ITTEN, JOHANNES. *The Art of Color.* New York: Van Nostrand Reinhold Company, 1973.

KUPPERS, HARALD. *Color: Origin, Systems, Uses.* New York: Van Nostrand Reinhold Company, 1973.

MUNSELL, ALBERT H. *Grammar of Color: A Basic Treatise on the Color System of Albert H. Munsell.* New York: Van Nostrand Reinhold Company, 1969.

———. *Munsell System of Color Notation.* Baltimore: Munsell Color Co.

SMITH, CHARLES N. *Student Handbook of Color.* New York: Van Nostrand Reinhold Company, 1965.

TAYLOR, GORDON RATTRAY. *The Natural History of the Mind.* New York: Elsevier-Dutton Publishing Co., Inc., 1979.

VARLEY, HELEN (ed). *Color.* New York: The Viking Press, 1980.

THE INTERIOR ENVIRONMENT

TWO

The Interior Environment

The Interior Space

Most people view the home as a static place, a reference point. The term *homestead* implies an unchanging refuge. Although the home is our basic source of protection and sustenance, it continues to evolve with changes in our needs and in our patterns of living. The interior environment is the stage upon which our lives are acted out; it influences our interaction with one another; it reflects our personalities, our goals, and ourselves.

Hotels, motels, apartments, condominiums, and hospitals are classified in the *Dodge Reports* as residential design, using the definition to mean any place where one spends the night. This means, in essence, that the dividing line between residential and commercial design is narrow and that most aspects of interior design covered in this book can be applied to both residential and commercial design.

Modern architects and designers have emphasized the importance of designing the home to meet the problems of people in contemporary society. To Gustav Stickley, a home could be simple, small, and inexpensive as long as it met the physical, mental, and moral needs of its occupants and harmonized with its surroundings (Fig. 6.1a).[1] Frank Lloyd Wright sought to provide an uplifting environment for people by designing homes from the inside out (Fig. 6.1b). It was from this idea that the term *organic* (growth out of the nature of the object), became associated with Wright. Le Corbusier also held the belief that homes should meet the specific needs of their occupants. Marcel Breuer developed the *bi-nuclear* or two-centered house to challenge the specific housing problems of the twentieth century.

In interior design, the arrangement of space has become more important than the amount of space. The use of multi-purpose spaces has become part of the solution to the problem of smaller homes. The living room (which replaced the old-fashioned parlor) and the dining room can be replaced by one multi-purpose room. A studio apartment encompasses all the activities of life (Fig. 6.2). The combination living- dining-kitchen area is popular in the Pacific Northwest. The resulting open plan appears more spacious than a closed plan and allows for a more diversified use of the space. But the area must still be divided into zones for privacy, food preparation, personal hygiene, entertainment and group activities, and storage.

These same space contraints also apply to commercial spaces. For example, many offices are planned using modular components to divide the space. Office landscaping, first developed in the 1960's in Germany by the Quickborner Team, creates an environment based upon communication and work flow. Its flexability has made it popular world-wide, and, as a result, many interior design firms specialize in it today.

The Open Plan

Early American homes were built on an open plan: one room served for all family activities. As the colonists began to tame the frontier and wealth increased, homes with several rooms came to be built. By the Victorian Period, rooms for very specialized purposes were typical: the library, the billiard room, the gallery, the ladies' sitting room, the saloon (for music and dancing), and the card room. Gradually, living patterns have changed and today an informal style is typical even of trend-setting homes. With this change, the open plan, which Ballie Scott and Wright used so frequently, has re-emerged. Between 1907 and 1916 the parlor vanished and the living room merged with the hall and the library to become the hub of family activity.[2] Wright's Usonian house, exhibited in New York, brought the open plan to the public's attention.

In the open plan, space continuously flows from one zone to another. Space may not be assigned to specific activities; the inhabitants move themselves to participate in these activities. Often several activities may take place in one space at different times (Figs. 6.3, 6.4).

Open planning is especially suited to people who enjoy frequent interaction, but it does have disadvantages. Unless sound and sight buffers are planned, the space may be noisy and lacking in privacy. Careful placement of furniture and other objects is necessary to seg-

---

[1] Gustav Stickley, "The Craftsman's House: A Practical Application of All the Theories of Homebuilding Advocated in this Magazine," *The Craftsman,* **XV** (Oct. 1908), 78.

[2] Mary Jo Weale, James Croake, and W. Bruce Weale, "Whatever Happened to the Parlor? A Look at Housing Changes from 1840 to 1972," *Self, Space and Shelter* (San Francisco, Calif.: Canfield Press, 1977), pp. 415–421.

Figure 6.1a
A corner of the living room in Stickley's farm house. From The Craftsman *(Oct. 1908).*

Figure 6.1b
An early house by Frank Lloyd Wright. From House Beautiful *(Aug. 1908).*

Figure 6.2
This studio apartment combines a kitchen, dining and conversation area in a small, well-planned, functional space. Interior designer: Emy Leeser. (Courtesy of Belgian Linen Association)

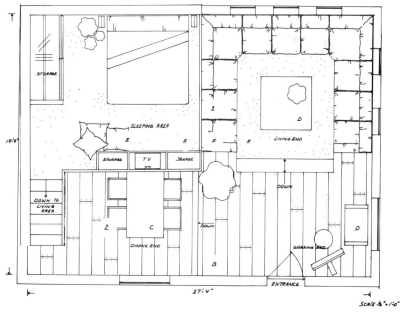

Figure 6.3
A modern open plan combines a sleeping loft over the kitchen-dining area. The entire space, only 27½ feet by 19 feet, affords a comfortable living and working space. Interior designer: William Branch Storey. (Courtesy of Barcalounger)

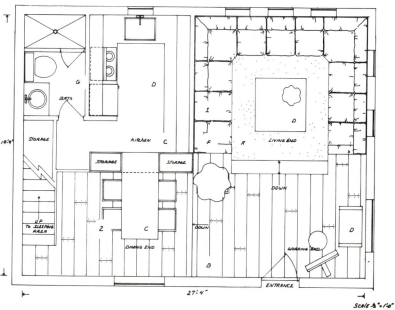

regate activities and to create visual interest (Fig. 6.5).

The Closed Plan

The closed plan is the division of space into separate rooms for specific activities. This plan may be perferred when there are different generations within the same house, when the occupants desire privacy, or when there is a need to close off portions of the house for work or play, to save energy, or to control noise.

It is usually easier to arrange furniture in rooms rather than in an open space, because there is more wall space (Fig. 6.6). The closed plan limits change because it is less flexible and appears smaller than an open space of comparable size.

Personality is a factor in space utilization. Individuals who are greatly dependent upon interaction with others do poorly in small, enclosed areas. Under such circumstances they may begin to display signs of tension, intolerance of the behavior of other family members, agitation, and general restlessness. Individuals who have a low need for interpersonal interaction do very well in limited space. When they desire to concentrate attention, they prefer a smaller room, avoiding the possible interruptions found in a larger room. The gregarious individual, on the other hand, welcomes the possibility of such distraction.

Division of Space

Biological Space

Biological space is that required for the daily requisites of life: renewal (sleeping and sex), food preparation (kitchen), and personal hygiene (bathroom and laundry). In Breuer's binuclear plan, the house is divided into two wings: one contains facilities for renewal and personal hygiene (private spaces); the other, facilities for food preparation, entertainment, and group activities (public spaces). Other houses have bedrooms and bath separated

MUTIPURPOSE ENVIRONMENT
(FAMILY ROOM / KITCHEN / DINING)

Figure 6.5
A multi-purpose environment designed for a young career couple. The free flow of space allows dinner to be prepared while conversation continues. The family-room area is defined by the area carpet, and the television is placed near the fireplace. Interior designer: Robert J. King. (Courtesy of Barcalounger)

from the noises of the inside and outside though not in a separate wing; still others have bedrooms and bath on a separate floor.

Renewal

Bedrooms constitute renewal space and are essentially designed for sleeping, sexual activity, and dressing. Since bedrooms are normally isolated from the rest of the house and from visitors, they are often neglected. This was not always the case, however. In earlier periods, beds were a status symbol. The ancient Romans had beds of silver and bronze; during the region of Louis XIV, seventeen-foot beds were richly upholstered in the most luxurious of fabrics shot with silver and gold; some of the great houses in England had a bed in every room and guests were often received with the host and/or hostess in beds.

In seventeenth-century America, beds were often merely wooden frames with strips of rawhide stretched across them to support the bedding, or just piles of straw on the floor. Early household, inventories, however, mention feather mattresses, and imported bedsteads were highly prized. Bedrooms were often combined with the dining room, the parlor, and the hall and the parlor-bedchamber, for example, survived until the early twentieth century. In New England, the custom of bundling provided privacy and warmth for a courting couple: the family sat by the fire and the young people were tucked into a jack bed with a board in the center to keep them separate.

The space allocated to the bedroom today depends upon the use to which it is put. If the room is used primarily for sleeping, comparatively little space is necessary, but if it is used for watching television, reading, or even bathing, a larger space is needed (Fig. 6.7 and Plate 20). Sleeping space may be built into the wall (Fig. 6.8), concealed in a cabinet (Fig. 6.9) or shaped imaginatively like a sneaker (Plate 21). A bed may be placed in an otherwise unusable space because little head room is required (Fig. 6.10).

The main item of furniture in the bedroom is, of course, the bed. It should be placed first when the room is being planned. Bedside tables on each side of the bed with light sources for reading or for night-time emergencies are important, and the light switches should be easily reached from the bed. The bedroom should be insulated from household and outside noise and well ventilated. Storage

Figure 6.6
A dining room need not be large, if the ceiling is as high as the one in this room, creating an illusion of more space. (Courtesy of Kirsch Co.)

for clothing should include at least five feet of hanging space for each person as well as shelf space, and drawer or bin space. If a dressing area is included in the room, there should be a place to sit down, a mirror and a light for applying cosmetics, and a full-length mirror—not just for checking one's appearance but also because increasingly health-conscious Americans realize that it is more effective than the bathroom scale for estimating proper body weight (Fig. 6.11).

Health awareness is also making the bedroom an exercise area where one can do morning and evening calisthenics free of the restraints of clothing and in much less than the time required to go to a gym or health club. The floor of a bedroom used for exercise requires padding and carpeting.

Many couples pay considerable attention to the bedroom as the prime area for sexual expression. Some clients request large mirrors on the walls surrounding the bed and even on the ceiling. The waterbed is reputed to enhance sexual behavior, but requires a sturdy floor to support its weight. Stereophonic equipment provides appealing mood music.

The bedroom should be protected both visually and acoustically from the rest of the house. Visually protection may be provided by variation in levels (Fig. 6.4), by halls, by

Figure 6.7
With space for reading and conversation, the bedroom can become the pivotal point of the home. Walls and bed in this luxurious bedroom are covered with linen, a fabric that has natural acoustical and insulation properties. The carpet is an antique Aubusson. (Courtesy of Belgian Linen Association)

Figure 6.8
Climbing into bunks built into the wall makes bedtime inviting to children. The wallpaper is tough and scrubbable. (Courtesy of Wallcovering Information Bureau)

other continuous noises are more readily adjusted to in sleeping than in waking hours. Most individuals adjust within a few days even to noise that is unpredictable or irregular, but assaultive noise during waking hours may result in increased depression, diminished well-being, and even suicide.

Children's Space

Young children's bedrooms, usually a combination play-sleeping-study area, are generally close to the parent's bedroom. The space must be versatile so that it can be adapted to the rapidly changing needs of the child. The room should have easy access to a bathroom and mirrors, and clothing storage at a convenient height should be provided. As the child grows older, more play space is required (Fig. 6.12); when the child enters high school, study space becomes more important. Space should be provided for the things children like to collect; blackboards for writing and drawing; and corkboards for the pinning up of cherished items.

As childrens' interests change and they become more or less, gregarious, space should be provided for storage, for grooming, and for music. Ideally, entertainment space for teenagers can be provided in the family area.

Children are not often involved in the design of their rooms, but even young children should be consulted. Children have definite ideas and should be guided to express them.

Color schemes and furnishings for children's rooms should not be too bright or heavily patterned, but durable and easy to

partial or complete walls, or by location in a separate wing of the house. Acoustical separation can be achieved by buffer zones (closets, built-in storage, or halls), by insulation of the walls, or by the use of surface materials such as wall carpet or fabric.

Noise control in the bedroom is important; however, if external noise is a problem, rooms should be arranged so that conversation and study areas (dens, libraries) are placed farthest from the noise. Industrial noise usually diminishes after working hours, while highway and

Figure 6.9
A bed concealed in a cabinet allows the floor space to be used for other purposes during the day. (Courtesy of Charles Eames)

Figure 6.10
A bed placed under a slanted ceiling allows use of otherwise unusable space. An old packing space serves as a bedside table. (Courtesy of Groundworks, Inc.)

Figure 6.11
The mirrored wall not only
expands space but helps to
observe proper body weight.
(Courtesy of Binswanger
Mirror Company)

Figure 6.12
Play space, with both
climbing and slide
equipment, is provided for
in a child's bedroom.
Student design: Steve
Louis, Pratt Institute.

hyperactive, too much color stimulation may lead to disturbed behavior. On the other hand, the slow child can benefit from bright, stimulating colors, just as depressed adults and elderly people do.

All too often, however, the child's bedroom is seen by the designer as an area in which the restraint exercised throughout the remainder of the house can give way to the creative, wild, or whimsical aspect of the designer's own personality. Such aspects of the designer's personality are better expressed in less critical areas of the interior.

The amount of space allotted to the renewal area depends upon the size of the house, the number of occupants, as well as their ages, their cultural background, and their personal preferences.

Food Preparation

Historical Background

The kitchen reflects changing societal patterns. It began as the center of family life and was the province of the wife and daughters. Today the kitchen is regaining its position as the center of family life, although it is no longer solely the domain of the wife: with dual family breadwinners, many kitchen tasks are shared.

Early kitchens were not designed for convenience, although they had to accommodate food preparation, visitors, and even play ac-

maintain. Carpets, bedspreads, and window hangings should be able to withstand rough handling and be soil-resistant.

Close attention to the use of color in children's rooms will be beneficial for their behavior. Bright and exciting colors stimulate activity and are beneficial for children until about the age of two (Plate 5); thereafter, however, normal children may find bright and vibrant colors over-stimulating: they may have difficulty in settling down at bedtime, and they may become argumentive, irritable, and rebellious. For the child who tends to be

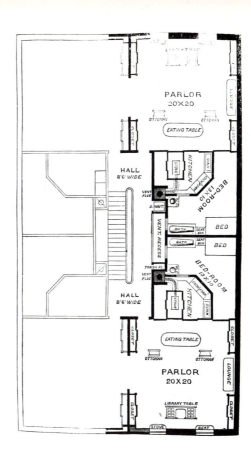

Figure 6.13
A plan by the Beecher sisters for two apartments with a central utility core.

tivities. During the long winter months, family members kept warm in front of the big, open fireplace. Kitchen tasks were never-ending and seldom shared: water was pumped by hand and carried into the house for cooking and cleaning; soap was made by boiling animal fat and lye made from wood ashes; candles were usually made at home; because there was no refrigeration, root cellars and ice houses (the ice cut from winter ponds and stored in sawdust) were used to keep foods as cool as possible, while larders and pantries were used to store nonperishables.

Gradually circumstances changed and by the middle of the nineteenth century, the Beecher sisters, advanced for their time, were the first to advocate better kitchen-planning and a central utility core, with the "close packing of conveniences"[3] saving time, money, and labor (Fig. 6.13). The advice of the Beecher sisters went unheeded for over fifty years; until women entered the work force and domestic servants became unavailable.

In the latter part of the nineteenth century, the open fire for cooking was replaced by the wood, coal, or gas stove. By 1884 there were inside water pumps and by 1890 the icebox was on the market. Enamel ware followed in 1900. Laundry, washed in the kitchen or basement, was put through hand-cranked wringers. By 1908 primitive electric stoves with temperature control became available, but they were impractically slow. Washing machines with agitators were on the market, but they had to be filled, emptied, and refilled by hand, and the laundry had to be hand-dipped into starch and bluing. The icebox was now stored on the screened back porch (screens were an innovation of this period) and the kitchen shrank to about two-thirds its former size during this decade (to about 11′ × 15′). Studies of kitchen efficiency began to be undertaken.

In the decade after World War I, with more and more women seeking employment outside the home and fewer domestic servants available, there was a demand for more efficiency in the kitchen so tasks could be simplified. Breakfast nooks became popular for quick meals and standardized cabinets were introduced in 1922. Kitchen appliances and re-

frigerators were now available in "decorator colors" as well as in white.

In the 1930s and 1940s, utility in kitchen design became increasingly important. A garage door off the kitchen simplified food flow from car to kitchen to table. The kitchen began to regain its status as the hub of family activity and islands were built in the center for extra work space. An informal kitchen-eating area replaced the breakfast nook. Kitchen cabinet space began to decrease after the proliferation of neighborhood markets and widespread ownership of cars made the storage of large quantities of food unnecessary.

New inventions and appliances deluged the market in the 1950s. Kitchens became triangular, hexagonal, and trapezoidal—and increasingly efficient. Garbage disposals, component stoves, warming trays, electric knife-sharpeners, and cooking utensils that doubled as serving dishes were now available along with freezers, dishwashers, and washers and dryers. Freezers and the two-car family made monthly shopping popular. By the 1960s convenience prevailed, with cordless appliances, microwave ovens, and the smooth glass cooking top by Corning. Food preparation was supplemented by a growing $3 billion frozen-food industry and the fact that families were eating out more often. By 1982 members of the average family were eating more than one third of their meals away from home.

Other changes will be reflected in the kitchen of the 1980s. These will be spurred in

[3] Catherine E. Beecher and Harriet Beecher Stowe, *The American Woman's Home or Principles of Domestic Science* (New York: J. B. Ford and Co., 1869), p. 83.

part by the interest in natural foods and in gourmet cooking. Not only have tastes become more sophisticated, but both men and women are sharing the cooking chores. Moreover, mini-meals are in focus now with family members eating at different times and often on the run.

New appliances such as food processors and speciality cooking aids are becoming prevalent in the home. Other additions include new energy-efficient appliances: more effectively insulated refrigerators and stoves that prevent the escape of warm and cool air; air-dry cycles on dishwashers; and convection microwave ovens, which operate on a fraction of the energy required by conventional ovens; and magnetic cooking devices.

Magnetic reactance—or, as it is sometimes termed, *induction cooking*—is as different from the standard method of heating food as is microwave cooking. A solid-state power-supply module raises the frequency of conventional electricity and creates an alternating magnetic field that heats the cast-iron or steel utensils placed atop the cooking surface. Because the magnetic field heats the utensil rather than the stovetop, the food within the utensil is more rapidly heated, and the stove receives only the heat transferred from the utensil. There are no burners to clean, so meal preparation can be shortened. Instant temperature changes, from simmering to boiling, are possible.

The kitchen has swung full circle from the living/sleeping/working and birth and death room of the pioneers to the cold, white machine of 1920s, and now back to the kitchen/family room where study, recreation, eating, cooking and laundering all take place (Plate 22). It was only in the early part of this century that the kitchen range was hailed as a labor-saving breakthrough. Today's computer-controlled appliances and ovens are a far cry from that first range.

The future will require even more adaptation to changing household size. Census reports show that 51 per cent of the country's 73 million households are now made up of no more than two people, as compared with 41 per cent in 1960; 21 per cent of all households consist of a single person (in the 1970's alone, there was a 40 per cent increase in the number of persons living alone). By 1985 this is expected to increase to 30 per cent of all households. Over half of all adult women are working full time. The shapes and functions of the kitchen must be redesigned to reflect these social trends.

The most dramatic evolutionary development in the home since the advent of indoor plumbing is the computer. By the close of the 1980s a computerized kitchen will be as necessary as a refrigerator. The computer, no matter where it is located in the home, has a variety of uses: it can keep track of the type and quantity of food on hand and can order automatically from the grocery when supplies are low; it can report which menus might be appropriate to a given occasion, particular to nutritional or medical needs, to individual tastes, or to the number of calories already consumed that day and the amount of physical energy expended.

The computer can be programmed to begin cooking various dishes at different times, to lower the heat, to defrost dessert in time for a seven o'clock dinner. It can determine the amount of food to be prepared by an electronic computation of earlier consumption rates for specific food. It can instantly report meal costs in relation to purchase prices and to the time required for preparation and cleaning up. Other purchases or preparation methods can be instantly compared for better efficiency. The computer is able to activate such appliances as the dishwasher and even automatically clear a table and place used dishes and silver into a dishwasher.

Kitchen Planning

Perhaps no other room in the household has stimulated more research into its use and efficiency than the kitchen. Studies have centered on the tasks performed, the design and placement of work centers, and the relationship of such centers to one another and to changing patterns of living. The sale or resale of a house is more dependent upon the quality of the kitchen than upon that of any other area of the house. Money spent in remodeling the kitchen will probably increase the value of the home whereas money spent on other areas may or may not.

Before beginning the kitchen plan, the designer should determine what type of room is needed and how it will be used. This can be accomplished by asking certain questions:

1. Will the cooking be done by one person or by several people?

2. Will the cooking be done for one person or for a family unit?
3. Is the cooking gourmet cooking, plain family cooking, quick-meal preparation, or a combination of these?
4. Is entertaining with food common and for how many guests?
5. What number of dishes and utensils need to be stored?
6. How often are groceries purchased and for how many? What storage facilities will be required?
7. Where will the kitchen be in relationship to the eating area(s)?
8. Will the kitchen be combined with another room, such as a family room?
9. What other tasks will be performed in the kitchen—entertaining? menu-planning? sewing? laundry?
10. Will cooking be done while young children are entertained or watched?
11. Is saving steps important?
12. Are there any unusual requirements?

Time-and-motion studies by the U.S. Department of Agriculture, Cornell University, and the University of Illinois, along with manufacturers of kitchen equipment, such as Poggenpohl, have determined how a well-planned kitchen contrasts with one that is poorly planned or too large. Poggenpohl made a series of photographs of the cook with a strobe light attached to her, and found that forty-six working days per year could be saved in a well-designed kitchen of the right size.

A kitchen should be aesthetically pleasing as well as efficient. The heights of the cabinets and work surfaces, the work triangle, and the relationship of the work centers to one another, to the eating areas, and to outside access should be planned to meet the physical needs of the user. For most tasks (except those that require force) counter tops should be approximately three inches below the elbow height when the arm is flexed. In an existing kitchen, especially tall or short users should have one counter raised or lowered to the correct height. In addition, the kitchen should be located near an outside entry to facilitate grocery delivery, and should be accessible to outside living spaces and play areas (if there are young children in the family). Cooking and eating on the deck or patio and in the backyard continue to be popular and the exit from the kitchen is the most convenient route for carrying food into and out of the house. Easy access to a bath and the laundry are essential and, of course, eating areas should be near to facilitate dining and entertaining. It has been found that families who have kitchen eating spaces do not use their dining rooms and the elimination of the dining room, or its combination with another room, can save space.

Work Centers

Work centers used to be limited to the clean-up or sink center, the cooking center, the mixing center, and the refrigerator center. With the proliferation of new appliances for the kitchen, and changes in eating habits, this has drastically changed. There may be several centers for cooking. Energy-saving ideas are numerous and include extra insulation on gas stoves, induction units, convection ovens (in which a flow of hot air is directed onto food by a fan, cooking it as much as 30 per cent more rapidly), special dishwashing cycles, faucet attachments which reduce water flow, and microwave ovens. The old-fashioned cast-iron range which uses wood or coal with hot-water coils is making a comeback in new-fashioned versions. Part of a kitchen counter may be constructed to make room for an herb garden (Fig. 6.14). Other kitchens have indoor barbeques. Work centers should be carefully planned to prevent wasting space and energy, and they should be logically arranged according to their use.

Kitchen storage should be accessible, and frequently used items should be easy to remove and store. Food storage may be concealed behind doors. Wall cabinets should have low door pulls; base cabinets, high pulls. Factory-made cabinets may be of wood, laminated plastic, or metal. Custom-made cabinets

Figure 6.14
Part of a kitchen counter may be constructed to make room for an herb garden cultivated in removable trays. (Courtesy of Tile Council of America)

Figure 6.15
A rotary tower with 17 spice jars and 5 sauce containers makes them accessible. The spice cabinet attached to the door. (Courtesy of Poggenpohl)

Figure 6.16
A corner unit with swivel shelves utilizes the "dead" space in inaccessible corners. The lower shelf swings out with the door, but the upper shelf is turned separately by hand. (Courtesy of Poggenpohl)

Figure 6.17
The waste bin can be installed under the sink. As the door opens, the waste bin cover automatically opens. (Courtesy of Poggenpohl)

Figure 6.18
A bottle cupboard has been a feature of French and Swiss kitchens for years. This one holds oil, vinegar and wine bottles. Smaller bottles and packages are housed in two wire baskets on top. (Courtesy of Poggenpohl)

may be of wood. A kitchen should contain a minimum of ten linear feet of wall and base cabinets in addition to cabinets under the sink and over the range and the refrigerator. Wall cabinets are twelve to thirteen inches deep and twelve to thirty-six inches high, and base cabinets are about twenty-four inches from the front of the counter to the wall and thirty-six inches high, with the addition of the counter top. This means that countertops are frequently too high for many women and some adjustment needs to be made for maximum comfort. Specialized cabinets include revolving shelves (Fig. 6.15), tray and lid storage, pull-out swivel storage (Fig. 6.16), waste bin storage (Fig. 6.17), built-in bottle storage (Fig. 6.18), spice storage (Fig. 6.15), pull-out staple storage (Fig. 6.19), and a pull-out serving cart.

Counters may be of laminated plastic, stainless steel, glass ceramic, or wood. Different surfaces are necessary in different areas of the kitchen. Laminated plastic, durable and easily maintained, comes in many patterns, finishes, and colors. Because it is not impervious to knicks and burns, it should not be used for chopping or hot dishes (Plate 22 has a red laminated plastic counter and a wood chopping counter). Glass ceramic is an excellent surface near the range because it is heat-proof. Ceramic tile makes a good cutting surface but dulls knives. A stainless steel counter, although expensive, is easily maintained, moisture-proof, and will not crack, chip, or break. It is advantageous next to the sink and range (Fig. 6.20). Wood makes an excellent chopping and cutting surface, although it is not moisture-proof and can be burned by hot pans (Plate 22). There also can be some difficulty in cleaning a rough surface, and sanitation is a consideration in the kitchen.

Kitchen floors should be easy to clean. Vinyl is excellent: easily maintained and resistant to grease, while cushioned (or "child-proof") vinyl is soft enough to prevent falling glasses from breaking and to make standing more comfortable. Carpeting and carpet tiles are comfortable although more difficult to maintain in areas of frequent spillage. Some carpets are stain-releasing, however, and individual carpet tiles may be replaced if stained or burned.

Flagstone, quarry tile, brick, and wood floors are sometimes used in kitchens that are also family rooms. These surfaces, although attractive and easy to maintain, are very hard: standing on them for long periods is tiring.

The Work Triangle

The work triangle is the area enclosed by an imaginary line connecting the refrigerator, the cooking area, and the sink. The perimeter of the triangle should not exceed twenty-five feet, to prevent wasted motion (Fig. 6.21a). Work centers opposite each other should be no more than five feet apart.

The U-shaped Kitchen

The U-shaped kitchen is the most efficient and functional of kitchen plans (Fig. 6.21b). It is compact, and thus reduces the number of wasted steps (ten feet should be the maximum at the base of the U). The center of this space may include a work island—sink, counter, or eating area. The end of the U may also include a leg to divide the kitchen from the family room (Fig. 6.22).

The L-shaped Kitchen

The L-shaped kitchen is adaptable to any interior (Fig. 6.21c). It can form an efficient work triangle and diverts traffic to some extent. The sequence of centers should be planned: from storage to clean-up to cooking to service. The open end may be used as an eating area and as a divider between the family room and the kitchen (Fig. 6.23).

Figure 6.19
This storage space for food is open on both sides and pulls out with the flick of a finger. (Courtesy of Poggenpohl)

Figure 6.20
A built-in stainless-steel drainboard is part of the sink unit. The built-in worktable lies flush against the cabinet when not in use. (Courtesy of Poggenpohl)

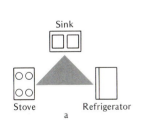

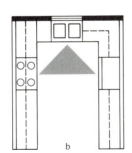

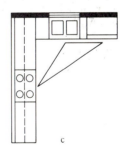

Figure 6.21
Kitchen Plans
a. Work triangle
b. U-shaped
c. L-shaped
d. Corridor
e. One-wall
f. Round

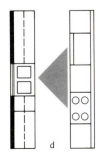

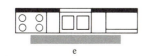

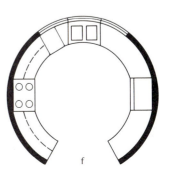

Figure 6.22
The U–shaped kitchen may include an eating area at one end. This one is of solid mahogany with silver-colored metal edges. The kitchen is one step lower than the eating area. (Courtesy of Poggenpohl)

should be placed in the center with the refrigerator and stove at opposite ends (Fig. 6.24).

The Kitchen-in-the-Round

An open-type kitchen similar to the U–shaped kitchen is the kitchen-in-the-round, especially suitable for garden-type or country kitchens (Fig. 6.25). Its main disadvantage is that appliances, usually rectangular, must be custom-fitted into its circular spaces.

With any of the open plans, social interaction is a factor. If the individual who will work in the kitchen enjoys the company of others or needs to closely supervise others, then the open kitchen is an asset. Those who find the presence of others in the kitchen area a distraction may find the corridor and U–shaped kitchen more suitable to their needs.

Clean-up Center

The sink or clean-up center is placed in the center of the kitchen, between the cooking and storage centers. It is the most frequently used area, used for washing fresh fruits and vegetables, disposing of garbage, providing water for cooking and mixing, and washing dishes and hands.

The Sink

Single, double, or even triple sinks may be selected, depending upon the needs of the user. Sinks are available in stainless steel or colored porcelain, and in step-down models (useful for the preparation of fresh foods). Extra accessories include spray hoses, single-lever faucets, water-saving devices, detergent dispensers, and an under-sink heater to deliver hot water from its own tap for instant drinks and soups and for food preparation (Fig. 6.20).

The Garbage Disposer

The garbage disposer is attached under the sink (the upper level in step-down models) and may be the continuous-feed type or the batch-feed type, which operates only when the lid is closed (a safety feature desirable in houses with small children).

The Dishwasher

The dishwasher is generally built in under the counter on the left side of the sink (Fig. 6.25). A disposer included in the dishwasher eliminates extensive scraping and rinsing.

Figure 6.23
This English L–shaped kitchen has an eating area in the open end. (Courtesy of Hygena, Ltd.)

The Corridor Kitchen

The corridor kitchen is efficient in terms of utilization of space, but if doors are placed at either end traffic may become a problem (Fig. 6.21d). Maximum counter space can be placed in the smallest space in the corridor kitchen. Corridor kitchens, best for long narrow rooms and typical of many apartments or condominimums, allow only one person to work at a time. The corridor should be at least six feet wide. A counter eating space may be placed at one end (Plate 23).

The One-wall Kitchen

The one-wall kitchen is most satisfactory for small open-plan houses and apartments (Fig. 6.21e). Prefabricated units can be concealed behind doors. The work pattern is difficult in this type of kitchen because counter space and storage space are usually lacking. A nearby closet is helpful for storage. The sink

Figure 6.24
A studio kitchen. The table forms an island.
Photograph by Bill Margerin. (Courtesy of Hardwood
Institute)

Most dishwashers are twenty-four inches wide.

The Trash Compactor

The trash compactor, placed to the right of the sink, mashes boxes, bottles, and cans into a solid bundle and needs be emptied only about twice a week.

Counters

A twenty-six-inch counter with built-in drainboard is needed to the left of the sink, with a twenty-four-inch counter to the right.

Storage

Storage is needed in the clean-up area for detergents, dishcloths and towels, scouring pads, vegetable knives, trash basket, cutting board, and any other items regularly used in this area.

The Mixing Center

The mixing center may be located between the storage center and the clean-up center or next to the cooking center. Sufficient electrical outlets as well as enclosed storage space should be provided for such small appliances as food processors, blenders, and mixers. This area should include space for cookbooks and perhaps a menu-planning center (Fig. 6.23). The mixing center is used for the preparation of foods for cooking as well as for the storage of leftovers (Fig. 6.23).

Counters

Counters four to six inches lower than the standard thirty-six inches are preferred for the use of appliances. The counter should be at least thirty-six inches long if several appliances are included in the kitchen.

Storage

The storage area should include space for condiments, dry foods, staples, packaged foods, and cookbooks, as well as for pans, bowls, and the many implements and small appliances used to prepare and store food.

The Cooking Center

The cooking center is ideally located near the mixing, sink, and serving areas. It requires

Figure 6.25
A kitchen-in-the-round is very similar to the U–shaped kitchen and can be wasteful of space if not carefully planned. (Courtesy of Cabinets by Kemper)

storage space for pans and cooking utensils as well as for cooking and serving. The final preparation of the meal takes place in this area, which means that it gets heavy use the last thirty minutes before the meal is served.

The Range

A built-in oven and drop-in cooking counter top require more space than a free-standing range, but built-ins offer more flexibility in placement (Fig. 6.23). The oven should be the self-cleaning or continuous-cleaning type. The self-cleaning pyrolytic oven removes soil by high heat; the contin-

Figure 6.27
A ventilating fan removes odors, humidity, and grease from the kitchen. (Courtesy of Poggenpohl)

Figure 6.26
The perfect solution for the hostess who wants to cook and enjoy the company of her guests at the same time, is the serving and flambé trolley. It has an electrical outlet, two drawers, bottle- and glass-holders, five spice canisters as well as a dish compartment. (Courtesy of Poggenpohl)

heat-resistant. A cutting board is a desirable addition in this area (Plate 22).

Counters

Storage is required for cooking utensils and for serving dishes for hot foods. These pieces can be hung on the wall or suspended from the ceiling above the counter. A wooden holder for knives is both convenient and necessary if knives are to be kept sharp. Placing knives in a drawer is dangerous—and a certain method for ruining their cutting edges. There should be a drawer for spatulas, ladles, and other implements required for cooking.

The Storage Center

The refrigerator and freezer are the main components of the storage center. This area is usually located at the end of the kitchen next to the mixing or clean-up center.

The Refrigerator and Freezer

Refrigerators may have many special features which include humidity-controlled drawers for leftovers; specialized storage; controlled temperature zones for various types of foods; ice-makers; water- and ice-dispensers; no-frost devices; adjustable, cantilevered shelves; and rollers (for easy mobility). The freezer may be a free-standing unit or part of the refrigerator (Fig. 6.19). Freezers can contribute greatly to waste as well as to savings unless frozen foods are carefully purchased and used. The contents of the freezer should be known at all times, and meals should be planned for effective utilization of frozen foods. The home computer is most useful in itemizing freezer contents, planning meals with existing supplies, and indicating what purchases are necessary to complement existing supplies of frozen foods.

Counters

The refrigerator should open into the adjacent storage area near an unloading-loading counter on the latch side, and it should be near an outside exit for easy unloading of groceries. Counters should be at least eighteen inches wide.

Storage

The storage area should include space for containers for refrigerator storage, for freezer supplies, for bottles, for foil, and so on.

uous-cleaning oven has a special finish that breaks down splatters and grease during normal use. Temperature sensing probes, rotisserie, griddle, grill, automatic memory and timer, and special broiler devices are other options. A microwave oven may be built-in, portable, or part of a free-standing range. A warming drawer is convenient for meals to be eaten at different times or for frequent entertaining. Also convenient is a serving and flambé trolley (Fig. 6.26).

Ventilation

Ventilation equipment to remove smoke, heat, odors, and moisture should be installed over the cooking surface or near it. A vented hood, equal to the width of the cooking top and set about thirty inches above it, removes odors, smoke, grease, heat, and moisture. Exhaust fans in the walls, the ceiling, or a window remove odors, smoke, moisture, and heat and may be used in addition to a hood. If it is impossible to vent directly to the outside, a hood and fan with filters may be used to remove odors, grease, and smoke (Fig. 6.27).

Storage

Twenty-four inches of counter space should be provided on either side of the cooking surface. The counter area to the right should be

Figure 6.28
A lavish Florida bathroom allows its owners to work, bathe, and relax in the sun. The stairs lead to a private roof garden. The oval tub is white marble. Antiques adorn the bath, including a Louis XV desk, an Empire mirror, and the ceiling chandelier. (Courtesy of Sherle Wagner International, Inc.)

The Serving Center

The serving center should be adjacent to the cooking center (and is often integrated into it) and to the eating center (Fig. 6.22).

Counters

A counter twenty-four inches wide is sufficient for a family of four. A pass-through facilitates serving if the eating area is not in the kitchen.

Storage

Storage should be provided for dishes, flatware, small appliances used at the table (such as the toaster, waffle iron, broiler, and coffeemaker), table linens, paper napkins, and condiments. If the eating area is in a separate room, cabinet space should open to each side.

The Eating Center

The eating center is frequently included in the kitchen. It may be an island, a counter leg (Fig. 6.20), a counter (Fig. 6.22), placed in the open end of the U– or L–shaped kitchen (Fig. 6.23), or in front of the one-wall kitchen (Fig. 6.24). Kitchens which include an eating area eliminate the need for a separate dining room. An eating counter for snacks or breakfast should be fifteen inches deep.

Personal Hygiene

Private bathroom facilities are a comparatively recent development. The Minoan and Roman civilizations had public baths with piped hot and cold running water, but during the Middle Ages, the Crusaders brought back shocking reports of Turkish baths. Somehow, the early Church had equated personal hygiene with sensual delights, sex, and sin, and taught that it was holy to ignore dirt and body care. Eating and drinking were considered more important than bathing. Public baths, called stews or bordellos,[4] spread by the end of the fourteenth century—for curative or sensual purposes—but only lasted until the close of the sixteenth century because they

were believed to spread venereal disease.[5] In colonial Philadelphia it was against the law to take a bath more frequently than once a month, and it was considered heresy when Benjamin Franklin advocated bathing twice a week. It was not until the nineteenth century, when the Victorians rediscovered washing, that public baths were again opened in England.

Today the bathroom has become increasingly important and is one expression of a larger social movement. It is not considered a sin to pamper one's body and there are very lavish bathrooms (Fig. 6.28) that allow their owners to work, bathe, and relax in the sun. A bathroom may become an atrium (Fig. 6.29), or have a Jacuzzi whirlpool bath (Plate 24). A bath may be large (Fig. 6.30), or simple.

Very little research has been done on the bathroom, except for that of Alexander Kira

Figure 6.29
Greenery thrives in the warm, moist air of the bathroom, making it into an atrium. The watercloset and bidet are low, fitting the needs of the body as determined by Kira. (Courtesy of Kohler Co.)

[4] Vern and Bonnie Bullough, *An Illustrated Social History of Prostitution* (New York: Crown Publishers Inc.), 1978, p. 123.

[5] Alexander Kira, *The Bathroom: Criteria for Design* (Ithaca, N.Y.: Cornell University Center for Housing and Design), Research Report No. 7, p. 3.

Figure 6.30
This large bathroom has a king-sized fiberglas oval tub with a whirlpool device. The plants and wall hanging add texture to the luxurious interior. (Courtesy of Kohler Co.)

Figure 6.31
Seating space on the tub is a safety feature. The bidet at the right facilitates perineal cleansing. (Courtesy of American-Standard)

tubs (Fig. 6.31) may have a place to sit down and the combination tub-shower (Fig. 6.32) has controls at a convenient level and a place for soap, towels, and sitting.

One interesting recent development is the composting toilet designed to save water. This was first suggested by the Beecher sisters in 1869. They quote the director of the Earth Closet Company as saying that

> the waste of more vital elements of the soil's fertility, through our present practice of treating human excrement as a thing that is to be hurried out to sea . . . or in some way put out of sight and out of reach, is full of danger to our future prosperity. . . . The elements we take from the soil in the form of food must be returned to the soil to replenish it.[7]

The Clivus Multrum (Fig. 6.33 and 6.34), a Swedish composting toilet, is very similar to the old earth closet referred to by the Beecher sisters.

A powder room, near the living area, is an added convenience, if money permits. It may be elaborate (Fig. 6.35), or it can be a small space, enlarged by mirrors (Plate 25). The powder room should not be placed in full view of the hall or the living area, for bathroom functions are private, and the door should not open so as to risk hitting the per-

at Cornell University, whose studies indicate that most bathroom equipment is inadequate, owing in great measure to embarrassment about bathroom activities.[6] He has suggested new designs for bathroom fixtures, and many of these have been incorporated into bathroom equipment today. For example, bath

---

[6] Alexander Kira, *The Bathroom* (New York: The Viking Press, Inc., 1979), pp. 23–26.

[7] Catharine E. Beecher and Harriet Beecher Stowe, *The American Woman's Home* (New York: J. R. Ford & Co., 1869), p. 404.

Figure 6.32
The shower features storage space for towels and soap and controls placed at a convenient level. The skylight provides natural light and privacy. (Courtesy of American-Standard)

Figure 6.33
The Clivus Multrum toilet installed in a bathroom. (Courtesy of Clivus Multrum USA, Inc.)

Figure 6.34
The Clivus Multrum, which transforms all organic material from the kitchen and bathroom into humus for fertilizer without the use of water, has been available commercially in Scandinavia for over ten years. It saves about 100 gallons of water daily (for a family of four). The digesting chamber must be installed in a basement or crawl space under the house. (Courtesy of Clivus Multrum USA, Inc.)

Figure 6.35
Books line the walls of this powder room, utilizing otherwise wasted space. (Courtesy of Kohler Co.)

son using the facilities or exposing him to public view.

The minimum size for a full bathroom is five feet by seven feet, but this size allows little but the bare essentials. A small bathroom may be increased visually by the use of a mirrored ceiling and mirrored walls (Fig. 6.36). If only one bathroom is included in a home, it should be compartmentalized so that more than one

person can use it at the same time (Plate 19). Twin tubs and wash basins can be used by two people (Fig. 6.37), and could serve a courting couple as a "bundling" bath.

The bathroom should be easily accessible to all the bedrooms; if two baths (considered necessary for a family of four) are planned, one should be located off the master bedroom. The master bathroom might include a couch

Figure 6.36
The illusion of space is created by mirrors in this tiny powder room. A chaise percée conceals the watercloset. (Courtesy of Sherle Wagner International, Inc.)

Figure 6.37
Twin sinks and tubs make this a special master bathroom. The ledges beside the tubs hold bathing paraphernalia. Towels are stored on the raised platform behind the tubs. (Courtesy of Tile Council of America)

Figure 6.38
A country bath with lounging space on the right. The twin sinks are installed in a Queen Anne style cabinet. (Courtesy of Kohler Co.)

for lounging, and a bidet (Fig. 6.38). The bidet is unpopular in the United States, Kira believes, because it has sexual connotations. This is unfortunate since it would simplify anal-genital cleansing and enhance personal hygiene.[8]

Bathrooms require soft ambient light as well as task lighting around the mirror for shaving and applying cosmetics. Storage must be included for towels, soap, and grooming supplies. Kira found that a minimum of one square foot of storage space is required near the washbasin for each person (Fig. 6.39). A locked cabinet for storing medicines is necessary when there are young children in the household.

Bathrooms may contain additional features, such as the Habitat by Kohler, in which heat, sun, rain, steam, and wind add a new dimension to enjoyable living. Heat lamps, sun lamps, spray heads, a steam generator, and warm circulating systems make many activities possible (Fig. 6.40).

The sauna is another possible addition to the bathroom. Popular in Scandinavia for many years, it is a dry-heat bath in a well-insulated room lined with untreated, kiln-dried soft wood heated by igneous rocks. The humidity is controlled by the application of water to the rocks (Fig. 6.41). Towels and water may be stored outside the room (Fig. 6.42).

The bath has even moved outdoors. Hot tubs, employing hydro-jets to heat the water to about 105 degrees, are very popular. They have a pump, filter and heater and are most often constructed of redwood. They are not used for cleansing but for relaxation. The next decade will see major changes in the bathroom. Increasingly bathroom design is making up for years of neglect arising from societal prudishness.

The bathroom can serve many of the present functions of the bedroom. A large carpeted area can be used for exercising, for sex,

[8] Kira, *The Bathroom, op. cit,* pp. 23–26.

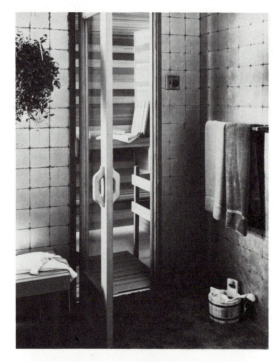

Figure 6.42
Towels and water are stored outside this prefabricated sauna room. (Courtesy of Metos Sauna, Inc.)

Figure 6.43
A combined sleeping bath and whirlpool. (Courtesy of Kohler Co.)

and for meditating. The privacy of the bathroom and the fact that it is often locked contributes to the versatility of this room. Parents can withdraw from conflicts with the children and, if the conflict is very intense, a longer stay with magazines, radio, stereo, television, sauna, whirlpool, or bubble bath can ease tension (Fig. 6.43).

Bathroom colors can be bright but their effect on skin color should be considered. Warm colors improve skin tones while cool colors may make the skin appear sallow. White has often been used in the bathroom since it reflects up to 90 per cent of the light. Wall finishes should be easy to clean, because the bathroom is a frequently used room. Ceramic tile (Fig. 6.44) is easily wiped clean. If space permits, the bathroom is an excellent location for laundry equipment. These compact laundry units fit neatly into a bathroom (Fig. 6.46).

Laundry

The laundry area should ideally be near the source of soiled items and the storage of clean ones—near or in the bathroom or near the bedroom. It may, less ideally, be placed near or in the kitchen (Fig. 6.45); however, noise from the washer and dryer can make conversation and concentration difficult.

The laundry should have ambient and task lighting and a ventilation fan to rid the room of excess humidity. Counter space for sorting dirty items, for pretreating badly soiled items, and for folding clean items should be about the height of kitchen counters (Fig. 6.46). The counter surface should be stain- and water-resistant. If there are small children in the household, the laundry area should have shelves or locked cabinets for storage of laundry supplies. If a dryer is not included, the laundry equipment, should be close to a drying area. The washer and dryer can be placed side by side (Fig. 6.45) or stacked (Fig. 6.46) if space is at a premium. Wall outlets should be three feet from the floor and storage for an iron and ironing board should be convenient. The return to natural fibers is giving renewed importance to ironing.

Entertainment and Group Space

The entertainment and group space in a home is the area where the occupants gather before and after dinner, for informal activities, for watching television, for parties, and for recre-

Figure 6.44
A luxurious bathroom with adjoining atrium. The carefree ceramic tile makes it easy to maintain. (Courtesy of Tile Council of America)

Figure 6.45
A washer and dryer placed off the kitchen. (Courtesy of Whirlpool Corporation)

Figure 6.46
A stacked washer and dryer are conveniently located in the bathroom. To the left is storage space for laundry supplies and folded items. The front of the shelf unit drops down to provide folding space. (Courtesy of Whirlpool Corporation)

Figure 6.47
A multi-purpose room inspired by the American Southwest: rough stucco walls, overhead beams, and a ceramic tile floor. The Mexican secretary to the left is handcarved. The hand loom testifies to the owner's love of weaving, and the baskets hold her yarns. Interior designer: Mary Jane Maher. (Courtesy of Tile Council of America)

ation. This area is the control center of the house, receiving traffic throughout the day.

In Tudor England and in the medieval houses of Europe, the great hall was the space in which all activities were carried on, including sleeping (except for the master and mistress of the house). In seventeenth-century America, family activities typically took place around the fireplace where the cooking was done. Today the kitchen has again become the center of family life and is often combined with dining and family areas. Limited space and a desire to return to more simple forms of daily existence have sparked the need for a multi-purpose room. The living room, used infrequently, is often wasted space and in fact has taken the place of the Victorian parlor as the room saved for guests. An all-purpose room for living, eating, entertaining, and even cooking is much more practical. A multi-functional room may combine a conversation area, a reading area, dining space, and a hobby area (Fig. 6.47).

A home without a multi-purpose room can often make use of otherwise wasted space. An

unfinished basement can, with careful planning, be converted into a versatile room suitable for a variety of activities (Fig. 6.48). An attractive dining nook, a breakfast or snack bar, a study, and a family room can be created in an unused basement space (Fig. 6.49). Sleeping, conversation, and dining areas may be combined in one room, at different levels for definition (Plate 8).

A family room should have a conversation area with sufficient space for the comfortable seating of the usual number of occupants and guests. The arrangement, usually square or circular, should facilitate conversation without the need to rearrange seats and should be less than ten feet across. It should include tables on which to place cups, books, and magazines, and ambient lighting with some lamps. A warm-color carpet and neutral colors create a comforting atmosphere which invites conversation (Plate 26). An outdoor area may be planned as an extension of the interior (Fig. 6.50).

A space may be designed to be inviting for many activities: conversation, reading, and

Figure 6.48
An unfinished basement space that was the catch-all for a typical family's paraphernalia, now converted into the multi-functional space shown in Fig. 6.48. (Courtesy of Armstrong Cork Co.)

Figure 6.49
The poorly used space in Figure 6.48 was made into an attractive basement family room. The breakfast/snack bar is delineated by fluorescent lighting integrated into the suspended ceiling which also hides the overhead pipes and ducts. (Courtesy of Armstrong Cork Company)

just relaxing (Plate 27). The requirements for a reading area are good light, either natural or artificial, coming from the side; a comfortable chair; and acoustical protection from household noises and traffic.

Television, an integral part of Western culture, requires careful space planning. Seating should be arranged so that the screen can be seen at no more than a sixty-degree angle. The television screen should be at the eye level of a seated person, and ambient light is helpful. Fabrics and carpet can provide acoustical control for the room, and the space can also double as a study (Plate 28).

Game areas require light and relative freedom from noise. They should also be sound insulated because extensive noise may be generated in this space. A game and music area may be planned as a dual-purpose area, with space for an extra guest provided (Plate 29).

Other kinds of recreation can be provided for in a multi-purpose room. Conversation, dining, hobbies, and even swimming can be provided for (Plate 30). The swimming pool is an example of a theme around which an entire house can be built. Because the functional aspect of the theme must precede beauty, the pool should be used as frequently as other functional features of the house, such as the bathroom or the kitchen. Unlike other design features, however, a pool cannot be easily relocated or removed, and—like other esoteric design features—it may make resale of the house difficult.

Dining Areas

Dining is an activity that brings family and friends together. Entertaining indicates hospitality and almost always involves the serving of food. When families visited each other during the early part of this century, a meal was nearly always served, no matter what time of the day.

The main dining area should be adjacent to the kitchen and the living area. A multi-purpose room visually increases the space for all activities and makes it possible to extend the dining space into the living area when serving large groups of people. A dining area may be adjacent to a terrace, bringing the inside and outside together, and the size of the space may also be increased by the use of a mirrored back wall (Plate 42). The dining area may be a light airy space created in a multi-purpose room by the use of a plexiglass and glass din-

Figure 6.50
An inviting redwood-and-glass solarium and adjoining deck seems to float in the treetops on this hilly site. The greenhouse-inspired solarium is a natural extension of the living room and has a hand-made Mexican tile floor. Convenient redwood shelves for plants and drinks are built into the railings. Architect: Jack Johannes. Photograph by Karl Riek. (Courtesy of California Redwood Association)

Figure 6.51
A separate dining room is desired by some families and this simple room answers that need. (Courtesy of Tile Council of America)

ing table (Plate 4). The living area may be designed as a multi-purpose space, appropriate for entertaining friends and for personal enjoyment of art, books, and music (Plate 31).

The living pattern of some families profits from a separate dining room, especially if they entertain frequently (Fig. 6.51). In the dining area there should be at least two feet between the backs of chairs and nearby walls for passage. The lighting should be warm, glare-free and focused on the table. A surface on which to place utensils and food, and convenient storage for dishes, should also be provided.

Outside Group Spaces

Outside group spaces can extend the living area, and provide a cool place to retreat (Plate 39). Areas for croquet, shuffleboard, badminton, putting, and archery can also serve as sanctuaries, as can a solar pool and social area (Fig. 3.14).

Transitional Spaces

Entryways and Foyers

The entryway to a house sets the mood the owners desire. It is analogous to the initial posture which the individual presents upon greeting another person. It can be formal or casual, firm or relaxed, ineffectual or affectionate, soft or hard, bright or dull, austere or lavish. It sets the tone for the design and interaction to follow.

The main entry is the one most frequently used. It should have a closet for guests, a powder room or lavatory, and direct access to the living area. The space should be large enough to accommodate several people. This ranges from a minimum of five feet by five feet to an ideal of eight by ten feet. The entry should be friendly and welcoming (Fig. 6.52). It may extend the outside to the inside (Fig. 6.53). Plants are a welcome addition. There should be acoustical and visual barriers between the entry and private areas (Fig. 6.54). The floor should be of some durable and easily cleaned material, such a vinyl or ceramic tile.

The service entrance should be easily accessible from the driveway or carport and should lead to the kitchen or laundry. Frequently this entrance also serves as the family entrance. It should be at least four feet wide and should have ambient light from the wall or ceiling.

Figure 6.52
A well-lit entry makes it easy to identify guests. Two closets are provided on either side of the door for coats. (Courtesy of Westinghouse)

Figure 6.53
A continuation of the flooring material used outside creates a flow of space into the entry. (Courtesy of Franciscan Tile)

Figure 6.54
The staircase to the private areas of the house is housed in the entry. (Courtesy of American Olean)

Storage

In addition to the storage space required in each area of the house for specialized items used in that space, storage space is required for out-of-season items and seldom-used items (winter clothing, blankets, luggage). One solution is an inexpensive storage wall made up of cubes (Plate 32). Stack-up storage units can provide space for books, records, serving pieces, and even clothing (Fig. 6.55), and can be open or closed. Storage can be provided for a living environment or for art objects (Fig. 6.56).

The Plan

The average home today contains less than 1400 square feet of space. If the space is to be used to its best advantage, each area should be capable of being used for several functions. For example, conversation, dining and sleeping areas may be placed on different levels and grouped around a central fireplace (Plate 8), creating a multi-purpose area to serve as bedroom, living room, and dining room. The di-

Figure 6.55
This inviting room has a wall of stack storage units for books, records, and clothing. The modular seating pieces cluster around the small tables for casual dining or lounging. (Courtesy of Workbench)

Figure 6.56
Primitive African artifacts are displayed on open storage shelves. Interior designers: Harry Schule and John MaCarville. (Courtesy of Royal System, Inc.)

Plate 1
Unique houses are becoming too expensive for most people but they can be a joy to live in. Interior designer: Anne C. Houle. Photograph by Michael Decoulos.

Plate 2
Designer Bob Rubenstein has created a warm interior in a large living area by using a high shag carpet, leather sofa, and deeply textured upholstered chairs. Multiple paintings contrast with the coral rock walls. Photograph by Les Rachline.

Plate 3
There are many textures to enjoy in this room: old wood, rough stone, and the smooth surface of the floor. (Courtesy of American Olean Tile Co.)

Plate 4 (Opposite)
A light, airy dining space is created at one end of a multi-purpose area with a plexiglas and glass dining table and chrome dining chairs covered in plaid Haitian cotton. Interior designer: Bob Rubinstein. Photograph by Les Rachline.

mensions of each space are appropriate to its function. When physical space is small, psychological space can be increased by placing less emphasis on the size of the space and more emphasis on its volume. For example, two-story space appears larger than a single-story space of equal size (Plate 33). Glass walls (which blend the interior with the exterior), atriums, skylights, interior gardens, clerestory windows, and fewer objects, patterns, and prints also give the illusion of a larger space.

Traffic Flow and Clearances

Halls, corridors, and stairways should be allocated as little space as possible. They are traffic routes and circulation should be directed from the entrance of the house through short, direct routes to other areas. Traffic should not cut through conversation areas, the kitchen, or any functional space. Doorways should be placed as close to the corners of rooms as possible to facilitate furniture arrangement.

Making the Plan

The requirements of the interior space plan can be ascertained in six steps:

1. Determine space requirements by gathering information.
2. Develop alternative solutions.
3. Select the final solution.
4. Develop the design.
5. Present the design.
6. Evaluate the solution.

Information Gathering

The interior designer should help the people using the space to analyze their needs and requirements. The development of an environmental matrix is an aid in ascertaining those requirements (Fig. 6.57). Some requirements will answer more than one need. For example, a sound baffle will provide sound control for reading, watching television, listening to music, studying, writing, and perhaps entertaining. Ambient lighting is required for all activities in the living room, but task lighting is required for reading, in the kitchen, and in bedrooms. By listing all the requirements of each activity, those that overlap can be determined. If, for example, an apartment is being planned for a client whose business requires him to entertain clients at home, a list should be made of the minimum space needed, the facilities required, and the special needs and interests of the occupant (Fig. 6.58).

	Counter space	Shelves	Desk space	Hard-surface floor	Carpet	Comfortable seating	Extra seating	Table and chairs	Specialized storage	Enclosed storage	Ambient lighting	Task lighting	Sound baffle	Visible baffle	Wall space
Entertaining	x				x	x	x	x	x	x	x	x	x	x	
Reading						x						x	x		
Dining	x							x			x	x			
Television						x			x		x				
Food Preparation	x	x		x					x		x	x	x	x	
Art Collection		x									x				x
Music													x		
Conversation						x					x				
Writing			x												
Space for visitors								x	x	x	x	x			

Figure 6.57
An environmental matrix for the apartment in Figs. 6.58 and 6.66.

A. Maximum space .... 450 m³
B. Client Facilities Requirements ....
- living/social/entertainment area
- dining area—seating for 8
- food preparation area with service entrance
- master bedroom with private bath
- guest bedroom with private bath
- visitor half bath
- office space for two persons

C. Special Requirements ....
- the apartment user is gregarious and entertains frequently . . . space must be provided for formal dinner parties and cocktail parties for up to 50 guests.
- client has extensive collection of 20th century art and antiques that will be displayed.
- The apartment must be easily maintained.

D. Other client interests ....
- music
- scuba diving
- auto racing
- likes late night television movies.

Step 1.   Determination of space requirements

Figure 6.58
Determination of space requirements for the apartment in Figs. 6.67–6.74. This project was done in metric. The design and drawings in Figs. 6.67–6.74 are by Randy Allen Clark, student of Professor Peter Munton, Florida State University.

Alternative Solutions

The second step in the planning of interior space is to develop a human spatial organization plan. Bubble-flow diagrams, developed from the information gathered, show spatial relationships among the required spaces, the relationship of the spaces between each other, their relative size (although not to scale), and the traffic patterns connecting the spaces (Fig. 6.59). These diagrams may be used to illustrate several possible solutions.

Selection of the Final Solution

At this point, a final solution that best meets the client's needs is selected (Fig. 6.60), enlarged, again studied. Primary and secondary circulation patterns are added to the bubble schematic (Fig. 6.61), and the bubble schematic is converted into a conventional two-dimensional floor plan (Fig. 6.62). Sometimes it helps to place the schematic over a 2 × 2 grid to define the plan and work from the inside out. Adjustments frequently have to be made on the grid. The designer should remain as abstract as possible, using the grid as a starting point and arbitrary mean. At this point, the

Figure 6.59
Bubble schematics help to develop alternative solutions. (Courtesy of Randy Allen Clark)

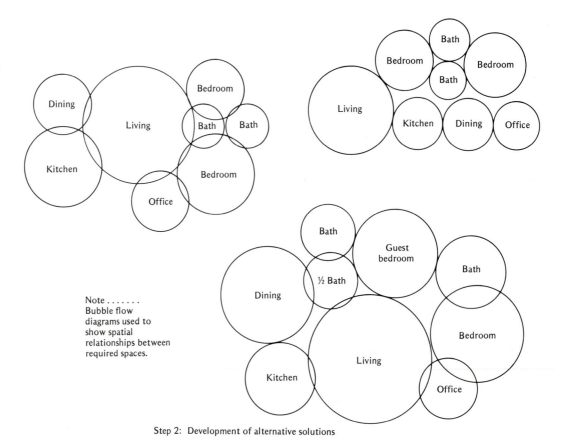

Note . . . .
Bubble flow
diagrams used to
show spatial
relationships between
required spaces.

Step 2: Development of alternative solutions

Figure 6.60
Selection of the final solution. (Courtesy of Randy Allen Clark)

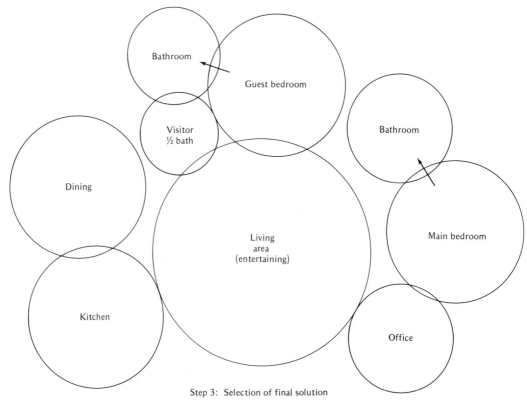

Step 3: Selection of final solution

Figure 6.61
Primary and secondary
circulation schematic.
(Courtesy of Randy Allen
Clark)

Bath

Bedroom

Bath

Bath

Dining

Living area

Bedroom

Kitchen

Office

| Primary circulation |
| Secondary circulation |

Step 4: Design development

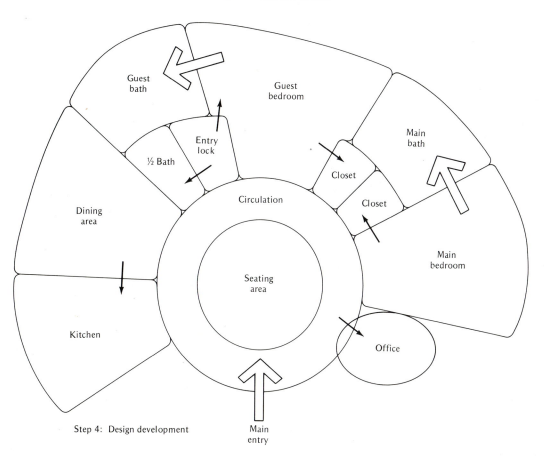

Figure 6.62
Conversion of bubble
schematic into a
conventional
two-dimensional floor plan.
(Courtesy of Randy Allen
Clark)

Guest
bath

Guest
bedroom

Entry
lock

½ Bath

Main
bath

Closet

Closet

Dining
area

Circulation

Seating
area

Main
bedroom

Kitchen

Office

Step 4: Design development

Main
entry

Figure 6.63
Further development of the plan, with windows, doors, and some large pieces of furniture indicated. (Courtesy of Randy Allen Clark)

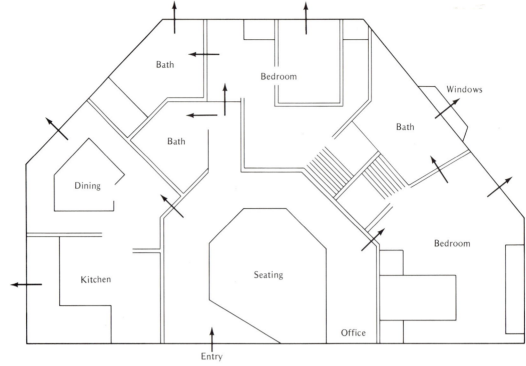

Step 4: Design Development

Figure 6.64
Quick pen-and-ink sketch of an exhibition kiosk executed to convey the feeling of the various spaces in one continuous drawing. (Courtesy of Shung M. Louie, Pratt Institute)

square footage of each area may be estimated as the outline of the final plan emerges.

Models are invaluable in the clarification of how users will move through the space. They help in graphically illustrating clearances and the relationship among spaces. Models may be simple or elaborate. The designer then analyzes the changes that need to be made and that can be made. Light, ventilation, and traffic patterns determine to a great extent how the space can be used. Several questions should be asked at this stage:

1. How large will each space be?
2. What shape should each space be?
3. How will the space appear?
4. What factors affect the function of the space?

The designer should make a rough sketch indicating placement of the entry and windows and any other architectural details that affect the space (Fig. 6.63). Perspective sketches also help in making decisions; These can be quick pencil or ink sketches (Fig. 6.64). At this point, a rough sketch of the furniture arrangement should be made (Fig. 6.65). Furniture, carpet, fabrics, and paint colors can now be selected.

Final Presentation

The final presentation boards should include floor plans (Fig. 6.66) and swatch boards (Fig. 6.67). If they are appropriate to the scope of the project, final perspectives may be made (Figs. 6.68a, 6.68b). Elevations may be used to clarify architectural details (Fig. 6.69). Detail drawings are necessary for built-in features or furniture (Fig. 6.70).

Evaluation of the Solution

After it is completed and in use, the solution should be evaluated. An evaluation aids in solving space problems and in preventing fu-

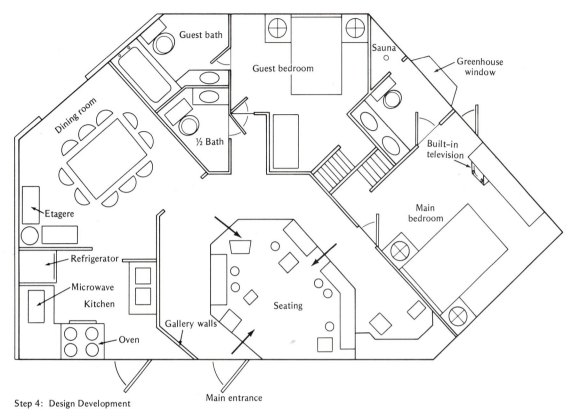

Guest bath

Guest bedroom

Sauna

Greenhouse window

Dining room

½ Bath

Built-in television

Etagere

Main bedroom

Refrigerator

Microwave

Kitchen

Seating

Oven

Gallery walls

Main entrance

Step 4: Design Development

Figure 6.65
A floor plan indicating the arrangement of furniture, the placement of windows and doors, and so on. (Courtesy of Randy Allen Clark)

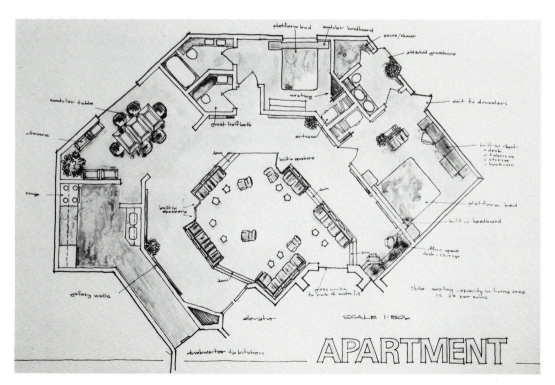

APARTMENT

Figure 6.66
Final floor plan. (Courtesy of Randy Allen Clark)

Figure 6.67
*Support board for
apartment. (Courtesy of
Randy Allen Clark)*

Figure 6.68a
*Bedroom and adjacent living
area designed and rendered
in watercolor by Nancy
Rohrig. (Property of
Alderman Studios, Inc.,
High Point, North
Carolina)*

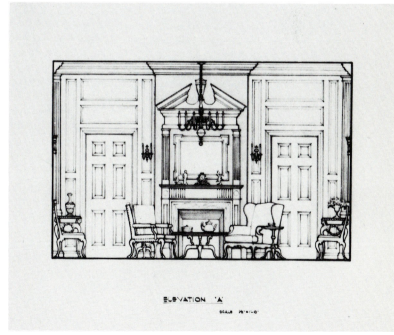

Figure 6.69
Elevation by Wilson Lau Huang Sam, student of Professor John Huff, University of Georgia. Lighter lines used for the panelling make it seem to recede into the background; darker lines for the mantle and furniture make them appear closer to the viewer.

THE INTERIOR ENVIRONMENT   **113**

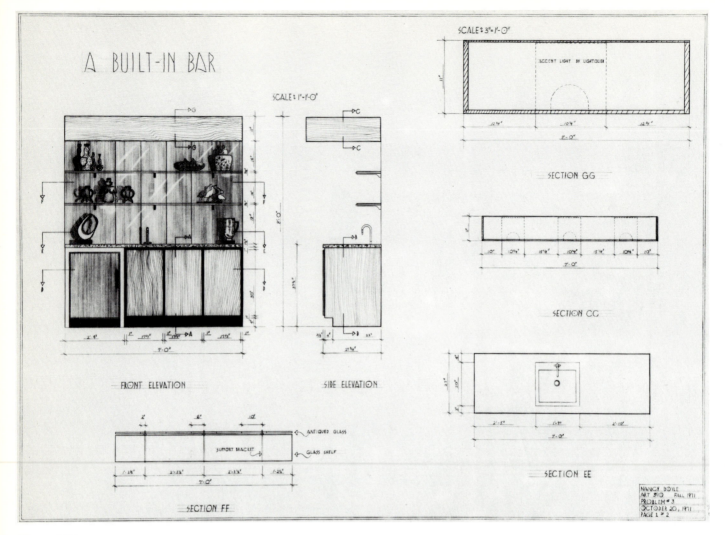

Figure 6.70
Elevations and sections of a built-in bar by Nancy Boyle, student of Professor John Huff, University of Georgia.

ture problems. Too often, this step is neglected and the space is designed and never considered again. Students at Florida State University, using a Semantic Differential, evaluated space before and after it was redesigned and found that well-designed spaces have a positive effect on the people using them.[9]

Glossary

Bi-Nuclear. Two-centered house plan developed by Marcel Breuer.

Biological Space. Space required for the daily requisites of life, such as sleeping and sex, food preparation and personal hygiene.

Chaise Perceé. A decorative covering for a toilet, usually in the Rococo or Neoclassic style.

Closed Plan. Division of space into rooms, enclosed by walls.

Entertainment and Group Space. Space in which occupants gather before and after dinner and for parties and recreation.

Open Plan. Definition of space by means other than walls.

Organic. Growing out of the nature of the object.

Personal Hygiene. Activities connected with bathing, laundry, and so on.

Transitional Space. Entryways, foyers, and storage space.

[9] Ann W. Danford, "An Appraisal of Selected Redesigned University Facilities." Unpublished master's thesis, Florida State University, 1972; Ann Whiteside, "An Assessment of Changes in Perception of Selected Redesigned University Facilities at Florida State University." Unpublished master's thesis, Florida State University.

Bibliography

BEECHER, CATHERINE E., and HARRIET BEECHER STOWE. *The American Woman's Home or Principles of Domestic Science.* New York: J. R. Ford and Co., 1869.

BULLOUGH, VERN and BONNIE. *An Illustrated History of Prostitution.* New York: Crown Publishers Inc., 1978.

Danford, Ann W. "An Appraisal of Selected Redesigned University Facilities." Unpublished master's thesis. Florida State University, 1972.

Conran, Terence. *The Bed and Bath Book*. New York: Crown Publishers, Inc., 1978.

———. *The House Book*. New York: Crown Publishers, Inc., 1974.

Kira, Alexander. *The Bathroom*. New York: The Viking Press, 1979.

———. *The Bathroom: Criteria for Design*. Ithaca, N.Y.: Cornell University Center for Housing and Design. Research Report No. 7, undated.

Newmark, Norma L., and Patricia J. Thompson. *Self, Space and Shelter*. San Francisco, Calif.: Danfield Press, 1977.

Kron, Joan, and Suzanne Slesin. *High-Tech*. New York: Potter, 1978.

Panero, Julius. *Anatomy for Interior Designers*. 3rd ed. New York: Whitney Library of Design, 1962.

Whiteside, Ann. "An Assessment of Changes in Perception of Selected Redesigned University Facilities at the Florida State University." Unpublished master's thesis. Florida State University, 1974.

Aakas, Spiros. *Lifespace*. New York: Macmillan Publishing Co., Inc., 1977.

The Background Environment

Walls, Ceilings, and Floors

The walls, ceilings, and floors of a house form the background for its occupants, providing protection and privacy and creating inner spaces within the house by determining the size and shape of each room. They reduce noise and conceal insulation, plumbing, and electrical wires. The materials used for walls, ceiling, and floors may be dramatic and important in themselves or totally nondescript. These large areas can create a mood and an atmosphere and integrate all the elements of the space into a unified whole.

Walls and Ceilings

In homes built before the twentieth century, walls were stationary and served to support the structure of the house, literally holding up the ceiling. They were thick and made of strong materials to keep out the heat and cold. The depth of the window openings in the Edmonston-Allston house, built in 1920 (Fig. 7.1), indicates the thickness of the walls. Today interior walls are seldom structural; often they are non-load-bearing walls that merely divide space in some fashion (Fig. 7.2). These walls may extend only part of the way to the ceiling, or they may be moveable or free-standing. A fireplace, seating unit, storage, or counter space may be built into or onto a wall (Fig. 7.3). Walls may have openings through which visual space flows freely from one area into another (Plate 34).

Materials used for walls and ceilings may be opaque or transparent, rough or smooth, patterned or plain, and of interior or exterior materials. Walls and ceilings may be made to appear active or passive depending upon the material covering them. They may be of fragile materials or of durable, maintenance-free materials. They may absorb or reflect both light and sound (Figs. 6.7 and 7.4).

Paint

The appearance of walls is changed more frequently than any other part of the house. This is because they can be transformed quickly and inexpensively with paint or wall coverings. A painted wall graphic, for example, can transform a work area (Fig. 7.5). Paint is one of the least expensive and most easily applied of wall coverings. New synthetics, such as vinyls, acrylics, and polyurethanes, have made it possible to cover almost any wall with a tough, washable surface. Paints are available in a wide variety of colors and finishes. Paint not only adds color to a space, it also provides a uniform surface.

Wallpaper

Wallpaper, which has been used since about 200 B.C., is a nonrigid material that can be used to cover the walls in any room in the house. It conceals cracks and flaws and can make a room appear larger or smaller, formal (Fig. 7.6) or informal (Fig. 7.7). Wallpaper in plain colors, textured or smooth, resemble paint. This paper is particularly good for walls in poor condition; however, the walls should first be covered with lining paper for best results. Wallpaper is priced by the single roll (which covers thirty to thirty-six square feet), but is usually sold by the double or triple roll.

Wallpapers come in many kinds of patterns. These can be machine-printed with a rotary press and a series of cylinders; silk-screened or hand-screened,[1] in a process in which a squeegee is used to apply paint; or block-printed, in another hand process involving wooden blocks. One of the patterns that has been used for many years is the traditional floral. A pattern designed by William Morris in 1892 is still available today, although smaller in scale (Fig. 7.8). Stripes are another pattern that has been in use a long time (Fig. 7.9). Scenic wallpapers may open up a room (Fig. 7.10), giving a view to a room without one. Bold designs should be used with care (Fig. 7.11). Grasscloth is another kind of wallpaper that hides wall defects (Fig. 7.12). Cork, a durable wall covering, adds warmth to the interior and also controls sound, although it is more expensive than many wallpapers (Fig. 7.13).

Fabric may be used to cover walls and provides acoustical control as well as color, pattern, and softness (Plate 35). Fabrics may also be stretched over walls or coated with vinyl and hung like wallpaper. Carpet can further tie together walls, floor, and furniture (Fig. 7.14).

Plastic wall coverings are of two kinds; one, a plastic-bonded wallpaper, is washable but will stain; the other, a plastic-coated wallpaper, is both washable and stain-resistant. Foil papers, composed of a thin sheet of flexible

---

[1] Wallpaper sample books are hand-screened, and all but the most expensive wallpapers, are machine silk-screened. This causes a variation in color so paint should not be matched to the wallpaper sample book but to an actual memo sample of the wallpaper. Memo samples are samples sent from the manufacturer to the designer.

Figure 7.1
*The front drawing room of
the Edmonston-Alston
House in Charleston
features the deep walls
typical of the 1820s.
(Courtesy of Historic
Charleston Reproductions)*

Figure 7.2
*The bedroom headboard is also a free-standing wall.
Interior designer: Paco Munoz, Spain. (Courtesy of
Solid Fuel Advisory Service)*

Figure 7.3
*The open feeling of this room is provided by the
"onion" fireplace set in a plexiglas wall. Interior
designer: Paco Munoz, Spain. (Courtesy of Solid Fuel
Advisory Service)*

Figure 7.6 ▶
*(Opposite, bottom) A sophisticated apartment, with a
signed Tiffany lamp, is enhanced by the use of a
wallpaper mural. Photograph by Yuichi Idaka.
(Courtesy of Jack Denst Designs, Inc.)*

Figure 7.7
A casual, informal country look is created with wallcoverings. (Courtesy of Jack Denst Designs, Inc.)

Figure 7.8
William Morris's famous Chrysanthemum pattern has been reduced in size for today's contemporary interiors. (Courtesy of Sanderson)

Figure 7.9
Stripes combined with a stylized pattern are printed on pewter mylar. Photograph by Yuichi Idaka. (Courtesy of Jack Denst Designs, Inc.)

Figure 7.11
The solid gold figure of Tutankhamun as a child, wearing a pleated kilt, inspired this Art Deco design. A smaller version appears in the coordinating fabric. (Courtesy of Perceptive Concepts, Inc., and Simmons Co.)

Figure 7.10
A Lake Placid mural gives a view to a room without one. (Courtesy of Environmental Graphics)

metal or mylar (a mirrored finish on a paper backing), can be printed with opaque or transparent colors (Fig. 7.15). Some papers are embossed; others are engraved with etched rollers. Some papers are strippable—that is, they have been treated with a chemical that makes them tear-resistant. Strippable paper can be removed from the wall without being wet, an advantage when repapering (Fig. 7.16). Vinyl laminates are also available and even woven fabrics can be laminated.

Rigid Wall Coverings

Rigid wall coverings consist of tiles, rigid materials (such as chalkboard, pegboard, and plastic laminate), brick (Fig. 7.17), glass, mirrors, and paneling. Tiles, either matte or glossy, may be used to cover the wall or as a panel or an accent. There are plastic tiles, vinyl tiles, ceramic tiles, copper tiles, stainless steel tiles, mirror tiles, terracotta tiles, quarry tiles, and porcelain-coated steel tiles. Tiles reflect noise rather than absorbing it and can create an acoustical problem, but they are moisture-proof and durable. They vary widely in price, depending upon the material used and upon whether they are hand- or machine-made.

Chalkboard, pegboard, and plastic laminate may also be used for walls. Chalkboard is particularly good in children's rooms, for it can be written on to their hearts' content. Pegboard is an excellent choice for kitchen, game room, or storage area. Plastic laminate is durable, easily maintained, and available in a variety of colors and patterns.

Paneling is available in solid wood, plywood, or veneers. Printed finishes resembling wood applied to gypsum board, and plastic laminates that look like wood, are also available. Paneling is warm and natural in appearance, easily maintained, and relatively durable (Fig. 7.18). It may be affected by moisture and

Figure 7.12
Grass cloth is always irregular when applied to the wall, for the material is composed of natural fibers. Furniture designer: Milo Baughman. (Courtesy of Thayer Coggin, Inc.)

Figure 7.13
Cork, although expensive, provides excellent acoustical control. (Courtesy of Armstrong Cork Co.)

Figure 7.14
Carpet ties together the seating units and the floor. Interior designer: Ed Secon. (Courtesy of Workbench, Inc.)

Figure 7.15
The large-scale mural is printed in blue on gold mylar, and is also available on black patent vinyl or plexiglas. Photograph by Yuichi Idaka. (Courtesy of Jack Denst Designs, Inc.)

water, however, and some types will crack or chip.

Glass is another wall material. It can be used for sliding doors, window walls, or glass blocks. Glass blocks are strong and they deflect light in interesting patterns. Mirror walls brighten and lighten a space and add depth; however, they are easily broken and relatively costly (Fig. 7.19).

Ceilings

Ceilings have a profound effect on the temperature, acoustics, and lighting of a room, yet they are often a neglected part of the interior design. High ceilings are cooler in hot cli-

Figure 7.16
This is a scrubbable, strippable wallcovering. (Courtesy of Wall Covering Bureau)

mates; low ceilings make rooms easier to heat in cold climates. Ceilings can be made of sound-absorbing materials. (Fig. 7.20). They can be painted in light or neutral colors, to reflect light into the interior, and they can even be made a source of light themselves (Fig. 7.21). Ceilings can be mirrored, increasing the perceived volume of the space and reflecting the light (Fig. 7.22). Ceilings that vary in level add interest to the interior and delineate spaces for different functions (Fig. 7.23). Ceilings with exposed beams can lend a rustic air to the interior (Fig. 7.17). Wood may be left its natural color or stained and used in an exposed ceiling (Fig. 7.24). Ceiling tile in a wood-grain plank may also be used (Fig. 7.25). A cathedral ceiling carries the eye upward and increases the apparent size of the space (Fig. 7.26). Ceilings of all kinds should always be well insulated to prevent heat and cooling losses.

Floors

Floors constitute the third background area; a large area, they define interior space and receive the greatest amount of use. Floors are for walking and occasionally for sitting, for insulation from the cold, for quietness, and for beauty. Floor coverings constitute a large part of the budget and should be selected carefully.

Figure 7.17
This old painted brick wall makes a beautiful background. (Courtesy of Groundworks, Inc.)

Figure 7.18
Pecan paneling is warm and natural in appearance.
(Courtesy of Georgia-Pacific)

Figure 7.19
Mirrored walls increase the size of this small bathroom.
(Courtesy of PPG Industries)

Figure 7.20
An acoustical ceiling in the bathroom reduces noise. Interior designer: Thomas Hills Cook.
(Courtesy of Armstrong Cork Co.)

Figure 7.21
Lights behind a translucent panel bathe the kitchen in a warm glow. (Courtesy of Evans)

In ancient times, floors were made of closely packed earth. Gradually stone and marble and finally wood came to be used. Today, choices for floor coverings range from hard materials to soft ones, with each having specific advantages and disadvantages.

Before selecting floor coverings, several basic questions should be answered:

1. *What kind of wear will the floor receive?* Floors that receive hard wear should be durable. Floors should be able to support furniture without cracking, chipping, or denting, and they should not be marked by ordinary traffic.
2. *What kind of maintenance will be required to keep the floor attractive?* Tests indicate that carpets are easier to maintain, but hard-surface floor coverings may be preferred for a variety of reasons, such as appearance, appropriateness, or color. Neutral colors or patterns conceal soil and are easier to maintain than dark or very light colors. Stain-resistant or stain-releasing surfaces simplify care.
3. *How much noise or quietness is desired?* Floors covered with carpet or with a resilient, cushioned material are quieter and more comfortable to walk upon. Floors can also be insulated so that they absorb noise (a desirable feature in high-activity spaces, in households with young children, or in apartments).
4. *Should the floor be hard or soft?* In some areas (as in a mud room or utility room), a hard surface may be more desirable. The amount of standing and walking required in the space should be the primary factor in the selection of a floor covering.
5. *How safe is the floor covering?* Safety should always be a consideration. Some surfaces are slippery when wet or waxed and should not be used, particularly in households in which there are older people. High-traffic areas should also be safe for walking.
6. *What kind of atmosphere is desirable in the house?* Some floor coverings are more formal in effect than others. Some suggest the outdoors. Some floor coverings, such as Italian or Mexican tiles, are indicative of a specific country. Floor color is also a factor: some colors are bright and sunny, while others are somber; the light reflectance of the floor color can affect the amount of electricity consumed, for lighter floors make the interior brighter; a warm color may create psychological warmth, while the warmth of wood represents a sentimental link with the past.

Figure 7.22
The mirrored ceiling and walls add a feeling of spaciousness. The watercloset is concealed behind a mirrored door. (Courtesy of Sherle Wagner International, Inc.)

THE BACKGROUND ENVIRONMENT 125

Figure 7.23
A ceiling of differing heights adds interest to this space. Interior designer: François Catroux. (Courtesy of Solid Fuel Advisory Board)

Figure 7.24
A stained open ceiling can complement a room. (Courtesy of Kirsch Co.)

Figure 7.25
Ceiling tiles are available in a wood-grain plank. (Courtesy of Armstrong Cork Co.)

7. *What is the cost of the floor covering?* The initial cost of a floor is high, and so is its replacement cost. Durability as well as initial cost should therefore be considered, and the time and energy required to maintain the floor.

Hard-Surface Floor Coverings.

Hard-surface floor coverings are divided into nonresilient and resilient surfaces. The nonresilient types are stone, marble, terrazzo, slate, ceramic tiles, quarry tiles, flagstone, and brick. Ceramic tiles are very durable and have been used for centuries (Plate 33). Slate is elegant and may be used in many areas of the interior (Fig. 7.27).

Improved production methods and new materials have been responsible for the increased interest in hard-surface floor coverings. Vinyl is available in almost any color,

Table 7.1
Hard Surface Nonresilient Floor Materials

Material	Description	Use	Advantages	Disadvantages
Concrete	smooth or textured; colors may be added to mixture before pouring or it may be painted	hard-wear areas; patios; showers; may be covered with other materials	inexpensive	hard, cold
Brick	many textures, colors, and sizes; buff, browns, yellows, reds, grays	hard-wear areas; country kitchens; hearths	can be used both inside and outside	expensive; grease will penetrate; transmits cold and dampness; hard and noisy
Slate	nonporous; dark blue to greenish-gray	foyers; inside and outside; hearths	long-wearing; elegant appearance	hard and noisy; very expensive; slippery when wet
Flagstone	flat stones, either cut or natural shape; grays, beige, browns	high-traffic areas; hearths; inside and outside	durable; easily maintained	very expensive; cold and hard
Marble	wide variety of colors: natural, beige, green, black, veining	high-traffic areas; bathrooms	elegant; long-wearing	cold and hard
Terrazzo	marble chips in concrete; limited selection of colors	foyers; baths; patios; high-traffic areas	maintenance-free; hard-wearing	hard; slippery when wet; noisy
Ceramic and Quarry Tiles	clay-fired; unglazed or glazed; surface-patterned or textured	many areas; used for effect	tough and impervious to stains and grease	cold; hard; noisy
Wood	over 100 kinds used; many colors; may be stained or painted; can be laid in many patterns	anywhere	can be sanded and refinished; warm, beautiful; permanent	fairly hard; noisy

Table 7.2
Hard Surface Resilient Floor Materials

Material	Description	Use	Advantages	Disadvantages
Asphalt Tiles	wide range of muted colors	concrete subfloor; any floor; areas of heavy use	inexpensive; can be used anywhere	can be cracked or dented; some not grease proof; very hard; noisy; slippery when wet or waxed
Vinyl Asbestos	wide color range	any indoor area	inexpensive; stain-resistant; wears well; easily maintained; may be dented by furniture	hard and noisy
Rubber Tile	wide color range, some marbleized	kitchen; bath; utility; children's rooms; family room	Soft; quiet; very resilient; resists most stains	may be damaged by grease and oils; moderately easy to maintain; difficult to lay; rubber heels will mark
Cork Tile	light to dark brown	areas of light use; not for kitchen use	very resilient; quiet and comfortable; provides good insulation	expensive; chips at edges; fades in sunlight; dents
Vinyl Cork	light to dark brown	areas of light use; not for kitchens	resilient; richer color; provides good insulation; easy to clean	less expensive than cork; easier to clean than cork; not as resilient as cork, easily dented
Sheet Vinyl and Vinyl Tiles	wide color and pattern range	any interior floor; counters	easily cleaned; resists most household materials; resists chipping; built-in luster; tough; waterproof	expensive

pattern, and texture and can appear either informal or formal. Vinyl can also simulate other, less functional floor materials and, with a cushioned back, makes walking or standing more comfortable.

Wood remains the most popular hard-surface floor covering. More than one hundred kinds of wood are used for floors, although red oak and white oak are the most popular. Wood is durable, but requires more maintenance than other types of floors. Its appearance can be restored by sanding and refinishing (Fig. 7.28). Wood comes in narrow planks, either tongue-and-grooved or butt-jointed; random-width planks; and parquet (Fig. 7.29). Wood may be left natural or stained or painted; it may be impregnated with plastic and irradiated (this must be done at the factory), or stenciled. It is warm looking, although noisy and hard to walk on, and gives an interior a certain character, depending upon what kind of finish is used. Irradiated woods need a minimum of care (Tables 7.1 and 7.2).

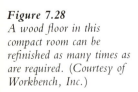

Figure 7.29
This unusual floor consists of slices of mesquite in a natural finish. (Courtesy of Kentucky Wood Floors)

Soft Floor Coverings

The history of soft floor coverings is a long one. Tomb records from ancient Egypt show that patterned fabrics were used on the floor before the thrones of the Pharaohs. Rugs were mentioned in the Bible and by ancient Greek writers. Scandinavian fishermen wore Rya rugs (long-pile wool rugs) as protection against the cold and sea spray. During the Middle Ages and in Tudor England, dried grasses and rushes were spread upon the floor, with the bottom layers remaining as long as forty years, and the top layers sprinkled with sweet-smelling herbs to kill the many odors. Rugs were often used for table coverings, for they were too valuable and scarce to be used on the floors. Rugs made in Persia before the fourth century B.C. were intricate and elaborately knotted, indicating a long rug-making tradition. Persian rugs of silk and wool were exported to Europe from about the sixteenth century. Turkish rugs, made by domestic weavers rather than by court weavers, were also exported and much in demand. In 1608 a carpet manufactory was established in the Louvre. The Aubusson manufactory was established in 1743, with only women permitted to weave the carpets. Savonnerie carpets were first made in Beauvais in 1780. The revocation of the Edict of Nantes in 1685 forced many Huguenots to leave France and come to Brussels and Flanders; later, Flemish emigrants helped to establish the English carpet industry. The first horizontal Brussels loom was erected at Wilton, England. By 1800, there were 1000 carpet looms at Kidderminster where carpets are still made today. In 1755, Axminster carpets were first made by female weavers. Hand looms were in use until 1839, when power looms were adapted to carpet weaving. From that time, carpet making spread rapidly all over the world.

Terms The terms *carpet* and *rug* are often used interchangeably, but there are differences between the terms. *Carpeting* refers to the textiles used in both rugs and carpets; *rug* refers to a standard size piece of carpeting, bound or finished at the edges; and *carpet* is cut from a roll of carpeting, ranging in width from twenty-seven inches to more than eighteen feet. *Broadloom* refers to carpeting woven on a broad loom, or a loom over six feet wide.

Wall-to-wall carpets unify a room, making it appear spacious and luxurious, and require less maintenance than hard-surface floors or floor coverings. Wall-to-wall carpet is suitable for all rooms in the house and is even used in some outside areas. Installation adds to the cost, however. Area rugs can be used over wall-to-wall carpets or hard-surface floors. They accent an area or define spaces in an interior (Fig. 7.30). Oriental, Rya, and hand-woven rugs are examples of area rugs. Carpet tiles (Figs. 7.31 and 7.32) can be easily laid and replaced in areas of high traffic. They are available in felted squares, printed patterns, shag, and heavy gauge.

Fabrication Methods Carpeting is made in a variety of methods, machine-made and hand-made. Machine methods include tufting, weaving, knitting, needle-punching, and flocking. Hand processes include tufting, braiding, hooking, crocheting, shearing and hand-tying (Figs. 7.33 and 7.34).

About 90 per cent of the carpeting made today is *tufted* (Fig. 7.35). Tufted carpets are

made on large multi-needled tufting machines. The yarn is stitched through a preconstructed backing to form a loop or tuft. Frequently the back is coated with latex to hold the tufts in place. This is the most inexpensive and rapid rug-making process. It is possible to vary pile height, to cut or loop the pile; and it is possible to vary pattern and surface texture.

The *knitted* carpet is faster to make than a woven carpet but slower to make than a tufted carpet. The backing is constructed when the carpet is made. The process involves different sets of needles that loop the backing, stitching and pile yarns together. Most knitted carpets are solid or tweed with varying pile heights or an even pile.

Woven carpets are of three kinds: *velvet, Wilton* and *Axminster*. The velvet method of construction is the least complicated. Velvet carpets usually come in solid colors, although occasionally a tweed effect may be achieved. The Wilton carpet is made on a Jacquard loom which can handle up to six different-colored yarns. The Axminster is made in a wide variety of colors and patterns.

A method similar to hand-hooking is *needle-punching*. It was first used for indoor-outdoor carpets, but is now used for indoor carpets as well. Hooked needles are used to interlock fibers into the backing. The fibers are then compressed into a felt-like carpeting.

Flocked carpets resemble a dense cut-pile velvet. Short fibers are electrostatically embedded into an adhesive-coated backing.

Oval or round *braided* carpets are commercially made of strips of fabrics. The strips may also be crocheted together.

Hooked rugs are made by pushing tufts of yarn or fabric through a woven backing on which a design has been drawn. The loops may be cut or left uncut.

Hand-tied or *hand-knotted* rugs are made in Spain, Portugal, India, Pakistan, Morocco, the Soviet Union, Turkey, Iran, Afghanistan, Japan, China and Hong Kong. They are the descendants of Oriental rugs. They can be made in any size, shape, color, or pattern. *Hand-tufted* rugs, made in Puerto Rico, Hong Kong, and Japan, are also available in any size, shape, color or pattern. They are made with a hand-tufting gun which shoots the tuft into the backing (Fig. 7.33).

Carpet Backing The carpet backing serves as foundation for the carpet as well as securing the pile yarn. It also provides strength, stiffness, and weight, helps to keep the carpet flat, and absorbs sound. Many carpet backings are coated with latex, which further secures the yarns and helps to prevent skidding. Materials used for backing are jute, cotton, and polypropylene. Polypropylene is lighter in weight than the other two, will not mildew or absorb moisture, and will not shrink.

Figure 7.31
Carpet squares are used to create wall-to-wall carpeting in this L-shaped multi-purpose room. (Courtesy of Armstrong Cork Co.)

Figure 7.32
Carpet squares offer the do-it-yourselfer an easy installation method with professional results. (Courtesy of Armstrong Cork Co.)

Figure 7.33
An example of hand tufting. Rug designed by Fran Murphy, interior designer. Photograph by Les Rachline. (Courtesy of Lorenzo, Inc., Miami)

Table 7.3
Carpet Fibers

Fiber	Description	Resilience	Soil resistance	Upkeep	Advantages	Disadvantages
Wool	standard by which other fibers judged; soft, warm, luxurious; matte appearance	excellent	good	may stain	dyes well; excellent appearance	expensive; not water-/sun-resistant
Nylon	dull to lustrous; warm, comfortable	excellent	good	easy	high abrasion resistance; nonallergenic; will not mold or mildew; good colors; can be made static-resistant	sun degrades; pills
Acrylic	warm, fluffy; resembles wool	excellent	excellent	easy	good resistance to abrasion; nonallergenic; excellent sun resistance	pills when new; static in low humidity
Polyester	soft, luxurious; resembles wool	good	excellent	excellent	good abrasion resistance; good colors	pills when new; some problems with crushing
Olefin	some luster; waxy feel	good, if construction controlled	excellent	easy	nonabsorbent; non-static; nonpilling; colorfast	moisture lies on surface; color and design limited
Cotton	soft	fair	poor	excellent	dyes well; less expensive than other fibers	not too durable

Figure 7.34
Craftsman shearing a custom rug at Lorenzo, Inc., Miami. Photograph by Les Rachline. (Courtesy of Lorenzo, Inc., Miami)

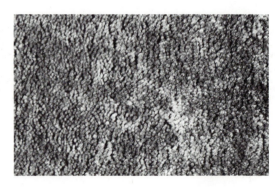

Figure 7.35
The tufting method was used to make this plush carpet. It was autoclave heat set. The fiber is 50 per cent polyester and 50 per cent spun nylon. (Courtesy of Armstrong Cork Co.)

Carpet Padding Padding underneath carpets and rugs cushions the surface, lengthens carpet life, increases sound absorption, and provides walking and standing comfort. Materials used for padding are natural hair and fiber blends and foam and sponge rubber. Rubber padding is more resilient and moisture-resistant, but it will disintegrate with age; hair and fiber blends will mildew and mat with age, but they do not transfer color to the carpet and they resist impact. Carpet padding of the correct type can prolong the life of a carpet by 50 per cent.

Installation There are two methods of installing carpet (except carpet tiles). The carpet may be stretched to pretacked strips of plywood attached to the walls of the room. This results in a smooth surface. In the second method, the carpet is glued directly to the floor without a cushion.

Finishes of Edges Area rugs have a finished edge of some type. The *beveled* edge is merely a cut edge. The *serged* edge is formed by cotton yarns (which should match the face yarn) sewn on the raw edge. Some edges are

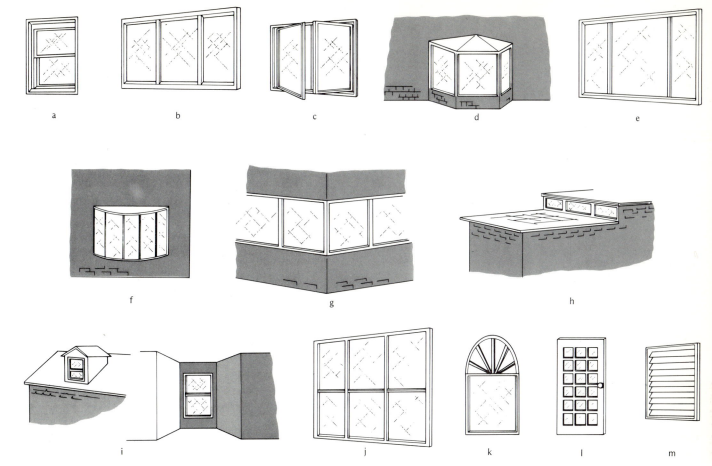

a   b   c   d   e

f   g   h

i   j   k   l   m

Figure 7.36
Window types
a. Double-hung
b. Ranch or strip
c. Casement
d. Bay
e. Picture
f. Bow
g. Corner
h. Clerestory
i. Dormer
j. Window wall
k. Arch
l. French door
m. Jalousie

bound with a fabric that matches the face yarns. A woven carpet may have a *self edge,* in which the warp threads are tied off. Edges may also be *fringed.*

Selection of Carpeting Carpet is selected for interior floors for a variety of reasons. It is comfortable to walk on; it effectively insulates against cold and sound; and it adds a dimension of safety, for one is less likely to slip on a carpeted floor (Table 7.3).

Windows

The word *window* comes from the Norse word, *wind-eye,* and early windows were high slits, kept securely fastened to protect the occupants of the dwelling from attack and to keep them as warm as possible. Animal skins, oiled paper, or cloth were placed over them to keep out drafts. In Tudor England, glass was available in small pieces only, and windows were made with small, often diamond-shaped panes. Gradually, as larger pieces of glass were produced, windows became larger. The world was now visible from the windows, which were often bays with window seats built into them. As more textiles became available, they were often hung at the windows.

Today, more people are realizing that the main function of a window is to expand interior space. This is especially important because, with rapidly increasing building costs, interior space is growing smaller. Windows are also the primary source of natural light and ventilation for an interior. Window coverings serve to reduce glare, and to soften, regulate, or filter natural light; they can also block out heat and cold; protect carpet and furniture from sun, hide an undesirable view, absorb sound, camouflage undesirable architectural features, extend or accent wall colors, and unify walls and windows. Studies at the Illinois Institute of Technology by Dix and Lavan indicate that roller shades can reduce heat loss 25 per cent in winter and allow 50 per cent less heat to enter in the summer months.

Types of Windows

Window glass is either movable or fixed in the frame. Fixed windows do not open. Movable windows come in several types. The *double-hung* window has two sashes which slide up and down (Figs. 7.36a and 7.37). It is inexpensive, easy to install and to operate; it does not sag or warp; it can be weatherproofed and may be opened from either the top or the bottom. Only half the window may be opened at one time, however, and when it is open, there

Figure 7.37
A double-hung window opens from the top and the bottom. These are covered with fiberglass-mesh shades, which deflect the hot rays of the sun, while permitting one to look out (but not to see in) during the day. Shutters are used at night for privacy. (Courtesy of Window Shade Manufacturers' Association)

arrangements and window treatments. The *corner* window (Figs. 7.36g and 7.39) may or may not open. The *window wall* (Fig. 7.40) is formed by a strip of double-hung or fixed windows (Figs. 7.36e and 7.36j). *Bow* windows may be of the double-hung or casement type, but are usually fixed (Figs. 7.36f and 7.41). Curved bow windows do not project as much as bay windows do. Floor-length drapery is unsatisfactory for this type of window.

The *casement* window has a single or double sash that slides or is hinged and swings inward or outward by means of a crank (Figs. 7.36c and 7.41). In the latter type, the entire window can be opened and ventilation can be directed by the angle of the opening. This window is difficult to weatherproof, however, and provides no protection from the rain (Fig. 7.41). Casement windows that open in interfere with furniture arrangements; those that open out are dangerous if they open onto an area where people may walk. The *awning* window has three or more horizontal sashes, hinged at the top, which swing outward by a crank mechanism. They offer draft-free ventilation and do not admit rain, but they are difficult to seal. The *jalousie* is similar to an awning window, except that its horizontal sashes are narrow (Figs. 7.36m and 7.42). They project only slightly from the wall, but they are difficult to weatherproof and to clean. *Dormer* windows, which may be double-hung, project at right angles over a pitched roof and form an inside alcove (Fig. 7.36i). The dormer extension has a roof of its own. *Ranch* or *strip* windows, set high in the wall (Fig. 7.36b), are functional and allow furniture to be placed beneath them. They slide or open in and out (Fig. 7.43).

Fixed windows do not open. Composed of a single piece of glass or of several panels, they are inexpensive to install but can be difficult to clean and may present a problem in the control of heat and light. Fixed windows come in several types. The *picture* window is composed of a large sheet of glass with one or more fixed panes at the sides that may be adjustable (Fig. 7.36e). *Clerestory* windows are windows at the top of a wall above an adjacent roof. Usually left uncovered (Fig. 7.36h), they admit light while retaining privacy. *Skylights* are ceiling windows; they retain privacy while admitting both sun and moonlight, never interfere with furniture arrangements, and take up no usable wall space (Figs. 7.44 and 6.50), but the only view through a skylight is the sky and perhaps some tall trees. (The concrete

Figure 7.38
A bay window adds space to an interior. This bay is curtained with sash curtains and draw draperies. Interior designer: Shirley Regendahl. (Courtesy of Belgian Linen Association)

is no protection from the rain. Double-hung windows are difficult to clean from the inside and may stick when painted.

There are many kinds of double-hung window styles. The *bay* window projects outward from the wall at ground level (Figs. 7.36d and 7.38), forming a recess in the interior wall. Bay windows provide abundant light and ventilation but may render difficult furniture

Figure 7.39
A corner window opens up a space. The floor is quarry tile. (Courtesy of Tile Council of America)

Figure 7.41
Casement windows are assembled to form a gracefully curved bow. (Courtesy of Caradco Wood Windows)

Figure 7.42
Jalousie windows on a glassed-in-porch. (Courtesy of Tile Council of America)

Figure 7.40
This house in the trees has large window walls to take advantage of the view. Architects: Roland/Miller Assoc. Photograph by Barbeau Engh. (Courtesy of California Redwood Assn.)

tube in Fig. 2.3 serves as a skylight and also catches the heat in winter.) *Arched* windows are frequently found in older houses (Figs. 7.36k and 7.45). The arch is usually left uncovered. *French doors* are windows set in wood door frames (Figs. 7.36l and 7.46). They are usually hung in pairs and covered with sash curtains.

Location of Windows

Picture windows formerly were placed at the front of the house, where the view was usually unattractive. Today, they are placed where there is a view, if possible. Privacy is an important factor in window placement. Other factors are light, ventilation, heat and cold, furniture placement, and ease of maintenance. Heat and cold can be somewhat controlled by exterior awnings, shutters, or louvres, as well as by roof overhangs. In summer, the sun is steep-angled, rising in the northeast and setting in the northwest; thus the house requires protection from these rays. In the winter, the sun is at a lower angle and an overhang will not prevent its rays from entering. This can also be a method of passive solar energy, if masonry or concrete is used for they retain heat. Solari's house in Arizona illustrates the angle of the skylight which catches the winter sun and keeps out the summer sun (Fig. 2.3).

Window Treatments

Rich, complicated drapery treatments with swags, tie-backs, and sheer glass curtains at

Figure 7.43
Strip or ranch windows allow great flexibility in furniture arrangement because furniture can be placed beneath them. They admit light but assure privacy. Interior designer: Allen G. Scruggs. (Courtesy of Tile Council of America)

the windows were once fashionable (Fig. 7.47). Today, the keynote is often simplicity (Fig. 7.48), and windows are often left uncovered. Ideally, window treatments should make interesting patterns in the interior, filter light, cut glare, expand interior space by admitting exterior views, and block out heat and cold.

If the view outside the window is unattractive, window treatment—fabric, shades, shutters, or blinds—can create a center of interest in addition to providing privacy (Fig. 7.49). The shape and placement of the window can be disregarded: window treatments can extend to the ceiling and beyond the dimensions of the window itself. Transparent glass curtains, shades, draperies, and shutters can be used alone or in combination.

Shades

Window shades may be opaque (Fig. 7.49), or translucent (Fig. 7.37), plain or textured. Opaque shades (some are vinyl-coated) control heat and glare and provide privacy at night. Block-out or room-darkening shades completely shut out the light in the daytime. Shades with fabric laminated to them (Fig. 7.49) may match other fabric in the room.

Figure 7.44
Skylights as they appear on the roof. (Courtesy of Bruce Weale)

Figure 7.46
A French door may be curtained with sash curtains, attached at both top and bottom. (Courtesy of Wallcovering Industry Bureau)

Figure 7.45
The lower part of an arched window can be curtained and the top left open. (Courtesy of Tile Council of America)

Woven wood shades (Fig. 7.50) let in more light and do not provide as much privacy at night, but they have an interesting texture and pattern. *Roman shades* are woven-wood or cloth blinds that fold horizontally when raised (Figs. 3.33 and 7.25; 7.54, Plate 45). They are usually mounted on a *cornice board,* a wooden board with a shape lower edge. Soft fabric mounted on a vertical tape makes *Austrian shades.* They fall in graceful, scalloped folds (Fig. 3.44). Often the fabric is sheer (Plate 35).

Shutters

Shutters were a popular treatment for windows in Colonial times because they kept out the cold and did not require scarce textiles. They may be one piece, or open in sections for large windows (Fig. 7.18). Louvered shutters permit adjustment of light levels. Shutters allow light to stream in during the day yet be completely shut out at night (Figs. 6.6, 7.18, 7.28).

Venetian Blinds

Venetian blinds, used in Colonial homes, are still used today (Fig. 7.51). The early examples were made of wood, but today blinds are also available in metal and plastic. Vertical blinds can be shaped to fit openings of various kinds, control light from side to side, and are easier to maintain because they do not collect as much dust as horizontal blinds.

Draperies and Curtains

Draperies and curtains are the most common kind of window treatments. They control light, provide privacy, absorb sound, insulate against heat and cold, and protect carpets and upholstery fabrics against fading. They can minimize or conceal architectural defects and they can be used to change the apparent size and shape of windows. For example, draperies hung from the ceiling by carrying the eye upward, make the window and the ceiling appear taller (Fig. 7.52). Draperies and curtains that blend with the wall color make the room appear larger and can increase the importance of the outside view (Fig. 7.53). On the other hand, draperies of contrasting color and/or patterned material direct attention to the window treatment rather than to the view (Fig. 7.54).

Draperies and curtains may be stationary or may open and close. *Curtain* usually refers to a stationary, lightweight, translucent or trans-

Figure 7.48
Because of the privacy afforded by the level of this second-story bath among the tree tops, these windows were left uncurtained. (Courtesy of American Olean Tile Co.)

Figure 7.51
Venetian blinds provide privacy and control light. (Courtesy of Armstrong Cork Co.)

Figure 7.52
The sheers draw on a ceiling traverse rod and the tie-backs are stationary. The eating area is defined by a rug. Interior designer: J. David Polk. Photograph by Harold Davis. (Courtesy of Kirsch Co.)

Figure 7.53
Draperies that match the wall color make an interior appear larger. Architect: Ronald Sorce. Photograph by Jessie Walker. (Courtesy of Kirsch Co.)

Figure 7.54
Draw draperies combined with a woven-wood Roman shade call attention to the window treatment. Notice the stenciled design on the floor. Interior designer: Morley Smith. (Courtesy of Kirsch Co.)

Figure 7.55
Casement windows in this nursery open inward. (Courtesy of GTR Wall Coverings)

Figure 7.56
A Roman shade, tie-backs, and an upholstered cornice complete this window treatment. (Courtesy of Belgian Linen Association)

pinch-pleated and hung on a stationary or *traverse rod* (on which curtains may be drawn to either end or to one side). Glass curtains provide privacy during the day, but not at night. Fabrics selected for glass curtains should be resistant to sunlight and are usually more attractive in soft pastel colors for light filtering through will pick up the color of the fabric. *Casement curtains* are transparent, translucent, or opaque open-weave fabrics. Casement curtains usually have an open weave (Figs. 3.40 and 6.55). Occasionally the terms *glass curtain* and *casement curtain* are used interchangeably. A separate lining left open by day and closed for privacy at night, may be used with glass curtains; this requires a double traverse rod.

Sash Curtains Curtains hung on a rod on the window sash or stretched between two rods at the top and the bottom of the window are called *sash curtains* (Fig. 7.38). These curtains are appropriate for windows or doors (Fig. 7.46).

Café Curtains *Café curtains* are hung in tiers, one or more, with or without a valance. They may be gathered or pinch-pleated and are hung from the rod with rings, clips, or hooks. Because café curtains are usually hand-drawn, the fabric should be easy to care for. Café curtains are functional because one or more tiers may be kept open or half-open (Figs. 3.38 and 7.7).

Tieback Curtains Tieback curtains are fabric draperies tied back and fastened to the side of the window frame or to the wall with fabric, cords, chains, or other decorative treatments (Figs. 7.4 and 7.24). Some have ruffles while others are tailored. Crisscross curtains are tieback panels that overlap one another at the top (Fig. 7.55).

Draw Draperies *Draw draperies* are mounted on a traverse rod (Figs. 3.21, 7.53, and 7.54). The traverse rod can be recessed into the ceiling or painted to match the color of the wall or window frame, or it can be more decorative (Fig. 3.39). One-way draw rods draw only to the right or to the left; on two-way draw rods, the drapery meets in the center of the window. Custom-made multiple-draw rods are also available.

Valances The *valance* is a gathered or pleated strip generally of matching fabric at

parent fabric (Fig. 3.52) that filters rather than shuts out light. *Draperies* usually refers to a heavier, opaque fabric, frequently lined, hung at the sides of the window, that may or may not draw (Fig. 7.54). Draperies and curtains extend from the ceiling or the top of the window to the sill, to the bottom of the apron, or to the floor.

Glass Curtains Thin, sheer materials that hang over the window are called glass curtains (Fig. 7.52). They may be shirred onto a rod or

Figure 7.57
An upholstered lambrequin surrounds the window in this living room. Furniture designer: Milo Baughman. (Courtesy of Thayer Coggin)

the top of the drapery or curtain. It conceals the hardware (Figs. 3.33, 3.51, and 6.52), and also increases the apparent height of the window. Café curtains may have a scalloped or gathered valance (Fig. 7.7). A *festoon* is a valance suspended between two sides of the drapery (Fig. 7.1). A *swag* is a draped valance that cascades down one or both sides of the window, giving it a formal effect (Fig. 7.47).

Cornices A *cornice* serves the same purpose as a valance, but is made of wood, metal, or fabric (Fig. 7.56). Cornices often have a decorative lower edge trimmed with molding, fringe, or braid (Fig. 7.25). A *lambrequin* is similar to a cornice but it extends over the top and both sides of the window (Fig. 7.57). It may be painted or covered with fabric.

Lined Draperies Draperies are lined for several reasons. The lining creates a unified appearance from the outside, protects the drapery fabric from fading, adds weight that makes the drapery hang better, and insulates

Figure 7.58
Lined draperies being fabricated for a hotel. In this example, the lining is laminated to the back. (Courtesy Hilmar Skagfield, President, Skandia Draperies Manufacturing Company, Tallahassee, Florida)

the interior against both heat and cold. Lined draperies cost more than the unlined, but the cost is usually worthwhile (Fig. 7.58).

Glossary

Austrian Shades. Soft fabric mounted on vertical tape and falling in soft, graceful folds.

Bay Window. Three or more windows that projects from the wall.

Bow Window. Curved bay windows.

Braided Carpet. Oval or round carpet made of strips of braided fabric.

Clerestory Window. Windows at top of wall above an adjacent roof line.

Corner Window. Windows at the corner of a building.

Cornice. Wood, metal, or fabric-covered decorative finish at top of window.

Flocked Carpet. Carpet that resembles a thick pile velvet.

Dormer Window. Window that projects at right angles from a pitched roof and makes a small inside alcove.

Double-Hung Window. Window with two sashes that slide vertically.

Curtain. Stationary, lightweight, translucent or transparent fabric that filters the light through the window.

French Door. Windows in a wood door frame, usually hung in pairs.

Hand-Tied Rug. Hand-knotted rug.

Hand-Tufted Rug. Rug made with a hand-tufting gun that shoots tuft into backing.

Hooked Rug. Rug made by pushing tufts of yarn or fabric through a woven backing.

Knitted Carpet. Carpet made at the same time as the backing, with different sets of needles to loop the backing, stitching, and pile yarns together.

Lambrequin. Painted or fabric-covered cornice that extends over the top and sides of the window.

Load-bearing Wall. Wall that is part of the basic structure of a building.

Needle-Punching. Hooked needles mechanically interlock fibers into the backing of this carpet which is then compressed into a felt-like carpet.

Picture Window. Large window (usually does not open).

Ranch Window. Strip of windows set high on the wall.

Roman Shades. Panels of stitched or press-pleated fabric or of woven wood that fold horizontally.

Shutters. Louvered wooden window covers.

Skylight. Glassed aperture in the ceiling.

Strip Windows. (See Ranch Windows).

Tufted Carpet. Carpet made on multi-needled machines that stitch the tufts through a preconstructed (and frequently coated) backing.

Valance. Decorative strip matching drapery fabric that hides the hardware.

Window Wall. Glass wall.

Venetian Blinds. Blinds of wood or metal that can be opened to adjust the light.

Woven Carpet. Velvet, Wilton, or Axminster carpet made on a loom.

Bibliography

CONRAN, TERENCE. *The House Book.* New York: Crown Publishers, Inc., 1974.

EVANS, HELEN MARIE. *Man the Designer.* New York: Macmillian Publishing Co., Inc., 1973.

FAULKNER, RAY, and FAULKNER, SARAH. 4th ed. *Inside Today's Home.* New York: Holt, Rinehart and Winston, 1975.

HARRIS, CYRIL M. (ed.) *Historic Architecture Sourcebook.* New York: McGraw-Hill Book Company, 1977.

Mussallem: The Oriental Rug. Jacksonville, Fla.: Mussallem Oriental Rugs, Inc., 1977.

SCOTT, JOHN S. *A Dictionary of Building.* Baltimore: Penguin Books, 1964.

WHITON, SHERRILL. *Interior Design and Decoration.* 4th ed. New York: J. B. Lippincott Company, 1974.

ZAKAS, SPIROS. *Lifespace.* New York: Macmillan Publishing Co., Inc., 1978.

The Textile Environment

Textiles add a unique dimension to the environment. They are pleasant to handle and may range from soft to hard and from smooth to rough. Textiles have been a part of life for centuries. The peoples of the Near East had a knowledge of flax ten thousand years ago and fragments of linen fabrics have been found in the ruins of the homes of Swiss lake dwellers, which date from about 5000 B.C. Wool fabrics were used in Mesopotamia in 5000 B.C.

Textiles have played a part in man's economic history as well, and their production has been affected by political, cultural, military, and religious events. They helped to make possible the rise of city-states in medieval times. England's growth as a commercial center was directly tied to the production of textiles, the first industrialized craft. Silk, discovered in China about 2460 B.C., was a coveted import: it ranked with jewels and spices in value. Even in modern times, textiles have had a strong economic impact. Beginning in the early 1960s, synthetic fibers replaced many natural ones. Industries involved in the production of natural fibers began a widespread decline. Recently, however, as the price differential between natural and synthetic fibers narrowed, there has been a trend back to natural fibers.

Textiles serve to humanize the interior and to relate architecture and furniture to human scale. They soften the lines of today's box-like houses and unify the furnishings of a space (Fig. 8.1 and Plate 35). They define the function of a space, control acoustics, and absorb or reflect light. Changing the textiles in a space can modify the whole effect of the interior. Textiles are pliable and easily draped or fitted to the rounded shapes of upholstery (Fig. 8.2). They are relatively inexpensive and thus easy to replace. In addition they may be cleaned. Textiles are beautiful in themselves and enjoyable both to view and to touch.

Selection of Textiles

Textiles are of primary importance when the designer considers the personality or life style of the client. Textiles can directly reflect the client's emotional needs, contributing to the type of environmental contact that is specifically desired by the client. The fabrics selected should mirror the client's personality, not that of the designer.

Individuals who do not perceive surface texture in the inkblot test of personality tend to deny emotional needs. They will be perceived as "stand-offish" by others and may be emotionally cold or distant. Although they have friends, they tend not to care for close, intimate relationships. They are uncomfortable with the discussion of feelings or the initiation of sensuous behavior. Frequently they are formal or stiff in manner. They tend to prefer hard surfaces, and crisp fabrics with little textural depth.

The inkblot test is not given to clients by interior designers but it is generally easy to recognize clients with such personalities by their stilted or military manner. However, a person can be very outgoing and still have these emotions and design desires. This kind of person knows many people but does not have many close friends. He may enjoy being surrounded by people, but feels very uncomfortable if physical contact or intimate conversation is initiated. The difference between this personality and the former will be reflected in factors such as color as well as texture. The former prefers subdued tones. The latter prefers bright colors which are usually emotionally charged, such as orange,[1] and likes the emotional impact of high-load color, light, and sound combined with hard surfaces.

Individuals at the other end of the emotional spectrum, who on the inkblot test see rich textures, and can perceive a tactile surface from a glossy photography, usually desire intense emotional contact and support. At the extreme emotive end they are very dependent individuals who weep or feel threatened by any hint of loss of emotional support. They desire soft, deep textures and want to be surrounded by these kinds of fabrics.

Other emotion-filled individuals who are not extremely dependent may still desire warm intimate contact with such fabrics. These people like to relate closely to family and friends and want to share intimate thoughts, personal feelings, and physical contact. An interior filled with rich fabrics reflects their personalities and facilitates their intimate contact with others. Low-load, hard-surface textiles are offensive to these people. Just as they seem to have an insatiable capacity for expressing and receiving emotion, so too they

[1] Color and personality are discussed in detail in Chapter 5.

seem to have a boundless desire to be surrounded by warm, soft, deep-textured textiles.

Textile considerations are usually considered in terms of the larger group of people who fall between these extremes. For this group, design flexibility is the rule. Under some circumstances they may desire emotional sharing; under others, they may not. Design can enhance a specific interior so that it becomes suitable to these varying needs. Conversation areas should contain heavy woven fabrics, or unwoven but deeply textured fabrics, patterned or plain, which suggest warmth and intimacy (Fig. 8.3). Hard-surfaced, stain-resistant patterned fabrics are appropriate for the less intense interpersonal contact typical of outer offices and waiting rooms, the game room, and television rooms (Fig. 8.4). Many would also benefit from experiencing soft, rich textures in the bedroom, the living room, and office sanctuaries. For spaces designed for physical activity, light interaction, and nonpersonal exchange—such as the kitchen, entertainment rooms, the bathroom, the laundry room, the workshop in the home and public areas in offices—hard-surface textiles, patterned or plain, are appropriate.

Terms

Certain terms will be used in the course of this discussion:

Crimp: the natural, mechanical, or chemical irregularity of a fiber, or the waves or bends that occur along its length.

Crock: the rubbing off of dye from a fabric, particularly linen.

Fabric: all cloths.

Fiber: the thread or filament that is the fundamental component of textile yarn. To be spinnable, fiber must have strength, flexibility, cohesiveness, a certain uniformity, and a sufficient ratio of length to breadth. Fabrics may be made of one fiber or of a combination of different fibers. Staple fiber is short and must be combined with others to form a yarn.

Filament: a continuous fiber, such as silk

(natural); a man-made fiber which is extruded through a *spinneret* from a solution.

Heat-setting: the shaping of fabric to a certain dimension or shape. Permanent press or pleats are heat-setting processes.

Hydrophilic: adjective used to describe a fiber that readily absorbs moisture.

Hydrophobic: adjective used to describe a fiber that does not absorb moisture.

Loft: the ability of a fiber or fabric to spring back to its original shape; the *compressional resiliency* of a fabric. Permanent high bulk fabrics have more loft.

Man-made fibers: synthetic fibers made from natural sources (rayon, acetate and triacetate, glass, metal, rubber, azlon) and nylon, polyester, acrylic, olefin, saran, spandex, anidex.

Natural fibers: fibers that are found in animal, vegetable, or mineral sources (wool, silk, cotton, linen, asbestos).

Specific gravity: a term used in determining the weight of a fiber (its density) in relationship to its bulk. Nylon is lighter than wool; and glass fibers are the heaviest.

Spinneret: a metal nozzle-like apparatus through which a man-made fiber is extruded.

Fibers

Certain properties of fibers—some of which can be changed or improved by mechanical, chemical, or thermal treatments—are considered to determine its wearability and its suitability for textiles:

Abrasion resistance: the ability of the fiber to resist rubbing. A tough, pliable, smooth surfaced fiber will be more abrasion-resistant than a rough fiber. Nylon is more abrasion-resistant than any other fiber, with wool about in the middle, and cotton and rayon least abrasion-resistant.

Absorbency: the ability of a fiber to take up moisture. Wool is very absorbent, and olefin is nonabsorbent.

Staple fiber: a fiber that varies in length—a number of which must be spun before being made into a textile. Man-made staple fibers are cut into short lengths.

Textile: originally used to describe only woven fabrics, but now used to refer to all cloths; *fabric* and *textile* are interchangeable.

Thermoplastic fiber: a fiber that softens with the application of heat. Synthetic fibers are all thermoplastic, or sensitive to heat, as are silk and wool to a certain extent. Thermoplasticity makes heat-setting possible, but damage will occur at high temperatures.

Chemical resistance: the ability of the fiber to withstand the effects of solvents, bleaches, detergents, alkalis and acids. Because pollution contains alkalis and/or acids, chemical resistance may be a factor in the selection of fabrics.

Durability: the ability of the fiber to withstand the stresses of normal use and to withstand varying degrees of tension without rupturing.

Dyeability: the ability of a fiber to absorb

Figure 8.4
Hard-surface textiles are best for a game room, where personal interaction is light and usage is heavy. Architect: Harry Wenning. (Courtesy of Tile Council of America)

Figure 8.5
The wool fibers tufted by scouring have to be separated before the wool can be combed. The carding machine teazes out the fibers and removes impurities, such as burrs. The wool is then removed from the final doffer (bottom right corner) and gathered into a long, even band called a sliver. (Courtesy of The Wool Bureau, Inc.)

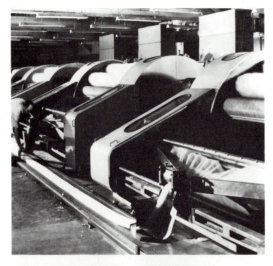

Figure 8.6
A worsted spinning frame. (Courtesy of The Wool Bureau, Inc.)

dye; the less absorbent a fiber, the more difficult it is to dye.

Elasticity: the ability of a fiber or fabric to return to its original size after it has been stretched.

Insect and mildew resistance: the ability of a fiber to withstand the damage caused by moths, insects, and mildew. A protective finish may increase this ability: for example, wool may be moth-proofed.

Luster: the ability of a fabric to reflect light; the smoother the fiber and the weave, the more light will be reflected from the fabric.

Resiliency: the ability of a fiber to resume its original form after creasing, stretching, and twisting. A good crease-resistant fabric is easily cared for and requires little or no ironing.

Stability: the ability of a fiber to retain its shape. Wool, for example, will shrink; it has less stability than nylon, which will not. It is particularly important to remember for window treatments that fabrics that are not dimensionally stable will sag and/or shrink.

Static buildup: the accumulation of static electricity in a fabric. Some fibers are good conductors of electricity, so static electricity does not build up in them; others are not, and therefore require an antistatic finish. Static build-up causes fabric to discharge electricity and to retain soil.

Natural Fibers

Natural fibers are of three types: *protein fibers* (wool and silk), *plant fibers* (cotton and linen), and *mineral fibers* (asbestos). Asbestos is valuable in fireproofing clothing, theater curtains, and so on, but, due to its cancer-causing characteristics, must be used with care. Its use is so specialized that it will not be discussed in this book.

Wool

Wool comes from the protective coat of sheep, one of the first animals to be domesticated. The Babylonians wore woolen garments as early as 4000 B.C. In 1000 B.C. the Phoenicians were engaged in wool trade. The finest source of wool, from the Merino sheep, was introduced into Spain about 800, and the Spanish jealously guarded these sheep until about 1600. By about 800, the French and English were engaged in the wool trade and in 925 a wool-dyers' guild was established in Germany. In 1340, there were over 30,000 workers in the Italian wool trade. In 1748, a wool-carding machine was introduced in Bristol, England. By 1820, there were twenty-four woolen mills operating in New England (Fig. 8.5).

Wool is an absorbent, resilient fiber used to make woolen or worsted fabrics. Woolen fabrics, made of thick, fuzzy yarns, are flexible and soft, with a medium to bulky texture. Worsted textiles, made from tightly twisted wool yarns are crisp, firm, and smooth-surfaced (Fig. 8.6). Wool has a natural crimp which makes it resilient; it is easy to dye (Fig. 8.7), felt, and (because it is thermoplastic) to shape.

There are several processes wool fiber must undergo before it is spun. It is *scoured* in large tubs with soap and water to remove soil and lanolin, its natural grease. It may be dyed at this point (Fig. 8.7). Then it is *carded* to straighten the fibers and remove any impurities. The wool is then formed into a thick rope of fibers known as a *sliver* or *roving* (Fig. 8.5). After this, it is made into a woolen or worsted yarn.

Wool does not burn readily, but it is affected by alkali solutions, so that washing with detergent will damage the fibers. Wool will shrink and, unless treated, is susceptible to damage by moths, but deteriorates very slowly. It is often used in combination with other fibers to achieve surface texture and special effects (Fig. 8.8). Upholstery fabrics, carpets, rugs, and draperies are often made of wool or of wool blends.

Silk

Silk, the protein fiber from the silkworm cocoon, is known to have been used in China as early as 2700 B.C. The secret of silk was closely guarded and many people thought it was a plant fiber. But about 552, two Nestorian monks stole some silkworm eggs and mulberry leaves, and thereafter silks were available in Byzantium and the rich fabrics were much in demand for ecclesiastical garments. By 1100 Italy had become a silk center. Lyons and Rouen were silk centers until 1685, when the revocation of the Edict of Nantes drove many Huguenot silk workers into exile. England then became a silk center. By the nineteenth century, there were many silk manufacturing centers in Europe.

Silk is a smooth, resilient fiber, light in weight and of medium absorbency. It dyes well, achieving a beautiful depth of color, and it has a soft luster. Silk deteriorates somewhat more rapidly than wool and is affected by strong light. Alkalis tend to weaken the fiber, although it does not burn readily. Silk fabric is luxurious and drapes well. It is soil-resistant and tough, but its high cost prohibits its widespread use. However, it is often blended with other fibers. Silk fibers are used in drapery and upholstery fabrics and occasionally in Oriental rugs. Some of the fabrics made of silk fiber are damask, brocade, velvet, and brocatelle.

Cotton

Cotton is a cellulosic fiber, obtained from the seed pod of the cotton plant. It was known

Figure 8.7
The wool is often dyed at the top stage. Here a batch of tops, *contained in perforated cylinders, is being lowered into a radial flow-dyeing machine. The lid is then secured in position and the dye is pumped through during the automatically timed cycle. (Courtesy of The Wool Bureau, Inc.)*

Figure 8.8
New surface textures and new effects in woolen cloth can be achieved by using fancy yarns. This composite fancy yarn is being produced from three separate ones on fancy twisting frames, and will then be utilized in both woven and knit fabrics. (Courtesy of The Wool Bureau, Inc.)

in Egypt and India as early as 3000 B.C. Pieces of cotton fabric dating from about 1200 B.C. have been found in Peru. By 800–900 A.D., cotton fabrics were being made in Japan and Spain. Cotton plantations were an important part of the economy of Virginia by 1650. In 1769, the invention in England of the spinning

Figure 8.9
The singeing, scouring, bleaching, and mercerizing of cloth prepares it for piece-dyeing. (Courtesy of American Textile Manufacturers' Institute)

Figure 8.10
The flax seed, planted early in the spring, grows to three feet. The plants are harvested by machine: pulled, not cut. Stalks are bundled and threshing machines remove the seeds, which are used for linseed oil. (Courtesy of Belgium Linen Association)

jenny and frame by Arkwright and Hargreaves made the production of cotton fabric the first industrialized craft. By 1793, the first cotton mill was built in Rhode Island.

Cotton is an inexpensive fiber, hydrophilic (absorbent) and easily laundered. It has low luster, but the process of *mercerization* adds luster to it. (Fig. 8.9). It lacks resiliency and flexibility, but wash-and-wear finishes can counteract its tendency to wrinkle. It is highly flammable, but flame-resistant and flame-retardant finishes can control this characteristic to a great extent. Cotton is used for scatter rugs, curtains, and upholstery. It is often blended with man-made fibers.

Linen

Linen is a bast fiber from the stalk of the flax plant. It is difficult and expensive to process, and therefore expensive for the consumer. Flax was known in the Near East about 8000 B.C. and remnants have been found in Swiss lake ruins dating from about 5100 B.C. Linen is mentioned in the Old Testament as being used for the robes of Egyptian princes. Greek males wore linen tunics during the time of Homer, and the Roman priests wore them in the last years of the Republic. Linen and woolen cloth was used during the Middle Ages, and fine linen was highly valued. Linen was woven in Ireland about 1000 and improved with the arrival of French weavers after the revocation of the Edict of Nantes. Linen is manufactured extensively today in Belgium, England, Scotland, and Ireland (Fig. 8.10).

Linen is a strong fiber with natural body. It has thick and thin fiber bundles. It wears evenly and for a long time, but it has low resiliency and wrinkles easily unless treated with a crease-resistant finish. Linen is undamaged by insects, alkaline solutions, or dry-cleaning solvents. It is very hydrophilic, but it has less affinity than cotton for dye. It also *crocks*. Linen, although high in price, may be an economical fabric owing to its durability. It is used for draperies, slipcovers, upholstery, wall hangings, and as background for needlework.

Man-made Fibers

Man-made fibers differ from natural fibers, in that they are produced in the laboratory (Fig. 8.11). Rayon and acetate, are produced from cellulose, a natural raw material. Glass and metallic fibers are produced from naturally occurring nonfibrous materials. Other fibers, such as nylon, polyester, acrylic, modacrylic and olefin are synthesized from chemical compounds. They are called synthetic fibers.

Rayon

Rayon, made from regenerated cellulose, was the first man-made fiber. In 1884, Hilaire de Chardonnet, a Frenchman, produced rayon by the nitrocellulose method. Between 1890 and 1892, two other processes, the viscose process (the major one in use today) and the cuprammonium process, were discovered. The fiber was named *rayon* in 1924. At first the fiber was stiff, with high luster and low resiliency, though low in cost. New treatments have improved rayon. It is stronger, but still very weak when wet. It lacks the elasticity of other fibers, but blends well with many of the new synthetics. It is absorbent, dyes easily, and is inexpensive to produce. In 1954, solution-dyed rayon became possible. Rayon is still flammable; it still will shrink, and it has a low resistance to wrinkling (unless treated), to light, and to mildew. Rayon is a versatile fiber, however, and is used for both knitted and woven fabrics including draperies, curtains, slipcovers, bedspreads, upholstery, floor coverings, and decorative pillows. Some trade names for rayon are: *Avril, Zantrel, Cupioni, Jetspun, Enkrome, Coloray, Fibro, Bemberg, Fortisan,* and *Avicron.*

Acetate and Triacetate

Acetate was first discovered in 1894; triacetate, in 1869. They were commercially produced in the 1930s and 1940s. By 1951, they could be solution-dyed. Both are low-cost fibers with a nice body and drape. Triacetate is more resistant than acetate to sunlight and high temperatures. Both are luxurious in appearance; weak when wet; nonabsorbent (and thus subject to static buildup). They are used for knit fabrics, drapery backing, upholstery, and shower curtains. Some trade names for acetate are *Avisco, Chromspun, Estron, Celenese, Celara,* and *Acele;* some of those for triacetate are *Avril, Rhonel,* and *Arnel.*

Glass

A silk weaver first wove glass fibers in 1840. In 1893, lamp shades of glass fibers and silk were exhibited at the World's Columbian Exposition in Chicago. It was not until the late 1930s, however, that Owens-Corning made Fiberglas. It is soil-resistant, totally noncombustable, strong, nonabsorbent, and unaffected by mildew, moths, sunlight, or chemicals; and it helps to insulate against noise, heat, and cold. But because glass fibers are completely nonabsorbent, they are difficult to dye, and they break when abraded or flexed, although a coating of thermoplastic resins enables them to resist wear to some extent. Glass fibers can cause skin irritation in some people. They are used primarily for draperies. Trade names for glass fabrics are *Fiberglas, Beta Fiberglas, Vitron, Uniglass,* and *Pittsburg PPG.*

Metals

Ancient weavers used metallic fibers made from silver, gold, bronze, and copper, but the fibers were soft, frangible, and tarnishable. In

Figure 8.11
The spinneret, from which synthetic fibers are extruded in a liquid chemical form. (Courtesy of American Textile Manufacturers' Institute)

addition, they were abrasive. About 1940, it was discovered that a thin layer of metal could be laminated between two layers of thermoplastic film. It thus became possible to dry clean or wash metallic fabrics without damaging the metal fibers; moreover, the fabrics were now impervious to high temperatures. In another process, developed later, metal particles were laminated to a polyester film. Metalized mylar, first made in 1957, is used to weave fabrics. Some tradenames for metallic yarns are *Lurex, Chromeflex, Malora, Lamé,* and *Nylco.*

Thermoplastic Fibers

Thermoplastic, or heat-sensitive, fibers have certain characteristics in common, some of which are advantages and others disadvantages:

1. They have low moisture absorption, which makes them resistant to spots, easy to wash and quick to dry, and facilitates spot-removal, but it renders them difficult to dye and contributes to static buildup in them.
2. They will melt at high temperatures or when touched with a hot iron or cigarette. This makes them easy to heat emboss and set creases, but also makes the same heat embossed creases difficult to remove. They have a durable shape and generally resist creases which are not heat embossed.
3. They are resilient and resist wrinkling.
4. They resist insects and mildew.
5. They are abrasion-resistant, but most will pill, especially when new.
6. Their strength when wet or dry is approximately the same.

THE TEXTILE ENVIRONMENT   **149**

Plain

Twill

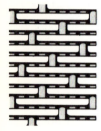

Satin

Knit

Non-woven

Figure 8.12
Fabric construction
a. Plain weave
b. Twill weave
c. Satin weave
d. Knit
e. Nonwoven fabric
(Courtesy of American Textile Manufacturers' Institute)

Nylon

Nylon, the first synthetic fiber, was discovered in 1928 by Du Pont, but it was not commercially produced until 1939. Only after World War II did nylon become available in any quantity to the public. Stretch nylon (Helanca) became available in 1954, and solution-dyed nylons in 1956.

Nylon is strong, resilient, elastic, stable, abrasion-resistant, and transparent. It is the lightest in weight of any fiber and it has all the characteristics of thermoplastic fibers. It has certain disadvantages, however. It is susceptible to sun, to stains, and to acids. Carpeting and upholstery are made of nylon, but nylon window fabrics are not satisfactory because sunlight will damage them. Trade names for nylon are *Helanca, Antron, Cadon, Enkaloft, Cumuloft, Vectra,* and *Qiana.*

Polyester

Polyester was patented in England in 1940 and produced commercially in the United States in 1953. It is a wrinkle-resistant, abrasion-resistant, resilient, and strong fiber. It is also resistant to sunlight when used behind glass. Like nylon, however, it absorbs oil and will pill. Polyester has good press retention either wet or dry. It is often blended with cotton. Its major uses in the interior are for draperies, curtains, and carpeting. It is also used as a fiberfill in pillows and furniture padding. Some trade names for polyester are *Dacron, Kodel, Fortrel, Trevira,* and *Quintess.*

Acrylic

Acrylic was discovered in the 1930s and produced by Dupont in 1950. It is a lightweight, very resilient fiber. Its bulkiness and loft make it suitable for pile fabrics and those resembling fur. Acrylic fabrics will burn, but are unaffected by sun and mildew. Acrylics are used for sheer curtains, draperies of all weights, and carpets, including indoor-outdoor types. Trade names for acrylic are *Orlon, Acrilan, Creslan, Zefran,* and *Zefkrone.*

Olefin

Olefin fiber was first manufactured in Italy in 1954, and then in the United States in 1960. It is a very light fiber with high insulation properties. It is strong, and it resists abrasion, static buildup, and pilling. It will not stain, but neither will it dye particularly well. Olefin is excellent for carpets (indoor-outdoor or kitchen carpets), and is used for upholstery fabric (though it may tend to stretch if used in long strips). Some trade names for olefin are *Herculon, Vectra, Polycrest,* and *Tuff-lite.*

Non-woven Fabrics

Felt

Felted fabrics were probably the first kind of fabric to be made. Felt is a mat of wool formed by the interlocking scales of the wool in a process that utilizes pressure, heat, and moisture. One felted material is *tapa cloth,* a decorative textile made by Oceanic people. The bark of the paper mulberry tree is steeped in water until it is pliable, then pounded together, bleached in the sun, and dyed with vegetable dyes in bold, abstract patterns. Other felted materials are needle-punched, the fibers made to cohere with solvents, pressure, heat (in the case of thermoplastic fibers), or spraying (Fig. 8.12e).

Woven Fabrics

Spindles for spinning yarn were in use by 4000 B.C., and weavers are depicted on the walls of Egyptian tombs and on Greek vases. By 1188, a dyers' guild was organized in Germany and about a hundred years later a weavers' guild was established in Florence. By 1200 there were silk mills in Europe and Barcelona had become a textile center. The spinning wheel was invented about 1530; the knitting machine, about 1589. By 1733, when the flying-shuttle loom was invented, textiles were being produced in almost all countries. Roller-printed cotton fabric was first manufactured in 1759 (Fig. 8.13). The first spinning mill was established in England in 1771. Developments were rapid after that: the spinning jenny was invented in 1777; the spinning mule, in 1779; the power loom in 1785. The Jacquard loom invented in 1801, made intricate patterns possible (Figs. 8.14, 8.15, 8.16, 8.17, 8.18). In 1816, the first circular knitting machine came into use, followed in 1826 by the mechanical loom. Weaving is a process in which two or more sets of yarns are interlaced at right angles to each other. The *warp,* or lengthwise yarn, is usually of better quality and higher twist, and therefore stronger and less apt to stretch than the *filling.* There are three basic kinds of weaves: plain, twill, and satin.

Plain Weave

In a plain weave, each filling yarn is interlaced at right angles to the warp yarn (Fig.

Figure 8.13
Rotary-screen printing is one of the newest and fastest methods for printing fabrics, combining a number of advantages of the older screen- and roller-printing processes. Dye is forced through a pattern of holes in the cylinder screen and the cylinder is rolled over the cloth imprinting it. (Courtesy of American Textile Manufacturers' Institute)

8.12a). Percale, muslin, calico, gingham, and chambray are plain weaves. Plain-weave fabric is usually smooth, although different-colored yarns may be used for the warp and the filling, and the fabric may be printed. A plain weave may be *ribbed,* an effect produced by the use of different-size yarns for the warp and the filling. Ribbed fabrics include broadcloth, poplin, bengaline, and ottoman. The *basket* weave is a plain weave in which there are two or more yarns used for the warp and the filling. Basket-weave fabrics include monk's cloth and oxford cloth.

Twill Weave

In a twill weave, the filling yarns go over and under the warp yarns to form a diagonal pattern. Twill-weave fabrics include tweeds, gabardine, ticking and drill (Fig. 8.12b).

Satin Weave

Floats, yarns that are interlaced at widely spaced intervals, make the smooth, lustrous surface of the satin weave (Fig. 8.12c). Satin, sateen, and chino are examples of satin-weave fabrics. Satin-weave fabrics do not wear as well as plain-weave or twill-weave fabrics because the long floats may catch on rough edges.

Variations of these weaves are also used for interiors. *Double-weave* fabric is made by weaving together two separate layers of woven fabric. The front of double-weave fabric may be different from the back, so that the fabric can be reversible. A *pile* fabric is one that has cut or uncut loops on its surface. Velvet, plush, corduroy, friezé, and velveteen are examples of pile weave. In *leno* weave, two sets of warp yarns are interlaced with a set of filling yarns. Marquisette is an example of leno-weave fabric. Elaborate designs are possible with the use of the *Jacquard* (zaka:r) *loom* (Figs. 8.14, 8.15, 8.16, 8.17, and 8.18), which combines plain, twill, and satin weaves. Each yarn is controlled separately by a card that controls the pattern. Brocade, damask, brocatelle, tapestry and matelasse (matlasje) are all woven on a Jacquard loom. *Laces* and *nets* are formed by knotting and twisting yarns.

Knits

Knits are formed by interlocking two loops of yarn (Figs. 8.12d and 8.19). Knits resist wrinkling, stretch, and can be made to fit unusual shapes. Many knits, of which Helanca nylon knit is an example, are used in the interior.

Figure 8.14
Point paper drawing of a document print from France used as a guide in card-cutting for a jacquard design. (Courtesy Margaret D. Nelson, Design Consultant)

Figure 8.15
The most intricate woven patterns are produced on the Jacquard loom. The fabric pattern is imposed on cardboard by a series of punchholes. This man is cutting the cards for the design in Fig. 8.14. Yarns are dropped into the punched holes that guide the Jacquard design. (Courtesy of Margaret D. Nelson, Design Consultant)

Figure 8.18
The Jacquard loom can produce the most intricate patterns. This is for upholstery. (Courtesy of American Textile Manufacturers' Institute)

Colors and Patterns

Dyeing

Yarns may be dyed before or after they are spun, or after they have been woven or knitted into fabric. *Solution-dyeing* is the most permanent form of coloring synthetic fibers for the color is added to the solution before the fiber is extruded from the spinneret. The process produces uniform color and, if production is high, is inexpensive. *Stock-dyeing* is a parallel method for dyeing natural fibers before they are spun. The results are excellent, but the method is expensive. *Yarn-dyeing* is the most usual dyeing method: the yarns are dyed before being made into fabric (Fig. 8.20). In *piece-dyeing,* the yarn is dyed after it has been made into fabric. Piece-dyeing is economical, but the dye does not penetrate the fiber as well as in other dyeing methods.

Batik-dyeing is a hand process in which hot wax is placed on the fabric to prevent the dye from reaching that part of the fabric. After the fabric has been immersed in the dye solution, the wax is removed from the fabric. The process may be repeated a number of times. *Tie dyeing* is another hand method in which the fabric is securely tied with thread to prevent parts of the fabric from coming into contact with the dye.

Printing

There are various methods of printing fabrics. In *block-printing,* one of the earliest, wooden

blocks cut in a pattern were loaded with dye paste and stamped onto cloth. Some patterns required up to one hundred blocks. Block prints were popular in England and France before machine-printing methods were developed. *Screen-printing* is a stencil process in which a fabric screen, formerly silk but now nylon or polyester, is stretched over a frame and some areas on the fabric are blocked by the screen to prevent the dye from reaching them. A rubber squeegee is used to press the dye paste through the screen. A different screen is used for each color. *Machine-screen or Buser printing* is a mechanized version of screen-printing; another is *rotary-screen-printing,* in which a cylinder is the screen and controls one color and pattern area.

The *roller-printing* method is similar to that used for printing a newspaper. It is the most common technique and utilizes copper rollers etched with the design (Fig. 8.13). A separate cylinder rolls the dye paste onto the etched cylinder (a separate cylinder for each color). The process is inexpensive and makes possible very fine-line prints. The *transfer-printing* process is similar to that used for applying decals. The pattern is printed with disperse dyes onto a wax paper and then transferred onto the cloth with applied heat and pressure. The dyes are absorbed into the fabric as they change from a solid to a gaseous state.

In the *discharge-printing* process, areas of color are bleached out and may even be replaced with another color. The *burnout-printing* process is similar, except that the cloth, not the color, is removed. For example, heavier yarns might be burned away leaving a fabric which is translucent in some areas and opaque in others. The *warp-printing* process, which involves printing the warp fibers before they are woven into cloth, results in a shadowy print.

Finishes

Finishes fall into three categories: mechanical, chemical, and thermal. Some finishes treat the fiber; others (functional finishes) impart a special property to it.

Mechanical Finishes

Mechanical finishes result in a physical change. *Brushing and shearing* is a mechanical finish: revolving cylinders covered with brushes raise the loose fibers from the surface of the fabric and short knives shear off the

Figure 8.20
Dyed yarn is being unloaded from an automated dye machine after it has been package-dyed. (Courtesy of American Textile Manufacturers' Institute)

short fiber ends; this produces a smooth, low pile. *Calendering* may be a cold or hot process; in the cold process, pressure is used; the hot press process is a thermal process. The fabric of cotton, linen, rayon, silk, or man-made fibers is passed through cylinders under heat and pressure to produce a smooth, polished surface. The *embossing calender* produces flat or raised designs on a thermoplastic fabric by the use of heat. *Crabbing,* which involves setting the warp and filling yarns at right angles by agitation in hot and then cold water, running the fabric through cylinders, and drying it, is used on wool. *Decating (decatizing)* is applied to woolens to set the length and width of the fabric and to produce a lustrous surface; the fabric is wound tightly on rollers and then subjected to steam.

Beetling, a process used on linen in which the fabric is pounded with wooden hammers to flatten the yarns and make the weave appear less open, makes the fabric softer, more absorbent, smoother, and more lustrous. *Fulling,* a shrinking process using agitation, moisture, heat, and pressure, is applied to wool to produce a closer weave and more bulk.

Glazing is applied to cotton fabrics: they are made more lustrous and stiff by being saturated with starch, glue, or resins and then run between smooth hot rollers under pressure.

Napping is a mechanical method of producing a low, soft, fuzzy pile: the fabric is moved under cylinders which have small hooks to pull up some of the fibers. *Tentering* is applied to all fabrics to give them an even width: the fabric is held by parallel sets of clamps, treated by moisture and dried or heat set and rolled onto bolts.

Flocking, in which short fibers are attached to the fabric by an adhesive to make a pile, may be applied by vibration, which builds up a static charge, or by passing the fabric through an electrostatic field. *Sizing,* applied to cotton fabrics, adds weight to fabric and gives it a firm hand:[2] the fabric is saturated with resin, starch, or glue, and then dried and calendered.

Chemical Finishes

Chemical finishes are those resulting from a chemical reaction. *Bleaching* produces white fabrics and prepares fabrics for dyeing and printing. Fibers, yarns, and fabrics may all be bleached, and the chemicals applied vary with the fiber. *Mercerization* (Fig. 8.9) of cotton and some rayon fabrics increases strength, improves dyeability, and adds luster. The fibers, immersed in sodium hydroxide, swell and untwist, becoming rounder, more lustrous, and more absorbent.

Thermal Finishes

Some mechanical finishes (such as *calendering, decating,* and *tentering*) are thermal in part, but *singeing* is thermal only. Fabric of cotton, wool, and man-made fiber is rolled rapidly over an open gas flame to burn off the free projecting fiber ends from the cloth surface; the process produces a smooth fabric surface.

[2] Hand refers to the feel of a fabric.

Functional Finishes

The first functional finishes, designed to increase resistance to wrinkles, were developed in the late 1930s in Great Britain. Today finishes are applied to make fabrics release soil, resist insects and bacteria, and resist abrasion. Functional finishes make it possible to use more fabrics for the interior than ever before. Most of these finishes are chemical in nature.

Abrasion-resistant finishes enable a fabric to resist wear. For example, a coating of thermoplastic resin applied to fabrics made of glass fibers enable them to resist abrasion. *Antibacterial finishes* render fabrics resistant to mildew and other fungi. *Soil-repellent* or *soil-release finishes* are particularly important in upholstery and carpets. Some fibers, such as polyester and cotton durable press, attract soil, and when the fibers are coated or impregnated with chemicals, they become less absorbent.

Many synthetic fibers are susceptible to electrostatic buildup but *antistatic finishes* help to control this susceptibility. *Durable-press finishes* prevent wrinkling and help fabrics to retain their shape; however, many of these finishes weaken the fiber. *Flame-retardant finishes* enable a fabric to resist burning or to burn more slowly. Some of these finishes, however, are removed by washing, or the dry-cleaning process and they may stiffen a fabric. *Moth-repellent finishes* protect wools and fur fabrics.

Fabrics may also have a *waterproof* or *water-repellent finish* applied to them. Wax dispersions, silicones, metals, and resins are the agents used to produce these finishes. Water-repellent finishes are of varying degrees of durability, but they prevent soil from being absorbed by the fabric.

Fabrication Methods

There are a number of fabrication methods that have been developed recently. These include the shuttleless loom which moves the filling yarns (without carrying them back and forth across the warp yarns by shuttles) by powerful water jet. These looms are faster than conventional looms and require fewer workers.

Another fabrication method is lamination. This is accomplished by fastening two or more layers of fabrics together with adhesive or heat. This method makes fabrics more wrinkle-resistant, easier to clean (if laminated to a film), warmer without too much weight (lamination of fabric to foam), or make it possible to use a fragile fabric (by laminating to a stronger one). The lamination of a thin layer of foam or other material serves to *insulate* a fabric, particularly important in draperies used in cold climates.

Types of Fabrics

Very Sheer Fabrics

Very sheer fabrics are usually made from synthetics, cotton, silk, or wool, and are suitable for curtains and table coverings.

Bobbinet: a fine net with a six-sided mesh; usually available in pale colors, natural or white.

Filet: hand-made square-mesh knotted lace with the pattern filling in the squares; available in white, cream, or solid colors.

Marquisette: leno-weave fiber; available in solid colors or printed or woven patterns.

Ninon: very thin, smooth, plain-weave fabric; available in solid colors, stripes, or shadowy patterns.

Organdy: plain-weave cotton with a crisp hand.

Dotted Swiss: sheer and crisp plain-weave fabric with spaced pattern of dots or figures; available in plain colors, often with constrasting dots.

Theatrical gauze: open-weave linen or cotton fabric with lustrous texture; available in plain colors.

Voile: soft, sheer, open-weave fabric of crepe-spun yarns (yarns with a matte finish and slight stretch); usually available in pale colors.

Sheer Fabrics

Sheer fabrics are usually translucent. Used alone at windows they provide privacy in the daytime, but not at night.

Casement cloth: any sheer drapery fabric in a plain or figured weave.

Fiberglass: a man-made fiber of glass extruded in continuous filaments; fabrics made from it range from sheer to heavy, translucent to opaque.

Film: nonfibrous waterproof fabric; thick or thin, plain or printed, smooth or textured; used for upholstery and wall coverings.

Muslin: plain-weave fabric of uncombed cotton; ranges from light to heavy, sheer to coarse; bleached or unbleached, dyed or printed.

Osnaburg: rough, coarse open-weave plain cotton fabric; light to heavy in weight; colored or printed.

Pongee: plain-woven raw silk with broken crossbar texture caused by irregular yarns (imitations are available in cotton and synthetics); usually ecru-heather in color, but may be dyed; also called tussah, antique taffeta, or douppioni (see Glossary).

Sheeting: plain-woven cotton of various weights; may be dyed or printed; traditional cloth for printing.

Silk gauze: plain-weave fabric with slight variation in threads.

Light-weight Fabrics

Light-weight fabrics may be of cotton, wool, silk, or synthetic fiber and are used for draperies, wall coverings, and slipcovers. Some examples may be used for upholstery if heavy enough.

Antique satin: a fabric made like a sateen but with a slub (a heavy area in a yarn) filling that produces a dull and uneven texture; used for drapery and upholstery.

Broadcloth: a ribbed cloth of cotton, wool or synthetic fibers used for draperies.

Calico: plain-weave cotton printed with a small, regular pattern.

Challis: plain-weave wool or synthetic fabric, usually printed with small floral designs.

Chambray: plain-weave cotton or linen with frosted appearance; available in wide color range.

Chintz: plain-weave glazed cotton often with printed design, produced by the application of resin and calendering.

Drill: diagonal twill-weave cotton; very strong.

Faille: plain-weave formed by cramming extra yarns in one direction with flat transverse ribs.

Gingham: yarn-dyed fine cotton or synthetic woven in check, stripe, or plaid pattern of two or more colors.

Homespun: slubby single ply yarn—water marked appearance.

Linen: plain-weave fabric of flax.

Moiré: wavy, watery pattern on ribbed weave produced by pressure and heat.

Oxford cloth: durable fabric in basket or twill weave.

Piqué: ribbed or honeycomb waffle fabric in plain weave.

Poplin: plain weave fabric warp-faced with fine crosswise ribs. The warp yarns finer than filling yarns.

Rep: plain weave with raised, rounded lengthwise or crosswise ribs.

Sateen: filling face fabric, usually of mercerized cotton, in satin weave (used for lining drapery).

Satin: warp-faced satin weave with high sheen.

Shantung: dense plain-weave silk or synthetic fabric with uneven, slubbed filling yarns, similar to pongee.

Taffeta: crisp, plain weave with filling heavier than warp resulting in slight cross-ribbing.

Medium-Weight Fabrics

Medium-weight fabrics are made of heavy fibers of cotton, flax, synthetics, silk, or wool. They are suitable for upholstery and heavy draperies.

Bark Cloth: originally referred to a felted cloth from tropical countries made from the soaked and beaten inner tree bark, but now usually refers to a barklike textured fabric (popular for draperies).

Brocade: a Jacquard patterned cloth with raised designs (resembling embroidery) produced by a supplementary warp or filling.

Brocatelle: a satin-faced jacquard patterned cloth similar to brocade in which a supplementary filling yarn creates a raised design that appears embossed; the background is usually a twill weave.

Burlap: loose basket-weave fabric with heavy, coarse texture.

Canvas: dense plain- or twill-weave cotton fabric.

Damask: reversible woven fabric with flat patterns produced by contrasting warp-face and filling-face fabrics.

Denim: warp-faced twill-weave fabric of cotton or blends, usually with dyed warp and natural filling.

Duck: plain- or ribbed-weave fabric, similar to canvas, but lighter in weight.

Hopsacking: loose plain- or basket-weave fabric of cotton or blends.

Monk's Cloth: coarse and heavy basket-weave fabric.

Sailcloth: plain-weave fabric similar to duck, but lighter in weight.

Serge: twill-weave solid-color fabric with diagonal rib on both sides.

Terry Cloth: uncut pile fabric, plain or jacquard weave, very absorbent.

Ticking: strong, heavy twill-weave cotton or linen with colored warp stripe or simple design.

Heavy Fabrics

Heavy fabrics are used for upholstery, draperies and wall coverings. Most must be dry cleaned.

Bouclé: plain- or twill-weave fabric of novelty yarns looped to produce pebbley surface.

Corduroy: cut-pile cotton or synthetic fabric with supplementary filling yarns producing ribs.

Expanded vinyl: plastic-stretch upholstery fabric with knit fabric back; stretches to fit contours of object.

Felt: nonwoven fabric of wool, rayon, and synthetic fibers intermeshed by heat, moisture, and agitation.

Frieze: warp-pile fabric with uncut loops or loops cut to form a pattern.

Matelasse': double-woven fabric woven on Jacquard loom with pattern repeat resembling quilted or puckered surface.

Needlepoint: woven on Jacquard loom to imitate hand-made needlepoint; ranges from small (petit point) to large (gros point).

Plush: cut-pile fabric with higher, less dense pile than velvet or velour; may imitate animal fur.

Tapestry: fabric, with raised design formed by warp yarns carried on back of fabric, woven on Jacquard loom; heavier than brocade or damask.

Tweed: woolen fabric in twill or soft, regular weave with rough texture from yarn and with several colors combined.

Velour: short-, stiff-pile fabric resembling velvet

Velvet: fabric with short dense pile; may be plain, printed or patterned.

Velveteen: cotton or synthetic fabric similar to velvet.

Glossary

Abrasion Resistance. The ability of a fiber to resist rubbing.

Absorbency. The ability of a fiber to take up moisture.

Azlon. Fiber produced from corn, milk, or soybean proteins.

Batik-Dyeing. A hand-dyeing process in

which hot wax is used to prevent the dye from penetrating parts of the fabric.

Beetling. A method of pounding linen that flattens the yarns and adds luster.

Bleaching. A process by which gray goods are whitened.

Block-Printing. A printing process in which wooden blocks are cut into a pattern, loaded with dye paste, and stamped onto cloth.

Brushing. A method of finishing a fabric to raise the fibers so that the construction of the fabric is concealed.

Burnout-Printing. A process in which areas of the cloth are removed to make a pattern translucent or opaque.

Calendering. A finishing process, either hot or cold, in which the fabric is passed through cylinders under pressure to produce a polished surface.

Cellulosic Fabric. A cotton, linen, jute or rayon fabric made from plant sources.

Chemical Resistance. The resistance of a fiber to certain chemicals.

Crabbing. A process in which the warp and filling wool yarns are set at right angles by agitation in hot and then cold water and then the fabric is run through cylinders and dried.

Crimp. The irregularity of a fiber or the waves or bends that occur along the fiber length; may be natural, or mechanically or chemically induced.

Cramming. The forcing of extra warp or filling yarns into a fabric during the weaving process.

Decatizing. A process by which the length and width of wool fabric is set and a lustrous surface produced.

Discharge-Printing. A process of printing fabric in which areas of color are bleached out and replaced with another color.

Double-Weave Fabric. Reversible compound fabric with two sets of filling and two sets of warp yarns held together by one of the warp or filling yarn at intervals.

Doupponi. A silk yarn resulting from the reeling of a yarn from two sets of cacoons grown together (slubby texture results).

Durability. The ability of a fiber to withstand normal stresses and varying degrees of tension without rupturing.

Dyeability. The ability of a fiber or fabric to absorb dye.

Elasticity. The ability of a fiber or fabric to return to its original size after it has been stretched.

Embossing Calander. A finish produced by patterned rollers and heat on a thermoplastic fabric.

Fabric. A general textile term for cloth, tapestries, carpets, and so on.

Felt. A nonwoven fabric made by intermeshing by solvents, needle-punching, agitation, heat or moisture.

Flocking. A process in which a fabric surface is covered with short fibers by adhesives, vibration or the electrostatic method.

Filament. A continuous thread, such as silk, or a man-made fiber which has been extruded through a spinneret.

Fulling. A process in which wool is shrunk by agitation, moisture, heat, and pressure to produce a closer weave and more bulk.

Glazing. A finish applied to cotton fabrics to make them more lustrous and stiff by saturating them with starch, glue, or resins and then running them between smooth hot rollers under pressure.

Hand. The feel of a cloth; its tactile qualities.

Heat-Setting. A process by which thermoplastic fabrics are stabilized under controlled heat to reduce shrinkage and stretching.

Hydrophilic Fiber. A fiber that readily absorbs moisture.

Hydrophobic Fiber. A fiber that does not absorb moisture.

Jacquard Loom. A loom used to weave complicated patterns by use of punched cards.

Loft. The ability of a fiber or fabric to spring back to its original shape.

Luster. The ability of a fabric to reflect light; depends on smoothness of fiber.

Machine-Screen Printing. A mechanical method of screen printing, sometimes called Buser printing.

Man-made Fiber. A fiber derived from the laboratory.

Mercerization. A process, using caustic soda, by which fabric is strengthened and its luster increased.

Napping. A mechanical method of producing a low, soft, fuzzy pile in which the fabric is moved under cylinders which have small hooks to pull up some of the fibers.

Natural Fiber. A protein, plant, or mineral fiber.

Non-woven. A mat of wool held together by wool scales made to interlock by the application of pressure, heat, and moisture.

Piece-Dyeing. A method of dyeing a fabric after it is made.

Pile Fabric. A velvet-like fabric with cut or uncut loops.

Pill. A ball of fibers on a fabric caused by abrading the surface.

Protein Fiber. Wool or silk.

Resiliency. The ability of a fiber to recover from creasing, stretching and twisting.

Roller-Printing. A method for printing fabric utilizing copper rollers etched with the design.

Rotary-Screen Printing. A method for printing fabric in which a patterned cylinder prints the pattern as the fabric moves under it.

Roving. A spun yarn after it is drawn and twisted.

Scoured. The washing of wool with soap and water to remove soil and lanolin.

Screen-Printing. A stencil process in which a fabric screen is stretched over a frame and the areas which will not be printed are blocked to prevent the dye from reaching them; several screens may be used; a rubber squeegee is used to press the dye paste through the screen.

Singeing. A process in which fabric is passed over an open gas flame to burn off the projecting fiber ends from the cloth surface.

Sizing. A finishing process in which starch is applied to cloth to give it body.

Solution-Dyeing. The more permanent form of coloring synthetics; the color is added to the solution before it is extruded as a fiber through the spinneret.

Specific Gravity. The weight of a fiber in relation to its bulk.

Stability. The ability of a fiber to retain its original shape.

Static Buildup. A phenomenon which refers to the electrical conduction of a fabric. Static build-up causes fabrics to discharge electricity and to retain soil.

Staple Fiber. A short fiber used to form a yarn.

Stock-Dyeing. A method of dyeing natural fibers before they are spun.

Spinneret. A metal nozzle-like apparatus through which a man-made fiber is extruded.

Synthetic Fibers. Fibers made in the laboratory, such as nylon, acrylic, polyester, and so on.

Tendering. A process, designed to give fabrics an even width, in which the fabric is held by parallel sets of slamps and then dried and rolled on bolts.

Thermoplastic Fiber. A heat-sensitive fiber.

Tie Dyeing. A hand-dyeing method in which the fabric is securely tied with thread to prevent certain parts of the fabric from coming in contact with the dye; the process may be repeated several times.

Transfer Printing. A method similar to that for applying a decal in which the pattern is printed with disperse dyes onto a wax paper which is then transferred to cloth with heat and pressure.

Warp-Printing. A method of printing the warp fibers before they are woven into fabric.

Weaving. A process in which two or more sets of yarns are interlaced at right angles to each other.

Yarn Dyeing. A method of dyeing yarns before they are made into fabric.

Bibliography

Evans, Helen Marie. *Man the Designer.* New York: Macmillan Publishing Co., Inc., 1973.

Hollen, Norma, and Jane Saddler. *Textiles.* New York: Macmillan Publishing Co. Inc., 1964.

Joseph, Marjorie L. *Introductory Textile Science.* New York: Holt, Rinehart and Winston, 1966.

Larsen, Jack Lenor. *Fabrics for Interiors.* New York: Van Nostrand Reinhold Company, 1975.

Montgomery, Florence M. *Printed Textiles.* New York: The Viking Press, Inc., 1970.

Quimby, Ian M. G., and Polly Anne Earl. *Technological Innovation and the Decorative Arts.* Winterthur Conference Report 1973.

Sulahria, Julie, and Ruby Diamond. *Inside Design.* New York: Canfield Press, 1977.

Vanderhoff, Margil, Lavina Franck, and Lucille Campbell. *Textiles for Homes and People.* Lexington, Mass.: Ginn and Company, 1973.

The Furnished Environment

Furniture is available today in a vast array of styles which will answer any need or purpose and suit any pattern of living or working. Furniture may be austere or luxurious, traditional or contemporary, of natural or man-made materials, free-standing or built-in. Before a client decides what kind or style furniture to buy, certain basic questions should be considered.

Furniture Selection

1. *Is the furniture flexible in function?* The home or office is divided into separate areas designated for various activities. No longer is it practical to buy furniture suitable for only one purpose. Multi-purpose furniture may be used in several areas of the interior or for more than one purpose.
2. *Is the furniture comfortable?* Comfort is related to sitting and sleeping and all connected activities. For example, a table without leg room or one that is too high or low is uncomfortable. The age of the person using the furniture should also be considered. Floor pillows and low furniture may accommodate a young person, but may be too uncomfortable for older persons. Seats that are too soft may also be unsuitable for the very young or the elderly.
3. *How durable is the furniture and is it easy to maintain?* Well-made furniture will withstand hard use, require fewer repairs, and last longer. But long-lasting furniture may not be appropriate for clients who plan to discard it within a few years. Ease of maintenance depends upon the finish, the material of which the piece is made, and—if the piece is upholstered—the fabric. The weave and fiber of the fabric will make maintenance difficult or easy and determine wearability. Fabrics may last as long as twenty-five years or less than one.
4. *Is the furniture in scale with the interior?* Traditional furniture is often too large for the small rooms of a modern home. Furniture should be in scale with the room and with the other objects in it. Furniture selected for a particular space should not interfere with the functions planned for that space. In the Victorian Period, for example, too much furniture was crowded into rooms without regard to its use.
5. *Is the furniture guaranteed?* Will the manufacturer or the vendor replace the furniture or compensate the buyer if something goes wrong?
6. *Will similar pieces be required in the future?* Although it is no longer fashionable to buy furniture in sets, it may be that similar pieces may be desired later. This is one advantage of open-stock styles, although even such styles are not available indefinitely.
7. *Are there children or pets in the household?* The presence of children or pets requires more durable fabrics, weaves, and finishes.
8. *Is entertaining frequent and does it include overnight guests?* Frequent entertaining requires furniture that will serve more than one purpose—a sofa hide-a-bed, for example.

Wood Furniture

Wood has been used in furniture construction for centuries. It is easy to work, to shape, and to finish. Wood is easy to maintain and to repair. It is pleasant to touch, lends warmth to the interior, and comes in a variety of textures, grains, and colors. It is durable, readily available, and hard-surfaced. When the wood selected for the piece is appropriate, and when it has been aged and dried correctly, the piece will last almost indefinitely.

There are some disadvantages to wood furniture: it will shrink and split if the wood has not been properly seasoned; it is vulnerable to insects, scratches, decay, fire, and humidity. Solid wood, a term meaning that all exposed surfaces are of a particular solid wood, may sometimes warp or crack even when properly maintained. Solid wood may be carved and turned; is easy to refinish, and has no joining lines as veneer does, but it is usually more expensive than veneer.

Wood Types

The terms *soft* and *hard wood* refer to the relative absorptive qualities of various woods and to variations in their structure. *Softwood* is from conifers, trees that keep their leaves or needles all year long. It is more utilitarian than beautiful and is used mainly for construction. Some examples are pine, fir, cedar, redwood, spruce, and hemlock. Softwoods grow more rapidly than hardwoods, are easier to work with, and less expensive. They are also lighter, and have a more open, coarse, and less attractive grain. *Grain* is the arrangement and quality of fibrous tissue in wood. Softwoods are less durable, do not take a fine finish, and cannot be intricately shaped.

Hardwoods are deciduous; that is, they come from trees that lose their leaves seasonally. Hardwoods, such as mahogany, walnut, birch, maple, rosewood, ebony, fruitwood, and oak have provided the majority of cabinet woods throughout history. They are strong, and are less likely than softwoods to warp or dent. They have a natural beauty and luster and take a finish well. The colors of hardwoods vary; highly colored hardwoods will lose their color when exposed to light and air, and all woods tend to darken with age.

Wood products are also used for furniture. *Hardboard* is manufactured from tiny, thread-like wood fibers bound together with lignin, the natural cohesive in wood. It is widely used as a core for veneers, for mirror backs, and for drawer bottoms.

The first known use of *plywood* was in 1500 B.C. in Egypt. Hardwood plywood may be a five-ply panel or a three-ply panel. Plywood may be made with a variety of cores and ply material such as kraft paper, metal sheets, aluminum foil, or plastic foam. The layers are held together by a urea-formaldehyde glue. Plywood is used in many kinds of furniture and is stronger than a comparable piece of solid wood.

Particleboard is made of wood flakes and resin binding agents hot-pressed or extruded into panels one eight of an inch to two inches thick. Hot-pressed panels are generally used in furniture and are best suited for the cores of very large table tops or for other special needs. The surface is flat and smooth, warp-free, hard, and dimensionally stable. It may be wood-grained, stained, lacquered, or overlaid with plastic laminates, veneers, and vinyls. Particleboard is less expensive than plywood or hardwood, but it is extremely heavy and this can be a disadvantage in some cases.

Inexpensive Oriental plywood, bonded to a printed plastic film (as for inexpensive table tops), is also available. The decorative grain is printed on the substrate and then coated with plastic and baked, or it may be printed by four-color presses onto the underside of polyvinyl chloride film which is laminated to the substrate. One method used for legs, moldings, and shapes but impossible with wood veneers, involves a printed photographic wood image covered with a six-mil vinyl film. This material can be embossed with graining or gentle distressing.

An *irridated wood* is also available. It is impregnated with plastic and irridiated and is many times harder and more abrasion-resistant than untreated wood. It has higher compression strength, bending strength, and shear strength. It has a satin-like finish; it will not splinter, warp, or twist; and it is hard, smooth, and almost indestructible.

Cutting Methods

The manner in which wood is cut determines the grain that is visible. *Plain-sawed* or *flat-cut* wood is cut with the blade at right angles to the log, an economical method. *Quarter-sawed* wood is cut from a log which has been sliced into quarters.

Veneers

Early Egyptian and Oriental craftsmen used *veneers* — thin sheets of wood, generally finer than the base wood, which are glued to a plainer, stronger wood or other material. Veneered plywood is stronger than the same thickness of solid wood. Veneers are more economical because they can be used to cover inexpensive woods. They may be made of fragile wood, impossible to use as solid wood, but they are less subject than solid wood to warping and shrinking, nor will they split or crack as solid woods do. They also facilitate the matching of grains. Veneers are available in large pieces and can be applied to curved, irregular areas. They cannot, however, be turned or carved or sanded for refinishing.

The identification of veneers is based on the section of the tree from which the veneer sheet is cut. A veneer is cut by mounting a log segment, a *flitch* to a log bed. The bed moves the log against the knife, which cuts a veneer slice on each downward stroke. *Plain-sliced veneers* are cut parallel to a line in the center of the log. *Quarter-sliced veneers* are cut from a quarter of the log at right angles to the growth rings. *Rotary* veneers are cut by a lathe knife in continuous sheets around the log. *Half-round* veneers are sliced from half the log, while the *rift-cut* is cut perpendicular to the medullary rays in oak to produce a parallel grain pattern.

Certain figures are named for the part of the tree from which they are cut. *Crotch veneer* is obtained from below the forks of a large tree, where the trunk is joined by large branches. The area below the forks is a distorted growth pattern, which is V−shaped, swirling, or feather-like. In a large mahogany tree, this pattern may extend six feet. Crotch veneer is usually matched to form a pattern.

Burl veneer is obtained from tree trunks on which large excrescences or wart-like growths have formed. The fibers are irregularly arranged and eyes or undeveloped buds are characteristic. Walnut, ash, cherry, yew, elm, and birch are some of the woods from which burl veneers are made (Fig. 9.1). *Butt-wood veneer* is cut from that part of the tree at which the trunk and large roots join. Cross figures, mottle figures, and curly grains are the result of this joining, and walnut is the usual wood from which butt-wood veneer is cut. It is similar to burl wood, but is thought to be caused by a fungus. The effect, usually in maple, is a series of circles.

Furniture Woods

Ash, a moderately hard, tough, creamy white, wood, has a coarse texture and a straight grain. It is easy to bend and has been used in chairs. Burl ash is particularly attractive. Ash is at present used for furniture frames. It is cheaper than more durable hardwoods.

Beech is a pinkish-tan, moderately hard wood that bends easily (it was used by Thonet in his bentwood furniture). It has a fine uniform texture and a straight grain, but is subject to wood worms. It is used extensively for the concealed portions and curved parts of furniture, and for rocker runners.

Birch, a very common wood found in both Europe and North America, is used as a substitute for mahogany and walnut and for doors, interior trim, and floors. It ranges in color from creamy tan to reddish tan and has a fine uniform texture and a straight grain. It was formerly used for seating pieces and cabinets.

Cherry, a reddish-brown wood, has been used for cabinet-making in both the United States and Europe. It has a fine even texture and a straight grain. It does not shrink or warp to any extent and is a tough, beautiful wood. It is often used as a veneer.

Elm is a light reddish wood with a coarse, uneven texture and deep, interlocked grain. It is a strong, elastic wood with many burl grains. It is used for decorative veneers.

Hickory is a pinkish-tan wood used in turned chairs and now generally used in combination with other woods. Moderately strong, tough, and springy, it is the hardest, strongest native American wood. It is difficult to nail, however.

Figure 9.1
Olive burl credenza with a marble top. Furniture designer: Milo Baughman. (Courtesy of Thayer Coggin)

Figure 9.2
Maple table. Furniture designer: D. V. Sliedregt, architect (Amsterdam). (Courtesy of D. V. Sliedregt)

Lime, a wood that ranges in color from ivory to yellow but ages to brown in the air, is a fine, close-textured wood, excellent for carving and fine detailing. It was widely used by Grinling Gibbons and the many wood-carvers who imitated his work in the eighteenth century.

Mahogany is a reddish-brown wood with a straight, uniform fine texture and a close grain. Hard and heavy, it is well suited to carved furniture. Crotch-grained mahogany is often used for case pieces. Mahogany does not shrink or swell to any extent. It is used in its natural state, bleached, and dark-stained.

Maple, which usually has a natural finish, ranges from light cream to pinkish-tan. It is a hard, strong wood with an even texture and a straight grain. Many different figures are available, including buttwood, bird's eye, and burl. Maple warps and splits when nailed. It is often used for moderately priced, unpretentious furniture (Fig. 9.2).

Oak, one of the earliest woods used in England and the United States, is very hard, with a coarse texture and an open, straight grain. It

Figure 9.3
Oak lounge. Furniture
designer: Stuart John
Gilbert. (Courtesy of
Harter Corp.)

Figure 9.4
Vladimir Kagan's
shadowless light cabinet
is made of rosewood and
ebonized walnut. (Courtesy
of Vladimir Kagan)

Figure 9.5
Teak desk. Furniture
designer: Art Carpenter.
(Courtesy of Art Carpenter)

Figure 9.6
Walnut chair. Furniture
designer: Art Carpenter.
(Courtesy of Art Carpenter)

ranges in color from light tan to a dark brown. It is used for floors, wall panels, plywood, and both solid and veneered furniture (Fig. 9.3).

Rosewood is a dark purplish wood with a deep brownish figure. It is often used as a veneer (Fig. 9.4).

Teak, which ranges from yellow to brown, has a medium-coarse texture and a straight grain. It has a slightly soapy feeling (Fig. 9.5). It is strong and was used in Oriental furniture. Today it is used in Scandinavian furniture.

Walnut is a grayish-brown wood, medium-coarse in texture, with a straight grain. Walnut figures are particularly beautiful (Fig. 9.6). Walnut is a medium-hard wood, easy to carve, and was used extensively in the Restoration, Queen Anne, and Early Georgian Periods in England (Fig. 1.2).

Yew is a orange-brown wood, tough and resilient, with a fine compact grain. It is resistant to the furniture beetle and is a good cabinet wood because it also resists dents.

Finishes

Finishes are applied to wood to protect it against natural destructive forces, to facilitate maintenance, to enhance its natural beauty, to prevent it from darkening and drying out, and to achieve special effects. During the Tudor Period, furniture was painted to protect it from vermin, but later natural finishes were used.

Finishes are of several types. The *penetrating finish* sinks into the wood and produces soft, rich surfaces. Formerly finishes with a tung oil base were used, but these have been replaced by finishes with a synthetic resin base. These penetrating finishes are typically used on Scandinavian furniture. *Transparent finishes,* such as varnish, protect the wood against soil and enhance its grain and color. *Opaque finishes,* such as lacquer, which conceal the grain of the wood and give it a smooth, uniform color, are hard, and offer good protection against weathering, but are subject to scratches. *Glossy finishes,* such as glossy enamel, are smooth and lustrous and reflect light; they are also durable and easy to clean, but they tend to chip. *Matte finishes,* such as flat paint, are soft finishes that do not reflect light, but they are durable and easy to clean, although not as easy to clean as glossy finishes.

Finishes may be *distressed*—that is, subjected to an artificial aging process that involves striking the wood with chains and

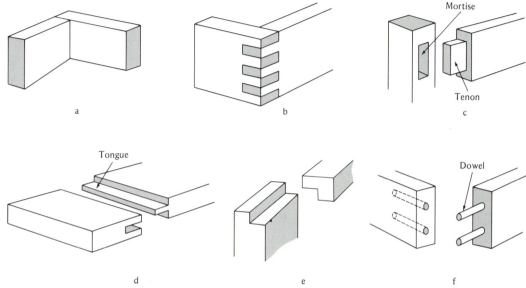

Figure 9.7
Joints
a. Butt
b. Dovetail
c. Mortise and tenon
d. Tongue and groove
e. Rabbet
f. Dowel or
double-dowel

hammers to gouge and nick it, and/or spraying it with paint to imitate worm holes and fly specks. *Antiquing* is an aging process achieved with paint or stain. A darker paint or stain is applied over a lighter one (or vice versa) and then rubbed off, to produce an effect resembling the patina of age.

Joinery

Furniture may be joined in a number of ways. Once cut, joints may be fastened with nails, rivets, screws, bolts, and/or glue. In early times, pegs and dowels were used for joinery. The *butt* joint, composed of two pieces of wood butted against each other and then glued, screwed, or nailed together (Fig. 9.7a), has been used since antiquity. It is seldom used today, for although it is the simplest joint, it is also the least satisfactory, as it will not take too much strain. *Dovetailed* joints (Fig. 9.7b) have wedge-shaped projections (*tenons*) on one piece and alternating grooves (*mortises*) on the other; these fit together to form a tight joint (Fig. 1.2). They are used on quality furniture drawers. In a *mortise and tenon* joint, one piece has a tenon, which fits into the mortise in the other piece. This joint is glued and used for the joining of stretchers to leg posts or seats to chair-back posts (Fig. 9.7c). *Tongue and groove* joints have a long, narrow, straight tenon the length of the board that fits into a corresponding mortise (Fig. 9.7d); they are often used for paneling and flooring. It differs from the mortise and tenon in that they extend the length of the board. A *rabbet* joint or

dado joint has a groove cut into one piece of wood into which the other piece of wood fits; it is held with glue, nails, and/or screws (Fig. 9.7e).

Joints are strengthened by various means. A *dowel* or *double-dowel* joint is one in which wooden or metal pegs or dowels are inserted into the joint to prevent slippage (Fig. 9.7f). A *spline* joint has a small piece of wood inserted into each piece of wood to reinforce it. *Corner blocks* or *corner braces* are braces inserted into the corners of joints for reinforcement; they are attached with glue, screws, and/or nails.

Metals

The first bronze and other metal furniture was made by the Greeks and the Romans. After the decline of their civilizations, metal was not used until the French Baroque Period, when ormolu mounts were used to ornament furniture and to keep the parts from separating. In both England and France, silver furniture was made, although much of it was melted down in later periods. In Renaissance Spain, wrought iron was used for table supports and ornamental detailing.

Metal was not again used to any great extent in furniture until the Victorian Period. A tubular metal chair, made by Grandillot in 1844, was painted and shaped to look like a wooden chair. Hollow wrought iron tubes (reinforced with glue or plaster to make them more durable) were used for tables and chairs

Figure 9.8
Contemporary brass bed. (Courtesy of Kirsch Co.)

Figure 9.10
Glass and bronze table. Furniture designer: Carl-Axel Acking, architect (Stockholm). (Courtesy of Carl-Axel Acking)

Figure 9.9
Iron enameled table with glass top. Furniture designer: D. V. Sliedregt, architect (Amsterdam). (Courtesy of D. V. Sliedregt)

Figure 9.11
The Allen screw caps on this chair designed by James A. Howell add interest to the center stretcher as well as hold the chair together. Photograph by: Tom Yee. (Courtesy of Howell Design Corp.)

Figure 9.12
Chrome and nickel are combined in this pedestal-base table. Furniture designer: Paul Evans. (Courtesy of Directional)

by Kitschelt of Vienna, who also cast a table of zinc. Both kinds of furniture were exhibited at the Great Exhibition in 1851. A metal rocking chair of tubular metal with a light seat was also very popular. Brass beds first became popular after Queen Victoria ordered one for herself at the Great Exhibition (Fig. 9.8).

Cast iron was a big industry in the Victorian Period. The Philadelphia firm of Wood and Perot was the first in the United States to use iron for decorative purposes; by 1853 they had over 3000 product patterns. Machinery made it possible to make delicate pieces of furniture from wire. Made in the Rococo style usually, they were charming and original (see Fig. 9.9 for an example of a contemporary table in enameled iron).

Metal is a very popular material for furniture today and new techniques make possible furniture of tubing, metal rods, wire, and flat pieces of metal. Aluminum (Fig. 9.16), stainless or forged steel (Fig. 9.11 and 9.14), bronze (Fig. 9.10), brass, chrome, and nickel (Fig. 9.12) are some of the metals used. Metals can be coated with enamel (Fig. 9.9) or chrome (Fig. 9.15) for protection. Joints are welded, shaped, riveted, and bolted. In many pieces, the screws are used as ornamentation (Fig. 9.11). The metal can be highly polished and reflective (Fig. 9.13). Even pipes can be used to make furniture (Plate 37). Metal is stronger than wood and less likely to show wear, but it requires more skill to repair.

Synthetics

During the Victorian Period, papier-mâché was used much as plastics are used today. The mixture of glue and waste paper was driven into oiled molds under pressure, dried, and baked. After the object was finished, it was lacquered, decorated, gilded and/or painted. The first plastic cellulose nitrate, marketed as

Figure 9.13
The Cityscape group is of highly polished metal. Furniture designer: Paul Evans. (Courtesy of Directional)

Figure 9.15
Chrome tubular railings enclose the sofas. The low table has an olive ash burl top. Furniture designer: Milo Baughman. (Courtesy of Thayer Coggin)

Figure 9.14
The dark verdi gres finish on forged steel makes a smart chair. Furniture designer: Cleo Baldon. (Courtesy of Terra)

Figure 9.16
The unicorn chair, designed by Vladimir Kagan, has a V–frame of mirror-finish cast aluminum. (Courtesy of Vladimir Kagan)

Celluloid, was discovered in 1858. It was highly flammable and not practical for many uses. Bakelite was discovered in 1907, when L. H. Baekeland began experimenting with phenol and formaldehyde. He discovered that after adding a catalyst, the compound, which could be molded and set, was hard and not flammable, nor was it affected by water and most acids.

Figure 9.17

Upholstery appears to float within the plexiglas frame of this chair. Furniture designer: Vladimir Kagan. (Courtesy of Vladimir Kagan)

Figure 9.19

Plastic is both functional and beautiful. Chair designer: Joe Colombo. (Courtesy of Kartell)

Figure 9.18

The "Bing-Bong Ball" chair is of stainless steel and acrylic sheet. Furniture designer: Eero Aarnio (Finland). (Courtesy of Stendig International, Inc.)

omy as steel, glass, and wood. They are less expensive than wood, more functional, and more durable. Plexiglas was first used in 1940 by Grosfeld House for tables and chairs, to imitate period furniture styles, but today the *see-through* material is exploited for its inherent qualities, resulting in light, airy furniture (Figs. 9.17, 9.18).

Plastic has many uses in furniture (Fig. 9.19). Drawers are made of plastic, plastic components are used for legs and case posts, and some manufacturers use plastics to imitate intricately carved parts. Melamine laminates were first produced in 1913 by the Formica Company, to serve as insulation for electric motors. Today, they are used for decorative table tops, and their durable surface makes them functional as well.

Rigid urethane foam is a material with great potential. It is sculptural, light-weight, stronger than wood, unaffected by age or temperature, buoyant, and resistant to mildew and insects; it also has good acoustical properties. Chairs of foam can be rigid or resilient and molded to body contours (Fig. 9.20). Foam must be covered with a fire-resistant material, however, for it is very flammable.

Pneumatic furniture can be inflated to the desired softness (Fig. 9.21). Some inflatable furniture is supported by a plastic or aluminum frame.

In the last ten years, many new plastics have become available. They may be foamed, formed, molded, folded, poured, sprayed, inflated, deflated, or vacuum formed. They may be transparent or opaque, hard or soft, lightweight and/or structurally reinforced, and colored, textured, or patterned. Plastics have become as fundamental to the furniture econ-

Figure 9.20
*Steel tubing and foam are
the materials in this chaise
lounge covered with stretch
fabric. Furniture designer:
Geoffrey D. Harcourt.
(Courtesy of Geoffrey D.
Harcourt)*

Figure 9.21
*This pneumatic group was
designed by Stephan Gip.
(Courtesy of Stephan
Gip)*

Figure 9.22
Smoked plastic storage units are functional. Furniture designers: Afra and Tobia Scarpa. (Courtesy of Stendig International, Inc.)

Types of Plastics

Two types of plastics are used for furniture: *thermoplastics,* which become soft when exposed to sufficient heat and harden when cooled; and *thermosetting plastics,* which remain rigid (reheating will not soften them). Some of the other types of plastics are used for coatings, table tops, and sculpture. Plastics are difficult (some are impossible) to repair and they are not biodegradable. The field is still new, however, and many people are working toward solutions of these problems (Fig. 9.22).

Upholstered Furniture

There are two kinds of upholstered furniture: *over-stuffed,* in which the stuffing is applied over the frame (Fig. 9.23); the *exposed frame* (*bergère*), in which certain parts of the frame are exposed and other parts are covered (Fig. 9.24). Upholstered furniture consists of *frame, springs, webbing,* and *filling or cushioning material.*

Frame

The frame should be of kiln-dried hardwood such as ash, birch, gum, maple, poplar, or elm, or of metal or plastic. Softwoods, such as pine, hemlock, fir, and spruce are unsatisfactory and may split when tacked. The frame should be securely joined, double-doweled with spiral-grooved dowels, and glued. Corner blocks of a secondary wood, or metal plates should be glued and screwed to the joints as reinforcement. Nailed frames are unsatisfactory.

Springs

Coil springs, hand-tied to prevent sagging or sewn to the webbing or stapled to the end slats, should be close together. At least twelve springs are required for a chair and about twenty-seven for a sixty-inch sofa. Individual muslin-pocketed springs are excellent (the Marshall unit type). Coil springs are covered with burlap as a foundation for the filling material. Steel-web horizontal link-type springs are also satisfactory, although less expensive. They do not require webbing and do not have to be tied although they are often connected

Figure 9.23
Mario Bellini designed this overstuffed grouping. (Courtesy of Stendig International, Inc.)

Figure 9.24
This open-arm love seat is designed in cherry by John Marcoux. (Courtesy of John Marcoux)

Figure 9.25
The pattern of the fabric should be carefully matched on upholstered furniture. (Courtesy of Kroehler)

Figure 9.26
A chair should fit the body and have a slightly angled back. Furniture designer: Ross Littell. (Courtesy of Stendig International, Inc.)

Figure 9.27
The dining table in this kitchen is the correct height: the legs of these seated at it do not touch the underneath side of the table. Furniture designer: Ico Parisi. (Courtesy of Ico Parisi)

by random rubber strands. They require a well-constructed frame to withstand their tension. Wooden slats and loose webbing with more than three inches between the strips is unsatisfactory.

Webbing

Linen or jute webbing, or rubber with steel fibers, or basket-weave jute is strong, durable, and resilient. Jute four inches wide is used for seats (red lines are woven into the jute to indicate the width), and three and one-half inches wide (with black lines woven in) for chair and sofa backs. The purpose of webbing is to support the springs and cushioning.

Filling

The cushioning material should be covered to prevent seepage through the cover. Various materials are used:

Dacron: highly resilient, but will flatten over time.
Foam rubber: latex, first used by Wright; retains its shape, but will deteriorate; not resistant to mildew; should be in solid sections.
Goosedown and feathers: best is mixture of 75 per cent goosedown and 25 per cent feathers.
Polyurethane: resilient and comfortable, long lasting; resists mildew.

Selection of Upholstered Furniture

Seams should be double-sewn and straight, with no loose threads. The fabric pattern, if there is one, should match on the body of the furniture, on each cushion, and on the furniture skirt (if there is one) (Fig. 9.25). A napped fabric should have the nap running in one direction. The grain of the fabric should be parallel with the construction lines. Reversible cushions distribute wear, and zippered cushion covers are easy to remove for cleaning.

The exposed wood parts should be of well-finished wood (Fig. 9.24), and the frame should be of hardwood, which will hold tacks well. Joints should be closely fitted, dowelled, screwed, and glued. Corner blocks should be screwed and glued. Metal reinforcements should be used where the arms meet the frame.

Upholstery Fabrics

In selecting upholstery fabrics (fabrics are discussed in detail in Chapter 8), certain questions should be considered:

How durable is the fabric? Balanced, close, and firm weaves, tightly woven fabrics, and tightly twisted yarns wear longer. Loosely woven fabrics are easily snagged. Synthetic yarns wear better than natural ones if the weave and yarn construction are the same. Fabrics with small all-over patterns such as tweeds, paisleys, and small prints tend to show soil less readily than solid colors.

Is the fabric suitable for its use?

Is the pattern in scale with the furniture and the interior?

Are there any allergy problems to be considered?

Are there pets or children in the household?

Is the cost of the fabric in the same category as the price of the furniture item?

Is a special finish required or available?

Furniture Selection

Seating Pieces

Seating pieces are used for many purposes: working, eating, studying, relaxing. The final evaluation of a piece is how comfortable it is when used. For a chair to be comfortable, the feet of the person sitting on it should rest on the floor, his legs should be relaxed, and he should feel no pressure on the knee area. The seat should be resilient and wide enough for some movement. The back of the chair should support the small of his back and both the seat and back should be tilted slightly backwards (Fig. 9.26). Seats come in all sizes and shapes and each should be carefully compared to its intended purpose desired before being selected (Plate 38).

Tables

The table is an essential part of the interior. The top is used for meals, games, study, and for the placement of lamps, magazines, books, and ashtrays. Most people prefer a surface beside each chair for convenience. Tables should provide enough leg room underneath (Fig. 9.27); they should be stable and stand firmly on the floor; and they should be the correct height for the intended activity.

Beds

Beds are one of the most important parts of the interior. They may be built into the wall (Figs. 9.28a and 9.28b), free-standing (Fig. 9.29), or they may do double duty as sofas (Figs. 9.30a and 9.30b). The most important

Figure 9.28a
A custom cabinet holds the Murphy bed, which is kept closed during the day. (Courtesy of Murphy Door Bed Co., Inc.)

Figure 9.28b
The bed pulls down at night. (Courtesy of Murphy Door Bed Co., Inc.)

Figure 9.29
A contemporary four-poster bed with a cane headboard is used in this master bedroom. Photograph by: Yuichi Idaka. (Courtesy of Jack Denst Designs, Inc.)

aspect of the bed is the mattress, which should be comfortable and should support the back properly. Mattresses are of innerspring construction, made of polyurethane foam, or filled with water. Mattresses should be selected with care: approximately one third of a person's life is spent in bed.

Interior Space Planning

Interior space planning is based upon the activities that will be carried on in a given space. Well-planned furniture arrangements will not require moving pieces frequently. In fact, if a room is disrupted after regular activities have been carried on in it, it is not well planned to begin with.

The needs of each household are unique to that family, just as office requirements are unique. There are no rules that can be followed in each case. Work habits, interests, and hobbies determine how a space will be used. Before the designer begins to plan an interior space, he should make a floor plan. It is usually preferable (except for very large spaces) to use a scale of one-fourth inch to a foot. The floor plan should indicate placement of doors, windows, architectural details, and phone and electrical outlets.

The next step is to determine the needs of the household members or office staff, and to list their personal preferences, ages, hobbies, and likes and dislikes, as well as the activities

that will take place in each room, and the furniture, storage, and special equipment required for each activity.

The third step is to cut out paper representations of furniture pieces to a fourth inch scale. Seating pieces should be in one color, case pieces and tables in another color, lighting in yellow, and plants in green. These pieces of paper can be moved about on the plan to develop the most logical and functional arrangement.

Fundamentals

There are a few fundamental principles of interior arrangements that must be kept in mind:

1. A comfortable, convenient room will be pleasant in appearance. The floor plan should be flexible, for a room will rarely remain static. Everyone needs a periodic change.
2. The plan should be as simple as possible.
3. Main traffic patterns into and through the space should be indicated on the plan with colored pencil. Major traffic lanes should be six feet wide; minor pathways, four feet. Approaches to the doors should be kept clear; furniture placed in front of them will obstruct circulation. Easy access to windows makes a room more usable.
4. Furniture should be so placed as to be approachable. Enough space should be left in front of pieces for them to fulfill their proper function. Each piece of furniture should be placed where it will accomplish its purpose most effectively. Reading areas should be located far enough from conversation areas to prevent an overlapping of activities.
5. The good architectural features of a space should be emphasized. A room with many irregularities needs more careful planning, and the furnishings should compensate for any irregularities. The most should be made of any view.
6. A logical pattern of furniture arrangement is important. Pieces should be placed for service, with the best use being made of the available space. The main conversation area should be inviting, so that normal conversation is possible, and the maximum distance between people should be no more than ten feet. Common sense is a great aid in arranging a

room for optimal use of the space. Pieces needed for a specific activity should be grouped, not scattered about the room. Records and equipment should be stored near the stereo, games near the game table, books close to the reading area, and magazines near a comfortable chair. The most frequently used area is often best situated near the main entrance of a room. Daylight should be utilized as much as possible. Available electrical outlets must also be considered in arranging furniture, for a reading area without a lamp is useless.

7. Important pieces should be positioned first, where they will appear best, so that they will not have to be moved. Large pieces should generally conform to the architecture of the space and be placed either parallel to the wall or at right angles to it. Violations of the basic lines of the space are disrupting. Chairs can be positioned at angles because they are relatively small. Upholstered chairs look better at an angle than straight chairs do.

8. Tall pieces of furniture seldom look good in corners. Furniture groupings can make good use of corners, but a lone chair located in a corner is lost. Corner space can be used for sectional pieces or curved units. Diagonal arrangements (unless small) should be avoided.

9. An area requires a center of interest. Large areas may require secondary centers of interest. These groupings should be separated. Some interesting or unusual centers of interest might be a large piece of furniture, an entertainment center, a painting or a piece of sculpture, a fireplace, or a view.

10. Furniture should fit the room; the room should not be fitted to the furniture. Room sizes are fixed, but furniture size and scale can be changed. The best arrangement is one in which the room and the furniture appear to be ideally suited to each other.

11. A well-designed room is balanced. Formal balance is no longer as popular as it once was, but even in formally balanced rooms, some asymmetry is necessary. Masses should be distributed so that the space feels right. Light, weight, pattern, color, wood, textures, and furniture must balance one another. A tall piece of furniture will help to balance a room if it is placed on a wall opposite a door rather than on the same wall as the door. A long sofa usually looks best on the longest wall.

Too much furniture at one end of the room can disrupt its balance. But furniture is only one component in the balance of a room. Empty spaces are another component. Empty spaces between groupings of furniture give an uncluttered effect to a room. Empty spaces should be included in groupings as well, but they should be smaller than those between groupings. Conversely, spaces should not be crowded with too much furniture. Each wall should balance and be pleasing to the eye and walls opposite each other should also balance visually. When working with floor plans, it is important to remember that furniture has height as well as width and depth.

12. A room should have unity and harmony of line, shape, scale, texture, and color. This does not eliminate the need for variety and contrast, which help to provide emphasis and interest. A particular mood or theme should be expressed in the space and the space should be planned so that it all works together.

13. Scale is a fundamental factor in the planning of an interior. Each piece of furniture must be related to every other piece of furniture and to the space as well. Groupings should be related in scale. For example, a small room needs small-scale furniture and fewer pieces if it is to appear as uncluttered as possible. Large pieces of furniture placed close to small, delicate ones destroy the scale. Large pieces of furniture in small rooms are best placed where they are not the center of attention.

14. Movement and rhythm are necessary in a room. The eye needs to move easily through a variety of lines and shapes, textures and colors. Continuity is achieved by a consistent use of line such as table tops the same height as chair arms. This is not only comfortable and useful but beautiful.

15. Furniture should be grouped according to its specific functions. Rarely is any piece of furniture useful alone; rather, it is useful in relationship to other pieces. Through effective grouping, the appearance of each piece is often enhanced. In a large room, purely decorative furniture.

may be used. In areas of limited space, each piece may have to be functional.

16. Almost any room is more pleasing if it conveys a feeling of spaciousness. Wall-hung furniture and pieces with legs seem to take less floor space than pieces extending to the floor. Wall-to-wall carpeting opens up a room, but area rugs divide it. If the center of the room is kept clear of furniture, the room appears more spacious.

17. Contemporary furniture has strong horizontal lines and a fairly constant height. This tends to make a room appear larger by carrying the eye around the room. The varying heights of traditional furniture pieces carry the eye up and down and accent the vertical lines in the room.

18. The requirements of a grouping should be carefully considered when areas are planned. A conversation center should seat about eight persons without requiring additional chairs from another area. Seating should be located so that it is easy to talk. A low coffee table, end tables, and lamps add much to the conversation center, and an area rug may serve to unify it. The conversation center should not be more than ten feet in diameter. Chair space must be about three feet deep with leg space about one and one half to two feet in front.

A reading area should include a good chair, a table, and a lamp. A chair and footstool require about six feet of space. A game corner with a round table and chairs requires about a space seven feet square. Eating tables require about two feet in length for each person, with two feet required behind each chair for passage.

Glossary

Antiquing. A paint or stain finish designed to give wood the patina of age.

Burl Veneer. Veneer of irregularly arranged fibers caused by wart-like growth on such trees as walnut, ash, cherry, yew, elm, and birch.

Butt Veneer. Veneer cut from that part of tree where trunk and large roots join.

Crotch Veneer. Veneer obtained from the area below the forks of a large tree or the point at which the trunk is joined by large branches.

Distressed Finish. A finish imparted by striking the wood with chains, hammers, and so on, to achieve the effect of age.

Flitch (flĭch). A mounted log segment from which a veneer is cut.

Grain. The arrangement and quality of fibrous tissue in wood.

Hardboard. A manufactured wood material made of tiny, thread-like wood fibers bound together with lignin, the natural cohesive in wood.

Hardwood. Wood from a deciduous tree (one that loses its leaves seasonally).

Irridated Wood. A wood that is impregnated with plastic and irridiated to achieve hardness and abrasion resistance.

Matte Finish. A finish, such as flat paint, without any shine.

Opaque Finish. A finish that conceals the wood grain.

Papier-mâché (pāy'-pur-mă-shāy'). A mixture of glue and waste paper driven into oiled molds under pressure, dried and baked, to make furniture and accessories.

Particleboard. A wood material made by combining wood flakes with resin binding agents and then hot-pressing them into panels.

Penetrating Finish. A finish that sinks into the wood.

Rotary Veneer. A veneer that is sliced in a continuous strip around the log.

Softwood. A wood from conifers (trees that do not shed their leaves).

Transparent Finish. A finish (such as shellac or varnish) that does not conceal the wood grain.

Veneer. A thin sheet of wood applied (generally) to a less expensive wood.

Bibliography

BACHELARD, GASTON. *The Poetics of Space.* New York: Orion Press, 1964.

CASSON, HUGH, ed. *Inscape, the Design of Interiors.* London: Architectural Press.

DAL FABBRO, MARIO. *Furniture for Modern Interiors.* New York: Van Nostrand Reinhold Company, 1955.

KOEHLER, A. *Identification of Furniture Woods.* Washington, D.C.: U.S. Department of Agriculture, 1926.

PELTON, B. W. *Furniture Making and Cabinet Work: A Handbook.* New York: Van Nostrand Reinhold Company, 1949.

SHAPLAND, H. P. *The Practical Decoration of Furniture.* 3 vols. London: Ernest Benn Ltd., 1926–27.

The Sound and Energy Environment

The Sound Environment

Noise in the environment is increasing at the rate of 5 per cent a year, particularly in the home, where many new labor-saving devices are being added. A comfortable sound level appears to be between 50 and 65 decibels. No sound standard has been developed because undesirable noises are more offensive than sounds associated with pleasant activities or with labor-saving devices. For example, although teenagers play the stero at an extremely loud 100 decibels, they apparently enjoy it. Also, few complaints are made to manufacturers about the noise level of appliances because many consumers corelate product efficiency with noise.

The calculation of noise is not based upon an arithmetic scale but, rather, upon a logarithmic scale: each increase of 10 decibels means that the noise is ten times louder than before. An increase of 20 decibels, from 70 to 90 means that the noise level is two hundred times louder.

When loud noises assault the eardrums, they may cause not only physical discomfort (actual pain occurs at 125 decibels), but also physiological changes: an increase in blood pressure and in heart rate, a slowdown of the digestive process (owing to a change in the rate of acid secretion in the stomach), a rise in cholesterol levels, and dilation of the pupils. Noise may have psychological changes as well, inducing fatigue, tension, nervousness, and depression. People who live near airports have a dramatically higher incidence of depression and sucide. This is also true for those who live in areas where the wind howls continuously.

A noise level of 90 decibels for eight hours a day, or a level of 115 decibels for only fifteen minutes a day, can cause hearing loss. Unaccustomed background noise at night (a cricket at 40 decibels or a barking dog a block away at 50 decibels) can disturb sleep, although lapping water and a scream of gulls at the beach (50 decibels) or the singing of birds in the woods (55 decibels) can be soothing and enjoyable. Radio and television are usually played at sixty decibels; conversation usually reaches about 70 decibels; a jet take-off reaches 112 decibels. Street noises are about 75 decibels, but a horn raises them to 90, as does the collection of trash; a siren raises them to 110, and on the Fourth of July they rise to over 100.

The kitchen is the noisiest room in the house (Fig. 10.1) because of its many appliances, several of which may be in use simultaneously. Sound levels are cumulative, so sound insulation (with materials such as thick, perforated panels and acoustical ceilings is essential. These materials can decrease sound up to 50 per cent. The selection of quiet appliances, placed on antivibrating rubber or cork or vinyl sound-absorbing pads and positioned away from walls or enclosed in cabinets, cuts noise considerably.

The separation of quiet from active areas in the interior and the use of halls, bookcases, and closets between rooms cuts down noise. Staggering doors breaks up sound waves, and solid flush doors insulate against sound more effectively than sliding doors. Noise control is particularly important in dining areas, for too much sound stimulation can interfere with digestion and cause tension and headaches (Fig. 10.2). Just as soft lights aid digestion and increase enjoyment of food, so do soft sounds. Thick padded carpeting, lined draperies, and upholstered furniture help to control sound (Figs. 6.7, 7.14).

The outside of the home should also be protected from distracting noises. In general, urban dwellers are subjected to more exterior noise than are those who live in the suburbs and in rural areas. People who live with constant city noise often require a more restful home environment with relatively little sound. Conversely, the rural dweller may enjoy lively conversation and music as a break from the usual quiet day. Urban exteriors can be protected from noise by trees, hedges, and garden areas, which absorb sound. A study conducted by the University of Nebraska and the U.S. Forest Service found that sound could be reduced by five to ten decibels when tall, dense belts of trees were planted.[1] This study was conducted for commercial purposes, but many of the findings can be adapted for residential use. Evergreens are favored for their year-round sound-absorbing qualities (they do not lose their leaves) and are best placed on the outer edges of the lot, nearest the noise source. Tall plants and grasses planted between the trees and the house will also absorb sound, but hard surfaces or stones conduct sound.

[1] David Cook, "Trees and Shrubs Can Curb Noise, But with Quiet a Few Loud 'Ifs'," *Landscape for Living,* (Washington, D.C.: U.S. Department of Agriculture, 1972).

Table 10.1
Decibel Level of Appliances

Appliance	Decibels
Blender	30–40
Compactor	70–80
Dishwasher	70–80
Dryer	50–60
Freezer	25–35
Food Processor	30–55
Garbage Disposal	80–100
Refrigerator	30–40
Vacuum	70–80
Ventilator (range)	80–90
Washing Machine	60–70

Figure 10.1
The kitchen has many noise-creating appliances but few soft surfaces to absorb the sound. Photograph by: Bill Margerin. (Courtesy of Hardwood Institute)

Figure 10.2
The carpet and chair cushions in this dining area absorb sound. (Courtesy of Armstrong Cork Co.)

Personality and Tolerance of Noise

Designers must be aware of the client's psychological tolerance for noise. An outgoing, sociable individual who has a loud voice and boisterous manner, for example, may be able to tolerate high noise levels in conversation, music, television, work and environmental sounds while another person, perhaps more introverted, may be disturbed by them. The extroverted individual could, however, profit from lower sound levels and find it easier to work, think, and plan in a more calm atmosphere.

For a particularly high-energy person, noise may result in an inability to finish tasks on time, in a tendency to promise more than he can possibly deliver or an inability to exercise good judgment. Even individuals who appear to thrive on noise would be wise to avoid high-decibel areas when they are tense, when they have a deadline, or when they are attempting to concentrate on a problem.

Children tolerate louder noises than adults do, but tolerate them less well as they mature. A slight lowering of the sound level for children and adolescents can have a sudden and dramatic calming effect. Teachers have long known that a noisy classroom is one that is low in productivity. When the sound stimuli are too great, the students become excited and hyperactive, experience difficulty in concentrating, and cause trouble. City schools and many offices also contend with the disruptive environmental sounds of traffic, planes, factories, and emergency equipment, and few are planned with sound-absorbing surfaces. Study areas in the home should be acoustically controlled to make concentration easier.

Too much noise is deleterious to health but often high-energy, outgoing people, such as adolescents, enjoy loud music and just plain racket and misjudge the subliminal effects of too much sound. Research indicates that although visual and auditory impressions can be received without conscious awareness, subsequent behavior reveals their impact. If too much noise is regularly present, it is often ignored, but its insidious effects can cause physical and emotional damage. These aspects of sound planning must always be considered in interior design.

Music

Although too much noise can be harmful, some subliminal sound can be beneficial.

Music is the best example of this positive phenomenon. It can instantly change the interior environment. It is so important that there are both national and international organizations for music therapy. Music can favorably influence the course of mental and physical illness as well as add enjoyment to the interior environment. Individuals diagnosed as manic, for example, when treated with music of gradually decreasing tempo, are often effectively calmed. Conversely, those who are depressed may respond favorably to a somber, slow tempo that gradually grows more lively. Soft background music is restful and conducive to eating, studying, working, relaxing, and conversing. Research suggests that quiet classical music improves learning in classrooms while rock music results in a poorer performance. These data indicate that some method of controlling the type and volume of music in the home and office is desirable. Soft background music, which is generally pleasant, may be replaced by more lively music during a party. The multitude of stereo systems available for homes today allows the owner to control the volume and type of music and to determine which areas of the home will receive it.

Sound-proofing between rooms and individual speaker controls is desirable. The same music played in speakers located in most rooms of the house is usually unsuitable: family members seldom have the same taste or emotional moods and seldom are engaged in identical activities at the same time. Music, like wallpaper, can cover a variety of flaws and should be considered a factor in the design of the home and office. It can mask exterior noise for example. Music, like light, is an instant mood setter. The designer should plan carefully for its inclusion in the interior environment.

The Energy Environment

Body Comfort Requirements

The normal human body generates heat to maintain its temperature of 98.6°F. (39.2°C.). At rest, this amounts to 400 British Thermal Units (BTU). A BTU is the amount of heat required to raise one pound of water 1°F. During stress or under heavy labor, the body may generate 1200 BTU per hour. Too rapid a heat loss results in feeling cold, while too slow a

loss results in feeling hot. Heat is lost in several ways:

1. Convection (by radiant heat transfer to a cooler surface)
2. Perspiration (by loss of moisture from the skin)
3. Conduction (by cool air moving about the body)
4. Respiration or breathing

In summer, cool surfaces surrounding the body accelerate heat loss while in winter warm surfaces (walls, windows, and floors) are required to diminish heat loss.

Humidity, or moisture in the air, also affects retention or loss of heat. A humidity increase in winter prevents evaporation; the higher the humidity, the slower the rate of skin moisture loss. If humidity can be maintained at 60 per cent in the winter, the body will remain comfortable at relatively lower temperatures. In summer a humidity level of 25 per cent or less causes moisture to evaporate quickly from the skin increasing comfort. Air movement and temperature must be controlled as well. Air velocities of about 25 feet per minute are most satisfactory, as are temperatures of 70–77°F. (21.1–25°C.). With the need for energy conservation, however, it has become necessary to develop methods of staying warm at temperatures of 62–68°F. (16.7–20°C.) and of staying cool at a temperature of 78°F. (25.6°C.).

In 1978, the Federal government cited research findings that suggested that individuals could be comfortable with interior temperatures as low as 54 degrees F. (12°C.). The government report, which was a recommendation to energy consumers, suggested that hats, sweaters, and even light gloves should be considered for daily wear within the home.

One problem with an arbitrary temperature control is that people of different ages require different temperatures to feel comfortable. Young children have a higher metabolic rate than adults do, and therefore require a lower room temperature to feel comfortable. Any adult who has visited an elementary school classroom will notice that when children are comfortable at the room temperature, the teacher is often wearing a sweater. As a person grows older and the metabolism slows down, temperature needs increase. Older people have the slowest metabolism and may not be able to keep warm at thermostat settings below 65° (18.3°C.). Hypothermia for this age group is a

Figure 10.3

The new energy-efficient, built-in fireplace has a stainless steel heat exchanger that returns 100 per cent more heat to the room than a conventional fireplace does. Heated air can even be diverted to adjoining rooms with optional ducts and fans. (Courtesy of Majestic Co.)

real danger even at temperatures of 70° (21.1°C.).

Most interiors when heated are drier than a desert, causing headaches, allergies, respiratory aliments, dry skin, and irritability, as well as the requirement for more heat. Consequently, many homes can benefit from lower room temperatures and higher humidity levels. Not only is physical comfort increased, but wood and leather are better preserved at lower temperatures and with humidity at about 30–40 per cent. If humidity is raised above 40 per cent, however, problems may arise from excess moisture.

One factor in planning the humidity requirements of a given space is the number of people who will normally occupy that area. People give off large amounts of moisture: the more people occupy a space, the higher the relative humidity. Some public buildings in the South are designed so that the body heat of the occupants plus the heat from the luminaires is sufficient to raise the temperature of the interior to comfortable levels in the cold months.

Fireplaces

The conventional fireplace is, unfortunately, impractical. It is expensive, and the heat it generates will not even replace the heat lost as the warm room air escapes up the flue. Little heat is radiated; instead, the heat is confined to the room in which it is generated. The fireplace creates drafts and often causes problems with central thermostatic controls. After the fire has died down, the flue must be left open, which further increases heat loss. Even when the fireplace is not in use and the flue is closed, heated house air is lost because it is impossible to close the flue tightly.

Clearly, a fireplace fulfills only emotional and design needs. To many it symbolizes warmth, comfort, and security; its soft light can be an important design component, and it creates a major center of interest even when not in use. For these reasons, fireplaces are often included in residential plans.

Formerly fireplaces were found in every room, for they were the only source of heat. Today, a fireplace is usually placed in the most frequently used family space, where it serves as a focus for social gatherings. Because fireplaces are generally large and centers of interest, they should be placed where furniture can be arranged in front of them. Until recently, they were usually placed on an outside wall, but with today's need for energy conservation, inside chimneys insure that any heat radiation will be kept in the interior.

The conventional fireplace can be adapted so as to retain its symbolic value and yet not result in heat loss. One method is to install a glass door, which not only markedly decreases heat loss but also provides safety from sparks. The "17 Hundred 90 Inn" in Savannah has a fireplace in twelve of its fourteen bed-

Figure 10.4
This cast iron enamelled stove can stand alone or against the wall. Interior designer: Jon Bannerberg. (Courtesy of National Coal Board)

rooms which blazes to life, summer or winter, at the push of a button. Its tempered glass shield keeps the heat from radiating into the room. Metal conducting pipes can replace the conventional grate, increasing heat radiation. These pipes draw in cool air from the room, allow it to flow around and over the fire, and expel the heated air through the top of the pipes back into the room (Fig. 10.3).

Prefabricated fireplaces, such as the Heatilator, are even more efficient. This heavy metal unit is similar to a small hot-air furnace and is usually installed inside the fireplace. Alongside the metal unit are air ducts which allow air to flow up and around the unit. This heated air is then forced out into the room around and above the metal unit by the natural movement of hot air or assisted by fans. The outlet for the heated air may be in a room behind or above the fireplace as well as in the same room.

Andirons, baskets, and grates are used in fireplaces to keep the fuel in place and for their ornamental effect. However, when heating pipes are not placed in the firebox, a fire laid directly on the brick floor is more efficient. A grate or basket makes the fire easier to start but makes it also burn more rapidly.

Fires need air to burn and the chimney should draw properly to prevent smoke from entering the room. Flues can be partly closed so that more heat is radiated without smoke coming into the room. Wood stacked in parallel rows tends to burn more slowly than cross-piled logs. Closing all doors, and closing heating ducts from the furnace into the room with the fireplace, will further reduce the amount of warm air drawn up the flue. Setting the house thermostat 15–20° lower then normal when the fireplace is operating effectively conserves warm air.

Wood-burning Stoves

Wood-burning stoves can be very efficient. One can enjoy the smell of burning wood without suffering the disadvantages of heat loss. Wood is also the only fuel source that can be harvested and replenished. It is cleaner and less expensive than coal, and more readily available than other fuel sources. The modern wood-burning stove is far superior to earlier models. Wood-burning stoves constructed as recently as 1970 were inefficient in both design and construction; the Franklin free-standing stove was even more inefficient.

The modern wood stove is airtight, heavy, and large enough to hold whole logs or large pieces of wood (Fig. 10.4). The result is a slow-burning fire which may need refueling only twice every twenty-four hours. Fuel savings of up to 80 per cent are possible with wood-burning stoves. Many new homes are being equipped with these stoves for heating and cooking. As gas, oil, and electricity become increasingly expensive and as shortages and blackouts become more frequent, coal and

Figure 10.5

Types of solar energy systems

10.5a Placement of the building on the site. Protection from the sun is provided (by deciduous trees) in summer, and from the winds (by conifers) in winter.

10.5b A passive solar system; direct gain with the sunlight passing through the south-facing windows.

10.5c A thermal storage wall which collects heat, named after Felix Trombe. Trombe walls may be concrete, brick, stone, or adobe.

10.5d A thermal storage unit composed of water barrels.

10.5e A thermal storage unit on the roof, most frequently used.

10.5f An attached sunspace (isolated gain) such as a greenhouse, atrium, or sunporch.

10.5g A convective loop, based on convective movement of the air; used in conjunction with solar collectors.

10.5h Natural ventilation or fans may be used to bring in cool night air.

10.5i A roof pond may be used to adsorb heat in the day and radiate it to the cool night sky; the pool should be shaded during the day.

10.5j Evaporative cooling is achieved in dry climates by the use of pools or sprays around the house.

10.5k The more a building is in contact with the ground the cooler it will be; building into the side of a hill or earth mounding is the easiest way to achieve this.

10.5l Natural ventilation can be achieved by properly positioned windows to take advantage of air movement.

(Illustrations courtesy of Peter Koenig, Associate Professor, Department of Interior Design, Florida State University)

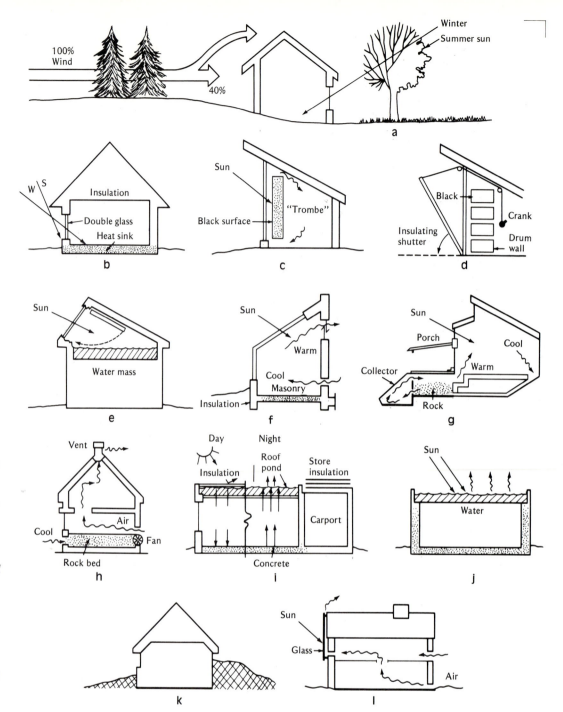

wood stoves are excellent back-up systems in case of emergency or even as replacements for conventional systems. Prefabricated chimneys are relatively inexpensive and can be integrated into the design of the room.

There are many books available on wood stoves and even a journal, *Wood Burning Quarterly Magazine*. Wood stoves can be used for cooking and if copper coils are run through the stove so that the water can circulate through the hotwater tank, hot water can be provided at no additional cost. A back-up electric or gas unit can be activated to maintain the desired water temperature when the stove is not burning.

Solar Energy

Solar energy has been utilized for hundreds of years. In 212 B.C., Archimedes, used mirrors to focus the sun's rays on the sails of Roman ships, and the intensity of the heat set the sails on fire. With the dawn of the Industrial Revolution, solar furnaces were designed which were capable of melting metals, including iron. The World's Fair of 1896 featured several solar engines adaptable to a variety of domestic or industrial functions. The Pueblo Indians of the southwestern United States used clay, mud, and stone for their dwellings, which absorbed the sun's rays effectively and thus gave

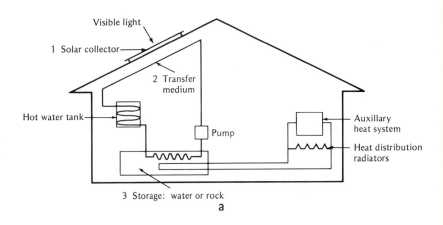

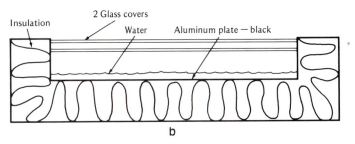

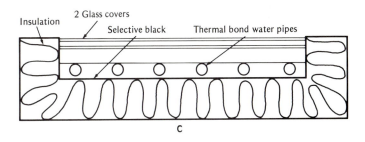

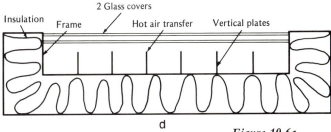

them "solar homes." Today, more than two hundred experimental solar homes have been constructed in the United States (Figs. 10.5 and 10.6).

Solar heating is past the experimental stage and is capable of furnishing up to 75 per cent of the heating needs of the home. (Except in equatorial areas, no solar system at present can supply all the heat required in the home.) A solar heating system consists of a collector, usually the large flat-plate type (Fig. 3.14); a storge tank for liquid or an insulated rock pile for heated air; various controls such as a differential thermostat to turn the pump or blower on and off when the collectors are hotter or colder than the storage; interconnecting pipes, ducts, and a blower (for air) or a pump (for liquid); and an auxiliary heat source, usually oil, gas, or electricity. The most common collector is a glass-X-14 or plastic-covered box with a copper, aluminum, or steel absorber plate to retain the heat. Liquid or air is used to collect the heat, which is then stored or used immediately.

Effective use of solar energy requires at least six hours daily of direct rays. The more direct the rays, the greater the heat potential. The angle of the sun and the average number of cloudless days are obvious considerations when determining whether or not a solar system is practical. Wind, rain, snow depth (collectors are operable with some snow, although not much), and the shape of the building in relationship to its site and the surrounding terrain are also factors to be considered.

Houses designed to use solar energy require a new orientation. Large solar collectors, the opening and closing of expanses of exposed glass, and different roof shapes affect the design of the house. Passive solar collectors, in the form of colored glass that replaces windows on the south side of the house, create new design problems. These thick colored glass collectors, usually five inches wide, are filled with water and occupy what would typically be window space. Even water filled colored bottles can be used in place of window panes to collect heat. These collectors have both a heating and a cooling function. During the day, when the direct rays of the sun might make the house uncomfortable, the colored glass and water shield the interior. At the same time, they are collecting the energy that will keep the house warm during the night.

Recent studies indicate that solar heat sys-tems are relatively expensive to install, but relatively inexpensive to operate. Solar collectors cost an average of $18 per square foot of heated area (1981). A solar heating system provides only two thirds of the required heat, but costs two to four times that of a conventional system because it must also be added to the conventional system. However, a study done at the University of New Mexico suggests that the cost of solar energy will be less expensive than that of gas or oil in over half the United States by 1985, owing to the more efficient, larger scale production of solar heating components and the increasing costs of oil and gas.

Figure 10.6a
Solar heating schematic.
10.6b A single fixed-plate collector.
10.6c A complex fixed-plate collector.
10.6d A vertical fixed-plate collector.
(Illustrations courtesy of Peter Koenig, Associate Professor, Department of Interior Design, Florida State University)

Table 10.2
Considerations in the Selection of Solar Heat

1. Initial cost of system; cost and availability of other fuels
2. Climate
3. Space and water-heating requirements
4. Availability of location for solar collectors and equipment

Solar energy is clean and it is unlimited, but at present few houses have incorporated it owing to design difficulties. However, with increased research, these design problems will probably be solved in the coming years.

Insulation

No matter what form of energy is employed for heating and cooling, proper insulation will result in savings. Most homes constructed before 1960 were generally poorly insulated; those with window air conditioners are almost certainly inadequately insulated. Proper insulation can save up to one third of heating and cooling costs, a large return for a relatively small investment.

Insulation requirements vary with climatic conditions. Generally more insulation against cold is required in the North, the Midwest, and the East, while more insulation against heat is required in the South and on the West Coast. A heating and cooling zone map, which indicates specific insulation requirements, may be obtained from the United States Department of Commerce.

R-values, shown on containers of insulating materials, indicate resistance to winter heat loss or summer heat gain, and also indicate the effectiveness of different insulation materials. The higher the R-number, the more effective the insulating capability. Insulation for exterior walls, attic floors, and ceilings typically consists of fiberglass, cellulose, or rock wool batts or blankets for new construction or foam or loose-fill materials which are poured or blown into existing houses. Rigid polyurethane foam panels are also used for new construction, but must be fully covered since the foam is very flammable. R-11 to R-13 is usually recommended by the Federal Housing Administration as a standard for exterior wall insulation. R-19 is the minimum standard recommended for attic floors or for top floor ceilings for new construction.

It is more difficult to determine the R-values for existing construction, but a rule of thumb suggests that about six inches of insulation equals R-11.

If energy is to be saved, insulation is also required for unheated areas such as garages and crawl spaces, as well as water pipes, and heating and cooling ducts. Other devices for energy conservation include calking and weatherstripping around doors and windows; double-glazed windows or storm windows; insulated draperies, and padded rugs. A lighted candle should be moved around window frame and sashes: if the flame is moved by outside air, insulation is needed. If a large coin can slide under a door, weatherstripping is required. Triple-glass combination windows (Fig. 10.7), or storm windows, can reduce heat or cooling loss up to 75 per cent.

Alternative Sources of Energy

Other types of energy, not yet commercially practical for homes in the United States, are being investigated. Wind and water power have been around for many years. Interest in them has been renewed because they are non-polluting and because conventional fuels are increasingly scarce and expensive. Units to generate wind power are available but expensive (a typical unit suitable for an average home costs about $23,000). Because wind is an undependable resource, a back-up system is necessary in most locations. Demand for this equipment would have to expand dramatically before the cost would decline.

Hydro-electric systems are also available for homes located near a rapid waterfall. The rate at which the water falls is a critical factor. For example, although the Columbia River is much smaller than the Amazon River, it has ten times as much potential electrical power owing to its rapid rate of fall. Hydro-electric-energy is relatively expensive and less dependable than conventional fuel. Both wind and water systems require storage for the electricity they generate. Unfortunately, the battery storage that meets this need is very expensive and requires time-consuming maintenance.

Other systems under investigation include geothermal energy extracted from the earth's interior, nuclear fission, and biological methods of changing waste materials into gas and oil. Waste can be a resource rather than a problem: it could be used to generate enough steam to fill 2-3 per cent of the nation's energy requirements. This method entails the

Figure 10.7
Triple-glass combination windows help to insulate the interior. (Courtesy of Caradco Wood Windows)

conversion of organic materials into methane by the anaerobic digestion process. An experimental plant in Bartow, Florida, converts manure from a thousand head of cattle to methane to supply the energy for a nearby meat-packing plant. A plant in Ames, Iowa, burns garbage to supply electricity, recovering over 90 per cent of the waste material. Pyrolysis is also used to convert garbage to such energy-rich fuels as gas and char (similar to charcoal). In this method, the waste is heated in the absence of oxygen. A fourth method of utilizing this energy source is to drill wells to tap the methane naturally produced in landfills.

The energy crisis has forced recognition of the necessity to conserve energy through the design, the construction, and the furnishing of the home. In the past, little attention was given to the insulating qualities of construction materials, the energy utilization of home appliances, or the efficiency of heating and cooling systems. Today, the designer must give these factors, as well as aesthetic considerations, top priority.

Glossary

Acoustical. Pertaining to sound, or to the sense of hearing.

British Thermal Unit (BTU). The amount of heat required to raise one pound of water 1°F.

Decibels. A unit of measurement for sound.

Humidity. The amount of moisture in the air.

Insulation. Materials used to protect buildings from loss of heat and/or cold.

Bibliography

ALVES, RONALD. *Living with Energy: Alternative Sources in Your Home.* New York, New York: Viking Press, Inc., 1978.

BLANDY, THOMAS, and DENIS LAMOUREUX. *All Through the House: A Guide to Home Weatherization.* New York, New York: McGraw-Hill Book Company, 1980.

CROWLEY, MAUREEN, ed. *Energy: Sources of Print and Nonprint Materials.* New York, New York: Neal-Schumsh Publishers, Inc., 1980.

Energy in America's Future: The Choices Before Us. Baltimore, Maryland: Johns Hopkins University Press, 1979.

Energy: National Geographic Special Report. Washington, D.C.: National Geographic Society, February 1981.

Energy: The Next Twenty Years. Cambridge, Mass.: Ballinger Publishing Co., 1979.

LOFTNESS, ROBERT L. *Energy Handbook.* New York, New York: Van Nostrand Reinhold Co., 1978.

Residential Energy Workbook. Tallahassee, Florida: Governor's Energy Office, 1980.

Woodstove Fireplace and Equipment Directory. Manchester, N.H.: Energy Communications Press: published annually.

The Green Environment

The growing of plants indoors is not new. In ancient Egypt unusual plants were imported and cultivated, and their drawings show potted plants being carried in processions. The ancient Greeks made beautiful plant containers and over five hundred plants are mentioned in their botanical records. The Romans grew exotic plants in containers in their atriums and had heated greenhouses with mica roofs where they produced out-of-season roses and lilies. During the Italian Renaissance beautiful gardens were common. In England and France, from the seventeenth century through the nineteenth century, citrus fruits were grown in orangeries or conservatories. French country families grew herbs and flowering geraniums indoors. The conservatory, or greenhouse, reached its zenith during the Victorian Period, when over five thousand species of tropical plants, including lush palms, feathery ferns, and flowering begonias were introduced into Europe.

Today, greenhouses are experiencing a worldwide rebirth, especially in the United States (Figs. 11.1a, and 11.1b). In the last few years, tremendous progress has been made in expanding the variety of available houseplants. The number of commercial greenhouses has increased (about 70 per cent of them are located in Florida) and sales of houseplants have increased over 600 per cent in the last five years. Worldwide exploration for new and unusual houseplants and new methods of propagation and hybridization have made it possible to bring indoors many plants formerly grown only in tropical jungles or in greenhouses.

The discovery of fluorescent light in 1938 made it possible to cultivate and bring to bloom many tropical plants, although a number of foliage plants can be grown with a simple spotlight. With so many new plants flooding the market from Central and South America, Africa, and Asia, the process of discovering which can be successfully grown indoors is frequently one of trial and error. In spite of numerous new instruction books, many plants are marketed before instructions are widely available. It is usually helpful to determine the plant's native habitat and then to apply this knowledge to the care of the plant. Many plants come from regions where rainfall is heavy, the soil rich in humus, and the light filtered through thick vegetation. It is just as well that these ideal conditions cannot be reproduced in the home, for some plants, such as Norfolk Island pine, might then grow two hundred feet tall, necessitating a hole in the roof.

Man obviously desires to surround himself with a green environment, perhaps because he is genetically programmed to a green landscape. As the concrete jungle expands and greenery disappears from the city and the suburbs, man finds the presence of plants reassuring. Plant-filled rooms reinforce the belief that home is a place of calm, refuge, and safety. Employers and city planners, realizing the effect plants produce, have increasingly included plants in work and public areas.

Plants are healthy to have around for they return vital oxygen to the air and, being composed largely of water, they raise humidity levels by combining expelled water vapor with air. In addition, plants appeal to man's aesthetic sense. They come in a variety of shapes, colors, textures, and sizes and are an asset to the design of the interior (Plate 41). Plants are an excellent learning medium, for the production and growth of life within the home is a natural teaching example for children, inducing an understanding of biology that came naturally on a farm but was lost when families moved to the cities.

Selection of Plants for the Interior

Today, there are many exotic plants available and their proper selection is an important aspect of interior design. First, the purpose for which the plant is desired should be determined. Some large specimen plants are literally green furniture and will stand alone in their own right. Plants can be used to create a center of interest or to emphasize or de-emphasize architectural details (Fig. 3.44). They can create a mood (Fig. 7.56) or an effect (Fig. 3.4) and can also divide space (Plate 42), or define areas within a room (Figs. 6.4, 11.2; Plate 43). A factor to be considered in selecting plants is the availability of natural light (Fig. 6.2) or the necessity for supplementary light (Figs. 3.7, 3.10, 11.3). Dark interiors need special lighting for plants (Figs. 7.24, 11.3), and blossoming plants require even more light than foliage plants do.

The size of the plant when fully grown must be considered (Figs. 3.15, 3.44, 7.19), for plants can take over an interior space (Fig. 3.30, 7.24). The amount of care the plant requires is also important (Fig. 6.14). This in-

Figure 11.1b
*Inside the greenhouse shown in Fig. 11.1a one sees a
sculpture by George Frederick Holschuh amid the
profusion of plants.*

Figure 11.1a
*The attached lathe house
has a sink and counter space
for potting plants. The
32-foot diameter greenhouse,
with its open center, is
used for entertaining.*

Figure 11.2
*Palms tolerate low light
conditions, grow slowly, and
need repotting about every
two to three years. (Courtesy
of Kroehler Co.)*

cludes the amout of pruning or pinching
needed to develop an attractive plant, the watering and fertilizing necessary, and the fragil-
ity of the plant (Fig. 6.5). Cold drafts can
injure plants, and most require a moist

atmosphere to achieve a lush growth (Figs.
6.29, 6.43, 7.1). As a general rule, blossoming
plants require more care than foliage plants
do. The color of the plant's leaves and flowers
is another characteristic to be considered

(Plate 41). Plants with beautifully colored leaves can add much to a room if they do not conflict with the interior colors; however, too many plants with unusual foliage may become overpowering.

Containers should be carefully selected. Size, portability, and material are all factors in the decision (Plate 44). Unglazed clay pots allow a plant to breathe, but if unglazed pots are used on the floor or on a carpet, they must be placed on a glazed or metal surface to prevent mildew.

Scale

Houseplants come in all sizes and shapes: large (Fig. 7.24), medium, and small; tall and thin; bushy and trailing (Fig. 7.25). Some grow rapidly; others, slowly. Plant size should be appropriate to the scale of the interior and to its furnishings: small plants, unless grouped together (Fig. 11.4), add nothing to large open areas, while fully grown trees will dwarf small rooms.

Figure 11.3
Supplementary lighting is provided by grow lights. (Courtesy of Westinghouse)

Figure 11.4
Small plants, such as African violets, can be grouped on a windowsill or plant stand. Interior designer: Frederick Twist. (Courtesy of Window Shade Manufacturers' Association)

Figure 11.5
Open shelves with plants
divide a living area. The
Ficus benjamina (at the
right) must be pruned to keep
it under control. The shelves
are Sherwood free-standing
units.

Figure 11.6
The Dracaena marginata at
the left rear, combined with
the fern, emphasize the
Egyptian feeling. (Courtesy of
Simmons Co. and Perceptive
Concepts, Inc.)

Figure 11.7
Ferns and hanging plants form a foil for the rectangular shapes in a kitchen. (Courtesy of Evans)

Use of Existing Features

Plants can define spaces and be used to delineate living and dining areas or entry and living areas without detracting from the spaciousness of the interior (Fig. 11.5). Plants used in this fashion are usually tall and slender or trained on a divider. Areas of a room can be enlivened and transformed when plants are backlighted or spotlighted. Plants can become a focal point in the interior and highlight or conceal a room's architectural features (Figs. 11.2 and 11.3).

Relationship to Backgrounds

Plants should blend with an interior and its furnishings (Fig. 11.6). Contemporary interiors provide an ideal background for dramatic plants with large leaves, while traditional interiors blend better with plants with smaller leaves. Delicate foliage shows up to advantage against bold backgrounds, but dramatic foliage, for example, a Rex begonia, may be a better choice against a small patterned background.

Plants can be used in any area of the home. Ferns and graceful plants provide an ideal foil for the functional shapes of bathroom and kitchen equipment and fixtures (Fig. 11.7). Plants add interest to stairwells and niches, and some type of plant can be found to fit into any space (Fig. 11.8). Often an indoor garden can become the focal point for the whole house. But caution is necessary for people with allergy problems. Even if one is not specifically allergic to mold, which is ubiquitous

Figure 11.8
The space under a stairwell is ideal for a plant collection. The white woodwork provides a background for the effective shadow patterns. (Courtesy of Westinghouse)

wherever plants exist, the mold will typically aggravate existing allergy problems. The mold spores are airborne so that isolating plants in one area of the house will not solve the problem.

Variety

With so many varieties of plants available today, it is relatively simple to combine different leaf shapes, colors, and sizes. Too many contrasts may seem overpowering, however.

Figure 11.9
Plants on the terrace blend with those in the interior, merging the two areas. (Courtesy of PPG Industries)

Figure 11.10
The staghorn fern (Platycerium) at the right is a medium-size plant, but a large schefflera (Schefflera actinophylla) is at the right in front of the window. The Ficus benjamina at the left, being open and lacy, does not appear large. (Courtesy of Ficks Reed)

Window sills are an ideal place for small plants that require lots of light (Fig. 11.4). Climbing and trailing foliage plants can be attractive in almost any room while requiring little space (Figs. 11.5 and 11.7). There is, however, a problem with watering, but this can be solved by taking the plant down, dipping it into a container of water, and then allowing it to drain in the sink. A few flowering plants add

beauty and interest to the interior and, if their bloom is seasonal, they may be rotated to private areas of the house when not in bloom.

Link with the Outdoors

Plants offer a link with the outdoors even for apartment dwellers. If a window opens onto an outdoor green area, plants can be selected to blend with the plants outside (Plate 45). Similar containers or floor materials can also be used to tie together the garden and the house, and the interior will appear larger for there will be no sharp dividing line between interior and exterior (Fig. 11.9).

Types of Plants

Plants selected for the interior should be able to tolerate low light, low moisture, and high heat. If possible, it is best to buy plants that are acclimatized to conditions in the home or office rather than to those in the greenhouse. These plants are usually found in a heavily shaded section of the greenhouse and are watered less frequently than usual, so that they experience less shock when placed in the interior.

Plant size and silhouette are two important considerations when selecting plants. Small plants are those under twelve inches in height, medium plants are those between one and three feet, and large plants are those over three feet. Small plants are suitable for hanging bas-

Figure 11.11
The Ficus benjamina at the left rear serves as green furniture. (Courtesy of PPG Industries)

kets, terrariums, table tops, and groupings, and may be used in combination with medium-size plants. Medium-size plants, which may be grouped with either small or large plants, are suitable for table tops and as accents. Large plants are usually specimen plants and function as accents, room dividers, and space definers (Figs. 3.30, 7.24).

Plants may also be selected on the basis of their silhouette. Some are bushy and may be either dense (the rex begonias) or lacy (the Whitmannii fern—Nephrolepsis exaltata [nē-frol'-e-pis eks-â-tā'-ta] "Whitmannii"). Others have an open silhouette (the false aralia—Dizygotheca elegantissima). Still others have a bold silhouette (the Dracaenas) and when spotlit, cast dramatic shadows on the wall (Fig. 11.10). Some plants give an Oriental effect (Fig. 7.28); others, a springlike one (Fig. 7.28). Lines may be curved (Fig. 7.39), angular (Fig. 7.53), cascading (Fig. 10.4), radiating (Fig. 7.48), or rectangular (Fig. 7.49). This discussion will deal with free-standing plants, trailers and climbers, and plant groupings.

Free-standing

Free-standing plants include indoor trees, large shrub-like plants, and plants with large leaves. These plants are usually grown for their foliage and require room light or a spotlight. They assume the role of green furniture and are seldom moved from their initial placement (Figs. 6.53, 6.54). They must frequently be shaped and pruned. These plants are often spectacular specimen plants, expensive when purchased fully grown (Fig. 11.11). Included in this group are palms (Figs. 3.15, 3.44), dracaenas (Fig. 3.4), ficus (Fig. 3.30), Norfolk Island pine, Araucaria—ar-â-kā'-ri-à (Fig. 7.49) and schefflera (Fig. 3.10, and 11.10).

Trailers and Climbers

Cascading trailers and climbers are used in hanging baskets and as room dividers. Flowering plants, however, will seldom flower under usual indoor light conditions; supplementary fluorescent light six to twelve inches away from the plant must be provided. Climbers and trailers (Figs. 6.29, 6.42, 6.50) fall within the medium- to small-size category and include such plants as ivys (hedera), wax plant (hoya) creeping fig (ficus pumila) rosary vine (ceropegia), philodendron (which also climbs), and wandering jew (tradescantia trad-es-kan'-shí-a). Some climbers include the kangeroo vine (cissus antarctica), grape ivy (Rhoicissus rhomboidea), and the true ivys (hedera). These plants must be pinched back regularly. The plants listed do not bloom but they are tough and easy to maintain.

Groupings

Grouping is healthy for plants, making them grow more rapidly. Small plants, rather insignificant alone, look better in groupings (Figs. 7.56, 11.12). Plants can be grouped according

Figure 11.12
*Simple pots, and an old iron kettle, were used for
these plants. (Courtesy of Westinghouse)*

to size, form, growth habits, texture, and perhaps even color. Similar plants of varying sizes can also be attractively grouped. Space for growth should be allowed between plants, which may make them look rather thin at first. Individual plants may be potted in groups, or several pots may be placed in a moist gravel-filled tray, which protects table surfaces and increases humidity. Plants may be placed in a large pot, a hanging basket, or a deep planter; with room for growth, they will not need frequent pruning or repotting.

Terrariums

In the latter part of the 1820s, Dr. Nathaniel Ward, a London physician, discovered that plants could be grown in closed containers. He also found that tropical plants, otherwise difficult to grow, flourished in these containers. He published his findings in the *Gardener's Magazine* in 1834, and as a result, decorative plant cases, known as Wardian cases, became an important feature of Victorian drawing rooms. These cases, actually miniature green houses, were self-supporting: the moisture taken up by the plants from the soil was released as water vapor; the plants absorbed oxygen during the night and expelled carbon dioxide during the day. These cases, ideal in chilly English Victorian homes, did not flourish in centrally heated American homes with large picture windows, for the combination of sunlight and heat turned them into death traps for plants.

The modern terrarium is a modification of the Wardian case. Terrariums can range from a four-inch cube to as large a unit as a four-foot coffee table. Terrariums may be used in any area of the house, although fluorescent lighting may be required in dark areas (incandescent lights are too hot). Terrariums are natural furniture and, protected from drafts and pollution, need relatively little attention.

There are many books written specifically about terrariums, and instructions for making them are beyond the scope of this discussion. Plants selected for terrariums should be relatively compatible and enjoy the same growing conditions. They should not require frequent pruning and/or replanting. Miniature African violets (*saintpaulia*—sánt-pâ′-liā) and *Sinningias,* small ferns and orchids, and begonias are appropriate. Pebbles, small pieces of bark, wood mosses, and wild plants such as partridge berry can add much to a terrarium. Terrariums can be used in almost any place in the interior, depending upon their size, and because they require little attention, they are an asset to the interior designer.

Display

Plants are always a focal point in the interior, so they must be used with restraint to prevent the room from being obscured by a mass of greenery. They must blend with the mood and effect created in the room, harmonize with the scale of the interior architecture and furnishings, and blend or contrast with the colors. Free-standing plants, such as floor plants or indoor trees, will be closely tied with the floor and carpet and the furniture surrounding them. Smaller plants, such as cacti and succulents, will be linked with the surface upon which they stand.

The container for a plant should not detract from the plant. Containers with strong colorful patterns should be used only for plants with dramatic foliage. Containers should also blend with the style of the interior, though some—clay, china, and earthenware pots, or baskets, metal containers, and Victorian wicker fern stands—can blend with almost any interior. Glass and chrome pedestals, simple fiberglass, chrome and stainless steel containers, and various wooden containers blend well with contemporary interiors. There are many containers for traditional interiors, such as dry sinks, whatnots, wooden stands, fire buckets, and soup tureens (Fig. 11.12). Plants grow best in clay pots with drainage holes;

these can be placed in more decorative containers with damp sphagnum moss between the pot and the sides of the container.

Many plants can be grown in water to which plant food has been added. Clear or colored bottles of almost any shape provide excellent containers. When clear containers are used the visible root system also provides interest. *Dieffenbachia, coleus,* English ivy (*hedera*) *spathiphyllum* and wandering jew (*tradescantia*) are easily grown by this method.

Some plants need special supports if they are to bloom, such as the wax plant (*hoya*). Trellises or wire, which will soon be hidden by the plant, work well, and some plants can be trained to cover chicken wire or sphagnum moss filled frames in interesting shapes. Still other plants need only to be anchored to a wooden support or tree fern post.

Selection of Compatible Plants

Light Requirements

One of the more crucial requirements for plants is light. Plants cannot grow in darkness. Light can be measured with the light meter on a camera or with a special footcandle meter. Low plant light is about 20–70 footcandles, equal to the light cast by reading lamps. Medium light is 70–200 footcandles, usually the amount of light some distance away from a window.

Over 200 footcandles is considered to be a high light requirement and plants requiring this amount must be placed near a window or lit by fluorescent tubes. Areas near windows receive 200–900 footcandles and two fluorescent tubes emit 600 footcandles when plants are placed about four or five inches away. Incandescent bulbs get very hot and may burn plant leaves, but cool bulbs such as theater marquee bulbs may be substituted.

Temperature and Humidity Requirements

Most indoor plants came originally from warm, steamy jungles (many at high altitudes), which had cool night temperatures. Daytime temperatures of about 85°F. (29.4C.) and night temperatures of no more than 60°F. (15.5C.) work best for most plants, with almost all plants needing a difference of at least 10°F. Plants require high humidity, and controlling humidity is one of the most difficult problems in the interior.

Humidity may be increased by misting the plants during the day. Morning and early afternoon are best, for misting in the late afternoon and evening encourages fungus diseases. Misters should deposit a fine film of water on the leaves but should not allow it to run down into the soil. A second method of increasing humidity is to place plants in pebble-filled trays the bottoms of which are kept filled with water that does not reach the bottom of the pots. Grouping plants will also increase humidity.

Soil and Water

Plants do better when they are planted in a sterile potting mix, such as a mixture of Canadian sphagnum peat moss, vermiculite, and perlite. A tablespoon of lime should be added to each quart of the mixture for all except acid-loving plants. Varying the amount of sphagnum peat will allow the mixture to fit the needs of various kinds of plants, including cactus. Books listing the various kinds of mixtures are listed in the bibliography.

Indoor plants are usually watered too frequently. They must be allowed to dry out so that the roots will be able to take in oxygen. If a plant ceases to grow, it is all too frequently because too much water has prevented the roots from obtaining oxygen. Plants grown in higher temperatures and actively growing plants must be watered more frequently, and all plants should be heavily watered periodically to leach out fertilizer salts.

Selection of the Right Plant

Indoor Trees

Tall plants, such as indoor trees, are generally used as green furniture or living architecture (Fig. 11.13). They are generally specimum plants and are often spotlighted. Examples are palms, *ficus, dracaenas, schefflera,* and Norfolk Island pine (*araucaria*). These plants can be used to relieve the starkness of contemporary interiors and as dividers.

Foliage Plants

Shrubs Shrubs or bushy foliage plants are excellent for filling an empty area in the interior. Most of them are easy to grow, tough, and (with some pruning) shapely. They also

Figure 11.13
The Dracaena fragrans carries the eye to the mural. Photograph by Yuichi Idaka. (Courtesy of Jack Denst Designs, Inc.)

yellow, and cream. With proper pinching, the *coleus* becomes a dense, compact plant suitable for a pot or hanging basket. The Ti plant (*Cordylined*-kôr-di-lī'-nē) is also easy to grow and is available in a variety of colors. The croton is a tough, beautiful plant with yellow, red, and green leaves on the same plant. It sometimes grows six or seven feet tall, making a dramatic statement in the interior.

Small-Leaf Plants Small-leaf plants, ideally suited for window sills or groupings, include the *peperomia,* which has thick leaves and should be allowed to dry out completely between waterings; the spider plant (*chlorophytum*) which has grassy green or white striped leaves; and the umbrella plant, (*cyperus alternifolius*), a relative of the papyrus of ancient Egypt, which can be obtained in varying sizes and can be grown in water as well as potting mixtures.

Flowering Plants

Many flowering plants will bloom indoors, although some require supplemental fluorescent light. These include begonias, African violets (*saintpoulia*), gloxinias, (*sinningia*—si-nin'-ji-a) *amaryllis,* and *bromeliads.* By far the easiest to grow are the bromeliads. Most bromeliads are epiphytes (an air plant, but not a parasite), and have a very shallow root system, depending upon the natural vase formed by their leaves to hold fresh water and nutrients.

A mixture of tree fern fiber and redwood bark is an excellent potting medium for these exotic plants. They will tolerate varying amounts of light and temperature and are seldom bothered by the usual pests. The leaves are beautiful by themselves but many bromeliads have a spectacular inflorescence as well. The plant blooms only once, after which it will send up off-shoots that continue the cycle. Bromeliads may be encouraged to bloom by placing them in a plastic bag for several days with an apple or by putting one-half a birth control pill in its throat. The ethylene gas from the apple of the hormone stimulates blooming in a mature plant in about four to eight weeks.

The *gesneriads* (jes-nē'-ri-à), which include African violets, gloxinias, *achimenes* (à-kim'-e-nēz), and *streptocarpus* (strep-tō-kär'-pus), require warmth, moisture, and filtered sunlight. African violets bloom all year round. Gloxinias will bloom twice a year under the correct

provide a background for groupings of smaller plants. Aralia (*araliaceae*), false aralia (*dizygotheca elegantissima*) *dieffenbachia, spathiphyllum, pittosporum* (*tobira*), *yucca, croton,* and *fatsia* are excellent shrub plants. Some—such as the *aralias, dieffenbachia,* and *yucca*—will even make indoor trees (Plate 45).

Large-Leaf Plants Numerous indoor plants have large leaves; some, such as the *Monstera deliciosa,* measure two feet across. Many of these plants are green, but others (such as the *dieffenbachia*) are varigated, or (like the *caladium*) have interesting leaf colors and patterns. Large-leaf green plants such as the *Monstera deliciosa,* aspidistra (as-pi-dis'-tra, or cast iron plant), and large-leaf philodendron, serve as backgrounds for other plants or as an island of greenery. Some varieties of *dieffenbachia* grow very large. *Caladium* hybrids, available in various colors of green, reds and white, can provide a center of emphasis in any room and are easily grown from tubers.

Colored- and Patterned-Leaf Plants Many plants have colorful leaves. Rex begonias have beautiful colored leaves and are relatively easy to grow if the humidity is kept high and if they are not over-watered. For ease of growing and sheer beauty of foliage, however, the *coleus* is an excellent selection, with leaf colors in shades of blue, green, red, bronze, brown,

Table 11.1 — Selected Plant Profiles for Interior Usage

Column legend:
- **Light requirements**: L–Low room, M–Medium or spot, H–Window or fluorescent
- **Moisture**: M–Constantly moist, D–Allow to dry out between waterings
- **Humidity**: O–No special, H–Extra humidity
- **Soil**: R–Regular mixture, C–Cactus mixture, O–No lime
- **Attention**: S–Slow growing, little care, P–Pruning or regular pinching, R–Repotting or repropagation frequently
- **Silhouette**: A–Bushy, C–Compact, L–Open or lacy, B–Bold
- **Line**: C–Curvilinear, A–Angular, R–Radiating, H–Hanging basket
- **Temperature**: O–No special, W–Warm, C–Cool
- **Effect**: F–Fill space, O–Bring in outdoors, S–Relieve starkness, A–Accent or center of interest, C–Contrast (texture or color), D–Dramatic shadows
- **Style**: M–Modern, T–Traditional, E–Eclectic, F–Formal
- **Usage**: P–Public, Q–Private or quiet areas, S–Service, such as baths and kitchens, D–Dividers and definers
- **Room sizes**: S–Small to medium, L–Large, H–High ceilings

Plant	Light	Moisture	Humidity	Soil	Attention	Silhouette	Line	Temperature	Effect	Style	Usage	Room sizes
Aloe	M	D	O	C	P	B	A	W	F,P,S,D	M,T,E	P,Q,S	S,L
Antherium	M–H	M	O	R	S	B	A	W	F,P,S,D	M,T,E	P,Q	S
Aspidistra	L	M	O	R	S	B	A	C	F,S	M,T,E	P,Q	S,L
Begonia	M	D	H	R	R	A–L	C–R	W	F,O,S,A,C	M,T,E	P,Q	S
Cacti	M	D	O	C	S	C	A	O	A,C,D	M,E	P,Q,S	S
Citrus*	H	D	O	R–O	S	A	A	C	F,O,S,A,C	M,T,E	P,D	L,H
Crassula	M–H	D	O	C	S	B	A	W	F,S,A,C,D	M,T,E	P,D	S,L
Dieffenbachia	M–H	D	O	R	S	L	A	O	F,O,S,A,C,D	M,T,E	P,D	L,H
Dracaena*	L–H	M	O	R	S	B	C	O	F,S,A,C,D	M,T,E,F	P,D	L,H
Fatsia	H	M	O	R	P	A	A	O	F,O,S,D	M,T,E,F	P,D	L,H
Ferns	L–M	M	H	R	S	A	R–H	W	F,S,A,C,D	M,T,E,F	P,Q,D	S,L,H
Ficus	M	D	O	R–C	S	A	A	O	F,O,S	M,T,E,F	P,D	L,H
Gesneriads	M–H	M	H	R	R	C	R	W	A,C	M,T,E,F	Q,S	S
Gynura Family*	H	D	O	R	R	A	H	W	S,A,C	M,T,E	P,Q,S	S,L
Impatiens	M	M	O	R	R	A	R	O	F,O,S,A,C	M,E	P,Q,S	S
Kalanchoe	M–H	D	O	C	P	A	R	O	F,S,A,C,D	M,E	P,Q,S	S
Palm	M	M	H	R	S	L	A	W	F,B,S,A,D	M,T,E,F	P,D	L,H
Peperomia	M	M	O	R	S	A	R	O	S,A,C	M,E	P,Q,S	S
Pilea	M	M	H	R	R	L	H	W	S,A,C	M,E	Q,S	S
Polyscias	M	M	O	R	S	A	R	O	F,O,S	M,E	P	S
Sansevaria	L–M	D	O	C	S	B	A	O	F,S,A,C,D	M,E	P,S,D	S,L
Schefflera	M–H	D	O	R	P	B	R	O	F,O,S,A,D	M,T,E,F	P,D	L,H
Spathyllum	L–M	M	O	R	S	A	A	W	F,S,A,C	M,T,E,F	P,Q	S,L
Tolmiea (Piggyback)	L–M	M	O	R	R	A	R	W	F, S, A	M, T, E	P, Q, S	S
Tradescantia (Wandering Jew)	L–M	M	O	R	R	L	H	O	F,O,S,A,C	M,T,E	P,Q,S	S,L

*Heavy Feeder

conditions. *Achimenes* is an easily grown summer-blooming plant, and its rhizomes reproduce rapidly. *Streptocarpus* is another periodic bloomer.

Begonias are often grown for their colorful leaves, but the tuberous begonias are grown for their brilliant summer blossoms. *Semperflorens* (sem-pēr-flō'-renz) or "wax" begonias are almost everblooming with green to bronze foliage. These plants, which require little care, can be transplanted outdoors in the summer.

Amaryllis bulbs, which yield spectacular blooms, may be obtained to blossom almost any time of the year. They require little except light waterings and they can be saved for bloom the next year.

Palms, Ferns, and Succulents

Palms, a reminder of Victorian times, lend a graceful air of elegance to both modern and traditional interiors. Palms require little attention, although most are slow growers. They tolerate shade and do not require large pots, but their roots should never be allowed to dry out (Plate 43). The *Howeia* (hou'-ē-à), or Kentia palm, the lady palm (*rhapis excelsa* ra'-pis), the parlor or *neanthe bella* palm and the fan palm (*chamaerops humilis*—ka-nē'-rops) are excellent choices for the interior.

Ferns are favorites for the interior and their graceful fronds are a link with the past, particularly the Victorian period, when ferns were a part of every home. They require little sun but they must have humidity to survive. Most like to grow until their roots completely fill the pot. Some of the best ferns to select are the bird's nest (*asplenium nidus*—as-plē'-ni-um), certain tree ferns, the asparagus fern (*asparagus plumosus*, not a true fern), and holly ferns (*crytomium folcatum*). Other ferns, such as the maiden hair (*adiantums*) and the brake of *Pteris* (tē'-ris) ferns, contain so much moisture in their leaves that they are almost impossible to maintain in the interior unless placed in a fern case or a terrarium.

Succulents and cacti tolerate neglect and can endure low light and humidity. Cacti range from the Easter and Christmas cactus to the desert cactus. Many are so small they can be planted in a dish garden while others grow too large for the interior. A number of cacti have beautiful blooms year after year.

Succulents, plants with thick leaves which store water, need watering infrequently. These plants include *sansevieria* (san-se-vre'-ri-à) or mother-in-law's tongue, *Aloe, Kalanchoe* (kal-an-kō'-ē) and *crassula* (jade plants). Most of these plants thrive when planted in shallow bulb pots.

In selecting plants for the interior, the purpose of the plant or plants should be determined first. The floor plan can be used to estimate how much light will be received by different areas of the room, and which plants may therefore be used in various areas.

It is often helpful to cut out circles of green paper to determine the final placement of plants on the floor plan. For those who enjoy a busy environment with many items of various shapes and sizes, plants are ideal.

Glossary

Conservatory. A greenhouse for preserving plants.

Green Furniture. Large green plants used in the interior.

Humus. The organic portion of the soil.

Orangery. Originally a greenhouse in England used to raise oranges, later used as a greenhouse, usually attached to the great house.

Terrarium. A closed container for growing plants.

Wardian Case. A closed case for growing plants, discovered by Dr. Nathaniel Ward, and an important feature of Victorian drawing rooms.

Bibliography

CROCKET, JAMES UNDERWOOD. *Flowering House Plants.* New York: Time-Life Books, A Division of Time, Inc., 1973.

————. *Foliage House Plants.* New York: Time-Life Books, A Division of Time, Inc., 1972.

ELBERT, VIRGINIE F., and GEORGE A. *The Miracle Houseplants.* New York: Crown Publishers, Inc., 1976.

————. *Plants that Really Bloom Indoors.* New York: Simon & Schuster, Inc., 1974.

GAINES, RICHARD L. *Interior Plantscaping.* New York: Architectural Record Books, 1977.

KRAMER, JACK. *Garden Rooms and Greenhouses.* New York: Harper & Row, Publishers, 1972.

WALLACH, CARLA. *Interior Decorating with Plants.* New York: Macmillan Publishing Co., Inc., 1976.

WRIGHT, MICHAEL. *The Complete Indoor Gardener.* New York: Random House, Inc., 1974.

THE HISTORICAL ENVIRONMENT

Cave drawings over twenty thousand years old indicate that humans have always been interested in the decoration of their dwellings. The images of animals and people incised, painted, and sculpted on cave surfaces reveal that early humans were keen observers. It is probable that this early art had symbolic and magical rather than aesthetic functions. Many of the carvings are believed to be part of a magic ritual which, it was believed, would produce a successful hunt. Symbolism remained an important element in design through the Classical and Gothic Periods. Interior design is as ancient as the oldest dwelling units, the caves, but the profession of interior design is relatively new and only recently has environmental space been studied scientifically.

This survey of interior design will begin about five thousand years ago, with the Egyptians. The basic items of furniture used by these ancient people are still in use today. Platforms (beds and tables) continue to be used for sleeping and eating, and boxes (stools and chests) are still used for storage and sitting. A common thread runs through all periods: an ancient Egyptian table looks much like today's Parsons table, and columns from ancient Greece have been used in almost all periods.

Since the beginning of civilization, certain moods have enveloped whole groups of people at a given time, manifested in certain design characteristics that, taken together, produce a style. The development of a particular style is tentative at first, beginning with simple structural forms which are gradually enriched. When people begin to tire of the same forms, however, the style begins to disintegrate into extremes and becomes heavily over-ornamented. For this reason, styles are best at their midpoint and least attractive near their end. Specific beginnings and ends of a style are difficult to establish because styles tend to merge into one another. Often provincial or country styles lag behind the court or city styles. It is frequently more important to develop a time sense for styles rather than rigidly to memorize dates.

Styles are often affected by physical conditions and by climate. Hard materials such as granite and basalt were used by the early Egyptians, resulting in simple, incised designs; later this stylistic tradition was continued when sandstone and limestone were used. The Greeks, on the other hand, used soft limestone and marble, which allowed them to carve realistic sculptures in the round. In dry, hot Egypt, houses were built of mud bricks with small slit windows to keep out the heat. In Italy and Greece, where rain is abundant, porticos evolved. In England long galleries developed so that the members of a household could have a place to walk during the winter months.

Geography and trade can also affect styles. The Egyptians, isolated by water, desert, and mountains, lived in relative security. An art of great splendor developed, which remained relatively unaffected by most outside influences for nearly three thousand years. The Greeks, forced by their barren, rocky land to import most of life's necessities, were subject to many outside influences. Trade brought about an exchange of ideas and goods between Rome and other lands, spreading Roman influence.

Scientific inventions have been significant factors in some style changes. The invention of gunpowder quickly made the castle obsolete and more gracious living became possible when the manor house replaced it. The invention of the printing press and the subsequent printing of design books made possible the diffusion of design ideas.

197

Historic and political events were key factors in the growth of some styles. The French came to the forefront in furniture and interior design when their military expeditions into Italy convinced them that they should have beautiful furnishings like the Italians to make life more pleasant. They stole furniture to take back to France and Louis XIV and his court became patrons of the arts.

Obviously economic and social conditions also contribute to the evolution of a style. Beautiful and elaborate architecture and furniture would not have been possible without the direction of a ruling class and the labor provided by slaves and common workers in the ancient world. The wealthy ruling class of France made possible the creation of beautiful art and furniture through its patronage. It has been suggested that England lost the lead in furniture design in the Victorian Period, when the uneducated middle class increased in numbers, influence, and power.

Religion can also modify styles. In Rome and Greece, before the Christian era, the house served the family as a temple for observance of religious rituals. Because the family wealth was largely represented by the land and the dwelling unit, the home became the center of most family functions. The land took on a sacred quality because the family members were buried there. Even after the birth of Christ, the house was the center of religious activity, with the oldest male in the family conducting religious services.

During the Gothic Period the lack of communication and protection made the Church the center of life. By this time, much of the religious ritual of the family was, for the most part, organized into formal group services. The church, as a patron of the arts, stimulated art, architecture, and interior design until the end of the Renassance. In fact, religious persecution in France resulted in the loss of many fine craftsmen who fled when Louis XV revoked the Edict of Nantes. Through these craftsmen, French design spread to Holland and to England.

A study of the relationships among materials, climate, geography, science, history, commerce, social conditions, and religion will aid us in understanding the development of architecture, of interior design, of furnishings, and of style. This discussion will not be concerned with a cross-section of society, however, but rather the people of influence and affluence —the "style-makers." No sexist reference is intended when a style is referred to as masculine or feminine. The authors are simply reporting how society was and are not evaluating it or justifying it.

The Ancient World

Any study of a past civilization from its artifacts must obviously miss much of the reality of that culture. Yet it is clear that each civilization had a pattern of development not unlike that of others. Each civilization developed an architecture, furniture styles, and accessories based largely on the materials indigenous to its geographic area or provided by trade and commerce, and on the availability of cheap labor. The Egyptians, the Greeks, and the Romans, for example, had a social structure characterized by a ruling class or elite, a plentiful source of forced or cheap labor, a religious tradition that encouraged skilled artistic performance, and a desire to achieve immortality through their buildings and possessions.

Egyptian (3100–311 B.C.)

Historical Background

To understand modern architecture and furniture, it is necessary to go back to the civilization of ancient Egypt. Many art traditions began with the Egyptians. The ancient Egyptian was in tune with his environment, using mud bricks and stone, the materials at hand. He ate off tables and slept in beds, as we do today. Perhaps the most characteristic feature of Egyptian furniture was the animal-shaped leg (Fig. 12.1a). This leg form was later modified by the Greeks, the English, the French and the Americans.

The Egyptian was a fine craftsman who accomplished much with his limited tools. The art of inlay, which appears later in many periods, was one of his greatest achievements. He was an outstanding weaver, making fabrics as fine as mosquito netting. He excelled at furniture-making, using the same joinery in use today: the dovetail, the mortise and tenon, and the tongue and groove. Vegetation supplied the motifs for his designs, which were rigidly systematic arrangements of plants native to his country, such as papyrus, lotus, lily, date palm, reeds, and a kind of leaf-like maize—some of which continue to influence modern design (Figs. 3.5, 3.51, 7.11).

The Egyptians were romantic, and artistic. Many tombs are filled with light-hearted figures or painted scenes and jokes or remarks. This magnificent civilization, which developed from a farming community beside the Nile, was protected by the sea and desert. Adapting to their environment, the Egyptians cooperated in controlling the annual flood of the Nile so that everyone might reap the benefits. The flood controls allowed for the tilling of crops and the domestication of animals. The nomadic life of previous generations became unnecessary. Families laid claim to the land and produced sufficient qualities of crops and animals for their own consumption and trade. Home, furniture, and interior design became an integral part of life.

Architecture

Pyramids

The pyramids, the most lasting architectural achievement of the Egyptians, contain the smallest amount of useful space in proportion to their size of any buildings known. Imhotep was the architect of the first pyramid at Sakkara, in which stone blocks (some of which weighed fifteen tons) were fitted together with extreme precision. Although his stepped pyramidal-shaped structure was soon dwarfed by the three pyramids at Gizeh, Imhotep was worshiped as a god centuries after his death. The great pyramid of Cheops at Gizeh, the largest man-made structure ever raised from a level footing, has about three million limestone blocks. Free citizens (who were idle due to the flooding of the Nile) were drafted to build the pyramids. Working in gangs of about twenty, it is believed by some authorities that they hauled the blocks up ramps of sand or earth and set them in place. After the pyramid was complete, it was covered with a casing of fine, dressed limestone to form the sloping sides (this outer casing has almost disappeared).

The interior of the pyramids also illustrates an outstanding engineering achievement. Enormous granite slabs roofed the compartments and stone sealing plugs were placed in the tombs to protect the mummy and the rich treasure from grave robbers.

Temples

The Egyptian temple also provided several innovations. There was a strong directional flow, with the temple becoming smaller towards the inner rooms, and a large, high entrance door and inward sloping pylons. Several explanations have been given for the inward slope of the walls toward the top: perhaps the idea came from the pyramid shape; perhaps it was the most effective way of combating the piles of sand resulting from

Figure 12.1a
Egyptian child's armchair with cove seat, lattice work beneath the seat and lion's-paw front and rear legs. The claws are ivory and the feet are placed on disks.

Figure 12.1b
Low Egyptian chair with animal legs in front and back. Inlaid ivory and ebony ornament the back.

Table 12.1
Relationship of Important Furniture Periods to the Egyptian Period

Greek	Roman
650–30 B.C.	753 B.C.–365 A.D.

the frequent sandstorms; or was due to the structural stability of the canted walls.

Trabeated (or post and lintel) construction with limestone roof slabs was used in the temples. As a result, spans could be only about eight to nine feet. Narrow chambers were avoided by using free-standing supports at regular intervals. The *hypostyle hall,* a covered hall, was built so that the roof rested on columns; frequently the two central rows were higher than the sides to allow more light into the interior. Because early supports were probably bundles of reeds, these were imitated in stone. Often leaves enfolded the bottom of the column shaft, just as they might in nature. The capitals of the columns imitated the closed buds of the lotus, the open lotus, or the bell-shaped flower of the papyrus, and the surfaces were carved or incised. Clerestory windows let the only light into the dark interiors.

Obelisks (äb'-e-lisk) were an important adjunct to temple design. Many were cut from red granite, with smoothly tapering planes and hieroglyphic inscriptions, they were sometimes over a hundred feet tall. They were floated down the Nile to their destination, just as the blocks for the pyramids were. A double row of sphinxes, sometimes over three miles long, lined the approach to the temple. The sphinx also appeared on Egyptian furniture, copied later by the Greeks and the Romans, and still later by the French in the Empire Period. The huge statues of the seated pharoah erected in front of the temple pylons were also typical. Ramses II had his architect carve sixty-foot statues out of the sandstone at Abu Simbel.

Interiors

Palaces served as self-contained cities where the pharoah lived. Large and imposing, with space for courtiers, servants, and animals, they were complicated, enclosed buildings composed of many small rooms around a large open court and were designed to keep the ruler from close contact with the people.

Because of his preoccupation with life after death, the Egyptian concentrated his efforts on building tombs and temples and gave little attention to other architectural forms. Houses and shops were made of sun-dried bricks, with flat roofs and small slit windows to keep the sun out—the same type of construction used in that area today. Everything was whitewashed. The interior of a typical dwelling consisted of a small court, a large central living room, and two or three small rooms, such as a kitchen and a workshop. Stairs led to the roof. Larger homes has *clerestory* (kli(é)r-stōr-ē) windows under a roof raised above the house. The main entry was capped by a *cavetto* (ke-vet'-ō) cornice (a quarter-round, concave molding decorated with vertical leaves) with a *torus* (tōr'-es) molding (a convex, semicircular molding). This detail was later repeated in furniture. Great importance was given to gardens, probably owing to the shortage of water, and there were elaborate systems of pools and irrigation ditches. Running water and inside sanitary facilities were common, even in humble homes. Floors were of a special hard plaster gaily painted with flowers, plants, birds, and fishes. Ceilings were blue, and brightly painted columns supported the roof.

Accessories

The making of *faience* (fā-än(t)ś) earthenware was an art in which the Egyptian excelled. Made of powdered quartz and coated with a vitreous paste, faience ware was fired to a glass-like shine in almost all colors. Accessories were important in the home, and elegant vases were produced for home use and for export—glass making was brought into Egypt about 1480 B.C. Egyptian painters were remarkably skilled with a paint similar to tempera, a mixture of mineral pigments and water with wax or glue as a binder. Carbon was used for black; ochres for brown, red, and yellow; powdered malachite for green; and chalk or gypsum for white. On stone surfaces, decorations were incised and painted with brilliant symbolic colors added in flat tones.

Art

Egyptian paintings and carved reliefs made use of the *convention of the broadest aspect,* or the law of frontality. This emphasized the significant and disregarded the nonessential. The head, arms, and legs of the subject were

Table 12.2
Characteristics of Egyptian Furniture

1. It was rectilinear, with straight lines predominating.
2. Animal legs, in a natural position with the feet resting on a cylinder or drum, were used as supports.
3. Chairs and beds (elongated chairs) had low square or rectangular backs, and wide, low seats which later were coved or curved.
4. Ornamentation was geometric or plant-inspired with rich overlay and inlay in various materials.
5. Colors were bold and symbolic.
6. The stool was the common seating piece, with chairs being the most important pieces of furniture and rare even in wealthy homes.
7. Chests were numerous, and used for storage of clothing and linens.

Figure 12.1c
Egyptian folding stool of ebony inlaid with ivory, with legs terminating in duck's heads. The seat is wood painted to resemble leather.

shown in profile, the eyes and torso in full-face view—without any indication of the muscular contortion that would have resulted if the pose had been assumed by a living model. These conventions were meant to convey a symbolic message.

Available materials, such as granite, basalt, and dolomite were very hard, and so much sculpture was simply carved and figures were shown in rigid poses, devoid of expression. Hair was carved in a long bob, not to follow fashion, but to keep the head from being broken off.

Furniture

The first records of constructed furniture are Egyptian. The Egyptians had to import timber from Lebanon and Syria or use small irregular pieces of wood joined in a patchwork pattern, for their small trees did not provide large planks. Furniture parts were joined with flat dowels, clamps, pegs, lacing, dovetailing, mortise and tenon, tongue and groove, and mitering. Early coffins, although hardly furniture, illustrate that craftsmen nearly five thousand years ago could cut a groove and fit panels. The Egyptians perfected the mortise and tenon.

The amount of furniture in Egypt was more than sufficient for comfort, although it was limited in terms of today's needs. Even the common people had some crude furniture. Important as a status symbol, ornamental de-

tail was lavishly applied to the pharoah's furniture, and much of it was covered with gold foil, becoming an instant source of wealth to thieves in later centuries.

The bull's leg and lion's leg were the most popular supports, with forelegs used in the front and rear legs in the back (Fig. 12.1a). Legs were probably lashed to a frame by wet leather thongs which would shrink and tighten when they were dry. Struts were often used to support chair backs (Fig. 12.1a). Upholstery was unknown in Egypt, but pillows and covers were placed on chairs for comfort. Egyptian seats were low for two reasons—the people themselves were only about five feet tall and they were used to squatting (Fig. 12.1b). The Egyptians also had folding stools (Fig. 12.1c). Gesso, or a chalk base, was used as a ground for painted scenes on chests (Figure 12.1d). Later we will see that Egyptian influences are particularly pronounced in the Regency and Victorian Periods in England and the Empire Period in France.

Greek (650–30 B.C.)

Historical Background

Greek art and architecture originated in a land vastly different from Egypt. Greece was a land of hard limestone mountains and deep valleys with fertile pockets of land where olives and grapes grew. It was impossible for a single ruler to govern this country, as the pharoah had Egypt, so city-states developed. The sea, with its winding coastline, connected the scattered cities. Because the Greeks could not produce enough food for themselves on the

Figure 12.1d
This Egyptian chest has hieroglyphs inlaid around the borders, openwork hieroglyphs of ebony and gilded wood, and bronze hinges.

Table 12.3
Relationship of Important Furniture Periods to the Greek Period

Egyptian	Roman
3100–311 B.C.	753 B.C.–65 A.D.

rocky soil, they traded wine and olive oil for what they needed. This trade and their colonization of distant lands spread their civilization.

Many people believe that the Greeks had an instinct for making beautiful objects, but this was not the case. They were logical, observing, imaginative people who sought perfection. Self-control, moderation, and individual freedom were important concepts.

Most Greeks were simple agrarian people and, except for the wealthy few, they lived simply and modestly. Household necessities, such as bread, cloth, and clothing, were made at home. Few people lived in sophisticated centers like Athens. Businesses were small; in fact, there was only one establishment employing more than a hundred workmen in Athens. There were individual perfumers, potters, tanners, and shoemakers who worked in tiny, suffocatingly hot workshops. The potters and blacksmiths depicted on Greek vases worked naked in order to keep cool. Houses, crowded together on small streets, had few sanitary arrangements, but outdoor living most of the year compensated for the absence of elaborate clothing and household furnishings.

Greek arts were designed to appeal to the intellect. Art was seen as real and a part of the spirit. Beauty was defined by exquisite proportions and graceful lines. The national character of Greek art differed from that of Egyptian art. Greek architecture and sculpture was reserved almost exclusively for temples and public buildings. Almost every Greek activity —art, architecture, and literature—had religious significance, and such now secular institutions as the theater and the Olympic Games developed from sacred ceremonies. The Greeks felt the presence of their gods everywhere and often religious feeling was indistinguishable from civic feeling. The Acropolis was both a sacred place where gods resided in the temples and a kind of municipal museum where the laws passed by the assembly were engraved on stones amid the temples.

The Greek drama began as a religious rite.

Theaters were outdoor auditoriums where large audiences sat upon stone benches.

Greek sculpture was highly developed and marble was abundant. Because the Greeks admired the human body, their sculpture delineates physical perfection, incorporating freedom of motion and accuracy of detail (Fig. 12.2). Statues were usually painted—red lips, glowing eyes of precious stones, and artificial eyelashes. Over the years these colors have faded in the damp climate to a chaste white but eyelashes and stone eyes may still be seen on a few examples. Sculpture of marble or limestone carved in relief had many small *moldings* (Fig. 12.3). Relief means that the pattern projected from the face of the stone, and the highlights, shades, and shadows produced by these projections were more important than the addition of color. *Moldings* are decorative treatments on edges and surfaces.

Pottery was probably the most important minor art. Functionalism was an important criterion. Once a form proved suitable, it was seldom varied. Proportion and unity were important in Greek design. Pictorial motifs— scenes of the Olympic Games and from everyday life—adorned many vases. This art has provided future generations with information about Greek clothing, furniture, and artifacts, for fabrics and wood deteriorated in the wet climate and most bronze articles were melted down.

Architecture

Early Greek designs were dependent upon Egyptian influences for form and ornament, but the Greeks quickly perfected what they borrowed and discarded the Egyptian stiffness to evolve original forms and designs of their own. The influence of the Greeks has probably been more widespread than that of any other civilization, and Greek architecture, motifs, and sculpture have served as models to other cultures for centuries.

The Greeks originated the orders for the column: the Doric, Ionic and Corinthian (Fig. 12.3). The capital at the top is the most characteristic feature of the column and gives it its name. Columns have been used in many periods, as have *pilasters* (pi-lăs′-tar) which are, decorative projections from the wall having the proportions, details, capital, and base of the column. The Greeks frequently placed their columns on a high block, called a *stylobate,* which the Romans enlarged into the

Plate 8
The conversation, sleeping, and dining areas of this room are all on different levels grouped around the fireplace. The smoke outlet is a pyramid covered with mirror foil. Lighting accentuates the different levels and defines the contours of the wall dining table. Interior designers: Elisabeth de Lestrieux and Jan des Bouvrie, Netherlands. (Courtesy of Bayer AG)

Plate 9
The warm reds in this interior by Charlotte Finn balance the large areas of blue. Photograph by Tom Yee. (Courtesy of Charlotte Finn Interiors, Inc.)

Plate 10
Blue is used in this high-key cool monochromatic color plan. Soft shapes and mirrors increase the size of the space. Interior designer: Antonello Mosca, Italy. (Courtesy of Bayer AG)

Plate 11
The warm middle-key reds in this monochromatic kitchen-living room create a cozy atmosphere where family life centers. Interior designer: Ritva Lehmusvuo, Finland. (Courtesy of Bayer AG)

Plate 12
Unequal areas of color in the light high-key monochromatic Japanese bathroom create more interest. Burnt orange predominates. The light orange of the wood, the next largest area of color, is picked up by the pattern of the fabric and the screens. The third area of color, the deeper orange of the fixtures, is the smallest. (Courtesy of Kohler Co.)

Plate 13
Blue and yellow-orange create a complementary color plan in this Swedish bedroom. Blue predominates in this interior (on the floor, ceiling, bedspread and upholstery) but the yellow-orange also flows throughout the room. Interior designer: Ingald Andersson, Sweden. (Courtesy of Bayer AG)

Plate 14
The red of the wall and the orange of the wood combined with blue create a split complementary color plan. (Courtesy of Kirsch Co.)

Plate 15
Blue and orange combined with red and the greenery create a double complementary color plan in the elegant conversation area. The blue of the walls predominates; the red used on the throw and pillows is next in importance, followed by the orange of the wood and the Hindu figure and the green of the plants. Interior Designer: Carlos Ojinaga, Spain. (Courtesy of Bayer AG)

Plate 16 (Opposite, top)
Interior designer Charlotte Finn has created a bedroom using the analagous color plan of yellow-green, blue-green and yellow in the flowers. Photograph by Tom Yee. (Courtesy of Charlotte Finn Interiors)

Plate 17 (Opposite, bottom)
This triadic color scheme could have been worked out by using the method illustrated in Fig. 5.9. Interior designer: Charlotte Finn. Photograph by Tom Yee. (Courtesy of Charlotte Finn Associates)

Plate 18
*Blue-violet, green, yellow-orange, and red create a tedtradic color plan in this
multi-purpose room. Hexagonal forms are combined with a small pool for interest.
Interior designer: Marianne Burton, Belgium. (Courtesy of Bayer AG)*

pedestal. The *pediment* (pĕd'-a-mant) is another Greek feature, which consists of the triangle formed at the front and rear of the building by the cornice and line of the roof. It was also used in later periods over doors and fireplaces.

Many Greek ornamental forms were borrowed from vegetation, such as the *acanthus* (a-kan(t)'-thəs) *leaf* and the *anthemion* (an-thē'-mē-ən) a conventionalized honeysuckle or palm-leaf ornamentation. Ribbons, garlands, the spiral, the *fret,* the *rosette,* and the *guilloche* (gil-ōsh'), were used in later periods: the *fret* is a geometric pattern of interlacing and interlocking lines; the *guilloche* is made of double interlacing circles; the *rosette* is a floral design with petals emanating from a central point. The *arabesque* (ar-ə-besk'), a design which combined plant forms such as vines and acanthus leaves with scrolls and spirals, also developed in Greece. Mythical and fanciful animals were represented: the *griffin,* a monster with a lion's body and the head and wings of an eagle, and the *chimera* (kī'-mir-ə), a dragon-like creature, were first used by the Greeks.

The rainfall made necessary a *portico* and a *colonnade* with roof extensions. The portico was a porch supported by a row of marble columns. Greek architecture was basically functional and the columns were used for support, not just for decoration.

The Greeks developed the wooden *truss,* a triangular support for a wide roof span. This was substituted for the stone lintel, eliminating interior columns and making it possible for walls to be placed further apart.

Greek buildings were built using one of three orders of architecture: Doric, Ionic, or Corinthian. The chief differences among them lie in the capitals of the columns. The *Doric* order, the oldest and simplest, is a baseless fluted column with a large square block, the *abacus,* on top, and a curved molding, the *echinus,* underneath. The *Ionic* capital, lighter in appearance and more elaborate in detail, has two large volutes, or spirals (based on the nautilus shell). The *Corinthian* order, the most slender, graceful and elaborate, has two rows of vertical acanthus leaves below four small volutes applied to a bell-shaped form. The Corinthian column is light, delicate, and rich in appearance. The lower portions of both the Ionic and the Corinthian columns are treated with a series of moldings called *bases.* The *entablature* the horizontal beam that is carried

Figure 12.2
Finely sculptured Greek marble statue.

Figure 12.3
Small relief frieze ornamentation and Ionic capitals.

by the column, is composed of the cornice (a series of moldings) at the top, the *frieze* (frēz), (the central portion, the wide flat surface frequently enriched with some form of carving), and the *architrave* (är'-ka-trāv) (the lower portion or lintel). The column, entablature, pedestal, and pediment have served as a constant

Table 12.4
Charactertistics of Greek Furniture

1. Proportions were beautiful.
2. Ornamentation was simple.
3. Fabrics were rich.
4. The Klismos chair was an original form.
5. Stools were common.
6. Rectangular, three-legged tables were typical.
7. Couches were long, straight, and usually high (requiring footstools).

source of inspiration for architecture, interiors, and furniture.

Temples

Greek houses have not had as great an impact on design as have Greek temples although it is believed that early wooden houses were the models for stone buildings. Greek temples represent a most important architectural legacy: their forms have been copied throughout the world, particularly in the governmental buildings of the United States and Europe. European capitals, such as Vienna, display abundant evidence of Greek design. The American Federal Period was inspired by Greek architecture. It is somewhat unfortunate that Greek classical architecture has been so extensively copied; because the temple was built to house the gods, little concern was given to the interior, making temple architecture.

The *Parthenon* (Pär′-thə-nän) the most celebrated Greek temple, was completed in 430 B.C. Many adjustments were made to correct optical illusions: the vertical features actually lean inward to counteract the appearance of leaning outward; the corner columns are slightly heavier and closer together than the inner ones; horizontal lines (stylobates, cornices and architraves) are convex; and flutings diminish in width as they rise. *Entasis* (éntəsis) the slight convex curving of vertical columns, was used to make columns appear straight. All these adjustments were to achieve optical harmony and to counteract the effects of perspective and foreshortening.

Located near the Parthenon, within the Acropolis (ə-kräp′-ə-lĭs) is the *Erechtheion* a highly complex Ionic temple with caryatid porches. *Caryatids* (kar-ē-at′-ed) are human figures used as supports. Later examples of the caryatid can be seen in furniture, especially in Italy and France during the Renaissance.

Furniture

The Greeks lived plainly and had sparse, simple furnishings. Accurate representations of these exist on vases, reliefs, and carvings of chairs, stools, couches, tables, chests and *stele*. Interiors were enriched with coverlets and cushions of richly embroidered silks, and bril-

liantly colored rugs. Greek furniture itself has seldom been copied, with the exception of the *Klismos* (kliz′-mōs) chair.

Many Greek motifs were revived in the Renaissance, however, and again in the eighteenth century in France, England, and America. Columns, caryatids, pilasters, entablatures, pediments, and other architectural motifs were applied to credenzas, bookcases, and large pieces of furniture. Columns were used for furniture supports. Many classical motifs appear in the furniture of such English designers as Sheraton, Hepplewhite, Adam, and Hope. By the end of the nineteenth century, the Greek Revival was in full swing and many Victorian examples may be seen in both England and America.

Most Greek furniture was made of maple, olive, boxwood, cedar, and oak, and some pieces were inlaid with precious metals and ivory. Ancient Greek books mention the use of a wax finish on the wood. The seasoning of the wood, the joinery, and the finishing were of the same high quality as those of the Egyptians.

Chairs and Seating Pieces

The most famous Greek furniture design is the Klismos chair (Fig. 12.4a). It had no Egyptian antecedent and rose slowly from the ground in a slow, continuous crescent curve. The back is a crest rail supported by two or three uprights at the shoulder. Some backs, set at an extremely oblique angle, were probably used for lounging. The seats were usually of plaited leather thongs with a cushion placed over them for comfort. The legs were steamed and then bent to their bold curving form. *Fielded panels* (panels defined by applied moldings), were often used on the legs, with exposed dowel heads for ornamentation.

The most common type of seating used by rich and poor alike in home, workshop, *palaestra* (pe′-ləstra), and schoolroom, was the stool or *diphros* (Fig. 12.4b). It had a rectangular seat with four legs, turned or straight, sometimes joined by stretchers. Many times the rounded top of the legs merged with the horizontal seat frame in one unbroken surface. Greek examples were much more graceful than Egyptian ones had been. The stool become the prototype of similar European stools for the next two thousand years.

The throne chair, a dignified and stately chair reserved for gods, goddesses, and

Figure 12.4a
Greek Klismos chair with concave back and splayed front and back legs, fielded panels, and plaited leather thongs for the seat.

princes, was synonymous with royal power. It was provided with a footstool, and its legs were often joined with stretchers and terminated with an animal's paw or rectangular or flat circular disk turnings. Seats were of plaited leather with a cushion. Dignitaries at the theater sat in throne chairs of marble which often had lion's-paw feet.

Beds

The bed, or *klini* (klē'-nē) was adapted from the Egyptians although it no longer had the vertical footboard and small separate headrest (Fig. 12.4c). It was used for reclining at mealtimes as well as for sleep at night. It was an important piece of furniture, usually six feet long, and relatively high. Some had low headboards with a Klismos back. For dining and banquets, embroidered mattresses and luxurious cushions were used, and for sleeping perfumed linen or wool bedclothes were added. Legs were rectangular, turned or animalform. Motifs used on the klini were appliqués in silver or bronze of busts or heads of dogs, mules, or horses. Footstools were necessary to mount the high couches as well as the throne chairs.

Tables

Tables, or *trapezai,* were more commonly used by the Greeks than by the Egyptians (Fig. 12.4d). They were placed beside the *klini* to hold food at meals. These individual dining tables were light, plain, and low enough to be pushed under the couch after a meal. Tops were oblong, round, or rectangular. Only three legs were used, often connected by high stretchers, making them ideal for uneven ground. Legs were perpendicular or oblique, tapering or curved, with lion's-paw or deer-hoof feet.

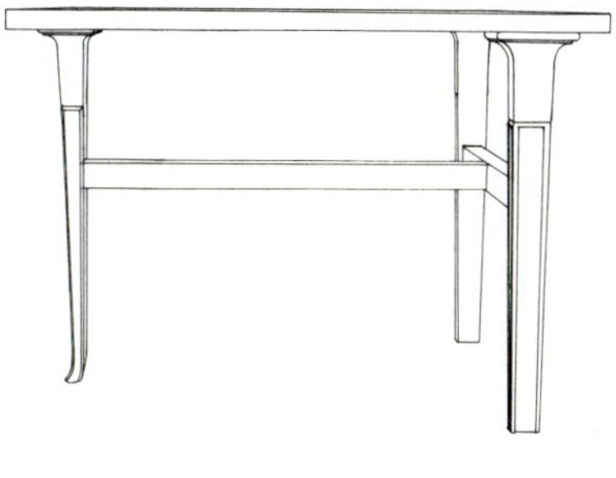

Chests

The general form of the Greek chest, boxlike and rectangular with paneled sides, was developed in Egypt. Chests were used to store clothing and household linens (Fig. 12.4e), and were also used as seats. Some were *polychromed* (painted in several colors), and embellished with metal or terra-cotta bas reliefs of legendary figures and animals. Feet were usually simple prolongations of the corner posts. Sometimes lion's-paw feet were used. Strings were wrapped around knobs on the lid and the box for lifting and carrying it. Com-

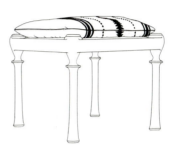

Figure 12.4b
Greek stool with rectangular seat, four turned legs, and seat cushion.

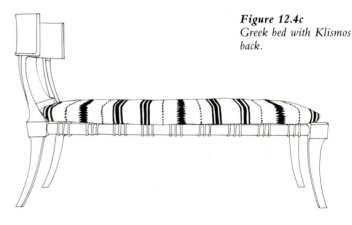

Figure 12.4c
Greek bed with Klismos back.

Figure 12.4d
Three-legged Greek table.

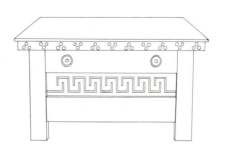

Figure 12.4e
Greek chest for storage and seating with bas-reliefs and fret design.

plex shelving was not used; vase paintings show that the Greeks hung their possessions on the walls, making cupboards and sideboards unnecessary.

The Greeks had a propensity for developing all facets of their lives to the fullest and for displaying that development. The Greeks strove to develop the body as well as the mind. Sculpted figures were handsome and physically well developed. The males showed great strength, particularly in those muscle groups that assist in lifting, throwing, and fighting. The women were strong and full-bodied. Greek design reflected this desire for physical and mental perfection.

Roman (753 B.C.–365 A.D.)

Historical Background

The Romans were very different from the Greeks or Egyptians. The Egyptians and the Greeks were scattered over a somewhat ill-defined area, but united by origin, language, culture, and religion. The roads from Rome led to distant areas outside Italy. Rome granted citizenship to many people scattered from the British Isles to the Sahara and from the Atlantic to the Red Sea. The Romans organized Europe and though modern ideals of law, art, drama, mathematics, and sports come from the Greeks, modern roadways, bridges, postal services, town planning, codifications of law, and engineering come from ancient Rome. The Romans believed that people in many lands should be united under one rule, and the Roman government was a representative system closely resembling that of the United States and other Western democracies today.

Architecture

The Romans adopted Greek architectural forms and developed a complete architectural vocabulary. The city became most important, with its multiplicity of houses, markets, baths, libraries, temples, theaters, triumphal arches, and squares. The Romans used brick, stone, or concrete to enclose large spaces and to make arches. They built roads everywhere to tie the Empire together. These roads, always direct paths, provided the foundation for many of modern Europe's main thoroughfares. Built to allow rapid military movements, these roads quickly became busy arteries of commerce and travel and helped to spread Roman

civilization. The arch was also used for bridges and aquaducts (used to bring water to the cities). The Roman arch is still in use today.

The Romans, an active and aggressive people, loved strength and power, luxury and comfort. If a Roman general won a battle or a new territory, he could request a formal triumph procession in the capital. These took place outside the city limits and large impressive arches were built to commemorate them. Other arches, such as the Arc de Triomphe in Paris and the St. Louis arch which was designed by Eero Saarinen, are examples of modern arches. Similar arches, built by the Romans, still stand in downtown Rome.

Inventiveness and a desire for comfort made the Romans demand sanitary facilities, hot and cold running water, and central heating. After the fall of Rome, these essentials disappeared for over a thousand years. The Romans built many public institutions for recreation, exercise, and amusement. Roman baths sometimes covered an area of more than twenty acres, and were fitted with reading rooms, running tracks, and enclosed swimming pools. Many of today's health spas are fashioned after these baths.

The Greek influence can be seen in Roman architecture. The Colosseum is a Roman adaptation of the Greek amphitheater and today's astrodomes are modern versions. The spreading of Greek architecture throughout the Western world was one of the most important Roman contributions.

The Roman use of Greek architectural orders is most important. The Roman orders were lighter in proportion than the Greeks, and two orders were added, the *Tuscan* and the *Composite*. The Roman Doric order, infrequently used probably because of its plainness, had a slender column, additional moldings, and a base. The Roman Ionic column had smaller volutes than the Greeks (sometimes four were used instead of two), and no ornament on the *necking* below the volutes. The most common Roman order, which had been infrequently used by the Greeks, was the Corinthian. The capital of the Roman column was slightly smaller than that of the Greek, and the character of the acanthus leaves was different. The Tuscan order was very similar to the Doric order, except that it had no fluting. The Romans combined the Ionic and Corinthian orders to make the Composite, with a capital that had volutes and foliation.

The dome, an arch rotated about its center, was one of the most important Roman contributions to architecture. The dome required a thick supporting wall without windows. The Pantheon, built about 120 A.D. is an excellent example of this. Its dome, a semisphere of brick and concrete, is 142 feet in diameter and the thick supporting walls are fifteen feet in depth. A window twenty feet in diameter at the dome's apex lights the interior dramatically, while reducing the weight of the dome. It is not known exactly how the building was erected, but it is believed that hidden within the walls is an elaborate framework of brick arches that support the dome's weight. Ickworth, a late Georgian house in England, and Monticello, designed by Jefferson, make use of the dome *coffers,* which are sunken ornamental panels. These were first used in the interior of the Pantheon dome.

Another Roman influence is the *basilica,* the building that housed the Roman law court. A rectangular building, it was divided into an open central space or nave, with aisles on either side. The central portion was a story higher than the rest, with windows in the upper walls, and on one of the narrow sides was an *apse,* a semicircular or angular extension where the Praetor might administer justice. When the Christians were allowed to worship openly, they wanted a building which could be respected and the basilica was particularly suitable to the processional form of worship. The altar was placed where the judge's seat had been, thus carrying the Roman tradition into the Christian Church.

The Romans developed a durable, lightweight concrete to execute their designs, and protected the concrete with tiles or brick. They strove for grandiose effects, so bulk and lavishness were extremely important to them.

Interiors

Romans made their homes the centers of their lives and homes became more luxurious as fortunes grew. The interior of the Roman house followed a general plan and was divided up into several sections. The *atrium* the central hall of the house, had a large opening in the roof, the *compluvium,* which lighted the house and allowed rainwater to be caught in a great pool below (the *impluvium*). Guests entered the atrium through the vestibule, which often had a mosaic floor. The *tablinum* at the end of

Table 12.5
Relationship of Important Furniture Periods to the Roman Period

Egyptian	*Greek*
3100–311 B.C.	650–30 B.C.

Table 12.6
Characteristics of Roman Furniture

1. Designs were variants of Greek models.
2. Furniture was massive and elaborately decorated.
3. Inlay, veneering, and carving were used.
4. Turned legs, animal feet, sphinxes, and Griffins were popular.
5. Tables used for display and for eating.
6. There was little underbracing of legs.
7. Chair backs were concave.
8. Architectural features were incorporated in furniture.
9. Three-legged tables and pedestals were popular.
10. Rich fabrics and cushions were used.

the atrium was a sanctified area and contained the nuptial bed and the dining table. There were small rooms off the atrium called *cubicula* (cū-bi'-cū-la). Kitchens and wine rooms were also included in the Roman home. The court, the *peristylium,* was lined with columns around a garden featuring statues and pools of water. Interior walls were plastered and frescoed (a technique in which paint is applied to wet plaster). Subjects included landscapes, mythological scenes, and scenes from everyday life. Stuccoed details, bas-reliefs, statues, and friezes were also used. The floors were paved with stone in middle-class homes; poorer homes had only dirt, while wealthy families used marble or mosaics.

Furniture

Our knowledge of Roman furnishings is dependent upon wall paintings and reliefs, occasional references to furniture by Latin writers, and actual pieces of furniture from Roman homes preserved in lava at Pompeii and Herculaneum. In many ways our knowledge of Roman furniture supplements our knowledge of Roman civilization.

Roman values were so similar to those of the Greeks that it was natural that design in the two cultures should be similar too. The importance of the family was paramount in both cultures. Each family member was val-

Figure 12.5a
Roman armchair throne.

Figure 12.5b
Roman throne with fantastic, winged figures placed on a dais.

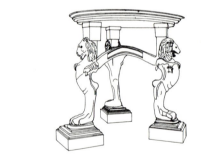

Figure 12.5c
Pompeiian table with monopodia; frequently copied in the Empire and Regency Periods.

Figure 12.5d
Sturdy table from Pompeii with fanciful figures carved on each end support.

were valued as family possessions to be passed onto succeeding generations. The material goods of the family, therefore, had to be worthy possessions that would serve well for the present, favorably represent past generations, and provide a continuum with the future.

Seating Pieces

Greek seats, couches, and tables were popular in Rome and so similar in shape that it is often difficult to distinguish Roman from Greek examples. Roman furniture, however, tends to be heavier in proportion than Greek furniture. Richly cushioned seats with carving, veneering, or inlay reflected the Roman's love of luxury. Upholstery was unknown to the Romans, but loose covers, hangings, and pillows were used. These were of wool, linen, and silk, with designs woven into the cloth in purples, greens, scarlets, and golds. Interesting motifs ornamenting the furniture included the *monopodia* (män-ə, pōd′-ē-a) a lion's head, leg, and paw later seen in Regency furniture), human figures, cupids, swans, rams' heads, and horses.

Two types of thrones used by the Greeks, one with turned legs and one with rectangular legs, were copied by the Romans. Several fine examples of thrones with turned legs (legs shaped on a revolving wheel—a lathe) appear on Roman wall paintings. The Romans' own contribution was an armchair throne (Fig. 12.5a). These thrones with solid sides became popular for official occasions and were heavier and more grandiose than their Greek prototypes. Thrones had a variety of ornamentation, but the basic form remained more or less the same: a round or rectangular back with solid sides often terminating in front in animal or monster forms (Fig. 12.5b).

The stool remained an important piece of furniture. Two popular styles were derived from the Greeks: the *diphros* (dī′-frōs) with four perpendicular turned legs, and the *sella curulis,* which influenced many later periods and had curved, X-crossed legs which were two seimcircles. Benches were regarded as the seats of the poor and were usually simple in design. Stone benches lined walls and were often used by students listening to lectures.

In the atrium a strong box for valuables, made of wood sheathed with iron, was frequently mounted on a heavy block of stone to which it was attached by an iron rod.

The entertainment room opened on the

ued in his own right apart from the economic contribution which he could make. Home design facilitated family interaction. The table became more than a dining convenience: it was a place where family matters were discussed and decided. Items within the home

atrium, but for private entertaining draperies were pulled across the opening. The furniture consisted of couches, tables, and stools. The couch was a versatile piece used for sleeping, dining, and other entertainments. The decorated couch was the most costly item in the house: made of gold, bronze, ivory, and/or silver, it was ornamented with inlay and relief. It might have a curved headboard and/or footboard, and the *fulcra* (ful'-kra). Favorite motifs for the fulcra were animal heads and busts of satyrs. The mattress was supported on interlaced leather thongs or metal cording. The height of the couch varied, depending on its use; some required a footstool.

Tables

With their great love of possessions, the Romans used tables for display as well as for eating. Four types of Roman tables can be distinguished and recognized as derived from Greek examples:

1. A rectangular table with four legs
2. A round-top table with three animal-shaped legs
3. A pedestal table with a round or rectangular top
4. A rectangular-top table resting on two solid transverse supports

The rectangular table, which the Greeks found so functional, continued to be used by the Romans, who ornamented the plain, perpendicular legs. The Greek table with a round top and three animal-shaped legs was used a great deal in Pompeii (Fig. 12.5c). Typical examples are decorated with heads of lions, panthers, or swans. The table resting on a single pedestal, found rarely in Greece, was a Roman development. Some tables had a plain column for a base, and for outdoor use there was a sturdy table with a rectangular top and solid decorated slabs attached to the short ends (Fig. 12.5d). The supports were made of marble and the top was marble or wood. Supports terminated in various figures of animals or monsters such as *satyrs* (sāt'-er) (a figure of a man with the body of a horse) and griffins (grif'-ən).

Miscellaneous

Other furnishings used by the Romans were shelves, cupboards, and sideboards to display the numerous ornaments so highly prized by them. Shelves were attached to the wall and sideboards had a table-like surface below an upper shelf. Cupboards were similar to those in use today, with shelves inside the doors opening from top to bottom. Tripods, which held various items, were also popular.

The Romans made a major contribution with their feats of engineering and their dissemination of Greek influences throughout the world. They were interested in utilitarian designs—large concrete buildings, straight roads, arches, and domes. The interiors of their homes were luxurious and Roman furniture, adapted from Greek models, was heavier and more ornate than the Greek. Roman furniture, however, eventually became too comfortable and too soft, as did the people.

Glossary

Abacus (ăb'-à-kŭs).   The slab that tops a column.

Acanthus Leaf (a-kan'(t)-thəs).   A carved and painted leaf used as a ornamentation.

Anthemion (an-thē'-mē-ən).   A conventionalized honeysuckle motif used in both Greek and Roman ornamentation.

Arabesque (ar-ə-besk').   Intertwining lines based upon plant and animal forms.

Arch.   A curved span supported at the sides.

Architrave (är-kə'-trāv).   The lowest division of the entablature (corresponding to a lintel).

Atrium (ā'-trē-əm).   The central hall of the Roman house.

Basalt.   A hard dark stone, green or brown, used in Egyptian sculpture.

Basilica (bə-sil'-i-kə).   The building that housed the Roman court of law.

Capital.   The top portion of a column.

Caryatid (kar-ē-at'-ed).   A female figure used as a column.

Cavetto (kə-vet'-ō).   A concave molding, usually quarter-round.

Chimera (kī-mir'-a).   A mythical figure.

Clerestory (kli(ə)r'-stōr-ē).   Window placed in a wall above a roof.

Coffer.   An ornamental sunken panel in a (usually domed or vaulted) ceiling.

Colonnade.   A row of columns supporting an entablature.

Composite.   A Roman column that combined the Ionic and Corinthian orders to make a capital with both volutes and folliation.

Corinthian.   A slender, graceful column with two rows of vertical acanthus leaves below four small volutes, applied to a bell-shaped form.

Cornice. The uppermost part of the entablature.

Dome. A convex covering over a building.

Doric. The simplest order, with an abacus and an echinus.

Echinus (i-kī′-nəs). The convex molding supporting the abacus, sometimes ornamented with an egg-and-dart pattern.

Entablature (in-tab′-lə-chủ(ə)r). The architrave, frieze, and cornice supported by a column or used on a wall as ornamentation.

Faience (fã-ä(t)s). Earthenware made of powdered quartz, coated with a vitreous paste, and fired to a glass-like shine.

Fielded Panel. A panel outlined with an applied molding or sunken bevel.

Fret. Geometric pattern of interlacing and interlocking lines.

Frieze (frēz). A decorative band between the architrave and the cornice.

Gesso (jes′-ō). A highly absorbent white ground for painting.

Griffin (grif′-ən). A mythical monster with a lion's body and the head and wings of an eagle.

Guilloche (gil′-ōsh). A pattern of double interlacing circles.

Hieroglyphics (hi-(ə)-rə-glif′-ik). A system of writing used by the Egyptians.

Hypostyle (hī-pə-stīl′). A covered hall, with roof supported by pillars.

Incised. A carved pattern, made by cutting into the ground; the opposite of relief.

Inlay. The technique of inserting materials into a surface into which a design has been cut.

Inercolumniation (int-ər-kə-ləm′-nē-ā′-shun). The space between columns, at the lowest part of the shaft, measured as diameters of the column.

Ionic. An order which has two large volutes and carved borders.

Klismos (kliz′-mōs). A Greek chair, much copied in later periods, with a concave back rail and curved legs that splay out in both front and back.

Lintel. The horizontal support that spans an opening.

Obelisk (äb′-ə-lisk). A tapering shaft with four sides.

Order. A column including base, shaft, capital, and entablature.

Pedestal (ped′-əs-əl). A support for a column, a statue, and so on.

Pediment (ped′-ə-mənt). A triangular gable that finishes the ends of a sloping roof.

Polychrome. Paint in several colors.

Portico (pōrt′-i-kō). A covered colonnade that forms a porch.

Post and Lintel. A construction device that consists of a lintel resting upon two posts.

Relief. Raised ornamental detail which may be carved or applied.

Stele (stē′-lē). A grave marker of carved stone.

Stylobate (stī′-lə-bāt). The continuous base or steps upon which the columns of the Greek temple rested.

Torus Molding. A convex molding used on column bases.

Trabeated. Constructed by the post and lintel method.

Truss. A bracket or console used as a support.

Tuscan. A Roman version of the Doric column, without fluting.

Volutes. A scroll form used on Ionic and Corinthian columns.

Bibliography

Ancient Egypt. Washington, D.C.: National Geographic Society, 1978.

FLETCHER, SIR BANISTER. *A History of Architecture* 17th ed. New York: Charles Scribner's Sons, 1961.

HALE, WILLIAM H. *The Horizon Book of Ancient Greece.* New York: Doubleday & Company, Inc., 1965.

MALLAKH, KAMAL EL, and ARNOLD C. BRACKMAN. *The Gold of Tutankhamen.* Newsweek Books, 1978.

PERSNER, SIR NIKALAUS. *An Outline of European Architecture.* 7th ed. London: Jarrolds & Sons Ltd., 1963.

RICHTER, G. A. *Ancient Furniture.* New York: Oxford University Press, Inc., 1926.

TAYLOR, BOSWELL, ed. *Ancient Romans.* London: Brockhampton Press, 1970.

WHEELER, MORTIMER. *Roman Art and Architecture.* New York: Praeger Publishers, Inc., 1968.

The Middle Ages, Gothic, and Renaissance Periods

As man developed from the first to the eleventh centuries, he was hampered by the overthrow of Rome and its institutions of law and order. The growth of government was retarded and the breakdown of social, political, and educational institutions resulted in widespread poverty and ignorance. The strongest and wealthiest man in an area came to be regarded as its ruler. The church became a unifying force, as Christianity was diffused throughout the civilized world. The bishops were better educated and became rich from the tithes they collected. Ultimately the church became the source of education and the source of decorative arts as the monks in the monasteries had preserved many classical manuscripts. The Crusades, which originated in the desire to free the Holy Land, resulted in increased communication and commerce between countries.

The low worth of the individual was reflected in the lack-luster homes, furniture, and artifacts of the period. The Renaissance lifted people's dignity and self-esteem, causing artistic productivity to rise to new heights of aesthetic beauty and creativity.

The Middle Ages (1–15th Centuries)

Historical Background

Western Europe was in upheaval during the Middle Ages. The Turks had captured Greece and destroyed most of the Greek civilization. In general, most people in Western Europe during the Middle Ages lived in misery, usually in crude cottages on feudal estates. Churches served as centers of education and social life as well as of religion. Buildings were designed by the monks, untrained as designers, using the materials that were available, and the workers, the common people, contributed their labor.

Furniture

The furniture of the ancient world disappeared after the fall of the Roman Empire and did not reappear until the Renaissance, when furniture making was relearned. The wealthy of the Middle Ages lived in castles, which had scanty ornamentation. Murals added light and color, as did tapestries and wall hangings. Furniture was scarce, and few examples of it survived the turbulence of the period.

What few pieces there were often had to be taken apart for travel as the wealthy went from castle to castle to oversee their lands. The most popular item was the chest, which served as a receptacle for storage, a seating piece, and a table (Fig. 13.1a). It was usually ornamented with *chip carving,* which was chiseled or gouged and heightened with color.

Chairs were ceremonial and throne chairs were of stone, bronze, or wood. They were solid and massive, with coarsely rendered plant and animal forms. A few benches and tables, also movable, were used, with table tops supported by trestle supporting frames. Camp or *trussing* beds were transported but elaborate beds remained in castles with the hangings stripped when the owner left. Furniture was architectural in form (furniture had the characteristics of a building), and columns and *arcading,* a form of ornamentation consisting of piers supporting an arch form, were popular.

Byzantine (323–1453)

During the Byzantine Period, an important new architectural system of thrust and counterthrust was developed, producing a method of dome construction called the *pendentive.* The pendentive was an inverted, concave, triangular piece of masonry, which transmitted the weight of a dome to four heavy piers or supports. The bottom points of the triangle form a square; the upper sections, a circle. Hagía Sophia, built in Constantinople between 532 and 537 A.D., was one of the earliest and most famous of the churches built in the Byzantine style. Its dome, pierced by forty windows, is 107 feet in diameter, and the vaulted aisles are fifty feet wide with upper galleries.

The Byzantine builder was concerned mainly with the interior of the churches, which were of polychrome marble and decorated with *mosaics* (small squares of brilliantly colored glass or marble, usually, each less than one-half inch long, pressed onto a surface that had been treated with wet cement).

Homes of the rich opened onto courtyards protected from the street by a stone wall. Inside were pillared halls and elaborate interiors. Furniture pieces were few, although for the wealthy there were some elaborate chairs inlaid with gold and ivory. Influences of the

Table 13.1
Relationship of Important Furniture Periods to the Middle Ages

Roman	Byzantine	Romanesque	Gothic
753 B.C.–365 A.D.	323–1453 A.D.	800–1150 A.D.	1150–1500 A.D.

Table 13.2
Relationship of Important Furniture Periods to Byzantine Period

Roman	Middle Ages	Romanesque	Gothic
753 B.C.–365 A.D.	1–15 Centuries	800–1150	1150–1500

Table 13.3
Relationship of Important Furniture Periods to the Romanesque Period

Byzantine	Middle Ages
323–1453	1–15 Centuries

Table 13.4
Relationship of Important Furniture Periods to the Gothic Period

Byzantine	Renaissance
323–1453	Italy 1400–1650
	Spain 1400–1650
	France 1485–1643

Byzantine Period may be seen in the Gothic art of France and England after the Crusades, in St. Mark's in Venice, and in Ireland and Scotland, where they mingled with the Celtic arts.

Romanesque (800–1150)

The Romanesque Period, a time of experimentation with new modes of expression, was different in every country. There were many styles, distinct yet related. The designs, influenced by Byzantine art, were rough conceptions of Roman architecture adapted to present needs, and are reflected in the hundreds of churches that were constructed during this period.

The architecture, which emphasized structure, was composed of semicircular arches and horizontal lines. Churches, massive stone buildings with barren interiors, also functioned as fortresses. Buildings were solid and heavy, with thick walls, round arches, vaults, and buttresses. Sandstone and limestone sculptures instructed the illiterate masses. Interiors were dark and the development of a flexible, precise, and scientific building method-the Gothic style-increased interior light.

Gothic (1150–1500)

Historical Background

Life in the Gothic Period was rigid. Bishops, kings, queens, and men of noble birth lived in castles supported by the labor of their serfs. These serfs were obliged to render unto their lords the fruits of three days labor out of seven. Serfdom had almost disappeared by 15th century, however, but even after that, the lords continued to exercise control over the common people. The castle was the pivot of life, serving as stronghold and fortress. Castles gradually expanded into palaces and then into towns, which became trading centers. Town life began to flourish politically and economically through fairs and markets. Guilds, organizations similar to today's trade unions, developed. The feudal system died out and the mercantile middle class assumed importance. The business and spiritual affairs of the Church were controlled by bishops who, with their enormous power and wealth, made possible the building of great cathedrals.

The dwellings of the period were relatively unimportant. They had pointed arches over doorways and deeply recessed windows. Ceilings were high and huge fireplaces had funnel-shaped hoods that extended through the ceilings. The walls and paneling of the interiors were usually painted in colors. The most important room in the house was the great hall, where meals and entertainment took place. Floors were generally packed dirt strewn with rushes or straw, or occasionally covered with small Oriental rugs.

Cathedrals

Gothic cathedrals typified man's upward reach to God in the dark years of the time. As agriculture and the domestication of animals flourished, so too did the need to sell, trade, and export the resulting products. Towns and cities were built, and grew. With the growth of towns, people began to demand their own churches, buildings of which to be proud. The stem family supported the church and guaranteed its place. The land was passed on to the eldest son, and the other sons, with nothing to inherit, turned to the priesthood as a secure calling. The dearth of males left many females to serve the church as nuns. As a result, the power of the church was strong.

Architecture was the dominating art of the

period. Notre Dame, one of the first Gothic cathedrals (Durham 1093–1490, Bayeux 1200–1400, and Laon 1160–1225) was built in France between 1163 and 1250 and served as the prototype for many other cathedrals in England, Spain, Germany, and Italy.

The fundamental floor plan of the Gothic cathedral was the *Latin cross,* which has one arm longer than the other three (the length was usually four to six times longer than the width). The basic areas were the *nave,* the side *aisles,* the *ambulatory* and the *apse.* The *nave,* the central part of the church, was usually flanked by aisles and terminated in the *apse,* a semicircular extension at the east end. The *ambulatory* was a walking area, like an aisle, around the *apse.*

The *flying buttress,* necessary to carry down the internal thrust of the vaulting, made possible the soaring height of the Gothic cathedral. It was a half arch running from the building wall to an exterior stone pier. *Rose windows,* sometimes called wheel windows, added to the beauty of the church. The rose window was a circular window with *tracery mullions* radiating from a central point; stained glass, first used in Byzantine churches, filled in the areas between the mullions.

The cathedral at Chartres, built between 1507 and 1513, was a marvel of high Gothic architecture. The exterior was adorned with ten thousand sculpted figures to educate and frighten the masses (few could read). Often these included gargoyles (a grotesquely carved figure) and *mementoes mori.* The earliest carvings on Chartres (shär′-tr) have elongated figures with stylized folds on their robes and accentuation on vertical lines. The interior *quadripartite vaults* (rib vaults in which each bay is divided by two diagonal ribs into four compartments) rest on slim *piers* with four attached *columnettes.* The main ornaments of Chartres are the 176 stained glass windows, which include a rose window 44 feet in diameter. Other stained glass windows were dedicated to crafts, such as the furriers.

Amiens (ăm-ĭ-ĕnz), begun in 1220 and finished in 1228, is the largest Gothic cathedral in France (450 feet long by 150 feet wide) and a classic example of the high Gothic style. The imposing façade of Amiens, inspired by Notre Dame, is dominated by the high placement of the rose window. The massive twin towers, completed in the late fourteenth century, have three richly carved deep portals. The nave is

Table 13.5
Characteristics of the Gothic Cathedral

1. Pointed arch
2. Flying buttress
3. Clerestory windows
4. Rose window
5. Ribbed vaults
6. Stained glass
7. Tracery

140 feet high to draw the eye always upward, and windows occupy almost half the total height. The windows were so high that in the sixteenth century much of the glass fell out from the strain of its own weight.

Other characteristics of Gothic cathedrals are *clerestory* windows (first used by the Egyptians); *ribs* (used for decoration), *bosses* (ornamental projections covering the intersection of the ribs); *gargoyles* (rainspouts carved in grotesque human or animal head forms), and *tracery,* the ornamental work formed by the branching of the mullions in the upper section of Gothic windows. *Blind tracery,* used for decoration only, is an imitation of window tracery on a solid surface. In Y *tracery,* the mullion splits to form a Y, and is characteristic of the thirteenth century. *Flamboyant tracery,* from the fourteenth century, consists of flowing, flame-like lines. *Perpendicular tracery,* introduced in the fifteenth century and particularly important in the Tudor Period in England, consisted of upright, straight-sided panels at the top of the window.

The capitals of Gothic columns were *cubiform,* based on a square form with stiff leaf forms, important in the perpendicular Gothic style. *Crockets,* projecting carved ornaments in a bud or leaf shape, were used on the side of pinnacles and spires. *Corbels,* brackets set into the wall to carry a beam, were used in later periods as well.

Furniture

At this time the requirements of people were very modest. The wealthy still traveled from castle to castle, taking most of their furniture with them, except pieces too large to move. The few pieces of furniture that have survived were from the monasteries or castles. The poor had little furniture or very crude pieces, such as three-legged stools.

Chests and Tables

The chest was the most important and most widely distributed piece of furniture. It was used for storage and, if the top was flat, it was also used as a table, seat, and/or bed. Some were made of hollowed tree trunks,

Table 13.6
Characteristics of Gothic Furniture

1. It was architectural in form, with crude detailing.
2. It featured architectural motifs, such as arches, tracery, trefoil, quatrefoil, linenfold carving, and pierced carving.
3. Chests and seating pieces featured panel construction.
4. Chests were used for both storage and seating.

but most were made by panel construction, with loosely held panels for adaption to climatic changes. Ornamentation included chip-carved *roundels*, like the rose window (on the front of the chest in Fig. 13.1a); the *quatrefoil*, shaped like a four-leaf clover; the *trefoil*, three-lobed clover-like ornament; *linenfold carving* (Figs. 13.1b, 13.1c, 13.1d), which resembled folded linen; the *pointed arch;* and *tracery*. Some chests were set on legs to keep them off the damp floor (Fig. 13.1a, 13.1b) and strengthened with ornamental ironwork. Crude low-relief carvings of chivalric scenes and *arcading* (on the chair back in Fig. 13.1c) became popular. Portable writing boxes, with sloping lids and hinged tops, were used to store books and documents. Tables were usually of the pedestal type, but *draw tables* (with two end leaves that could be drawn out from beneath a center leaf) were made for the first time in this period (Fig. 15.4b).

Seating Pieces

The *stab-ended* stool was a stool with thick wooden ends. Some supports were shaped like buttresses. Some stools were **X**–shaped and had a folding top with a leather or cloth sling seat. The *curule* stool, a version of the Roman **X** stool was also popular.

Seating furniture was heavy and difficult to move and was seldom found except at court or in churches (Fig. 13.1c, 13.1d). These pieces included box-like, architectural chairs which were originally brightly painted and layered with gesso and gilt. (Fig. 13.1d). The *settle,* a bench with a back, was first made during this period (Fig. 15.1d).

Beds and Storage Pieces

Beds, draped with curtains which were drawn at night, usually occupied the corner of the living areas, the *great hall*. Many beds were large enough to hold six people. The term *bed and board,* a symbol of married life, originated in this period. The board was a *trestle table,* flanked by benches and stools. Cupboards had doors, which closed with simple wooden latches. *Presses* were used for clothing. Up until this time, storage pieces had not been enclosed. The closed variety were first used to hold church vestments. *Livery* cupboards, which had pierced openings for the circulation of air, were designed to store food (Fig. 15.2c).

The Renaissance

Italian Renaissance (1400–1650)

Historical Background

The Italian Renaissance began in Florence about 1400. The term *Renaissance* means *rebirth* and all of Italy experienced a tremendous expansion of artistic activity. Stimulated by the patronage of the popes and the powerful Medici family, beautiful buildings, magnificent art, and elaborate furniture and interiors were created. Artists bestowed the same attention on carved and painted furniture and interiors as on the façade of a palace or church. This revolution in thought occurred in a land where the scattered ruins of Rome were a constant reminder of its Classical heritage.

People began to make use of the knowledge which had almost been lost during the Middle Ages. They began to scorn the narrowness of medieval ignorance and superstition and dubbed the churches built during the Middle Ages *Gothic,* meaning barbaric, coarse, and

Figure 13.1a
Medieval storage chest (English) ornamented with chip-carved roundels.

Figure 13.1b
Storage chest with linenfold carving, from the Gothic Period.

crude. Individualism and secularism were replacing the ecclesiastical outlook, which had stressed the worthlessness of life on earth.

During the Gothic Period, Italy was a conduit for Oriental trade, and as a result of the Crusades and the travels of Marco Polo, it had become a center of commerce and banking. Scientific discoveries were conflicting with church doctrines and doubts arose in the minds of intellectual leaders. This new knowledge was spread by the invention of the printing press in the fifteenth century, and the time was ripe for a reaction against the past.

People were being challenged by new ideas and they needed new forms of expression to execute the new ideas. There was a new belief in the dignity and worth of the individual, and as social habits changed, they affected the function and character of dwellings. The medieval fortified castle was replaced by luxurious city and suburban villas. Comfort, convenience and beauty became more significant than strength and protection. Artists and architects concentrated on the use of Classical forms, such as the pedestal, the column, the pediment, the balastrade, and the entablature. Palatial dwellings and rich furnishings were designed to outshine one another in magnificance.

Architecture

The influence of antiquity was revealed in many Italian villas. In Florence, great stone palaces built up to the street foreshadowed the great classic banks of modern cities. A new phenomenon emerged, the architect, one who instructed others in the method of building, working on the drawing rather than the site. *Andrea Palladio* (päl-lä′-dyō) (1508–80) influenced the architecture of his time and inspired much of the eighteenth-century Georgian style in England and the Federal style in the United States. Palladio and Giacomo da Vignola (vē-nyō-lä) (1507–73) rediscovered and formulated the principles of classicism and standardized the proportions of the Roman architectural orders. Palladio's book, *Quattro Libri* (1570), was to become the ultimate source for architects for the next three hundred years.

Gardens with geometric beds of flowers banked by sculpted green hedges were set against a background of natural woodlands or trees. Pools, fountains, and cascades with statues and stone benches were used as integral parts of the formal architecture.

Table 13.7
Relationship of Important Furniture Periods to the Italian Renaissance

Byzantine	*Spain*	*France*
323–1453	1400–1600	Renaissance
		1485–1643
		Louis XIV
		1643–1700

Interiors

During the Renaissance in Italy there were two social classes, the peasants and the wealthy. The peasant had little or no influence on design during this period or later; it was, rather, for the homes of the wealthy that new designs were created. Our discussion will center on those homes.

Interiors consisted of smaller rooms than those of the Gothic castle, but were large in scale when compared to today's interiors. These interiors allowed the Italian's sophisticated understanding of primary colors full reign. If the walls were neutral, accessories and draperies in brilliant blues, purples, yellows, and greens were used. Interiors were ornamental, with walnut-, oak-, or cypress-beamed ceilings painted in vivid colors with a cartouche, medallion, or coat of arms in the center. *Coffered* ceilings (with sunken panels decorated with painted arabesques) and flat plaster ceilings were also used.

Della Robia's terra-cotta plaques were light blue with white relief ornament and small areas of other colors; his subjects included cherubs, human figures, wreaths, and garlands. *Pilasters* (flat-faced projections having the details, capital and base of a column) flanked paintings, windows, and niches. The *niche,* a functional or decorative recess in the wall, was one of the most popular built-in features of the room. Large paintings were incorporated into the architectural design. Windows were either square-headed or topped with a pediment. Black and white or colored floors were inlaid with checker or scroll patterns of tile, brick, or marble. *Terrazo* (a crushed marble mixed with cement) was used for floors and after 1600, elaborate patterns in rare colored woods were popular. Occasionally Oriental rugs were used. Fireplaces were ornamented with mantles.

During the Renaissance, ornamentation of rooms assumed almost as much importance as

Figure 13.1c
Gothic throne chair with linenfold carving on front, arcaded panel on back, and finials on top of chair posts.

Figure 13.1d
Gothic architectural chair with linenfold and high-relief carving.

Table 13.8
Characteristics of Italian Renaissance Furniture

1. It was large with rectilinear lines.
2. It featured classic motifs in high relief.
3. There were numerous pieces on low pedestals.
4. Seats were upholstered.
5. There was a variety of pieces.
6. Walnut was used almost exclusively, except for small amounts of oak, cedar, and cypress.
7. Furniture was used sparingly.
8. Silk textiles with large patterns were used for upholstery.

paintings. Furniture became less architectural and there was a sense of continuity between the structure and its ornament. Furniture was arranged in different ways in keeping with new social habits. There were more chairs of different types and seats were upholstered. Inventories show, however, that there were still very few pieces of furniture except for chests. The *loggia,* a room with an open area or colonnade on one side, appeared.

Furniture

During this time, a greater emphasis was placed on comfort for there was more social interaction and entertainment. Furniture was generally placed against the walls and made a dominant part of the wall composition along with wall plaques, busts, and paintings. Horizontal lines were emphasized and the furniture was rectilinear until the end of the period, when vigorous, high-relief carving included more curved lines. The Italian names for these pieces are still retained today.

Chests

The most important piece of Renaissance furniture was a hinged chest or storage box called a *cassone* (Fig. 13.2a). Its size varied from a jewel casket (Fig. 13.2b) to the almost immovable dower chest, and it often doubled as luggage. Inventories reveal that *cassoni* were used to store clothing and other items and as seats or tables. *Cassoni* were passed

Figure 13.2a
Italian Renaissance cassone with paw feet.

from one generation to the next and many have survived. Great ingenuity was applied to their ornamentation. Very popular at the beginning of the period was a classical architectural framework adorned with pediments, cornices, and moldings. Paintings of battle scenes, religious scenes, and Roman triumphs were included, along with friezes, swags of fruit, and flowers in gilt gesso. Later, carved and polished walnut *cassoni* became popular and some emulated antique sarcophagi, supported on lion's-paw feet and decorated with carved foliage or scenes from classical mythology.

Intarsia designs, incised and then inlaid with colored woods, bone, ivory, or shells, and *pastiglia* designs, bas-relief designs formed by thin layers of plaster over fabric, were also used. Some *cassoni,* fitted with a back and arms and called *cassapanca,* were forerunners of the sofa. They were usually set upon a dais and had loose cushions (Fig. 13.2c).

Chairs

Although chairs were not widely used, they began to assume more elaborate forms; simple benches, stools, and rush-seat chairs disappeared from all but the poorer homes. Ingeniously carved splats at the back of the chair were added, along with padded seats and high backs. The *sedia* was a square, straight chair with low stretchers or runners and rear legs that extended to form the back upright which usually terminated in an ornament (generally an acanthus leaf), or *finial* (Fig. 13.2d).

Finials continued to be features of furniture design in later centuries, and some chairs today feature finials. The Colonial period in America emphasized finials not only as ornamentation on furniture but also as an integral part of chandeliers (most often these were the centered, highly polished brass pendants which were the lowest hanging point of the lamp). Chair arms were straight or baluster-turned and the backs and seats were covered in leather, velvet, damask, or tapestry fastened by gilt nailheads and sometimes ornamented with silk fringe.

The *sgabello,* a light, rather uncomfortable wooden chair, was used for dining (Fig. 13.2e). Early examples had three legs, small octagonal seats, and stiff backs. Later ones had elaborately carved trestle or slat supports and backs. Low stools were also made with trestle or slat supports. *Certosina,* an ivory inlay, and

Figure 13.2b
Small Italian Renaissance cassone for storage of jewelry, with lion carved on top and lion's-paw feet.

Figure 13.2c
Italian Renaissance cassapanca on dais.

Figure 13.2d
Heavily carved Italian Renaissance sedia with a finial at top of back upright.

Figure 13.2e
Italian Renaissance sgabello with three legs and octagonal seat.

Figure 13.2f
Italian Renaissance Savonarola chair carved back, curved wooden slats, and solid arms.

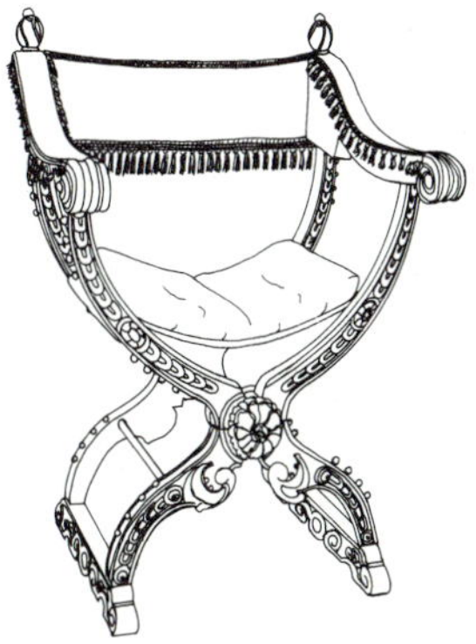

Figure 13.2g
Italian Renaissance Dante chair with heavily carved arms and legs, and velvet seat back.

intarsia were used to ornament chairs. There were two types of X–shaped chairs. The *Savonarola* (sä-vō-nă-rô′-lä) *chair*, named for a monk who was burned at the stake in Florence, was composed of curved wooden slats attached to solid arms, and a carved wood seat and back panel (Fig. 13.2f). The *Dante* (dăn′-tē) *chair*, more frequently pro-

duced today, had heavily ornamented arms and legs and a seat and back panel of cloth or leather (Fig. 13.2g).

Tables

Tables came in all sizes. The *refectory table*, which probably originated in the monasteries, typically had an oblong top of a single wal-

Figure 13.2h
Italian Renaissance refectory table with turned baluster supports on a carved pedestal.

Figure 13.2i
Italian Renaissance credenza on a base, ornamented with relief carving.

nut plank supported by elaborately carved trestles, dwarf Doric columns, or turned baluster forms with either plain or carved stretchers (Fig. 13.2h). Small occasional tables had hexagonal or octagonal tops supported by carved pedestals or scrolled supports and edges finished with ornamental molding.

Because houses and even grand palaces did not have special rooms for eating until the nineteenth century, dining tables were rather simple boards on trestles covered with a cloth that reached to the floor. Seating was on *sgabelli* or stools, which had three or four splayed legs. On great occasions, however, chairs were brought for important guests.

Other Pieces

Cabinets and cupboards were also in use. The *credenza,* most popular (Fig. 13.2i), was set on a carved base; it had two or three drawers with doors beneath, and was ornamented with carving or intarsia.

The bed, or *letto,* was a massive structure. Often placed on a base, it had a paneled headboard and footboard and occasionally a tester. The canopy and draperies were of rich, large-patterned velvets, silks, and damasks; large-patterned brocades were introduced during the latter part of the period. Except for the bed, bedrooms were sparsely and simply furnished.

Accessories

Accessories consisted of framed pictures and small mirrors, pedestals for statues and ornaments, bookcases, vases, hanging shelves, the *torchère,* (a table made to hold a candle or lamp), and candlesticks made of wood or iron. Art played such an important part in the lives of Renaissance noblemen that even the most insignificant household item was designed with care. Italian interiors were admired and imitated throughout Europe and Italian craftsmen were much in demand. About 1659, the Renaissance style in Italy began to decline; political, financial, and cultural influences moved to France and later to England.

Spanish Renaissance (1400–1600)

Historical Background

Renaissance styles were first introduced into Spain in the fifteenth century, but it was not until the beginning of the sixteenth century, when Spain became the dominant power in Europe, that the real influence was felt. Many of the special characteristics of this style reflected the influence of the Moors, who held portions of Spain from the eighth century until 1606, when they were finally overthrown, and who had dominated cultural life in Spain for eight hundred years.

Spain was affected by many other cultures, including the Italian, the French, the English, the Indian, and the Chinese.

Many pieces of furniture were imported into Spain, so the discovery of an old piece of furniture in Spain does not necessarily indicate it is of Spanish origin. Charles V invited foreign craftsmen to make furniture for his splendid court, but actually the visiting artisans learned more than they taught, for Spanish metalwork and Moorish inlaying were superb.

Design development was also affected by geography and climate. Spain is a mountainous, arid country in which isolated groups developed different interests and customs, and were united by religion rather than by economics or politics. Emotional qualities dominated the wealth and power of the Spaniards.

Spanish design was masculine and furniture and interiors of a crude beauty were created but without the elegance and simplicity of the Italian forms with which they were allied. Women were expected to sit rigidly upright on cushions or to retire to bed, for there was no furniture which permitted lounging. Spanish furniture is characterized by harsh simplicity and strength in materials and execution.

Architecture

The art of Spain largely ecclesiastical, and the cathedrals drew muralists, mosaicists, weavers, sculptors, and metal workers. The cathedrals of the period had an almost incredible wealth of ornamentation: sculptured alabaster, polychromed woodwork, gilded wrought iron grills, silver altar pieces, and marble tombs. Under the patronage of the Church, Spanish painting became significant, with El Greco and Velázquez most important. The Inquisition, which began in the late fifteenth century, maintained the power of the church but also attempted to crush freedom of thought and creativity that questioned fundamental scientific or religious beliefs.

Mudejar Style (1200–1600)

The *Mudejar* style is a mingling of Moorish and Christian details superimposed over Gothic then Renaissance forms. An important structural feature was the horseshoe-shaped *Moorish arch,* the origin of which is unknown. The arch, a three-quarter circle, springs directly from the column's capitals. Oriental craftsmanship and techniques such as inlay and the use of precious metal predominate. Geometric forms—such as stars, crescents, crosses, hexagons, octagons—and interlaced work were used on the doors and ceilings.

The Moors, excellent mathematicians, used complicated geometric patterns because the Koran forbade the copying of natural forms. Squares and rectangles were usually avoided and originality in the design of the surface ornamentation was pronounced. Geometric ornamentation was well adapted to wood, tile, weaving, plasterwork, and it was accentuated by brilliant reds, greens, blues, white, silver, and gold.

The Moors were responsible for the development of the arabesque, which probably originated from the Assyrian tree of life.

Plateresco (1475–1550)

The Plateresque (or early Spanish Renaissance) style takes its name from the word *platero,* or "silversmith," or *plateria* (silverwork).

Beaten, embossed, stamped, and plain silver were used to ornament furniture. Florid designs were typical in Gothic and Renaissance designs. Some furniture pieces were constructed completely of silver. The use of silver in furniture was forbidden by royal edict in the late sixteenth century. The Plateresque style, considered by many to be the most beautiful Spanish style, is typified by its lacy ornamentation, exuberant details, and Moorish carvings.

Desornamentado
(Dāz'-orn'-ə-men-tə'-dō) (1500–1659)

The influence and close adherence to Italian Renaissance designs became more pronounced through the influence of the architect Juan de Herrera (1530–97), a pupil of Michelangelo. In his work, classic forms with unornamented, austere surfaces dominated. Architecture during this time was extremely severe and barren and a reaction occurred against it led by José de Churriguera (1665–1725) and his family.

Churrigueresco (1650–1750)

While the Churrigueresco (chŭr-i-ga-resk-kō) does not really belong in the Spanish Renaissance Period, it is often classed there because of its influence on Latin America. It was an opulent design with a disregard of Classical rules and was primarily exterior. Led by the Churriguera family of architects, the style was bold and large in size, and continued in vogue until Philip V, Louis XIV's grandson, came to the throne in 1700, bringing French influences. Long after it disappeared in Spain, its influence continued in North America.

Interiors

Spanish interiors combined Moorish and Renaissance detail, and even plain plastered houses were enriched with wood, wrought iron, and tile accents. Doors were of heavy wooden panels, topped with the Moorish arch. Rooms were long and narrow with exposed painted beams in the ceiling or shallow wooden panels forming intricate geometric patterns. Doors and windows were deeply recessed, with wrought iron grills and heavy wooden shutters or Venetian blinds. Floors were of tile or brick laid in geometric patterns. The dado below the plain or painted plastered wall was also of tile. Framed paintings, tapestries, and leather coverings ornamented the walls, and rugs covered the floors. Leather and

Table 13.9

**Relationship of Important Furniture Periods
to Spanish Renaissance Period**

Italy	England	France
Renaissance 1400–1650	Tudor 1485–1558	Renaissance
	Elizabethan 1558–1603	1485–1643
		Louis XIV 1643–1700

wooden chests were used for clothing storage. *Majolica,* bronze, and copper were typically used for cooking and eating utensils. *Majolica* was a stamped and painted pottery covered with a tin enamel glaze in bright colors.

Walnut was the most important wood until after Phillip II depleted the forests to build the Spanish Armada; then pine became the most frequently used wood. The Spanish were the first to use mahogany as a cabinet wood (about the middle of the sixteenth century).

Furniture

Much Spanish furniture was primitive. The cabinetmaker's art was subservient to the skill of the inlayer. Strength and stability of construction were increased by the use of wrought iron bracing. As early as 1515, the Spaniards in Granada had a law regulating furniture workmanship and materials. Chairs were taxed and had to be stamped with a city mark. By 1502 *Cordovan* leather, forbidden to be falsely labeled, was in demand in Europe and England.

Very little furniture was used in the interior, but when it was, it was placed formally against the walls. Benches were usually built in or attached to the walls, and cushions and straw mattresses were numerous, especially in the women's quarters. A platform at the end of the main public room held two elaborate seats of honor for the master of the house and his wife. Chairs and benches were covered with velvets and silks (the latter were first made in Spain about 700). Many Spanish items of furniture are still called by their Spanish names.

Chairs

The *sillon de chadera* (or hip-joint chair) was the Spanish version of the Dante or Savonarola chair (Fig. 13.3a). It frequently appeared top-heavy because the upper part was often larger than the lower part. Inlaid ivory star motifs, arabesque designs, and decorative nailheads were typical. A decorative *boss,* or projecting ornament, was often placed where the curule legs intersected. Heavy fringe, luxurious tassles, and upholstery were used on these chairs.

The most typical chair was the *sillon frailero* (or monk's chair). This chair (Fig. 13.3b) was rectangular, with a leather, velvet, or damask seat and a back ornamented with decorative nailheads. The legs extended above the seat to

form arms at the front and, at the rear, back supports, which often ended in a finial. Low stretchers braced the legs and the broad front stretcher was often decorated or pierced. Chiseled grooves, like fluting, often ornamented the legs and front apron.

The *ladder-back chair* with the uppermost back slat richly carved and larger than the others, was also popular. Legs and stretchers were turned and the top front stretcher often repeated the design of the back. The seat was usually rush.

Benches

A long bench with a hinged top was used for seating and storage. These benches might be ornamented with finials, turned spindles, and heavy carving, or they might be left very plain. The plain bench, called a *monastery* or *sacristy bench,* was made of two planks, one serving as the seat and the other as a back, and had trestle legs and wrought-iron bracing. The benches were often upholstered with rich fabrics and fringe attached with decorative nailheads.

Tables

Tables were important items in the Spanish Renaissance. Usually they had long, plain surfaces with square-cut edges and a long overhanging top. Tables had either lyre-shaped trestle bases (similar to Italian examples), or four legs—column, spool, or disk-turned (Fig. 13.3c). Both the legs and the trestle were

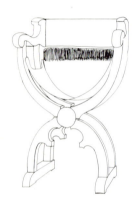

Figure 13.3a
Spanish Renaissance version of the Dante chair with a boss at the intersection of the curule legs and fringe ornaments on the back.

Figure 13.3b
Monk's chair from Spanish Renaissance with fretted front splat, legs extending above seat to form arm supports and back legs, and low stretchers at sides and back.

Table 13.10
**Characteristics of Spanish
Renaissance Furniture**

1. It had heavy proportions and was rectangular.
2. It was structurally simple, lacking the architectural details used in Italy.
3. It featured iron braces and mounts and exposed nailheads.
4. It was large, masculine, brilliantly colored (often to mask inferior workmanship).
5. Tooled or plain leather upholstery was used.
6. Walnut was the most important wood, then pine.
7. Motifs included short chiseled grooves, geometric patterns.
8. Legs were splayed or slanted.
9. Iron and silver rosettes, stars, and shells were used as ornaments.

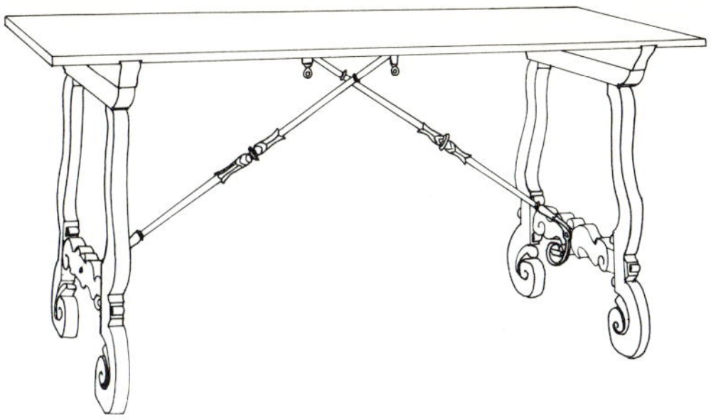

Figure 13.3c
Spanish Renaissance table with plain top and lyre-shaped trestle base. Wrought iron bracing of trestle.

splayed and braced with curving wrought iron.

Vargueño The *vargueño,* or writing cabinet, was a Spanish Renaissance innovation (Fig. 13.3d). It was a chest or hutch with a hinged writing surface that rested on pull-out supports. Drawers and secret compartments were in the interior. The upper and lower sections were always made separately and handles on the upper section made it easier to carry (Fig. 13.3e). The drawers and doors were ornamented in geometric patterns with inlaid wood and ivory. Many examples had pierced metal mounts with red velvet set behind them. A lock, keyholes, and a large bolt of wrought iron completed the top. The base had trestles or turned legs, braced with wrought iron.

Papelera The *papelera* was a smaller chest, without the hinged lid, used to hold paper and writing materials. Ivory inlay, shells, fluting, rosettes, and architectural detailing were used on the papelera. Tables or bases similar to the ones holding the varqueño were typical.

Storage Pieces

Storage pieces, called *armaria,* served as closets. Ornamented with geometric patterns, some armaria were built in two sections and decorated with moldings and turned spindles. Doors were elaborately carved in geometric shapes and stylized animal feet rested on the floor.

The storage chest, or *arca,* was made in all sizes and woods. Sometimes it was inlaid or carved, or had metal mounts with a leather or velvet cover (Fig. 13.3f). Depending upon its size, it might be mounted on a separate stand. Inside the lid might be interwoven geometric or arabesque patterns.

Beds

Spanish beds were made with and without corner posts, which might be twist-turned. Some beds had separate painted headboards of turned piers and arcades. Draperies were very important and rich fabrics with fringe and tassels were widely used.

Brazier The *brazier* was a brass, iron or copper pan on legs. It held hot charcoal or olive stone embers and was used for heating or perfuming with lavender sticks. This piece was so indispensable that there was usually

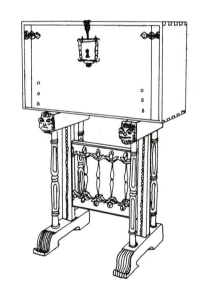

Figure 13.3d
Spanish Renaissance varqueño, open, to reveal ornamental interior in geometric patterns of inlaid wood and ivory. Writing surface supported by pull-outs.

Figure 13.3e
Spanish Renaissance varqueño made in two sections, with lock, hinges, and keyhole of wrought iron.

Figure 13.3f
Spanish Renaissance arca ornamented with relief carving.

one in every room. It was set on a platform with wooden or metal supports.

Glossary

Ambulatory (am-byə-lə-toŕ-ē). An aisle behind the altar in a church.

Apron. The structural part of the table underneath the top or of a chair directly under the seat at right angles to the top or seat; often ornamented.

Apse (aps). The semicircular termination of the church, usually the chancel (where the altar is placed).

Arcade. Adjoining arches with columns between as supports.

Blind Tracery. Tracery on a solid surface.

Boss. The projecting or hanging ornament at the intersection of the beams in the Gothic church or of chair legs.

Buttress. A masonary support built against a wall to counteract the outward thrust of the vault behind it.

Cassapanca. A cassone or chest fitted with back and arms and usually placed upon a dais, used in Renaissance Italy.

Cassone. A hinged chest or jewelry storage box used in Renaissance Italy.

Certosina. An inlaid pattern of ivory used in Renaissance Italy.

Chip Carving. Simple, low-relief carving achieved by chipping out the wood.

Cloister. A covered, frequently vaulted, passageway.

Corbel (kór-bəl). Brackets set into the wall to support a beam.

Credenza (kri-den′-zə). An Italian Renaissance sideboard.

Crocket (kräk′-ət). Projecting carved ornaments in bud or leaf shape used on the side of pinnacles and spires.

Cubiform (kyü′-bə-form). A capital based upon a square form with stiff leaf forms important in the perpendicular Gothic style.

Curule (kyu̇(ə)r′-ül). Semicircular legs based on a X created by the intersecting curves (resembles a C placed on an inverted C).

Draw Table. A table with two end leaves, stored under a center one, that pull out to lengthen the table.

Egg and Dart. A molding with dartlike points separating egg-shaped forms.

Finial (fin′-ē-al). The ornament that terminates a post or pediment.

Flamboyant Tracery. Consisted of flowing, flame-like lines.

Flying Buttress. A half arch that connects the building wall to a stone pier and carries the external thrust of the vaulting; used in Gothic cathedrals.

Gargoyle (gär′-goil). Rainspouts carved in fantastic human or animal head forms; used on Gothic cathedrals.

Grotesque (grō-tesk′). Fantastic masks or monsters (the originals were rediscovered in Italian grottos as ornaments.)

Intarsia (in-tar′-sē-ə). Italian Renaissance designs inlaid with colored and scorched woods, bone, ivory and shells.

Linenfold. A carved ornamentation, resembling folds of linen popular in the Gothic Period.

Loggia (Läj′-(ē)ə). An area which had an open colonndade on one side.

Majolica (mə-jäl′-i-kə). A stamped and painted pottery covered with a tin enamel glaze in bright colors (Spanish Renaissance).

Mosaic (mō-zā′-ik). Pattern formed by colored glass or stones pressed into wet cement.

Mullions (məl′-yən). The horizontal and vertical bars separating window lights (glass).

Nave. The central part of the church, usually flanked by aisles.

Niche (nich). A functional or decorative recessed space in the wall, first used in the Italian Renaissance.

Pastiglia (pa-stig′-lē-ə). Bas-relief (low-relief) designs formed by thin layers of plaster over a fine fabric.

Pendentive (pen-dent′-iv). A system of thrust and counterthrust developed during the Byzantine Period: an inverted, concave, triangular piece of masonry transmitted the weight of a dome to four heavy supports.

Perpendicular Tracery. Consisted of upright, straight-sided panels at the top of the window.

Pier. A column-like support for arches in a Gothic church.

Pilaster. A column (load-bearing or not) that projects from the wall and has the capital, base, porportions, and details of the classical column.

Quatrefoil (kat′-er-foil). A stylized four-leaf clover used in Gothic ornamentation.

Refectory Table (ri-fek′-te-rē). A table, originally used in monasteries, with a top formed by a single wood plant supported by elaborately carved trestles (Italian Renaissance).

Ribs. Arched supports for a vault.

Roundels (raùn-dəl′). A carved ornament resembling a rose window.

Rose Window. Wheel-shaped windows of stained glass with tracery mullions radiating from a central point.

Settle. Benches with a high back and arms, usually with storage under the seat.

Sgabello. An Italian Renaissance light wooden dining chair.

Side Aisles. The passageways on either side of the main body (nave) of the church.

Splay. A leg that flares out, either back or front.

Stretcher. The connecting crosspiece of chairs and tables.

Terrazo (tə-raz′-ō). A mixture of crushed marble and cement first used in the Italian Renaissance.

Terra-cotta. Baked, colored with painted, and glazed clay ornaments used first in the Italian Renaissance.

Torchère. A small table to hold candles or an oil lamp.

Tracery. The pattern formed by the branching mullions in the upper sections of a Gothic window.

Transept (trań(t)s′-ept). The part of the church which crosses the nave at right angles near the aspe of the building.

Trefoil. A three-lobed clover-like ornament.

Vault. An arched roof used in the Gothic Period.

Vargueño. A Spanish Renaissance chest with a writing surface, hinged at the bottom, that rested on pull-out supports.

Y Tracery. The mullion splits to form a Y.

Bibliography

BAUMGART, FRITZ. *A History of Architectural Styles.* New York: Praeger Publishers, Inc., 1970.

BECKWITH, JOHN. *Early Medieval Art.* London: Thames & Hudson Ltd., 1964.

BEVAN, BERNARD. *History of Spanish Architecture.* New York: Charles Scribner's Sons, 1939.

BRANNER, ROBERT. *Chartres Cathedral.* New York: W. W. Norton & Company, Inc., 1969.

BUENO, LUIS PEREZ, and RAPHAEL COMENECH. *Antique Spanish Furniture.* New York: Towse, 1965.

BURCKHARDT, J. *Civilization of the Renaissance in Italy.* New York, N.Y.: Oxford University Press, 1944.

BURR, GRACE H. *Hispanic Furniture.* New York, N.Y.: Hispanic Society of America, 1964.

BYNE, A., and M. S. BYNE. *Spanish Architecture of the Sixteenth Century.* New York: G. P. Putnam's Sons, 1917.

CLARK, KENNETH. *The Gothic Revival.* Baltimore: Penguin Books, 1964.

EBERLEIN, H. D. *Interiors, Fireplaces and Furniture of the Italian Renaissance.* New York, N.Y.: Architectural Book Publishing Co., 1916.

———. *Spanish Interiors Furniture and Details from the 14th to the 17th Century.* New York: Architectural Book Publishing Co., 1925.

FLETCHER, BANISTER. *A History of Architecture on the Comparative Method.* 17 ed. New York: Charles Scribner's Sons, 1961.

HARVEY, JOHN. *The Gothic World, 1100–1550.* London: Batsford, 1947.

PEVSNER, NICOLAUS. *An Outline of European Architecture.* New York: Penguin Books, 1943.

SCHOTTMULLER, F. *Furniture and Interior Decoration of the Italian Renaissance.* New York: Brentano's, 1921.

The French Periods and the Biedermeier Period

The printing press was an important factor in the development of French design. The dissemination of pattern books, made possible by the printing press, helped artisans to copy models and to improve their furniture and accessories. The invention of gunpowder made castles less secure and turned attention to the development of living spaces for beauty and comfort. Exploration and military forays into other countries, made easier by the invention of the compass, opened the eyes of French invaders to the art and design of other cultures and started fierce competition for artists' services.

The rivalry among members of the ruling class, expressed in the number, the quantity, and the beauty of their acquired possessions, did more than anything else to elevate the state of art and artisans in France.

French Renaissance (1485–1643)

Historical Background

In 1495 the first of a series of French military expeditions into Italy gave the French an opportunity to see magnificent Italian palaces filled with splendid furniture and art. They took home not only objects, but the realization that furnishings and interiors could make life more pleasant. French noblemen became patrons of the arts. During the reign of Francis I, a great patron of the arts, Leonardo da Vinci and Benvenuto Cellini came to France to work on commissions under his protection.

Italian motifs, Spanish marquetry, and German and Flemish designs were gradually assimilated by the French, with Italian Renaissance forms dominating by 1610. The change from Gothic to Renaissance forms was slow, for artisans resisted. At first Renaissance architectural details and motifs were added to Gothic structural forms, but gradually Gothic forms were replaced by those of the Renaissance.

In 1598, Henry IV brought peace between Catholics and Protestants and by the Edict of Nantes kept many French Huguenot artisans from leaving France. The Edict gave the Huguenots freedom to worship their religion. It was revoked in 1685 by Louis XIV and over 100,000 Huguenots (many accomplished artisans) fled France and went to Holland, England, and Germany. Workshops were established in the Louvre for sculptors, cabinet-makers, and goldsmiths to revive the decorative arts. Italian products no longer had to be imported and, under Louis XIII, art began to develop a distinctly French flavor. The Renaissance paved the way for French leadership in design and the arts for the next two centuries.

Architecture

The châteaux of the Loire (lwəhr) Valley, such as Chambord, combined both Gothic elements with Renaissance details. Exteriors were still medieval in appearance with such military features as flanking towers, round turrets, and moats, although these no longer served a useful purpose. High dormer windows framed by pilasters and surmounted by pediments were added, and façades were decorated with niches and medallions. Sculptured chimneys were added as the period progressed. The pointed Gothic arch was replaced by a rounded one. Exteriors became symmetrical, combining angular and curving motifs, and including terraces. Fontainbleau (fõn'-t'n-blō), transformed by Francis I (1515–47) from a hunting lodge into a great palace, influenced decoration throughout Europe with its sumptuous, architectural interiors. Henry IV (1589–1610) began to bring order out of the chaos of medieval cities. As society changed, under Louis XIII (1610–43) the flourishing nobility and bourgeoisie built luxurious homes, such as the Palais du Luxembourg in Paris (1615–24), the Château du Coulommiers (1613—)and the Châteaux de Blerancourt (1614–19).

Interiors

French Renaissance interiors were dominated by towering fireplaces with heavily carved mantles. The overmantle was ornamented with classical columns or pilasters and niches. Rooms were cold in winter owing to the drafty fireplaces and hot in summer because the fires were never allowed to go out (matches were unknown).

Gradually the great hall was replaced by more formal rooms, creating a need for additional furniture. Rooms were still dark, even though larger, symmetrically spaced windows allowed more light into the interior. Stone or plaster walls with wooden *wainscots* were painted or hung with tapestries or Cordovan leather or adorned with family portraits. Beamed ceilings were gradually replaced by coffered ones and floors were laid in *Delft*

Figure 14.1a
This French Renaissance chest on a stand with human finials has twist-turned legs.

Figure 14.1b
This French Renaissance chest on platform is ornamented with masks on the upper front panels, bosses on the lower panels, and a boss in the lower center; Corinthian columns are placed on the sides (ca. 1550).

(dĕlft) *tile,* marble squares, or costly wood *parquetry* (pär'-ka-trē). Niches to hold statues were an integral part of the interior decoration.

The bedroom became the center of private life and the bed the most important item of furniture. Married couples and ladies, fully dressed in bed for warmth received guests who sat on folding stools or cushions. Brussels tapestries were used on the walls and as upholstery or bedcovers.

Furniture

There was a scarcity of ornamented furniture during the early Renaissance in France. People primarily used chests, beds, and a few chairs; however, as the period progressed and prosperity grew, more pieces appeared. Furniture was massive and elaborately carved with marble, metal, or tortoise-shell inlay, but towards the end of the Renaissance it became austere. Two innovations of the period were fixed upholstery filled with horsehair, and the development of the *armoire* (ar-mwahr') (or clothing wardrobe). Horsehair is still considered to be an excellent fill throughout northern Europe, although its expense is making it more rare. The armoire is also still in use throughout Europe. Only the most modern homes and hotels have built-in closets. The demise of the armoire is not so much a result of design efficiency as a result of the loss of skilled cabinetmakers. The use of ebony veneers late in the period was responsible for the word *ébéniste* (literally "worker in ebony"), which designated the high-quality cabinetmaker.

By the sixteenth century, furniture joints were hidden, making it possible to ignore the division between panels and to ornament the entire surface of a piece. Inventories reveal that there was an abundance of fabric-covered furniture, and rich, colorful fabrics were thrown over chairs, tables, and chests.

Marquetry, the insertion of contrasting materials into veneers, appeared, and rules governing the technique were laid down by the guilds. In marquetry, both the field and the pattern are cut at the same time, and in some companion pieces the field and the pattern were reversed. Wood surfaces were also incrusted with stones, metal, and mosaics.

Chests

Coffers or chests were made until about 1650, when they were replaced by the fore-

Table 14.1
Relationship of Important Furniture Periods to the French Renaissance Period

Italy	Spain	England	America
Renaissance 1400–1600	Renaissance 1400–1650	Tudor 1485–1558 Elizabethan 1558–1603	Early American 1608–1720

Table 14.2
Characteristics of French Renaissance Furniture

1. It was massive, heavily carved in high, sharp relief.
2. It was made of shiny well-polished oak or walnut; ebony veneer appeared late in period.
3. Chairs had throne-like backs, straight arms.
4. Chairs had turned ball, spiral or baluster legs with bun or Flemish-scroll feet.
5. Marquetry of colored wood, tortoise-shell, gilded metal, mother-of-pearl, ivory was used.
6. Pieces had fixed upholstery of embossed Cordovan leather, velvet, needlepoint or petit-point, damask; fringe trim.
7. Motifs included olive, laurel, or acanthus leaves; foliated scrolls, arabesques; rosettes; cartouches; medallions; shells; chimera, griffins, lozenges; grotesques; caryatids.
8. Furniture joints were concealed.

runner of the commode (Fig. 14.1a). They followed the Italian style and many were not portable, being placed on a platform (Fig. 14.1b). Every surface was elaborately carved, and carytids, columns, or pilasters were added. Some chests were covered with leather and others were gilded or ornately studded with brass nails. Even at the court, many low chests were still used as seats.

Stools and Benches

Stools, with or without backs, were used throughout the Renaissance. Some had hinged seats with a storage chest underneath (Fig. 14.1c). Turned legs and upholstered seats were typical. Because there was no separate dining room, folding stools were often used.

Beds

Beds were too monumental to be moved and had elaborately carved headboards, posts, and cornices, and heavy testers. The bed was designed to be an integral part of the room and was adorned with fringes, braid, tassels, and luxurious fabrics. Often the fabrics were more impressive than the bed itself. The emphasis on the bed was probably not a manifestation of sexual preoccupation, as it is today; rather, the bed was a symbol of wealth and leisure. Rest from toil was appreciated by all classes. The bed was the ultimate symbol of rest and relaxation, far removed from the straining realities of existence that daily faced the masses.

Chairs

Chairs had high paneled backs (Fig. 14.1d) until the middle of the sixteenth century. Then they became lighter (Figs. 14.1e, 14.1f), backs were lowered, and both backs and seats were upholstered. The tall, slender back was

Figure 14.1c
A French Renaissance stool with turned legs, upholstered seat, and H–shaped stretchers.

Figure 14.1d
French Renaissance chair with linenfold carving below the seat and a separate cushion.

Figure 14.1e
An upholstered French Renaissance chair with scroll supports for the arms.

Figure 14.1f
An upholstered sidechair with shaped legs that foreshadow the cabriole leg.

Figure 14.1g
A French Renaissance chair with columnar legs and low stretchers; the head carved in the medallion on the back is outlined with curving foliage.

Figure 14.1h
This architectural trestle-end table is ornamented with caryatids and further supported by arcaded columns; the frieze is ornamented with gadrooning.

usually ornamented with a head in profile enclosed in a medallion encircled by curving foliage (Fig. 14.1g). Stretchers, close to the floor at the beginning of the period, were gradually raised. Armless chairs were popular for women because they accommodated their exaggeratedly full skirts (Fig. 14.1f). The most important chair was the *caquetoire,* or conversation chair: the seat was considerably wider in front than in back, and the arms curved inward from the front to the back. The legs were usually baluster-turned, or slender columns terminating in bun feet. This chair might be compared to the Italian *sgabello.* For the first time, cane was used as a material for furniture.

Tables

Tables often had columnar legs (Fig. 14.1h), or rested on trestles. The stretcher was low and heavy.

The Baroque Period: Louis XIV (1643–1700)

Historical Background

Louis XIV became king of France in 1643, at the age of five, but it was not until 1661 that he personally ruled. Louis resolved to restore the power and prestige of the throne and to make his court the center of artistic life. In spite of the many jealousies and intrigues surrounding him, he made France the undisputed leader in art, architecture, and design. Other courts throughout the world tried to emulate his style. Louis XIV was known as the "Sun King," and his motif was a sunburst. The style associated with his reign was called *le grand siécle,* or "the grand century." The strict etiquette and formal ceremonies which surrounded the king and the court made every activity involving the king a ceremonial event that was witnessed by his retinue and thus every room became a public room.

Early in Louis' reign, Nicholas Fouquet (foo-keh′) (1615–80), Minister of Finance, introduced a centralized system for the development of the decorative arts when he built Vaux-le-Vicomte (vō-le-vikɔ̃it) (1657–61). This splendid château surpassed all the royal palaces, so Louis jailed Fouquet for building it with public funds and set about building Versailles (vĕr-sī′), a structure that would never be surpassed. Jean-Baptiste Colbert (col-bāre′) (1619–83) who succeeded Fouquet, coordinated the development of the decorative arts with Charles LeBrun (luh-brœN′) (1619–90) the Art Director of France. Many art industries were given royal encouragement during this period, and Colbert protected them with

Table 14.3

Relationship of Important Furniture Periods to Louis XIV Period

England	America
England	*America*
Elizabethan 1558–1603	Early American
Jacobean 1603–60	1608–1720
Restoration 1660–1702	

Table 14.4

Characteristics of Louis XIV Furniture

1. It was monumental, with exaggerated, massive classic forms.
2. It was elegant rather than comfortable, although upholstery was used.
3. It featured straight lines with some compass curves, and rectangular, symmetrical structure.
4. Oak, walnut, some lime and pearwood were used, with inlays of zebra, tulipwood, kingwood.
5. It featured underbracing and solid construction until stretchers were eliminated late in period.
6. It featured carving and boulle marquetry as well as gilding and parcel gilding of silver and gold (gilding applied to part of ornamentation) inlay, lacquer, painting.
7. Straight legs became curved as the period progressed.
8. Table tops were of marble and stone mosaics.
9. Chairs had high backs.
10. Marble-topped console tables with elaborately carved understructures were placed against walls.
11. Motifs included sunburst (head with rays surrounding it); double L in oval; satyr mask; C and S curves; dolphins; sphinxes; lion's head and claws; ram's head or horns; acanthus, laurel, or olive leaf; rinceau (scroll ornament); lozenges; flowers, fruit, birds, butterflies, palmettes, and water-lily leaves irregularly scattered; human or allegorical figures; ancient weapons.

subsidies and tariffs. He also regulated prices and exercised quality control. The Gobelins (gŏb′-uh-lĭn) was purchased and transformed into workshops where tapestries, furniture, and accessories were made under LeBrun's direction. In the Louvre (lōō-vr′) workshops, a cabinetmaker, André Charles Boulle pro-

duced furniture for the king and court, perfecting a method of marquetry using tortoiseshell, pewter, and brass.

The French Baroque style, which grew out of exaggerated Roman forms, was one of grandeur. The monumental scale of rooms and their furnishings was coordinated with rich symmetrical ornamentation and sharp color contrasts. It was an interior style, rather than an exterior one, with three distinct demarcations: the early period, when Italian influences were more important; the middle period, when the style was at its height and at its best; and the last part, when Louis' influence dwindled. Toward the end of Louis XIV's reign, the king's tastes became austere. Paris rather than Versailles became the center of society and the Régence began.

Architecture

The architecture of the Baroque Period is characterized by its vast scale, rectilinear outlines, and use of classical details. Versailles was built to house ten thousand people and was a city in itself. Colbert assembled artists, designers, architects, and master craftsmen to build it. Its park and gardens, lakes, and canals integrated nature with the palace, and it became the prototype of town planning. Construction began in 1661 and was in progress for almost ninety-five years. Louis did not move his court to Versailles until 1682. Originally a hunting lodge, Versailles consists of two long wings emanating from a central block. It is a quarter of a mile long, covers 6183 acres and has 2143 windows, 67 stairways, and 352 chimneys; the stables had room for 2400 horses and 200 coaches.

Every room in Versailles was planned as a public room and was lavishly decorated. The rooms had massive proportions, and walls, ceilings, and ornamentation were coordinated with the furnishings. Furniture was still placed next to the wall, because most activities took place while people were standing. Colors were rich and vivid and some of the combinations were violet and red or silver and gold or red and green. Light colors were used on some walls to emphasize the gilding, and toward the end of the period, a feminine influence was first seen when pastel colors began to appear. Large plate-glass mirrors were used, and many walls were painted with historical or legendary scenes. Some Chinese wallpaper was imported and Chinese themes appeared in

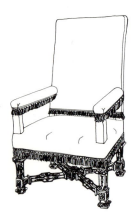

Figure 14.2a
This Boulle design Baroque cabinet is ornamented with putti (small cherubs) and trophies combined with marquetry on a brass ground.

Figure 14.2b
This Baroque upholstered chair has an X–shaped stretcher and is trimmed with fringe.

Figure 14.2c
This Baroque upholstered chair has light scroll-shaped legs and a curved X–shaped stretcher.

domestic wallpapers. These wallpapers can still be found throughout Europe. (The Schönbrun the summer palace of the Hapsburgs in Austria, features Chinese wallpaper in many of the rooms.)

Architectural details, such as columns, pilasters, and entablatures were popular. Heavy sculptural moldings with a cornice were used around the high windows and deep-relief sculptural moldings, often with foliage and cherubs, were used around the doors. Some Aubusson (ō'-bü'-sôn') and Savonnerie woven-wool carpets with the emblem of Louis XIV, usually a double L, were used. Floors were of parquetry in the grandest rooms and of stone or black and white marble in the halls. Crystal or carved wooden chandeliers, *gueridons* (elaborate candlestands), wall brackets, and torchères (tɔrʃɛːr) furnished light and decoration.

Furniture

Monumental furniture had to be designed for the massive interiors. It was usually placed against the wall—where it stayed, because it was too heavy to move. It was designed for elegance rather than comfort. Sitting was a ceremonial ritual with a throne-like chair for the king, and stools for members of the lesser ranks.

André Charles Boulle

The development of French cabinetry resulted in large part from Boulle's influence.

He was appointed master cabinetmaker to Louis XIV in 1672, and with his four sons designed magnificent furniture inlaid with brass, pewter, horn, German silver, and tortoiseshell (Fig. 14.2a). Marquetry patterns were cut from sheets of these materials. Boulle perfected this technique and furniture made in this manner in later periods was called Boulle furniture. He employed twenty cabinetmakers and bronzeworkers in his Louvre workshops and made furniture for the king, for the nobility, and for foreign courts. Boulle also designed parquet floors, inlaid panels, and mirrored walls. He perfected *ormolu* (or'-ma-lü'), or gilded bronzework, in which moldings and motifs were applied to furniture to ornament it as well as to brace and protect it. Ormolu is typical of later French furniture, changing in scale, subject matter, and motifs.

Chairs and Sofas

Chairs were upholstered and had tall rectangular backs, arms that curved downward and *gained legs* (legs that resembled pillars narrowing towards the bottom) with carved, molded bun (Fig. 14.2b) or lion's-paw feet. Later in the period, the scroll-shaped or cabriole (kab'-rē-ōl) leg was used for the first time. The word *cabriole* came from the French *cabrioler* ("to leap"). It was a conventionalized wood animal leg with a knee, ankle, and foot; it curved outward toward the knee and in again in an S shape. Heavy carved X– or H–shaped (Fig. 14.2b) stretchers were typical, and arms and stretchers were sometimes curved in S–shaped curves. Walnut was the usual wood and it was painted or gilded. The backs of chairs were completely covered with fabric. Chairs were enriched with ormolu.

The *seggiolone* was a large, imposing chair of gilded wood. Confessional chairs, which developed about 1673, were upholstered, had wings to hide the sitter's face, and were used by priests. They had open arms like the *bergère* of the eighteenth century.

The *fauteuil* (an upholstered chair with open arms) was also used (Fig. 14.2c). *Gossips* were low-backed chairs which developed near the end of the period. Cane chairs were imported for the wealthy.

Storage Pieces

Storage pieces were large and elaborate and were frequently ornamented with Boulle marquetry (Fig. 14.2a). The cupboard, made as imposing as possible, was a symbol of status among the ladies. The bookcase cupboard was not just a collection of shelves but, rather, an imposing piece of furniture often with glass doors (glass had begun to be manufactured in large sheets). The *commode* became the most important piece of furniture, although the term was not used until the end of the period (Fig. 14.2d). It was heavy, with compass curves, ormolu, and marquetry topped with a massive marble top. The most important storage piece was the *armoire* (ar-mwahr′) (Fig. 14.2a), usually of ebony veneer with Boulle panels on the front. Some cabinets were set on stands supported by gilded caryatids. Coffers, or chests, which had been very popular in earlier periods for transporting goods, ceased to be used except by provincial people.

Tables and Desks

Tables were massive and many were gilded, inlaid, or of stone mosaic (Fig. 14.2e). Some silver tables were made by LeBrun. Tables generally had massive stretchers connecting the pillar or scroll legs. Marble, stone mosaic, or wood tops ornamented with marquetry were common. Small specialized tables were made in walnut with turned baluster (băl′-ŭs-tēr) legs and matching stretchers. The *cabaret* (kăb′-à-rĕt) table was the forerunner of the tea table. Console tables, decorated on three sides with a fourth side attached to the wall, began to be used (Fig. 14.2f); these were often surmounted by tall mirrors. The *bureau,* or writing table, which came into use about 1650, had drawers, was elaborately ornamented with marquetry or gilding, and was frequently surmounted by a mirror.

Beds

Beds were primarily the work of the upholsterer. As pieces of furniture they had no artistic value, but the wealth of the family was often marked by the richly draped embroideries and textiles that completely concealed the wood. Most beds had four posters, but the *duchesse* bed had only two rear posts with a tester (canopy) that ran the full length of the bed. The daybed was large enough to seat two or three people (Fig. 14.2g) and later became the settee (Fig. 14.2h).

Accessories

Accessories were numerous and consisted of mirrors with carved and gilded frames, torchères and gueridons to hold candles and candlebra, and small decorative objects, such

Figure 14.2d
This Baroque Boulle commode has ormolu mounts and a shell motif.

Figure 14.2e
This Baroque table, carved and gilded with a figured marble top, has pillar legs.

Figure 14.2f
This console Baroque table has the curved lines that foreshadow the Rococo Period.

Figure 14.2g
This Baroque daybed could seat two or three people.

as clocks, statues, and vases on pedestals. Tall clocks were also popular.

The French Régence (1700–30)

Historical Background

The French Régence was a transitional style, a reaction against the majestic formality of the Louis XIV Period that marked the change from a rectilinear to a curvilinear style. The features of the style are either modified Louis XIV forms or rudimentary Louis XV forms, and are not unique to the Régence; in fact, it is difficult to characterize Régence furniture. The Régence began fifteen years before the death of Louis XIV and lasted through the Duc d'Orleans' regency.

The death of Louis XIV released the court from its strict formality and turned its attention to luxury and comfort. More intimate forms of living demanded smaller homes with specialized rooms for music, conversation, and quiet activities, such as reading. Smaller, lighter, movable furniture was required. Home furnishings became a source of pride and even country dwellers began to demand specialized furniture for the interior. Curves were introduced (Fig. 14.3a), which softened the rectangular appearance of Louis XIV furniture.

Jean Antoine Watteau (wah-tō′) (1684–1721) the painter, was very influential in interior design. His charming, playful scenes of the shepherds and shepherdesses appealed to the aristocracy, and mirrored the spirit of the times. They were a complete reversal of LeBrun's sumptuous, formal style in the Baroque Period.

Interiors

The popularization of the decorative arts led noblemen and wealthy members of the bourgeoisie to ornament their homes in the new style. Richness was still a characteristic, but graceful, curved lines began to appear. Flat curved paneling with curved corners and ribbons and foliage embellishments became typical. Structures remained solid and heavy, but new curves introduced a playfulness, and the influence from the Orient added light-hearted motifs. The Régence so blended the styles of Louis XIV and Louis XV that it is impossible to divide them.

Furniture

Guilds

The *guilds,* which were in effect closed corporations, kept standards high. There were two important guilds, that of the *menuisier,* (the chairmakers) and that of the *ébénistes* (the cabinetmakers). Young boys of twelve or thirteen were apprenticed to a master for six years without pay, then became assistants if their work was satisfactory. After three to six years, an assistant submitted a piece of his furniture to a jury; if the work was satisfactory, he became a master. Duties were regulated much as in unions today: *ébénistes* and *menuisiers,* for example, were not allowed to carve furniture or make ormolu. Juries also inspected shops regularly, confiscating inferior furniture and imposing fines on the maker.

Cabinetmakers

There were two famous cabinetmakers during this period: *J. A. Meissonier* (meh-sō-nyeh′) (1815–91) and *Charles Cressent* (1685–1768). Meissonier was appointed designer to Louis XV, two years after the end of the Régence. He was the inspiration for Thomas Chippendale, and the originator of the Rococo style. Cressent, the greatest cabinetmaker of the period, was famous for the ormolu and chased metalwork on his furniture. In fact, he was fined three times for making the metal mounts for his furniture, because it was against guild regulations. Cressent, a student of Boulle, used floral ornamentation, cupids, garlands, and monkeys for his ormolu.

Chairs

Chairs were the first furniture pieces to reveal the change in style. They became lighter, easily movable, and more comfortable. Backs were lower though still straight (Fig. 14.3a). Cabriole legs were ornamented with a shell or acanthus leaf on the knee and stretchers disappeared or were Z–formed. Chairs were upholstered or caned and wood was natural walnut, or painted and gilded. The wooden

Table 14.5
Relationship of Important Furniture Periods to the French Régence Period

France	England	America
Régence 1700–30	Queen Anne 1702–14 Early Georgian 1714–50	Early American 1608–1720 Georgian 1720–90

Table 14.6
Characteristics of Régence Furniture

1. Carved or cabriole legs appeared.
2. Stretchers disappeared as period progressed.
3. Chair top rails and side rails became slightly curved.
4. Arms were set back.
5. Pieces were smaller and less bulky.
6. Design was less symmetrical.
7. Surface ornamentation increased and ormolu trim appeared.
8. Elegant, light cross banding and colorful exotic veneers were used.
9. Oriental influence appeared.

Figure 14.3a
A Régence chair with cartouche-shaped back, padded manchette, and ornamental carving, has the cabriole leg that was beginning to appear at this time; its arms are set back to accommodate the full skirts.

framework of the chair was visible and curved at the top. Arms, straight or scrolled, were set back to accommodate the ladies' full skirts. The square seats of the Louis XIV period lasted until about 1720, when they were replaced by curving seats.

Tables and Commodes

Free-standing tables no longer had cross-stretchers. They had baluster, pedestal, or cabriole legs with hoof or scroll feet (*à pied de biche*) (Fig. 14.3b). Elegant commodes of rare wood veneers with beautiful ormolu trim were typical of this style and remained massive and heavy (Fig. 14.3c). Straight lines were almost completely eliminated and cabriole legs were typical.

Figure 14.3b
A Régence table with bronze mask and bronze female heads at the corners.

Miscellaneous Pieces

Hinge-topped writing desks appeared, along with grandfather clocks. The sides of the Régence armoire were gracefully curved and covered with exotic wood veneers with cross-banding.

Régence furniture cannot be placed in a single category, for it is a combination of the Louis XIV and Louis XV styles. It is important as the forerunner of the Louis XV Period, rather than for the development of outstanding pieces.

Figure 14.3c
The front of this Régence commode with bronze masks and ormolu is ornamented with geometric marquetry.

The Rococo Period: Louis XV
(1730–60)

Historical Background

The reign of Louis XV was one of comfort and luxury for the nobility and the wealthy upper classes. Wars, poverty, and poor living conditions, however, contributed to the dissatisfaction of the lower classes and ultimately led to the French Revolution. Louis XV, interested in fashion, mistresses, and hunting and gambling, paid little attention to matters of state. The Rococo Period was characterized by frivolity and excessive luxury. Louis, a political failure, presided over an administrative system marked by confusion and corruption. The Church remained powerful, but religious belief declined and many high church officials led very worldly lives.

In spite of widespread censorship, philosophers, such as Voltaire (1694–1773) and Rousseau (1712–78) criticized society, government, and the Church. Newspapers and periodicals multiplied to satisfy the taste of a growing reading public and cafés became popular places to discuss current issues and ideas. Men began to question the political and social structure, while the wealthy indulged themselves in intimate dinner and theater parties, practiced social refinements, and collected Oriental art.

French artists, such as Watteau, François-Boucher (boo-sheh′) (1703–70) and Jean Honore Fragonard (fra′-gô′-nar′) (1732–1806), influenced design because Louis encouraged and protected the best artists. Women acquired greater freedom in this period, owing in part to one of Louis' mistresses, Madame de Pompadour, a woman of great culture and refinement, who had quickly learned court manners and then transformed the court itself. An educated woman, she commissioned paintings and furniture. She is the key to French taste during the period. This is the first period to be influenced by women and that influence is apparent in the size of furniture, its ornamentation, and the popularity of pastel colors.

Architecture

Architecture was affected least by the Rococo style. Symmetrical façades were simplified and ornamentation was restrained: buildings had simple moldings around large windows, delicate cornices, and wrought iron railings. Proportions were subtle and the design was graceful and light. Many modest mansions, châteaux and town hôtels were built, and they usually enclosed a private courtyard. The Petit Trianon, built as a retreat for Madame Pompadour, with its classical columns, simple proportions, and square plan, belongs in reality to the Neoclassical Period that followed.

Interiors

Interiors, the most important aspect of the Rococo style, were planned with intimate special-purpose rooms. The dining room, however, did not appear until the Louis XVI Period. The size and shape of rooms varied according to their function. Pastel painted panels with curved moldings replaced the marble and stucco walls of the previous period. Pastoral or mythological scenes, decorative chinoiseries (shēn-wäz-a-rē′), and/or Rococo ornamentation in low relief, often gilded, were placed asymmetrically within the panel. Wallpapers were popularized by the middle classes, who could not afford the ornate paneling, and flocked papers imported from England.

Parquet patterns continued to be popular for floors and were often covered with patterned carpets in soft colors. Fireplaces, the main source of heat, had richly ornamented mantles and the trumeau, or overmantle, combined paneling, a mirror, and painted ornamentation. Rich draperies blended with or matched upholstery fabrics.

Furniture

High-quality furniture is typical of the Louis XV Period, owing to government and guild control. The court and nobility demanded fine cabinetry and got it. The middle classes demanded simplified copies of the court styles, which will be discussed later as part of the French provincial styles.

The word rococo (ro-co′-co), a combination of the French words rocaille ("rockeries" or "grottoes") and coquille ("cockleshell"), is synonymous with the Louis XV style. Meissonier, who worked in the Régence Period, is credited with developing the style, for he published a book of designs that used the shell as an ornamental motif. The ornate furniture was light, graceful, and curved to fit the human body. Curved lines were particularly noticeable in chair backs and legs, commodes,

Table 14.7
Relationship of Important Furniture
Periods to the Louis XV Period

France	England	America
Louis XV 1730–60	Early Georgian 1714–50	Georgian 1720–90
	Middle Georgian 1750–70	

Table 14.8
Characteristics of Louis XV Furniture

1. Furniture was feminine, graceful, humanized in scale.
2. Emphasis was placed on curved lines, particularly for legs.
3. Cabriole legs had no stretchers.
4. Pieces were smaller, lighter, hence readily movable.
5. Walnut, mahogany, and fruitwood were used, as well as cane, rush, and straw.
6. Ornate ornamentation included carving, inlay, ormolu, painting, polychrome, gilding.
7. Many new pieces were introduced or made in quantity for the first time.
8. Pastel upholstery fabrics were used.
9. Motifs included assymetrical broken curves, flowers, twisted scroll, shells, singeries (monkeys), chinoiserie, musical instruments (violin, horn, tambourine), love symbols (cupids with bow, quiver, and arrows; burning hearts), wreaths, pastoral scenes, trophies (decorative arrangement of battle symbols), flowers and animals).

and textile patterns. There was an emphasis on asymmetrical balance rather than formal balance.

There were also many influences from the Orient and many French interpretations of Oriental designs. Oriental lacquer work was also imitated, and known as *Vernis Martin,* for the Martin brothers who excelled in it.

Many pieces of special-purpose furniture were developed or made in quantity for the first time. These pieces are still in use today, although in different styles, and seldom thought of as being an innovation of the Louis XV Period. Sofas, lunch tables, the drop-leaf desk, tall narrow chests of drawers, and many new kinds of game tables first appeared in this period. This resulted in great part from the growing importance of women and the desire to cater to their comfort. But, though women were catered to and treated with deference, they were not considered equal to men. Although there were a few exceptions, women had no direct political influence. They were treated with extreme courtesy, but were not highly regarded for their

intellectual capacities. The male was the superior sex who, in all his benevolence, treated women kindly but not equally; chivalry was still practiced and the strong always reached down to assist the weak. The deference of designers and craftsmen towards women during this period is not to be construed as a recognition of equal rights for women; on the contrary, this patronizing only reinforced the idea of male superiority.

Chairs

Chairs were easily moved and usually had padded arms set back from the front to accommodate women's clothing. Cabriole legs usually ended in a scroll foot (Fig. 14.4a), and there were no stretchers. Backs were curved to fit the body and the exposed framing was heavily carved. There were two important upholstered armchairs, the *fauteuil* (Fig. 14.4a) and the *bergère* (Fig. 14.4b). The *fauteuil* had upholstered arms that were open underneath; in the *bergère,* which was larger than the *fauteuil,* the upholstery enclosed the sides beneath

Figure 14.4a
This Rococo fauteuil with manchettes has cabriole legs with carved knees and a cartouche-shaped back.

Figure 14.4b
The upholstery on this Rococo bergère with manchettes and carved knees is attached with nailheads.

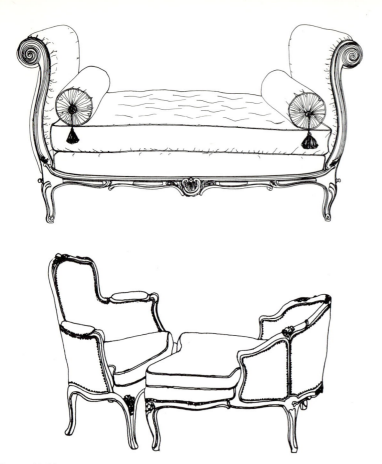

Figure 14.4d
A Rococo duchesse brisée of carved walnut: the chair is combined with an extended longue rest.

Figure 14.4e
A Rococo gilded console table with cabriole leg and shell motif.

the arms, and the cushion was loose. The *voyeuse* was a straddle chair, in which the sitter faced the chair back and rested his arms on the upholstered top rail. Upholstered armless sidechairs and cane kitchen or desk chairs were also used. The *cabriolet* was a small chair with a concave back and cabriole legs.

Sofas

The social life of the period made people vie with one another to have the most beautiful furniture and contributed to the development of many pieces, among them, several types of sofas. The *canapé* (Fig. 14.4c) was a small, two-seat sofa with an exposed frame. The *marquise,* a completely upholstered small sofa similar to a love seat or a wide *bergère,* developed to accommodate the wide skirts of the period. Many other types of sofas appeared. The *lit de repos* was a daybed, as was the *chaise longue,* an upholstered chair with a long seat for reclining. The *duchesse-brisée* was a chaise longue with a separate foot rest (Fig. 14.4d). The *confidante* had three seats attached to a single unit, with the two end seats smaller and separated by arms from the center section.

Tables

Tables were made for a variety of uses; they were simple and light and were finished on all sides so that they could be used anywhere in the room. These included the bedside table (*table de chevet*), the dressing table with drawers that opened to reveal a mirror (*table à coiffer*) the make-up table (*coiffeuse*), the serving table (*desserte*), a small table with a gallery (*bouillotte*), the game table (*table à jeu*), a sewing table (*tricoteuse*), and a table with several drawers (*petite commode*). There were no dining tables as yet, but plain, large round or trestle tables were used for eating and were completely covered with a cloth. Consoles, tables attached to the wall and having only two front legs, were numerous (Fig. 14.4e).

Desks

Many desks were developed in the Louis XV Period. The *bureau plat* (Fig. 14.5a), or table desk, which had developed earlier, became very popular and is still in use today in many offices. The drop-leaf desk (*bureau à dos d'âne*) was new with its slant top and absence of drawers. The rolltop desk (*bureau à cylindre*) was extremely popular (Fig. 14.5b) and the famous *bureau du roi* (king's desk) took nine years to finish. A small lady's desk, with a cabinet top and drawers with a drop front, was called the *bonheur du jour*.

Chests

The versatility of chests was discovered during the Louis XV Period, and the commode, a low chest of drawers, was the most typical (Fig. 14.5c). A framework of oak or pine was covered with veneers or marquetry panels, or portions of lacquered folding screens imported from the Orient. French lacquer or Vernis Martin often had an irridescent appearance. Other ornamental details included paintings, porcelain plaques, ormolu or ivory and mother-of-pearl inlay. The *semainier,* introduced in this period, was a tall narrow chest with seven drawers, one for each day of the week.

Cupboards

The *encoignure* was a corner cupboard and many were built into the room. The armoire continued to be used for clothing storage.

Beds

Beds, which usually had a canopy, were of two important types: the *lit duchesse* and the *lit d'ange* (angel bed). They were usually placed with one side against the wall and were painted white and green, blue, pink, or yellow. The *duchesse* bed (without posts) was covered by a large tester attached to the wall at one end: The angel bed had a smaller tester supported at the back by posts but with none in the front.

Accessories

Accessories were important and included plate-glass mirrors. Sèvres (seh'-ve) porcelain vases, portrait busts, *Celadon* (se-la-dō') vases from China, and Vincennes (vĭn-sĕnz') soft paste figurines and serving pieces. There were numerous mantle clocks in exotic animal shapes, wall clocks, and tall case clocks. Porcelain and marble candelabra and candlesticks were used, along with gilded wall sconces. There was also a wide variety of decorative boxes to hold writing and sewing materials, perfumes and cosmetics.

Textiles

Beautiful textiles in curvilinear prints or wavy stripes of silk brocade, damask and velvet, Aubusson tapestry, petit-point and needlepoint were fashionable. *Toile de Jouy* (twahl-de'shōō-wē') made by Christophe-Phillippe Oberkampf (1738–1815), was popular: it was a natural or white linen or cotton fabric hand-blocked in one color with pastoral scenes.

Cabinetmakers

Charles Cressent continued to work through this period, and was best known for the ormolu work on his pieces. The two most famous cabinetmakers of the Louis XV Period, Jean François Oeben (d.1765) and Georges Jacob (made Maître-Ébéniste, 1784) worked primarily for Madame de Pompadour.

The Neoclassic Style: Louis XVI (1760–89)

Historical Background

The Neoclassic Period began in 1760, fourteen years before the death of Louis XV. Louis XVI and Marie Antoinette, married at sixteen, were immature, inexperienced, and indifferent to people outside their court. They began their reign in a country which had already been rendered financially insolvent by the loss of its American colonies, the expense of its partici-

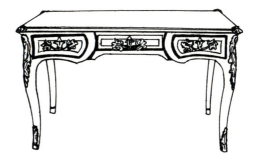

Figure 14.5a
A Rococo bureau plat with bronze mounts.

Figure 14.5b
This Rococo bureau à cylindre (or rolltop desk) has a bronze gallery, floral marquetry, and bronzes on the feet of the restrained cabriole legs.

Figure 14.5c
This Rococo commode has a bronze masque in the center, marquetry, ram's-head ornament at the top of the cabriole legs and scroll feet.

pation in the American Revolution, and widespread internal corruption.

France was divided into three classes: a small group of nobles who owned most of the land, the major source of wealth; a second, group, the clergy; and a third group, the bourgeoisie, composed of all other members of the society including merchants, professional men, artisans, farmers, and peasants. Only members of the third group paid taxes but only they had access to wealth through commerce. In actuality, the only nobles with great

Table 14.9
Relationship of Important Furniture Periods to the Louis XVI Period

France	England	America
Louis XVI 1760–89 (Actual reign 1774–89)	Middle Georgian or Chippendale 1750–70 Late Georgian or Adam 1770–1810	Georgian 1720

Table 14.10
Characteristics of Louis XVI Furniture

1. Classical influence was dominant.
2. Pieces were lighter, more feminine and delicate; scaled for human comfort.
3. Design was symmetrical, with straight lines and geometric forms.
4. More furniture was painted.
5. Cabinets and commodes were rectangular in shape.
6. Hardware on case pieces had drop ring handles framed by circular motifs.
7. Seating pieces were upholstered.
8. Legs were rectilinear, gaine (a pedestal leg which tapers towards the bottom), fluted, turned, and quiver-shaped, or spindle-shaped and fluted.
9. Chair backs were rectangular, square, oval, or medallion.
10. Bronzework was at its height, but metal mounts were subdued.
11. Ornamentation was delicate and graceful; it included marquetry and ormolu.
12. Motifs were derived from Greek sources and from nature: classical orders, fruit, flowers, laurel wreaths, garlands, ribbons and bowknots, mythological scenes, shepherds and shepherdesses, caryatids, trophies, hunting and music symbols, arabesques, running motifs such as guilloche, beads, leaf bands.
13. Furniture and architecture of rooms were designed to match.
14. Mahogany was the major wood, though some ebony was used.
15. Numerous innovations appeared, such as dining tables, combination secretary and chest-of-drawers, cylinder desks, mechanical furniture, and furniture with metal tops.

wealth were those at court. Many rural nobles were almost poverty-stricken.

It was during this time that the spirit of republicanism began to flourish and discontent with court scandals and the monarchy became universal. Thomas Paine's political tracts and the American Revolution further increased the spirit of nationalism. When in 1787 Parliament refused to ratify a land tax, the revolution was underway. From this point, resistance to and disrespect for both government and the monarchy developed. When the disastrous harvest of 1788 caused the price of bread to rise beyond the reach of even the middle classes, the people rebelled. The storming of the Bastille was followed by the execution of the monarch and his queen, and the ensuing reign of terror led finally to the execution of the revolutionary leaders by their followers.

Architecture

Architecture was the first art form to reflect the Neoclassical style. Buildings, stripped of all but pure Greek forms or Roman interpretations of them, had simple proportions and restrained elegance. In 1762, the architect Jacques-Ange de Gabriel (gah-brē-ĕl') (1698–1782) began to build the Petit Trianon as a *folie,* or summer château, for Madame de Pompadour, although historically it is more closely associated with Marie Antoinette. Gabriel was inspired by the delicate forms unearthed by the excavations of Pompeii and Herculaneum in 1748. Archaeology was a fashionable subject and by the time Louis XVI came to the throne, Greek architectural details and ornament, or Roman copies of them, had come to dominate interior and exterior design.

Interiors

Interior architecture and furnishings are the most important aspects of the Neoclassical style. Proportions were light and refined, retaining intimacy and charm, but with an emphasis on straight lines and geometric forms. Ovals, ellipses and circles, which were usually segmental, were the only curves used.

Wide and narrow panels of painted wood or plaster, covered with rich fabrics or wallpaper or filled with mirrors or paintings, were symmetrically arranged. Slim panels on the walls, called *boiseries* (carved woodwork picked out in gilt) were popular. Doors and windows had rectangular or elliptical panels over them and were symmetrically arranged, with flatter more austere moldings, such as the egg and dart. The *trumeau* (overdoor or overmantel paneling filled with paintings or mirrors) was frequently seen. Color prints and paintings were popular.

Ceilings were usually flat and decorated with simple classical motifs, with a large glass chandelier in the center. Rooms with high ceilings had an entablature crowning the paneling; rooms with low ceilings had a simple cornice or a cove.

Fireplaces continued to be used in every

room and had low marble mantels with rectangular mirrors over them. In the aristocratic homes full draperies of crimson or yellow damask, lampas or satin, were elaborately ornamented with swags, trimmings, and tassels. The feminine influence continued and life was less formal. Pale colors were popular. Hall floors were of marble while parquetry covered with Oriental or French carpets was used in other rooms.

Furniture

Furniture again came under the influence of architecture. It was symmetrical in both form and ornament, had light, refined proportions, and was scaled to the human body. Straight lines and geometric proportions replaced the curves of the Louis XV Period. The design of buildings, interiors, and furnishings of this period easily adapted to the rediscovered Greek style. Political upheaval and world unrest created a desire for stability, symmetry, and regularity in design.

Chairs and Settees

Chairs had rectilinear legs, fluted vertically or spirally or turned and quiver-shaped, with a cube at the top decorated with a rosette or acanthus leaf. The frame was ornamented with classical elements carved in a running pattern. *Manchettes* (padded arm rests) were typical and the arms ended in a volute (Fig. 14.6a, 14.6b). Armposts curved inward or were straight and baluster-shaped, and were usually joined to the top of the leg. Seats were semicircular, circular, or straight. Upholstered backs were square, rectangular, oval, or medallion-shaped. Chairs were painted Trianon gray or white, gilded, or left natural.

There were several types of chairs: the *fauteuil,* the *bergère,* the *voyeuse,* and the *open-back chair.* The *fauteuil* (Fig. 14.6b), with a square or medallion back that did not extend to the seat rail, was often slightly concave; a settee was often designed to match. The *bergère* (Fig. 14.6a) had closed sides and a loose-cushion seat, a square or gondola-shaped back, or was winged. Some *bergères* had caned backs and sides. The *voyeuse* was popular too. The open-back chair (Fig. 14.6c), used in dining rooms, had a caned or leather seat with a lyre back (Fig. 14.6c), or hoop back (the latter had uprights and top rail in one continuous arch).

The *canapé* usually had eight round, tapering legs, and the back, usually rectangular or

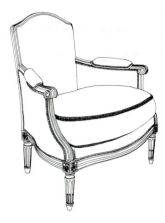

Figure 14.6a
This Neoclassic bergère has manchettes, upholstery attached with nailheads, and fluted legs round in section.

Figure 14.6b
A small Neoclassic chair with tapered back and turned and fluted legs.

Figure 14.6c
A Neoclassic strapwork-back chair with fluted column-like uprights and fluted legs.

occasionally curved, often did not extend to the seat rail. When it did, there was a seat cushion and the arms had closed sides.

There were four versions of the chaise longue, all of which were upholstered: a one piece version; a version made in two pieces of equal length, which looked like two small chaise longues; a version which was made of two unequal pieces, combining a bergère and

Figure 14.6d
The sides of this Neoclassic chest of drawers with marble top and brasses ornamenting the ends widen toward the back, and the legs are fluted and tapered.

Figure 14.6e
This Neoclassic period secrétaire (fall-front desk) is of mahogany veneer. Caryatids ornament the front, bronzes ornament the feet, and a brass gallery finishes the top. The lower columns are fluted.

Figure 14.6f
This Neoclassic secrétaire has Wedgwood plaques inserted into the upper portion, a brass gallery, a cylinder top, and fluted legs.

Figure 14.6g
A Neoclassic bureau plat.

a bench seat; and a three-piece version, which was two *bergères* with a stool between.

Commode

The commode assumed great importance in this period. It was usually rectangular (Fig. 14.6d), although occasionally crescent-shaped, and had a marble top. Underneath the top was a frieze, which often was a shallow drawer. The front was divided into three sections, with the center of each section made of elegant marquetry framed by a bronze molding. Sometimes doors concealed the drawers. Open mirror-backed shelves with a gallery were occasionally used at the corners to display china. The ornamentation of the front ignored the horizontal division of the drawers. The *chiffonniere* (ʃi-fɔ-ne), a five- or six-drawer commode first used in the Louis XV Period, had a brass gallery. The cabinet, which was intended to house collections of precious objects, was an item of furniture used only by the very wealthy.

Secrétaires and Desks

The *secrétaire* had a fall front (a drop lid) that concealed the interior shelves and drawers (Fig. 14.6e). The two lower doors also concealed drawers and compartments for valuables. The secrétaire frequently had a brass gallery top with a shallow drawer beneath, decorated like a frieze. Caryatids or fluted pilasters were used at the corners.

The rolltop or *cylinder-top desk* continued to be popular in this period (Fig. 14.6f). The top was often ornamented with Wedgewood plaques and a brass gallery, while stretchers connected the legs. The *bonheur du jour* was especially designed for a woman. It often had a white marble top and a brass gallery. Some had roll tops, but a pull-out shelf, a drop-shelf, or a drawer with a writing-board top were usual. The *bureau plat* remained the most popular office desk (Fig. 14.6g). It was a rectangular table with four fluted legs, often decorated with bronze mounts. The top was usually covered with Moroccan leather attached by a bronze frame. There were two or three shallow drawers beneath the top and small pull-out flaps.

Tables

Many tables used in the Louis XV Period continued to be made, except that the style changed (Fig. 14.6h). There were some innovations, however. The *bouillote* (bwa-lōte′)

table, used for various card games, was popular with the nobility. Small and circular and mounted on four round fluted legs, it was usually made of veneered mahogany, had a pierced bronze or brass gallery edge with a marble top, and a paneled frieze that was fitted with two small drawers and two pull-out candle slides. The *trictrac* (trik-trak) *table* was a backgammon table with a removable top that had one side covered with leather and the other covered with *baize* (a loosely woven fabric with soft filling yarns); inside was the backgammon board, and space for candles, dice, and counters.

The console table continued to be made and was usually supported by two legs, with a stretcher between the legs. It was either rectangular or shaped like a half-moon. Dining tables were first introduced in this period and followed the design of other tables.

Mechanical Furniture

Many items of mechanical furniture were developed during the Louis XVI Period, and the most popular was a chair which converted into a toilet. The mechanism of mechanical furniture was usually excellent.

Beds

Alcoves, still built in for some beds, were ornamented with symbols of love. The bed was usually painted soft gray or white and had matching bedspread, hangings, and upholstery (Fig. 14.6i). Legs usually tapered, with classical orders. There were several kinds of beds, the most common one being the angel bed, which had a low headboard and a lower footboard, only two posts, and a tester fixed to the back wall and ceiling that extended over part of the bed. The side draperies, which extended to the floor, were tied back. The *duchesse* bed was similar except that the tester extended over the entire length of the bed. The *polonaisse* (pɔ-lɔnɛ-ɛːzʹ) bed was placed lengthwise against the wall, and had a dome-shaped tester, made as part of the bed, and a headboard and footboard of equal height.

Cabinetmakers

George Jacob (zhah-cōbeʹ) founded a dynasty of cabinetmakers during this period. *Jean Henri Riesener* (1734–1806), a Parisian cabinetmaker of German birth and a pupil of Oeben, designed many pieces of furniture for Marie Antoinette. *Martin Carlin, Adam Weisweiler* made Maître-Ébéniste (1778), and *David Roentgen* (1743–1807) were also leading *ébénistes*.

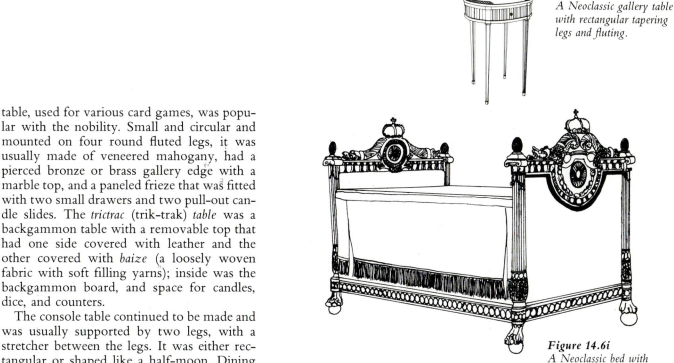

Figure 14.6h
A Neoclassic gallery table with rectangular tapering legs and fluting.

Figure 14.6i
A Neoclassic bed with fabric-covered ends and fluted supports.

Directoire (1795–1804)

Historical Background

The years after the French Revolution were chaotic. The contents of palaces and châteaux were destroyed, and the contents of Versailles auctioned off for pennies. When the guild system was abolished, there was no method of enforcing standards, so less careful methods of workmanship resulted. Many craftsmen, lacking clients during the Revolution, fled from France or turned to other forms of employment. Finally the National Convention appointed the painter *Jacques Louis David* (dahveedʹ) (1748–1825) and an *ébéniste, Jean Henri Riesener* (1734–1806) to decide what was worth saving from past designs. George Jacob (made Maître-Ébéniste, 1784), however, is credited with the creation of the Directoire style. Although he had been a court designer, through his friendship with David he remained a favored cabinetmaker. The designs of this period were a subdued, severe version of the Louis XVI style. Because the period is so short, however, there are few examples of architecture and interiors and comparatively few examples of furniture.

Interiors

The most important characteristic of Directoire interiors is their simplicity. Paneling continued to be used, but with little carving, although painted decoration and wallpaper were popular. Colors were gaudy when compared to those of the preceding period, with

Figure 14.7a
A Directoire chair influenced by Neoclassic design.

Table 14.11
Relationship of Important Furniture Periods to the Directoire Period

France	England	America
Directoire 1795–1804	Late Georgian 1770–1810	Georgian 1730–1800

stronger hues and contrasts. Monochromatic colors were used for many decorations. Walls were often draped with textiles, such as toile de jouy. Revolutionary subject matter replaced the rustic scenes and figures of the Louis XVI period. Broad stripes were popular, and damasks, silks, and brocades continued to be used. Windows were elaborately draped with valances surmounted by a military framework of lances and spears.

Furniture

The furniture of the Directoire Period represented a meld of Greek and Egyptian styles. Early pieces had simplicity and charm, but later examples were austere and weighty, and

Table 14.12
Characteristics of Directoire Furniture

1. Solid mahogany or painted wood was used.
2. Design was austere, severe, and heavier than that of the preceding period.
3. Forms were angular with few rounded corners.
4. Pieces were less well constructed than those of preceding periods.
5. Greek and Roman forms were used: throne chairs, tables and legs, *klismos* back, volute-shaped chair backs, outward-curving sofa arms, forward-curving front legs and backward-curving rear legs, curule legs with X–shaped supports, folding seat frames, straight-rising arm rests, claw-shaped legs, one-piece rear leg and upright.
6. Greek and Egyptian styles were blended.
7. Motifs included revolutionary symbols (liberty cap, tricolor, piled pikes, clasped hands, fasces [a Roman bundle of rods enclosing ax], cross, sword, spade and bonnet, spear, trumpets, drums), agricultural symbols (plough, flail, scythe, sheaves of wheat), Greek symbols (star, lyre, lozenge, vase, key, tripod, torches, swan), Egyptian symbols (lotus, lily, papyrus, palm, reed, lion's head [for chair and table supports], sphinx, pyramids).
8. Ornamentation was applied and inlaid and included carved legs and posts, friezes and borders, pilasters, metal mounts, and porcelain plaques.
9. Innovations included the méridienne, a day-bed for reclining.

Figure 14.7b
A Directoire chair with Roman curule legs.

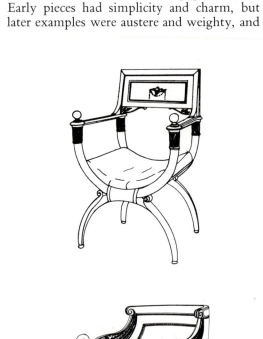

angularity replaced the slender, graceful forms of the Neoclassic Period.

Chairs and Seating Pieces

Chairs were influenced by Greek, Roman (Fig. 14.7b) and Egyptian motifs, while retaining some Louis XVI influence (Fig. 14.7a). The arm rest on the Directoire chair was straight and sometimes ended in a scroll or a swan (Fig. 14.7c). Upholstery was very tailored in most Directoire examples.

The *méridienne* was used by women for reclining. Upholstery was either horsehair, silk, velvet, or brocade.

Figure 14.7c
This Directoire Consulate chair is painted and accented with black and gold; its arms terminate in swans and its legs are fluted.

Tables and Case Pieces

Table tops of marble, alabaster, or *porphyry* (a type of marble) were supported by tripod or pedestal bases. Brass galleries were often used. The desk and chest were often combined into one piece and the most popular chest had three to four drawers. Commodes were also common. Most of these examples were simplified Louis XVI styles until late in the period.

The Empire Period (1804–15)

Historical Background

The French Empire Period was dominated by the personality of Napoleon Bonaparte. Thousands of French aristocrats had lost their lives during and following the Revolution. Foreign wars had drained the economy, and financial affairs had deteriorated. Napoleon's military victories brought him to power. In 1804 the French Senate voted him Emperor. In the coronation ceremony, Napoleon placed the crown upon his own head, and then crowned his beautiful wife, Josephine, whose charm had already captivated French society.

The glittering Napoleonic Era lasted only eleven years, but before it fell in 1815 the style to which it gave rise dominated all aspects of French art. The motifs of Napoleon and Josephine were seen in fabrics and ormolu. Napoleon, seeing himself as a modern Caesar, turned to the grandeur of ancient Rome as a source of inspiration and used the arts as instruments of his glorification. No art escaped Napoleon's influence. He dictated a majestic style and the Empire Period remains the only period in which a style did not evolve naturally, but was dictated by a monarch. Its influence was felt throughout the world.

Interiors

The Empire style is reflected in furniture rather than in interiors. However, during the Revolution many interiors had been destroyed and much reconstruction was necessary. *Charles Percier* (1764–1838) and *Pierre Fontaine* (1762–1853), government architects, became the official arbiters of the Empire style. Their work was severe and strongly influenced by Pompeii, as expressed in their plates from *Recueil de décorations intérieures*.

New rooms were larger than those of the Louis XVI Period. Many were square or had

Figure 14.8b
This Empire fauteuil, ornamented with carving and bronze mounts, reflects the Egyptian influence.

semicircular ends. Walls were plain painted plaster with a soft glossy finish, and were covered with wallpaper or with stretched or loosely draped fabric held with nailheads and tassels. Some walls had painted friezes. Cornices were often gilded. Ceilings were flat and some had stars or a center rosette. Marble mantles were supported by columns, pilasters, or caryatids. Columns and pilasters were used over doors, windows, and mantles. Windows and alcoves were elaborately draped with tassels and fringes. Valances, jabots, and swags were common. Floors, either parquet or black and white marble squares, were frequently left uncovered to preserve the antique look. Occasionally Oriental rugs were used. Harsh colors were common in fabrics and wallpapers and included greens, magentas, golds, browns, and blues.

Furniture

Empire furniture, like Empire interiors, tended to be austere and heavy. Many flat surfaces of mahogany were common until Napoleon banned the use of mahogany for royal furniture in 1810.

Chairs and Seating Pieces

Chairs had heavy, simple lines, often with saber legs (Fig. 14.8a) or legs, like those of Egyptian furniture, resembling the front and back legs of animals (Fig. 14.8b). A variation of the Greek *klismos* chair was also popular (Fig. 14.8c). Chairs often flared back at the top (Fig. 14.8d) and sometimes formed a scroll shape (Fig. 14.8d). Winged Egyptian heads were also popular (Fig. 14.8b).

The Roman curule form was frequently seen in stools (Fig. 14.8e). Sofas were also

Figure 14.8a
An Empire chair with saber legs and dolphin supports for arms.

Figure 14.8c
An Empire chair with klismos back and Egyptian-style ornamentation and lotus legs.

Figure 14.8d
This Empire sidechair has pierced Egyptian ornamentation on the rolled back.

Figure 14.8e
An Empire curule stool.

Table 14.13
Relationship of Important Furniture Periods to the Empire Period

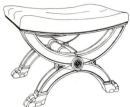

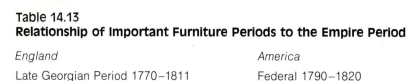

England	*America*	*Germany*
Late Georgian Period 1770–1811 Regency 1811–30	Federal 1790–1820	Biedermeier 1800–50

Figure 14.9a
A classical Empire sofa with swan and swags.

Figure 14.9b
This Empire table with three animal legs and feet on a pedestal is copied from a Pompeian example.

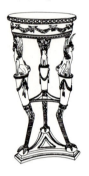

Figure 14.9c
An Empire table with columnar legs and marble top.

Figure 14.9d
This Empire dressing table has lyre-form legs with brass strings, candleholders, mirror, and flame finials.

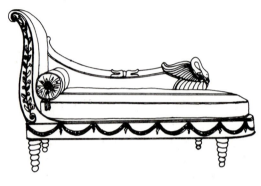

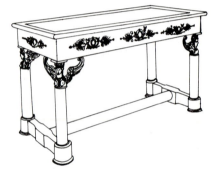

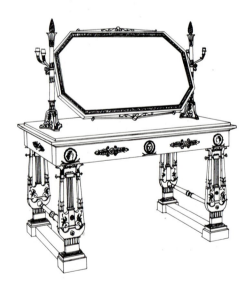

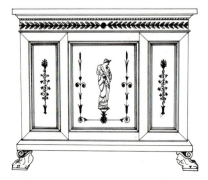

Table 14.14
Characteristics of Empire Furniture

1. Pieces were massive and heavy with stiff curves and monumental proportions.
3. Mahogany was used until 1810 when oak, beech, elm, maple and lemonwood were used.
3. Glued construction replaced dowels.
4. Pieces were symmetrical and uniform in appearance.
5. Ornamentation included heavy, flat surfaces of plain wood; bronze supports, inlay, mounts; silver inlay; some low-relief carving; gilding; extensive use of scrolled curve; few moldings.
6. Motifs included Napoleonic devices (wreaths of oak leaves tied with ribbons, bees, the letter *N*, swan, wreath encircled with stars), military symbols (tripods, victory emblem, eagle, helmeted warriors, Roman chariots, weapons), Egyptian symbols (palm leaves, sphinx, ancient heads with headclothes, lotus, lotus capitals, obelisks, pyramids, hieroglyphics), and classical symbols (caryatids, sirens, marine horses, griffins, horns of plenty, arabesques, acanthus leaves, garlands, husks, laurel leaves, heads of Hermes and masks of Bacchus, amphorae, chimeras.
7. Curved legs were used on chairs, with the front curving outward and the rear curving to the back like a saber (saber leg); or caryatid, chimera, turned, pillared, curving, or griffin shaped legs.
8. Feet were plain, paw, claw.
9. White marble was replaced by colored marble, malachite, mosaic.
10. Few new forms appeared: the sleigh bed (often made in one piece); a dressing table with drawer, mirror and candle holders; bookcases with glass doors; a pedestal-base round table, and a three-legged round table.

made along classical lines, with winged swans and garlands as ornaments (Fig. 14.9a).

Tables

Tables were the most characteristic item of furniture. Many had round tops. Some were almost direct copies of Pompeian examples, with three animal legs and feet (Fig. 14.9b). Others had rectangular tops of colored marble, malachite, glass, mosaic, and porcelain (Fig. 14.9c). Bedside tables, wash stands, tripods, and other small tables were used.

Figure 14.9e
An Empire dressing table with classical motifs.

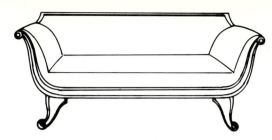

Figure 14.10a
A Biedermeier sofa with saber legs.

Case Pieces

The dressing table (Fig. 14.9d) with the lyre leg (with brass strings), candleholders, and a mirror, was a new form. Dressing tables also had classical motifs (Fig. 14.9e). These were all heavy pieces and very unlike any French designs before or since. Many case pieces did not have hardware on the drawers, so that surfaces were flat and uninterrupted. Handles, when used, were small rosette-shaped knobs or loose handles attached to round back plates.

Beds

Beds were made to be placed with one side against the wall and massive *sleigh beds* were very much in vogue. Many ladies' beds were draped, tent-like, in lavish fabrics. They were never placed in alcoves as had previously been the case.

Accessories

Mirrors had plain frames and several were used in each room. Some were large and free-standing and others were portable. Mantel clocks in bronze and marble, painted porcelain vases and gilded, antique bronzes, Grecian pottery, and torchères were popular.

Biedermeier (1815–48)

Biedermeier furniture, which originated in Austria and Germany, is included in this discussion for it was an outgrowth of the French Empire period. It was a forerunner of modern furniture and marks a time when the opportunity arose for functional furniture to develop in keeping with the new mechanization.

Historical Background

Biedermeier combined the French Empire style with traditional German peasant furniture design, resulting in a quaint and simplified style. The name arose from a comic character, Papa Biedermeier, a symbol of the middle class, who had definite ideas about comfort and contentment. The furniture and interiors will be the only aspects of this style discussed.

Furniture

Biedermeier furniture combined many Empire shapes and motifs with German painted peasant furniture. It was simple, with brass mounts, painted black or gold or ornamented with simple marquetry patterns. There was little carving, and classical lines were softened with curves influenced by peasant designs. Many small pieces were produced in local woods, with an occasional piece in mahogany. As in French Empire furniture, glue was substituted for more substantial joinery, and there were occasional structural problems.

Rooms were casually arranged, usually with a round pedestal table in front of a sofa surrounded on three sides by *klismos*-type chairs. The deep, rectangular sofa had a high back and ends, and was supported on saber or straight legs (Fig. 14.10a). Some sofas were curved to fit into niches. Chairs often had square backs with the lyre, swag, urn, or Prince of Wales feather, or a plain splat (Fig. 14.10b). Some had curved backs with saber legs and were simple and graceful (Fig. 14.10c). Upholstery was of striped velvet and silk, which frequently matched the draperies.

Most case pieces were practical and included sideboards, china cabinets, writing cabinets and drop-front secretaries (Fig. 14.10d). These had somewhat heavy classical columns, pilasters, and moldings. Commodes occasionally had lion's-paw feet and lion's-head pulls. The furniture was simple, and the best pieces compare favorably with eighteenth-century English designs.

Figure 14.10b
A Biedermeier chair with rounded back and tapered legs.

Figure 14.10c
A Biedermeier chair with saber legs and curule back.

Table 14.16
Characteristics of Biedermeier Furniture

1. It had classical lines, with some curves.
2. It was for the middle class rather than royalty.
3. It had painted ornamentation or simple marquetry to imitate carving.
4. It had many plain surfaces.
5. Medium size furniture with more functional pieces, such as chairs.
6. Types and pieces were limited.

Table 14.15
Relationship of Important Furniture Periods to the Biedermeier Period

France	England	America
Empire 1804–20	Regency 1811–30	Federal 1790–1820
	Victorian 1830–1901	Victorian 1820–1900
		Greek Revival or American Empire 1820–60

Figure 14.10d
A Biedermeier library table.

French Provincial (1650–1900)

Historical Background

French provincial furniture was the furniture of the landed gentry, the middle classes, and the weathier peasants. In addition, many nobles had châteaux or manor houses in which the ornate, fragile furniture of the period appeared out of place. The simpler French provincial furniture evolved to fill their needs. Rural craftsmen did not have fine tools or sophisticated skills, but they did have a deep sense of pride that resulted in the production of fine-quality, timeless furniture of local woods.

Because rural craftsmen continued to make styles long after they had ceased to be fashionable in Paris, provincial furniture is extremely difficult to date. French provincial furniture often combined styles from the French Renaissance through the Empire Period, with the Louis XV style the strongest influence because it was lighter and easier to fit into the small farmhouses. The Louis XIV style was too expensive and complicated to be copied by rural craftsmen, but it engaged public interest in fine furniture and inspired craftsmen to develop the necessary skills. Louis XVI styles were not widely copied because rural craftsmen could not reproduce its fine detailing but Louis XVI ornamentation was applied to Louis XV pieces. The cold and rectilinear Directoire and Empire furniture was seldom copied.

Architecture and Interiors

The typical country farmhouses were made of stone, with oak or hardwood frame, a centered chimney, and steeply pitched slate, board, or straw roof. Three-panel casement windows with shutters on each side were typical. The barn was placed under the house or beside it so that the warmth generated by the animals would help heat the house and that their care during inclement weather would be facilitated. This efficient and convenient arrangement is still common today.

At first there was just one room, where the family worked, ate, slept, and played. Gradually houses became larger, although the kitchen, with its open-hooded fireplace rising to the wood-beamed ceiling, remained the center of the house. Walls were of rough white plaster or, occasionally, paneled. Frequently they were stenciled to resemble wall-paper. Panel moldings were simple, with curved forms at the top and bottom of the frame. There were no cupboards, closets, or storage areas. For this reason, the armoire became the most important family possession and, in some provinces, was placed in a separate bedroom. Furniture was arranged around the walls so that it appeared to be part of the interior architecture. In colder areas, beds with wooden doors were built into the walls for warmth and for protection against the night air. Desks, a status symbol, indicated that the owner could read and write and were used by both the bourgeoisie and the landed gentry.

Furniture

There were five main styles of French provincial furniture, each associated with the province in which it was produced: Normandy, Provence, Burgundy, Brittany, and Alsace. Economic, social, and climatic conditions played an important role in the development of these furniture styles. The furniture was made of local woods, with ornamentation carved directly into the solid surface, which was then waxed.

Normandy

The province of Normandy, close to Paris and to the English Channel, was more strongly influenced by Louis XVI designs than any of the other provinces. Oak furniture was typical of the province, although some mahogany and ebony were imported. The nature-loving people of Normandy used delicate carved floral motifs such as the lilac, the elagantine, the marguerite, and the rose. Brass and copper locks and hinges were typical.

Provence

Provence, a wealthy southern province, was the gateway to Italy and the Orient, from which came bright textiles, lighter furniture such as ladder-back chairs and settees, and a greater diversity of forms. Delicate low-relief motifs included subtly curved baskets, vases, urns, and native flora, such as wheat sheaves, bunches of grapes, pine cones, and olive branches. The ornamentation was always subordinate to the furniture design. Pieces were made of walnut or painted with scrolls and mottoes.

Burgundy

Burgundy, almost in the center of France, was a wealthy cultural center. Farmhouses

Table 14.18
Characteristics of French Provincial Furniture

1. Designs tended to be simpler, less expensive to produce, larger, and heavier than those of the Parisian styles.
2. Featured curvilinear construction, restrained curved panels, small cabriole legs.
3. Styles were combined, with Louis XV more popular; change was slow.
4. Pieces had delicate or high relief carving into solid wood, few veneers; moldings important.
5. Cane backs and rush seats were common.
6. Simple metal mounts of steel and brass were used.
7. Stretchers were used.
8. Legs were spiral and baluster turned.
9. Feet were scroll, bun, ball.
10. Motifs included native flora, baskets, vases.
11. Comfort was important with many small seating pieces popular.
12. Tie-on cushions were used rather than upholstery.

were large, and furniture was massive. Burgundy craftsmen were proficient, producing deeply incised carving in conservative designs. Leather upholstery was often used.

Brittany

Brittany, an isolated northern province, had little contact with the outside world. The people lived rugged, seafaring lives. Nevertheless, their designs were often very original. Their strongly religious life was reflected in motifs taken from bell towers, altars, and windows. In addition, floral designs were common. Their oak furniture, made with turned parts, was sturdy.

Alsace

There was a greater variety of furniture produced in Alsace. It was also the most unusual because of its proximity to Switzerland and the Rhine region. It most closely resembled the designs of neighboring Burgundy. The rather massive style was symmetrical and typically had baroque ornamentation in marquetry panels. The double heart, the *fleur de lis,* and the two-headed German eagle were popular, along with bouquets of marguerites, tulips, carnations, roses, and vines. Often the legs were splayed. Polychrome ornamentation reflected the Swiss influence.

Armoire

The armoire, usually a dower gift, was the most important piece of furniture, usually made of oak or occasionally of walnut. There were two styles: one was tall with two doors (Fig. 14.11a); the other was in two parts with a recessed upper section (Fig. 14.11b). Brass, sometimes in punched patterns, was a common ornamentation. Hinges were often large with elaborately fretted *escutcheons* (ĕs-kŭch'-ŭw). Carving and occasionally painting was used in Provence and Alsace.

Other Storage Pieces

Storage pieces were numerous and graceful. Buffets sometimes resembled the armoire, with a recessed upper section and several doors in the lower part. Others were smaller, and were really narrow cupboards without

Figure 14.11a
A two-door French provincial armoire in the Rococo style.

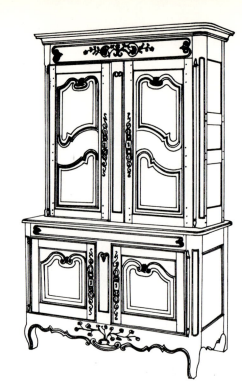

Figure 14.11b
A French provincial armoire with recessed upper section in the Neoclassic style.

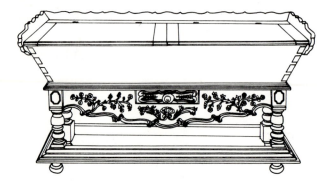

Figure 14.11c
A French provincial panetière.

Figure 14.11d
This French provincial chair has pierced splat and cabriole legs in the Rococo style.

shelves. Oak, walnut, and fruitwoods were typically used. The commode often had a bombé front with serpentine outlines and S–shaped doors. It might be four feet long and three feet high, with two or three drawers, or it might be about twelve inches across, set on high slender legs, and have several drawers.

Numerous small pieces of furniture were developed for convenience such as the *panetière* (a wall breadbox) or the dough-mixing table designed to double duty as a dining table (Fig. 14.11c). Tall case clocks were very popular and were the counterparts of the English and American grandfather clock.

Chairs

The first chairs were high-backed and straight. They gradually became light and graceful (Fig. 14.11d). They were made of local woods, had straight or cabriole legs often with S– or H–shaped stretchers, and ladder-, lyre-, or curved backs either upholstered or of cane (Fig. 14.11e). Rush seats were common. Upholstery usually had floral motifs. The *fau-*

teuil chair (Fig. 14.11f), was more common than the bergère (Fig. 14.11g).

Glossary

Armoire (ar-mwahr′). A large wardrobe.
Angel Bed. A bed with a partial canopy supported at the back by posts.
Baize (bāz). A loosely woven fabric with soft filling yarns.
Baluster Leg (băl′-ŭs-tẽr). A turned spindle used as a chair leg, stretcher, and so on, usually with a vase or urn shape.
Bergère (bair-gair′). An armchair with closed arms.
Boiserie (bwazri′). A carved panel used as woodwork, often gilded.
Bouillotte Table (bwa-lōte′). A small circular table with a gallery, used for games.
Bonheur du Jour (bən-ur′-du-zuːr). Small lady's desk with drop front and cabinet top.
Boulle Work. Inlay technique of Charles André Boulle, who used tortoise shell, brass, silver, or pewter.
Bureau à Cylindre (būr-o′-ă-silē′-dr). Roll-top desk.
Bureau du Roi (būr-o′-du′-rwa′). The king's desk, which took nine years to make.
Bureau Plat (būr-o′-plă). Table desk.
Cabriole Leg (kab′-rē-ōl). A convention-alized wooden animal leg with a knee, ankle, and foot that curved outward toward the knee and in again in an S–shape.
Cabriolet Chair (kab-rē-ə-lā′). A small chair with concave back and cabriole legs.
Canapé (kan′-ə-pē). A sofa with an exposed frame for two people.
Caquetoire (kăke-twa′). A conversation chair with the seat wider in front than in back and the arms curved inward from front to back.
Celadon Vase. A Chinese porcelain vase of a light grayish-green color.
Chinoiserie (shēn-wāz-a-rē′). French versions of Oriental designs.
Coffer. A small chest for traveling.
Coiffeuse (kwa-fyrz′). A make-up or dressing table used in the Rococo and Neoclassic Periods.
Columnar Leg. A leg turned to resemble a column.
Commode. A low chest of drawers or cabinet.
Console Table. A table with two front legs which was attached to the wall.

Cylinder-Top Desk. A rolltop desk.

Delft Tile. A blue glazed tile with a white background made in Holland.

Desserte. A small serving table or sideboard.

Dolphin. A sea mammal used as an ornamental detail.

Duchess Bed. A bed without posts, with a large canopy extending over the entire bed and attached to the wall at one end.

Duchesse-Brissée (dū-chess′ brē-ṡa′). A chaise longue with a separate foot rest.

Ébéniste (eb-e-nēst′). A "worker in ebony," a term used to designate a master cabinet-maker.

Encoignure (ākan-ūr′). A corner cabinet.

Escutcheon (is-kach′-an). A decorative plate for a keyhole, knob, or drawer pull.

Fauteuil (fotœːj). An armchair open underneath the arms.

Flemish Scroll Foot. A scroll ending to an S– or C–shaped leg.

Fleur de Lis (flard-al-ē′). A conventionalized iris.

Flocked. Finely powdered wood which was adhered to the surface with glue.

Foliated Scroll (fō′-lē-at-ed). Gothic ornamentation using flowing leaves.

Folie (fo-lē′). A pseudo ruin in the classical or Gothic style.

Gallery. A metal or wooden rail around table edges, tops of desks, and so on.

Gobelins (gŏb′-uh-lĭn) A tapestry factory that became an art-producing factory under Louis XVI.

Le Grande Siécle (le grãːd sjɛkl). The Louis XIV or Baroque Period.

Griffin (grĭf′-ən). A mythical animal with the body of a lion, and the head and wings of an eagle.

Gueridons (geridɔ̃). Elaborate candlesticks.

Guild. An organization whereby cabinet-makers were regulated, such as a union today.

Hôtel (otel). A townhouse.

Lacquer. An Oriental finish, very shiny, made from the resin of the lac tree.

Lit de Repos (lē-də-rəpo′). A daybed.

Maître-Ébéniste (mā′-tr-eben-ēst′). A master cabinetmaker.

Manchette (mã-shet′). Padded arm rest.

Marquetry (mär-ka-trē′). The insertion of materials into a veneer to make a pattern.

Marquise (mär-kēz′). An upholstered small sofa with closed arms.

Menuisier (mənyizje). A craftsman who made furniture out of solid wood.

Méridienne (meridjēn). A sofa with one end higher than the other.

Needlepoint. A cross-stitch embroidery on heavy canvas.

Ormolu (or′-ma-lü′). Sometimes spelled or-moulu, a gilded bronze applied to furniture to prevent it from pulling apart and as ornamentation.

Palmette (pal-met′). A palm-like ornament.

Panetière (pan-trē′). A French provincial dough box.

Parcel Gilt. Partly gilded.

Parquetry (pär′-ka-trē). An inlaid wooden floor.

Petite Commode (pet-ēte′ kə-məd). A small table with three drawers.

Petit Point (pet′-é pwē′). A very fine needlepoint.

Pied de Biche. Scroll leg or hoof foot.

Polonaisse Bed. A bed placed lengthwise against the wall, with a dome-shaped tester and a headboard and footboard of equal height.

Porphyry (por′-f(ə)-rē). A type of marble.

Putto. A young boy similar to a cupid.

Ram's Head. The head of a ram used as an ornamental detail.

Rinceau. Scroll ornamentation.

Rocaille. A word meaning "rockeries" or "grottoes," from which the word Rococo was developed.

Rosettes (rō-zet′). A word meaning little roses.

Satyr Mask (sāt′-er). A part-animal, part-human figure.

Secrétaire (sək-re-tair′). A desk.

Semainier. A very narrow seven-drawer bedroom chest.

Singeries (sēzri′). A decorative detail combining the monkey in human activities, often combined with chinoiseries.

Sun King. Louis XIV.

Table à Coiffer (tabl-a-kwa-fer′). A dressing table.

Table à Jeu (tabl-a-Zɸ′). A card table.

Table de Chevet (tabl-de-shə′-vā). A night table.

Toile de Jouy (twal-de-shoo-wē′). A cotton textile hand blocked in one color on a white or cream background.

Tortoise-Shell. The back plates of a sea turtle flattened and joined together under pressure and heat; used as inlay by Boulle.

Trictrac Table (trik′-trac). A game table for backgammon.

Tropheries. A carved, painted or inlaid ar-

Figure 14.11e
This French provincial sidechair has cabriole legs and cane seat and back in the Rococo style.

Figure 14.11f
A French provincial fauteuil, with upholstery attached with nailheads, manchettes, and cabriole legs.

Figure 14.11g
This French provincial Neoclassic bergère was less common than the fauteuil.

rangement of flowers, musical instruments, spears or weapons, and so on.

Trumeau (trū-mō′). Overdoor or overmantel paneling filled with paintings or a mirror.

Vernis Martin (vair-nē′ mar-tē′). A type of imitation Oriental lacquer developed by the Martin brothers.

Vitrine (ve-trēn′). A glass-fronted curio cabinet.

Voyeuse. A conversation or straddle chair in which the sitter faces the chair back and rests his arms on the upholstered top rail.

Wainscot. A wooden lining applied as paneling to walls.

Bibliography

Aronson, Joseph. *The Encyclopedia of Furniture.* 3rd ed. New York: Crown Publishers, Inc., 1965.

Bajot, Edouard. *Encyclopédie du meuble du XV siécle jusqu'à nos jours.* Paris: C. Schmid, 1901–9.

Blunt, Anthony. *Art and Architecture in France, 1500–1700.* Baltimore: Penguin Books, 1954.

Boger, Louise Ade. *The Complete Guide to Furniture Styles.* Rev. ed. New York: Charles Scribner's Sons, 1969.

Cooper, Douglas, ed. *Great Private Collections.* London: Weidenfeld and Nicolson, 1963.

Gebelin, François. *The Châteaux of France.* New York: G. P. Putnam's Sons, 1964.

Goodwin, P. L., and H. O. Milliken. *French Provincial Architecture.* New York: Charles Scribner's Sons, 1921.

Guerber, A. *A Short History of France.* New York: W. W. Norton & Company, Inc., 1946.

Hayward, Helena, ed. *World Furniture.* New York: McGraw-Hill Book Company, 1965.

Hickley, F. Lewis. *A Directory of Antique Furniture.* New York: Crown Publishers, Inc., 1953.

Hourticq, L. *Art in France.* New York: Charles Scribner's Sons, 1917.

Kimball, F. *Creation of the Rococo.* Philadephia: Philadelphia Museum of Art, 1943.

Longnon, H., and F. W. Huard. *French Provincial Furniture.* Philadephia: J. B. Lippincott Company, 1927.

Pegler, Martin. *The Dictionary of Interior Design.* New York: Crown Publishers, Inc., 1966.

de Ricci, S. *Louis XVI Furniture.* London: Wm. Heinemann Ltd., 1913.

Verlet, Pierre. *The Frick Collection.* New York: Whittenborn, 1956.

———. *Le Style Louis XV.* Paris: 1942.

Viaux, Jacqueline. *French Furniture.* New York: G. P. Putnam's Sons, 1964.

Viollet-Le-Duc, Eugene Emmanuel. *Dictionnaire raisonné du mobilier français de l'époque carlovingieen à la Renaissance.* Paris: Morel, 1858.

Watson, F. J. B. *Louis XVI Furniture.* London: B. T. Batsford, 1960.

English furniture styles evolved as an expression of the artist's creativity rather than as an outgrowth of the needs of the user. Each designer-artist was encouraged to express his individual preferences through competition with other designer-artists and by improving upon, or being influenced by, earlier fashions. The political or religious fortunes of the English rulers who supported these artists and designers were also significant in the advancement or retardation of particular furniture styles. For example, Oliver Cromwell forbade ornamentation, but with the restoration of the monarchy and the ascent of Charles II to the throne, furniture became highly ornamented and reflected French influence. English designs inevitably reflected the religious or political trends of their times as well as the creativity of their designers.

These artisans who served as designers to the king or queen were not exclusively in the service of the monarchy, as artisans in France had been; they served other clients, but to be able to add "Designer to His Majesty, the King," or "Her Majesty, the Queen," was very beneficial and deemed an assurance of quality.

Transitional Periods (1485–1603): Tudor (1485–1558) and Elizabethan (1558–1603)

Historical Background

The Renaissance came late to England. At the close of the fifteenth century, Henry VII, the first Tudor monarch, came to the throne by right of conquest. The most important monarch during the Tudor Period, however, was Henry VIII (1509–54), a well-educated man who enjoyed jewels and rich clothing.

The period was a time of royal pomp and pageantry. Elaborate garments encrusted with jewels were common at court, although manners were rough and boisterous. The contrast between rich and poor was extreme; however, medieval modes of living were thrust aside and a new class of wealthy merchants was developing and the middle class was growing. The power of the church decreased with the dissolution of the monasteries by Henry VIII between 1536–39, and it lost control of education, politics, social services, secular life, and its land—the release of which stimulated domestic building and created a new class of landowners, particularly between 1558–1603.

During this period merchandise was sold at weekly markets and semiannual fairs. Guilds, similar to modern trade unions, gained in strength for craftsmen of all kinds, although most were more interested in selling their wares than in maintaining high standards of workmanship. The printing press had made more books available, but illiteracy was still widespread among the lower classes.

A surge of creative energy was released when Elizabeth came to the throne. After the defeat of the Spanish Armada in 1588, England controlled the seas, and began a period of expansion and increased foreign trade. Sir Walter Raleigh, Sir Francis Drake, and Captain John Smith were involved in exploration and colonization with monetary gain as its purpose. The English people began to demand a greater voice in government and more freedom and independence, as evidenced by the Puritan movement. It was also a time of cultural development and the golden age of English literature.

By the end of the sixteenth century there were about four million people in England. Most of them lived in the country, although there was already a movement toward the towns. London, an incredibly dirty city by today's standards, was said to be the cleanest city in Europe, but raw sewage ran down the centers of the streets and perfumes were used liberally by the wealthy to cover the stench. Plague was common, even in the smaller towns.

Tudor Period (1485–1558)

Architecture

The taste of the English people was conservative. After Henry VIII's break with the church, Italian Renaissance influences decreased, and Gothic styles, particularly the perpendicular style, which dominated English architecture from 1377 to 1485, were modified and very intricate patterns were combined with new forms in a distinctly English fashion. This style was noted for large windowed spaces, by slender vertical lines perpendicular on moldings and ornamentation, and by tracery (Fig. 15.1e). The Tudor Gothic style was characterized by the use of a flatter arch, called

Table 15.1
Relationship of Important Furniture Periods to the Tudor and Elizabethan Periods

England	Italy	Spain	France
Tudor 1485–1558	Renaissance 1400–1600	Renaissance 1400–1650	Renaissance 1485–1643
Elizabethan 1558–1603			

the *Tudor* or *four-centered arch,* plainer vertical windows, and brick, which replaced stone as the standard building material.

For the first time, there was a concern for human scale and an interest in the exterior of a building; more secular buildings, such as hospitals and schools, were built by the state, rather than the church. Houses of *half-timber* construction (in which a timber framework is filled in with brick, stone, plaster), *wattle-and-daub* (a mud or clay coating over a screen of interlaced wooden rods), brick, and stone replaced the *crenellated* (notched-parapet) castle. Half-timber construction was an early version of prefabrication: the framework was built on the ground, the timbers numbered (with Roman numerals) and raised to position, and then the filling added. The upper stories overhung the lower ones to protect them from dripping water, to protect passersby from slops thrown from the upper windows, and to add more space.

With the discovery of gunpowder, fortified castles were no longer practical and the square country house, built around an inner courtyard, evolved. These had larger glass windows divided into triangular panes or *lights* with lead *mullions* (dividers). Polygonal bay windows, with built-in window seats, and *oriel* windows were common. The second-story oriel window was supported by underbracing or by a *corbel* (bracket). Beautiful grounds and gardens surrounded the country house. Palaces provided a new standard of living, different from castles. When Cardinal Wolsey built Hampton Court in 1514, he required five hundred servants to take care of it, forty-six of whom attended to his personal needs. Italian Renaissance motifs were popular and Italian craftsmen were employed to do the palace ornamentation. Doorways and fireplaces utilized the Tudor arch. Brick was frequently used decoratively, as in the criss-cross (*diaper*) pattern. Chimneys, a Tudor innovation, were tall and decorative, with each one having an individual design.

Gatehouses were an important feature of palaces and great houses. These tall brick or stone structures were usually flanked by octagonal shafts at the four corners and had an oriel window above the main entrance arch.

Henry VIII, encouraged by Cardinal Wolsey, invited to his court foreign scholars, craftsmen, and artists, who brought new influences and designs. English buildings were somber and vigorously individual, and lacked the symmetry and restraint of their foreign models.

Interiors

Before the Tudor Period, all household activities had taken place in an open, drafty, all-purpose great hall which had a fire in the center of the room and a hole in the roof for the smoke to escape. During the Tudor Period, however, smaller rooms off the great hall began to appear, and simple fireplaces of terra-cotta or brick, surmounted with a Tudor arch, were built into the walls. The great hall remained an important room, however: large and rectangular, it had wooden partitions at one end, behind which was the *screens passage,* a space that separated the kitchen and kept drafts from entering. Above this area was the *minstrels' gallery,* where the musicians played. Banners, arms, and armor decorated the walls.

One of the most beautiful characteristics of early Tudor interiors was the *fan-vaulted* ceiling, sometimes ornamented with *pendants* (elongated crosses which hung down), and *filigree,* a delicate openwork design cut in wood, stone, or metal.

The *hammer-beam truss,* the typical domestic roof, was composed of massive beams which projected horizontally and were connected by arched Tudor braces. Smaller rooms frequently had a plain timber support system. Flat plaster ceilings were first used about 1500. At first plaster was used only between the beam supports; later it covered the beams. A decorative network of geometrically patterned ribs was the usual design, with pen-

Table 15.2
Characteristics of Tudor Furniture

1. Fine-grained oak, radially cut to prevent warping was the chief wood; it was difficult to work.
2. Design was utilitarian, rectilinear, crude, and boxy; comfort was not particularly important.
3. Pieces had low stretchers to keep rushes on floor.
4. Construction was simple: panel and frame with mortise and tenon joints held by wooden pegs.
5. Pieces were painted for protection against vermin, smoke, and weather.
6. Carving was rough: Gothic tracery, linenfold, chip carving, romayne work, Tudor rose, lozenge, medallion.
7. The chest was the most important item of furniture.
8. Chairs were rare, and indicated owner's status.

Figure 15.1a
A joined Tudor chair with linenfold carving.

dants often added at the main intersections of the ribs. Between the plaster ceiling and the wainscoting there was often an ornamented band called a *frieze,* an Italian Renaissance influence.

Well-seasoned oak paneling and plaster were first used as insulation during the Tudor Period. Rectangular panels were placed in a framework of long horizontal rails and short vertical pieces. A *linenfold* pattern (relief carving resembling folded linen) was typical (Fig. 15.1a). Floral carving and *romayne work* (carved heads or medallions encircled by vines in the Italian style) (Fig. 15.1b) were also used. Often the designs were picked out in red and gold, which has since worn away. Paneling provided the main wall ornamentation, for furniture was sparce and paintings were not hung on the wall until the seventeenth century. Brilliantly colored tapestries or painted cloths (a less expensive substitute) were in great demand in the homes of the wealthy for they were decorative and also added warmth.

Tudor floors were of stone or clay on the ground level and were covered with loose rushes sprinkled with sweet herbs (to mask odors). The upper layer of rushes was changed occasionally but the lower ones remained on the floor for as long as forty years. Upper floors were of wood and were left uncovered.

The kitchen in the great house was large and separated from the other rooms. Food had to be prepared for seventy to eighty people at each meal, making a huge fireplace necessary. The fireplace usually had a Tudor arch.

Corridors were unknown; rooms led one into the other. Staircases were unimportant and of the *newel* type: spiral stairs that wound around a central newel or post. They had narrow, poorly lit stone or oak steps. Some staircases were on the outside, a tradition carried over from earlier periods.

Furniture

Furniture was scarce in the Tudor Period and fine possessions were the prerogative of the rich. Until about the middle of the sixteenth century, pieces were boxy, crude, and generally painted for protection from vermin, smoke, and weather. Oak was the most widely used wood, but was difficult to work with the methods and tools of the time. Conversion of oak logs to planks was done on the spot since the trees were so large.

Seating Pieces

Chairs were rare and uncomfortable. Often the only chair in the house was the *chair of the estate,* which was used by the master of the house as a symbol of his authority (Fig. 15.1a). Sometimes a slightly smaller version was used by his wife. (In fact, the word *chairman* developed from this use.) Chairs were sturdy and virtually immovable. They were placed on the dais in the great hall, behind the *table dormant,* and the *cloth of the estate* was hung behind the chairs. Chairs were usually of the *wainscot* va-

Figure 15.1b
This Elizabethan caquetoire has a low stretcher, a high narrow back, a romayne medallion carved in the center of the back, curved arms, and a seat wider in the front.

Figure 15.1c
A Tudor slab-ended stool.

riety, also called *joined* or *box* chairs (Fig. 15.1a). They were made by a joiner (rather than by a carpenter), who used the panel and frame technique, with the back of the chair looking like a wainscot panel. These box chairs often had a storage compartment under the seat. As the period progressed, the solid panels underneath the seat and arms were opened up and low stretchers were added to brace the legs.

The *caquetoire* chair, derived from the French gossip's chair, was lighter than the wainscot chair and had a seat narrower at the rear, a tall, narrow, carved panel back, arms that curved inward from the front to the back, and stretchers to brace the legs (Fig. 15.1b). *Lozenge* (Fig. 15.1d) or diamond-shaped

motifs and romayne work ornamented the back.

The *curule* or X–chair was derived from ancient Roman models. Decorative nailheads were often used along the edges of the frame and a medallion was placed at the center of the X in front. A *finial,* or terminating knob, finished the armrest.

Upholstery was unknown, but small cushions were used on seats. The triangular seat, or *thrown* chair (so named because its parts were turned on a lathe), was first made during this period, but became more popular later, during the Elizabethan Period. These chairs were made by turners who fitted the members of the chair into sockets.

Stools were the most common seating pieces and early ones had slab or simple board ends (Fig. 15.1c). Window seats were built in, with under-seat storage, and benches (a long version of the slab stool) fixed to the walls. The settle (Fig. 15.1d) developed from the window seat: it included a storage area and its high back provided protection from drafts.

Chests

Chests were generally used for seating as well as for storage and were the most numerous pieces of furniture. As elsewhere, they were used as luggage and as portable furniture. Early chests were crude, made of planks held by iron bands pinned or nailed together. These were gradually replaced by panel and frame chests made by a joiner. Elaborately carved panels were typical (Fig. 15.1e). Sometimes smaller boxes were placed inside and the front panel of the chest opened outward for convenience. This led to the development of the chest of drawers in the next century.

Tables

The *table dormant,* used by the master of the house and his family, stood on a dais at one end of the room. The master and his guests sat with their backs to the wall, so conversation was almost impossible (Fig. 15.2a). Servants sat at trestle tables, which could be stacked out of the way when not in use. These tables consisted of a large board that rested on two trestles or uprights usually linked by one or two stretchers held in position by removable oak wedges (This is how *board* came to mean a person's food supply). By the middle of the Tudor Period, the trestle table was replaced by a table with legs and stretchers, with the latter used to keep the feet off the cold, damp, rush-

Figure 15.1d
This Tudor settle has a storage compartment inside the seat and ornamental lozenges carved on the back.

Figure 15.1e
A Tudor chest with elaborately carved panels with Gothic tracery designs.

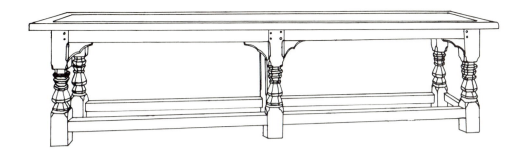

Figure 15.2a
A table dormant with low stretchers from the Tudor Period.

Figure 15.2b
This low-hutch Tudor table has linenfold carving on the front and sides.

covered floor. The *draw table,* which developed about the middle of the century, had layers so constructed that the lower leaves could be pulled out at each end and the upper portion would drop down between them, doubling the table area; the leaves were supported by runners. Another space saver was the chair table, with a rectangular or circular back hinged so that it folded down horizontally over the arms to make a table. A third space saver was the hutch table (Fig. 15.2b), a serving table with a cupboard that was placed against the wall and used as a side table.

Storage Pieces

The *aumbry,* a piece used only in the Tudor Period, was designed for food storage and had pierced carving for ventilation on the front (Fig. 15.2c). The name was derived from the alms box which was used in churches to collect food for the poor.

The word *cupboard* was used in this period to designate a storage unit for food, or a piece used to display silver serving pieces, or a locked piece in which silver was kept. Cupboards usually had shelves and occasionally doors (Fig. 15.2d).

The *press* was a tall storage unit used for storage of linen or clothing. Full-sized desks had not developed, but there were some portable desks used for the storage of expensive books and writing materials.

Beds

Beds were the most costly item in the home, largely because of the expensive textiles

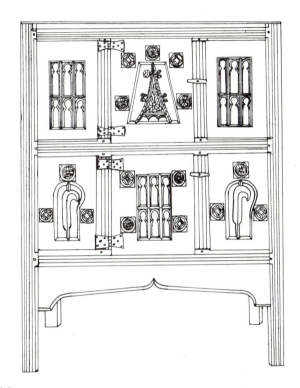

Figure 15.2c
*A Tudor aumbry with pierced openings for ventilation, a wooden latch, an **A** design in the front, and the Prince of Wales feather in lower sections.*

Figure 15.2d
This Tudor cupboard has arcading on its front panels and foliated scrolls.

used to cover them. They were built against the wall and were a structural part of the room. Some had three wooden sides and curtains on the fourth, while others had a canopy that hung from the ceiling. Later headboards were added. All but the very poor owned feather mattresses.

Elizabethan Period (1558–1603)

Architecture

Domestic building increased during the Elizabethan Period and the first modern homes were built for both pleasure and comfort. The classic H–plan or E–plan (said to be in honor of the Queen) was used and the houses had carefully designed, simple exteriors with a central entrance and two side wings. Cut stone, brick, timber, and plaster, oak, and large windows were typical of Elizabethan dwellings. The style of building was determined by the owners of large estates as they followed the models of the Italian designer *Andrea Palladio* (pahl-lah′-dee-ō) (1518–80). Because these designs had been filtered through Holland and Germany, they were more robust than the originals and lacked Palladio's purity and grace. However, they were charming and well-suited to the Elizabethan Period. One of the more important architectural features was the emphasis on symmetry.

Houses were built by master masons, carpenters, and craftsman, usually working on the contract system, which paved the way for the development of trained architects in later periods.

Townhouses were still built using half-timber construction, but because the building of the navy had depleted the forests, the use of stone and brick increased.

Many Englishmen built great houses in the hope that the Queen would visit during her summer travels. A mansion was required to house her entourage of several hundred people. The expense of this entertainment almost bankrupted many hosts. These great houses, unlike the timber-framed houses in town, were quite different from those of the Tudor Period. Symmetry was achieved by matching windows, gables, and chimneys on each side of the house. Classical features were added for decoration. Two wings were added to the central section to produce an H–shaped house; this was gradually extended into an E plan with two side wings, a center entrance, and a porch with classical columns and capitals.

Interiors

Houses were more compact and symmetrical inside as well as out. Oriel and bay windows were still used and *bow* or semicircular windows were added, but glass panes were still small. Inside classical columns and pediments began to surmount doorways and fireplaces. The great hall, declining in importance as special rooms developed, was now only one story, served as an entry rather than as a main room, and was frequently replaced by two large reception rooms; the door was placed in the center instead of behind the screens. Dining rooms, private rooms, and chambers were added but the greatest change was the popularization of the *long gallery,* which had appeared during the Tudor Period though it was not widely adopted until the Elizabethan Period. The long gallery extended the length of the house and the outside and end walls had a series of windows with cushioned window seats. Some galleries were over 170 feet long, and had two or three fireplaces on the long inside wall. The long gallery was used for family gatherings, entertainment, leisure activities, and exercise in winter.

Fireplaces became a focal point of the interior. They were very large—often too large for the room—and made of stone, plaster, or marble. They were flanked by pilasters with *strapwork* carving above. Strapwork, a design of interlacing, curving bands that formed arabesque patterns and resembled a plaited-leather design, was combined with caryatids, animals, fruit, scrolls, and classical elements to create a splendid effect.

It was during the Elizabethan Period that the stairway became an object of beauty and importance in the house. There were two types: the *dog-legged* stairway had short flights of ten steps, with each flight flanking the preceding one, and wide landings to accomodate the full skirts; the *openwell* stairway had short flights that progressed at right angles to one another. Hand rails were mortised into large posts (newel posts) at the top and bottom and were surmounted by finials in fantastic animal shapes or human forms, urns or balls. Both stairways had smaller turned posts, called *balusters,* between the newel posts.

Walls were paneled but often had large panels divided into five small ones with intricately carved or inlaid designs. *Double arcading,* a series of adjoining arches with supporting columns, was also used (Fig. 15.3d). Paneling was wider and no longer carried to the ceiling, but covered three quarters of the wall height where plaster or a wooden frieze met it. Rich vermilion, dark green, and olive were used to paint the designs.

Ceilings were plaster and had a flat or semi-elliptical center with covered sides. They became more elaborate as the century progressed and motifs included strapwork, classical motifs, swags, scrolls, dolphins, fruit, and plaques. Many ceilings were painted.

Floors were covered by plaited rush mats; carpets were still rare. When available, carpets were used as coverings for windows, tables, or furniture. Many carpets were imported from Turkey or Persia, although embroidered or *turkey-work* carpets (constructed of knotted pile with a cross-stitch that was cut open) were made from about 1575. This was the age of embroidery and women embroidered carpets as well as clothing, book-bindings, purses, and upholstery.

Norwich was a cloth trade center and many workers from the Netherlands, fleeing from religious persecution, stimulated the production of new designs. Woolen tapestries with Biblical or mythological subjects embroidered in silk and gold were popular.

Accessories included Chinese porcelains, tin glaze earthenware, pewter, and glass articles. Silver objects, displayed by the wealthy, were regarded as a safe way of keeping wealth.

Furniture

Furniture pieces were more plentiful in the Elizabethan Period and were considered prize possessions. Often the owner's initials and the date were incorporated into the design. Furniture was somewhat lighter in appearance, with a profusion of carving, although most pieces had developed from Tudor counterparts. Oak was still the favorite wood, but other woods were occasionally used. Lightly padded, fabric-covered furniture was used near the end of the period. Wax replaced painted finishes.

Chairs and Other Seating Pieces

Chairs had straight, rectangular backs and seats, low, heavy stretchers, and straight feet;

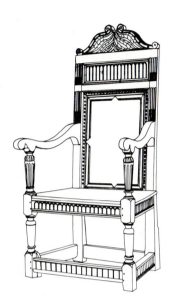

Figure 15.3a
An Elizabethan wainscot chair with simple geometric carving, turned legs, fluted arm supports, and low stretchers.

they were not yet contoured to the body. The wainscot or joined chair was open beneath the seat with slightly curving arms ending in a scroll (Fig. 15.3a). The front legs were turned

Table 15.3
Characteristics of Elizabethan Furniture

1. Oak was the basic wood, but walnut, chestnut, birch, fir, holly, cedar finished with bee's wax; and ebony inlay were also used.
2. Furniture was no longer painted.
3. Pieces were heavy, massive, rectilinear, but lighter than Tudor designs.
4. Construction was improved.
5. Ornamentation was lavish, irrespective of technical quality; carving was vigorous and in high-relief.
6. Furniture was a prized personal possession; the owner's initials and the date were often included in the design.
7. Furniture was more plentiful.
8. Motifs included cup and cover (bulbous form from Dutch melon bulb, top was carved with gadrooning and bottom with an acanthus leaf; top of support was a crude Ionic scroll form), inlay with floral and chequer patterns, strapwork, grotesques, caryatids, swags, leaves.
9. Stretchers were low and heavy.
10. Chairs were not contoured to body; they had straight backs and seats.
11. Chests were the most common and useful item of furniture.
12. The court cupboard was an innovation.

Figure 15.3b
This Elizabethan caquetoire chair has low stretchers, and a lozenge design on the high narrow back.

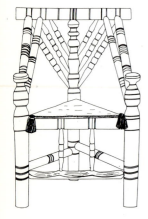

Figure 15.3c
An Elizabethan thrown or turned chair with triangular seat and squab cushion.

Figure 15.3d
This Elizabethan Glastonbury chair folds, and has arcading and lozenges on the back.

columns or balusters (similar to those used on staircases) and were usually extended to support the arms; the rear legs were plain. Cresting or elaborate carving decorated the top rail, and floral inlay, arcaded panels, strapwork, and carving ornamented the back panel. Extensions of the back rail above the top rail, called *ears,* were common. Sometimes the front legs and arm supports were fluted. The *apron,* or band of wood beneath the seat of the chair, might also be carved.

The *caquetoire,* a lighter joined chair, still had a high narrow back, although less widely curved arms than it had had (Fig. 15.3b). The thrown or turned chair, seen in the Tudor Period, was now very popular. All parts of the chair were turned except the seat (Fig. 15.3c). There were usually three uprights, and a thin cushion (known as a *squab cushion*) was placed on the triangular seat (Fig. 15.3c). The spindles of the chair fit into the sockets of the support parts. It is believed that this chair was of Byzantine origin.

The *curule* or X–chair was lightly padded and, by the end of the century, was completely upholstered. The seat and back were wider and the armrests, extending beyond the uprights, ended in a scroll. A folding chair, called the *Glastonbury chair,* was derived from Italian models: the back was ornamented with lozenges, arcadings, a *guilloche* pattern (a motif composed of interwoven circles), and other typical Elizabethan motifs (Fig. 15.3d).

Stools were no longer the slab type but were similar to chairs, with four stretchers (Fig. 15.4a). Joined stools often had turned and carved *splayed* legs. They were sometimes made in matching sets and became more important as eating arrangements changed. There was a separate dining room and the lord and lady now sat at either side of the table, with guests at the sides on stools. The arrangement symbolized the power structure in the family, with the most important members occupying the ends.

Tables

As dining habits changed, the table dormant ceased to be used. More common was an elaborate draw table (Fig. 15.4b): the apron beneath the table top was ornately carved or inlaid with a *chequer* pattern and the legs were the bulbous cup and cover form, which mirrored the puffed sleeves of Elizabethan costume. The acanthus leaf from antiquity be-

came more ornamental and was used in a vine-like design as well as on the cup and cover. Sometimes table tops were inlaid, or a piece of turkey-work was thrown over them when they were not in use. Stretchers continued to serve as foot rests. Some tables were used as a buffet against the wall and had storage compartments beneath them. Large tables were needed because the Elizabethans had numerous dishes of food at each meal. Smaller game and embroidery tables with simple turned legs began to appear; their round and square tops had inlaid geometric designs, strapwork, and other patterns.

Cupboards and Chests

An important innovation of the Elizabethan Period was the *court cupboard* (Fig. 15.5a). The word *court* comes from a French word meaning *short*. These cupboards, seldom over four feet high, were used to display silver serving pieces and dishes. The court cupboard had two or three open shelves with an ornate cup and cover, or animal- and human-shaped front supports (the rear ones were straight). The fronts of the shelves were elaborately carved or had geometric inlay. The *livery cupboard* was similar to the court cupboard except that the upper section had doors. Often the sides were *canted* (or slanted). The *livery,* the food and drink for the day, was stored in the upper section. The *press cupboard* was a taller closed cupboard with two sections, the lower one of which had shelves inside and was used to store clothing and linens.

Portable writing desks were more common and were in box form with a slanted, hinged top with a ledge to hold paper and writing implements. Chests were still the most common and useful objects of furniture. The better ones were framed with three to four panels in the front and decorated with carving and inlay; the end panels were not ornamented.

Beds

Beds were the most expensive item of furniture and had large footposts, usually with bulbous supports, that stood independently at the foot of the bed (Fig. 15.5b). Sometimes a bench connected them. The headboard and canopy were of heavily carved wood. Luxurious curtains of velvet, embroidered silk, and tapestry (of cotton or wool in middle-class homes) were drawn about the bed at night. Screens were also used to prevent drafts.

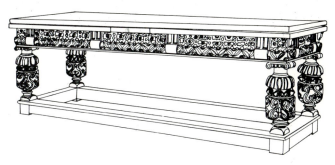

Figure 15.4a
An Elizabethan stool with turned legs and low stretchers.

Figure 15.4b
An Elizabethan draw table with cup and cover, and an Ionic capital and gadrooning on the upper part of the cover.

Figure 15.5a
This Elizabethan court cupboard has a cup and cover with Ionic capital; the top is carved with gadrooning and the lower part with an acanthus leaf.

Figure 15.5b
The Great Bed of Ware, made in the Elizabethan Period, has feet (ornamented with lozenges) detached from the foot of the bed, arcading on the back panels, strapwork on the tester with a mask in the center, and gadrooning and acanthus leaves on the cup and cover. It slept about eight to ten people.

Jacobean Period (1603-49)

Historical Background

The Jacobean Period was comparatively anticlimactic, and religious and civil strife dominated England. The period was named after James I, the first Stuart monarch, but included Charles I as well. James I was interested in the art and culture of the Italian Renaissance and appointed *Inigo Jones (1573-1651)* as Surveyor-General of Royal Buildings. Jones introduced true Palladian architecture into England. Charles I, lover of art and splendor, continued as Jones' patron. He brought the French influence into the court when he married the sister of Louis XIII. It was during this time that the groundwork was laid for later social, political, and economic changes. This period also marks the final merger of English Gothic designs with those of the Italian Renaissance.

Architecture

Life was difficult during the Jacobean Period and great numbers of townhouses remained much as they had been before the Tudor Period. However, many new manor and great houses were built throughout the countryside. Brick and stone were used, for James I forbade the use of timber, which was in short supply. By 1625 brick sizes were standardized.

There were two types of architecture. The Jacobean was an extension of the Elizabethan: houses were more symmetrical, with longer, lower lines, smaller windows, and greater areas of plain wall; ornamentation was *mannered,* and perspective and scale were manipulated. In the second half of the century, the Palladian or Italianate style developed, growing out of the drawings and paintings of Palladio, whose work continued to be widely studied even after his death in 1580.

Inigo Jones (1573-1652)

Inigo Jones introduced the Palladian style into England. He had studied Palladio's works in Italy, and in 1615 became Surveyor-General of Royal Buildings. He introduced the concept of architect as planner and supervisor of construction. He spent much of his time working on royal buildings and *court masques,* which were extravagantly produced plays. Actually much of Jones's work was only in drawings, for there was little money for public building during his years under royal patronage. Jones regulated the details of the house with a system of mathematical proportions relating each element to the whole. Large Italian windows ran evenly along the front, plain chimneys were visible above the roof line, and exterior outlines were clean and simple.

The Queen's House at Greenwich (1616-35) was the first classical building begun in England. Jones's most famous building, the Banqueting House in Whitehall (1619-22), was the first completed classical building; it had two orders on its severe classic exterior: Ionic on the lower story, and Composite on the upper.

Interiors

Customs were changing in the Jacobean Period, the desire for comfort increased. Anthony Van Dyke (1599-1641), a Flemish painter and student of Peter-Paul Rubens (1577-1646), brought an informality to the portraits which were now hung on walls. Textiles became more important and the first tapestry factory was established at Mortlake. In contrast to the severe exteriors, interiors were luxurious.

Long corridors were used in most buildings, and rooms were placed symmetrically. Rooms, especially in Jones's buildings, were carefully proportioned in relationship to one another. The great hall was now only one story high and growing smaller as more and more of its functions were taken over by the dining room, the drawing room, the library, the study, and the private chambers. The long gallery was on the first floor and the bedchamber, serving as both sleeping and sitting room, was on the second. As yet, no feminine

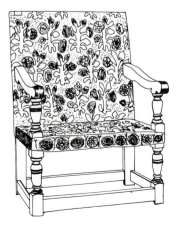

Figure 15.6a
A Jacobean chair upholstered in turkey-work, with turned legs and low stretchers.

Table 15.4
Relationship of Important Furniture Periods to the Jacobean Period

America	France	Italy	Spain
Early American 1608–1720	Renaissance 1485–1643	Renaissance 1400–1600	Renaissance 1400–1650
	Louis XIV 1643–1700		

influence had appeared in the interior; rooms were masculine, large and formal.

The wainscot remained popular, although panels were now cut across the grain and fitted together with beveled edges and a raised center. Jones was partial to white plastered walls, but they could be carved and painted in the Elizabethan fashion or inlaid with patterns. Classical orders and pilasters were used around windows, doors, and fireplaces, and to separate rooms into bays. Framed paintings often matched the wall paneling.

Ceilings were made of decorated plaster in a strapwork design or with ribs emphasized at their intersections with pendants. The more classical ceilings had a central circle, oval, or rectangle, often filled with a painted scene, and outer sections divided by ribs. Classical moldings with swags and acanthus-leaf designs were popular. Floors were of tile, flagstone, slate, or stone on the lower stories and of irregular oak planks on the upper ones. Plaited rushes or, more rarely, imported Turkish or Persian carpets or turkey-work covered them.

The large fireplace remained the focus of the room and was ornately designed, with Flemish, German and French ornamentation, including thick, curving strapwork, broken pediments, caryatids and grotesques, paintings, coats of arms, or an occasional scene carved in plaster or stone. Mantels often had curving bands beneath and consoles that supported them. Doors were flanked by pilasters surmounted by rounded arches or broken pediments. Windows were tall and rectangular, with larger panes of glass and cushioned window seats. By 1610, stairs had shorter flights, broader treads, and profuse carving. The first large circular stairway was in the Queen's House at Greenwich. The solid newel posts had ornate finials with massive handrails and turned balusters.

Furniture

Furniture remained large, rectangular, and crude and was mainly utilitarian. Motifs were restrained and there was more emphasis on comfort. Oak was still the most frequently used wood, but walnut and beech were now common. Stretchers were placed higher because rushes no longer covered the floors. Wooden knobs or ivory rings were used on drawer fronts.

Chairs and Other Seating Pieces

Chairs were more numerous and lighter in weight, with tall, straight backs, arms that curved downward, narrower wooden seats, and legs that were turned, fluted, or columnar (Figs. 15.6a, 15.6b, 15.6c). Feet were plain and stretchers were turned or plain and higher off the floor. Carving was more ornate and some inlay was used. Upholstery, such as turkey-work, was often nailed to the frame (Figs. 15.6a, 15.6d), or frequently made to cover the chair completely (Fig. 15.6e). Cushions were

Table 15.5
Characteristics of Jacobean Furniture

1. Pieces were large, rectangular, utilitarian.
2. There was more emphasis on comfort.
3. Oak was the most frequently used wood, but some walnut and beech was used.
4. Stretchers were higher off the floor.
5. There was more ornate carving (lower relief) and inlay, and more restrained design; scale and ornament were related.
6. Motifs included lozenges, lunettes, fluting, chip carving, guilloches, split-spindles, urns, scrolls.
7. Legs were baluster, fluted, columnar; feet were straight.
8. Upholstery was nailed to the frame; more cushions were used.
9. Innovations included the gate-leg table.

Figure 15.6d
This Jacobean upholstered chair trimmed with fringe and nailheads has twist-turning on legs and stretchers.

Figure 15.6b
This Jacobean Wainscot chair has an acorn finial, guilloche ornamentation on the upper back, an arcaded panel back, and turned legs. The stretchers are higher than those of earlier models.

Figure 15.6c
This Jacobean Farthingale chair has an upholstered back and seat attached with nailheads, and a loose cushion; the back legs are straight, and the front ones columnar-turned.

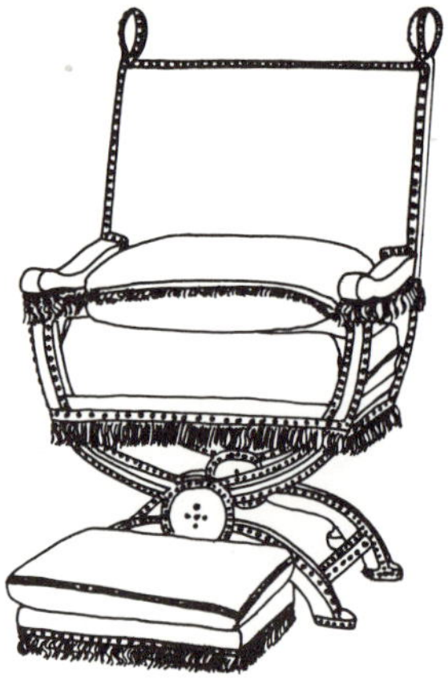

Figure 15.6e
The frame of this curule or
X–*shaped Jacobean chair is
entirely covered with fabric;
the design reflects the
influence of the Italian
Renaissance.*

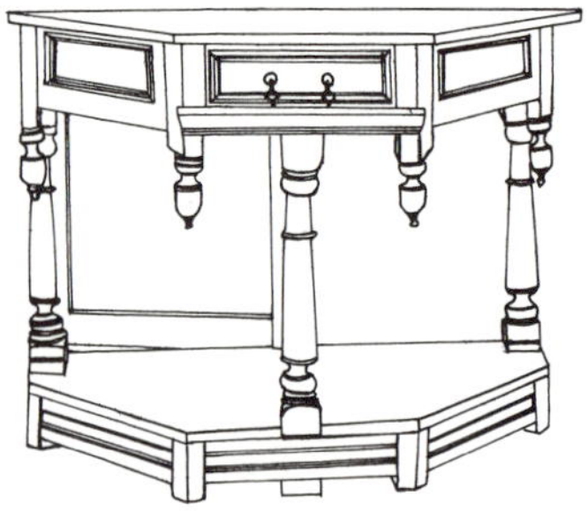

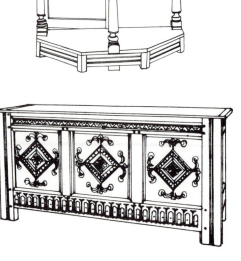

Figure 15.7a
*A Jacobean gate-leg table
with teardrop handles, acorn
pendant drops, octagonal
top, and columnar legs.*

Figure 15.7b
*A Jacobean chest with
geometric designs.*

Figure 15.7c
*A Jacobean high chest with
panel front and lozenges
carved on the upper panels.*

than examples except that the back panel was more elaborately carved with floral designs, arabesques, and arcading. The *lunette* (a half-moon shape) and *split-spindles* (half of a turned ornament) were also popular. The chair had a *cresting* (carving on the top of the back), and the front legs were turned. The *farthingale* chair (Figs. 15.6c, 15.6d), which got its name from the hoop worn under skirts, was armless, low-backed, and had a heavily padded seat usually of turkey-work.

Two lighter and more movable provincial chairs developed: the *Yorkshire* and the *Derbyshire* chairs. They were armless, and had turned legs, top and middle back rails. The **X**–frame chair (Fig. 15.6e) became more comfortable, with an upholstered seat, back, and frame. It often had a matching footstool and both chair and footstool were ornamented with fringes. The settle continued to serve as a hard, uncomfortable sofa, and lighter joined stools, which did double duty as small tables, were popular.

Tables

The draw table and many other types of tables were in use. An innovation of the period was the gate-leg table, which had one or two folding leaves supported on pivot legs (Fig. 15.7a). Tops were round, square, oval, or polygonal.

Chests

Chests continued to be numerous, still serving as seating pieces and for storage (Fig. 15.7b). The same kinds used in the Elizabethan Period were popular, and were ornately decorated (Fig. 15.7c). A dresser or chest of drawers with paneled front and bun-shaped feet appeared late in the period.

Beds

The bed continued to be the most important item of furniture. It was comfortable, with massive, carved posts, tester, and headboard.

Commonwealth Period 1649–60

At the end of the Jacobean Period there was a bloody civil war in England; Charles I was executed, and the Puritans under Oliver Cromwell were in power from 1649–1660. This was a puritanical period when designs were severe and starkly functional. Carving

of velvet, cloth of gold or silver, silk, or embroidered fabrics.

At least one joined chair for the head of the household was now owned by all but the very poorest of families. It was similar to Elizabe-

Table 15.6
Relationship of Important Furniture Periods to the Commonwealth Period

France	America
Louis XIV 1643–1700	*Early American 1608–1720*

and inlay were replaced by severe applied moldings. Few pieces of furniture were made —except for chairs, for it was believed that every man should have a chair to sit upon.

Restoration Period (1660–1702): Carolean Period (1660–89) and William and Mary Period (1689–1702)

Historical Background

After the death of Cromwell, the house of Stuart was restored and Charles II came to the throne. Charles II, who had been living on the Continent, had formed his taste at the court of Louis XIV, his first cousin. He introduced French furniture into England, and was a serious patron of the arts, science, and the theater. He also brought back the extravagant, idle court life. Later, when James II came to the throne, his openly professed Catholicism made him unpopular, and he was forced to flee to France. William, Prince of Orange, and his wife Mary, daughter of the exiled king, were then invited to rule England. William brought many Dutch influences into England, while Mary brought the craze for collecting Delft pottery and porcelain.

Many changes occurred in England during this time. The revocation of the Edict of Nantes had brought Huguenot artisans from France (some via Holland) to England. Coffeehouses became popular meeting places and diaries, such as Evelyn's and Pepys' give us a full account of the life of the times. The plague killed about 20 per cent of the population and the Great Fire of London in 1666 destroyed the central business district and many churches. This stimulated the building of homes and created an increased demand for furniture. A wealthy middle class of merchants was firmly established, and large landowners built many luxurious country houses.

Architecture

Architecture during the Restoration period was eclectic, due in part to the court's exile in Holland and France. Building activity increased, because little had been done during the Cromwellian Period. The style was a French adaptation of the Roman High Baroque, with lavish, sculptural curves.

Dwellings were well planned, with a front doorway in the center flanked by one or two windows. Chimneys were in pairs and dor-

Table 15.7
Relationship of Important Furniture Periods to the Restoration Period

France	America
Louis XIV 1642–1700 *Régence 1700–30*	*Early American 1608–1720*

mers appeared on the roof. Gradually the gable disappeared. The over-all effect was massive, with a repetition of forms, domes, pediments, and entablatures. Finials, pilasters, and urns were popular exterior motifs. The materials in use were red brick and Portland stone; the Portland stone had a silvery cast.

Christopher Wren (1632–1723)

Christopher Wren dwarfed all other architects of the period and continued to dominate architecture until his death in the Early Georgian Period at the age of 91. He firmly established the profession of architect, which Jones had earlier introduced into England. Wren, an astronomer and physicist, dominated both royal and church designs with the practicality of his scientific mind. Constantly seeking new forms, he consolidated the Roman style producing classical building suited to England. He was one of the first city planners, but after the Great Fire of London, his fine geometrical plan for a new city, with main thoroughfares linking public buildings, was turned down because property owners objected to it. However, he designed over fifty city churches of originality.

Other Architects

Hugh May (1622–1684), *Nicholas Hawksmoor (1676–1734)*, and *William Talman (1650–1720)* were also important architects whose designs were somewhat similar to those of Wren although they were completely overshadowed by him.

Table 15.8
Characteristics of Christopher Wren's Architecture—Restoration Period

1. Red brick buildings were combined with Portland stone quoins (stones placed at the corner angle of building).
2. Roofs were tiled, straight-line.
3. Projecting cornices were added.
4. Doors and windows were symmetrically arranged.
5. Structures were massive, with repetition of forms.
6. Details included entablature, pediment, and pilasters.
7. Wren style in domestic building was established, although he designed few residences.
8. Scientific training enabled him to design sound, unified structures.

Figure 15.8a
This Carolean side chair has twist-turned legs and scrolled feet, a caned seat, a tall, straight back, and crown cresting that matches the stretcher carving.

Interiors

By now the interior was completely symmetrical, with stairs and a fireplace in the great hall, which had become a vestibule. The dining room and the main reception room occupied the front of the house. Private rooms, card rooms, and the long gallery were on the first floor, but bedchambers were almost always on the upper floors. Corridors were used extensively, and houses were two to four stories high. An interesting feature of the period was the placing of life-size painted cardboard male and female figures in a room so it would not appear empty when entered. Stairs had broad, shallow treads which became steeper as ceilings became lower. Marble and stone were used in the finest houses. Balusters were vase-shaped or *barley-sugar twist,* a turning that resembled twisted rope (Fig. 15.8a).

Walls had wide panels in natural-finish oak or walnut, or were covered with Chinese wallpaper or fabric, or painted to resemble marble. Naturalistic carvings were used around the fireplace, over doors, and as trim around mirrors and paintings. Ceilings were between twelve and twenty feet high. Decorative plaster with high-relief oval, circular, or rectangular designs in the center, which contained paintings, were surrounded by a frieze, cornice, and border. Naturalistic, well-proportioned ornamentation was typical.

Fireplaces became simpler and more dignified and were often made of marble with a deep carved, acanthus-leaf *bolection* molding (a rounded, projecting molding with naturalistic, high-relief carving surrounding it). Doors were framed by architraves and broken pediments and often had framed paintings above. Windows, of the large casement type until 1685, were replaced by sash windows with twelve rectangular panes or lights. Heavy, voluminous draperies with valances were in vogue.

Floors were of marble, tile, or flagstone on the lower stories and of polished oak above. Parquetry floors (an inlaid wood floor with a geometric pattern) were used after 1680. Although large rugs were still rare, small rugs were in use.

Grinling Gibbons (1648–1721)

Wren and *Grinling Gibbons* were linked closely in interior design, for Gibbons carved many of the ornamental decorations for Wren's buildings. Gibbons changed the vogue from plaster carving to wood. His material—soft lime, pear, or boxwood—made possible high-relief, deeply undercut, naturalistic carving. Gibbons' carvings, and those of the men who emulated his style, were used for trim around windows, doors, fireplaces, and paintings. His motifs included fruit, flowers, foliage, birds, animals, garlands, and swags.

Wall and Ceiling Painters

The ceiling centerpiece and walls of large interiors were frequently painted with allegorical, mythological, and Biblical scenes. *Antonio Verrio* (1634?–1707) an Italian painter who had worked in Italy and France, was invited to England by Charles II, who became his patron. He was a rapid, skillful painter, although often in his haste his drawing, composition, and colors suffered. *Louis Laguerre* (1663–1721) came to London in 1684 as Verrio's assistant after being apprenticed to Le-Brun. His work was more restrained and of a richer quality than Verrio's.

Furniture

Walnut became the dominant wood during the Restoration period. Veneers were now used and wood grain became an important as-

Figure 15.8b
This William and Mary chest on a stand, or highboy, has inverted cup turned legs and pear-drop pulls; the shaped stretcher matches the curves on the apron.

Table 15.9
Characteristics of Restoration Furniture

1. Walnut replaced oak after 1680; ebony and fruit woods were used for inlay.
2. Fine workmanship developed.
3. Pieces were lighter in scale, simpler in shape, easier to handle.
4. Comfort became a consideration: slanted chair backs and increased padding were introduced.
5. Pieces had more curves, with hooded or double-hooded tops with molded cornices on cabinets, shaped aprons.
6. Foreign influences included use of bun feet, inverted cup, pierced splat back (Dutch); ornate Louis XIV **X**–stretchers, cane backs and seats (French); lacquer with Oriental scenes as motifs (Oriental); scroll foot, spiral turnings (Spanish).
7. Scroll leg appeared first, then the inverted cup, and finally beginnings of the cabriole leg.
8. Pieces had large, unbroken surfaces of richly grained walnut.
9. Innovations were numerous: wingback chair, padded settee, chest of drawers, chest-on-chest, lowboy, highboy, bureau cabinet, kneehole desk, slant-top desk.
10. Ornamentation included floral and seaweed marquetry (Fig. 15.9a), gilded gesso, lacquer, veneer, stringing (insertion of thin layer of wood or metal to outline design).
11. Motifs included flowers, foliage, cupids, scrolls, serpentine curves, twist turning, acanthus leaf, caryatids, husks, shell (at end of period).

pect of furniture. The influence of French and Dutch styles brought about the introduction of decorative furniture. Lighter and more refined (owing to new working methods) new furniture pieces appeared, as well as new ornamental methods. Chair backs began to slant, for the first time, although they were not contoured to fit the body until the Queen Anne Period.

A new leg form (Fig. 15.8b) developed called the *inverted cup* (it resembled its name) and towards the end of the period, a tentative *cabriole leg* with a hoof foot, a conventionalized animal leg, appeared (Fig. 15.8c). The wingback chair, the chest of drawers, the padded settee, the slant-top desk, the bureau cabinet, the kneehole desk, the chest-on-chest, the lowboy, and the highboy (a chest mounted on

a stand) were innovations of the period. New methods of ornamentation included *japanning,* an English imitation of Oriental lacquer; *gesso,* a paste used to make three-dimensional decorations, which were then gilded (Fig. 15.8d); and *marquetry* (the insertion of different woods and materials into veneers) in floral designs. Cane was introduced for seats and backs of furniture (Fig. 15.8a, 15.9b), as were pear-shaped glass drop handles.

Chairs and Other Seating Pieces

Chairs became more comfortable and lighter in weight. Sidechairs had high, slanted backs, which caused a structural weakness in some examples. Seats were smaller. The Flemish scroll foot, which flared in the front with the scroll shape in the back (Fig. 15.8a), and a scroll foot were used at first, with an occasional melon-shaped foot. Ball- and bun-shaped feet were popular in the latter part of the period (Fig. 15.9b). Twist turning was used for stretchers and back rails (Fig. 15.8a). Upholstery was padded for comfort and fabrics became richer. Cane was also a popular material for both seats and backs (Fig. 15.8a, 15.9b). The pierced splat back appeared (Fig. 15.8c).

Figure 15.8c
A William and Mary sidechair that shows Dutch influence has a pierced splat back and a forerunner of the cabriole leg with hoof foot.

Figure 15.8d
The upper part of this Carolean cabinet is of Oriental lacquer; the gilded, ornately carved stand has scroll feet; the caryatids, flowers, and foliage are of gilded gesso.

Figure 15.9a
Figure 15.9a
This William and Mary
secrétaire or cabinet on a
stand has bun feet, a
pull-out shelf for writing,
and *seaweed marquetry*.

Figure 15.9b
A *melon-footed* William and
Mary sidechair with caned
back and seat, matching
cresting and stretchers.

Figure 15.10a
The stretcher on this
Carolean wing chair with
S–shaped legs and scrolled
feet; front stretcher is
carved in *cyma* curves.

longer). *Marquetry* made very beautiful designs possible: field and design were cut at the same time making one exactly the reverse of the other. Floral, *seaweed* (an arabesque pattern), *oyster* (a circular design formed by cutting across the grain of woods [Fig. 15.9a]), and *stringing* patterns (a narrow inlay of contrasting wood or metal) were used. Furniture aprons were shaped and sometimes stretchers matched this shaping (Fig. 15.8b). Many tall pieces had four legs in front and two behind. Brass pear-shaped drops served as hardware (Fig. 15.8b).

The chest of drawers, an innovation, was of walnut veneer ornamented with geometric panels and split spindles. Near the end of Charles II's reign, chests were mounted on stands and called *highboys*. These were tall, dignified pieces, but many did not survive because the upper part was too heavy for the delicate stand (Fig. 15.10c). Usually they had lacquered fronts, but those made during the reign of James II were plain. Lowboys, which matched the highboy, were made near the end of the period (Fig. 15.10d).

Secretaries on stands were made in two pieces so they could be taken up narrow stairways to the second floor. Some had pull-out shelves for writing, and others had fall fronts, supported on each side by a chain. Inside were numerous pigeon holes for storage of writing materials (Fig. 15.10e). The kneehole and slant-front desks were also innovations. Sometimes a kneehole desk with a mirror over it was used as a dressing table.

The wingback chair, called a sleeping chair, protected the sitter from the drafts (Fig. 15.10a). It had a high back with side wings, was padded and upholstered, and had curving stretchers with scroll feet. The settee, with a double curved back, resembled two wingback chairs attached in the center. X–shaped stretchers with a finial in the center were typical. Stools were similar to chairs and were caned or upholstered.

Tables

The many types of small tables reflected changing social customs, and included tables for cards, tea, chocolate, and coffee. The gateleg table continued to be popular and often several were used in a dining room instead of one large dining table (Fig. 15.10b). Octagonal tables and candlestands often had twist or baluster tripod bases. Long tables, which served as sideboards, were still in vogue.

Case Pieces

Case pieces, such as chests, cabinets, and desks, were among the most innovative pieces of the period. Ornamentation was elaborate. *Coromandel* (cor-o-man′-del) *screens* were imported from the Orient and cut in pieces to make tops and fronts of various cabinets. An English lacquer technqiue, called *japanning,* was also used, although English designs were not as delicate or well executed as the Oriental. *Gesso,* a white mixture of chalk and glue, was applied to wood, layer by layer, then incised or carved and gilded with *water gilding* (best quality) or *oil gilding* (which lasted

Beds

Tall beds, (some were eighteen feet tall) remained the most important and most expensive piece of furniture. Hangings around the bed, topped with a valance, matched the draperies, and French ostrich plumes ornamented the corners of the carved wood tester. The headboard was usually low and carved.

Cabinetmakers

The Restoration Period brought the advent of the cabinetmaker in England. *Daniel Marot* (1661–1752), a French cabinetmaker who was William's leading designer, had fled France with the Revocation of the Edict of Nantes. William became his patron in Holland and Marot came to England with him. His furniture, in the Louis XIV style made for the wealthy and elite, was characterized by elaborate ornamentation, such as carving, gilding,

Plate 19 (Above, left)
This bath and shower in-the-round, designed by Fabio Lenci, received the Sixth Annual Resources Council Product Design Award. It combines a cylindrical see-through shower cabin atop a giant circular bathtub. In the back wall of the shower are compartments for accessories, mirror, thermostatic mixer controls, handspray, and a coiled holder and warmer for towels. (Courtesy of Hastings Tile and Il Bagno)

Plate 20 (Above, right)
The walls in this master bedroom are upholstered in silver-gray twill. The silk spread is reflected in the ceiling of twill and grey glass. The many sound-absorbing surfaces make the room ideal for sleeping, and built-in storage is ample. Interior designer: Tony Guido. Photograph by Les Rachline.

Plate 21 (Right)
The sneaker bed, a signed piece of art, is a happy, nontraditional approach to a child's private haven. Lace up the laces and forget about a bedspread. Interior designer: Austin Bernstein. Photograph by Les Rachline.

Plate 22
Memories of long ago are evoked by this warm, friendly kitchen with its brick wall, hanging baskets, and copper pans. It can be used for entertaining as many as ten people. Interior designer: Ann Houle. Photograph by Michael Decoulos.

Plate 23
The corridor kitchen, planned for an English bachelor, is very efficient although traffic can be a problem. (Courtesy of Hygena Ltd.)

Plate 24
A beautiful whirlpool bath to pamper the body, with a lounge area nearby. Architect: John Seals, AIA. Interior designer: Mary Lou Stern, Wyatt Interiors. (Courtesy of Jacuzzi Whirlpool Bath, Inc.)

Plate 25
A small space using a stainless steel vanity, one quarter of a pie shape, becomes a visual circle with the use of mirrors. Interior designer: Tony Guido. Photograph by Les Rachline.

Plate 26
The irregularly shaped walls of this room were created by white rough plaster on metal lathing to create a cave effect. The flush-mounted chandelier is added for an icicle effect. The sofa is a Milo Baughman design. Interior designer: Renée Marshall. Photograph by Les Rachline.

Plate 28
Built-in storage in this den houses the television and includes a drop-front desk. Interior designer: Bob Rubinstein. Photograph by Les Rachline.

Plate 29
This game and music area in a south Florida condominium is insulated from the formal living area. Interior designer: Austin Bernstein. Photograph by Les Rachline.

Plate 30
The circular pool creates a center of interest in a triangular second-floor space. Concrete, laminated girders, rafters, and roof decking are the construction materials. Ascent to the upper story is by a stairway encircling the pool, which has portholes strategically placed for underwater viewing. Furniture designer: George Nakashima. Architect: Alfred Browning Parker. Photograph by Les Rachline.

Plate 31
The Mexican tile floor, Oriental rugs, and African and Pre-Columbian artifacts of this multi-purpose living area reflect the taste of the designer-owner. There is a gracious space for entertaining friends and for personal enjoyment of art, books, and music. The dining area is close by. All the materials are natural and for the creativity of the occupant. The dining chairs are designed by Marcel Breuer. Interior designer: Austin Bernstein. Photograph by Les Rachline.

Plate 32 (Below, left)
Green predominates in this living room in a triadic color plan with touches of yellow-orange and red-violet. Simple cubes are used to create a storage wall. Interior designer: Terence Whelan, Great Britain (Courtesy of Bayer AG)

Plate 33 (Below, right)
This two-story weekend house on Fire Island has an open plan, with living areas clustered around an open two-story space in the center. Architect: Earl Burns Combs. (Courtesy of American Olean Tile)

Figure 15.10b
A William and Mary gate-leg table with turned legs and Spanish feet.

Figure 15.10d
A William and Mary lowboy that shows Louis XIV influence.

Figure 15.10c
A Carolean cabinet with Oriental lacquer work on an ornately carved and gilded gesso stand; the finial on the stretchers matches the finials on top.

Figure 15.10e
A William and Mary éscritoire with fall front, twist-turned legs, and bun feet.

seaweed marquetry, and lacquerwork. A publication of a book of his designs extended his influence. Marot's furniture was primarily intended for the court, but other cabinetmakers were influenced by him in their designs for the wealthy middle class.

Gerritt Jensen designed furniture over a long period, from the reign of Charles II through that of Queen Anne. He employed Boulle's techniques, and used marquetry, japanning, and metal inlay. A number of other fine cabinetmakers—*Andrew Moore, C. Coxed, T. Woster, John Grumley, Samuel Bennett, Hugh Granger*—worked during the Restoration Period.

Queen Anne Period (1702–14)

Historical Background

The Queen Anne Period was the first modern furniture period in England, a period in which furniture adaptable to contemporary use was made. The Queen Anne style has been copied in many later periods. Queen Anne ruled over one of England's most brilliant periods, but she herself was not interested in art, literature, or the theater. The Stuart line ended with Anne, for she left no heirs. She was dominated by her childhood friend, Sara Churchill, the

Duchess of Marlborough, most of her life, and the great palace of *Blenheim* was built for Sara's husband.

Out of England's six million people, there were only two or three hundred who were educated about the arts and design and who were considered the elite. It was for these

Table 15.10
Relationship of Important Furniture Periods to the Queen Anne Period

France	America
Louis XIV 1642–1700	Early American
Régence 1700–30	1608–1720

people that the great houses were built and the finest furniture and accessories made. The middle class lived well, however, and many women could read and write. Many middle-class homes were filled with excellent, comfortable furniture, paintings, and books. Middle-class families sent their sons to universities and built manor houses in keeping with their new social position.

Social customs changed rapidly during the Queen Anne period. Coffee houses (males only) continued to be gathering places and diaries vividly portray the life of the times. The Queen Anne period was a time in which the Empire expanded and prosperity was general. Education was available to most people and the wealthy began to collect large libraries. Women played cards and met for tea while men gambled, hunted, dueled, and socialized in the coffee-houses.

Architecture

The architectural style of the Queen Anne Period was English Baroque, but more plans were made during this period than were executed. Most completed great houses were ostentatious rather than comfortable and convenient. Symmetry continued to be most important in the planning of the house with function a low priority.

A large house, an indication of social status, often had as many as forty people living in it —parents and children, unmarried relatives, grandparents, and servants. From this period on, houses were constantly remodeled to make them more "modern," so many exteriors and interiors are a combination of more than one period.

The English Baroque style is characterized by a central block with wings. *Rusticated* stone (a roughened stone with recessed edges) was a typical construction material.

The most important building of the Queen Anne Period was *Blenheim Palace,* the only English palace which is not a royal or episcopal dwelling. It was built for John Churchill, Duke of Marlborough, to commemorate his victory over the armies of Louix XIV at Blenheim. Blenheim Palace, England's answer to Versailles, is an angular Baroque building 856 feet wide—a monument rather than a comfortable home. The architect, *Sir John Vanbrugh* (1664–1726) refused to consider cost (it ran about three times the estimates), and he and the Duchess never got along. Finally he was excluded from the building and *Nicholas Hawksmoor* (1661–1736) finished it after his death. The building has a central block with a Corinthian portico and pediment, and the wings spread out around the court. The east wing, the kitchen court, finished first so that the family could live in it, is balanced by the stable court. Both wings are connected to the central block by colonnades with Doric columns.

Architects

Wren continued to work, although he had outlived his period. His buildings remain outstanding examples of his inventive genius, however, with their harmony of interior and exterior and their adaptation of the Louis XIV Baroque style. He continued to work on St. Paul's Cathedral until it was completed in 1710.

Sir John Vanbrugh, the builder of Blenheim, was of Flemish extraction. He had been an adventurer and dramatist before he became an architect. He probably owes much to the technical assistance he received from Nicholas Hawksmoor, who had been Wren's assistant. Vanbrugh's best work was large in scale, when he could create dramatic effects.

Nicholas Hawksmoor changed from Wren's classical style to the Roman Baroque after working with Vanbrugh. He was an outstanding assistant, and some of his original designs, influenced by both the Roman and medieval periods, were very individual.

Craftsmen

Exterior details became more important in this period, and in addition to Grinling Gibbons, whose marble and bronzework designs were carried out by his assistants (his work in these media was mediocre), other craftsmen became known.

Caius Gabriel Cibber (late 17th century) sculpted heavy Baroque figures with classical heads. He was Danish and had visited both Italy and Holland before coming to England to work. *Jean Tijou* (late 17th century c. 1712) a French Huguenot smith, designed light,

Table 15.11
Characteristics of Queen Anne Furniture

1. Furniture was lighter, more refined, with unpretentious lines; human scale was considered.
2. Workmanship was superior.
3. Pieces were curvilinear in shape (chair backs, legs, seats, and aprons) and ornamented.
4. Pieces were comfortably padded, shaped to fit the body.
5. Wood included French and Italian fine-grained walnut veneers; some ash, fruitwoods, elm, beech, yew; surface beauty and figure of wood was most important.
6. Carving was low-relief, delicate.
7. The cabriole leg was the chief characteristic, with pad, club, or slipper foot; the ball-and-claw foot became popular after 1712.
8. Stretchers were eliminated.
9. Motifs included shell, broken pediment, cyma curve (S–shaped), husk, pendant, cabochon (round or oval ornament).
10. Foreign influences included cabriole leg, spoon back, ball-and-claw foot (Oriental); shell motif and curves (French).
11. Chairs had open-splat backs, were spoon-shaped in profile, had fiddle, vase, and parrot forms.
12. Seats were horseshoe-shaped or curved, often with upholstered seat rail.
13. Veneers were applied in $^1/_{16}''$ strips over oak or other secondary woods.
14. More furniture was upholstered.
15. Broken pediment and bonnet tops on secretaries
16. Innovations included Windsor, corner, reading and porter chairs; commode.

graceful iron railings, gateways, and screens that influenced interior design.

Interiors

The interiors of the Queen Anne Period were similar to, although plainer than, those of preceding periods—a reaction to the elaborate ornamentation of the past. The layout was classical, as were the proportions and decoration. Stairs were open string, of marble or stone in great houses, with a wrought iron balustrade.

Walls were vertical panels of oak above the *dado rail* (earlier called a wainscot) and horizontal panels below. Classical proportions were now correct. Some entire walls were painted with Biblical or allegorical scenes, or covered with wallpapers or fabric between the dado and ceiling. Ceilings varied from twelve to twenty feet, depending upon the formality of the room, and were more restrained, with shallow, delicate ornamentation that became more rococo near the end of the period. Paintings, similar to those of the walls, were common on the ceilings of great houses. In addition to Verrio and Laguerre, *Sir James Thornhill (1676–1734)* painted many walls and ceilings. He used delicate forms and was an excellent draftsman.

Floors were of wide polished oak boards with small carpets. It was not until 1701 that carpets were first woven in England. Inlaid floors in geometric or floral patterns were seen in the great manor houses. Fireplaces became less important and plainer, with marble or glazed Dutch tiles surrounding the opening.

Doors were paneled, surrounded by a bolection molding topped by a carved architrave and pediment. Sash windows were now in common use although window seats were retained. Long, voluminous draperies with valances were tied back during the day.

Furniture

Domestic furniture, no longer confined to the elite, was designed to meet the needs of the home rather than those of the palace. It was made of walnut and characterized by fine workmanship, comfortable padding, and shaping to fit the body, which gave it a luxurious feeling.

Chairs and Other Seating Pieces

Queen Anne chairs, with beautiful curved lines, were well designed and well executed of imported French or Italian walnut. The spoon-shaped back (in profile) was more comfortable than the straight back because it was shaped to the body. The open splat lightened the appearance of the chair back. The S-shaped cabriole leg, the most important characteristic, made possible the elimination of stretchers because it distributed weight more effectively and gave the chair greater stability. The shell motif, carved in low relief, appeared on the knee, the cresting, and the apron of the chair, often with a husk beneath it. Chair backs were lower and the top rail was rounded; many had no cresting. The front part of the chair seat was rounded and narrow in the back. The *club* or *pad* foot (a flat,

Figure 15.11a
A Queen Anne corner chair with club feet.

Figure 15.11b
A Queen Anne lowboy with bat-wing brasses, slipper feet, and cabriole legs.

Figure 15.11c
A Queen Anne chair with vase back, pierced splat, cabriole legs, and club feet.

Figure 15.12a
A Queen Anne Windsor chair with pierced Gothic baluster splat and hoop-shaped back.

Figure 15.12b
This modern Windsor Scandinavian chair was designed by Hans Wegner.

Figure 15.12c
This modern Windsor chair, similar to a captain's chair, was designed by George Nakashima.

Figure 15.12d
A Windsor chair with comb back and turned legs.

rounded, or disk-shaped foot) was common (Fig. 15.11a). Occasionally a *slipper* foot was used (Fig. 15.11b) and, after 1712, the *ball-and-claw* foot, probably of Chinese origin (carved to resemble a claw grasping a ball), occasionally appeared. It was more popular in American furniture than in English.

Chair backs were open and resembled a *fiddle* or *vase* (Fig. 15.11c), or were *parrot backs,* (the negative space between resembles the splat and the side and top rails a parrot). The S—shaped curve was found on chair backs, aprons, or as underframing of the arms.

The most important innovation of the Queen Anne Period was the *Windsor chair,* which has survived to the present virtually unchanged. It had a solid wood saddle-shaped seat or one of rush with cabriole or turned legs pegged into sockets in the seat. The back legs were *splayed* (slightly angled outward). The

Figure 15.12e
A Windsor chair with hoop back.

back, except in very early examples, had turned spindles, uneven in number. It is believed that the chair originated around High Wycombe, the center of England's chair-making industry, in the late 1600s. The early Windsor chair often had a *hoop back,* cabriole legs, and a pierced Gothic baluster splat (Fig. 15.12a). The Windsor chair has been adapted for modern use by such contemporary designers as Danish designer Hans Wegner (Fig. 15.12b) and George Nakashima (Fig. 15.12c). Other types of Windsor chairs have a *comb back* with turned legs (Fig. 15.12d); a *hoop back,* in which the back rail and the uprights form a continuous curve or hoop (Fig. 15.12e); an *arch back* (Fig. 15.12f), and a *fan back* (shaped like a fan). Many other styles of Windsor chairs developed in England and America in later periods.

Figure 15.12f
A Windsor chair with arch back.

The *wing chair* continued in use, with arms and wings which flowed gracefully outward (Fig. 15.13a). The *corner chair,* similar to Queen Anne side chairs with arms, was made to fit into a corner and the sitter could sit facing either to the left or the right (Fig. 15.11a). The *reading chair* was made so that the sitter straddled the seat and faced the rear to read. An elaborate piece of furniture was the enclosed *porter's chair,* which frequently had a storage compartment underneath the seat.

Stools remained popular and were used for extra seating (Fig. 15.13b). Some had loose cushions while others were upholstered. *Love seats,* less than four feet in width, were used in drawing rooms. They had low backs, and arms similar to those the wing chair. Double chairs or settees sometimes had as many as four chair backs and were similar to side chairs.

Tables

Tables, a necessity with so many men and women gambling, often had holes for money and corner pieces to hold candles. Legs were cabriole and the top was usually *chinoiserie* (or Chinese-like) needlework. Tea drinking became popular and stimulated the development of numerous small tables (Fig. 15.13c). Drop-leaf tables continued to be used for dining or for breakfast in the bedchamber. Another type of drop-leaf table, the *handkerchief table,* was square when open but triangular when the flap was closed, so that it would fit into a corner (Fig. 15.13d). The *flap table* had pull-out sides to hold up the flaps on each side of a fixed center section. Other tables included the

Figure 15.13a
A Queen Anne wing chair with gracefully outward-flowing wings, cabriole legs, and pad feet.

Figure 15.13b
A Queen Anne stool with drop seat, cabriole legs, and pad feet.

Figure 15.13c
A Queen Anne tea table with pull-out ends, cabriole legs, and small club feet.

tilt top (with the top that could be dropped vertically), which had a *pie crust* or scalloped edge.

Case Pieces

The *commode* was a small, low storage unit with a lid into which a mirror might be fitted (Fig. 15.13e). *Bracket feet* (with a curved inner edge and a straight corner edge) were typical. Numerous cabinets and chests were required for the increasing amount of clothing. Some consisted of two chests mounted one on top of the other. *Slant-top desks* (Fig. 15.13f), *secretaries* (Figs. 15.13g, 15.13h), and *bureau bookcases,* similar to the highboys of the Restoration Period, were in demand. These might be flat on top, have a *broken scroll* or *swan-neck*

Figure 15.13d
A Queen Anne handkerchief table.

Figure 15.13e
This Queen Anne commode has a mirror inside the lid and bracket feet.

Figure 15.13f
A Queen Anne slant-top desk with cabriole legs and pad feet.

Figure 15.13g
The drop-front Queen Anne double-dome secretary with escutheons rests on slides when open.

Figure 15.13h
A Queen Anne lacquered secretary has a drop front that rests on slides, a broken-arch pediment, and flame finials.

pediment (a pediment composed of two S-shaped curves open at the center), or a *double-dome top* (Fig. 15.13g) with a shaped finial between the domes. These pieces were often *japanned* or finished with Oriental lacquer (Fig. 15.13h).

Beds

Beds increased in importance, for ladies often received guests while in bed (to keep warm). Usually the bed had four slender posts with little visible woodwork, similar to that of Restoration Period, and had velvet or damask hangings.

Cabinetmakers

Hugh Granger, active between 1690 and 1706, specialized in case furniture, using geometric panels and floral marquetry patterns with inlaid lines. Coxed and Worster continued to work, and modernized old-fashioned mirror frames and made candlestands with mirrored backs that intensified the candle-light. They used burl wood (which gave a knotted effect when sliced into veneers) darkened with burned oil to emphasize the grain, and pewter inlay. *Samuel Bennett* was a master at laying veneers to form a symmetrical pattern.

Early Georgian Period (1714–1750)

Historical Background

The Hanover line began with George I, a German who had so little interest in England that he continued to speak German after he ascended the throne. During his reign (1714–27) and that of George II (1727–60), peace and prosperity made possible many developments in architecture and furniture design.

Times were still hard and there was little regard for education by the lower classes. Sanitation was almost nonexistent and magic charms were believed by many to cure disease. The average life expectancy was less than forty-five years. The rich over-ate because it was fashionable to be obese, while the poor starved. Entertainment was largely confined to the home (travel was very hazardous), and consisted of musicales and card parties. Public entertainments tended to be violent: hangings, bear-baiting, and cock-fighting were popular. Women were still not considered worthy of education and this assisted male dominance.

Conditions in the Early Georgian Period were conducive to the growth of large estates and the building of great houses. The Early Georgian Period is often referred to as the golden age of English architecture and many of the elegant squares in London were built during this time. Economic conditions improved with the importation of American raw materials and the export of finished goods to the Americas (this suppression of American industry was an important cause of the American Revolution).

London became the center of a thriving furniture industry, and the lifting of the import duty on mahogany in 1747 stimulated its use. There were two types of furniture shops in London: the craftsmen's shops, where fine furniture was made to order, and the merchants' shops, where furniture made by others was sold. The many furniture design publications enabled rural artisans to copy London styles.

Table 15.12
Relationship of Important Furniture Periods to the Early Georgian Period

France	America
Régence	Early American 1608–1720
Louis XV 1730–60	American Georgian 1720–90

William Hogarth's (1697–1764) keen perception and genre scenes were an accurate reflection of the times.

Architecture

When the works of Palladio and Inigo Jones were revived during this period, somewhat as a protest against Baroque excesses, Roman classical motifs and designs dominated the architecture. *Colin Campbell* (d. 1729) was one of several architects who published treatises laying down the canons of the Palladian style. His *Vivtruvius Britannicus* (1718) compared English classical homes with Palladio's work and became an important influence on the design of country houses and villas both in England and in America. Many country houses were based on Palladio's Roman villa plan, with a central block balanced by wings. Palladian motifs, such as segmental arches, and small plain windows topped by pediments, domes, and classical orders became popular.

William Kent (1685–1748), a painter and decorator until 1730, was encouraged to become an architect by *Lord Burlington* (1694–1753), his patron. Kent, immensely popular (he even designed dresses with classical orders for his female friends), was the first Englishman to design furniture for a specific architectural setting. He also began the vogue of making the gardens an extension of the house, with winding paths, grottoes, statuary, and seating areas for relaxation.

Other important Palladian architects were *James Paine* (1716–89), *Vanbrugh,* and *John Wood* the elder (1704–54), who designed Bath and *John Wood,* the younger (1728–81) who completed it. Bath was the most elegant resort of the period, a city of crescents and squares.

Interiors

Interiors had a rectangular plan with an imposing hall in the center. The rooms, large and well-proportioned, included a dining room,

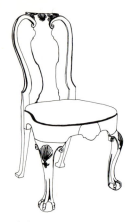

Figure 15.14a
An Early Georgian decorated Queen Anne style chair of parcel gilt walnut with ball-and-claw feet; the shell on the cresting matches that on the knee.

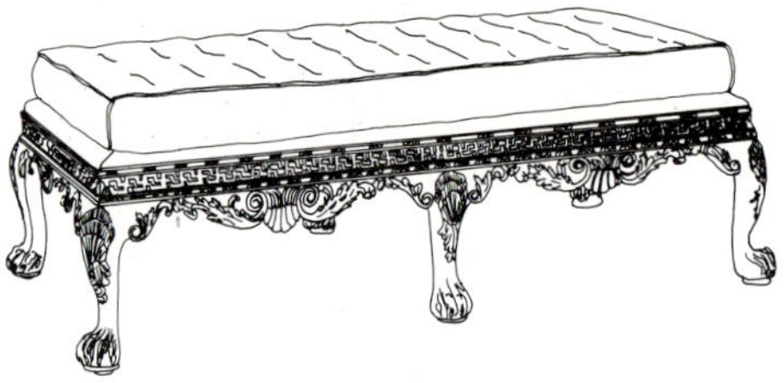

Figure 15.14c
An Early Georgian satyr mask chair with masks on the splat, knees, and apron; lion's-paw feet, eagle-head detail on the cresting rail.

Figure 15.14b
An Early Georgian lion style bench with paw feet, scroll and shell motifs.

Table 15.13
Characteristics of Early Georgian Furniture

1. The heavy Baroque style was popular until 1730, when Rococo began to be popularized.
2. Major ornamentation included elaborate carving, marquetry, and gilded gesso.
3. Woods included walnut until 1735 (native woods continued to be used by rural artisans); imported mahogany after 1735 (available in wide, long boards; easily worked; wormproof; took high polish).
4. Lacquered furniture was popular until 1750.
5. Motifs included lions' heads, masks, eagles' heads and spreading wings, shells, satyr masks, capitals, egg-and-dart, broken pediments, acanthus leaves.
6. Palladian style: designs were improvised to imitate ancient furniture and were influenced by Jones' architectural details and Marot's furniture; ornamentation included classical orders and human masks; proportions were heavy; designers were architects, resulting in integration of architecture and furniture; William Kent was the chief designer.
7. Rococo style: light, fanciful, influenced by interior details rather than architecture; featured continuous curves and structural ornamentation, with laminated wood used to create structural curves; motifs included birds, animals, plants, rocks, shells; major designers were Matthias Lock, Thomas Chippendale (known by 1750), William Kent.
8. Kent style: dominated furniture design between 1727 and 1740; massive, large-scale, heavy furniture well suited to spacious rooms; motifs included broken pediments, floral and fruit festoons, acanthus leaves, eagles, lions' heads, human masks, shells, Greek fret, swags, feathers, sphinxes, cupids; featured heavy cabriole legs with ball-and-claw or hairy-paw feet; frequently used gilded gesso over pine; reflected Venetian influence; marble table tops; eclectic designs: Baroque, Gothic, fantasy, Roman influences.

perhaps two drawing rooms or salons (which varied in size), a library, bedrooms, and a living room. The kitchen and servants' quarters were not considered in the planning (and would not be until William Morris' Red House was designed in the Victorian Period). Kitchens were usually placed in basements and servants' rooms in the attic. Bathrooms were nonexistent; chamber pots or outside fa-

cilities were used. Most rooms were not arranged for function but rather for effect.

The dominant feature of the room was the fireplace. The wood or marble mantels usually had as overmantel a painting or relief sculpture. Walls had rectangular panels separated by pilasters, and were painted white or cream and accented with gilding. Some were covered with fabric or wallpaper above the dado. Blue and red rooms were also popular. Niches to display statuary became more popular in later periods. Ceilings had a cornice and stucco relief ornamentation with classical details or, later, rococo motifs. They were painted white, with perhaps some gilding.

Doors and windows were framed with pilasters and surmounted by pediments. Rectangular paneled doors were typical. Windows had heavy draperies looped back with tasseled cords. Patterns and colors of fabrics and carpets were coordinated. Cotton printed fabrics in a wider color range were more readily available for the block-printing process had been improved, and cotton was imported from America as part of a triangular trade pattern (molasses to Africa, slaves to America, and cotton to England). Chintzes were popular coverings for both windows and walls. Floors were of polished wood, covered with patterned carpets in important rooms. Carpets, such as the *Wilton,* were available and were made on Jacquard looms in floral patterns.

Accessories

Accessories became increasingly important and included silver and plate (a convenient way to store wealth), pottery and porcelain (displayed on plate rails around the room or in cabinets), and *Delft* (imported from Holland). By this time, nearly a hundred glasshouses were in operation producing clear glass. Pictures, statuary, and small pastoral pottery figurines were also popular, even in middle-class homes.

Furniture

Furniture was arranged to enhance the elegance and enormous size of the rooms. Furniture retained the outlines of the Queen Anne Period, but gradually lost its Louis XIV characteristics and began to resemble the Rococo style of Louis XV. Walnut, which remained an important wood in rural areas, was in the cities replaced by mahogany after 1735. Lacquered furniture, extremely popular until

Figure 15.14d
An Early Georgian cabochon and leaf sidechair with the cabochon and leaf on the knee, and ball-and-claw feet.

around 1750, was available in red, black, green, and yellow.

There were several styles of furniture: the *Palladian,* the *Rococo,* and the *Kent.* Chairs were further grouped according to substyles: the *decorated Queen Anne* (Fig. 15.14a), the *lion* (Fig. 15.14b), the *satyr mask* (Fig. 15.14c), and the *cabochon and leaf* (Fig. 15.14d).

Chairs

Chairs, available in many types, were no longer used just by the rich. Within the house, chairs were increasingly used by women. As middle-class women enjoyed more furnishings, marketing possibilities were greatly expanded.

Early Georgian chairs, larger and stronger than Queen Anne styles, retained the heavier cabriole leg. Foot styles included the *club, duck, cloven hoof, claw and ball, hairy paw, lion's paw,* and *scroll* (after 1725). Splats were pierced and ornamented with rich carving. Armposts were set back on the seat rail and this, combined with wider, horseshoe-shaped seats, made it easier to accommodate the full skirts of the women.

Side and arm chairs, used in dining rooms, generally had *drop-in* seats. Upholstered armchairs, now overstuffed, had lower backs than dining chairs, with padded arms and cabriole legs. The back was slightly raked and had a serpentine arch. These were used in both bedrooms and sitting rooms. Leather was used for upholstery, as was the discarded embroidered clothing of both sexes.

Substyles The *Decorated Queen Anne* chair style, popular from 1714 to 1725, was heavier and more solid than its predecessor (Fig. 15.14a). It was ornamented with elaborate carving and the arms frequently ended in eagles' heads (often incorrectly attributed to the American designers). Motifs were carved lions or satyr masks, shells, honeysuckle, husks, acanthus-leaf foliage and pendants, rosettes, foliated scrolls, dolphins' heads, and scaled legs (around 1723). Gilded chairs were common. More decorated Queen Anne chairs were made than those of any other style.

The *Lion Style* chair (1720–35), had a lion's hairy-paw foot clutching a ball (Fig. 15.14b). Between 1725 and 1745 the eagle motif was popular.

The *Satyr's Mask* (1730–40), replacing the lion's head on furniture, appeared on the arms

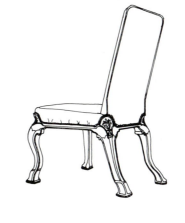

Figure 15.14e
This Early Georgian sidechair was designed by William Kent.

Figure 15.14f
An Early Georgian settee with heavy ornate carving, gilded, designed by William Kent.

and knees of chairs, and the legs and aprons of tables (Fig. 15.14c).

About 1735, the *Cabochon and Leaf* appeared and lasted until the Middle Georgian Period. This oval convex ornament resembled a cut gemstone, and was usually surrounded by leaf forms (Fig. 15.14d). The shell and acanthus leaf were modified and influenced by French designs.

William Kent's chairs and settees (Fig. 15.14e), influenced by elaborate, over-ornamented, and gilded Venetian models (Fig. 15.14f), were also gilded or *parcel gilded* on a white background (only parts of the design were gilded). His wing chairs often had the arms extended to the wings, so that they appeared to be one continuous piece. Kent was particularly noted for his mirror frames,

Figure 15.14g
An Early Georgian mirror with feathers and masks, heavily gilded, designed by William Kent.

Figure 15.15a
This Early Georgian reading chair on casters has pull-out candleholders; the sitter faced the rear.

Figure 15.15b
This Early Georgian double chair has a drop-in seat, cabriole legs, ball-and-claw feet, and a shell motif on the knees and apron.

which were heavy and typically ornamented with gilded feathers and masks (Fig. 15.14g).

Thomas Chippendale (1718–1779), well known by 1750, had by 1754 brought out his famous pattern book, *The Gentleman and Cabinet Maker's Director,* which contained designs for the three Chippendale styles: Gothic, Chinese, and Rococo. Chippendale was apparently not too concerned over the merit of his designs; he was willing to make what the public wanted. The Middle Georgian period is often referred to as the Chippendale Period.

The reading chair, with a horseshoe-shaped crest rail supporting an adjustable book rest and pull-out candleholders, was made so that the sitter faced the rear (Fig. 15.15a). These chairs, now on casters, were simpler in design than most other pieces. The *corner* or *roundabout chair* also continued to be made, and was fitted with a slip seat and had a high back usually upholstered in leather. These chairs were often seen in barber shops. The hall chair or hall settee, not meant for comfort, was designed for people who were waiting to see the master of the house (Fig. 15.14f). Kent's style was widely copied. The enclosed *porter's chair,* upholstered in leather, continued to be used. The Windsor chair increased in popularity and was used both in coffeehouses and in gardens. Most had a spindle back of some kind and were made of a mixture of woods.

Other Seating Pieces

The *double chair* closely followed new chair designs but continued to be uncomfortable for it had a drop-in seat or was unpadded (Fig. 15.15b). However, an upholstered settee with thin cushions, was used in both reception and sitting rooms (Fig. 15.15c). Benches were designed for window recesses or garden areas and often had a serpentine-shaped seat.

Tables

Early Georgian tables, inspired by French designs, were heavy with architectural details. Many had marble tops. Swags, Greek frets, masks, feathers, and satyrs appeared on the apron underneath (Fig. 15.15d). The extension dining table was composed of a center table and detachable semicircular end tables. The long dining table, typically Baroque in style, had a marble or *scagliola top* (scăl-yō'-luh), an imitation marble made of marble chips, color, and plaster).

The console table, a shelf-like table attached permanently to the wall and usually made in pairs, was a permanent part of the room (Fig. 15.15e). It had only two front legs, scroll feet, and was ornamented with caryatids, cherubs, or masks. *Pier tables* were gilded, heavy, and ornate, and were made in pairs to be used be-

Figure 15.15c
An Early Georgian upholstered settee with cabriole legs, shell motif on the knees, and ball-and-claw feet.

Figure 15.15d
An Early Georgian hall table of painted and gilded wood with architectural details, mask, swags, and scrolls.

Figure 15.15e
This Early Georgian gilded console table with marble top, satyr mask, and scroll feet is attached to the wall.

Figure 15.16b
An Early Georgian secretary with swan-neck pediment, bombé front, and paw feet. Pilasters ornament the sides of the upper section.

Figure 15.16a
This Early Georgian bookcase has a broken-arch pediment with a head in the center, bracket feet, and a pull-down front supported by slides.

tween windows, usually with mirrors over them.

Massive side tables gradually declined in popularity and were replaced by small mahogany tables around 1740. These also had marble tops, friezes, and scrolled legs with female heads. Card tables continued to be made and served as side tables, pier tables, or tea tables.

Because tea was increasingly popular even though very expensive, tea gardens and special rooms in the home for tea drinking appeared, as well as small "china" tables. Some of these tables were oblong with cabriole legs, ball-and-claw feet and fretted galleries; others had tripod bases with pie-crust edges or galleries to prevent the tea implements from falling off.

Chests, Cabinets, and Stands

Copies of Italian Renaissance chests were made, with Renaissance detailing and large hairy-paw feet. Bookcases, architectural in character, were richly molded with broken or swan-neck pediments (Fig. 15.16a). Some lower parts had a bombé front with a swelling convex curve on the sides (Fig. 15.16b) and bracket or paw feet. The tallboy and chest-on-chest replaced the chest after 1725 (Fig.

15.16b). Often the upper part had canted (slanted) or fluted corners (Fig. 15.16c). A flat frieze was common at the top after 1735.

Many types of storage pieces from earlier periods remained in use, such as the dresser, the lacquered chest, and the clothes press or wardrobe. Stands were used to hold vessels for washing, and often had a tripod base.

Figure 15.16c
An Early Georgian chest-on-chest with ogee bracket feet.

Figure 15.16d
An Early Georgian torchère with heavy Baroque detailing.

Torchères or candlestands were ornate, in keeping with other designs (Fig. 15.16d).

Beds

Because audiences were no longer held in bed, beds decreased in importance. They had lighter proportions and were made of richly carved mahogany with tall, slender *reeded* posts (rows of convex moldings similar to fluting in appearance). Beds continued to be draped with rich fabrics.

Cabinetmakers

William Kent was widely copied by other designers. *William Hallett* became a fashionable designer, as did *John Gunley* and *James Moore.*

Middle Georgian or Chippendale Period (1750–70)

Historical Background

The Middle Georgian Period is the first furniture period to become known by the name of the designer. Thomas Chippendale (1718–79) so dominated the period with his publication, *The Gentleman and Cabinet Maker's Director* (1754, 1775 and 1762), that all furniture in the style, whether made by Chippendale or not, bears his name.

The power and prestige of England increased in this period, and there was domestic peace, although George II paid little attention to national affairs and George III presided over the loss of the American colonies.

The theater became popular again and fairs developed into general markets. Spas and resorts, such as Bath, were increasingly popular.

A few newspapers appeared, with some advertisements, and bookshops were opened. The growth of mercantile prosperity made it possible for more people to own fine furniture.

Hogarth continued to paint, using satire as he saw fit, and his engravings were very popular. *Thomas Gainsborough (1727–88)* was in great demand for his portraits and landscapes, and *Sir Joshua Reynolds (1723–92)* became the most successful painter of society portraits. *Benjamin West (1738–1820)* became the first American painter to become successful in England.

Architecture

Architecture was a continuation of that of the Early Georgian Period, with a preference for the Palladian style, and many architects went to Italy to study the original designs. The Gothic Revival, (usually spelled *Gothick* to distinguish it from the real Gothic style), was popularized by *Horace Walpole (1717–97)* when he built *Strawberry Hill* (1749) with its medieval towers, long galleries, and asymmetrical interior plan. The Gothic Revival was primarily an interior style. During this period, early Greek and Roman influences dominated, and the Palladian style gradually became more romantic. In the 1750's *Robert Adam* and his brother went to Greece to measure and draw ancient buildings, and Adam designs came to dominate the Late Georgian Period. The Middle Georgian Period, a transitional period between the curvilinear Rococo styles and the classicism of the Adam brothers, was an era of residential design rather than one of public buildings. It also marks the beginning of the apprenticeship system for the study of architecture.

Architects

Isaac Ware (d. 1766), while not a great architect, is remembered for his books *Palladio* (1738) and the *Complete Body of Architecture* (1756), which pointed out that even Palladio could make mistakes. *Henry Fitchcroft's* (1697–1769) work illustrates the extremes to which the Palladian style was taken. *Sir Robert Taylor (1714–88)*, originally a sculptor, was also a traditional Palladian architect.

Interiors

Palladian, Rococo, Gothic and Oriental motifs were popular, and many interiors combined

Table 15.14
Relationship of Important Furniture Periods the Middle Georgian Period

France	America
Louis XV 1730–1760	American Georgian
Louis XVI 1760–1789	1720–1790

elements of all of them. The typical house was rectangular, with a central hall off which opened the living room, the dining room, the drawing rooms, and the library; bedrooms remained on the second floor.

Interiors were usually ornamented with French Rococo motifs in plaster stucco on both ceilings and walls, rather than with paneling. Stucco was painted in light colors with gilded C and S scrolls, dainty shells, festoons, and floral designs. Wallpaper, with hand-blocked chinoiserie designs, was popular. Bedrooms continued to be draped with rich fabrics.

Ceilings typically had naturalistic stucco ornamentation, although Gothick interiors had simulated vaults and ribs. Fireplaces, still the focal point of the room, were of heavily carved marble, or of gilded and/or painted wood or stucco, with gilt-framed mirrors or paintings often incorporated into the design. Floors of polished wood were covered with *Axminster* and *Kidderminster* carpets, in addition to Wiltons, although they were still very expensive. The production of printed cottons, woven in Manchester and printed in London, was stimulated by the invention of copperplate printing in 1752, which made fine designs possible, and the invention, by *Richard Arkwright* (1732–92) of the spinning frame.

Accessories

Sheffield silverplate was invented in 1742, making cutlery and hollow ware more readily available. Delftware, stoneware, and creamware pottery were all popular with *Wedgwood creamware,* perfected in 1763, coming into demand in later periods. Glass, increasingly light in weight and proportions, had refined, delicate designs.

Furniture

The furniture designs of the period, as has been noted, were dominated by *Thomas Chippendale,* who opened his famous shop in St. Martin's Lane in 1753. His dark mahogany furniture was characterized by rich carving, the primary ornamentation. He used no turned elements, but cabriole legs with a ball-and-claw foot or straight legs (with stretchers) were typical of his designs. Chippendale was influenced by the Queen Anne and Early Georgian styles as well as by Louis XV and Oriental motifs.

Table 15.15
Characteristics of Chippendale Furniture

1. Mahogany was the chief wood, except on gilded furniture (usually deal).
2. Heavy carving was the chief surface ornamentation: carved pierced splats, carved aprons and skirts on chairs, cabinets, and tables.
3. Furniture legs were not turned.
4. Backs were carved and pierced, three-rung ladder, with bow-shaped cresting rail.
5. Seats were upholstered over seat rail, or drop seat.
6. Commodes had serpentine, kettle base (swelling), or bow front.
7. Case piece corners had pilasters or fluted quarter-columns; broken pediments were used.
8. Rococo (or French) influences included curvilinear silhouette, cabriole leg with ball-and-claw foot, bow-shaped chair cresting rail, naturalistic carving, Oriental motifs, ribbon (ribband)-back chair.
9. Chinese influences included Oriental wallpapers, carpets, porcelain, and accessories; rectilinear shapes; geometric lattice or fretwork; scroll work and Oriental motifs, such as long-necked birds, bullrushes, bells, monkeys, pagodas, dragons; legs square in section; carved and pierced fretwork; bamboo-like carving; ornamentation included carving, lacquer, japanning, gold leaf, painted Oriental scenes and motifs over lacquer, free-standing fretwork.
10. Gothic influences (from 1750) included legs square in section; wood or simulated stucco paneling with Gothic arches; carved motifs such as pointed arches, rosettes, diamond-shaped patterns, flowers, lacy fretwork.
11. Neoclassic influences included rectilinear shapes; such motifs as fluted legs, classical figures, vases, acanthus leaves.
12. Designs were often a blend of styles.

Chairs

Chairs were the most typical pieces of Middle Georgian furniture. They had a carved open-work splat attached to the back seat rail or a three-rung ladder back. There were two leg forms: the cabriole with a ball-and-claw foot (Fig. 15.17c), and the straight leg (Figs. 15.17a, 15.17b). The arms were curved, flaring out at the ends with supports slanting inward where they joined the arm. Most backs had square outlines with a serpentine-shaped top rail. The *Chinese back* had open fretwork, bamboo-like carving and/or a pagoda-shaped top (Fig. 15.17a). The *Gothic back* was arched and pointed, with tracery (Fig. 15.17b). The *Ribbon* or *French back* had interlaced carving

Figure 15.17a
A Chinese Chippendale chair with pagoda back and open fretwork.

Figure 15.17b
A Gothic Chippendale chair with Gothic arches and tracery.

Figure 15.17c
A ribband-back (Rococo) Chippendale chair with cabriole legs and ball-and-claw feet.

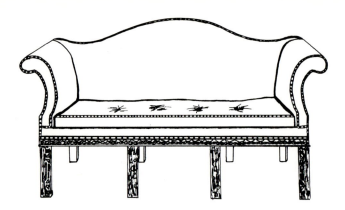

Figure 15.17d
A Chippendale camel-back sofa.

Figure 15.17e
A Middle Georgian tripod table with brass gallery.

Figure 15.17f
*A Middle Georgian
partners' desk with
lion's-head masks and brass
rings.*

and C-scrolls (Fig. 15.17c). The *ladder back* had three shaped, pierced parallel rungs. The knees of the cabriole leg were ornamented with floral carving, leaves, or a cartouche (oval or rectangular partially unrolled scrolls) (Fig. 15.17c). Seats were of the drop-in type or had upholstery covering the seat rail.

Settees and Other Seating Pieces

The double- and triple-chair settee continued to be popular and usually had ornamented legs in front and plain ones behind. An upholstered settee was also made in the Chippendale style. Those with a hump in the center were called *camel-back sofas* (Fig. 15.17d).

Tables, Desks, and Case Pieces

Small tables were increasingly popular, and a small drop-leaf table called the *Pembroke* was used as a breakfast table. Game tables, which had folding tops, were common. Also, many small tripod tables were in demand (Fig. 15.17e), some with piecrust edges and others with tilt tops, square tops, or gallery tops. Hall tables were often gilded and heavily carved.

Desks were popular and those made for two people (called *partners' desks*) had drawers on either side (Fig. 15.17f). Ornamentation might include lions' heads, caryatids, or pilasters. Other desks, similar to those of earlier periods, had a drop front. Large, architectural bookcases often had a broken-scroll pediment,

and mullions (in various patterns) and glass in the upper part (Fig. 15.18a).

Richly ornamented commodes were popular in England as well as in France and were used in the drawing room. Some were lacquered with Chinese scenes while others were of beautifully figured wood (Fig. 15.18b).

Beds

The most important bed of the period is the Chippendale Chinese bed, an example of which can now be found in the Victoria and Albert Museum in London (Fig. 15.18c). It was japanned in red, black, and gold with Chinese detailing.

Cabinetmakers

Many cabinetmakers enjoyed a good business during this period. Chippendale's chief rivals were *William Vile* and *John Cobb,* who designed furniture in both Baroque and Rococo styles. Vile was the cabinetmaker and Cobb the upholsterer (the partnership of upholsterers and cabinetmakers was common).

Several books of design were published in this period. *Matthias Lock,* a fine carver and designer believed to have been employed by Chippendale between 1754 and 1768, published five books of designs. *William Ince* and *John Mayhew* published a book of furniture designs, with notes in both French and English, and their firm became well known.

Late Georgian Period (1770–1811)

Historical Background

The Late Georgian Period marks a time of great change. The American and French Revolutions brought violent changes, but the Industrial Revolution, which manifested itself in England earlier than in any other country, changed England far more. At the beginning of the period the country was rural; at the end,

Figure 15.18a
A Middle Georgian architectural bookcase with swan pediment and Gothic mullions.

Figure 15.18b
A Chippendale lacquered-Chinoiserie commode with husk ornamentation.

Figure 15.18c
This Chinese Chippendale bed is japanned in red, black, and gold, and has Chinese detailing, dragons, pierced fretwork, and a brass gallery at the top.

Table 15.16
Relationship of Important Furniture Periods to the Late Georgian Period

France	America	Germany
France	*America*	*Germany*
Louis XVI 1760–89	American Georgian 1720–90	Biedermeier 1800–50
Revolution 1789–99	Federal 1790–1820	
Directoire 1799–1804		
Empire 1804–20		

it was changing to a modern industrial state. Inventions included the steam engine, mechanical looms, and the spinning jenny and frames that made possible the first practical cotton mill. Cottage industries were replaced by mills and factories. The change from a rural-agrarian society to an urban-industrial society significantly influenced family patterns, and the changes in those patterns, in turn, affected home design.

Women, even those of the aristocracy, were not the models of decorum their portraits suggest. Language was blunter than that of today. Both sexes indulged in snuff-taking, though women did not smoke. The wealthy created an atmosphere of gaiety in pleasure gardens, where they picnicked, strolled, or listened to concerts. Everyone played cards, and reading was a favorite pastime. There were more newspapers than there are today and a new literary genre—the novel—evolved. The first English dictionary was compiled by Dr. Samuel Johnson.

The upper classes had their portraits painted by such artists as Reynolds, Gainsborough, *George Romney* (1734–1802), and *Sir Thomas Lawrence* (1769–1830). In 1768, the Royal Academy was formed, which helped to raise the status of artists. Watercolor was introduced in this period, becoming a popular and typically English medium in later periods.

Architecture

Palladian architecture had enjoyed a long period of popularity and naturally people were becoming bored with it. This desire for a change, combined with the research on Greek, Roman, and Etruscan antiquities (particularly those of Pompeii and Herculaneum), inspired architects; the Classical Revival began. Architecture began to feature Corinthian façades with columns and pilasters and often an Ionic portico; slender pilasters appeared on either sides of the doors; roof balustrades and classic ornamental details such as the egg and dart,

anthemion, and dentils in low-relief became popular. The exterior, often of stucco, was finished and painted to resemble stone. Many squares, crescents, and terraces were built.

Architects

Robert Adam (1728–92) one of four sons of the Scottish architect, William Adam, studied in Italy four years; by 1770, many architects were following his designs. He unified the design of the exterior, interior, and furnishings. Like Frank Lloyd Wright in the twentieth century, he was an innovator and did not allow clients' tastes to dominate his own understanding of good design. The publication of *The Works in Architecture of Robert and James Adam* (in 1773 and 1822 and again after his death) increased his fame. He knew and was influenced by *Giambattista Piranesi* (1720–78), the Venetian architect who made superb etchings of Roman antiquities. Adam's own designs were carefully modeled on classical originals.

Sir William Chambers (1723–96) was the official architect of the period. His conservative buildings were based on Roman designs.

James Wyatt (1746–1813), initiated Adam's classical work while *Henry Holland* (1745–1806) designed in a simplified Adam style, and is most famous for his Greco-Roman villa at Brighton.

Gardens

Gardens were an important part of domestic design by this time. *Humphrey Repton* (1752–1818) was the best-known landscape designer. *Lancelot ("Capability") Brown* (1715–83) also was influential. At first gardens were formal, with lawns, lakes, hedges, summerhouses, and pseudo-ruins. Gradually, after the turn of the century, they became less formal, with winding paths and informal plantings.

Interiors

The interiors of the Late Georgian Period were splendid and dignified, with comfort and

Table 15.17
Characteristics of Late Georgian Furniture

1. It was rectilinear in shape, extensive use of straight lines.
2. It was smaller in scale than Chippendale furniture.
3. It featured small-scale, fine moldings.
4. It was graceful, although many pieces were fragile.
5. Legs were straight, tapered, without stretchers.

Adam

1. Designs were based on classical Italian designs.
2. Furnishings and interior were unified; furniture was architectural.
3. Mahogany with light woods was used.
4. Furniture was gilded and parcel-gilded.
5. Motifs included paterae, festoons, honeysuckle, frets, husks, banding, stringing.
6. Ornamentation included fluting, marquetry, painted panels by Kauffmann and Zucchi.
7. Chairs had wheel, shield, rectilinear, Louis XV, and Louis XVI backs.
8. Chair legs were slender, square in section with spade foot, or round with paterae in block at top.
9. Sideboard (an Adam innovation) had straight or serpentine front.
10. Commode was semicircular.
11. Damask upholstery was used.

Hepplewhite

1. Designs were based on Adam's; pieces were small.
2. Curves were used to soften straight lines.
3. Mahogany with exotic wood bandings was the chief wood; satinwood was popularized.
4. Furniture was gilded and parcel-gilded.
5. Motifs included Prince of Wales feather, husks, drapery, urns, wheat blossoms, vases, floral designs (smaller than Adam's, low-relief).
6. Ornamentation included French-style mounts, fluting, reeding, painted motifs, satinwood inlay.
7. Chairs had shield, medallion, hoop, interlacing heart, camel, and oval backs.
8. Chair legs were often square in section, spade or no foot; round leg had ring on upper section.
9. Sideboard had concave ends.
10. Commode was semicircular, like Adam's.
11. Upholstery was silk and satin, leather and linen, plain and striped.
12. Cabinets and chests had curved bracket feet.

Sheraton

1. Designs were a refinement of Hepplewhite's but furniture was smaller than Adam's or Hepplewhite's.
2. Lines were straight; rectilinearity was emphasized.
3. Mahogany with lighter woods was used.
4. Furniture was painted rather than gilded.
5. Motifs included swags, drapery, urns, elongated vases, classical devices.
6. Ornamentation included marquetry, veneers, porcelain plaques.
7. Chairs had rectangular backs.
8. Legs were turned, reeded or fluted; round legs in section had small turned feet.
9. Sideboard had ends convex.
10. Commodes had ends convex.
11. Upholstery was striped damask.
12. Tambour desks, mechanical furniture, twin beds were introduced.

convenience frequently sacrificed to appearance and symmetry. The important rooms, the entrance hall and reception rooms, were placed at the front of the house on the first floor. Bedrooms were on the upper floors; the kitchens were not even a consideration; and bathrooms were outside (even though Cumming invented the water closet in 1775). Circular, octagonal, and square rooms were common, and furniture of the same shape as the room was chosen. Every item in the interior was related to the over-all design.

Walls were pale pastel, in greens, blues, pinks, creams, and lavenders, with low-relief stucco ornamentation emphasized with gilt. French or Chinese wallpapers (which were copied by the English) were light in color. Ceilings (also pastel) had low-relief plaster ornamentation which had been pressed into boxwood molds and attached while still damp. The centerpiece, an oval or circle, perhaps painted with a scene, was connected to the cornice with decorative details, such as anthemions, medallions, swags, rosettes, cupids, dolphins, acanthus leaves, sprays, or scrolls. Details were picked out in gilt. The carpet motifs often echoed the center ceiling design. Polished wood floors were typical except in the entrance halls, where tile, flagstone, marble, or scagliola was used. Linoleum was first used on floors in this period.

Fireplaces, of marble or scagliola, were surmounted by gilt-framed mirrors, molded stucco panels, or paintings, and the openings becoming smaller as the century progressed. Doors, surmounted by cornices or a frieze, were of polished mahogany panels with brass hardware. Sash windows had wooden frames, and bow windows became popular. The staircase, often illuminated by a skylight, was wide and often circular, with an iron balustrade and a mahogany handrail.

Figure 15.19a
*An Adam wheel-back chair
with tapered legs and
spade feet.*

Figure 15.19b
*This Adam chair with
round back is surmounted by
cresting and surrounded by a
fluted molding, sphinx
ornament the back of the
seat; an extension of the
fluted front legs supports the
padded arms; the back legs
are flared.*

Figure 15.19c
*An Adam chair with Prince
of Wales feather and
drapery on oval back; patera
in block at the top of the
fluted legs; and fluting
on apron.*

Accessories

Accessories became more important. Silver was influenced by Adam's classical motifs and proportions. Many porcelain factories, such as those at *Chelsea, Derby, Bow,* and *Worcester,* were in production. *Staffordshire, Wedgwood,* and *Spode* pottery was in demand. Wedgwood *jasperware,* in blue, lavender, green, pink, yellow, and black, had white bas-relief figures designed by the sculptor *John Flaxman* (1755–1826). High-quality cut glass was also extremely popular.

Furniture

Late Georgian furniture had an architectural quality about it. The craftsmanship was superb and flat surface ornamentation, such as marquetry and painted panels, was typical. Low-relief gilded gesso and jasperware panels and medallions inserted into the wood surface were also common. Mahogany was the favorite wood, although after 1785 satinwood became popular. Furniture was graceful, with no underbracing or stretchers. Smaller in scale than Chippendale furniture, it had fine, small-scale moldings and classical motifs. Chairs were the most typical pieces of furniture produced during this period.

There were three styles of furniture during the period, each of which was named for a designer: *Adam, Hepplewhite,* and *Sheraton.* As is the case with Chippendale furniture, however, the name refers to the style and not necessarily to the maker. Actually Adam only designed furniture and there are no authenticated pieces made by Hepplewhite or Sheraton.

Figure 15.20a
An Adam bookcase cabinet with urn marquetry, dentil molding at top, and spade feet.

Figure 15.20b
This Adam commode with ram's-head on corners and vase marquetry has a Greek fret design on the feet.

Figure 15.20c
An Adam semicircular commode with marquetry swags, vases, and foliage; acanthus leaves on feet.

Figure 15.20d
An Adam sideboard with stringing, a curved front, tapered legs, and spade feet.

Robert Adam (1728–92)

Although architecture was his primary profession, *Robert Adam* was also a furniture designer. He never made furniture, but employed craftsmen, such as Chippendale, to execute his designs. He designed the interior from top to bottom: ceilings, walls, and furniture. His style was based on classical designs from ancient Rome. Adam was a modifier rather than an innovator.

Adam chairs had graceful tapering legs with *wheel* (Fig. 15.19a), *rectilinear, lyre,* Louis XV (Fig. 15.19b) or Louis XVI backs. Chairs were often gilded or parcel-gilded. Inserted into surfaces were *bandings* and *stringings* of veneers. Legs were usually *fluted,* and round or square in sections. Many were surmounted by a block with a *paterae* (pat-er-æ'), (an oval

or round disk usually with a rosette in the center) on it (Fig. 15.19c). Upholstery was silk damask in light colors. Larger pieces of Adam furniture were architectural and had cornices, friezes (Fig. 15.20a), and even pediments, making them appear like small buildings. These were ornamented with classical motifs or panels painted with mythological or allegorical scenes by *Angelica Kauffmann* (1741–1807) and her husband *Antonio Zucchi* (1726–95). Adam was particularly fond of the commode. It usually had a straight front with concave sides (Fig. 15.20b) or was semicircular (Fig. 15.20c). The feet were carved, with ormolu mounts. The *sideboard,* an Adam innovation, had a straight, serpentine, or semicircular front (Fig. 15.20d). On each end of the sideboard were placed urns or knife boxes, which

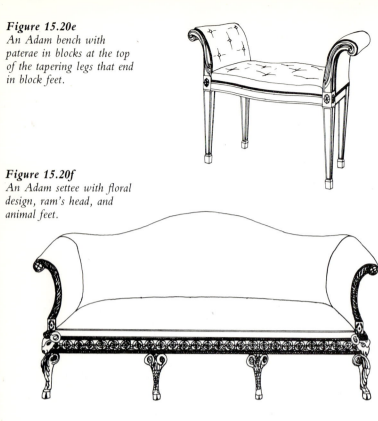

Figure 15.20e
An Adam bench with paterae in blocks at the top of the tapering legs that end in block feet.

Figure 15.20f
An Adam settee with floral design, ram's head, and animal feet.

Figure 15.20g
An Adam mirror with bow ornament, husk ornamentation, swags, and candleholders below the mirror.

matched the table. The urns held water to wash silver, for tableware was in short supply. The sideboard frequently matched the architecture of the room. Adam window seats (Fig. 15.20e) and sofas (Fig. 15.20f) were also popular. Adam mirrors were an addition to many interiors (Fig. 15.20g).

George Hepplewhite (d. 1786)

George Hepplewhite (died 1786) is a puzzle: it is not even known if there was a designer of that name. A George Hepplewhite apparently

died in 1786, however, and his widow, Alice, published *The Cabinet Maker and Upholsterer's Guide,* although the designs she included in it may have been made by two other men, using a *nom de plume.* Nevertheless, there is a style known as Hepplewhite, which was greatly influenced by Adam and is noted for its grace and small scale. Straight lines are softened with curves.

Chairs were the most typical Hepplewhite pieces. The most common back was the *shield* (Fig. 15.21a), which became very popular in the United States during the Federal Period. The back was not connected to the seat, except at the side rails, making it fragile and subject to breaking. These chairs often had a finely carved *Prince of Wales feather* (Fig. 15.21b) at the center of the splat. Hepplewhite chairs also had *medallion, oval, hoop, interlacing-heart* and *camel* backs (Fig. 15.21c). The elements inside the backrails, in addition to the Prince of Wales feather, were urns, drapery, and radiating bars (oval back). Ornamentation consisted of low-relief floral designs, vases, husks, and classical motifs. Gilding and marquetry were common. Legs were fluted or reeded (Fig. 15.21b), and were either square in section with a spade foot (Fig. 15.21b) or round with a ring on the upper section. The Hepplewhite settee was similar to chair designs and was upholstered in striped fabrics. (Fig. 15.21d). The sideboard was usually concave at the ends. *Tambour* furniture was an innovation in England. It was a desk, similar to a roll-top desk. The roll top consisted of thin strips of wood glued to a piece of fabric. The commode was semicircular with marquetry motifs, similar to that designed by Adam. Hepplewhite used *French bracket* feet (Fig. 15.21e) on case pieces. There were many small Hepplewhite tables, such as the *Pembroke,* and tops were rectangular (Fig. 15.21f) or oval (Fig. (15.21g). Also included was a sewing table with a bag attached beneath the top to hold supplies. Mirrors were also included in *The Cabinet Maker and Upholsterer's Guide* (Fig. 15.21h).

Thomas Sheraton (1751–1806)

Thomas Sheraton, who wrote the *Cabinet Maker and Upholsterer's Drawing Book* (four parts of which were published between 1790 and 1794) and the *Cabinet Dictionary* (1803), never had a workshop but was influenced by Hepplewhite designs. He refined them by utilizing the straight line to a greater extent. His

Figure 15.21a
A Hepplewhite shield-back chair with raked-back legs, slim tapered fluted front legs, and spade feet.

Figure 15.21b
A Hepplewhite chair with Prince of Wales feather, fluted legs, and block feet.

Figure 15.21d
A Hepplewhite confidante with striped upholstery.

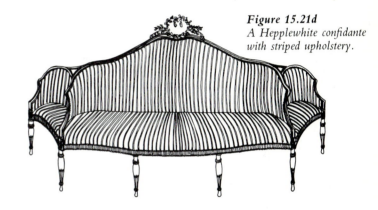

Figure 15.21c
A camel-back Hepplewhite chair.

Figure 15.21e
A Hepplewhite breakfront bookcase with French bracket feet.

Figure 15.21f
A Hepplewhite Pembroke table with classical designs in marquetry on the top and drop leaves.

Figure 15.21g
An oval Hepplewhite
Pembroke table with swags
and paterae in marquetry.

Figure 15.21h
A Hepplewhite mirror with swags, urns, and ribbons.

Figure 15.22a
A Sheraton sofa with
polychrome ornamentation,
and high-set arms.

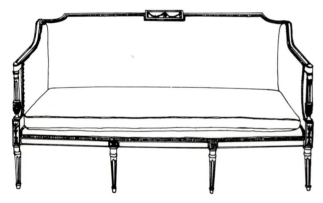

Figure 15.22b
A Sheraton desk with
stringing and casters.

Figure 15.22c
A Sheraton kneehole desk.

designs had a light and delicate look. He was also responsible for the designs of many pieces of mechanical furniture and was the first to introduce twin beds. His drawings influenced many English cabinetmakers and especially Duncan Phyfe in the United States.

Sheraton furniture is of very high quality and relatively small. Chairs usually had rectangular backs with an urn, Prince of Wales feather, drapery or baluster. Upholstery was usually striped. The legs, fluted or reeded, were turned and round in section with small turned feet. (Fig. 15.22a). Commodes and sideboards had convex ends. Ornamentation consisted of veneers, marquetry, and porcelain plaques. *Tambour* desks were another Sheraton specialty. Sheraton also designed writing desks (Fig. 15.22b) and kneehole desks (Fig. 15.22c). He was particularly competent in the design of large furniture pieces; for example, his very tall pieces tended to be narrow, for balance. Even though Sheraton's furniture was very fragile in appearance, it was sturdy. *Fancy chairs* in the United States were derived from Sheraton designs. Sheraton also designed mirrors (Fig. 15.22d).

Regency Period (1811–1830)

Historical Background

Vast economic and social changes occurred during the Regency Period. The population was becoming increasingly urban, and technological advances such as the invention of the gas street light (1814), the safety lamp for miners, the camera (1816), and the steam press (1814), as well as the opening of the railroad stimulated industry.

This was also a time of diminished parental influence. The autocratic family, with the oldest male in charge was patriarchal in structure,

Figure 15.22d
A Sheraton convex mirror surmounted with an eagle.

Table 15.18
Relationship of Important Furniture Periods to the Regency Period

France	America	Germany
Empire 1804–20	Federal 1790–1820	Biedermeier 1800–50
	Victorian 1820–1900	
	American Empire or Greek Revival 1820–60	

but the foundations of that structure were being shaken. In poor families, children as young as nine worked as many as twelve hours a day to help support the family. No longer could the patriarch's rules bind the dependent offspring to his arbitrary command. Yet there was little open rebellion and most children stayed close to their parents even when they had families of their own.

When George III became mad in 1811, due to an illness now known as *porphyria,* his son, a promiscuous, self-indulgent, and egotistical man became Prince Regent. One thing at which the Prince excelled was spending vast sums of money. A playboy, he made Brighton, already a fashionable seaside resort, his home. The one building that mirrors his taste and embodies the Regency style is the Pavilion at Brighton.

During this period, fashion became an art form and Beau Brummel was the epitome of style. He was not only the most fashionably dressed man of his time, but he was also fastidiously clean at a time when regular bathing was almost unheard of. There was also a renewed interest in the theater, as well as the first real effort to control crime (the police force was organized), and to reform society (a task undertaken by the evangelical sects).

Watercolor was a popular medium and caricatures, cartoons, and book illustrations offered artists an additional way to earn a living. Popular Regency subjects were picturesque landscapes, genre paintings (scenes of everyday living), and animal paintings. *Joseph Turner* (1775–1851), the best watercolorist of the period, refused to paint in the prevailing style, creating a feeling of luminosity (light) in his works.

Architecture

Interest in architecture declined during the Regency Period. This was partly owing to the Industrial Revolution, which was bringing new wealth to a middle class that had neither the time nor the inclination to cultivate artistic taste. Few great country houses were built but small dwellings, terraces, and crescents became fashionable. Many of these houses were of stucco painted to resemble stone, or of plain or glazed brick, with bay windows and bowfronts. Row houses, in crescents or terraces, formed a single palatial unit and were in the Greek Revival style, with cast iron railings. The other style of architecture was the Picturesque, which really marked a transition between the Greek and the Gothic Revivals.

The *Royal Pavilion* at Brighton is an example of this latter style. *John Nash* (1752–1835) the architect, borrowed many styles from exotic sources, including the Chinese, the Hindu, and the Gothic. The original Pavilion had been a Palladian villa; to this Nash added an immense onion dome surrounded by smaller onion domes that surmounted the bow windows on the wings. The delicate pierced stonework in Indian-style tracery added to its brilliance when the building was lit by the new gas lamps in 1818. The interior of the Royal Pavilion at Brighton was unusual too. Oriental in feeling, it included hand-painted Chinese wallpapers, a water-lily chandelier, a chandelier held in the claws of a silver dragon with four gilt dragons holding lotus-shaped lamps, palm-tree columns, Chinese murals, black and gold lacquered furniture, and a crocodile chaise longue. The building was restored in the 1950s and is an excellent example of a royal folly.

Interiors

The general plan of the Regency interior was light and open, designed to accommodate a more informal style of living. Large folding doors separated rooms. Front bow and bay windows extended interior space for the first time since the Jacobean Period, and concentrated light at one end of the room. Doors and tall sash windows were framed with a simple architrave molding. Light striped or delicate flowered draperies of silk, linen, or chintz were tied back. Light striped or flocked wallpapers sometimes matched the drapery fabrics. Fireplaces were less important than they

Table 15.19
Characteristics of Regency Furniture

1. Form, lines, construction, and finish were simple.
2. Many pieces were rectangular.
3. Mahogany and rosewood were the chief woods.
4. There were rapid changes in style for sake of change.
5. Many items of patent (mechanical) furniture appeared.
6. Furniture was machine-made, so it became more readily available.
7. Design rather than comfort was the chief criterion.
8. Influences included French Empire (Boulle work, brass mounts), Egyptian (monopodia, sphinx, crocodile, snake, lotus), Chinese (imitation bamboo, mandarin, pagoda, dragon), Greek and Roman (*klismos,* tripod, **X**−shaped and curule stool, swan, dolphin, scroll, classical motifs), Gothic (tracery and arch).
9. Ornamentation included little carving (owing to expense), spiral and vertical reeding; chased ormolu and brass ornamentation such as inlaid bandings, lions' feet, casters, wire trellises on doors of case pieces.

Figure 15.23a
A Regency table with monopodia.

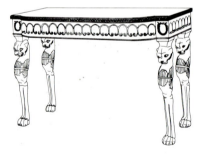

Figure 15.23b
A Regency klismos style chair with boldly curving rear legs and scroll arms; casters on front legs.

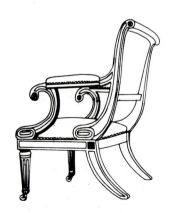

had been and were framed with white or black marble mantles. Often convex mirrors were placed over them.

Floors of polished wood were covered with rugs that had a floral centerpiece and outer border. Ceilings were of plain plaster, except in the homes of the wealthy, who retained the low-relief plaster ceilings popularized by Adam. When a chandelier was used, there was a central decoration. Iron balusters, plain, **S**− or scroll-shaped with mahogany handrails, were typical.

Accessories were numerous and included silver in many bizarre designs, pewter (used in the kitchen), porcelain, Wedgwood pottery, and glassware. Costly glass chandeliers, wall sconces, and torchères (similar to classical examples) were used in larger homes. Gas lighting was too experimental to be widely used.

Furniture

Furniture, inspired by the French Empire style, was further influenced by the immigration of French cabinetmakers to England at the time of the French Revolution. A further important influence was the invention of the woodworking machine, which made possible mass production of straight-line furniture.

Included in this period were Chinese, Egyptian, Gothic, Indian, Roman, and Greek influences. Furniture was severe and simple, of mahogany or rosewood, and ornamented with brass mounts. One of the most important characteristics was the *monopodia* (mon-o-po′-di-a), a table support composed of the head, chest, and foot of a lion (Fig. 15.23a).

Thomas Hope (1770–1831)

Thomas Hope, a wealthy banker, was the most important designer of the Regency Period. He traveled extensively and in 1807 published a book of his designs, *Household Furniture and Interior Decoration.* His became known as the English Empire style. Furniture and interiors were developed from these designs for his home, Deepdene, which he opened to the public. The influence of his friend, Charles Percier, one of Napoleon's architects, can be seen in his work. Hope's furniture was also influenced by Egyptian forms and motifs (such as the lotus, the sphinx, and the chimera) and classical motifs. His designs were severe and followed ancient examples more carefully than did those of other designers. He included the curule and **X**−form legs for chairs, which were low and had cane or striped upholstery seats. There were many circular, pedestal tables with metal paw feet, and torchères.

George Smith

George Smith, who worked with Hope, published *A Collection of Designs for Household Furniture* (1808) and *Cabinet-maker and Upholsterer's Guide* (1828). His designs, inspired by the Greek, Roman, Egyptian, and Gothic styles, were also strongly influenced by the designs of the French Empire Period. Like Hope, he designed chairs with low seats. Upholstery was in bright colors with ivy and lotus motifs. He designed many circular tables on a *plinth* (plain pedestal) with paw feet. He also included in his book complete guides for furnishing rooms.

Sub-Styles

The Regency Period is divided into sub-styles, such as the *Greek Revival,* the *Egyptian,* and the *Chinese.* Greek Revival furniture was made of rosewood or mahogany with brass mounts and moldings. The *klismos* chair, and the **X**–shaped and curule bases on both stools and chairs were extremely severe in form with large areas of unbroken space accented by bold curves (Fig. 15.23b). Motifs included lyres, reeding, anthemion and acanthus-leaf designs, lion's-paw feet, and the monopodia (copied almost exactly from examples in Pompeii). Ebonized bandings were often used.

The *Egyptian style,* which became popular after Napoleon's campaign in Egypt, was made of mahogany or satinwood with ormolu mounts, brass casters, and cane seats. Tapering and fluted sheaths representing bundles of reeds and lotus, hieroglyphics, crocodiles, sphinxes, lions' heads, and female heads were typical motifs (Fig. 15.23c).

Furniture in the *Chinese style* was usually of japanned or lacquered ebony, carved to represent bamboo (Fig. 15.23d). Typical motifs included palm trees, dragons, pagodas, and Oriental scenes.

The *Gothic style* really became most popular during the Victorian Period. Motifs such as French window tracery and the Gothic arch were used on some pieces.

Chairs and Seating Pieces

Chairs usually had low, caned, or wood seats with curved and tapering front legs (Fig. 15.23e). Some examples had lion's-paw feet. They were often a mixture of styles, with the

Figure 15.23c
A Regency Chinese chair with snakeskin carving and casters on feet.

Figure 15.23d
A Chinese style Regency chair carved to resemble bamboo.

Figure 15.23e
A Regency sidechair with cane seat, spiral fluting, and saber legs.

Greek and the Egyptian being the most popular. When arms were used, they were set high on the back and had scrolled ends or lion's head-terminals. Back rails were slightly curved to fit the body. Cushions were of striped fabrics or of fabrics with delicate floral designs. Brass or wood stringing was sometimes used.

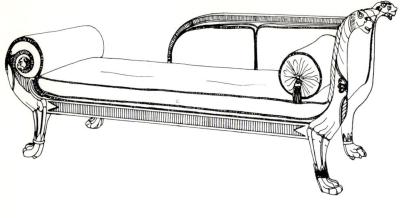

Figure 15.23g
A pedestal-base Regency table with round top, star brasses and casters.

The convex, circular mirror, the most popular type, was hung over the fireplace. It was usually crested with an animal or eagle (often incorrectly thought to be an American innovation). The frame was gilded and carved. Rectangular mirrors were used over pier tables and fireplaces. They were generally separated into sections by caryatids.

The *pianoforte*, the forerunner of the piano, replaced the harp and the harpsichord. It was beautifully proportioned and ornamented with brass inlay.

The Victorian Period (1830–1901)

Historical Background

The Victorian Period was strongly influenced by Queen Victoria, who early in life was taught the meaning of duty and the importance of a rigid schedule. She lived a very private domestic life and after Prince Albert's death in 1861 went into a seclusion that lasted, nearly unbroken, until her own death in 1901.

The Victorian Period was characterized by peace and prosperity, but it was also a time of expansion. The population of the British Isles doubled and the shift from rural to urban areas was massive. Unplanned cities sprang up and slums were numerous.

The Victorian Period was also marked by exciting technological advances. There was a general belief in progress and an optimistic view that perfection could be obtained. England's national pride was at its height. When Victoria ascended the throne in 1837 there were only about five hundred miles of railroad track, but by 1847 there were three thousand miles. This expansion of the railway system increased travel, trade, and communications. The invention of the bicycle too helped to change customs. How could a chaperone manage to follow a young couple on bicycles? Hoops and bustles had to give way to a simpler cycling costume for women, and clothing became more practical.

The Industrial Revolution had become an accomplished fact: furniture, carpets, household items, and accessories were all mass produced. But it was not until the end of the century that household servants began to rebel against their ceaseless labor and it was even later before women began to demand mechanical labor-saving devices in the home. Bissel invented the carpet sweeper in 1876 but it was 1902 before Booth invented the vacuum

Stools had an **X** or curule frame and leather, cane, or upholstered seats. Settees were common. Most popular was a light-weight Grecian couch with curved rolled ends and back, and short outward curving lion's legs and paws. Casters were common (Fig. 15.23f).

Tables

Tables were of three types: one type had a round or octagonal top on a pedestal base (Fig. 15.23g); another had four legs at the corners (Fig. 15.23a); and a third had a central pedestal with two legs at each end. Sofa tables had drop leaves and drawers under the central portion. Library tables were also common. Small work tables were either tripod or had four legs. Some had silkwork pouches underneath.

Sideboards

Sideboards were very massive and had knife boxes and urns at each end. Brass inlay was common, and some were even fitted with plate warmers. The *chiffonier*, which was first used in England during the Regency Period, was a sideboard with two doors that had brass lattice work on a pleated silk back; the top half was used to display porcelain.

Miscellaneous Pieces

Bookcases were of various kinds, with wall-hung or circular or revolving or rectangular shelves. They were often enclosed with brass-trellis doors.

Table 15.20
Relationship of Important Furniture Periods to the Victorian Period

America	Germany
Victorian 1820–1901	*Biedermeier*
Greek Revival or American	1800–50
Empire 1820–60	
Historical Revivals	
1840–1901	

cleaner. Even though Edison discovered electric light in 1879, it was not until after the turn of the century that it came into general use.

Art was changing and individualistic portraits were painted by *John Singer Sargent* (1856–1925) and *James Whistler* (1834–1903), a fine colorist and an American, also became involved in interior decoration. *Aubrey Beardsley* (1872–98) did many original drawings that later influenced the development of the Art Nouveau Movement.

The novelty and excitement of the industrial age spawned an era of exhibitions in the second half of the nineteenth century. The first of these was the *Great Exhibition* of 1851. The exhibitions created competition among furniture manufacturers, who attempted to outdo one another with strange blends of styles, none of which was suited to modern living. It quickly became apparent that material prosperity was unrelated to good design. Even designers who had an opportunity to improve taste seem to have been more interested in displaying virtuoso models of monumental scale rather than in designing models for everyday use. The furniture they produced was known as *exhibition furniture*.

The United States declined to send furniture to these exhibitions. Instead, United States craftsmen sent functional domestic equipment, such as water pails, tools, adjustable school desks, and household implements. These were the most beautiful objects in each show. Because materials were plentiful and labor scarce in America (the opposite was the case in Europe), designs had to be simple and functional. Also, Americans were unfamiliar with traditional forms and techniques and were forced to develop a new technology.

Architecture

The most important architectural style of the Victorian Period was the *Gothic Revival,* which developed out of the Romantic Move-

ment of the early nineteenth century. Gothic motifs were used as ornamental detail. *John Ruskin (1819–1900)*, a Victorian art critic, popularized the "high moral value" of this style in his books and frequent public lectures. Some typical Gothic castles were built, such as Belvoir Castle by James Wyatt and the ecclesiastical style, similar to Gothic cathedrals, was used for churches. More people were traveling, owing to the expansion of the railway system, and many Gothic-style hotels were built. Most domestic homes were large and required at least three servants for their maintenance. Some of the houses were pseudo-half-timber or pseudo-Elizabethan in style.

The other prevalent style, the *Classical Revival,* was used mainly for museums and monuments. It was less popular than the Gothic and had classical details such as orders and heavy proportions. These buildings were solid and square; examples include the Victoria and Albert Museum and the Bank of England. This style ceased to be important about 1910.

The outstanding building of the period and the first prefabricated one was the *Crystal Palace,* built in about eight months to house the Great Exhibition of Machinery, Science and Taste (1851). The designer, *Joseph Paxton* (1801–1865), who had formerly designed greenhouses, was the first to recognize the aesthetic properties of glass and iron. The building had a modular framework of metal girders. It was economical to build, elegant, and light. It was also the first building without applied ornamentation.

William Morris (1834–96) began the transition from the Gothic Revival to the Modern Movement, by building his home, the *Red House* (1861), a solid brick home designed by Philip Webb. The unpretentious red-brick structure was a landmark in the domestic architecture of England. Exterior ornament, though Gothic, was used sparingly, for the emphasis was on the balance of mass. The irregular plan was practical and informal with such innovations as the movement of the kitchen from the basement, windows in the servants' quarters that opened onto the garden, the use of English materials and craftsmanship, and plain surfaces with simple ornamentation. The interior was furnished with simple, medieval-style furniture.

The Art Nouveau Movement was not important in England, except for the graphic arts of Beardsley, and the attempt by *Charles Ren-*

Figure 15.24a
A bentwood Vienna café chair designed by Michael Thonet.

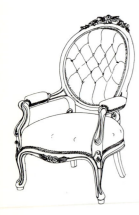

Figure 15.24b
Rococo style Victorian furniture elaborately carved and with tufted back.

Figure 15.24c
A Rococo style balloon-back Victorian chair.

nie Mackintosh (1869–1928) in Scotland to integrate it with vertical architectural structures (see Chap. 18).

Interiors

Many new types of rooms developed during the Victorian Period, including rooms for smoking, billiards, and plants (the conservatory). Servants' rooms were enlarged. Because home entertainment was a custom, large rooms with high ceilings continued to be popular. The narrow, tall houses were not labor-saving, however, and required many unnecessary steps.

The walls in Victorian homes were covered with wallpapers; these were imported until the middle of the period, when domestic production could meet demand. Patterns were at first hand-blocked, later roller-printed, in floral, scenic, and geometric patterns. Paintings of all kinds were hung on the opulent wallpapers.

Polished wood floors were covered with rugs and carpets made by Aximinster, Wilton, and Kidderminster in flamboyant floral patterns, scrolls, scenes, and imitation Oriental designs. Cheap copies of these carpets were also available in painted felt. The high ceilings were light or white and usually had a center ornament. Sash windows were common (plate glass was introduced in 1840) and were draped with heavy velvet or *rep,* a plain-weave fabric with a corded effect, that hung from brass rings on mahogany rods. Later, printed cotton and chintz fabrics became popular. Colors were bright—and even strident after the discovery of analine dyes by William Perkin in 1856.

Fireplaces were necessary for heat. Ornamental iron grates held the coal, and mantels in various styles had decorative mirrors above them. On stairways, stone or wood treads were frequently carpeted in brown. Iron balustrading with carved mahogany handrails were typical. Light remained poor, with gas lamps, chandeliers, and candles widely used until after 1880, when electric lighting was introduced.

The Victorian room was cluttered with furniture and accessories. Traffic patterns were obscured and often the function of a room was difficult to determine by its furnishings. Books, such as *Hints on Household Taste,* by *Charles Eastlake* (1793–1865) were written to assist the lady of the house with the interior

decor, and as the period progressed arrangement of rooms became somewhat simpler.

Elegant greenery was used and included potted palms, ferns, and aspidistra. Other accessories included pottery and china (often displayed on plate rails around the tops of walls), classical figures, glassware, and silver. Many strange and unusual accessories were made, such as wreaths of human hair, shells, and feathers.

Furniture

Victorian furniture, a combination of historical styles made in dark wood, relied upon a profusion of structural and decorative curves. Many styles and combinations of styles were popular, but the four most important were the *Classical,* the *Rococo,* the *Elizabethan,* and the *Gothic. Italian Renaissance, Turkish,* and *Oriental* designs were also used and were frequently combined with other styles. New materials and technology made possible many of the new shapes.

New Materials

Many new materials were developed during the Victorian Period. *Tubular metal* was introduced in 1833, and this ultimately resulted in the manufacture of the tubular brass bed. A brass bed displayed at the Crystal Palace was ordered by Queen Victoria, which created an instant demand for this item. The production of *cast iron* was also a big industry. It was used not only for yard accessories but also for balconies, porch balustrades, fountains, and delicate furniture.

Papier-mâché was introduced from the Orient, although it was made by the French in the early 1700s. It was made by driving a mixture of paper cuttings, glue, and size into oiled molds under pressure, then drying and baking it. It was then used much as plastics are today. Complicated pieces of furniture could be made, which were then lacquered, inlaid with mother-of-pearl, gilded, and painted. At the height of its popularity, some very large pieces of furniture (including a piano) were made by *Jennens and Bettridge.*

Michael Thonet (tŏn'-ĕt) (1796–1871), a German cabinetmaker, pioneered the use of laminated *bentwood* softened with steam (1836–40). He got the idea while watching workmen use steam to soften wood for wheels. His first furniture pieces, made in a shop in Boppard, Germany, were in the Biedermeier style. An Aus-

Table 15.21
Characteristics of English Victorian Furniture

1. Exaggerated interest in historical styles, combined indiscriminately.
2. Design degenerated.
3. Furniture was machine-made (furniture craftsman virtually disappeared after 1880).
4. New materials and technology included tubular metal, cast iron, papier-mâché, bentwood, laminated wood, coil springs (overstuffed furniture).
5. Curves were considered necessary for comfort; corners were rounded.
6. Pieces were massive, with heavy proportions.
7. Woods were dark: mahogany, oak, rosewood, ebony.
8. Ornamentation included inlay, paint, carving.
9. Motifs included Classical, Rococo, Gothic, Renaissance, Oriental, Turkish, miscellaneous.
10. Finishes included lacquer, paint, gilding.

trian Chancellor saw his work at a trade fair and invited him to Vienna (1842). Thonet wanted to produce furniture for the mass market and moved to what is now Czechoslovakia. After seven years, he set up the first known furniture assembly line. By 1847 he was able to manufacture his chairs commercially, making him one of the first large industrialists. After the Great Exhibition of 1851, when his furniture was internationally acclaimed, it was in great demand. (He received a patent on his technique in 1856.)

The classic *Vienna cafe chair* (1849) was made of steamed bentwood rods, was easily shipped (in six pieces), and was assembled with screws. It was strong, light in weight, and inexpensive. This chair is still available today (Figs. 15.24a and 18.20c). Corbusier used a version of it (*Arm Chair #89*) in many of his interiors which further popularized the style. In 1869, Thonet made the bentwood rocker. Laminated wood techniques were perfected by John Henry Belter in the United States (see Chap. 16).

Technological developments such as the *coil spring* made possible comfortable, overstuffed furniture. Mechanical furniture pieces also developed, and these were basic to the evolution of contemporary furniture.

Rococo Style

The Louis XV or Rococo style of Victorian furniture was the most popular. Pieces were elaborately carved and gilded with an excessive use of curved lines (Fig. 15.24b). Motifs included shells, scrolls, feathers, swirls, and other devices from the Louis XV Period. The ornamentation was structural rather than applied (Figs. 15.24b, 15.24c). The *balloon-back* chair (Fig. 15.24c) was an example of this style. The Rococo style was most frequently seen in drawing room or boudoir chairs (Fig. 15.24d).

Gothic Style

The Gothic style (Fig. 15.24e) was characterized by the use of dark oak, and angular Gothic motifs combined with carved floral motifs. These pieces were tall and uncomfortable. Many of the design reformers were partial to Gothic designs, which were popularized by the Pre-Raphaelites (see Chap. 18).

Elizabethan Style

The Elizabethan style of furniture was ornamented with strapwork and faceted carving, and was often assembled from old pieces of carving. Renaissance details were frequently combined with this style (Fig. 15.24f). This furniture was the essence of the Romantic spirit (Fig. 15.24g).

Figure 15.24d
A Rococo style Victorian boudoir chair with scroll foot and casters.

Figure 15.24e
A Gothic style Victorian chair with Gothic motifs; the cushion has tassels at each corner.

Figure 15.24g
A Victorian Renaissance sideboard with carved details.

Figure 15.24f
An Elizabethan or Renaissance style Victorian chair with twist turning, cabriole legs, and cane seat.

Figure 15.25a
A Grecian style Victorian chair.

Figure 15.25b
This Victorian roundabout seat reveals Turkish influence.

Figure 15.25c
An Egyptian style Victorian chair with cove seat, and lattice work on the back and under the seat.

Classical/Greek Style

Grecian-style furniture was made of mahogany and was usually simple and sturdy (Fig. 15.25a). Pedestals in the form of classical columns were used in dining rooms, and some sofas similar to those of the Empire period were used.

Miscellaneous Styles

There were many pieces of furniture made in a combination of styles, including the Turkish, the Oriental, and the Egyptian (Figs. 15.25b, 15.25c). Furniture of bamboo and simulated bamboo was particularly popular between 1870 and 1890. Overstuffed furniture was very popular but often the upholstery overpowered the design and smothered the structure. Ottomans and overstuffed sofas were also in vogue.

Glossary

Agate Ware. A marbled earthenware made of different-colored clays.

Aniline Dye. A dye obtained from a coal-tar derivative.

Apron. A band of wood just under the seat of a chair, the top of a table, or the base of a cabinet.

Arcade. A series of adjoining arches with supporting columns, often used as a decorative detail on the backs of chairs or on chests.

Aumbry (also *ambry* or *almery*). An early food-storage cupboard with a pierced door.

Ball-and-Claw Foot. A foot carved to resemble a claw (probably of a dragon) clutching a ball.

Barley-Sugar Twist. The ornamental spiral turning used in the Restoration Period.

Bay Window. A window that projects from the exterior wall.

Bellflower. An eighteenth-century carved motif resembling a vertical chain or swag of bell-shaped flowers (similar to the husk design)

Bentwood. Wood which is softened by steaming and then molded.

Bevel. A slanted edge on a mirror or panel.

Block Print. Fabric printed by the use of carved wooden blocks.

Bobbin Turning. A leg that is turned to resemble a small series of bulbs.

Bombé. A commode, bureau, or chest with a convex base.

Bonnet Top. The arched top of clocks, highboys, secretaries, and so on.

Bow Window. A curved window that projects from an exterior wall.

Box Chair. A chair crudely made in the shape of a box.

Broken Pediment. An interrupted pediment with (often) an ornament between the two pieces.

Bun Foot. A slightly flattened ball foot.

Burl. A wartlike growth which produced a knotted pattern in the veneer cut from it.

Cabochon. A convex oval ornamentation found most often on the knee of Early Georgian Period legs.

Camelback Sofa. An upholstered sofa, usually Chippendale, which is higher at the centerback than the sides.

Cane. A flexible seat material woven from rattan palm.

Canted. Slanted or angled edge.

Cartouche. An oval or oblong shape used as ornament.

Casters. Small wheels on the legs and bases of furniture, used in the Victorian Period.

Chair-Table. A chair which converts to a table, either round or rectangular, when the back is dropped to a horizontal position. It is supported by the arms, and was used in the Jacobean period.

Club Foot. A flat, round pad foot used on the cabriole leg in the Queen Anne Period.

Comb Back. A type of Windsor chair back resembling the Spanish comb.

Confidant. A sofa with attached seats at either end placed at a diagonal; popularized by Adam and Hepplewhite.

Coromandel Screen. A Chinese paneled screen with bas-relief patterns on rich, dark lacquer.

Cornucopia. The horn of plenty with fruits and flowers pouring forth, used as a decorative detail.

Court Cupboard. A short cupboard with open shelves used during the Elizabethan and Jacobean Periods to display plate.

Crenellation. Originally battlements but later a parapet with alternating indentations used on English houses as ornamental detail.

Cresting. The carving on the top rail of the back of a chair or settee.

Cyma. A double S-shaped curve.

Dado. The lower part of the wall (two to three feet) delineated by a molding.

Dentil. Ornamental detail resembling teeth.

Derbyshire Chair. A Jacobean English country chair with inward scrolls on the top of the back uprights, an arch-shaped back, and a cross-rail.

Diaper. A diamond pattern in brick.

Draw Table. A three-leaved table with two end leaves stored under a center leaf.

Dog-Leg Stair. A stairway in which each flight flanks the one below.

Dome Bed. An eighteenth-century bed with a dome-shaped tester.

Ebonize. The staining and polishing of wood to make it appear to be ebony.

Escutcheon. The metal plate that fits over the keyhole of a chest or door.

Exhibition Furniture. Very large furniture designed for the exhibitions popular from 1851 to 1900, and never intended for domestic use.

Fan Vault. A vault overlaid with radiating ribs that form a fan pattern.

Farthingale Chair. An upright, upholstered armless chair popular in the Restoration Period; named after the hoop women wore under their skirts.

Filigree. A lacy, delicate design pierced in metal, wood, or stone.

Finial. The ornament at the end of a pediment, an intersection, or a post.

Flap Table. A table with a fixed center slab and two side leaves supported on slides; often called a *drop-leaf table*.

Fall Front. A writing cabinet with a drop-front for writing.

Flemish Scroll Foot. An S or C form found on Flemish, Dutch, and English furniture feet.

Fluted. A series of parallel, grooves cut into a column or a furniture leg.

Field Bed. A small arched-canopy bed named for the bed used in the field by army officers.

Four-Centered Tudor Arch. A pointed arch with a low rise.

French Polish. A highly glazed Victorian furniture finish that emphasized the grain.

Gable. The triangular portion of a wall at the end of a pitched roof.

Gadrooning. A band of oval forms carved in relief.

Gallery. A brass or wooden rail used to edge tables and sideboards.

Gate-Leg Table. A table with one or two fold-down leaves, usually supported by movable legs.

Gilding. The use of gold leaf or gold dust to ornament furniture and emphasize architectural details.

Girandole. A many-branched, usually mirrored, wall candle sconce.

Glastonbury Chair. An Elizabethan folding chair based on Italian designs but mistakenly named for a chair at Glastonbury which the abbot used.

Gothick. A spelling of *Gothic* used in the eighteenth century and popularized by Horace Walpole when he made his home, Strawberry Hill, into a "Gothick castle."

Griffin. (often spelled *griffon* and *gryphon*): A mythical animal with the head, wings, and forelegs of an eagle and the hindquarters of a lion; revived as ornamental detail in the Late Georgian and Regency Periods.

Guilloche. A motif composed of interwoven circles.

Half-Timber. (sometimes called *timber-frame*): A timber framework filled with wattle and daub, plaster, brickwork, or stone; used in the Tudor and Elizabethan Periods, and imitated in the Victorian Period.

Hall. (Sometimes referred to as the *great hall.*) The main living room in Tudor, Elizabethan, and Jacobean houses; usually had a dais at one end and was entered through the screens passage.

Hall Chair. A wooden chair placed in the hall for servants.

Hammer-Beam Truss. An English Renaissance arched roof that rested upon wooden brackets.

Handkerchief Table. A triangular table with a triangular drop leaf that fit into a corner of a room.

Harewood. A wood, frequently dyed, used in the eighteenth century for inlay and marquetry.

Hock Leg. A broken curved leg ornamented with carved spiral scrolls at the sides of the knee.

Hoof Foot. A foot that resembled an animal hoof; used with the cabriole leg.

Hoop-Back Windsor Chair. A Windsor chair in which the top rail and uprights form a continuous curve.

Husk. A representation of an oak husk which was used to create an ornamental pattern, popular during the Late Georgian period.

Hutch Table. A low serving table with storage.

Inverted Cup. A leg form resembling an inverted cup, popular during the William and Mary Period.

Jappanning. An English imitation of Oriental lacquer.

Jasperware. An unglazed stoneware with white classical designs on blue, green, lavender, pink, or black background, introduced by Wedgwood.

Joined Chair. A chair made by joiners.

Joiners. A Craftsmen who joined furniture with joints, glue, and/or dowels.

Joinery. The assembling of furniture with joints, dowels, or glue.

Kneehole Desk. A desk with solid sides with storage space and central leg room.

Ladder-back Chair. A chair with horizontal slats on the back.

Lacquer. An Oriental finish made from the resin lac from the lacquer tree; hardened and polished to a high gloss.

Lattice. A diamond-shaped or fretwork pattern.

Lights. Window panes.

Livery Cupboard. A court cupboard used to store food.

Long Gallery. A long room in Elizabethan and Jacobean houses used for exercise and work during the winter months.

Lozenge. A diamond-shaped motif popular in the English Renaissance.

Lyre Form. The curving outline of a lyre, used in the Late Georgian period; the strings of the lyre were usually brass.

Lunette. A half-moon shape.

Marlborough Leg. A straight, grooved leg with a block foot.

Marquetry. Inlaid veneers.

Medallion. An oval or circular frame enclosing an ornamental motif.

Minstrels' Gallery. The place where the minstrels sat in the great hall.

Monopodium. A form resembling a lion's head, chest, and paw, used as a support; especially popular in the Regency Period and revived by Thomas Hope.

Morris Chair. An easy chair with a wooden frame and adjustable back designed by William Morris & Co.

Mounts. Ornamental metalwork; e.g., handles, escutcheons, and drawer pulls.

Newel Post. The post at the end of the rail on a stairway.

Newel Stair. A circular stair that winds around a circular newel.

Niche. A functional or decorative wall recess; used by Adam.

Nonesuch Chest. A chest with an inlaid pattern representing the Nonesuch Palace built for Henry VIII in the Tudor period.

Ogee. A molding made of two S—shaped curves meeting at a point and used on pediments, aprons, or bracket feet.

Ogee Bracket Foot. A bracket foot with a reverse S—shaped curve.

Open-Well Stair. A stairway with flights at right angles to one another surrounding an open space.

Oriel Window. A bay window supported by brackets; used in the English Renaissance.

Overstuffed. Heavily upholstered furniture with a concealed frame.

Ovolo. A convex molding which is quarter round in section.

Oyster Veneer. A veneer with a circular figure.

Pagoda. A temple design used by Chippendale on his Chinese styles.

Papier-mâché. A paper pulp that was

molded, baked, and lacquered; popular during the Victorian Period.

Parcel Gilt.   Partly gilded furniture.

Parquetry.   An inlaid geometric floor pattern.

Parrot Back.   The negative parrot-shaped space between the splat and the side and top rails of the chairs and settees of the Queen Anne Period.

Partners' Desk.   A desk with space for two people to sit facing each other; used in the eighteenth century.

Patera.   A small round ornament used as ornamentation in the Late Georgian Period.

Pedestal Support.   A decorative base for furniture or stands.

Pembroke Table.   A small breakfast or occasional table with drop leaves.

Pendant.   A hanging ornament used on Renaissance ceilings and later on furniture.

Perpendicular Style.   A late English Gothic style used in the Tudor Period; characterized by slender vertical lines.

Petit Point.   Fine needlepoint with about twenty stitches to the inch.

Piecrust Table.   A tripod table with a scalloped edge.

Pier Table.   A side table made to be placed against a wall; often had a mirror over it.

Pierced Splat.   The openwork design in the center splat; appeared in the William and Mary Period.

Pompeian Style.   Regency rooms ornamented in the style discovered in Pompeii.

Porcelain.   A fine, hard, translucent ware, first made in China in the thirteenth century.

Porphyry.   A red, green, or purple marble.

Porter's Chair.   A chair, found in the English country house, with enclosed sides so that a servant sitting near the door was protected from drafts.

Portland Stone.   A white or creamy limestone, found on the island of Portland, popularized by Christopher Wren.

Press.   A clothing storage unit.

Prince of Wales Feather.   The ostrich feather adopted by the Prince of Wales; used as ornamentation in the Late Georgian Period.

Quoin.   Dressed stone or brickwork on the corners of a building.

Rake.   An inward slant or slope; the opposite of *splay*.

Ram's Head.   A classical motif used by Adam.

Reeding.   Semicircular convex moldings; the opposite of *fluting*.

Rent Table.   A pedestal table, usually with a circular top, with drawers painted or inlaid with letters to keep accounts; popular in late Georgian period.

Ribband Back.   (Sometimes called *ribbon back*.) A light, rococo decoration used by Chippendale to resemble ribbons.

Roll-top Desk.   A tambour desk with a curved top.

Romayne Work.   Carved medallions and/or heads used in the English Renaissance.

Rosette.   A carved, painted, or molded rose.

Rush.   Grass scattered on stone floors in the Tudor Period.

Saber Leg.   (Also called *sabre*) A splayed Grecian leg on Regency seating pieces.

Satyr Mask.   A motif used on Early Georgian furniture.

Scagliola.   An imitation marble made of marble chips and plaster of Paris.

Sconce.   A wall light.

Screens Passage.   The entrance that kept drafts from the great hall.

Seaweed Marquetry.   An arabesque pattern of leaves and seaweed used in the William and Mary and Queen Anne Periods.

Settle.   An early unpadded seat with arms and a high back.

Shell Motif.   A motif popular in the Queen and Chippendale Periods.

Sidechair.   An armless chair.

Side Table.   A table with a decorative front, positioned in front of a wall.

Slab-ended.   A board-ended chest or stool.

Slant-front Desk.   A writing desk with a slanted front and a hinged lid.

Slipper Foot.   A club foot with a pointed toe, popular during the Queen Anne Period.

Sofa Table.   A Late Georgian table made to be placed behind the sofa; usually had drawers and often two flaps.

Spade Foot.   A short square foot which is tapered, sometimes called a therm foot.

Spanish Foot.   A foot that is an inward curving scroll.

Spindle.   A long, slender, turned rod.

Splay Leg.   An outward flaring leg.

Split Spindle.   A spindle, cut in half lengthwise, and then applied to the furniture as ornamentation.

Spode.   An underglazed blue transfer-printed ware.

Spoon Back.   The concave back of Queen Anne chairs, inspired by the Chinese.

Squab Cushion.   A loose thin cushion used in the Renaissance.

Stoneware. An opaque, heavy pottery made from a siliceous paste.

Strapwork. A pattern of curving, interlacing bands used in the Renaissance to ornament ceilings, fireplaces, and so on.

Stretcher. The horizontal support for legs of chairs and tables.

Stringing. A narrow metal or wood inlaid outline mainly on case pieces.

Swag. A festoon in imitation of fabric or floral motifs used as a decorative motif.

Swan-neck Pediment. A broken pediment made of two scrolls.

Table Dormant. The table used by the master of the house in the Tudor Period; it was placed on the dais in the great hall.

Tallboy. A chest-on-chest, usually with two small drawers at the top and six large ones below.

Tambour Desk. A roll-top desk with small pieces of wood or reeds glued on a canvas backing which forms the roll top.

Teardrop Brasses. Teardrop-shaped drawer pulls.

Tent Bed. A four-poster bed with a tester resembling a tent top.

Tester. A flat, paneled, and/or carved wooden canopy used on four-poster beds.

Tilt-top Table. A table with a hinged top.

Therm Leg. A tapering leg used in the Late Georgian Period, usually decorated with inlay or carving.

Therm Foot. A spade or tapering block foot.

Trafalgar Chair. A regency saber-leg chair with a scrolled arm.

Tripod Table. A small tea table with a central support with three legs.

Truckle Bed. A trundle bed or a bed kept under a full-sized bed when not in use.

Trumpet Turned. A leg form with a flaring end, used in Restoration styles.

Tudor Arch. A four-centered arch.

Tufting. Upholstery tied in a pattern to create little pillows, most popular during the Victorian Period.

Tudor Rose. A Renaissance motif resembling the five-petal rose set in the center of a circle; it symbolized the marriage of Henry VII to Elizabeth of York.

Turkey-Work. Fabric or rug with a knotted pile.

Turned Chair. (Also called *thrown chair*.) A Tudor chair constructed of many turned members and usually with a triangular seat.

Twist Turning. A sprial turning used in the Restoration Period.

Veneer. A thin slide of wood, usually decoratively grained, glued to a less expensive wood.

Wainscot. A close-grained oak paneling which may continue to the ceiling; popular in the Tudor period.

Wainscot Chair. A chair named for the back panel which was named for a piece of wainscot paneling.

Wattle and Daub. Interlaced willow or hazel rods coated with mud or clay and used for building houses in the Renaissance.

Wardrobe. A hanging cupboard and clothes-storage unit.

Water Leaf. A broad, unveined leaf carved in low relief in the eighteenth century.

Wedgwood. Jasperware.

Wheat Ear. A carved, painted, or inlaid decorative motif resembling an ear of wheat; used in the Late Georgian Period.

Wheel-back Chair. A chair with spokes radiating from a central boss or patera; used particularly by Adam.

Wing Chair. A fully upholstered easy chair with wings to protect the sitter from the draft.

Yorkshire Chair. A small, provincial Jacobean chair with knob-turned wooden legs and straight uprights that ended in an inward turned scroll.

Bibliography

ARONSON, JOSEPH. *The Encyclopedia of Furniture.* New York: Crown Publishers, Inc., 1965.

BOGER, LOUISE ADE. *The Complete Guide to Furniture Styles.* New York: Charles Scribner's Sons, 1969.

The Connoisseur Period Guide to the Houses, Decoration, Furnishings, and Chattels of the Classic Periods. London: Connoisseur. 1956–58.

EDWARDS, RALPH, and L. G. G. RAMSLY, eds. *The Connoisseurs Complete Period Guides.* New York: Bonanza Books, 1968.

GIBBS-SMITH, C. H. *The Great Exhibition of 1851.* London: The Victoria and Albert Museum, 1950.

MACQUOID, PERCY, and RALPH EDWARDS. *Dictionary of English Furniture from the Middle Ages to the Late Georgian Period.* London: Country Life Ltd., 1954.

PEGLER, MARTIN. *The Dictionary of Interior Design.* New York: Crown Publishers, Inc., 1966.

PENDEREL-BRODHURST, et al. *Glossary of English Furniture of the Historic Periods.* London: John Murray, 1925.

PEVSNER, NIKOLAUS. *An Outline of European Architecture.* New York: Penguin Books, 1943.

SYMONDS, ROBERT W., and B. B. SHINERAY. *Victorian Furniture*. London: Country Life Ltd., 1962.

WANSCHER, OLE. *The Art of Furniture*. New York: Van Nostrand Reinhold Company, 1966.

WELLMAN, RITA. *Victoria Royal*. New York: Charles Scribner's Sons, 1939.

YARWOOD, DOREEN. *The Architecture of Britain*. New York: Charles Scribner's Sons, 1976.

———. *The Architecture of England*. London: B. T. Batsford, 1963.

———. *The English House*. London: B. T. Batsford, 1956.

American Architecture and Interior Styles*

It was inevitable that the early American colonies would absorb the English heritage. Its influence was spread by the colonists' great dependence upon the furniture, clothes, and tools imported from England. As an American merchant class emerged and the new colonies developed the ability to manufacture the necessities of life, this dependence upon England and the Continent gradually diminished.

A new patriotism, unknown to the early settlers, was fostered by freedom from political or religious persecution. This patriotism kindled ingenuity and inventiveness that allowed them to achieve the self-reliance and independence necessary to break political and economic ties with the mother country.

Early Colonial Period (1608–1720)

Historical Background

The first permanent settlement at Jamestown in 1607 was followed by two unsuccessful attempts by the British to establish colonies before the Mayflower finally landed in 1620. After the landing, settlements increased rapidly. Colonists came to America for a variety of reasons: to seek economic opportunity, to secure freedom of worship, and to acquire land. Difficult conditions made shelter the first priority, then land had to be cleared and crops planted and cultivated. A running battle against the Indians, the elements, accidents, and sickness demanded so much effort that little time was left to cultivate the arts.

The economy was based upon agriculture and as early as 1612, tobacco was cultivated in Jamestown. Some trades and industries, such as fishing, lumber, ship-building, and iron manufacture, were gradually added; later such crafts as the making of furniture, glass, pottery and metal developed. The social center of the community was the church, and strict laws governed behavior. Harvard College was founded in 1636, though it was not until 1647 that a public school system was established. News was spread by word of mouth, by post riders, and by the town crier. The first newspaper, the *Boston Newsletter,* was founded in 1704. Early American literature had a strong religious tone, although there were a few books about colonial life. A few untrained artists called *limners* traveled about the country earning their living by painting portraits of wealthy colonists.

Governors were elected by the people or appointed by the king. Legislatures resembled the English Parliament, although any laws they passed had to be approved in England. The right to vote was limited to male property owners, and usually to one religious group. The social structure was similar to England's (except America had no hereditary aristocracy). It consisted of an upper class or gentry (rich merchants and planters), a middle class (farmers, shopkeepers, teachers, and craftsmen), and a lower class (indentured servants and slaves).

Architecture

Frame Dwelling 1620–1700 (Fig. 16.1)

The earliest colonists lived in single-room dwellings (with perhaps a sleeping loft) that had a wood frame, a thatched roof, and end chimneys of sticks and mud. The builders were immigrants, mostly of peasant origin, who understood the technique of frame construction and knew how to build simple structures. Harsh conditions dictated that dwellings be quickly constructed, so there was no time for details. Using Iron Age tools, the builders hewed timbers into frame, joined them by mortises and tenons, and insulated the dwelling with clay. Glass was rare, so window openings were shuttered against the elements. Shingle roofs were soon substituted for thatch, but the dangerous stick and mud chimney (responsible for many fires) persisted long after other primitive features disappeared. Wood was used in America for, unlike the case in England, it was plentiful. The frame dwelling was simple and all the living areas—hall, parlor, bedchamber and kitchen—existed within a single space.

Family interaction was greatly affected by house structure, for there were often as many as ten people living in the limited space. Children, parents, grandparents, and even unmarried aunts and uncles shared the same quarters. It is certainly no wonder that exchanges were restricted and inhibited among the various relatives. The lack of sexual privacy, for example, helped to foster prudish and restrained behavior.

* Most of the houses in this chapter and some of the historical material was developed by Tim Bookout, Professor of Interior Design, Georgia State University.

Table 16.1
Relationship of Important Furniture Periods to the Early Colonial Period

England	France
Jacobean 1603–60	Renaissance 1485–1643
Restoration 1660–1702	Louis XIV 1643–1700
Queen Anne 1702–14	Régence 1700–30
Early Georgian 1714–50	

Table 16.2
Frame Dwelling

Space:	Single room
Form:	Square
Colors:	Natural Materials
Texture:	Wood
Correlate:	Restricted, inhibited family exchanges

Medieval Frame Dwelling 1650–1700 (Fig. 16.2)

Seventeenth-century colonists drew heavily upon abundant timber to create dwellings in styles familiar to them. Although medieval in character and already going out of fashion in England at the time of their construction in America, these homes gave the settlers time to deal with the physical requirements of survival.

Most of these dwellings were clapboard-sided, with small casement windows of diamond-shaped pieces of glass leaded together. High-pitched roofs in gabled construction were covered with hand-made shingles. The second floor of these buildings protruded slightly beyond the first in English fashion, with wooden *pendrils* (the ends of the corner posts) under the over-hang. Fireplaces were generally in the center in the parlor and bed-chambers were on the second floor. Few of these buildings still exist but those that do (mainly in New England) are reminders of the lasting quality of timber construction.

This style of house was an exception to the more typical one-room construction that dominated in most areas. The larger plan allowed for more privacy and for increased personal space, although it frequently housed ten to twelve family members in addition to servants. It afforded family members some expression of individual personality, for a given area within the house was likely to contain and display the possessions of a single family member, the married couple, the children, and/or the relatives. As other national groups came to America, they brought influences from their native lands. Contrary to popular belief, the log cabin did not appear until about 1683, when it became an important factor in the expansion of the frontier. It was a Swedish tradition and first appeared in Delaware.

Cape Cod Dwelling 1690–1840 (Fig. 16.3)

The Cape Cod house was built by ship's carpenters to ride the sands and withstand the strong northeast winds. It was low (one and one-half stories) and wide, with a low-pitched roof with gable ends. The roof was very effi-

Table 16.3
Medieval Frame Dwelling

Space:	Hall and parlor plan
Form:	Irregular or rectilinear gabled construction
Colors:	Natural wood
Texture:	Clapboard, weatherboarding, timber framing
Line:	Horizontal or irregular
Correlates:	More privacy, greater personal space

Table 16.4
Cape Cod Dwelling

Space:	Symmetrical arrangement around central chimney
Form:	Rectangular
Colors:	Weathered gray
Texture:	Wood shingles or clapboards
Line:	Horizontal
Correlate:	Kitchen center of family life

Figure 16.2
A medieval frame dwelling,
1650–1700. This example
has an overhanging second
story with pendrils, a
high pitched shingle roof
and windows with
diamond-shaped panes
of glass.

Figure 16.3
A Cape Cod dwelling,
1690–1840. Board
pediments cap the door and
windows; the central
chimney serves both sides
of the house.

Figure 16.4
A salt-box dwelling, 1700–
70. This house has a
central chimney and
doorway; windows are
double-hung.

cient in shedding rain or snow, and the massive central brick chimney served as an anchor for the house. There were no dormers or projections of any kind. The front windows and those at the gable ends were capped with simple board pediments. The two-room-deep plan was arranged symmetrically around a central chimney stairway, which led to the upstairs bedrooms. The center of family life was the back kitchen, which extended the width of the house: here the family worked and the children played during the long winter days. Interior walls were painted white throughout the house to reflect the weak winter sun, and soft pine furniture was gaily painted for protection against the elements.

Salt-Box Dwelling 1700–70 (Fig. 16.4)

The salt box, with its two-story front and one-story rear, evolved from the practice of

Table 16.5
Salt-Box Dwelling

Space:	Symmetrical arrangement around central chimney, one room deep with room across back
Form:	Square base
Colors:	Natural materials
Texture:	Narrow clapboards
Line:	Horizontal
Correlate:	Close family life

Figure 16.5a
An Early Colonial chest, with bun feet, split spindles, and panels for ornamentation.

Figure 16.5b
This Early Colonial chest with three asters in center, split spindles, and turtle-back bosses, has a two-leaved tulip on each side.

Figure 16.5c
The drawers of this Early Colonial high chest of drawers with William and Mary inverted-cup legs are veneered walnut with herringbone border; the drops are pear-shaped, and the curves of the stretcher match those of the apron.

Table 16.6
Characteristics of Early Colonial Furniture

1. It was crudely made with few tools.
2. It was based on simplified versions of Jacobean and Restoration styles.
3. Pieces were smaller than English pieces.
4. Native woods were used, such as oak, pine, maple, hickory, cherry, and walnut.
5. Several woods were often combined in the same piece.
6. Legs were turned and straight.
7. Chairs had straight backs (ladder, banister, solid, and wainscot); rush or wood board seats.
8. Ornamentation was simplified and included turnings, chip carving, split spindles, painting, round or oval wood handles.
9. Motifs included guilloche, lunette, Tudor rose, arcaded panel, tulips, sunflower, acanthus leaf, strapwork.
10. Furniture was frequently dual-purpose.

ney. There were symmetrical front windows and simple board pediments over both windows and doors. The house was one room deep, with a lean-to (which added a room across the back). There were no windows in the back and a side door opened into the lean-to space.

Furniture

Furniture was the last priority of the colonists, because one room had to serve a multitude of needs, furnishings had to be dual-purpose. There were few cabinetmakers among the ranks of the early settlers. Designs were based upon simplified English provincial styles of the Jacobean and Restoration Periods.

Chests

The chest was the most common as well as the most important piece of furniture in the early American home. It was used as a trunk when traveling or for storage at home. It also served as a seat or a table. Early chests were boxes with hinged lids, resting flat on the floor or on extended end boards that served as legs. Gradually drawers were added and later the chest was decorated with scratching, carving, painting, and attached ornamentation, such as *split spindles* (Fig. 16.5a), moldings, or *bosses* such as turtle bosses, which were the shape of a turtle's back (Fig. 16.5b). The chest gradually evolved into a chest of drawers on

adding a lean-to at the rear. In the early examples, this addition could often be seen by the changed angle of the roof. The roof-line, similar in shape to that of the salt box in use at that time, gave the style its name. The house was a true square with a central doorway and chim-

Figure 16.5e
This Early Colonial court cupboard with foliated scroll design around top has a rosette and foliation in the center panel, a guilloche in the lower center strip, and a lunette design around the base; the sides of the upper section are splayed.

Figure 16.5d
This Early Colonial press cupboard in simplified Jacobean style has round wood door knobs; its sides are splayed, with turned supports and simple moldings.

feet. Brass pulls, usually in the *drop* style (Fig. 16.5c), were first made about 1675 to replace the early clothespin-type wooden knobs (Fig. 16.5b, 16.5d).

Highboys were chests of drawers on legs. Most show the influence of the Restoration Period, with *pear drops, inverted cup legs* (Fig. 16.5c), and X–shaped stretchers. *Court* and *press* cupboards evolved from the chest and were made in two sections so that they could be moved up the steep, narrow stairs. The press cupboard (Fig. 16.5d) held clothing and linen and was usually paneled and carved, in a simplified Jacobean style. The court cupboard, which reached the zenith of its development in the early 1600s, was the most ornamental piece of furniture in the early Colonial house (Fig. 16.5e): it had a door in the shelved upper section and was used to store eating utensils and wine and to display plate, the wealth of the household. It often had *splayed sides, split spindles,* and carved and paneled doors. Many typical motifs were carved on it such as *guilloches, foliated scrolls lunettes,* and *rosettes.*

The *scrutoire,* which developed from a chest-enclosed desk used for writing (Fig. 16.5f), had drawers below, a drop lid, and enclosed book-shelves above. *Corner* cupboards, designed to fit into the corner of a room, were also popular and continued to be through the eighteenth century.

Figure 16.5f
A double-dome slant-front Early Colonial desk with bun feet.

Figure 16.6a
A turned table in Early Colonial style has an ogee-curved apron and pendant drops.

Tables

Early tables were of the trestle type and were usually large, but after the meal was over the removable top was placed against the wall and the trestles were moved out of the way.

The frames were made of oak, but the boards were made of pine because it was unnecessary that they be strong.

Figure 16.7a
The front and rear legs of this Early Colonial wainscot chair-table are turned; a drawer is under seat.

Figure 16.6b
A drop-leaf gate-leg Early Colonial table with two turned legs.

Figure 16.6c
An Early Colonial table with butterfly support for flaps.

Figure 16.7b
An Early Colonial wainscot chair with turned front legs and stretcher.

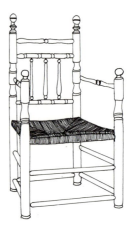

Figure 16.7c
An Early Colonial Carver-style turned chair with vase-shaped supports for arms with knobs.

Figure 16.7d
This Early Colonial banister-back chair with Spanish feet has fleur-de-lis and C–scroll on cresting; its legs are turned in vase, ring, and bulb pattern.

Figure 16.7e
An Early Colonial chair with spiral turning.

Later tables had turned legs (Fig. 16.6a) connected by stretchers, with a wide over-hang and drawers in the apron under the top. *Drop-leaf* tables with *gate-legs* (Fig. 16.6b), *butterfly flaps* (Fig. 16.6c), swinging arms, and pulls for the support of the hinged flaps were typical. Chair tables were also common (Fig. 16.7a).

Chairs

Because space was at a premium, dual-purpose furniture was common, with the chair-table most typical. Some of the earliest exam-ples combined the wainscot chair with a table that folded over the arms (Fig. 16.7a). Turned legs and drawers under the seat were typical. Other examples had square or round table tops.

The *wainscot chair* served as the seat of honor (Fig. 16.7b); it had a paneled oak back, curved arms and turned front legs with stretchers. The *Carver chair* (1650–1700) was turned and had a rush seat (Fig. 16.7c). The *banister-back* chair (Fig. 16.7d) and the *Brewster chair* were similar to the Carver chair. Some turned chairs were very ornate (Fig. 16.7e).

In the latter part of the seventeenth century, upholstered leather (Fig. 16.7f) or *turkey-work* chairs were introduced. About 1690 cane chairs were introduced that were more ornate and had the *Flemish scroll foot* (Fig. 16.7g). Restoration-style chairs with matching cresting and stretchers, upholstered in leather with nailhead ornamentation, became popular (Fig. 16.7h).

Beds

Beds were of the pull-down type at first; then the trundle bed was introduced. Later the four-poster bed was made to harmonize with the furniture. Mattresses were of straw, oak leaves, beech leaves, cattails, corn shucks, or feathers. Beds were corded with heavy rope.

Accessories

Treenware, objects made from wood (often burl) for the table, became popular. Stoneware was made in the late 1600s and ornamented with a transparent salt-glaze or a cobalt blue slip. Iron utensils were imported until about 1725. Pewter, also mostly imported, was made in the late 1600s and early 1700s in America and was called "poor man's silver." Silver coins were made into tableware, one way to store wealth. The centers of silver-making were Boston, New York, and Philadelphia. Styles were simple until about 1660, when relief ornamentation was used (gadrooning was most common). Brass was also imported, as was copper. Tinware was made in the early part of the eighteenth century and was light in weight, bright, and inexpensive. Textiles were mainly woven in the household; flax, cotton, and wool fibers were used alone or in combination.

American Georgian Period (1720–90)

Historical Background

During the American Georgian Period America was settled between Maine and Florida. Indian attacks had almost ceased making it possible for the country to become industrialized. In 1754 a Federal union was recommended. Although the colonies were not yet ready for this, it marked the beginning of a desire for home rule. In 1781, after the Revolution, the Constitution was signed and ratified.

In 1789 Washington was inaugurated as President. Patriotism swept the land. The economy was expanding both in the agrarian South and in the industrial North. The diverse society no longer had England's strong class system, but sexual mores included a double standard for the middle and upper classes. Children were numerous and educated at home until the age of fourteen when they were hired out, apprenticed, or, in the case of the wealthy, sent to private schools (if they were male). There was little demand for the arts, but journals and diaries were kept, and family portraits were in demand.

Architecture

The exterior of the house was symmetrical and imposing. Regional differences were less marked than in earlier periods. English styles

Table 16.7
Relationship of Important Furniture Periods to the American Georgian Period

England	France
Early Georgian 1714–50	Régence 1700–30
Middle Georgian 1750–70	Louis XV 1730–60
Late Georgian 1770–1811	Louis XVI 1760–89

Table 16.8
Ways in Which European and English Style Influences Came to America

1. Trade with London and the importation of furniture and architectural components, such as brass hardware, candeliers, scenic wallpapers, and so on
2. The travels of gentlemen who became familiar with the architecture of England, Italy and France
3. Books on Italian Renaissance architecture, theory and composition, particularly Palladio's book
4. The many handbooks published for use by carpenters

predominated, however, in spite of political differences. English and European influences came to America, with a ten- to fifteen-year lag, in several ways.

Queen Anne Style-Dwelling 1720–50 (Fig. 16.8)

In the Queen Anne style, active experimentation with the building surface gave rise to the diversity of classical motifs incorporated in the surfaces of these symmetrically organized buildings. Split pediments, large moldings, and arched and pedimented windows and doorways were only a few of the details characteristic of a Queen Anne façade. Although these details were not applied with historical accuracy, they were by definition part of the robust and active quality that gave the Queen Anne style its unique character.

The Queen Anne style reflected the wealth attained by a limited number of families. Those who could afford a home of this character lived a life quite different from that lived by the general populace. The wife directed and controlled the servants who cared for the house. These duties, even with a full staff of servants, occupied most of her day. The husband had little to say about the day-to-day op-

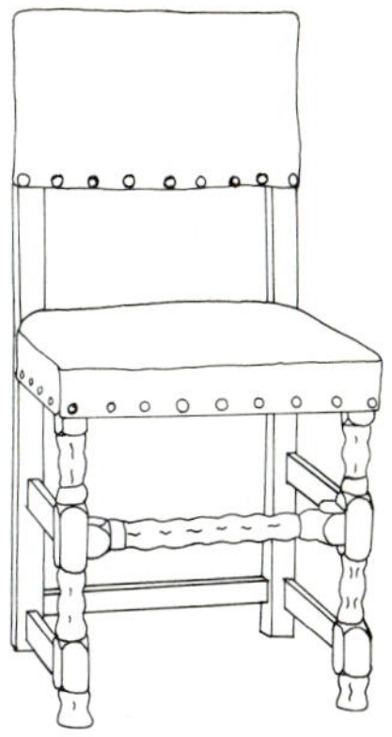

Figure 16.7f
An Early Colonial chair covered with leather attached with nailheads.

Figure 16.7g
This Early Colonial cane chair with X–shaped stretcher and Spanish feet has birds' heads on the corners of the back, and cresting is two birds' heads with beaks together; its legs are cup-shaped, and there are finials on the stretcher.

Figure 16.7h
This Early Colonial chair in William and Mary style with matching stretcher and cresting is upholstered in leather attached with nailheads.

Figure 16.8
A Queen Anne-style dwelling, 1720–50. A broken scroll pediment surmounts the door, chimneys are placed at each end of the hipped roof, and the dormer windows have triangular pediments.

Figure 16.9
A Late Georgian dwelling, 1750–80. The projecting entrance and door are surmounted with triangular pediments; a set of three Palladian windows is on the second floor over the door which has a fan light. Quoins at the sides and the projecting entrance and a string course which separates the stories are typical of this style. The hipped roof has a balustrade and end chimneys and there is a key stone over the sash windows.

Table 16.9
Queen Anne-Style Dwelling

Space:	Georgian plan
Form:	Rectilinear
Colors:	Terra-cotta and stone
Texture:	Brick, stone and weatherboard
Line:	Horizontal, symmetrical balance
Correlate:	Owners had high status

Table 16.10
Late Georgian Dwelling

Space:	Georgian plan
Form:	Square
Colors:	Terra-cotta, gray, stone white
Texture:	Brick, stone, stucco, weatherboarding, wood made to resemble masonry
Line:	Unified, symmetrical balance
Correlate:	Formal family roles

eration of the home: he was expected to tend to his investments, politics, or business outside the home. The families who owned such houses were considered the pillars of the community and even of the state and the nation, and were looked up to by those of lesser means.

Late Georgian Dwelling 1750–80
(Fig. 16.9)

Queen Anne houses combined a rectilinear plan with classical motifs. The Late Georgian house formalized these features into a more unified and vertical structure and expanded the use of classical details. These houses were most frequently built in Virginia and were strongly affected by English Palladian styles.

Doorways were surmounted by closed or broken pediments in the Queen Anne style, but they now projected in the Georgian style to give additional depth to the dwelling. Symmetry, still the most important characteristic, was heightened by the use of such features as dormers, hipped roofs, patterned brick surfaces, stone quoins at the edges of the buildings, and plain string courses separating the various stories. Classical entablatures and dentils expanded the depth of the cornices beneath the eaves. Doorways had a semicircular fanlight above, surmounted by a cornice and/or pediment.

As part of his education, the eighteenth-century gentleman and builder included travel in Italy to study the value of the Classical Period. Measured drawings from ancient ruins were published in pattern books to give Americans ready access to the latest European and English building styles for the first time.

Table 16.11
Characteristics of American Georgian Architecture

1. The exterior was symmetrical.
2. The entrance was imposing: wide paneled center door; classical orders, entablature, and mitered pediment.
3. A semi-circular fanlight window with ornamental tracery surmounted the door after 1750.
4. Sash windows (six lights over six lights) framed with architrave or triangular cornice were symmetrically placed: two windows on each side of door, five on second story.
5. Dormers, if used, were topped with arch or low-pitched gable.
6. Roof was hipped, gambrel, or low gable.
7. Form was square rectilinear, with moldings emphasizing horizontal lines and marking floor levels.
8. Quoins (corner stones) on masonry houses were emphasized by size, manner of cutting, joining, or texture.
9. Some houses featured a captain's walk (a flat roof deck) enclosed with balustrade, often with Oriental lattice work.
10. Plain, rectangular chimneys were placed on the ends.
11. Regional differences were less marked owing to improved communication.
12. Textures of wall surfaces (wood) were treated to resemble stone or brick.

As a result, the later eighteenth-century Georgian styles rendered classical motifs more elaborately and with greater historical accuracy. The formality of the style reflected the growing sophistication of upper-class Americans, and their increased desire to prove to Europe that American aesthetic expression was coming of age, even though its impetus was European. In architecture, America borrowed rather than imitated designs. The Georgian style was consistent with the formal family roles and the demeanor of its members prevalent at the time.

Interiors

The elegant American Georgian interiors were based upon English styles, but had a more pleasing simplicity. They combined the classically severe Palladian style with aspects of the Louis XV style. The interior was based upon a square plan, with an imposing central entrance hall that ran from the front of the house to the rear. Rooms opened off the central hall. The handsome stairways were quite large and sometimes ornate, with carved and polished mahogany handrails that swept into turned or carved newel posts.

Walls were now papered or paneled to replace the wainscoting of previous periods. Wallpaper was first imported from China in 1737 and produced in America after 1786. By the end of the period, there were over six hundred patterns available in twenty-six colors. Some paneled walls had stenciled patterns to imitate the more costly wallpapers. After 1735, interior woodwork was often painted to match the ground color in upholstery and drapery fabrics. Ceilings were plastered and, in the homes of the wealthy, typically had high-relief stucco ornamentation. Floors were of wide boards left bare in most homes or stenciled in patterns to imitate parquet, marble, or Oriental rugs. A few carpets were imported from the Orient until late in the period, when English carpets, such as Wilton and Axminster, became available.

The fireplace, no longer used for cooking, became smaller. The first ones were framed by a simple architrave and lacked a mantel shelf. Later in the period, elaborately carved mantels with matching overmantel (such as a large panel and architrave) were used. Pilasters usually flanked the fireplace.

Classical architectural details were used to trim doors and windows. Doors were often framed with architrave moldings and triangular pediments. Shutters, similar to today's Venetian blinds, were used at the windows for textiles were still rare and expensive.

Most details of the house—such as the panels, chimney pieces, and balustrades—were made on the site, although brass hardware, crystal chandeliers, and many fabrics were imported. Wall sconces and ceiling fixtures of tin, wood, and pewter were made in America.

Accessories consisted of mirrors (very similar to English examples), porcelain, silver (used as a form of money), pewter, clocks (made in America after 1722), needlework, and tea equipment.

Furniture

American styles were influenced by those in England, in spite of the many differences that divided the mother country from the colonies. In fact, very few French influences came to

Figure 16.10a
This American Georgian upholstered wing chair, with acanthus leaf on the knees of its cabriole legs, and ball-and-claw feet, is in the Queen Anne style.

Figure 16.10b
This American Georgian high chest of drawers with bandy (cabriole) legs, fan carving, and flame finials is in the Queen Anne style.

Figure 16.10c
This American Georgian settee with three pierced ladder backs and double-ogee-curved support, legs is in the Chippendale style.

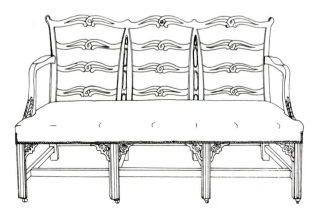

Table 16.12
Characteristics of Queen Anne Furniture—American Georgian Period

1. Lines were light, simple, graceful (Fig. 16.10a).
2. Legs, frames, skirts, aprons were curved (Fig. 16.10b).
3. Legs were cabriole in front, raked in rear (Fig. 16.10a).
4. Feet were pad, slipper (pointed), trifid (three-toed), ball-and-claw (later).
5. Chairs had fiddle, vase-shaped, yoke-shaped backs (spoon-shaped from side).
6. Ornamentation included carving, plain surfaces, line.
7. Motifs included scallop shell, leaf, scroll, pendant, flower, acanthus leaf.
8. Hardware included bat's-wing brasses (Fig. 16.10b).
9. Woods included walnut, cherry, maple; mahogany near end of the period.
10. Form and function harmonized.
11. Innovations included folding card table, Windsor chair.
12. Highboys were popular.

Table 16.13
Characteristics of Chippendale Furniture—American Georgian Period

1. The style was robust, with good proportions.
2. Legs were Marlborough (Figs. 16.10d, 16.10e) and cabriole.
3. Feet were ball-and-claw, scrolled toe, hairy-paw, straight.
4. Backs were pierced splat (Fig. 16.10d), ribband, Gothic (Fig. 16.10g), Chinese (Fig. 16.10f), ladder-back (Fig. 16.10c).
5. Ornamentation included elaborate carving, parcel gilding, veneering.
6. Motifs included cyma curve, carved shell, fan (New England), Gothic frets, pierced Chinese fretwork, cabochon, cartouche, tattered acanthus leaf, floral garlands.
7. Woods were mahogany, walnut, maple, cherry.
8. Innovations included breakfront bookcase, blockfront chest of drawers, serpentine-back sofa, china and Pembroke tables.
9. Small pieces reflected period's increasing wealth and included candlestands, and so on Fig. 16.11a.
10. Highboys (Fig. 16.11g) and matching lowboys (Fig. 16.11h) were popular.

Figure 16.10d
This American Georgian sidechair in Gothic Chippendale style with fret brackets has splats pierced to resemble a Gothic window.

Figure 16.10e
This American Georgian Martha Washington chair is in the Chippendale style.

Figure 16.10f
This American Georgian sidechair in Chinese Chippendale style has a pagoda on top, rope-and-bell design on the splat and legs.

Figure 16.10g
An American Georgian sidechair in the Gothic style, with back columns, Gothic arches, and cluster columns for legs.

America that were not filtered through England. By 1750, when England was already into the Late Georgian Period, styles in America combined elements of the Queen Anne through the Chippendale Periods. These two styles, with their beauty and simplicity, were the most popular ones.

Regional Furniture Differences

There were also regional differences in furniture and some of the famous centers were Philadelphia and the Delaware River Valley, Newport, New York and the Hudson River Valley, and Boston.

Philadelphia and the Delaware River Valley Philadelphia furniture was the most ambitious style, perhaps because the city was the seat of government. Chairs had ample proportions and were deeply and elaborately carved. There were no stretchers. Cabriole legs ended in *slipper, club,* or *trifid* feet, or *Marlborough legs* were used. Carved scrolls and volutes were typical on the splat. Case pieces often had ser-

pentine fronts. The best-known cabinetmakers from Philadelphia were *Thomas Affleck* (1740–95), who was known for his Chinese Chippendale designs and his use of the Marlborough leg; *John Folwell* (active 1771–79), who was known as "the American Chippendale" and who designed furniture in the Chippendale style for the Congress; *Benjamin Randolph* (active 1760–90), who was the most skillful in the Chippendale Rococo style; and *William Savery* (1721–88), who worked first in the Queen Anne style, using *intaglio leaves* (designs cut out of a surface so that the finished design is below the surface) on cabriole-leg knees, and who was skillful in the design of highboys.

Newport, Rhode Island Newport designers were partial to Queen Anne-style chairs and, in fact, few Chippendale chairs were designed there. The ball-and-claw foot, which appeared earlier there than elsewhere, was elongated and had slender talons which were

Table 16.14
Characteristics of Goddard and Townsend Furniture

1. Pieces were heavy, large, graceful.
2. Chairs were Queen Anne style; chests, Chippendale.
3. Motifs included shell (most typical), bracket foot with ogee curve (combination of concave and convex curve) and decorative scroll, urn finial with corkscrew flame, combination of two convex shells flanking center concave carved shell on blockfront, spiral carving, rosettes, pediments.
4. Front of case pieces were divided into alternating convex and concave panels with recessed center panel (Figs. 16.11b, 16.11c).
5. Woods included mahogany (primary wood), pine, cedar, chestnut.

Figure 16.11a
An American Georgian tea table with acanthus leaf on the knees of cabriole legs and ball-and-claw feet.

Figure 16.11c
This blockfront desk with relief and incised shell design, ogee bracket foot, and bat-wing brasses was designed by Goddard and Townsend in the American Georgian Period.

Figure 16.11b
This two-part American Georgian secretary by Goddard and Townsend has pilasters at the side fronts, ogee bracket foot, rosette at broken pediment, urn finials, and a block front.

Figure 16.11d
This American Georgian secretary in the Adam style has a bombé front, ball-and-claw feet, pull-out supports for the lid, pull-out candleholders, pilasters with Corinthian capitals, a rosette at the broken-arch pediment, and flame finials.

often undercut (an opening was carved between the talons and the ball). Newport furniture, although large and heavy, was graceful and beautifully finished. Dove-tailed joints were common. The most famous Newport designers were from two families whose members worked together for over four generations: the Goddards and the Townsends.

New York and Hudson River Valley New York furniture was heavy and sturdy, with solid proportions and bold curves. Low relief carved tassels were popular on the back splats of chairs, and gadrooning was common on skirts. The ball-and-claw foot was carved in a square, box-like shape. *Gilbert Ash* (1717–85) was a New York designer whose characteristic chair backs had interlaced scrolls enclosing a diamond. Cross-hatched *lambrequins*, reproductions of valance boards for draperies, were carved on the knee of cabriole legs.

Boston Slender proportions, fretwork, and japanning characterized Boston furniture. Cabriole legs terminated in ball-and-claw feet with angled side talons, or in hairy-paw or scroll feet. *Bombé*, (Fig. 16.11d) and block fronts without shells were typical on case pieces. *Benjamin Frothingham* (1734–1809), who lived in Boston, was known for his re-

Figure 16.11f
A comb back Windsor writing chair.

Figure 16.11e
A bow back Windsor chair with turned splayed legs, an uneven number of spindles.

Table 16.15
Comparison of English Georgian and American Georgian Furniture Styles

1. American styles lagged ten to fifteen years behind English styles.
2. American furniture relied more on beauty of line than on rich materials.
3. American pieces had less ornamentation.
4. Queen Anne motifs persisted longer in America.
5. American pieces combined Queen Anne and Chippendale styles, particularly the ball-and-claw foot on Queen Anne pieces.
6. The pad foot persisted longer in the United States than in England.
7. The American style was more faithfully Georgian; the English style combined Rococo, Chinese, and Gothic elements with classical forms.
8. Some American pieces—highboys with matching lowboys, block-front case pieces with shell carving—were not produced in England (Figs. 16.11g and 16.11h).
9. The American Windsor chair was lighter, more graceful.
10. Some pieces were typically American: the American Chippendale highboy with tall, scrolled pediment and well-carved drawers at top and bottom; the Philadelphia Chippendale lowboy with deep carved skirt, inset quarter columns, shell carving on drawers; matching high and lowboys.

Figure 16.11g
This American Georgian highboy in Chippendale style has bandy legs, fan-incised carving, fluted pilasters, and broken-arch pediment.

verse serpentine construction on case pieces (the center curve is concave). *John Cogswell* (active 1762–89) was the maker of some of Boston's finest bombé Rococo pieces.

The Windsor Chair

The Windsor chair was popular in America as well as in England. It was similar in shape to English versions although not as heavy.

Philadelphia cabinetmakers transformed English models into light and graceful chairs, inexpensive and functional. The Windsor chair first appeared in America about 1725 and had finely turned arm supports, slender spindles, stretchers, and legs. The quality of a Windsor chair was determined by the shaping of the saddle seat and the outward rake of the legs. The greater the number of the spindles (almost always uneven in number), the more valuable the chair: a nine-spindle chair was excellent while an eleven-spindle chair was exceptional. The Windsor chair (except the seat) was produced on a lathe (Fig. 16.11e). The legs were wedged into the seat while the joints were held by glue. Hickory, maple, and oak were the woods used to made these chairs in America. These comfortable chairs needed no upholstery, were light in weight and stable (owing to the splayed legs), and could be pro-

Figure 16.11h
This American Georgian lowboy in Chippendale style has heavily carved acanthus leaves on the knees of its cabriole legs, and ball-and-claw feet.

duced at a low cost (Fig. 16.11f). Many different types were made and they have remained popular since they were introduced.

During the American Georgian Period, low-back, comb-back, fan-back, and loop-back chairs were produced. *Andrew Gautier* of New York (active 1746–76) was a well-known craftsman who made them. Today they are still being produced, some by the Danish designer, Hans Wegner, and the American craftsmen, George Nakashima (Figs. 15.12b and 15.12c).

Comparison of English and American Georgian Furniture

American Georgian furniture differed from English styles in several ways; generally, it was simpler and less elaborately ornamented.

Federal Period (1790–1820)

Historical Background

Although American culture was strongly rooted in England, patriotism developed after the war of 1812. The burning of the White House by the British, and the American Revolution. The capital was moved to Washington and the White House became the President's home. During the Federal Period the new country was expanded. Florida was purchased from Spain in 1815, the year of Napoleon's defeat at Waterloo.

Inventions were numerous. In 1800, Whitney introduced a system of interchangeable parts that was eventually to lead to mass production. A machine saw that cut veneers was introduced in 1820. Commerce increased and the growing middle class was dominated by merchant groups. Transportation was improved by the construction of canals, roads, and railroads, and the frontier moved steadily westward.

Society was increasing in importance and Dolly Madison was becoming a famous White House hostess. Portrait and historical painting were popular and still-life painting was introduced. For the first time, women were deemed worthy of education.

Architecture

Architecture was dominated by the classical tradition. Sympathy for the French Revolution, combined with European travel and design periodicals, spread Continental ideas.

Table 16.16
Relationship of Important Furniture Periods to the Federal Period

England	France
Late Georgian Period 1770–1811	Directoire Period 1799–1804
Regency Period 1811–30	Empire Period 1804–15

Federal Style Dwelling 1780–1820 (Fig. 16.12)

After Jefferson became Ambassador to France, his work as an architect was influenced by the buildings he saw in Paris. Upon returning to America he began to remodel his Virginia home. His new designs for Monticello and his subsequent plan for the University of Virginia were marked by classical symmetry and Roman proportions. This restrained but formal organization of architectural details was quickly adopted by the gentlemen of the new Republic and became the first national style. Designs for the new capitol in Washington were Federal in character. Few Federal residences reached the level of significance or diversity of detail that Monticello and the White House had, but simpler Federal buildings were erected in the Northeast, the Southeast, and the Midwest well into the first quarter of the nineteenth century.

Federal architecture was characterized by symmetry of form and detail. A federal dwelling usually had two or three stories with a pedimented entrance with slender columns, which modestly projected from the face of the building. Chimneys projected through the roof at either end. The plan was an I or Georgian plan. Some houses had hipped roofs, often with a balustrade; others had a flat roof. American houses were smaller than their European counterparts.

Federal design was a timely and strong force in shaping the new United States. The style symbolized the growing strength and influence of the country. Although the average family never lived in such monumental dwellings, a new national pride was reflected in this restrained but classical style.

Interiors

The interior plan in the Federal Period was symmetrical: there was a central hallway and

Figure 16.12
*A federal-style dwelling,
1780–1820. The box
shaped house has a
balustrade which ornaments
the flat roof with chimneys
projecting through the roof
near the ends.*

Table 16.17
Federal-Style Dwelling

Space:	Georgian plan
Form:	Rectilinear
Color:	White
Texture:	Flat weatherboarding
Line:	Balance between horizontal and vertical
Correlate:	National pride

stairway, with many specialized rooms leading off the hall. Many oval, circular, and octagonal rooms were included along with traditional square and rectangular rooms. Walls were covered above the dado with geometric, floral, or pastoral French, English, or Chinese wallpapers (clipper ships regularly sailed to the Orient). Walls were also plastered and painted in robust colors. Pilasters were a frequent addition to walls, and classical moldings added a finishing touch at the wall's upper rim. Ceilings were high and usually painted in white or pastel colors. Classical motifs (swags and circular arabesques) were added around the center chandelier. Floors were made of wide and polished hardwood boards or of parquet, and sometimes covered with area carpets in geometric patterns.

Federal fireplaces were elegantly designed of grey, pink, or white marble, and usually had pilasters and caryatids on either side. A white wooden mantel, ornamented by a classical frieze (often with swags and bellflowers), surrounded the fireplace and a painting or mirror was placed above it. Taller doors and windows were surmounted by cornices or friezes and flanked by pilasters. Sash windows often had small rectangular panes, usually six over six. In some areas, windows were taxed, so occasionally houses would have some false windows, covered with black paint to appear

real, but not cut through to the inside; there was no tax on fake windows.

More cotton textiles were being used, particularly French and English prints, and subjects celebrating the independence of the United States. The development of the Jacquard loom in 1801 made possible elaborately patterned upholstery. Other fabrics included plain and patterned horsehair, sprigged and narrow-striped patterns (after 1800), and bold medallion designs in bright greens, gold, deep blues, and shades of red from crimson to rust. Textile printing was improved with the development of cylinder printing in 1770. Carpet and rugs were woven on power looms, and became more readily available.

Mirrors were one of the most popular accessories; many were convex, surmounted by a gilded frame that was topped with an eagle. Other mirrors included small dressing and shaving mirrors and full-length pier-glass mirrors for dressing. Banjo clocks (by *Simon Willard*) and shelf clocks were made in great variety. English and European pottery and glass, Chinese export porcelain, and American-made glass and china (which often had an American eagle pattern), were avidly collected.

Furniture

Federal furniture falls into two categories: the Early Federal style (which includes Sheraton and Hepplewhite and Ducan Phyfe), and the Late Federal style (in which Empire influences were popular). The styles came to the United States about a decade after they were popular in England, and French styles were filtered through England.

Inlay, the first sophisticated method of ornamentation used in the United States, was popular during the Federal Period. Most of the early furniture designs followed Hepplewhite and Sheraton styles; few were influenced by Adam.

Figure 16.13a
An Early Federal highboy with eagle ornament in center, urn finials, Gothic mullions, and tapered legs.

Figure 16.13b
A Federal tambour desk with pilasters at sides and center, swags on the tambour front, and bell-flower inlay on tapered legs.

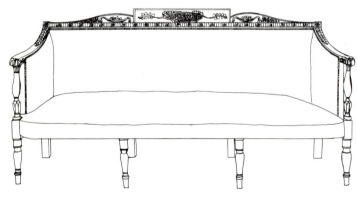

Figure 16.14
A Federal sofa by Samuel McIntire with a carved basket of flowers on the back, turned legs round in section, and carved drapery festoons.

Table 16.18
Characteristics of Federal Furniture

Early Federal Style

1. Proportions were delicate, refined, and small in scale.
2. Straight lines were used, with lightness and grace (Fig. 16.13a).
3. Principal ornamentation included veneers, ornamental inlays, carving, painting, brass inlay, tambour desk fronts (Fig. 16.13b).
4. Motifs included stringing, geometric patterns, oval and round paterae, shells, fans, flowers and leaves, bellflowers, husks, eagles (Fig. 16.16a), baskets (Fig. 16.14), cornucopias with fruit and flowers, fluting, Prince of Wales feather, drapery swags, sheaves of wheat (Fig. 16.16a), gouge-work, pineapples (Fig. 16.16d), spiral reeding (Fig. 16.15b).
5. Woods included crotch mahogany, bird's-eye maple, rosewood, satinwood, sycamore, walnut, ebony, birch, cherry (pine was a secondary wood).
6. Legs were turned, square or tapering; the Marlborough leg with spade foot was also used.
7. Feet: plain or spade (Figs. 16.13a and 16.13b).

Later Federal Style (influenced by English Regency and French Empire)

1. Designs were heavy, cumbersome (Fig. 16.15a).
2. More mechanical furniture was produced.
3. Ornamentation included brass mounts, larger amounts of plain wood, stringing.
4. Motifs included lion's paw (Figs. 16.15c, 16.15d), acanthus leaf (Fig. 16.15d), classical details such as Greek key and frets, scrolls, palmettes.
5. Woods included cherry, maple, birch (stained to resemble mahogany), mahogany (one hard and dark, another softer and redder).
6. Legs were concave on chair fronts and some backs (Figs. 16.15c, 16.15d), scroll, Grecian curve, cabriole.
7. Feet included animal feet (sometimes winged), snake feet (on cabriole legs), brass-ornamented or brass feet.

Figure 16.15a
A Late Federal chest (influenced by French Empire) with claw feet, drawers with swelling front, and a rosette at top of reeded column.

Table 16.19
Characteristics of Samuel McIntire Furniture

1. Design influenced by Hepplewhite or Sheraton style.
2. Motifs included baskets of fruit and flowers, horn of plenty, dishes of fruit, drapery festoons, laurel sprays, clusters of grapes, husk pendants, eagles, scrolls, fluting, rosettes, lovers' knots, cockleshell, bead moldings (Fig. 16.14).
3. Ornamentation included delicate carving.
4. Woods included mahogany, combinations of woods, bird's eye maple, and satinwood.
5. Chairs (Hepplewhite in style), had vase, shield or oval backs; richly carved frames; straight front legs with spade feet and carved back legs, or (Sheraton in style) square backs with delicate carving; some were similar to the French bergère.
6. Sofas (Hepplewhite in style) had curved backs, continuous carved top rails, and carved arms and legs, or (Sheraton style) rectangular backs with straight-forward projecting sides and carved arms, supported by turned and carved baluster, and backs carved with center ornamentation.

Cabinetmakers

Samuel McIntire (1757–1811) The seaport town of Salem, only a short distance from Boston, became rich from the China trade. Many wealthy Salem merchants had homes, interiors, and furniture designed by *Samuel McIntire* (1757–1811). McIntire followed by the styles of Hepplewhite and Sheraton, and was influenced by their publications as well as by that of *Batty Langely,* an English architect who published *Treasury of Designs* in 1740. Langley's houses were characterized by low-pitched hip roofs with balustrades and Adam-style decorative detailing.

Duncan Phyfe (1768–1854) Duncan Fife, a Scotsman, came to the United States at the age of fifteen and was apprenticed to a cabinet-maker a year later. He settled in prosperous New York and his fashionable clients soon made him wealthy. He also changed the spelling of his name to *Phyfe.* He was strongly influenced by Sheraton and, to a lesser degree, by Hepplewhite, but he also designed furniture in the style of the American Empire.

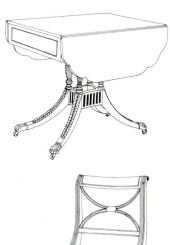
Figure 16.15b
This drop-leaf table on a pedestal base with four feet has a water-leaf design on the legs, claw feet and casters, and spiral reeding on the pedestal supports.

Figure 16.15c
A Federal chair with curule back, saber legs, paw feet and scroll at the front of the seat apron.

Figure 16.15d
This Federal chair in the Empire style has lion's-paw feet, scroll arms, and leaf on the knees.

Figure 16.16a
A Federal méridienne, designed by Duncan Phyfe, with saber legs, paw feet and casters, bow-tied sheaves of wheat carved on the apron, and rosette on the low end.

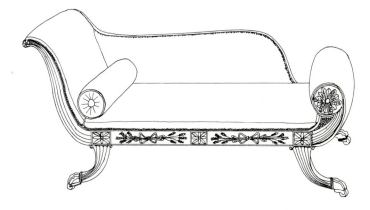

Figure 16.16b
A Federal lyre-back chair
by Duncan Phyfe, with
spiral reeded saber legs and
brass strings on the lyre.

Figure 16.16c
A tilt-top Federal Duncan
Phyfe pedestal table with
eagle support, casters on
metal feet, a mask on the
pedestal, and water-leaf
design on the legs.

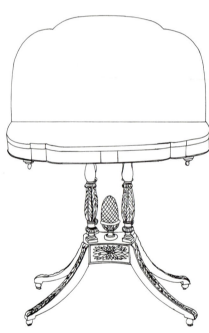

Figure 16.16d
A Federal Duncan Phyfe
tilt-top table with pineapple
finial, water-leaf design on
the legs, and leaves on the
pedestal supports.

Table 16.20
Characteristics of Duncan Phyfe Furniture

1. Pieces were small, like Sheraton's with slender arms and legs.
2. Construction was excellent, with fine dovetailing.
3. Curved lines were preferred over straight, but were subtle.
4. Proportions were superior.
5. Woods included mahogany from Cuba and Santa Domingo, satinwood, and rosewood (after 1830).
6. Ornamentation included low-relief carving (almost the equal of Chippendale's), incised detail, ornamental brasses, reeding, delicate turning, veneers.
7. Motifs included acanthus leaf (somewhat flattened), oak and water leaves, ribbon, Prince of Wales feather, egg and dart, wheat ear, rosettes, plums, cornucopias, drapery swags, crossed laurel branches, urn pedestals, lyres (Fig. 16.16b).
8. Top rails of chairs and sofas were carved, front and sides of seat rails were fluted, legs were incised.
9. Chair backs formed continuous curve with legs (Fig. 16.16b).
10. The Regency pedestal base was popular (Figs. 16.16c, 16.16d).
11. Finely proportioned brass mounts of excellent quality were used.
12. Pieces included chairs, sofas, tables; few sideboards, beds, footstools, and pianos; tables and sofas were often in sets.
13. Tables included gaming, sewing, Pembroke (with multiple curves on leaves), tripod, dining, dressing, library; casters were on most pieces (Figs. 16.16c, 16.16d, 16.16e).

Figure 16.16e
A Federal Duncan Phyfe
sofa with carved leaf
designs, bird's-head feet,
cornucopia designs on the
back and legs, and casters
on the feet.

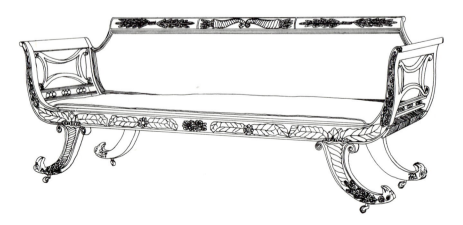

Phyfe followed fashion and if the public wanted a style, he produced it.

Some of the furniture innovations in the United States during the Federal Period include small folding tables, extension tables, sideboards, beds with decorated headboards and footboards, four-poster beds, a variety of shelf clocks and wall clocks and, chests of drawers.

The Victorian Period (1830–1901)

Historical Background

During the Victorian Period in the United States, there was a great contrast between the upper class and the middle class. Society had stablized by this time and there was a visible gentry. The general public was becoming more interested in glittering social functions. In fact, the rich were the only people worth reading or talking about.

Inventions were numerous: the telephone, the telegraph, the incandescent bulb, the typewriter, and the elevator came on the scene. The sewing machine was available in quantity after the inventors formed the Sewing Machine Trust in 1855. Paper dress patterns were introduced by Ebenezer Butterick in 1864. In 1870, there were seven women who had defied convention and become stenographers; by 1900, there were 20,000. Higher education for women was still unusual, but by 1889 there were approximately 11,800 women undergraduates and 180 women graduates attending college.

The entrance of women into the athletic world did much toward freeing them from their restrictive clothing and restricted lives. Bicycling, tennis, and golf demanded more freedom of movement than skating and croquet had. Bicycling was a national craze by 1893, in spite of a warning issued by the Boston Women's Rescue League to the effect that 30 per cent of "fallen women" had been bicycle riders. A new sport arrived with the advent of the automobile; driving was called "a game between man and machine" (women did not yet drive). It was hoped, ironically, that the advent of the automobile would rid the country of the terrible pollution caused by horses. Women were beginning to invade the masculine world by the end of the century, and Charlotte Perkins Gilman, a lecturer and writer involved in the labor and feminist movement, wrote in 1898 that only "by complete economic independence from the nearest male relative by birth or marriage can women throw off the fetters of tradition."

Immigration from many countries was making America "the melting pot of the world." It also manned the factories and made urban growth possible. Child labor was common, with children beginning work at the age of four or five. The "robber barons" were brought under some control by the Antitrust Act of 1890, and laws were enacted regulating workmen's compensation, working hours for women and children, minimum wages, and interstate commerce.

The arts were at their height, and writers such as Whitman, Dickinson, Lanier, Longfellow, Holmes, Whittier, Irving, and Poe were widely read. America began to develop its unique culture.

Architecture

Greek Revival-Style Dwelling 1815–40 (Fig. 16.17)

American sympathy with the Greek wars of independence and the existing prevalence of classical architectural motifs gave rise to the Greek style, which became the "American" style. Structures were deeper than they were wide; low, triangular, gabled, and pedimented porticos supported by large columns extended in front of the buildings. Sometimes the house would be surrounded by a columned portico or symmetrical wings that produced the effect of side aisles. Of the classical orders for columns (Doric, Ionic, and Corinthian), the Doric was the one used most frequently by American builders. Also it was the simplest for it required little or no hand carving and thus was more quickly fabricated. The front of the house was often surfaced with horizontal boards butted together which, when painted, had the smooth appearance of stone.

Table 16.21
Relationship of Important Furniture Periods to the American Victorian Period

England	*Germany*
Regency 1811–30	Biedermeier 1800–50
Victorian 1830–1901	

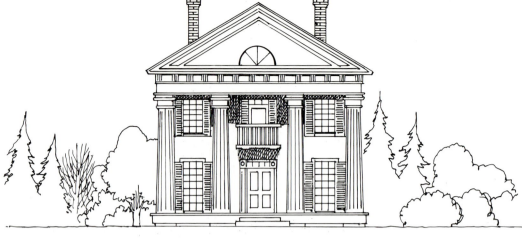

Figure 16.17
A Greek Revival-style dwelling, 1815–40. Doric columns on the portico give this dwelling the appearance of a temple.

Figure 16.18
A Gothic-style dwelling, 1830–1910. The Gothic-arched windows are tall, the gables are pointed, and the verge board is scalloped. The effect is vertical.

Table 16.22
Greek Revival-Style Dwelling

Space:	Georgian plan
Form:	Square, symmetrical balance
Color:	White
Texture:	Weatherboarding, paneling
Lines:	Unified, horizontal
Correlate:	Epitomized high level of recognition in society

Table 16.23
Gothic-Style Dwelling

Space:	L–plan
Form:	Square, assymmetrical
Colors:	Natural with contrasting trim
Texture:	Board and batten
Line:	Vertical
Correlate:	Family values shaped by home ownership as reward for hard work

Greek Revival houses were usually two and a half or three stories high, with tall, narrow first-story windows that extended to the ground and allowed access to the porch. Other windows were six over six.

Greek Revival architecture was favored in the Midwest and in the South after the 1830s; the homes of Southern planters were particularly large and imposing, with side chimneys and, frequently, separate kitchens (owing to the hot climate). This style appealed to those with lofty ambitions; it continues to capture the interest of Americans today.

Gothic-Style Dwelling 1830–1910
(Fig. 16.18)

The Gothic residential style was an American inspiration. Details based upon Gothic church architecture were added to modest residences both to give them significance and to link them with the past. The Gothic style persisted throughout the Victorian Period, particularly in the *cottage style* of many rural dwellings. The writings of *Andrew Jackson Downing* (1815–52) and the illustrations of *A. J. Davis* (1803–92) spread the cottage style throughout America. Sometimes referred to as *gingerbread* or *carpenter* Gothic, the decorative motifs varied widely with the taste and skill of the client and the builder. The romantic link with the past was, at best, "picturesque." The result was generally a modified frame home with the addition of tall Gothic-arched windows, scalloped *verge* or *bargeboard* (the ornamental board that finishes the part of the roof that overhangs the wall at the gable

Figure 16.19
An Italian Villa-style dwelling, 1845–1900. The inspiration for this villa was Mediterranean with its emphasis on square and vertical forms. Brackets support the cornices.

Table 16.24
Italian Villa-Style Dwelling

Space:	Irregular
Form:	Asymmetrical balance
Colors:	Light yellow, grays, melon
Texture:	Concrete, stone, terra-cotta
Line:	Vertical
Correlate:	Desire to hold fast to the past

end), and pieces of colored glass. Porch railings and aprons were finished with decorative patterns and medieval motifs were popular. The effect was vertical, emphasized by sharply pointed gables. Sometimes the casement windows had leaded diamond-shaped panes of glass.

The Industrial Revolution enabled the middle class to participate in the architecture of the period and this basically simple style, with its use of machine production, could have been economically available to even more Americans if their taste had not directed them to arches, scallops, and colored glass. Nonetheless, the American dream of home ownership was born; it fit well within the Protestant ethic, which promoted the value of hard work in securing happiness and the good life. Such motivation was passed from parent to child and became a prominent force in patterns of child rearing and family interaction.

Italian Villa-Style Dwelling 1845–1900 (Fig. 16.19)

Late nineteenth-century buildings were constructed in imposing styles tending toward the picturesque and borrowing from the style of Mediterranean villas. These buildings were generally a series of asymmetrical squares and vertical forms with attached towers, squared pillared porches and balconies; they were unified in material and design. Although generally constructed of masonry, they maintained a feeling of lightness in scale.

Architectural details were drawn from Italian models: rounded arches and triangular pediments for the tall, slender windows, and flat or low-pitched roofs. Balustraded balconies and deep bracketed cornices lent the second name, *Bracketed style,* to this style of building. Frequently incorporated in the façade were wood and stone details made to look like marble.

The Italian villa marked a confusing transition period when Americans, moving from the farms to the cities, were faced with new and frightening, yet exciting, aspects of life. Immersion into this new world brought forth a strong desire to retain the links with the past.

Mansard-Style Dwelling 1855–85 (Fig. 16.20)

Distinctive roofs characterized the *Mansard* style, sometimes called the *General Grant* style. The mansard roof had two slopes: the lower one was very steep and often covered with slate; the upper one was less sloping, and because it had four sides, there was no gable. Sometimes it was referred to as a *French* or *hipped* roof. Fancy shingles were also used as roofing material during this time. Dormer windows with rectangular, square, pointed, gabled, or domed tops pierced the roof. Columns and pilasters, with incorrectly proportioned classical orders, were used as ornamentation. Occasionally the porch had a balustrade. Cupolas and *porte cochères* (a porch that sheltered passengers descending from carriages) was often added. Sash windows and large bay windows were common. Frequently the yards were filled with cast iron deer, stags, and dogs.

Victorian Eclectic Dwelling 1870–1900 (Fig. 16.21)

Increasing industrialization by the middle of the nineteenth century and the rise of the middle class created a strong demand for decorative arts that would convey the appearance of

Figure 16.20
A mansard-style dwelling, 1855–85. Dormers pierce the mansard roof. Balustrades ornament the porches.

Figure 16.21
A Victorian Eclectic dwelling, 1870–1900. Many types of ornament were combined on this house. There is a porte-cochère on the left.

Figure 16.22
A Queen Anne Revival-style dwelling, 1877–1900. Windows with small panes were typical of this type of architecture as were bay windows and turrets.

Table 16.25
Mansard-Style Dwelling

Space: Rectangular
Form: Symmetrical balance
Colors: Gray, white, yellows
Texture: Weatherboarding, stone
Line: Vertical
Correlate: Emphasis on material values

Table 16.26
Victorian Eclectic Dwelling

Space: Irregular
Form: Irregular
Colors: Yellows, grays, red, white, contrast-
            ing trim
Texture: Wood, weatherboarding, board and
            batten
Line: Asymmetrical
Correlates: Uncertain occupation, location, and
            interpersonal relations

Table 16.27
Queen Anne Revival-Style Dwelling

Space: Irregular
Form: Irregular
Colors: Terra-cotta, brown, grays, white
Texture: Clapboards, shingles applied in pat-
            terns, smooth boards, brick chim-
            neys
Line: Irregular
Correlate: Irregular, unplanned life; large fami-
            lies

wealth and luxury. Machines were adapted to produce carved and routed multiple details, and houses became complex forms upon which to attach all manner of decoration. Without traditional or classical plans, irregular designs displaying all kinds of experimentation and technique were executed.

The most extravagant houses in this style were built by extremely wealthy urban families. But rural areas were not excluded from the fashion of adorning simple structures with brackets, colored glass, cupolas, towers, and/or verandas. This style represented the highest form of the picturesque and was the climax of Victorian taste. Rejection of this style was soon to come with the spread of the English Arts and Crafts Movement, which represented a return to sanity and a new honesty and order in the creation of buildings and products.

The Victorian Eclectic style was a further manifestation of the extent to which the movement into the urban industrial era unsettled Americans. Families in this period were as lacking in direction as was the architectural design of their homes.

Queen Anne Revival-Style Dwelling 1877–1900 (Fig. 16.22)

The Queen Anne Revival was inspired by the Romanesque buildings of *Henry Hobson Richardson*. They were picturesque, asymmetrical and built of smooth boards, shingles applied in patterns, or clapboards, rather than stone. Fluted brick chimneys were usually topped with large caps. The Queen Anne house usually had a high gabled roof pierced with dormers and round turrets with corner towers added which resulted in irregularly shaped rooms. Oriel windows and circular bay windows were common. Balconies were frequently added to the already over-ornamented exterior. Delicately turned spindles were used on both porches and balconies.

Classical Revival-Style Dwelling 1895 (Fig. 16.23)

The opening of the World's Columbian Exposition in Chicago in 1893 marked the grand climax of the nineteenth century and of progress in American building. The architects adhered closely to classical designs, and the "White City" (as it was called) cost over $26 million. This "mercantile classicism" was based upon Greek, Roman, and Italian Renaissance design. Louis Sullivan said the damage wrought by this style would last fifty years, and it almost did.

Many meetings accompanied the fair and at one session, Frederick Jackson Turner, a professor at the University of Wisconsin, read a paper entitled "The significance of the Frontier in American History." His thesis was that the American was a new man, not a transplanted European, owing his distinctive characteristics—coarseness and strength, inquisitiveness, practical inventiveness, a masterful grasp of material things, and a basic deficiency in artistic matters—to his unusual New World environment, which reflected the fluidity, simplicity, and perennial rebirth of primitive frontier society.

Industrialization had come of age, however.

Figure 16.23
A Classical Revival-style
dwelling, 1895. Ionic and
Corinthian columns
ornament the imposing
entrance of this house. It
has a hip roof with
balustrades.

Table 16.28
Classical Revival-Style Dwelling

Space:	Irregular
Form:	Asymmetrical balance
Colors:	White, natural materials
Texture:	Frame construction, stone
Line:	Horizontal
Correlate:	Badge of attainment for urban, status-conscious family

Skyscrapers, a feat of engineering, made possible denser American communities. Residential structures were becoming an assortment of historic and bizarre details, materials, and construction techniques.

Architects and builders at the turn of the century, trained in or influenced by the French architectural tradition, borrowed liberally from classical and Renaissance buildings, organizing their own structures in the Beaux Arts tradition. Grand in scale but pleasing to the eye, this new style was to fit the ideals of the many newly rich Americans who sought homes that were impressively classical in appearance but built for the comfort of their occupants.

Classical Revival houses were usually balanced, though not symmetrical in the organization of their detail. Decorative motifs drew heavily on the richly carved Ionic, Corinthian, and Composite Roman orders rather than on the simpler Doric style preferred by the Greeks.

The Classical Revival style, in large part a reaction to the Victorian Eclectic, served those who had successfully made the transition from rural to urban life. These families were a select few in an ambitiously evolving country.

Interiors

Cluttered rooms with obscure traffic patterns were the hallmark of a well-decorated Victorian room. The hall was the entry and included an umbrella stand, chairs, and a folding table—and often an impressive stairway. The parlor served as a special room for formal occasions and had highly polished mahogany furniture. Included were a satin or velvet upholstered sofa, an oval marble-topped table, an *étagère* or *whatnot,* and chairs. Opulent patterned carpets covered polished wooden floors and a chandelier (lit with gas or oil until electricity became available in 1880) hung from the center of the high ceiling. This room was saved for company but was frequently used because most entertaining was done at home. The dining room had a table with leaves, chairs, a hanging lamp or central chandelier, and perhaps a sideboard. Every room had a fireplace with a small mantle and a decorative mirror over it. Windows varied in size and number, but all were heavily draped with velvet trimmed with tassels.

There were many changes in the plan of the house from 1840 to 1901. One of the earliest reformers was *Catherine Ward Beecher,* who suggested, in her *Treatise on Domestic Economy* (1841), that the nursery, the parlor, and the kitchen should be on the same floor. Her advice went largely unheeded. Tall, narrow, three-story houses continued to dominate architecture. They had several porches, large entrance halls, a dining room, a drawing room, a saloon (for music and dancing), a billiard room, a gallery, a ladies' sitting room, four or five bedchambers, dressing rooms, a nursery, a conservatory (for plants), a kitchen, a scullery, a pantry, larders, a servants' hall, and a housekeeper's room. Usually wells, cisterns, and privies were located some distance from the house. If there were bathing facilities inside, the water usually had to be bailed out. *Godey's Lady's Book,* a women's "bible" after 1837, began a Model Cottage Department in 1846 but published clumsy and involved plans; however, the editor, Mrs. Hale, invited inventors to develop a washing machine to simplify housework. By the following year, the first practical model was on the market, but it sold for the then-astronomical price of $40. By 1855, the sewing machine, another celebrated family aid, was available, but women used their new leisure to over-ornament their clothing with machine-applied trimmings.

From 1857 to 1866, the Mansard style was popular, and most houses were planned for families of eight to ten members. Crude central heating was available by 1866 and multiple fireplaces began to disappear. Some critics suggested that the parlor serve as a living room, but no one seemed interested in this advice. In 1860, the first radiator was marketed, along with chimneys that made kerosene lamps safer and more effective. Bathtubs were even found in some plans by 1866, although all were located on the second floor. Because Benjamin Franklin's recommendation that everyone bathe twice weekly had been largely ignored, families without bathtubs did not feel greatly deprived. The outhouse was still in use and houses were planned without closets, making storage a problem even in the largest of homes.

Between 1867 and 1876 some comforts were added, such as bed springs and wool mattresses. Catherine Beecher and Harriet Beecher Stowe wrote in *The American Women's Home: or Principles of Domestic Science* (1869) that "time, labor, and expense" could be saved "not only in the building but in furniture and its arrangement," if conveniences were placed in one central area. Most plans by this time included bathtubs and laundry, storage for linens and food, a cistern and a well, an ice closet (for perishable foods), and a water or earth closet (advocated by the Beecher sisters), which were placed in close proximity in the basement. (Earth closets are again getting attention today, because they recycle wastes and save water.) The shortage of servants was a problem, and it was lamented that America was the only country in which "ladies" did their own work. *Andrew Jackson Downing,* in his book, *Cottage Residences* (1873), suggested that a hall-dining room would conserve space if the dining area portion could be closed off. By now closets were planned in kitchens, back halls, and bedrooms. Big porches and halls, which ran the length of the house, were typical. In 1871, it was suggested for the first time that color affected health and was as important as light, air, and drainage (*Godey's Lady's Book,* [1871]). Between 1877 and 1886, few changes were made, although in 1884 pumps were included in the kitchen.

The houses of the decade beginning in 1887 were still inefficient. The kitchen remained in the basement, which rendered inconvenient the serving of food. Household items were much in advance of floor plans. The icebox was on the market in 1890; enamelware, in 1895. But the house continued to be a subject of interest, and Tood Goodholme, in his *Domestic Cyclopedia of Practical Information* (1889), suggested that a sober effect in the house was the "test" of family refinement (muted colors and so on). The least important item in the bedroom was the bedstead, and he suggested that brass be used for family beds and iron for those of the servants. He suggested that carpet be omitted from the nursery, for "it will always smell," and he held a similar notion about curtains.

Few positive changes occurred in the plan of the house during the Victorian Period in spite of such writers as the Beecher sisters. Rooms remained large, with high ceilings, and were difficult to clean, which made household chores a trial. Yet, families remained relatively unconcerned. It was not until the twentieth century dawned and servants began to disappear that the plan of the home received the attention it needed to develop into a functional background for the family.

Furniture

Victorian furniture is a manifestation of the industrialization of the United States. Increased prosperity and widening distribution of wealth made it possible for more people to buy furniture, even though their taste was largely uneducated. The Victorian style, which was always in a state of flux, was adapted from those of earlier periods and was divided into several substyles.

Table 16.29
Victorian Substyles

1. Greek Revival or Empire 1815–50
2. Gothic Revival 1830–65
3. Louis XV (includes work of John Belter) 1845–70
4. Renaissance Revival 1860–80
5. Eastlake 1870–80
6. Oriental or Turkish 1870–1901
★7. Shaker (furniture sold between 1815–80)
★8. Art Nouveau 1890–1906

★ Discussed in Chap. 18.

Figure 16.24a
An American Victorian sideboard with swelling front, three upper drawers and three lower cupboards with acanthus-leaf design and melon feet.

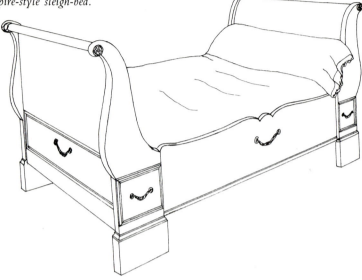

Figure 16.24b
An American Victorian Empire-style sleigh-bed.

Victorian furniture was made in a variety of styles. Carving and rich veneers were the chief types of ornamentation, although painting, marquetry, and inlay were used on the most elaborate pieces. Many American examples were similar to the English, except perhaps for the Eastlake influence (seen at the Philadelphia Centennial) and the work of John Belter; as a result, English examples will be referred to in some cases.

Greek Revival or Empire

The Greek Revival style was important in the United States for two reasons: first, Americans identified with the Greeks' struggle for freedom because they had so recently achieved their own; second, the Empire style was important not only in France, but throughout the world. In the United States, the style expressed itself primarily in architecture, with Greek mansions rising throughout the country, particularly in the South.

American Empire furniture, with its many straight lines, was easier to produce than French Empire furniture, and it was more durable. One of the most popular American Empire pieces was the sideboard, (Fig. 16.24a), typically rectangular, with flush drawers, and acanthus-leaf ornamentation, and legs ending in melon feet. The American Empire sleigh-

bed was much more simple than French versions (Fig. 16.24b). Pieces were always large, with applied carving in flowers and leaves, or a *pillar-and-scroll* design (a scrolled design with columns on each side). Crotch mahogany veneers, often with carving, were used for cornices and pedestals and on sofas. Split spindles were another applied detail. Bedposts, table legs, and pedestals were often turned, and carved bracket feet were typical on case pieces and sofas. Chairs frequently had saber legs. The tops of tables and sideboards were of white or richly colored marble. Some charming, simplified country pieces, without carving and with mushroom handles, were made in Wisconsin, Kentucky, Tennessee, Indiana, Illinois, and Ohio. New pieces in this style were the ottoman and the lazy susan.

Gothic Revival

One of those responsible for the shift to Gothic architecture and furniture was *Andrew Jackson Downing*. This easily recognizable style had Gothic motifs, which included arches; tracery in quartrefoils, trefoils, rosettes, and heraldic designs; carved cusps, spandrels, and crockets. The carving was medium-deep, but sharply cut. Incising, piercing, turning, and bold moldings were typical. The style is typically seen in chairs, mirrors, hall stands, whatnots, and small pieces. Tables and sofas were seldom made in the Gothic style (see Fig. 15.24e).

Architects often designed furniture to blend with their exteriors and these pieces were usually superior in both design and construction. Few country examples were attempted. Crotch-grain mahogany, rosewood, and black walnut were the most popular woods. The size of Gothic Revival furniture was average except that chairs had high backs that were pierced and carved.

Louis XV

Louis XV Victorian furniture, often called Rococo or Belter furniture, is the most attractive of the Victorian substyles (Fig. 16.24c). Light and graceful, it was recommended by Downing for parlors. These pieces had cabriole legs, S–scrolls and curves, naturalistic carvings of shells, flowers, birds and fruit combined with deep finger molding. Many mass-produced pieces competed with those made by such designers as Belter.

John Henry Belter (1800?–65) John Henry Belter, a native of Germany, was the leading cabinetmaker of the American Victorian period. Known mainly for his chairs, sofas, and tables, he established a shop in New York in 1844 and by 1858 employed forty apprentices. His furniture, popular until about 1860 when mass-produced furniture became readily available, was made by a secret lamination process using steam. He used from three to eighteen layers of rosewood and was able to create deeply carved curves without weakening the wood (Fig. 16.24c).

Balloon-shaped chair backs appeared in this style and were very popular in both open and upholstered styles. A triple sofa was an expanded version of this style. Lady-and-gentleman chairs appeared, matched in design, except that the lady's chair was smaller and armless. The Boston rocker (Fig. 16.24d) was also in vogue. The étagère, which replaced the whatnot in this period, had shelves flanking the mirror. Few large pieces, such as extension tables or sideboards, were made in this style.

Renaissance Revival

The Renaissance Revival was a heavy style of furniture, much more elaborate than Gothic Revival furniture. This was partly the result of

mass production, which made furniture flatter and heavier. The style first appeared in England and was displayed at the Great Exhibition of 1851. It was also shown at the Philadelphia Centennial in 1876. It was characterized by stiff outlines, broken arches, strapwork, bold moldings, raised cartouches, raised small panels or large panels framed with applied moldings, and such motifs as medallions, swags, flowers, fruit, animal heads, rosettes, and sporting trophies carved in medium or high relief. Most of the pieces in this style were made for the dining room, the library, and the bedroom. These included beds, case pieces, library and parlor tables, and large rectangular dressers on plinth or block feet.

Eastlake

Charles Eastlake, the chief proponent of good taste in this period, suggested in his book, *Hints on Household Taste,* that consumers were responsible for the poorly designed furniture available on the market. Eastlake did not design any furniture, but such a demand developed from his book that manufacturers designed an "Eastlake style" of furniture. Pieces were angular, of oak or black walnut, with little ornamentation except simple incising. Gingerbread edges on aprons and shelves were common (and easy to make with the new wood-cutting machines). The Centennial Exposition further popularized "Eastlake-style" furniture but the furniture had nothing to do with the style Eastlake recommended; the name was only a merchandising gimmick.

Oriental or Turkish

Every large house in this period had an *Oriental corner* with furniture of bamboo and wicker. The Oriental style was a minor phenomenon, for it was never used throughout a home. The style became popular during the Middle Georgian period, with Chippendale, and continued through the Late Georgian and Regency Periods, reaching its peak about

Table 16.30
Characteristics of John Henry Belter Furniture

1. Pieces were constructed of three to eighteen layers of highly polished laminated rosewood (from Brazil).
2. Rococo, curvilinear forms were accented by interwoven pierced scrolls; there were no straight lines.
3. The backs, knees, and seat rails of chairs were elaborately and deeply carved; backs were pierced.
4. Backs of pieces were faced with finished wood so furniture could be placed in the center of a room.
5. Pieces had one-piece concave backs.
6. Legs were cabriole with whorl feet.
7. Motifs included scrolls (both large and small); S–, C–, and cyma curves; pendent grapes; flowers, full-blown roses and lilacs; foliage; finger molding; tendrils; galleries (pierced); carved spandrels.
8. Pieces were carved and assembled by hand.
9. Parlor sets were matched.

Figure 16.24d
An American Victorian Boston rocker by Hitchcock.

1880. Mother-of-pearl inlays and Tiffany glass were used with it. Many authentic pieces were imported from the Orient, and upholstered chairs with a Turkish appearance were made possible by the invention of the coil spring.

Patent Furniture

There was a great interest in mechanical furniture during the Victorian Period. Many of these pieces were patented, for they were unique. These included swivel, reclining, and folding chairs, sofas and cupboards that converted into beds, and chairs that were also stepladders. The desire for novelty resulted in many innovative items of furniture, particularly in the United States, which had no long-standing history of hand-craftsmanship.

Glossary

Andiron. Horizontal bars, attached to decorative posts, that support fireplace logs.

Aster. Decorative carving, consisting of three flowers, on panels of Connecticut chests of the seventeenth and eighteenth centuries.

Balloon Back. An arched or hoop shaped chair back.

Bandy-Legged. A term used in the United States during the Colonial Period for the cabriole leg.

Boss. An oval applied ornament found on Colonial furniture.

Boston Rocker. A rocking chair of the Victorian Period; the seat curved up at the back and down at the front; the back was composed of vertical spindles.

Breakfront. An eighteenth-century bookcase, cabinet, or secretary, the central portion of which was recessed or advanced.

Brewster Chair. A chair of the Colonial Period that had a double row of turned spindles on the back and a rush seat.

Butterfly Table. A table with a hinged butterfly-wing-shaped support for the drop leaf (an American innovation).

Carver Chair. A wood turned chair with rear legs that formed continuous uprights with the back, horizontal and vertical spindles set between the uprights, and rush seat.

Cock Bead. A molding, semicircular in section, applied to the edges of drawers.

Corbel. A bracket used as support for a beam or on furniture.

Crown Glass. Window glass, made with a blowpipe, with a button or a bull's-eye center.

Dry Sink. A kitchen cabinet with storage space beneath the marble top for pitcher and washbasin.

Étagère (e-tazeːr′). A set of open shelves, such as a whatnot.

Fan Light. A fan-shaped window over the door, used by eighteenth-century architects.

Fancy Chair. A small, Sheraton style sidechair, often painted and gilded.

Fiddle-back. Chair splat that resembles a fiddle (based on the Queen Anne style).

Flame Stitch. A needlepoint design that depicts the waving outline of flames, popular in the seventeenth century.

French Bracket Foot. A bracket foot with a concave curve that gives the foot a splayed effect.

Gambrel Roof (găm′-brĕl). A gable-type roof with a lower slope much steeper than the upper one.

Hadley Chest. An early New England chest decorated with incised carvings and stained red or black.

Hipped Roof. A roof with a sloping end instead of a gable.

Horsehair. A Victorian upholstery material woven from the horses' tails and manes.

Jabot (zhȧ′-bōʹ). The cascading side pieces of a valance.

Mansard Roof (măn′-särd). A hipped roof with two slopes on each side, the lower slope much steeper than the upper one.

Martha Washington Chair. A chair of the Federal Period with open arms and a high upholstered seat and back.

Palmette. A motif similar to a stylized palm leaf.

Roundabout Chair. An American term for an English corner chair.

Sausage Turning. A method of turning that resembles sausage links.

Sleigh Bed. An American Empire bed with a high scrolled headboard and a slightly lower footboard.

Spandrels. A triangular wood section between a horizontal rail and vertical support.

Spool Turning. A method of turning which was derived from bobbin turning, used in the Victorian Period.

Summer Beam. A large beam that spanned the width of the Colonial home.

Trifid. A three-toed foot used in the American Georgian Period.

Whatnot. A highly decorated tiered display unit, popular in the Victorian Period.

Bibliography

BJERKOE, ETHEL HALL. *Cabinet Makers of America.* Garden City, N.Y.: Doubleday & Company, Inc., 1957.

BOLLES, A. S. *Industrial History of the United States.* Norwich, Conn.: the Henry Bil Publishing Co., 1879.

BRAZER, E. S. *Early American Decoration.* Springfield, Mass.: Pond-Ekbert Co., 1940.

BRUNNER, EDMUND DES, and WILBUR C. HALLENBECK. *American Society: Urban and Rural Patterns.* New York: Harper & Row, Publishers, 1955.

BUTLER, JOSEPH T. *American Antiques, 1800–1900.* New York: Odyssey Press (Publishing), 1965.

CESCINSKY, HERBERT. *English and American Furniture.* Grand Rapids, Mich.: Dean-Hicks, 1929.

CLIFFORD, C. R. *Period Furnishings.* New York: Clifford & Lawton, Inc., 1927.

COMSTOCK, HELEN. *The American Furniture: 17th, 18th and 19th Century Styles.* New York: The Viking Press, Inc., 1962.

———. *The Concise Encyclopedia of American Antiques.* New York: Hawthorn Books, Inc., 1958.

DREPPERD, CARL W. *New Geography of American Antiques.* New York: Award Books, 1927.

DOWNS, JOSEPH. *American Furniture: Queen Anne and Chippendale Periods 1725–1788.* New York: The Viking Press, Inc., 1967.

FITCH, JAMES MARSTON. *American Building.* Boston: Houghton Mifflin Company, 1948.

GOODFRIEND, ARTHUR. *What is America?* New York: Simon & Schuster, Inc., 1954.

HICKS, JOHN D., and GEORGE E. MOWRY. *A Short History of American Democracy.* Boston: Houghton Mifflin Company, 1956.

KIMBERLY, W. L. *How to Know Period Styles in Furniture.* Grand Rapids, Mich.: Periodical Publishing Co., 1912.

KOUWENHOVEN, JOHN A. *The Arts in Modern American Civilization.* New York: W. W. Norton Company, Inc., 1948.

LYNES, RUSSELL. *The Demoesticated Americans.* New York: Harper & Row, Publishers, 1963.

MARZIO, PETER C. ed. *A Nation of Nations.* New York: Harper & Row Publishers, 1976.

McCLINTON, KATHERINE MORRISON. *Antiques Past and Present.* New York: Bramhall House, 1971.

MUNFORD, LEWIS. *Roots of Contemporary Architecture.* New York: Van Nostrand Reinhold Company, 1952.

OTTO, CELIA JACKSON. *American Furniture of the 19th Century.* New York: The Viking Press, Inc., 1967.

WANSCHER, OLE. *The Art of Furniture.* New York: Van Nostrand Reinhold Company, 1966.

WHITON, SHERRILL. *Interior Decoration and Design.* New York: J. B. Lippincott Company, 1974.

WINCHESTER, ALICE, ed. *The Antiques Book.* New York: Bonanza Books, 1950.

Twentieth-Century American Homes*

The right to have a home of one's own has always been a fundamental part of the American dream. From its first architectural forms to those of the present, the shelter has represented a haven of security, a place in which to nurture the family, and a symbol of the roots put down in a community. The evolution of architectural styles has closely followed our industrial needs. As the desire to live in the suburbs or rural areas has grown, changes in house styles have made the home more functional, more innovative, and more adaptable to the owner's needs, to the topography of the site, and to the ecology of the area. As technologies improve, future homes will be even more aesthetically pleasing and efficient, and more nearly an extension of the behavior patterns and psychological needs of their occupants.

Architecture

Craftsman House 1900 (Fig. 17.1)

At the turn of the century, with an increasing number of Americans working in factories and the population of urban centers growing more dense, a new style of architecture was needed to meet the limitations of urban geography while providing a sense of country charm. Concurrently, the Arts and Crafts movement was developing in England in opposition to the dehumanizing effects of the Machine Age. In American this opposition manifested itself in the *Craftsman* style led by *Gustav Stickley,* who stressed the value and individuality of hand-made arts and crafts. His New York firm produced numerous plans and drawings for houses of honest and natural materials built to last a lifetime. This Craftsman style was as much a rejection of Victorian decorative motifs as it was a new means for constructing inexpensive but sound dwellings.

Craftsman houses were simple forms: usually of gabled construction, often faced with concrete and stone, they had extended front porches and arbors for plantings. Country houses in this style were often constructed of logs exposed on the interior as well as the exterior.

Europeans of some economic means at this time traditionally had two homes, a winter home in the city and a summer home in the hills. These homes may have been only five miles apart but they housed remarkably different patterns of living. When Americans began adopting the two-home pattern in the late 1800s and after the turn of the century, they began a design analysis that was permanently to change interior planning.

The principal house of these wealthy Americans was extremely inefficient. For example, the kitchen and the laundry were typically located in the basement; the single bathroom, used by family and servants, was located on the second floor. The domestic staff traveled unnecessary miles within the home each day doing basic chores, but it was of little concern to the family that the house was inefficient in terms of both time and energy.

The first summer homes in America resembled the winter residences in this respect. However, when the family moved to the summer home, only one or two of the domestic servants went along, the others remaining in the city to maintain the winter home. This decrease in staff meant that the women of the family had to do many of the chores—which led them to notice the inefficiency of home design. They began to demand step-saving houses; Stickley's Craftsman house, and then the bungalow, evolved from those demands.

The Bungalow 1905 (Fig. 17.2)

The bungalow, one of the first houses within the economic reach of middle-class Americans, grew out of the West Coast architecture of the Greene brothers, *Charles Sumner Greene* (1868–1957) and *Henry Mather Greene* (1870–1954). The precursor of the ranch house of the 1950s, it swept the country. Photography, beginning to come into its own, gave magazines such as *House Beautiful, Ladies' Home Journal,* and *Good Housekeeping* the opportunity to publish photographs of bungalow designs and plans, increasing the demand for them. The bungalow became an extremely popular style because it allowed families to move from brownstones and tenements into their own homes.

The bungalow was generally one story high with a slightly pitched shingle or tile roof. Columns of fieldstone, brick, wood, or cement supported the front porch. This self-sufficient home flourished and became an inspiration for efficiency in future house design.

* Most of the illustrations of the homes in this chapter were developed by Tim Bookout, Professor of Interior Design, Georgia State University.

Figure 17.1
The Craftsman House, 1900. A simple gabled house faced with concrete with an extended front porch and an arbor on the front.

Figure 17.2
The bungalow, 1905. A one-story house with a shingle roof with columns supporting the porch across the front.

Figure 17.3
A California Mission-style dwelling, 1920–30. A stucco house with a tile roof.

Architects had once concentrated on designing homes for the very rich but, as early as 1897, Frank Lloyd Wright was instrumental in the development of more efficient homes that utilized the central utility core the Beecher sisters had advocated.

The bungalow had no entry hall: the living and dining rooms opened into one another. The bathroom now was complete with tub, sink, and watercloset. The laundry remained in the basement, and the drying yard was in the back. The pantry, located between the kitchen and dining room, helped to block the transmission of kitchen noises, but was relatively inaccessible to the storage area in the basement. The advent of screens made porches more convenient both for sitting and for storage (the icebox was often placed on the back porch). By 1905, a desire for a simpler pattern of living had forced structural changes; by 1906, because space considerations were becoming important, several functionally related rooms were being combined into one and room size was decreasing.

The bungalow served to reunite families whose patterns of living had been changed by the Industrial Revolution. Families could recover some of their togetherness in the single dwelling that had typified America in its early agrarian period.

California Mission-Style Dwelling 1920–30 (Fig. 17.3)

The 1920s were a period out of which developed a number of architectural styles, including the California Mission style. The westward expansion of the last quarter of the nineteenth century and the twentieth-century entrance of the Southwestern states into the Union had stimulated an appreciation for native American architectural styles of wood and stucco with baked tile roofs. These were adapted by builders to urban settings, creating different, surprising homes in districts once typified by frame construction. California Mission-style homes were asymmetrical in design, reminiscent of their Spanish origins, and at their best appeared as though they had grown and been added to as the need arose.

Earlier Americans had moved cautiously

Table 17.1
Craftsman House

Space:	Somewhat open plan
Form:	Square
Colors:	Grays, browns, greens, earth colors, natural materials
Texture:	Log, concrete, natural wood frame
Family Correlate:	More cohesiveness

Table 17.2
Bungalow

Space:	Open plan
Form:	Rectangular with front porch
Colors:	Grays, browns, greens, earth tones, natural materials
Texture:	Wood, with shingles, tiles, field stone, cement, brick, or wood
Line:	Horizontal
Family Correlate:	Togetherness

Table 17.3
California Mission-Style Dwelling

Space:	Irregular plan
Form:	Asymmetrical, horizontal
Colors:	Natural stucco, yellow or gray or (occasionally) white, terra-cotta roof
Texture:	Rough stucco
Family Correlate:	Adventurousness

into the cities, attempting to retain as much of the old as possible. The California Mission style represented the expansive ambitions of more adventurous families. It was a symbol of the growth opportunities for the restless and the eager. The adoption of this style suggested that these families were not content with the tried and true, but were willing to venture into the unfamiliar. These families were also the ones who tended to encourage their children to look to industry as an exciting opportunity rather than a frightening unknown.

By 1920, industry's higher salaries were attracting many former domestic workers, so the increasing number of surburban and country houses were designed to be more compact and efficient. Women demanded functionality in design, and instead of housekeepers they became *"household engineers"* (*Ladies Home Journal* [1912]). Parlors had vanished and the living room had merged with the hall and the library to become the hub of family activity. It was a "discouragement to the . . . never closely chaperoned courtship of American youth and maid" thus a "prime cause of early marriage among the well-to-do" who sought privacy.[1] Some open plans for summer homes combined living and dining areas and Theodore Roosevelt's emphasis on health influenced the advent of sleeping porches. An additional lavatory appeared near the living room and, occasionally, a second bath. Kitchens disappeared from basements, room size decreased further, central heating replaced open fires, and mechanical devices replaced domestic servants. Breakfast nooks facilitated quick meals and in 1922 standardized kitchen cabinets began to be produced. The laundry, now next to the kitchen, contained a washing machine and an electric mangle, although the latter was never successful. "Decorator" colors were introduced into bathrooms to replace traditional white. Simplicity was the order of the day.

Colonial Revival-Style Dwelling 1920 (Fig. 17.4)

The wealth of the 1920s was manifested by the variety of architectural styles adapted from the English tradition. But after World War I, and before the Depression of the 1930s, the disenchantment with European strife produced a brief revival of American nationalism. One of the most popular styles was the Colonial Revival.

The 1876 Philadelphia Centennial Exposition had made the public aware of America's significance as a developing country; fifty years later, with the money from an industrial society, architecture was available in almost any style to please a patron's image of himself. Colonial architecture developed into an expanded twentieth-century form to meet the physical and emotional needs of a new America.

The Colonial Revival style borrowed heavily from the proportion and modest classical motifs which had existed in earlier structures. Small window lights, fan lights, Palladian windows, broken pediments, arches over doorways, pedimented and balustraded

[1] Robert C. Spencer, Jr., "The Hall," *House Beautiful*, Vol. 20 (Aug. 1908), p. 52.

porches, dormers, hipped roofs, and Ionic and Corinthian columns were found in this style.

Those who purchased the Colonial Revival house were looking beyond mere ostentation to a sense of belonging and a relationship to their American heritage. The families in these homes tended to be more conservative in their economic, political, religious, social, and educational views; but they were also an ambitious group, imbued with the work ethic and a belief in the supremacy of individual effort.

The interior of this house had fireplaces, door and window treatments, and wall coverings which had many Colonial characteristics. Water ran to the upper floors and the upstairs bath was attached to the master bedroom. Many of these homes displayed garland-ornamented basins and gilded infra-humans spouting water. There was also a greater tendency toward privacy and better interior design.

Half-Timber Dwelling 1920 (Fig. 17.5)

One of the most popular styles of the 1920s was the two-story half-timbered house, copied from those found in the English countryside. The frame, generally exposed and filled with plaster and stucco, was a strong contrast of light and dark patterning that suggested a structure of permanence and stability. These characteristics were important to the newly rich American who wanted to convey an image of landed gentry and to reflect the sophistication of a European heritage.

Although they borrowed heavily from the appearance of English dwellings, the American versions emphasized detail rather than structural accuracy. Slate roofs, half-timbered gables, diamond-shaped leaded windows, and solid panel doors were a few of the massive details used in achieving an "English" appearance.

The half-timbered house reflected the excitement and optimism of the 1920s. Families were adjusting to city life, the war that was to end all future wars was fading from memory and expanded economic opportunity appeared possible for most Americans. The difficulties of family adjustment to the rapid changes wrought by industrialization seemed less onerous. The direction of those changes was far from clear, but the sense of joy was obvious.

The interior of half-timbered houses was somewhat lighter due to more windows but they were still small owing to the elimination of the over-hanging roof as part of an "outdoorsy" trend. The popularity of the family

Table 17.4
Colonial Revival-Style Dwelling

Space:	Georgian plan
Form:	Rectilinear; symmetrical balance
Colors:	Weatherboarding, frame construction, brick
Line:	Horizontal
Family Correlates:	A sense of the American heritage and the work ethic

Table 17.5
Half-Timber Dwelling

Space:	Irregular plan
Form:	Irregular
Colors:	Dark woods, slate, white-washed stucco
Texture:	Half-timbered; natural, rugged texture
Line:	Vertical
Family Correlates:	Optimism and a sense of joy

Table 17.6
Tract House

Space:	Square plan
Form:	Asymmetrical on exterior
Colors:	Variety
Textures:	Variety
Line:	Unified
Family Correlates:	Cohesiveness, sense of unity and purpose

car encouraged relocating the garage alongside the house, although as late as 1913 women who drove this machine were considered a trifle "fast."

Tract House 1930–45 (Fig. 17.6)

The economic depression of the 1930s brought hardship to the middle class in America. In order to meet the increasing needs for shelter, houses had to be produced more inexpensively than before.

Prior to this time, with the exception of row houses, American residential dwellings had been conceived as individual units to meet individual demands. Tract housing provided a community concept of housing. Economics dictated that people buy smaller structures, but there was an increased demand for shelter with a lack of community resources to pro-

vide for it. Environmental planning around centers of industry produced houses similar in construction varying only in color and detail.

Tract houses were generally squarish in plan and one and one half stories high, utilizing attic space for living. The exterior varied from shingle to weatherboarding, often with stone or brick added around doorways and attached to single chimneys. These houses were usually constructed over basements that provided additional square footage and housed central heating facilities.

Europeans had a tradition of leasing a townhouse-like unit for perhaps a lifetime. Rarely did families change residence. A family grown unexpectedly large might seek a new house, but beyond such a requirement permanent location was a desire and expectation. Individual home ownership was not a European tradition or a popular ambition. The American tradition, however, included owning one's own home, but the economic realities of the 1930s made that ambition difficult to realize. Tract housing was an attempt to keep alive that American dream.

There was a sense of cohesiveness in families during the Depression of the 1930s that has since disappeared. For most families, finances were a major problem, and all family contributions were welcome. The money that children could contribute from babysitting, paper routes, lawn mowing, and odd jobs was

Figure 17.7
A ranch-style house,
1950– . This one-story
house has a large picture
window in the front.

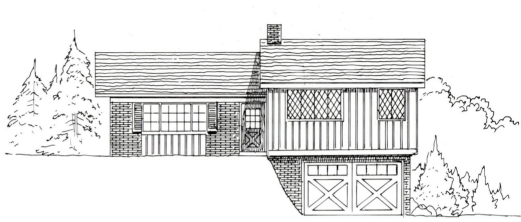

Figure 17.8
A split-level house, 1960s.
The garage of this
split-level house is on the
lower level with a family
room and patio in the rear.

often essential. Frequently, an older child would drop out of school if a job presented itself. The sense of unity and purpose that came from the need for the family to pull together built strength of character and dramatically reduced the incidence of emotional disturbance.

The self-confidence children developed from contributing to the family, whether from self-earned income or by assuming household chores in the place of working parents, laid a psychological foundation for adult emotional security. The work done by the children in the family often enabled a family to maintain a home or to purchase one of the new, relatively inexpensive tract houses.

The size of the house continued to contract. The editors of *House Beautiful* advised readers to "design as you live" (February 1934). The exterior was secondary to the basic plan. The hall entry was small and the upstairs bath was two thirds its former size. The master bedroom was for rest and sexual activity. Bedrooms were now very small. The condensed U–shaped kitchen, all-white, had a laboratory-like appearance. The housewife did most of the work (only 5 per cent of American households had servants). All kitchen floor space was utilized and some kitchens had islands in the center. An informal eating area replaced the breakfast nook, and the kitchen began to regain its status as the center of family activity. The basement and attic were eliminated, and large areas were designed for outdoor living. Family rooms were used for living while living rooms replaced the parlors of the Victorian Period. Although the World's Fair of

Table 17.7
Ranch-Style House

Space:	Rectangular plan
Form:	Rectangle
Colors:	Brick, terra-cotta, natural wood
Textures:	Natural
Line:	Horizontal
Family Correlates:	Beginning of break-up of the traditional family

Table 17.8
Split-Level House

Space:	Irregular plan
Form:	Irregular
Colors:	Browns, olives, wood colors
Texture:	Brick on first level, wood on second
Line:	Asymmetrical balance
Family Correlate:	Split between the generations in the family

1939 introduced a variety of new materials and techniques, these could not be utilized owing to the shortage of labor and of materials that accompanied World War II.

Ranch-Style House 1950–Present (Fig. 17.7)

After World War II, houses were more efficiently designed and the many household conveniences greatly altered the traditional female role. Women had more time to devote to their children. This unwittingly led to a pampering of children, which was to have an explosive impact upon society in the 1960s. Children were no longer required to do many chores about the house, or to contribute to family finances.

Parents who had grown up during the Depression wanted their children to experience none of the difficulties they themselves had faced. But children raised in a home where there is little opportunity to contribute become takers and develop little sense of worth. The resulting insecurity and emotional problems produced a generation of adults with little sense of purpose and a continued need to seek identity.

By the end of World War II, the American industrial complex was ready for conversion to the consumer production. The greatest necessity was for housing. Traditional styles of architecture were replaced by industrially functional forms, clean in line and efficient. The resulting form was the ranch style.

These houses were still tract houses however, increased family income made possible larger plots for one-story structures. For the most part, the new structures lacked traditional or classical details; instead natural materials were used to achieve a modern balance of plane surfaces. Brick was the most popular exterior material, used in a variety of colors. Increased income created a demand for two-car garages, now attached to the main structure. Roofs were flat or hip and large plate-glass "picture" windows were frequently centered in the façade.

Uniformity of construction was a standard building practice and valued by the postwar Americans as a symbol of unity and progress. But the break with traditional forms that personified the ranch style parallels the beginning of the break-up of the traditional family.

The Frank Lloyd Wright *Usonian* house was one-story without a definitive front or back which created a feeling of spaciousness and comfort. Wright popularized the open plan, the merging of indoors and outdoors (made possible by the availability of large panes of glass and central heating), and the use of light as a pleasure source. The open plan offered simplicity and warmth in one large gracious room containing kitchen, living, and dining areas. Often a music center was included. Privacy was a canon of this era and windows were meant to provide a view and

light, but were not meant to expose the family to the sights and sounds of their neighbors.

The idea that the "bedroom services you as you service the rest of the house" (*House Beautiful* [February 1954]), made it a multipurpose room, as it had been in earlier decades. Kitchen arrangements were triangular, hexagonal, and trapezoidal, and efficiency was increased by garbage disposals, component stoves, electric can openers, knife sharpeners, and cooking utensils that doubled as serving dishes. The home freezer made it possible to shop less frequently. Natural materials, such as wood, brick, and plants, made the interior more livable, and brought the exterior inside.

Split Level House 1960s (Fig. 17.8)

In the 1960s the American populace was restless, experiencing great social change. The older members of the middle class, satisfied with postwar prosperity, found themselves in conflict with the younger generation. Those who were raised in the Depression and who valued the security represented by their homes and families found their attitudes conflicting with the pervasive and seemingly rootless do-your-own-thing philosophy of the new generation. The problem of creating security and a personal identity in an almost totally urbanized society created strong social frustrations.

Builders were faced with the problem of designing structures that were individual in character but were cramped by diminishing available land. The look-alike houses of the 1950s were rejected for construction methods incorporating multilevel housing concepts with strong variations of form and materials. The split-level structures were not traditional in design, but they exhibited a variety of details and materials reminiscent of traditional construction.

The split-level house was not a true two-story house. The two- or three-foot difference between levels, though functionally difficult to maintain (clean, paint, or repair) provided psychological separation between occupants. For this reason, the split-level house nicely symbolized the split between generations. The house represented an attempt to express an uncertain individuality through a new kind of conformity and to further the search for basic values in a time of great personal insecurity. But the dissatisfaction expressed by families in this period resulted in split marriages and split families as well as split-level houses.

Unalloyed finishes and materials wove the

split-level house into its environment. Gardens, patios, and game areas were included on the outside but the interior accented "apartness." The bedrooms were separated from the center of family activity; the children's sleeping area featured recreational and study space; and the master bedroom was the least accessible room in the house. The master bath, typically one of two baths, was smaller than it had been, for bathing had become a daily routine, over as quickly as possible, and no longer a special event.

The living room was the family gathering place for conversation and passive entertainment, but the recreation room was the family play area. In the kitchen, convenience prevailed, with cordless appliances, microwave ovens, and other equipment (93 percent of American homes had electricity by 1967). Although 70 per cent of the family meals were served in there, the kitchen continued to shrink in size as food preparation was increasingly simplified.

Self-Affirmation 1970s (Fig. 17.9)

Although the house of the 1970s was smaller than earlier houses, and had fewer frills, it was sufficient for most families, for the divorce rate was nearly 50 per cent across the nation and reached almost 75 per cent in some localities. The birth rate continued to decline, and many couples were waiting until their late twenties and early thirties to have children. The larger families of earlier periods would have found these quarters much too cramped.

American families moved as often as five times in ten years, and the life cycle of dwellings greatly changed, as had the demands of the occupants. Recessive economic trends, which began in late 1979, dictated a reduction of square footage and of expensive details. For many families the cost of an individual dwelling had become prohibitive, single-family houses were giving way to multilevel unit-owned or unit-rented structures.

Americans underwent a time of soul-searching in the hope of establishing stronger values for the future. This attitude was one factor that helped to produce an architecture that was less personal than it had been and one that often turned inward as if to exclude the outer world. It was an architecture frequently more responsive to its own functional requirements than to those of its occupants. At the same time, popular taste set up a demand for

Table 17.9
1970s House

Space:	Irregular plan
Form:	Irregular
Colors:	Natural
Texture:	Wood
Line:	More height than breath
Family Correlate:	Individual expression

Table 17.10
Energy-Dictated Home of 1980s

Space:	Small, open space
Form:	Concealed, small, square, rectangular, or round
Colors:	Earth
Textures:	Often underground except for glass on one side
Line:	Concealed except for front
Family Correlate:	Individual survival

honest materials and textures (not substitutes). This took the form of a *"back-to-nature movement."* The result was a paradox. The thin veneer of paper photography, or the metal which replaced the traditional wooden stud only appeared to be wood. The most dramatic buildings styles began in the 1970s, with the increasing need for alternative energy sources; and function began to dictate form in the 1980s.

The emphasis in the 1970s was on the individual and not on the family unit. Self-expression was the rule and individual desires were primary. The house became smaller. Microwave ovens and eating counters made eating fast and usually solitary. By the end of the decade, one meal in every three was eaten outside the home. Some families never sat down to a meal together except on holidays.

Quite typically, both husband and wife worked and their schedules did not foster family unity. Children were often delivered to babysitters and day-care centers by one parent and picked up by the other. When the family was together, its members seemed to have little in the way of meaningful conversation, so the television area became the center of family life.

More single-parent families appeared as the stigma once attached to divorce gave way to the fashion of finding personal fulfillment. The attitude of letting children "do their own thing," however, was beginning to diminish

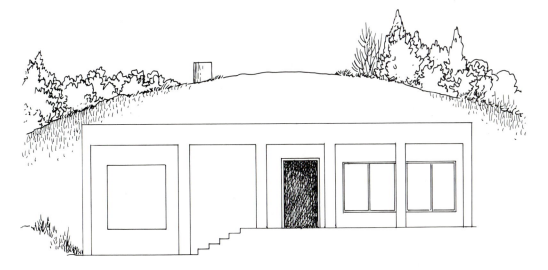

and there was a renewed demand for basic discipline.

The television room was important because it apparently occupied the children of parents who were too busy or not trained to meet the challenge of raising children. Children and adults felt little sense of belonging, and group therapy began to replace the interaction with family, friends, and relatives that earlier generations had known.

Space in the interior was not assigned for eating, sleeping, or entertaining. The occupants moved themselves rather than things. A touch of sybaritic elegance remained in the eclectic interior, however. Modular units allowed for the dispersion of kitchen centers throughout the home. Innovations, such as microwave ovens, magnetic stoves, small refrigerators, and trash compactors, were typical. The sexual thrust of advertising added to the importance of the bedroom and along with facilities for reading, writing, stereo, and television, a bathtub or Jacuzzi began to occupy space in this room.

Apartment houses and condominiums met the needs of the many small families that move, on the average, once every eighteen months. The developing unemployment problem of educated Americans fostered residence changes because individuals needed to live where jobs existed and then to move again when the job ceased to exist or when an opportunity for advancement presented itself.

Energy-Dictated Home 1980s (Fig. 17.10)

The energy crisis that developed in the 1970s will be the major influence on house design in the 1980s. Solar heat, with its glass- and water-storage panels, will give the house a different appearance. The underground house will become increasingly popular because it is naturally insulated against winter cold, summer heat, and sound. Respect for the environment, which de-emphasizes material things, will dictate smaller homes more sparsely furnished. This is fortunate for the sluggish economy will preclude the building of larger and more luxurious homes. Increasingly homes will be no more than 1000 to 1200 square feet in area, and will have scaled-down furniture. Single-family homes will still be in demand for home ownership is central to the American dream. Showers, because they require less water and are more sanitary than baths, will lead to the demise of the tub. Soaking will increasingly be seen as a luxury, usually indulged in a hot tub. Houses will still have at least two relatively small bathrooms, however.

There will be a greater interest in the structural and functional aspects of the house. Rugs will be partly replaced by tile or man-made soil-resistant materials. Rugs may also replace furniture in the living area: carpeted platforms will serve as seating units or tables. Sanitizers built into central vacuum systems will make cleaning relatively simple. Parascopic skylights, which allow the sun's heat to enter in the winter, but block it in the summer, will dot rooftops (Fig. 2.3).

Draperies will probably be replaced by one-way windows or by glass water containers that regulate the light entering a room and store solar heat. Thin metal blinds that contain solar heat collectors will become common, as will insulated shutters. Double-paned windows will be modified (shuttered, shaded, or made of different materials) on the south side of dwellings. These panes will contain an air space of several inches between them and will be filled with insulating beads to block the sun's rays and to guard against loss of heat. Houses will be climate-controlled, in spite of energy shortages.

Wood stoves will become the main source of heat for more and more homes. In northern states, more expensive heating systems will be used less frequently as solar energy and insulation complement the effect of the wood stove. Present-day wood stoves are vastly superior to those of the 1970s, being made of heavier-gauge iron and almost air-tight. They can be further modified: air can be drawn from outside the house directly into the stove with heatilators and fans circulating the heated air within the home. Even in the most fashionable homes the open fireplace will be replaced by a wood stove.

Copper tubing run through the stove can be used to heat water for household use. Wood, in spite of its atmospheric pollutants, will serve heating needs until nuclear power is more widespread.

A nuclear breakthrough at the University of Florida in 1978 has made atomic energy much safer, cheaper, and more readily available. Homes of the 1980s, beginning with apartments and condominiums, will utilize nuclear energy emanating from a common community source.

Efficiency and individual self-care through food centers will become a way of life. The shrinking size of the family, and the fact that more people are choosing to remain single, will contribute to this phenomenon. Several mini-meals a day will become the norm, because so many Americans are accustomed to eating "on the run." Eventually families will receive six-month supplies of food staples, often freeze-dried or partially prepared (one tenth of its normal weight), so cooking will take only a few minutes. However, a growing interest in nutrition and fresh food (one in every five family units now has a vegetable garden or grows fresh food in containers) will allow families to prepare food from "scratch" with the use of appliance centers.

Dishwashers will be included in every one-family home and high-frequency sound waves will do the cleaning, saving human energy and time. The completely self-sufficient home will eventually have its own power source, recycling waste (the composting toilet is available today) into energy and fertilizer. Saunas and exercise centers (because physical fitness is so important) will be emphasized.

With the increasing cost and decreasing supply of gasoline, travel will decrease drastically. More meals will be eaten in the home, and the home entertainment center, controlled by computer, will be a center of activity. This same computer will in time render unnecessary daily trips to the office. The direct line to the office will see the home office assuming the day to day tasks that now require presence at the place of work. The home computer will have a dramatic impact upon the home. Just as, at the advent of the Industrial Revolution, machines replaced the muscular strength of hundreds and even thousands of workers, so the computer will replace human cognitive and motor functions.

The computer will also contribute to the further disintegration of the family. Families could grow more cohesive from sharing chores, but the computer, by drastically reducing the need for such activities, will activate automatic vacuumers, or bath-, and kitchen cleaning devices, to assume accurate control of nutrition and billing, and even to remember and produce birthday and anniversary cards. The computer will contribute markedly to the ease of daily life, but it will also contribute to the impersonal atmosphere in the modern home: family members will interact more with the computer and less with one another.

The computer will affect all areas of modern life. Computer dating will take on new levels of sophistication: couples with similar interests can come into instant visual and auditory contact with neither having to leave his own home; initial meetings will be easier and more frequent as couples decide whether or not to pursue further contact. International chess associations will conduct matches at all levels. Participants will compete with someone on the other side of the world without leaving their homes. Similarly, other games will, through the computer, reach new levels of skill among the masses. Computer-assisted instruction with terminals on lines to universities and other learning centers will make it possible for people to earn college degrees without leaving home. In addition, most family business will be conducted through the home computer.

Further advances in automation will extend the period of adolescence to the late twenties. Children in post-World War II Western culture were noticably more dependent upon their families for physical survival. In pre-industrial America, even the three-year-old child made a work contribution. Before World War II, adolescents made a work contribution. Increasingly work contributions and, hence, acceptance as full-fledged members of society entitled to the respect that comes with that acceptance, are expected at a later age. Well-educated individuals may not join the work force until their middle thirties. They will probably remain dependent upon their families of origin until then.

There are some obvious implications for design that follow from these phenomena. The modern house will have to be flexible in structure and design to accommodate a family of parents and infants, parent or parents and children, and parents and adult children. As living-together arrangements become more popular, flexibility will be needed to meet the desires of many different adults who migrate through the same central core of family members. Not only are parents becoming more tolerant of their child living with someone of the other sex in the family home, but many parents too are living in the family house with mates they have not married.

A house with so many adults will require more automobile spaces, more bathrooms and closets. As families grow less cohesive, there will be less use for a living room or other gathering areas.

Apartments and condominiums will continue to meet the needs of families and individuals in search of employment, advancement, change in family size (through divorce or maturation) and the still longed-for "place of belonging." The rapid rate of cultural and technological change and the modification of the traditional family will necessitate changes in patterns of living. Housing will become more functionally adapted to individual needs, and solutions to spatial problems will be more aesthetically satisfying. As the limitations of the environment become more apparent, the Scandinavian attitude toward aesthetic appreciation will become more important: if it is functional, it has beauty.

Glossary

Modular Units. Units based upon a specific measure. These are flexible and can be fitted into a space with ease.

Usonian House. House planned by Frank Lloyd Wright which was a long, low rectangle with an open plan.

Bibliography

BLAKE, PETER. *Marcel Breuer: Architect and Designer.* New York: Museum of Modern Art, 1949.
———. *Marcel Breuer: Sun and Shadow.* New York: Dodd, Mead & Company, 1956.
FITCH, JAMES MARSTON. *American Building.* Boston: Houghton Mifflin Company, 1948.
GIEDION, S. *Space, Time and Architecture.* Cambridge, Mass.: Harvard University Press, 1947.
———. *Walter Gropius, Work and Teamwork.* New York: Van Nostrand Reinhold Company, 1954.
GOWANS, ALAN. *Images of American Living.* New York: J. B. Lippincott Co., 1964.
HILBERSEIMER, LUDWIG. *Mies van der Rohe.* Chicago: Paul Theobald and Co., 1956.
HITCHCOCK, H. B. *Built in USA.* New York: Museum of Modern Art, 1945.
———. *Built in USA: Post-War Architecture.* New York: Museum of Modern Art, 1953.
MASON, GRANT CARPENTER. *Frank Lloyd Wright to 1910.* New York: Van Nostrand Reinhold Company, 1958.
MOCK, E. *Built in USA: Since 1932.* New York: Museum of Modern Art, 1944.
RICHARDS, J. M. *An Introduction to Modern Architecture.* Baltimore: Penguin Books, 1959.

MUMFORD, LEWIS. *Roots of Contemporary Architecture*. New York: Van Nostrand Reinhold Company, 1952.

PETER, JOHN. *Masters of Modern Architecture*. New York: Bonanza Books, 1958.

SIRJAMAKI, JOHN. *The American Family in the Twentieth Century*. Cambridge, Mass.: Harvard University Press, 1953.

SMITH, G. E. KIDDER, and MARSHALL B. DAVIDSON. *A Pictorial History of Architecture in America*, Vol. 2. New York: American Heritage Publishing Co., Inc., 1976.

TEMKO, ALLEN. *Eero Saarinen*. New York: George Braziller, Inc., 1962.

WRIGHT, FRANK LLOYD. *Modern Architecture*. Princeton, N.J.: Princeton University Press, 1931.

Contemporary Developments in Furniture Design

English Reformers

The first design reformers lived during the Victorian Period, a time of rapid change and industrialization. In their search for identity, the Victorians demanded elaborate furniture designs based upon styles of the past. The pioneers in the design revolt, who were attempting to restore beauty to the home, blamed the disintegration of taste upon industrialization, although in reality it resulted from several factors: an increase in the wealth of the middle class, whose members became untrained arbiters of taste; the growing assembly lines of anonymous laborers; and the disinterest of manufacturers and merchants in good design. The expanding furniture industry was a factor in the disappearance of furniture craftsman. The technology of the Machine Age and new materials (tubular metal, cast iron, papier-mâché, bentwood, and laminated wood) made possible twentieth-century developments in contemporary design.

It is understandable that early design reformers hated and feared the machine. In fact, few reformers realized that simple, well-designed, machine-made furniture was possible. England's uncontrolled industrialization, with its pollution, exploitation of workers, and mushrooming city slums, was largely responsible for the loss of pleasure in work. Before the Industrial Revolution, the members of the family worked a farm or family business together. They were producers. Their product was a source of personal pride and strengthened the family bond. Industrialization meant departure from the family or at least the disintegration of the family as a productive unit. The impersonal factory, with its many independent operations, accelerated the loss of group pride. The individual became a consumer. His contribution to the family was indirect: money, and the goods produced by unknown others. Skill and pride in work were markedly diminished.

The reformers sought to return to medieval working conditions (similar to the guilds) and Gothic designs. They believed social reform to be a prerequisite to good design and a fulfilling life. The majority of the public disregarded these reformers, but the reformers nonetheless attempted to lead the masses toward good design by their writings and their work.

The growing strength of the masses, made possible through employment in industry, meant that no one need be subservient to the landowner. The individual's ability to seek independent economic survival in the cities, far from family ties or the beneficence of the wealthy, caused great disruptions in all social institutions—the church, the schools, the government, and the family. Once, each individual had known his place in an unchanging social order. Suddenly this time-honored order was disrupted and the social hierarchy was shaken. Women and children became less subservient; male authority and dominance was questioned. This was the end of an era and the beginning of a democratic revolution that is still in progress. With the death of the patriarchial society, so too died the premise that the strong and superior reach down to help the weak and inferior.

The new movement toward social and economic equality disturbed the old way of life. There was a longing for the former settled days when the common person "knew his place" and tradition meant security. The Gothic style reemerged in an attempt to return to a formal, familiar demarcation between aristocrats and the common populace. It was a symbol of the traditions that were being eroded with each passing day. An ever-increasing number of people could afford to have houses filled with furniture; hand-crafted Gothic designs, however, were still beyond the reach of all but the wealthy. Gothic style, therefore, served as one symbol of class distinction, even though this was not the intention of the reformers. The chair, for example, was reserved for the patriarch of the family, for it served to enshrine male dominance over women and children. Mass furniture production was thus one of the many factors which destroyed the traditional masculine dominance within the family and society.

August Welby Northmore Pugin (1812–52)

As early as 1836, *August Welby Northmore Pugin* suggested that modern buildings be adapted to modern life, thus becoming the first design reformer. He also integrated industrial methods with good design. Though Pugin's creative life was short (1836–46), he had an impact on later reformers though his caustic architectural criticism. He was a rare exception to the designers of his day, and his beliefs foreshadowed the principles of twentieth-century functional design. Although unacknowledged by John Ruskin, the art critic,

Figure 18.1a
A Pugin cabinet with Gothic detailing; linen-fold carving, foliated scrolls, and acorn finials, ca. 1847.

Table 18.1
August Welby Northmore Pugin (1812–52)

1. He was the first reformer.
2. He stressed functional design.
3. He accepted the machine.

Table 18.2
William Morris (1834–96)

1. He was influenced by Ruskin.
2. He believed social reform and good design must be united.
3. He was the most important person in the revival of decorative arts.
4. He raised the status of artisans.
5. He laid the groundwork for today's studio craftsmen.
6. He influenced later European and American designers.

Table 18.3
John Ruskin (1819–1900)

1. He was a very popular art critic, not a designer.
2. He dictated moral and spiritual (Protestant) design principles regardless of technical concerns.
3. He believed in visible construction based upon natural forms.
4. He believed the consumer held the ultimate responsibility for design reform.
5. He was convinced that geometric design, popular with some reformers, was an immoral compromise with technical production.
6. He believed Gothic architecture resulted in contented workmen.
7. His books, *Stones of Venice* and *Seven Lamps of Architecture,* helped form the philosophy of the Pre-Raphaelite Brotherhood and ultimately influenced many English design reformers.

and William Morris, the "father of modern design," his writings had a major influence on their design philosophy and that of the Pre-Raphaelite Brotherhood.

Pugin was converted to Catholicism at the age of twenty-three, a time when it was extremely unpopular to be a Catholic in England. He believed that function was an integral part of design and that design was a manifestation of God in a sinful world. This idea was founded on his contention that only a Catholic could design in a manner pleasing to God and one which best served people's needs. Design, prior to this time, had slighted function in favor of ornamentation and had given primary attention to the façade and to symbolism. This lavish ornamentation served as a subtle barrier between the rich and poor, for the buildings and furnishings of many of the institutions were more suited to the noble and wealthy (Figs. 18.1a, 18.1b).

William Morris (1834–96)

William Morris, painter, architect, poet, socialist, lecturer, and manufacturer of interior furnishings, was the man most responsible for the revival of the decorative arts in the nineteenth century. Morris was strongly influenced by *John Ruskin,* The Victorian art critic. Ruskin, disgusted with industrialization, believed that Gothic buildings, constructed without pretense, resulted in godly architecture and happy workmen. Ruskin was a tall, well-dressed Protestant, and his lectures were accepted by many of his listeners almost

as law. Ruskin's books, *Stones of Venice* and *Seven Lamps of Architecture,* formed the basis for the *Pre-Raphaelite Brotherhood.* This group believed that only painters before Raphael (actually, before the Renaissance) expressed honesty and sincerity in their work. They sought a return to the art and ideals of the Middle Ages, confident that the simplicity of nature could stop the dehumanization of life by industrialization. In reality, their ex-

Figure 18.1b
A Pugin Gothic style chair of carved oak, upholstered in leather, ca. 1840.

Figure 18.2a
A carved cabinet by Morris and Company, with painted decoration on the front.

Table 18.4
Beliefs of Pre-Raphaelite Brotherhood (1848)

1. The expression of genuine ideas.
2. The attentive study of nature in order to express it.
3. Sympathy with the "direct, serious, and heartfelt in previous art," excluding the conventional.[1]
4. The production of fine pictures and sculpture
5. The only honest and sincere painters were those before Raphael.
6. Return to art and ideals of Middle Ages would prevent dehumanization of man by man.

Table 18.5
Philip Webb (1831–1915)

1. He designed most of the early furniture produced by Morris & Company.
2. His early furniture was austere, massive, unornamented, rectilinear.
3. His later furniture was decorated with paintings or ornamented leather.
4. He designed the Red House for Morris.

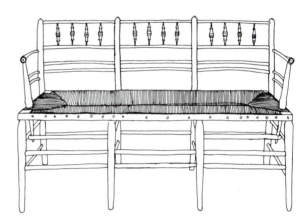

Figure 18.2b
This Sussex settee with rush seat, based upon country models, is one of the few inexpensive pieces of furniture manufactured by Morris and Company.

pressed ideals were self-deceiving attempts to maintain a society divided between the "have's" and the "have not's."

Morris, who joined the Brotherhood in the mid-1850s, was a creative craftsman in many media, which gave him a unique insight into design and quality control. Unfortunately, he was unable to separate design from historicism (designs based upon past styles) and was never convinced that beautiful objects could be produced by machine. He began to manufacture wall coverings, textiles (Fig. 7.8), stained glass, metal objects, and furniture in 1861. Even though he believed that furniture should be simple, well constructed, and priced within the reach of all, most of his firm's production was richly carved, inlaid, painted, and priced beyond the reach of all but the wealthy (Fig. 18.2a).

Morris attempted to preserve the positive aspects of the pre-industrial era without its class distinctions, but owing to the shortage of labor and the cost of production, his ideal was

[1] C. H. Ashbee, "Man and the Machine: The Pre-Raphaelites and Their Influence on Life, Part I," *House Beautiful*, **27** (February 1910), p. 75.

doomed to failure. His socialistic ideas (he believed that society should be reformed) prevented him from reaching his goal, but his design influence continued long after his death (Fig. 18.2b). He rekindled a love of craftmanship and pride in workmanship and laid the groundwork for today's studio craftsmen. Unfortunately, manufacturers of the period flooded the market with pseudo-hand-crafted items to capitalize on Morris's popularity, and his immediate influence was a negative one.

Philip Webb (1831–1915)

Philip Webb, an architect, was responsible for most of the early furniture designs of Morris and Company. His pieces were austerely medieval, rectangular, and without decoration (Figs. 18.3a, 18.3b). Webb later designed furniture with painted and gilded leather panels (Fig. 18.3c). He was responsible for the architectural designs of Morris and Company.

Figure 18.3a
A Philip Webb Gothic style table made by Morris and Company.

Figure 18.3b
A Webb designed medieval-style circular oak table manufactured by Morris and Company, ca. 1858–1859.

Figure 18.3c
A Webb cabinet with painted panels by William de Morgan made by Morris and Company, ca. 1865.

Figure 18.4a
A Godwin sideboard of ebonized wood, silver-plated fittings and insert panels of "embossed leather paper"; influenced by Japanese design, ca. 1877.

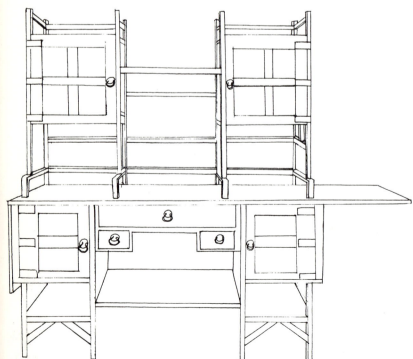

Table 18.6
Edwin William Godwin (1833–86)

1. He believed in integration of life and art; influenced by Ruskin.
2. He believed the architect should be responsible for interiors and furnishings.
3. His furniture was light, rectilinear, asymmetrical.
4. He was influenced by Japanese design, Morris Sussex furniture, Art Nouveau style.
5. His furniture was closer to modern furniture designs than that of any reformer.

Table 18.7
Charles Locke Eastlake (1836–1906)

1. He believed that simple design and unconcealed construction could be obtained inexpensively.
2. His *Hints on Household Taste* that took the responsibility for reform to the consumer, became influential in the United States and England.
3. His book resulted in manufacturers designing furniture to meet consumer demand which violated Eastlake's design principles (these designs were exhibited at the Philadelphia Centennial Exhibition in 1876).
4. He was responsible for "artistic" and "picturesque" craze in the United States.

Table 18.8
Charles R. Ashbee (1863–1942)

1. He was influenced by Morris.
2. He attempted to recreate medieval guild-like working conditions, but failed.
3. His typical furniture pieces had more than one craftsman working on them so many were less successful than they might have been.
4. He accepted the machine as part of modern life, abandoning Arts and Crafts doctrine.

Edwin William Godwin (1833–86)

Edwin William Godwin also sought to integrate life and art. Believing that furniture and interiors should be integrated, he designed both. His light, airy, graceful furniture, strongly influenced by Japanese design, was far ahead of its time (Fig. 18.4a). His book *Art Furniture, With Hints and Suggestions on Domestic Furniture and Decoration* (1877), showed examples of his simplified furniture, which was also related to the Morris Sussex chair and Art Nouveau styles. He did not copy Japanese art but used it for inspiration and as an opportunity to break away from historicism (Fig. 18.4b).

Charles Locke Eastlake (1836–1906)

Charles Locke Eastlake's fame rests upon a book he wrote, *Hints on Household Taste*, first published as a series of articles in 1864. By 1881 four editions had been published in England and six in the United States. Sharing a common interest in Gothic designs with Morris, he blamed the consumer for the poor designs available. He had little patience with fads and condemned change for the sake of change. He said.:

> So long as a thirst with mere novelty exists independently of all artistic considerations, the aim . . . will be to produce objects which by their singular form of striking combination of colors shall always appear new.[2]

The statement that good taste need not be expensive was revolutionary. Eastlake did not actually design furniture but believed that wood should be used for its intended purpose and should not appear to have been "squeezed through a pastry cone." He believed that furniture should be designed for its function with unconcealed construction and incised ornamentation. He deplored the rapid changes in style made possible by the machine and the unhealthy price competition that resulted.

Charles R. Ashbee (1863–1942)

Charles R. Ashbee, an important member of the English Arts and Crafts Movement, was also influenced by Morris's social commitment. He formed the Guild and School of Handicraft (1888) so that his pupils could apply art to industry. By 1904 about seventy men and boys were engaged in cabinetry and wrought-iron work as well as in other crafts. About this time, Ashbee tried to create medie-

[2] Russell Lynes, *The Tastemakers* (New York: Harper, 1954), p. 101–102.

val guild-like working conditions in the rural community of Chipping Camden so that a man could support his family while creating beautiful hand-made objects. He failed, for his workers had to be paid even though work was scarce and his designs were plagiarized by firms that could mass produce them less expensively.

Ashbee was influential in Europe and in the United States and *House Beautiful* had articles by Ashbee or about him between 1904 and 1910. He gradually ceased to reject the machine and wrote in 1901: "We do not reject the machine, we welcome it. But we desire to see it mastered." By 1910 he was convinced that modern civilization depended on machinery, and thus adopted one of the basic premises of the Modern Movement, which caused him to abandon the doctrine of the Arts and Crafts Movement.

Ernest Gimson (1864–1919)

Ernest Gimson, one of England's greatest artist-craftsmen, was strongly influenced by Morris. Although Gimson was an architect, his main interest was in furniture design and applied art. He, like many other reformers, rejected the machine; no power tools were allowed in his workshops. He started a furniture workshop in London with Sidney and Ernest Barnsley; later they moved to the Cotswolds, where many native craftsmen still worked (Fig. 18.5).

Figure 18.4b
A Godwin chair with light, rectilinear shape, influenced by Japanese design.

Figure 18.5
A cabinet designed by Gimson.

Table 18.9
Ernest Gimson (1864–1919)

1. He was one of England's greatest artist-craftsmen.
2. He inspired modern Danish designers.
3. He believed the designer and master craftsman were equally important.
4. His furniture was simple, with feeling for nature of wood; of unstained, unpolished oak, with unconcealed construction, particularly mortise and tenon joint, dove-tailed inlay, and visible dowels; ornamentation included black and white inlay, gouge cuts and chamfering (a beveled or angled edge), fielded panels, hand-wrought iron handles as part of the design.

Table 18.10
The Arts and Crafts Movement in England

1. It was the most important modern contribution to applied art.
2. It was a factor in development of Art Nouveau.
3. It was closely allied with Middle Ages in spirit, not form.
4. Reformers desired to re-establish status of craftsman, removing the barrier between fine and applied arts.
5. Guilds and societies were formed to reunite good design, skilled craftsmanship, and social reform; members believed creation of beauty was a debt owed to society, and opposed modern production methods.
6. Arts and Crafts Exhibition Society (1884) exhibited work of Morris, Gimson, Scott, Barnsleys, Voysey, and others between 1888 and 1914.
7. Its outgrowth of movement was revival of craftsmanship.

Table 18.11
Early Influences in the United States

1. The Shaker movement was the earliest influence: simple, functional and beautiful designs.
2. The Arts and Crafts Movement lasted until World War I: Mission furniture was a forerunner of contemporary furniture, the first "do-it-yourself" design.

One of Gimson's more important concepts was that a designer should give the craftsman a free hand in interpreting a design. Gimson, unlike many other designers, was not a skilled craftsman, yet he had a knowledge and understanding of craftsmanship and materials. Gimson, like Morris, wanted to make simple, reasonably priced furniture, but he never succeeded for he demanded expert craftsmanship.

Early Influences in the United States

Shakers

The earliest and most important influence on contemporary design in the United States came from the *Shakers,* a religious sect active from 1774 to the early 1900s. Their simple designs, governed by functional principles, had a great influence on Scandinavian design and are, in fact, still influential today. The four principles of Shakerism were: confession of sins, community of goods, celibacy, and withdrawal from the world. Nineteen colonies with about six thousand members were established in New York, Kentucky, Maine, Ohio, Indiana, and New Hampshire. There was a military orderliness in their community plans, their architecture, their manner of living, and the plain forms of their unornamented furniture.

The Shakers were outside the mainstream of design and their belief that all beauty not founded in use grows distasteful is an early statement of pure functionalism. They applied principles of form and function that were later advocated by Ruskin, Morris, Eastlake, Sullivan, and the Bauhaus designers. The Shakers, unlike Morris and the social reformers, did not fear the machine: their communities produced more inventors and mechanics per capita than other villages of comparable size. These inventions gave them time for spiritual growth. They welcomed improvements, and thought of artistic merit as an unsought by-product. The later Shakers (after 1870) lacked the dedication of the first Shakers and some worldly trends crept into their designs.

Shaker furniture was severe and plain, in harmony with the machine, and was an outward expression of their discipline and moral character. Its indigenous quality comes from their separateness from the cultivated traditions of the "outside" world.

The Shaker joiner was a fine craftsman with pride in his work. Shaker pieces were finely made and even backs were completely finished. The origins of Shaker designs can be

Table 18.12
Shakers

1. The basis of their society was horticultural, with small manufacturing plants in each community.
2. They used and accepted the machine.
3. Their craftsmen were governed by utilitarian principles; articles had to be required, functional, durable, and made of suitable materials.
4. Their influence, important in Scandinavian design, is still apparent today.
5. The characteristics of their furniture included:
   a. Low chairs, tables and stands.
   b. Many built-in storage pieces.
   c. Storage planned for specific items.
   d. Unenclosed drawers and drop leaves on tables.
   e. Finishes: light stains, varnish, or green, red, or yellow stain.
   f. Woods: local and suited for purpose (maple for slender articles under constant stress, ash and hickory for bentwood, pine for ease in working).
   g. Lightly tapered or rod-shaped legs, no feet.
   h. No eschutcheons and brasses; simple-turned pegs as drawer pulls.
   i. Sharply angled bracket feet on case pieces.
   j. Large wooden casters on beds for ease in moving.
   k. Exposed structural dove-tailing.
   l. Strong, but lightweight (chairs).
   m. Ball and socket on back posts of side-chairs so they could be tilted.

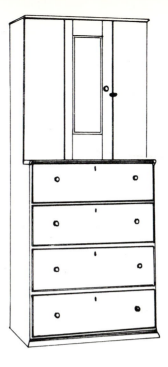

Figure 18.6a
A Shaker weave-chest or sill chest with narrow cupboard door, originally red.

Figure 18.6b
A Shaker table or lap desk of maple and pine, dark red.

found in the provincial colonial patterns of New York and New England. The splat back, the banister back, and the cabriole leg were too complicated to make and too ornate for Shaker beliefs (Fig. 18.6a). Only an absolute minimum of wood was used even though it was abundant; thus, their furniture achieved elegance (Fig. 18.6b).

The Shakers began to sell furniture about 1789 and their inexpensive, well-made slat-back rocking chairs (Fig. 18.6c) and three-slat chairs were in demand. In 1807 a Shaker chair cost seventy-five cents; by 1828 it had risen to $2.50. Prices ranged from $3 to $10 for chairs in the catalog of the Centennial Exposition in Philadelphia in 1876. Thousands of Shaker chairs were sold during the nineteenth century, but they were not particularly esteemed for most people of the time preferred the stylish Victorian furniture.

The Arts and Crafts Movement in the United States

The impact of the Arts and Crafts Movement in America lasted until World War I. Mission furniture, at the height of its popularity about 1909, was its most important development, a forerunner of American contemporary furniture. It was the first "do-it-yourself" furniture available to the public and made modern design available to almost all classes of people. Most *mission* furniture (Gustav Stickley used a small *m* to differentiate his style from that of the California Mission) built at home ended up as firewood, but Frank Lloyd Wright used some of *Elbert Hubbard's* (1856–1915) furniture in his houses. Stickley saw the machine as a necessity for mass-produced furniture and he designed for it. This explains why his furniture had such severe outlines and plain surfaces.

Figure 18.6c
A Shaker brethren's chair (larger than the sisters') which was stained red.

Figure 18.7a
A mission-style sofa by Stickley.

The American Arts and Crafts Movement began in Minneapolis in 1895. The first society, the *Chalk and Chisel Club,* was composed of woodcarvers and designers, but gradually other craftsmen were added. Cabinetwork was first exhibited at an exhibition in 1901. A Chicago Arts and Crafts group furnished a room in the *"true spirit"* of Morris— self-respect, love of one's work, and thoroughness in carrying out all parts.[3] Societies throughout the country were organized as a protest against prevailing taste and to infuse a spirit of creativity into art instruction in the schools.

Mission Furniture

The origin of Mission furniture is a point in controversy. Some authorities claim that Mission furniture is that made by the California Indians, while others claim that the work in old Spanish missions was improved upon and inspired by the work produced in England under the names *New Art, Craftsman,* and *Arts and Crafts* (W. L. Kimerly, *How to Know Period Styles in Furniture* [1912]). Gustav Stickley, the main Mission designer, wrote in *The Craftsman* (1909) that the idea of mission designs being based upon California Mission furniture was merely a clever advertising gimmick:

> The general belief is that the first pieces were discovered in the California Missions and that these served as models for all the "mission" furniture which followed. This is an interesting story . . . because of the commercial cleverness that saw and took advantage of the power of a . . . sentimental association. A number of years ago a manufacturer made two very clumsy chairs. . . . It was just at this time that the California Mission were exciting much attention, and a clever Chicago dealer, seeing the advertising value that lay in the idea, bought both pieces and advertised them as having been found in the California Missions. . . . The mingling of novelty and romance instantly pleased the

[3] Isabel McDougall, "A William Morris Room," *House Beautiful,* **13** (February 1903), pp. 169–77.

public and the vogue of "mission" furniture was assured.[4]

One thing that is certain is that Americans were ashamed of their lack of a heritage as early as 1851, when the American commissioner apologized because America "could not contest upon equal grounds with the nations of Europe" in furniture and decoration.[5] By 1890, people were tired of domestic and foreign critics telling them that the United States had no indigenous furniture style, and their cultural insecurity made them ready for Mission furniture.

The mission style appears to be an offshoot of the English Arts and Crafts Movement, and the accompanying taste for hand-made furniture, combined with the primitive seventeenth- and eighteenth-century furniture made by Indian neophytes in the Southwest Spanish missions.

In 1894 a chair created in a Spanish mission in California was sent to New York. Some furniture of ash and oak with exposed tenons and dowels was developed from this model and exhibited in Chicago. Mass merchandizers of furniture, capitalizing on the romantic associations of the West and the popularity of the romantic novel, *Ramona,* found the "mission" label a good sales incentive. This furniture was also called *Arts and Crafts, Quaint, Cottage, Roycroft,* and *Craftsman* during the period and Stickley and a few writers called it *mission* without capitalizing the word, thus denying any historical association.

Gustav Stickley (1858–1942)

Gustav Stickley, whose name is most closely associated with Mission furniture, quit school in the eighth grade to work in his uncle's chair factory. He worked in a long succession of chair factories, all formed by various members of the Stickley family. He operated a furniture store in Binghamton, New York, selling reproductions of Renaissance-Baroque and Colonial furniture until about 1900, when he completed his new lines of mission furniture.

Strickley, like many of the reformers in

[4] "How 'Mission' Furniture Was Named," *The Craftsman,* **16** (May 1909), p. 225.
[5] John A. Kouwenhoven "The Background of Modern Design," *An Exhibition for Modern Living* (Detroit, Mich.: The J. L. Hudson Co., 1949), p. 11.

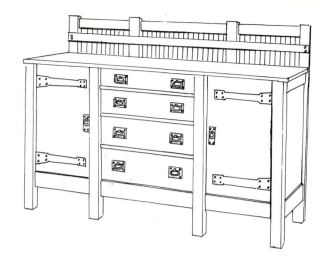

Table 18.13
Characteristics of Craftsman Furniture

1. Native woods included oak, butternut, maple, beech, elm.
2. Pieces were massive, boxy, plain, rectilinear.
3. Structural elements—such as mortise and tenon, key, dovetail joints—were visible.
4. Finishes were dark, dull; emphasis was on wood grain.
5. Large nailheads and hammered copper designs were the only ornamentation.
6. Leather upholstery (usually not attached) was treated to appear old.
7. Style was primitive and severe with simplicity of form but without beauty of form.

Figure 18.7b
A mission-style sideboard designed by Stickley.

Figure 18.7c
A mission chair designed by Stickley.

England, romanticized the Medieval Period. Ruskin's books convinced him that furniture and the decorative arts should express the contemporary life of the people. Morris's writings persuaded Stickley to stop using standard furniture patterns and finishes. He began to experiment with plant forms but was soon convinced that they were unsuitable for furniture. In 1898, he visited Arts and Crafts societies in England and Samuel Bing's *Art Nouveau* shop in Paris. Concluding that British inspiration was from the past and Art Nouveau was nonfunctional, he began applying fundamental principles of structure to the design of furniture suited to modern America (Fig. 18.7a). His plea for a democratic art came at a time when there was a worldwide drive for simplicity in art and life (Fig. 18.7b).

Stickley reflected the thought and action of an industrialized Western culture. Rural rigidity was being rejected. New forms of behavior, new materials, and new ideas were appearing daily, but many standard bearers of the past resisted change in every form. Stickley's creations met with widespread rejection; nonetheless he completed his new line of mission furniture, which emphasized structure and in which every part revealed, explained, and justified its existence. Mission furniture was massive, with hardware and leather treated to look green with age (Fig. 18.7c). It received a cool reception at the Grand Rapids Furniture Exposition, so Stickley introduced his furniture directly into the commercial market, an almost unheard-of action. He exhibited it at Arts and Crafts exhibitions and sold it by mail order from advertisements in

House Beautiful, Ladies' Home Journal, and *Popular Mechanics.* Stickley referred to his style as *Craftsman* furniture. He was inspired by Savonarola's belongings from the Renaissance Period, by Spanish mission houses, by Flemish and Tyrolean cottages, and by the Colonial kitchen.[6]

Stickley began publishing *The Craftsman* (1901–16) in 1902. It merged with *Art World* in 1916. This magazine, with its emphasis on functionalism, became the basic vehicle for the Arts and Crafts Movement in the United States. It led American taste in home furnishings, architecture, gardens, art, and sculpture. Included in it were house plans and designs for furniture, metalwork, and textiles. Stickley over-expanded his business, however, and the *Craftsman* empire collapsed in 1916. While in demand, he had been the leader of mass-produced modern furniture, and has been called the progenitor of functional furniture.

[6] Gustav Stickley, "The Structural Style in Cabinet Making," *House Beautiful,* **15** (December 1903), p. 587.

THE FRONT OF THE BRADLEY HOUSE

THE GARDEN FRONT OF THE BRADLEY HOUSE

THE BACK OF THE BRADLEY HOUSE

THE EAST SIDE OF THE BRADLEY HOUSE

Stickley was one of the early proponents of freedom from household drugery for women:

This is the age of opportunity for women. Her age-long limitation to the four walls of her own home, and to the duties and occupations that are conventionally "womanly" is past, and if she will she may be free to live as broadly in her mental and social life as does man, and to handle her own difficulties with the same general knowledge of life and its conditions as he brings to bear upon his. The only obstacle now in the way of her development is her own conservatism and reluctance to free her life from the unnecessary things that hamper it. When she is forced by the relentless pressure of circumstances into doing this, she will become the real home-maker—not the household drudge or the worried mistress of unsatisfactory servants, and the home over which she presides will fulfill all the beautiful possibilities implied in the home idea that has survived so much. . . . With the passing of the present complex conditions this conventional belief that leisure and indulgence in a home where she is sheltered from all contact with the world is the highest ideal of a woman's life, must pass also, and leave her free to develop as she will.[7]

[7] Gustav Stickley, "The Modern Home and the Domestic Problem," *The Craftsman,* **11** (Jan. 1907), pp. 452–457.

By today's standards his statement may fall short, but during his time he was a champion of woman's rights and of an egalitarian society.

Each month *The Craftsman* featured a "Craftsman Home." Stickley insisted that, to be happy in their surroundings, people must be aware of their needs and preferences and build accordingly. The home should be simple and plain, but it should meet the physical, mental, and moral needs of the occupants. Although Stickley was an iconoclast, he was also aware of the harmful effects of the transition from an agrarian to an industrial society. In the agrarian period, people had cooperated with nature: the sowing of crops and the domestication of animals had required a symbiotic relationship, and the environment and the people had been more nearly one. Death had not been a stranger and mutual respect for the environment was a necessity.

Stickley sensed this loss of human feeling for the environment as people moved to cities and became less dependent upon their crops and animals. The growing separation between humans and their environment led to a more self-centered existence. Such separation is artificial and totally unrealistic in view of the biological chain and its direct effect upon the quality of human existence. Stickley's insights on this point resulted in designs that blended the interior with the exterior environment. He believed that the home should be built of native materials, harmonize with its surroundings, and have open spaces conducive to family living. Built-ins were important as was the merging of the interior and outside. He advocated innovative and inexpensive building methods, such as wooden forms and concrete. In sixteen years, he had a tremendous impact on all aspects of the home.

Will Bradley (1868–1962)

Will Bradley, often referred to as the American Beardsley, was another advocate and designer of the Mission style in the United States. He was the highest paid commercial artist of the period and developed innovative book designs, layouts, and advertising formats. He tired of the Art Nouveau style around the turn of the century and changed to straight lines and geometric modules while retaining curvilinear Art Nouveau decorative details. Bradley built his home in the style of Stickley and C. F. A. Voysey. The influence of Morris and M. H. Ballie Scott is also apparent in his work.

Edwin Box (1863–1930), editor of the *Ladies' Home Journal,* commissioned Bradley to design a complete house with functional furniture to be featured in eight installments for the magazine. It was called the *Bradley House* (Figs. 18.8a, 18.8b). Bradley believed that directness, appropriateness, honesty, sincerity, and individuality were important elements in home design. He was antitradition and by *mission,* he meant *function.* His purpose was to inject imagination and taste into everyday articles. He used diamond-shaped window panes and curved lines in nonstructural and nonfunctional areas, but his structural lines were geometric. He used built-in furniture, ornamented in Art Nouveau style, as much as possible. His furniture was functional but, like Stickley's, uncomfortable. Bradley designed furniture for the *Ladies Home Journal* articles but did not make it. His beliefs were similar to Stickley's:

> To work in a severe and simple manner means the elimination of detail . . . as with straight-line furniture, beauty of design comes from beauty of line, good proportion, perfect balance, and color. . . . The method and the design is primitive, yet perfect workmanship makes perfect art.[8]

Elbert Hubbard

Elbert Hubbard (1856–1915), another designer of Mission furniture, was a successful author, printer, and businessman. He championed hand-craftsmanship, but also believed in modern industry. He visited Morris in 1894; impressed with Morris's *Kelmscott Press,* he founded the *Roycroft Press* a year later. Gradually other crafts were needed. First a bindery, then a leather shop, and by 1901 the catalog included a furniture line, including a Morris chair. The pieces were similar to the Mission style: simple, heavy, and made of oak and mahogany (Stickley did not use any imported woods, such as mahogany). At one time, Hubbard employed over five hundred men and women who made books, furniture, and objects of copper, brass, iron, silver, and

---

[8] *American Clap Book,* II (July 1905), p. 5 as cited by Crosby McDowell "Will Bradley and the Mission Style." *American Life: A Collectors Annual* (Watkins Glen, New York: The American Life Foundation, 1965), **V.,** p. 37.

The Nursery—By Will Bradley

leather. All the crafts were marked with the Roycroft name or with the orb-and cross trademark.

Hubbard was a master salesman, and companies throughout the United States sought his copywriting skills. His furniture industry began after furniture made for the Roycroft Inn was ordered by guests for their homes. Hubbard was not a furniture or craft designer, but it was his charisma that made him important to many Americans during this period. On May 7, 1915, Hubbard and his wife were drowned when the *Lusitania* was torpedoed. His son continued the business until he went bankrupt in 1938.

The Failure of Mission Furniture

Mission furniture failed because it was too archaic and primitive for luxurious living. Its designers were concerned only with simplicity of form, ignoring beauty, elegance, and comfort. Stickley, Bradley, and Hubbard illustrate the weakness of Art Nouveau and the Arts and Crafts Movement in the United

States. The public accepted ugliness in furniture because it was all that was available, or because it was admired as a false standard of beauty. A *House Beautiful* writer contended that over-decorated furniture was not merely a question of taste, but one of morals, because a "life of crime was founded on less."[9]

In 1905, *Good Housekeeping* published a poem, "Frenzied Furniture," which seems to illustrate the state of furniture design at that time:

When Gladys went crazy on Simple Designs
She said: "Do away with indefinite lines;
All foolish upholstered devices must go—
Plain, square Mission furniture—massive, you know."
I meekly, agreeably answered: "That's so!"

Then trouble began when a lumbering van
Brought furniture built on a mountainous plan,
Brought chairs elephantine with ponderous legs,
Brought tables like platforms with crossbeams and pegs,
Brought bungling brown sideboards and copper-hooped kegs.

A smoke-covered burlap was hung on the walls;
Great benches like battleships stood in the halls;
Plain, heavy plank bookcases, desks with sharp edges,
And sickly green "art-ware" in deep window ledges.

Simplicity frowned in aesthetical gloom
From every hallway, from every room;
We sat down to tables our knees didn't fit in,
On chairs too confoundedly simple to sit in.

Like giants about us the mighty Things sat
And bullied and browbeat our poor little flat,
Till pygmied and lost in this wonderous creation
We frequently raised the faint interrogation:
"Can this be Our Home or some new Railway Station?"

Then Gladys awoke to her error, and so
She turned to the style which they call "Art Noovo."

9 "Immoral Furniture," *House Beautiful,* **21** (April 1907), p. 17.

"For Nature," she said, "loves lithe, languorous curves
And tenuous tendrils and swivels and swerves."
I answered: "She does," though it got on my nerves.
So, our brown Mission furniture hustled away,
An "Art Noovo" outfit came to us next day:
A wallpaper figured with lilies and loops,
And cupboards like highly adorned chicken coops,
And armchairs suggesting cadaverous goops.

On "art bronze" tobacco trays lay my cigars;
Lank, taffy-shaped females on platters and jars,
Long, swan-maiden table lamps, stringly and swirly,
Gave all decorations a flavor quite girly.

One night as we lay in our serpentine bed
With querlicue carvings at footpiece and head,
We dreamed that the bureaus, increased by a million,
Were dancing an "Art Noovo" demon's cotillion
With armies of furniture quaintly reptilian.

A spider-like chiffonier first pirouetted
And near a fantastic art-curtain coquetted;
A crab-legged table, beginning to caper,
Traced out the designs on the snaky wallpaper—
A bookcase marked time with its tentacles taper,

A horrible chair, in the midst of the play,
Threw up its lithe arms and came hissing our way—
"O murder!" I cried in a cold perspiration
"O mercy!" screamed Gladys with wild intonation
And fell on her pillow in nervous prostration.

Then unto the telephone quickly I ran
And called Dr. Bottle, a sensible man,
Who giving poor Gladys a quick diagnosis,
Said: "Here is no use for my medical doses—
The patient's distemper is called "Art Noovosis."

"Remove from your house these delirious curves,
This eel-winding furniture, hard on the nerves,

Some old-fashioned couches and cushions are
    best,
Some soft, easy chairs where the muscles can
    rest—
For chairs, after all, are intended for rest."

And so, from that moment an era began
Of suiting our home to a rational plan.
"For really," said Gladys, "in parlor and den
One likes to feel human, at least, now and
    then."
I feelingly, earnestly answered: "Amen!"[10]

Art Nouveau (1892–1905)

Between 1892 and 1905 England was the leading country in the emerging Modern Movement, but soon after, the initiative passed to
Belgium (Art Nouveau), Holland (de Stijl),
Germany (the Bauhaus) and finally to the
United States. This movement of design leadership was probably owing to the decline of
the class structure in England at first. When
wealth was more evenly distributed as a result
of the Industrial Revolution, the demarcation
between the wealthy and middle class was not
so wide. The Modern Movement began to
embrace all levels of people and other nations;
Belgium at first, became active in it.

Art Nouveau was a result of a wide social
reaction which marked the end of one period
and the beginning of another. Its designers
were antitradition, antimovement, and no
longer looked to the past for inspiration.
These designers reflected a changing culture
and were a strong influence upon that change.
The rejection of form and function, which
typified agrarian culture, can be clearly seen in
their work. Their new creative attempts to design furniture that was in harmony with other
facets of change accompanying industrialization were usually unsuccessful. Their ideas
and intent inspired their followers further to
develop style that was useful and in keeping
with societal change.

The name *Art Nouveau* came from the name
of a shop in Paris. The owner, *Samuel Bing,*
called his shop *Art Nouveau,* meaning *the new
art.* Other names were *modern and style metro,*
named for the series of entrances for the Paris
metro by the architect Guimard, and *style
nouille* or *noodle style* for the sinuous interlac-

ing lines. Bing specialized in furniture and accessories in the Art Nouveau style; his shop,
the site of art exhibits, meetings, and lectures,
became a center for the new artistic expression. Art Nouveau was an effort to produce a
style unrelated to past styles, an art for art's
sake. It was based upon the flowing, asymmetrical lines of growing plant forms. Art
Nouveau designers were antinaturalists who
wanted elegance and a free, imaginative form.
It was a feminine style, strongly influenced by
Japanese designs and devoid of religious
themes.

The feminine note and the elimination of
religious themes in the Art Nouveau style was
a reflection of cultural change. Women were
beginning to be seen as more than male possessions. Their independence was growing
and their desires could no longer go unrecognized. Industry had freed them from the fixed
positions dictated in agrarian society. The
Church had supported the structure and
values of the extended family, which had
been characteristic of Western society for five
thousand years. When people moved from the
farms to the cities, new societal groups, independent of family and church, were formed.
Art Nouveau was, in large part, a response to
this changing society. Like the members of the
Arts and Crafts Movement, the Art Nouveau
designers rejected the use of the machine in
the production of their objects. Their designs
were finely crafted and many were handmade.

Considered an international style, Art Nouveau began in Belgium, the first country after
England to become industrialized. Brussels
became the center of the contemporary design
movement; creative artists were welcomed
and their work was exhibited in Brussels art
galleries. Publications about contemporary
design were widely available in Brussels. England, where Art Nouveau was considered
decadent, was the one country relatively unaffected by it.

One of the most important developments in
this period was the merging of form and interior. *Henri van de Velde,* a Belgian and one of
the leaders in the Art Nouveau Movement,
said:

The contours are firm and closed with
no projecting pieces, everything being
smoothed out in a fixed and continuous outline. . . . Art Nouveau . . . subjects the
individual ornament to the most meticulous
treatment, and presents it against a plain

[10] Wallace Irwin, "Frenzied Furniture", *Good Housekeeping,* **40** (July 1905), pp. 118–19.

Figure 18.9a
A Mackmurdo oak desk with emphasis on verticals and horizontals, ca. 1882.

background . . . and strove to place an ornament according to its function.[11]

Art Nouveau was a short-lived movement, but it was instrumental in developing the concept of looking toward the future and toward new ideas.

Arts and Crafts Designers Who Influenced the Art Nouveau Movement

Arthur H. Mackmurdo (1851–1942)

Arthur H. Mackmurdo was a proto-Art Nouveau designer of the Arts and Crafts Movement in England, one of the most original artists of his time, and unlike any other Arts and Crafts designer. He anticipated European Art Nouveau designs by ten years. He was the first to seek a new kind of design, one that was not symmetrical or based upon the designs of the past. Mackmurdo traveled widely and his sketches of stylized Gothic and Romanesque floral decorations and his interest in plant forms had a wide impact in the 1890s. His motifs for textiles, wallpapers, and title pages of books, with their undulating stalks, wind-swept character, and flame-like movements, were two-dimensional and largely confined to flat surfaces. When these are compared with Art Nouveau designs, a great similarity can be seen.

Mackmurdo's furniture designs were different from his other designs. His furniture was simple in construction and unornamented, its beauty based upon the strong contrasts of vertical and horizontal lines (Fig. 18.9a). He used flat patterns as ornamentation in carving—as in seaweed-like decoration on the back of a chair (Fig. 18.9b), or in metal hinges. These were forerunners of the Art Nouveau style.

Charles Francis Annesley Voysey (1857–1941)

C. F. A. Voysey was another English Arts and Crafts designer who influenced the Art Nouveau Movement. His simplified structural interiors led Art Nouveau designers away from floral exaggerations. Voysey was influenced by Mackmurdo, his teacher, as is apparent in his use of vertical lines, mushroom finials, and cut-out heart shapes (Fig. 18.10a). Voysey was known for his bright, simplified flat-pattern tulips and stylized trees interlaced

[11] Henri van de Velde, *Renaissance in Kunstgewerbe* (Berlin: Neue Ausgabe, 1901), p. 102.

Table 18.14
Arthur H. Mackmurdo (1851–1942)

1. A proto-Art Nouveau designer (although he rejected Art Nouveau).
2. His motifs included undulating, wind-swept, flame-like lines.
3. His furniture was simple and unornamented.
4. He emphasized contrasts of horizontals and verticals.
5. He used flat patterns as carving or metal hinges.

Table 18.15
Charles Francis Annesley Voysey (1857–1941)

1. His furniture was light, airy, plain, and severe.
2. His work reveals Japanese influence; use of vertical lines.
3. He used flat pattern in hinges, cut-outs on chairs.
4. His motifs included heart, tulip, stylized plants and animals, mushroom finials.
5. He designed wallpapers, textiles, furniture, and interiors.
6. He disliked Art Nouveau intensely.

Figure 18.9b
A Mackmurdo chair with seaweed-like waving stalks and undulating flowers, one of the first examples of Art Nouveau in applied art, ca. 1881–1882.

with birds and animals. The hinges on his cabinets were the primary attraction (Fig. 18.10b). Believing that realistic ornament was unsuitable for decoration, he treated plants and animals as mere symbols and subjected them to a linear movement suggestive of Art Nouveau.

Voysey's furniture was carefully designed, plain and severe, and revealed the Japanese influence so very important in the 1890s (Fig. 18.10c). His furniture was reproduced in English, German, and French design magazines and was widely copied. Both Mackmurdo and Voysey were firmly opposed to Art Nouveau, but their designs were very much Art Nouveau in style and some European Art Nouveau designers acknowledged their influence. Voysey's interiors inspired van de Velde and initially affected the designs of Mackintosh and Scott. His emphasis on simplicity and his use of white and delicate colors was unusual for the time.

The exteriors of Voysey's houses were characterized by asymmetrically placed windows, located according to the needs of the interior, plain white-washed walls, medieval-style buttresses, and oriel windows.

Figure 18.10a
A Voysey chair with rush seat and cut-out heart shapes on the splat, ca. 1899.

CONTEMPORARY DEVELOPMENTS IN FURNITURE DESIGN

Figure 18.10c
A Voysey arm chair designed in 1897.

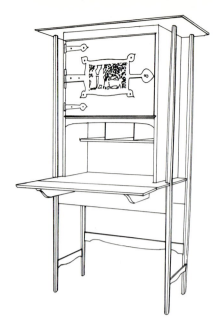

Figure 18.10b
A Voysey oak writing desk with copper hinges and pierced flat-pattern design of copper on the front, ca. 1896.

Figure 18.11a
A Baillie Scott oak music cabinet with colored inlay and metal relief, designed in 1898.

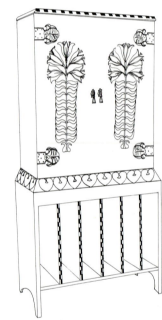

Table 18.16
MacKay Hugh Baillie Scott (1865–1945)

1. Structure was elementary in his furniture.
2. He used geometric and circular structural lines.
3. His motifs included stylized flowers, leaves, hearts.
4. He used both inlay and relief with colored woods, metals, ivory, mother-of-pearl.
5. Oak was his favorite wood.

Table 18.17
Charles Rennie Mackintosh (1868–1928)

1. He was the only English Art Nouveau designer.
2. His pieces had tall, slender, stem-shaped lines.
3. His furniture was rectilinear.
4. He used no upholstery.
5. The backs of his chairs were either very high or very low.
6. He believed structure determined the form of furniture.
7. His motifs were organic.
8. He designed furniture for a particular setting.

which devoted ten articles (four of them in color) to his work between 1894 and 1900. He designed houses, interiors, and furniture in Poland, Russia, Germany, and Switzerland as well as in England.

Traditional sources were the inspiration for Baillie Scott's motifs, but his ideas and his use of them were new and different. He stylized flowers and leaves, giving them a touch of Art Nouveau rhythm but not the sinuous linearity and asymmetrical force they later developed. He ornamented flat surfaces with elaborate stylized motifs, using colored woods, metals, ivory, pewter, and mother-of-pearl in both inlay and relief (Fig. 18.11a). Oak was a favorite wood of his, and he also used colored inlays and applied metal relief (Fig. 18.11b). Geometric and curved structural lines were common in his designs.

Charles Rennie Mackintosh (1868–1928)

Charles Rennie Mackintosh was a most creative designer, one of the first to design without using historical precedents. He produced an original interpretation of the Arts and Crafts ideal, combining the Celtic Revival, Japanese rectangularity and refinement,

Figure 18.11b
A carved oak chair designed by Baillie Scott; ornament is applied, ca. 1898.

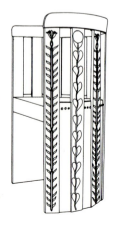

MacKay Hugh Baillie Scott (1865–1945)

M. H. Baillie Scott was another English Arts and Crafts designer who influenced Art Nouveau. Baillie Scott, an English architect, was one of the first to design small houses that were innovative works of art. He was influenced by the American shingle style; horizontal lines and low massing of exterior forms were common in his work. He favored an open plan, combining several rooms into a single area, and expanded space by using shutters and stained-glass openings into galleries and stairways. Built-in furniture was another device he used to open space, and recessed niches with a fireplace and built-in seating were characteristic of his work. His color sense was highly developed for the period and his work was widely published in the *Studio,*

Figure 18.12a
A Mackintosh oak dining chair with elongated forms,
ca. 1901.

Figure 18.12c
This chair, designed by Mackintosh for his own
apartment, reveals his emphasis on structural elements,
ca. 1900.

Figure 18.12b
A Mackintosh tea table in
white enameled wood, ca.
1900–1902.

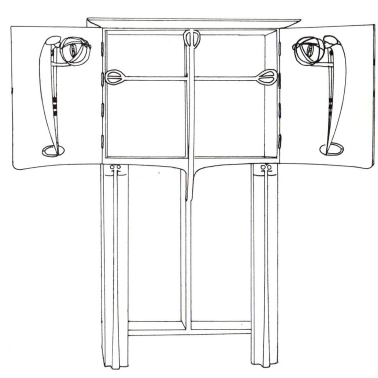

Figure 18.12d
A white-enameled cabinet
designed by Mackintosh
with female figures and roses
designed by the MacDonald
sisters.

and the reform spirit of the era. Mackintosh
was the only inventive architect working in
Great Britain in the Art Nouveau style. He
lived in Glasgow, where there was a great deal
of artistic activity in the latter part of the
1800s. Art Nouveau was given a deliberate
impetus there, although it was discouraged
elsewhere in Britain. In fact, Mackintosh does
not appear to have influenced English design
although his impact was strong in Germany,
Austria, and Belgium.

Mackintosh believed that construction determined the form of furniture. His designs
were rectilinear and made much decorative
use of structural elements. His furniture falls
into two classes: high-and low-backed. Both
look equally uncomfortable. Some chairs
were over six feet tall and were designed as
decorative elements for a particular setting
where vertical emphasis and formal elegance
were a requirement (Fig. 18.12a). His low-
backed chairs were well constructed and
sturdy, with wide drop-in or rush seats and
sloping arms. He never used deep, comfort-

able upholstery. Oak was his preferred wood,
stained and polished in dark brown or olive
green. Some pieces were painted stark white
(Fig. 18.12b) and then ornamented with organic motifs in colored glass, gesso, and repoussé metal by the MacDonald sisters. Ornamentation was oval, pierced squares and
crescents (Fig. 18.12c), or linear, swirling
dream-like figures (weeping figures, fountains
trickling blood, rose bowers, and flowing
draperies (Fig. 18.12d).

Art Nouveau Designers

Henri van de Velde (1863–1957)

Henri van de Velde, who considered himself a direct link with the English Arts and
Crafts style, helped to spread the movement
in Belgium, France, and Germany, and is considered the spokesman for Art Nouveau. Although he wrote about function and structural
clarity, his furniture designs show little evidence of these qualities. He designed both the
interior and the exterior of homes, and even

Figure 18.13a
This desk chair, with fluctuating lines broken by rectilinear construction, was designed by van de Velde, ca. 1896.

Figure 18.13b
A Jacaranda desk, designed by van de Velde, with sloping outer edges and butterfly ornamentation, ca. 1898.

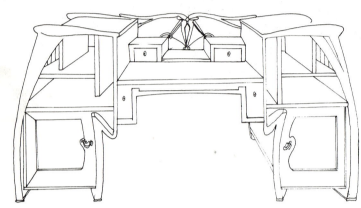

Figure 18.13c
This table, designed by van de Velde for his own home, has light, slat-like construction, ca. 1896.

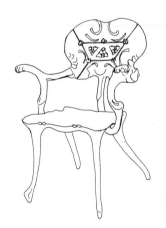

Figure 18.14a
A Gaudí chair with undulating skeleton-like lines, ca. 1898–1904.

Table 18.18
Henri van de Velde (1863–1957)

1. He believed in designing for machine production.
2. He held that form and construction must be determined by material.
3. His designs were heavy, complex, curvilinear.
4. His ornamentation depended upon line movement.

Table 18.19
Antonio Gaudí y Cornet (1852–1926)

1. His furniture had organic, undulating asymmetrical lines.
2. He used forms similar to that of the human skeleton.
3. His furniture lacks the appearance of stability owing to the movement of lines.
4. He used wood and iron.

Table 18.20
Émile Gallé (1846–1904)

1. He was most famous for glass accessories.
2. His furniture was based upon Rococo styles.
3. His ornamental details were inspired by natural forms: plants and flowers.

Table 18.21
Louis Majorelle (1859–1926)

1. He was inspired by traditional French motifs.
2. His symmetrical forms were inspired by plants and animals.

designed his wife's clothing. He wrote that "Ruskin and Morris chase ugliness out of man's heart, I, out of his intellect."[12] He held to a rational system of production, a judicious use of materials, and a form and construction determined by the material employed. Van de Velde believed in designing for machine production, although he was influenced by both Morris and Ruskin. According to van de Velde, the designer was responsible to the public for his designs and for the end products.

[12] Henry F. Lenning, *The Art Nouveau* (The Hague: Martinus Nijohff, 1951), p. 19.

Van de Velde's furniture was heavy, with complex, curvilinear patterns throughout, but became more rectilinear in his later years (Fig. 18.13a). He did not decorate his designs, but depended upon the line movement for beauty (Fig. 18.13b). His influence was exerted through his writings, rather than through his designs (Fig. 18.13c).

Antonio Gaudí y Cornet (1852–1926)

Antonio Gaudí y Cornet was one of the most creative and inventive Art Nouveau designers, working completely outside the European movement, in Barcelona, Spain. Most of his work reveals no historical influences ex-

Plate 34
A multi-purpose room is divided with red latticework to delineate the sleeping space. Interior designer: David Hicks, England. (Courtesy of Bayer AG)

Plate 35
Two hundred fifty yards of printed cotton tent the walls and ceiling of this rectangular room to focus attention on the antique stained glass insert. The lambrequin and Austrian shades are in matching fabric. Interior designer: Jill Weinberg. Photograph by Les Rachline.

Plate 36
A bachelor's penthouse
bedroom was designed so
that the large television
screen hidden in a cabinet
opposite the bed could be
viewed. Shades of gray are
combined in a neutral color
scheme. The headboard
and graphic are of Florida
cypress and suede and the
footboard and night tables
are of the same suede
combined with travertine.
The copper sconces were
constructed by a local
craftsman. Interior
designer: Jill Weinberg.
Photograph by Les
Rachline.

Plate 37
Furniture of pipes can be
used both inside and
outside. (Courtesy of Pipe
Dream)

Plate 38
Seats are used for many different activities: the Eames chair in the foreground is for lounging; the dining chairs for eating or study. Interior designer: Peg Walker. (Courtesy of Royal System, Inc.)

Plate 40
The palm is a focal point in the library; other plants repeat the green throughout the room. Interior designers: Harry Schule and John McCarville. (Courtesy of Royal System, Inc.)

Plate 41
Plants are available in all sizes, shapes, and textures: in the front row are different varieties of begonias with dracaena, dieffenbachia, cactus, palms and ficus in the rear. Plants supplied by Bob Mentelos, Fantastic Gardens, Miami. Photograph by Les Rachline.

Plate 42
This dining area adjacent to a terrace is small, but its visual size is increased by a mirrored back. The absence of window coverings and the use of green plants both inside and outside increase the flow of space. Interior designer: Gaston Herrera. Photograph by Les Rachline.

Plate 43 (Opposite)
Plants are massed in the living area of this penthouse apartment and are potted in ceramic containers that blend with the quarry tile of the file floor. Interior designer: Anita Breslow. Photograph by Les Rachline.

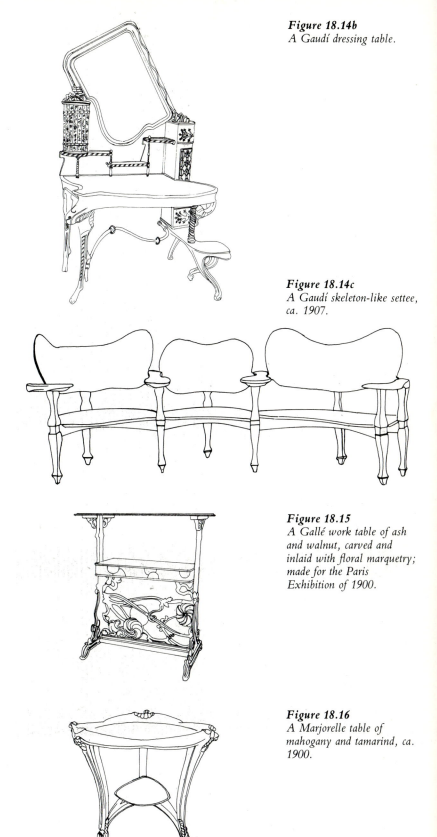

Table 18.22
Eugène Gaillard (1862–1933)

1. He was influenced by Rococo designs.
2. His motifs were abstracted whip-like plant forms.
3. He believed in functional furniture and in respect for the material used.

cept that of the Moors, who had occupied Spain for over eight hundred years. He used parabolic arches and often left the metal structure of his buildings uncovered. Gaudí designed the total building: exterior, interior, and furnishings. His furniture had undulating organic lines and was asymmetrical, and his chair designs have much in common with the human skeleton (Fig. 18.14a). The lines move as if they were alive and the furniture lacks the stability of most furniture pieces (Fig. 18.14b). His material was wood and iron and his furniture designs were for specific interiors (Fig. 18.14c).

Émile Gallé (1846–1904)

Two centers of Art Nouveau developed in France: Paris and Nancy. The Nancy school, the first to be established and the most comprehensive arts and crafts center in France, was closely alied to the Rococo style. *Emile Gallé* was the first great exponent of Art Nouveau in France. He was a botanist and his designs were inspired by plants and flowers as well as by Japanese designs. His main contribution was in glass-making, but his furniture was also important. He based his designs upon traditional styles such as the Louis XV, but his ornamentations were inspired by nature. A work table he designed for the 1900 Paris Exhibition (Fig. 18.15) is a good example of Gallé's development of the entire structure into branches which changed into blossoms.

Louis Majorelle (1859–1926)

Louis Majorelle, another Nancy furniture designer, was inspired by traditional French motifs, such as the cartouche, the serpentine front, ormolu mounts and the cabriole leg. His plastic forms were derived from plants and animals (Fig. 18.16).

Eugène Gaillard (1862–1933)

Parisian Art Nouveau was characterized by stylized nature-inspired ornamentation, more abstract than the designs from Nancy. *Eugène*

Figure 18.14b
A Gaudí dressing table.

Figure 18.14c
A Gaudí skeleton-like settee, ca. 1907.

Figure 18.15
A Gallé work table of ash and walnut, carved and inlaid with floral marquetry; made for the Paris Exhibition of 1900.

Figure 18.16
A Marjorelle table of mahogany and tamarind, ca. 1900.

Gaillard was one of the most pominent designers of furniture. He was greatly influenced by Rococo styles. He tended toward classical forms (Fig. 18.17). His motifs, which resem-

Figure 18.17
A Gaillard chair with classical French influence, ca. 1902.

Table 18.23
Georges de Flure (1868–1928)

1. His furniture was delicate, gilded, feminine.
2. He was influenced by the Louis XV style.
3. His abstract motifs were derived from plants and flowers.

Table 18.24
Hector Guimard (1867–1942)

1. His Paris Métro entrances were his most famous design.
2. His designs resembled plant growth.
3. He combined beauty and function.
4. He designed furniture for specific interiors.

bled swirling whip-like shapes, were abstracted plant forms. Gaillard believed in functional furniture, in respect for the nature of the material used, and in abstract ornamentation. After 1900, Gaillard's furniture became lighter, with straight lines.

Georges de Flure (1868–1928)

Georges de Flure was one of Bing's Parisian designers whose work manifests fine and delicate craftsmanship. He is one of the most significant French designers. His pieces (Figs. 18.18a, 18.18b) are labeled neo-Louis XV and are typically French in character. They were gilded and feminine in appearance. His motifs include abstracted plants and flowers.

Hector Guimard (1867–1942)

Hector Guimard was the most prominent French Art Nouveau architect. He is best known for his design of 91 entrances to the Paris Métro. Made of cast iron, his entrance structures had twisted glass roofs and raised eaves to catch the rain; the ironwork was bright green with orange panels inside and the pattern was picked out in white, green, or blue. Unlike many Art Nouveau designs, they were mass produced and manufactured in

Figure 18.18a
A sofa designed by de Feure, with abstract plant forms and gilded woodwork, ca. 1900.

modules. He also designed interiors with built-in furniture as well as free-standing pieces. His ornamentation was derived from nature and was characterized by gentle curves combined with a sudden whiplash form. His designs often resembled the curving lines of growing plants from the base to the top. He held that beauty and function had to be combined.

Early Twentieth-Century Architects

Frank Lloyd Wright (1869–1959)

Frank Lloyd Wright, America's greatest architectural genius, designed over a thousand buildings, wrote twelve books, gave several thousand lectures, received nine honorary degrees, accepted twenty-one gold medals and farmed 3,500 acres of Wisconsin land during his ninety years. Wright's philosophy of architecture was that human needs go beyond the need for comfort and convenience and that the spirit as well as the body must be nurtured. He believed that architecture and a democratic culture were indivisible.

Wright's chief goal was the creation of an uplifting environment, with the interior as his starting point. When he had selected the interior structural system and materials, the exterior followed in a consistently pleasing way. It was from this idea that the term *organic* became associated with Wright's work. His structures blended into the land, with no distinct divisions between the outside and the inside. Other architects had attempted to integrate the exterior environment into the interior of the house, but Wright sought harmony by extending the interior of the house to the exterior surroundings. Wright's treatment of space is one of his major contributions to domestic architecture. He removed boundaries and broke away from the traditional boxy room, by using diagonals, obliques, circles, and arcs. He used the open plan, making interior space continuous and flowing.

Wright designed and built in much of his furniture to blend with his architecture. He treated free-standing furniture, such as tables, benches, and chairs, as an integral part of the structure. Circular houses had circular tables and chairs and seats with arms shaped as segments of a circle. Box-like forms were used in

Figure 18.18b
A chair designed by de Feure with traditional French form, ca. 1901.

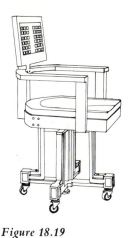

Table 18.25
Frank Lloyd Wright (1869–1959)

1. He designed from the inside out.
2. He popularized the open plan.
3. He made ornament an integral part of the structure.
4. He produced the illusion of unlimited space by the use of diagonals, glass, light, and asymmetry.
5. He related the house to the site, its materials, and its occupants.
6. He integrated parts to make a unified whole.
7. He used such innovations as wall-hung toilets, airconditioning, radiant heat, glass doors.
8. He designed furniture which was geometric, uncomfortable, and rectilinear but which paved the way for future developments.
9. He designed furniture for specific interiors, paralleling the shapes of the space.

Table 18.26
Le Corbusier (1887–1965)

1. He believed furniture was equipment, and the house a machine in which to live.
2. His utilitarian objects needed no ornamentation.
3. His chairs were designed for one of three purposes: conversation, reclining, comfort.
4. His storage units were designed to be built in, free-standing, or fitted against walls.
5. He designed furniture to fit into any of his interiors.

rectangular houses and hexagonal houses had polygonal forms. Ornamentation repeated the central motif of the house. Furniture was designed for a specific space.

Wright's furniture had characteristics in common with that of Mackintosh. It was geometric, uncomfortable, and unsuccessful (Fig. 18.19). Wright did not use upholstered pieces but, rather, padded cushions (he was the first to use latex foam, which he introduced into the Falling Water House in 1936). No furniture approximating the lines of Wright's architecture was available except for mission objects, which he occasionally recommended. Wright's chairs were uncomfortable because he believed that reclining was the natural posture for relaxation and that sitting was unnatural. He anticipated future furniture develop-

ments even though his furniture was unsuccessful.

Le Corbusier (1887–1965)

Charles Édouard Jeanneret, born in the Swiss Jura Mountains, adopted the pseudonym *Le Corbusier* from one of his ancestors. In 1910 when Picasso and Braque were painting interiors and exteriors of objects depicted simultaneously, Le Corbusier developed the interpenetration of inner and outer space. The simple, whitewashed peasants' houses in Europe influenced him to use white for both interiors and exteriors.

Le Corbusier wanted to communicate with the masses and he believed this could be done by using certain universal shapes which had developed through many civilizations, such as the wine bottle, the pipe, the column, and the flask; consequently, his furniture, considered part of his total design, has often been overlooked. To Le Corbusier, furniture was equipment divided into three categories: chairs, tables, and built-in storage. He believed that modern, machine-made art needed no ornamentation and that utilitarian objects had a beauty of their own. In 1927, he labeled the house "a machine for living in." He asked, "Why is furniture movable and need it be so? What actually is furniture, for what is it used? Where exactly ought it to be?"

Le Corbusier designed chairs for conversation, for reclining, and for comfort. The Basculant chair (Fig. 18.20a), designed for conversation, had a chromium-plated tubular steel frame, leather seat and back, and leather-strap arms. The chaise for reclining (Fig. 18.20b) could be adjusted by moving the entire seat unit (Fig. 2.2). The Grand Comfort

Figure 18.19
A Wright chair of metal designed for the Larkin building, the first metal office chair.

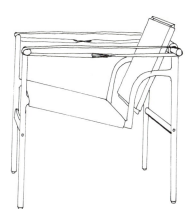

Figure 18.20a
Le Corbusier's Basculant chair with chromium-plated tubular frame and leather seat and back, and leather-strap arms, designed for conversation, 1929.

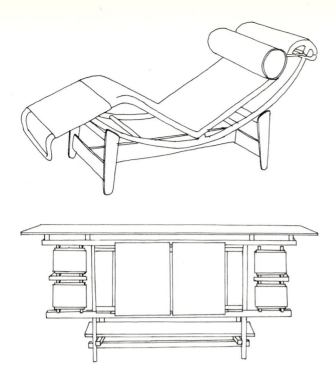

Figure 18.20b
A Le Corbusier chaise longue designed for reclining; made of chrome-plated steel tubes; leather upholstery; angle may be adjusted, 1927.

Figure 18.20c
A chair designed by Thonet and selected by Le Corbusier for use in his interior for the Paris Exhibition of 1925.

chair was an overstuffed chair based on the cube principle, with a comparatively small seating space. He also designed a chair that pivoted, but it was less popular than the others. The curve of its back was influenced by the Thonet armchair of 1870, which he used in the Paris Exhibition of 1925, *"L'espirit d'Art Nouveau,"* and other interiors (Fig. 18.20c). Le Corbusier designed standardized cabinets which could be free-standing or fitted against the walls, either blending with the walls or painted a bright color. He also built in open concrete shelves, which represented a new kind of furniture.

Le Corbusier's furniture was functional and fitted into any of his buildings. He designed basic chairs, tables, and storage units early in his career, but he did not concern himself with furniture again.

De Stijl (1917–29)

De Stijl originated in Holland after World War I and was the result of the breakdown in social values and the disillusionment and poverty that followed World War I. The movement lasted longer than other movements and helped to destroy the limitations imposed by tradition. The cubism of Picasso and Braque and the architecture of Wright affected the de Stijl Movement, which was marked by a close collaboration between painters, sculptors, architects, and designers.

Three elements formed the basis of de Stijl philosophy: the rectangle, saturated primary colors (red, blue, and yellow), and asymmetrical balance. The group was convinced that the

Table 18.27
de Stijl (1917–29)

1. It had no ties to the past.
2. It featured simple, square elements screwed together.
3. Rectangular cubic forms appear to bypass each other by joining of vertical elements.
4. A feeling of lightness was created with each part separate.
5. The furniture was more idealogical than comfortable.
6. The furniture was made to be mass-produced of standard components.
7. It affected architecture more than furniture.

achievement of universal harmony by total abstraction and simplification in art and design would help to transform a materialistic, individualistic society into an idealistic, socialistic one. The founder, *Theo van Doesburg,* began publishing the *de Stijl* magazine in 1917 to explain the theories of the *Constructivists,* as they called themselves.

The furniture of *Geritt Rietveld* (1888–1964) mirrored the paintings of van Doesburg and Mondrian, although the effect of de Stijl on interiors was minor compared to its effect on architecture and painting. In Rietveld's designs, there are no traditional influences. Rectangular cubic forms are placed tentatively close together, but appear to be unjoined, giving them a sense of lightness. The joining of the vertical elements makes them appear to bypass each other (Fig. 18.21a). Rietveld designed one of the first chairs to have lapped joints fixed with nuts and bolts. His furniture was uncomfortable (Fig. 18.21b), but he used

Figure 18.21b
Rietveld's red, blue, yellow chair, 1917.

new materials and solutions that were to affect later developments in design. Modern architecture, with its flat planes, rectangles, and squares and its informal balance was most affected by de Stijl designers. These designers stimulated a geometric system of design, with machine-finished standard elements so combined that construction was unconcealed.

Bauhaus (1919–33)

The *Bauhaus* was created in Germany in 1919 to function as a consulting center for industry. *Walter Gropius,* an architect, was its head. Each student was trained by two teachers, an artist and a master-craftsman. The program offered the student practical training as a joiner, a blacksmith, a stonemason, a potter, or a weaver, and an artist's understanding of form, color, and material. According to Gropius: "The Bauhaus workshops were really laboratories for working out practical designs for presenting everyday articles . . . [and] improving models for mass production."[13]

The machine was accepted at the Bauhaus and designs suitable for machine production were created. The study of the past was ignored and inventiveness was considered desirable. Gropius wanted to unite art and technology to create a new functional design. Many of the creative ideas of Bauhaus designers— abstract painting, metal furniture, and flat roofs—were soon accepted. At the Bauhaus, tubular metal furniture and stackable furniture was designed by Marcel Breuer, and chromium-plated steel furniture was designed by Mies van der Rohe. Other innovations included the use of metal tubing in lamps, the use of textures instead of ornamentation to contrast with highly polished surfaces, and the use of geometric forms adaptable to machine production in product design. When Hitler came to power, the Bauhaus was closed and its designers were dispersed. But the style became international. Its designers, who combined creative imagination with craftsmanship, gave the world a new understanding of functional design and a philosophical enhancement just beginning to be grasped by urban cultures throughout the world.

[13] Ruth Estella Hawthorne, "The Development and Critical Survey of Modern Trends in Furniture and Fabrics in the United States, 1925–1945," unpublished master's thesis, Michigan State College (1949), p. 32a.

Table 18.28
Bauhaus (1919–33)

1. Students were trained by artists and master-craftsmen.
2. Designs had no traditional basis.
3. Influences include
   a. Scandinavian designers influenced by Breuer, especially Aalto
   b. American designers influenced include Saarinen, Nelson, Eames, Bennet and Bertoia
   c. Plastic furniture which utilizes a material suitable for machine production
   d. Breuer's theories of air support for people influenced inflatable furniture
   e. Cantilevered, see-through furniture
   f. Geometric patterned textiles and rugs

The Bauhaus was significant in the development of a philosophy of aesthetics. The Bauhaus presented a new perspective developed specifically for the urban-industrial society. The idea that we must look for beauty in our everyday existence and immediate setting is still being discovered and brought to readers through many popular books. The Bauhaus designers recognized that just as beauty in an agrarian society was to be found in the sunrise, the trees, and the wild birds, so beauty in an urban society can be found in machines, buildings, and furnishings. A good example of this is the book, *High Tech,*[14] which illustrates the use of industrial materials in the home.

Marcel Breuer (1902–81)

Marcel Breuer, the son of a Hungarian physician, became the master of the Bauhaus carpentry shop at twenty-two, the youngest master there. Breuer's major interest at the Bauhaus was furniture design, but he conceived of furniture as an architectural form directly related to the human body (Fig. 18.22a). Breuer's favorite piece of furniture

[14] Joan Kron and Suzanne Slesin, *High Tech* (New York: Clarkson N. Potter Inc./Publishers), 1978.

Figure 18.22a

A folding chair designed by Breuer in 1921 and manufactured at the Bauhaus Carpentry Works.

Figure 18.22b
A Breuer wood chair designed in 1922.

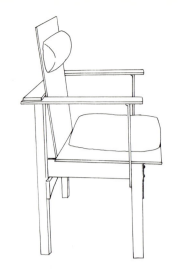

Figure 18.22c
Breuer's demountable Wassily chair, of chromium-plated steel tubing and canvas, designed for Wassily Kandinsky in 1925.

Figure 18.22d
The Cesca chair designed by Breuer of mirror-chromed steel, satin-finished ebonized wood, with cane seat and back, 1928.

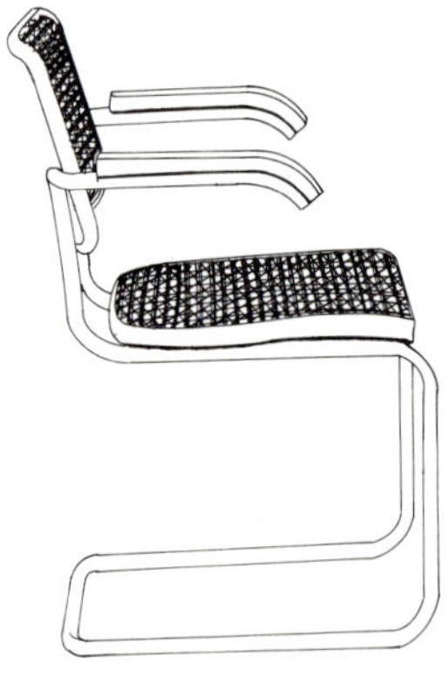

Figure 18.22e
Breuer's most organic design: his laminated bentwood Isokon chair, with base and seat strips of laminated wood and side frames supported by bent-plywood seat, designed in 1935.

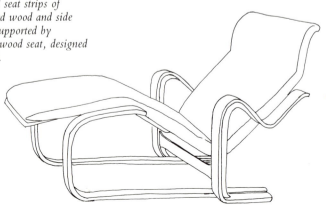

Table 18.29
Marcel Breuer (1902–81)

1. He believed that furniture is an architectural form in relationship to the human body.
2. His furniture was at first angular with straight lines, then gradually developed into flowing, organic forms.
3. He used bent frames, tubular steel, bent aluminum straps, bent plywood, and finally upholstered pads with wood-slat frames.
4. He used cantilever structure.
5. Structure is visible and tactile materials for upholstery.

Table 18.30
Ludwig Mies van der Rohe (1886–1969)

1. His architecture reflected the ideas of de Stijl, with bypassing planes, a continuous flow of space, and a relationship between interior and exterior.
2. His furniture was elegant, simple, unornamented.
3. His furniture was complementary to architecture with its exposed structure and cantilever construction

was the chair, which he felt expresses the human desire for comfort. Breuer considered furniture an autonomous form of architecture and for this reason did not attempt to relate it to domestic architecture.

Breuer's furniture, at first angular with straight lines (Fig. 18.22b), later developed into flowing, organic forms. He started working with straight slabs of plywood, then stretched canvas upholstery (Fig. 18.22c), caning in bent frames (Fig. 18.22d), bent plywood, and finally upholstered pads with wood-slat frames carefully fitted to the human body and curved into an **S**-shape (Fig. 18.22e). His frames were bent, tubular steel (Figs. 18.22d, 7.27; Plate 10b), then bent aluminum straps (Fig. 18.22f), bent plywood (Fig. 18.22e), and finally laminated, cut-out plywood sheets, In 1925, he designed the *Wassily* chair (Fig. 18.22c), one of the first tubular steel chairs, with a canvas seat and back under continuous tension rather than compression. The weight-bearing elements were sled supports (Fig. 18.22c). His *Cesca* chair, designed in 1928 and similar to an earlier design by Mies van der Rohe but more angular (Fig.

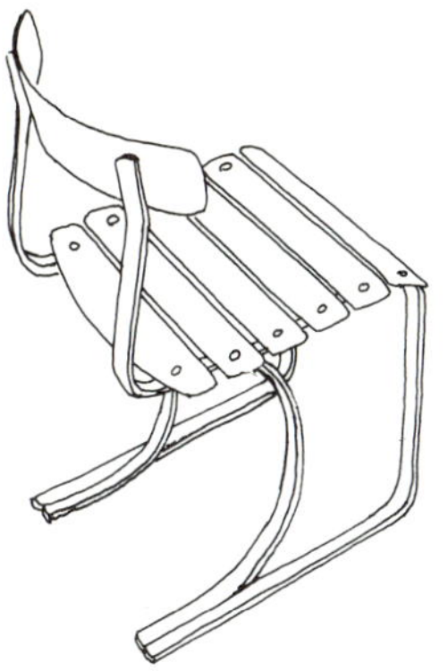

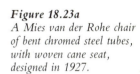

Figure 18.22f
A Breuer aluminum chair designed in 1933.

18.22c), was of polished chrominum-plated steel contrasted with cane where the body touches the chair. Another Breuer innovation was the glass-topped dining table, which made the form less bulky. In 1935 Breuer designed the *Isokon* chair, a reclining chair (Fig. 18.22e) of laminated bentwood and foam-rubber padding, his most organic design. This chair influenced Alvar Aalto.

Breuer laid the foundation for modern furniture design between 1920 and 1930, shaping the interiors of today. The chair was an easy, inexpensive vehicle for the exploration of the basic principles of architecture, particularly the cantilever structure. According to Breuer,

> The new kind of structure possible today—the cantilever structure—in its most expressive form is hollow below and substantial on top—just the reverse of the pyramid. It represents a new epoch in the history of man—the defeat of gravity.[15]

Figure 18.23a
A Mies van der Rohe chair of bent chromed steel tubes, with woven cane seat, designed in 1927.

He disagreed with Le Corbusier's theory that the house is a "machine for living," maintaining rather that functional needs are human and spiritual as well as physical. He liked to see structure and emphasized and developed it. He was also interested in the tactile quality and the nature of materials.

Ludwig Mies van der Rohe (1886–1969)

Ludwig Mies van der Rohe was older than Breuer but arrived at the Bauhaus later. He was the son of a German stonemason, and first became aware of the possibilities of modern technology while working for Bruno Paul, a skillful decorator and furniture designer. Mies opened his first architectural office before World War I and began to emerge as an original architect at this time. He was the first architect to use glass in an office building which had steel bones and a glass skin (1919). In 1922 he was building structures that reflected the ideas of Theo van Doesburg. In 1930 he succeeded Gropius as director of the Bahuaus. When the Bauhaus was disbanded, Mies came to the United States where he headed the Department of Architecture at the Massachusetts Institute of Technology between 1942 and 1950.

Mies designed his first chair for the 1927 *Exposition de la Mode* in Berlin (Fig. 18.23a),

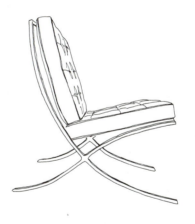

Figure 18.23b
Mies van der Rohe's Barcelona chair designed for the German Pavilion at the International Exposition of 1929, made of stainless steel and covered with leather upholstery.

using bent steel tubes and a cantilevered seat for an effect that resembled Thonet's bentwood furniture (Fig. 3.8).

In 1929 Mies designed his most famous and elegant chair, the Barcelona chair, for the German Pavilion at the International Exposition at Barcelona. The building and its furniture were the exhibit and the Barcelona chair was a work of art never meant for mass production. It is still used today in many modern buildings (Fig. 18.23b). Its unornamented, elegant form, with exposed construction, complements the interior. In 1930 he designed the Tugendhat House in Brno, Czechoslovakia, and two cantilevered chairs were the result (Figs. 18.23c, 18.23d). Until 1957 Mies's major income came from the chairs he designed in the 1920s; during the last twelve years of his life it came from his architectural endeavors.

Figure 18.23c
The Brno chair designed by Mies van der Rohe for the Tugendhat House, 1930.

[15] Peter Blake, "The Selective Eye of Marcel Breuer," *House Beautiful,* **109** (March 1967), pp. 154–55.

Figure 18.24
Ebony, macassar, and ivory cabinet designed by Ruhlmann in 1925.

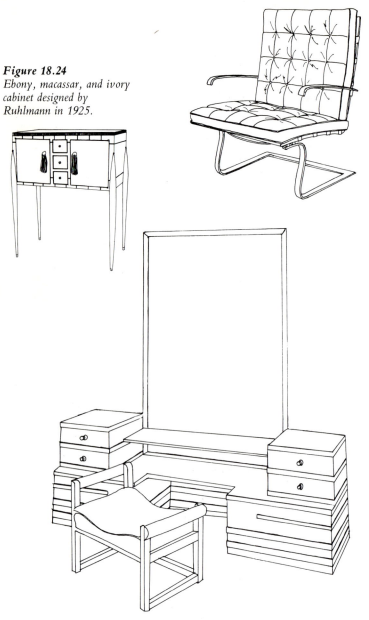

Figure 18.23d
Mies van der Rohe's Tugendhat chair, designed in 1930; frame of chrome-plated flat steel, leather strapping and upholstery.

Figure 18.25a
Black lacquer dresser with gold-plated metal trim, based upon skyscraper lines with sharp angles and flat, plain surfaces, designed by Frankl in 1929.

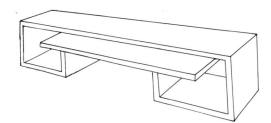

Figure 18.25b
Long, horizontal table designed by Frankl in contemporary Chinese style.

Art Deco (1918–35)

Art Deco, a classic style, developed in France. During the period after World War I, there were many innovations, such as the discovery

Table 18.31
Art Deco (1918–35)

1. The name is derived from the 1925 Exposition Internationale des Arts Décoratifs.
2. It was influenced by Russian ballet (colors), cubism, Bauhaus and Aztec temples (stepped shape).
3. Many materials were used, such as plastics, aluminum, formica, chromium-plated steel, mirrored glass walls.
4. All aspects of the interior and accessories were affected.
5. Lines were simple and rectilinear; furniture was symmetrical.
6. Pieces were designed for rational production.

of the atom, and the development of high-speed elevators, sound movies, radio, and the invention of a new concept of merchandising—the chain store. It was a period of frantic change: people were willing to test out new ideas; women were becoming increasingly liberated; the young were challenging their parental authority; and cars were becoming the universal method of transportation. Until the stock market crash in 1929 there was a high standard of living and money was spent lavishly.

Art Deco was given strong impetus by the appearance of the Russian ballet in Paris in 1909 with its brilliantly colored sets, cubism, and the Bauhaus. The stepped shape of Aztec temples also appears in Art Deco designs. It was a machine style, using new materials such as plastics, ferro-concrete, aluminum, formica, chromium-plated steel furniture and mirrored and glass walls. Hard geometric shapes and bold colors were used. Much attention was paid to lighting, which was often more decorative than functional.

The 1925 *Paris Exposition of Decorative Arts* brought together the new design trends in the hope that designers would adapt their designs to machine production without sacrificing artistic quality. There was an attempt to bring beauty into everyday life, as Morris had desired. No material was considered too impractical to use. Lines were simple and rectilinear, and furniture was symmetrical, with little ornamentation. *Émile-Jacques Ruhlmann* was the best French designer of the period. He used rare woods such as macassar and ebony often combined with ivory marquetry

Figure 18.26a
Klint's safari chair of dark or natural ash and canvas.

Figure 18.26b
Klint's beechwood chair, his only piece designed for mass production (1933), based upon French and Italian peasant furniture.

Figure 18.26c
A folding stool in ash with natural canvas seat and each pair of legs cut from a single round bar of wood, designed by Klint in 1933.

(Fig. 18.24), but he was uninterested in mass production and had little feeling for small, intimate spaces.

In 1926 several museums held exhibits of Art Deco (or Art Moderne) and later department stores placed it on display. *Paul Frankl,* who was designing furniture in the United States, wrote: "The contemporary style we can define only as a living, pulsating, transforming energy, changing before our very eyes, assuming forms which seem to elude definition."[16]

Frankl's first designs were based upon the skyscraper and were simple and tall, with sharp angles and flat plain surfaces (Fig. 18.25a). Later, when horizontal steel building structures were emphasized, Frankl designed furniture emphasizing long, low lines (Fig. 18.25b). He wrote in 1929: "Not only is the furniture today reflecting the architecture, but it [is] also . . . symbolizing one of the most important characteristics of today's life—speed."[17]

Art Deco furniture was a new style, designed with straight lines for machine production. It was made to go into the stark white interiors with the streamlined look of the period. All accessories were dictated by the style.

Modern Furniture Designers

Kåre Klint (1888–1954)

Kåre Klint was the great Danish innovator of the 1920s and 1930s, but not in the same sense as Breuer. Klint renewed rather than invented, adapting the best features of other periods and

[16] Betty Pepis, "Modern Moves Ahead," *The New York Times Magazine* (February 26, 1950), p. 36.
[17] "Strange Motifs in Furniture Design," *The New York Times Magazine* (April 28, 1929), p. 14.

cultures, such as Egyptian, Chinese, *eighteenth-*century English furniture, Italian country furniture, and ship's furniture. His forms were functional and timeless with stylistic characteristics eliminated.

Klint was executing sketches for storage units in 1916; in 1924 he was appointed head of furniture design at the Danish Academy. He attempted to standardize dimensions of storage units on the basis of function, an idea revolutionary at the time, but taken for granted by today's designers. The functional basis of modern furniture and the nature of materials were other points investigated at the school. He believed that the Bauhaus sacrificed much when it rejected the past and he had his students study all types of furniture, searching for functional elements, analyzing and examining their findings, and then working out new versions of the style. *Modern* to Klint was synonymous with that which was well done and consistent. He believed that there were no design problems which had not already been solved.

Klint's Safari chair is a classic design and has been used in many interiors (Fig. 18.26a). He also designed a chair based on French and Italian peasant furniture, his only piece intended

Table 18.32
Kåre Klint (1888–1954)

1. He renewed rather than invented, adapting the best features of earlier periods.
2. He developed standardized storage on the basis of function.
3. He believed that all design problems have been solved.

Figure 18.27a
Aalto's plywood chair, designed for the Sanitarium at Paimio.

Figure 18.27b
Aalto's armchair with laminated bentwood frame, one-piece, plywood seat and back, designed in 1934.

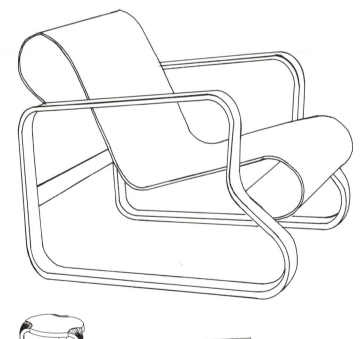

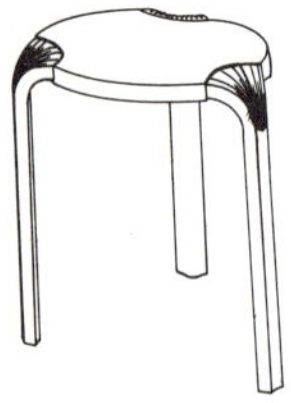

Figure 18.27c
A stacking stool with three legs designed by Aalto.

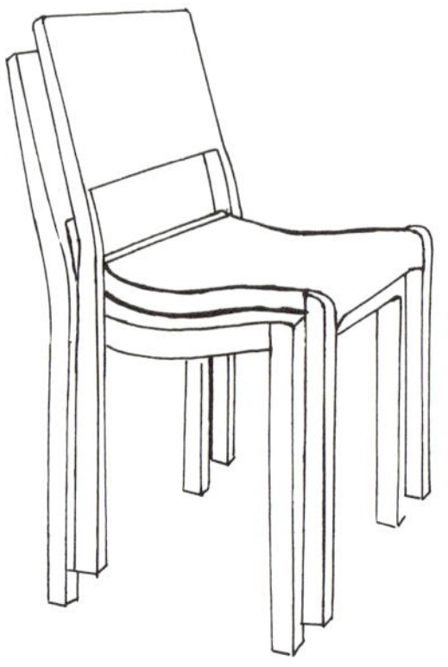

Figure 18.27d
Aalto's design for the first stacking chair.

Figure 18.26d
Klint's teak ship's deck chair (which folds into a compact block) with canvas-covered cushion, designed in 1933.

Table 18.33
Alvar Aalto (1898–1976)

1. He used plywood, which he believed was best suited to human needs.
2. He designed simply and elegantly, outside fashion influences.
3. He made well-designed modern furniture available at low cost.
4. He designed for machine production.

Table 18.34
Bruno Mathsson (1907–)

1. He designed chairs to fit the needs of the human body.
2. He used laminated bentwood and, later, tubular steel in organic shapes.

Table 18.35
Charles Eames (1907–78)

1. He was the most influential designer of contemporary furniture.
2. He won awards in the Museum of Modern Art Organic Design Competition and Low-Cost Furniture Competition.
3. He exploited the possibilities of molded plywood and plastic.
4. He designed light, comfortable, strong chairs.
5. He designed chairs that followed body contours.

for mass production (Fig. 18.26b). A folding stool with each pair of legs cut from a single round bar of wood (Fig. 18.26c) and a teak deck chair that forms a compact block when closed (Fig. 18.26d) are other Klint designs.

Alvar Aalto (1898–1976)

Alvar Aalto, a Finnish architect, derived his inspiration from his country and his love of wood, utilizing forms that suggest the shores of lakes and wooded areas. He was one of the great modern architects. In his furniture designs, he exhibited his knowledge of mass production methods (Fig. 18.27a). He used plywood rather than metal because he felt it was better suited to the requirements of the human body. Before beginning to design furniture, he studied the various angles of human posture, finally deciding that a single sheet of one-quarter-inch plywood was strong enough to support the body. In 1929, Aalto designed a

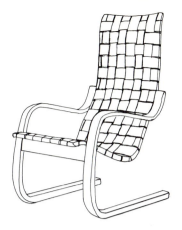

Figure 18.28a
Mathsson's easy chair of laminated plywood and webbing seat and back, designed in 1941.

Figure 18.27e
A plywood chair with webbing seat and back designed by Aalto.

Figure 18.28b
Mathsson's Jetson II swivel steel-base chair, upholstered in wood tweed edged with leather, 1967.

chair with a continuous plywood seat and back. An armchair with a laminated bentwood frame and plywood seat and back resulted (Fig. 18.27b). His coffee table or stool (Fig. 18.27c) has been copied many times and was the result of ten years of experimentation. The vertical, bearing portion was a small version of an architectural column. He also designed the first stacking chairs (Fig. 18.27d) and a plywood easy chair (Fig. 18.27e).

Aalto's creations made well-designed modern furniture available at low cost. His furniture was organic yet consistent with the needs of the machine. (Fig. 3.46).

Bruno Mathsson (1907–)

Bruno Mathsson, a fourth-generation Swedish cabinetmaker, is also interested in the needs of the human body. He designed chairs that made sitting effortless and comfortable, using laminated bentwood in the gently curving forms of growth patterns (Fig. 18.28a). In 1939, the Museum of Modern Art exhibited Mathsson's furniture with that of Breuer and Aalto. Mathsson has also designed a chair of tubular steel with a fabric sling featuring the same organic shapes (Fig. 18.28b).

Charles Eames (1907–78)

Charles Eames is considered by contemporary furniture designers to have been the most significant creative designer, and his designs have had the most impact on today's furniture.[18] He was active in many other areas of design, such as architecture, films, and toys; he also designed a splint for the wounded during World War II. His first chair (Fig. 18.29a), designed with Eero Saarinen, was of molded plywood; it won first prize in the Museum of Modern Art Organic Design Competition in 1940, but was not produced until after World

Figure 18.29a
Eames' chair, designed with Saarinen, won first place in the Museum of Modern Art's Organic Furniture Competition, 1940.

War II owing to the high cost of the molding process (Fig. 18.29b).

Eames was invited by the Museum of Modern Art to exhibit his furniture designs in 1946 in a one-man show and was given a research grant for the Low-Cost Furniture Competition sponsored by the Museum of Modern Art to develop a molded plastic chair. Eames's main objective was to develop reasonably priced, comfortable, strong yet light chairs that followed body contours and flexed with body movements. He developed a longue chair of polished aluminum (Fig. 18.29c), and a longue chair of Brazilian rosewood (Figs. 3.56, 18.29d; Plate 38). Eames' chair designs were light and could be placed in any position

[18] Mary Jo Weale, "Contributions of Designers to Contemporary Furniture Design," unpublished doctoral dissertation, Florida State University (1968), p. 945.

Figure 18.29b
This molded walnut plywood chair designed by Eames in 1946 was developed from the one shown in Fig. 18.29a.

Figure 18.29d
Eames' longue chair with Brazilian rosewood shell and imported leather upholstery.

Figure 18.29c
Eames' longue chair of polished aluminum.

Figure 18.29f
A molded plywood chair with metal legs and rubber shock mounts, designed by Eames in 1945.

Figure 18.29e
Eames' chair with formed wire seat, wire rod base, and metal legs.

Table 18.36
Eero Saarinen (1910–61)

1. He designed in relationship to the next largest context.
2. He believed plastic to be most appropriate because it was sculptural.
3. His womb and pedestal designs are his most famous work.

Table 18.37
Hans Wegner (1914–)

1. His furniture is a tool for the human body.
2. He works from models.
3. The Peacock, the Wishbone, and the Chair are his most famous designs.
4. His designs are homogeneous and timeless.

Figure 18.30a
Saarinen's Womb chair and stool with molded frame, designed in 1946.

in a space; they were of various colors (Fig. 18.29e). He exploited machine production, yet controlled it (Fig. 18.29f), and his designs received many awards. Eames also designed his own home, using factory-produced compo-

nents, such as structural beams, sliding doors, and windows. The criteria for inclusion of these components was attractiveness and suitability.

Eero Saarinen (1910–61)

Eero Saarinen, a Finnish architect and designer, moved to the United States in 1922 after his architect father, Eliel Saarinen, won second place in the Chicago Tribune building

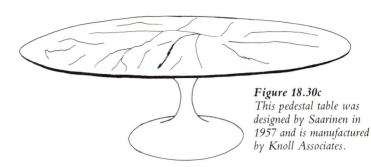

Figure 18.30c
This pedestal table was designed by Saarinen in 1957 and is manufactured by Knoll Associates.

Figure 18.30b
This pedestal arm chair with molded plastic seating shell supported on a porcelain-enameled aluminum pedestal was designed by Saarinen in 1958 and manufactured by Knoll Associates.

Figure 18.31b
The Wishbone chair, designed by Wegner in 1950, is of teak with a paper cord seat.

Figure 18.31a
The Chair designed by Wegner in 1949, is of teak with caned seat.

competion. After winning a commission to design Cranbrook Academy, Eliel moved the family to Michigan, where their home became a center for visiting architects, artists, and sculptors.[19]

Saarinen's interest in furniture began at sixteen, when he designed a bed for himself. He began designing furniture professionally when his family was asked to participate in building Kingswood School. Saarinen always designed an object by considering it in its relationship to the next largest context. A chair, for example, must be related to a room. He designed in plastic because he believed it to be the most appropriate medium for contemporary furniture. With plastic, sculptural solutions were possible. His first chair for Knoll Associates (1943) was of laminated plywood and his *Womb* chair (1946) had a molded shell and was intended for lounging (Fig. 18.30a). His most famous chair, the pedestal (1958), was designed to clear up the "slum of legs" in modern rooms (Figs. 18.30b, 18.30c). The

molded plastic shell was supported on a porcelain-enameled aluminum weighted pedestal (Fig. 18.30c). Saarinen received many awards for his furniture and architecture.

Hans Wegner (1914–)

Hans Wegner, a Danish cabinetmaker and architect, designs both custom and commercial furniture. His designs developed from a series of models, are timeless. According to Wegner, a "piece of furniture is a tool; it is made to be used."[20] His work became known in 1947 when he received wide publicity for his *Peacock* chair (Fig. 15.12b). The function of the chair and its material determine the curves of the Wegner chair. *The Chair* (Fig. 18.31a) and the *Wishbone* chair (Fig. 18.31b) are both sidechairs. His folding chair, influenced by hanging Shaker chairs (Fig. 18.31c), has been widely copied. He also designed a functional three-legged valet chair (Fig. 18.31d). Wegner's creations have been widely acclaimed and he has received many awards. His chairs are in the collections of twenty-two museums, including the Museum of Modern Art and the Metropolitan Museum of Art (Fig. 18.31e).

Finn Juhl (1912–)

Finn Juhl, a Danish architect and designer, began to design furniture when there was a

[19] Olga Gueft, "Saarinen," *Interiors,* 121 (November 1961), pp. 128–129.

[20] Oppi Untracht, "Chairs from Hans Wegner's Workshop," *Craft Horizons,* **15** (January–February 1955), p. 33.

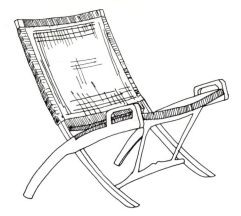

Figure 18.31c
A Wegner folding chair of fumed oak with cane seat and back, designed in 1949.

Figure 18.31e
A teak longue chair designed by Wegner.

Figure 18.32a
A teak easy chair with padded seat, back, and armrests covered with leather, designed by Juhl in 1949.

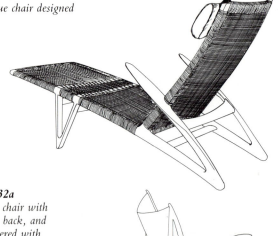

Figure 18.32b
Juhl's walnut chair with woven cane back.

Figure 18.31d
The three-legged Valet chair by Wegner has a seat that opens to hang pants on, a back for the coat, and compartments inside to hold miscellaneous items.

Table 18.38
Finn Juhl (1912–)

1. His sculptural designs have no ornamentation.
2. The backs and seats of his chairs are often separated, with the seat suspended in a square cage.
3. His joinery is beautiful.

its shaping and joining of the wooden parts. The separation between back and seat is often emphasized by the suspension of the seat in a square cage (Fig. 18.32a). Juhl's pieces are plain, unornamented, and made of teak, walnut, maple, and pine (Fig. 18.32b).

Developments in the 1950s and 1960s

World War II served to isolate American designers from European influences and their designs began to develop in either organic forms or free forms, the latter being abstract, amoeboid shapes. At the end of the war, many people returned to the furniture industry with knowledge gained in war industries that enabled them to bring many innovations to furniture design. By 1947, plastics, fiberglass, and resin-reinforced plywood were revolutionizing the furniture industry.

In January 1950, the Museum of Modern Art, in cooperation with the Chicago Merchandise Mart, began the Good Design exhibitions to stimulate the interest of designers, manufacturers, and retailers in good design. The Museum also sponsored the Low-cost Furniture Design competition to create an incentive for designers to develop well-designed, economically priced furniture. Many designers who had formerly worked in the

shortage of architectural commissions during World War II. He began to win prizes at that time and has continued to do so. He designs for mass production as well as for hand production. His sculptural furniture is noted for

custom-design field began to design furniture for the mass market.

Personal and family hobbies often determined the plans and furnishings of the American home. Americans were more mobile than they had been before the war, and because they liked the appearance of built-in storage, but wanted it movable, more flexible units became available. Many women, combining a career with homemaking, demanded easy-care finishes, multipurpose furniture, and "mechanical servants." World War II changed living patterns: rooms shrank in size and number, and had lower ceilings and fewer storage areas; open-plan areas were separated with screens and storage walls, a *George Nelson* (1908–) innovation.

Furniture designed by the avant-garde designers became widely copied by the end of the 1950s and "knock-offs" became accepted. There is no adequate way to protect an original furniture design, even today, because different materials can be used and small details can be changed.

During the 1960s, most magazines carried articles on contemporary furniture design. International furniture fairs began to be held as well, which gave the public a chance to see contemporary furniture design. Interfern is the British furniture show. The Scandinavian Furniture Fair and fairs in Frankfurt, Hanover, and Cologne are held yearly. An international exhibition rather than a trade fair, the *Milan Triennale,* was first held in 1921 and has awarded many gold and silver medals for outstanding furniture design. Other awards that have stimulated contemporary furniture design are those given by *Industrial Design,* the American Society of Interior Designers, and the Institute of Business Designers.

Furniture Designers Selected as Important by Furniture Designers Themselves

There are many competent furniture designers working today, and they are no longer primarily architects; most were trained for their profession. The majority of them are working in the countries of their birth; however, the number of designers working in the United States, Scandinavia, England, and Canada has increased over the number born there, while the number working in Germany, France, and Switzerland has decreased over the number born there. Approximately one third of the

Table 18.39
Major Influences on Furniture Designers[21] (in order of importance)

1. Scandinavian design and designers
2. Bauhaus
3. Charles Eames
4. Mies van der Rohe
5. Italian design and designers
6. English design and designers
7. Present United States design
8. Le Corbusier
9. Marcel Breuer
10. Oriental design
11. Eero Saarinen
12. French traditional design
13. Shaker design
14. Frank Lloyd Wright and American architects
15. Egyptian design
16. The present period in time
17. Art Nouveau

Table 18.40
Most Significant Furniture Designers[22]

1. Charles Eames
2. Hans Wegner
3. George Nelson
4. Arne Jacobsen
5. Joe Colombo
6. Eero Saarinen
7. Alvar Aalto
8. Edward Wormley
9. Mies van der Rohe
10. Finn Juhl
11. Milo Baughman
12. Poul Kjaerholm
13. Verner Panton
14. Marcel Breuer
15. Olivier Mourgue
16. Marco Zanuso
17. Harry Bertoia

designers have one parent in some art- or design-related field, and most come from a middle- or upper-middle-class background.[23]

Furniture designers participate in all areas of design from architecture to automobiles; few design furniture alone. Table 18.39 lists those designers who have had the most influence on furniture design in the order of importance designated by the furniture designers themselves.

Furniture designers were also asked to list the furniture design which had been most significant; their opinions are shown in Table 18.40.

[21] Mary Jo Weale, "Contributions of Designers to Contemporary Furniture Design," unpublished doctoral dissertation, Florida State University (1968), p. 928.
[22] Ibid., p. 930.
[23] Ibid., pp. 924–25.

Figure 18.33a
Aarnio's swivel Ball chair of fiberglass lined with foam rubber covered in red, orange, black, or white.

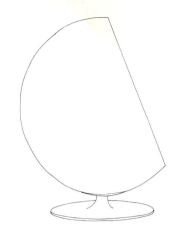

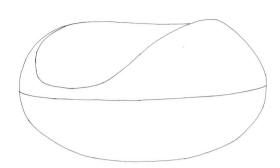

Figure 18.33b
Aarnio's Gyro chair of fiberglass.

Figure 18.34a
This high-backed upholstered chair with steel wire seat and back unit on steel rod base was designed by Bertoia and manufactured by Knoll Associates.

Figure 18.34b
Bertoia's steel wire chair on steel rod base, with seat pad, manufactured by Knoll Associates.

Figure 18.35a
Stella chair of preformed and bent plywood with leather upholstery designed by Colombo in 1962; a built-in spring between the seat and the base allows the seat to tilt with body weight.

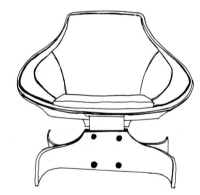

Figure 18.35b
Colombo's Elda chair, designed in 1966, and named for his wife, has a one-piece shell fiberglass frame with soft leather in a scooped-out seating area; the high shell back provides acoustical insulation.

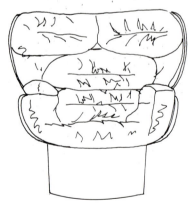

Figure 18.35c
Colombo's Supracomfort bent-plywood frame chair has removable cushions and tension springs beneath the upholstery that may be tightened for comfort.

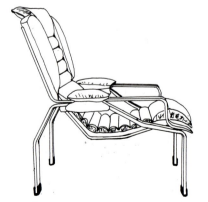

Plastics and new materials have been the strongest single influence on contemporary furniture design, according to furniture designers.[24]

The furniture designers discussed in this

[24] Ibid., p. 930.

Table 18.41
Most Significant Contemporary Furniture Design[25]

1. The plywood furniture of Charles Eames
2. All the furniture of Charles Eames
3. The metal furniture of Mies van der Rohe
4. The Barcelona chair of Mies van der Rohe
5. Scandinavian furniture
6. The metal furniture of Marcel Breuer
7. All the furniture of Eero Saarinen
8. The plywood furniture of Alvar Aalto
9. The action office of George Nelson

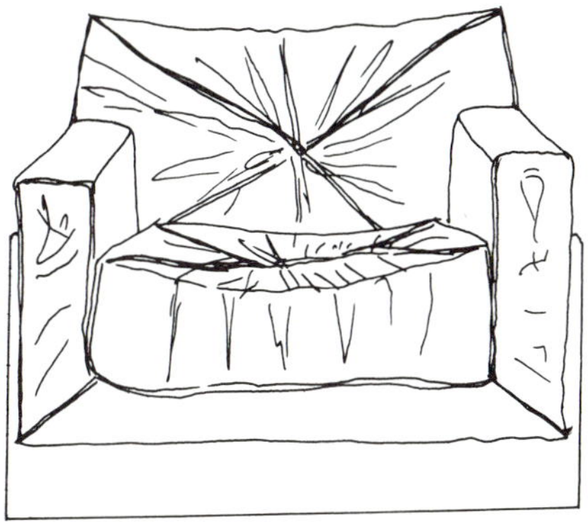

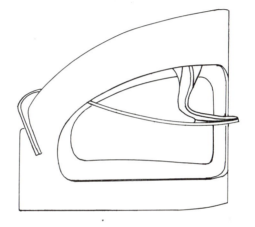

Figure 18.35d
Colombo's Golf-Club chair has a wooden frame box on casters and separate cushions; the back upholstery is anchored to the center of each cushion with a wooden button, and the frame is lacquered red, black, or white, 1966.

Figure 18.35e
Colombo's KD chair, a three-piece knock-down chair designed in 1963 of prestamped, interlocking, contoured, laminated plywood sections; painted.

section are not the only important ones, but they are those believed by their peers to have had the most impact on contemporary furniture design. They will be listed in alphabetical order. There are many other fine furniture designers, including hand-craftsmen, who are working today.

Eero Aarnio (1932–)

Eero Aarnio is a Finnish interior and industrial designer who was trained in the Institute of Industrial Arts in Helsinki. He has won numerous awards and is most famous for his fiberglass furniture such as the *Ball* chair (Fig. 18.33a) and the *Gyro* chair (Fig. 18.33b). Other furniture he has designed includes the Mustang group and *Bing-Bong Ball* chair (Fig. 9.18).

Milo Baughman (1923–)

Milo Baughman has probably done much to popularize good design by his designs for Thayer Coggin. He believes that the home is the place to discover taste in ourselves. He studied at the Los Angeles Art Center and the University of Maine. For some years he was head of the Design Department at Brigham Young University in Provo, Utah. He has designed chairs, sofas, longues, tables, case pieces, and all kinds of residential furniture (Figs. 3.8, 7.57, 7.12, 9.1, 9.15, Plate 26).

Harry Bertoia (1915–78)

Harry Bertoia, an Italian, emigrated to the United States in 1930. He became an instructor in metal-craft at Cranbrook, working there with Saarinen and Eames, where he designed furniture pieces in the 1950s. Believing that a chair should rotate and change, he used a steel wire frame (Figs. 18.34a, 18.34b). He then became a sculptor and never again designed any furniture.

Joe Colombo (1930–70)

Joe Colombo, an Italian architect, designed residential and contract furniture. He disliked decoration and believed that color was the only decoration needed (Figs. 3.23 and 9.19). His designs were dynamic and multipurpose. He designed many pieces (Figs. 3.23, 9.19), such as the *Stella* chair (Fig. 18.35a), the *Elda* chair (Fig. 18.35b), the *Supracomfort* (Fig. 18.35c), the *Golf Club* chair (Fig. 18.35d), and the *KD* chair (Fig. 18.35e).

Arne Jacobsen (1902–71)

Arne Jacobsen, a Danish designer and one of Denmark's best known architects during his lifetime, was trained at the Copenhagen Academy of Fine Arts. He was an architect who designed furniture for his architectural projects. Each piece had a purpose. For example, the *Egg* chair (Fig. 18.36a), designed to allow the sitter to view the life of the city, fits around the body, isolating the person from distraction. On the other hand, the *Swan* chair (Fig.

Figure 18.36a
Jacobsen's Egg chair, designed in 1961, swivels on an aluminum base.

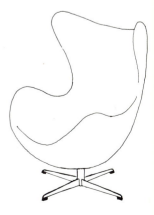

[25] Ibid., p. 931.

Figure 18.36b
Jacobsen's Swan chair, designed in 1958 for conversation, has a fiberglass shell, leather and foam-rubber padding, and aluminum swivel base.

Figure 18.37a
Kjaerholm's chair with matte chrome-steel frame and braided flag-line seat.

Figure 18.36c
Jacobsen's stackable Ant chair, pressure-molded beechwood with three metal legs, was designed in 1953.

Figure 18.38a
Mourgue's Djinn chaise longue, with steel tube structure covered with foam and jersey, manufactured by Airborne, designed in 1963.

Figure 18.37b
Kjaerholm's folding stool of matte chromium-plated steel with canvas (or leather) seat was designed in 1960.

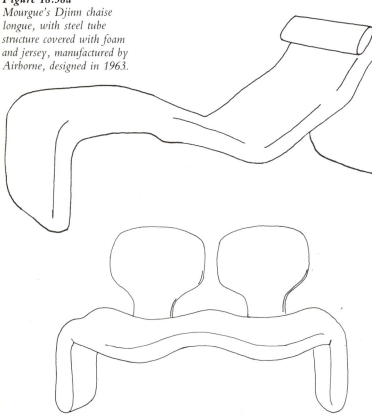

18.36b) was designed for people who want to enjoy conversation with each other. Jacobsen designed the *Ant* chair (Fig. 18.36c) of pressure-molded plywood with a metal base and three legs; the stackable chair is inexpensive, comfortable, and small.

Poul Kjaerholm (1929–)

Poul Kjaerholm developed the principle of using steel as the supporting element in furniture construction. He was trained at the Copenhagen School of Arts and Crafts, studying under both Klint and Wegner. His refined, simple furniture is beautiful from all angles. He works primarily in steel (Fig. 18.37a) and uses natural materials for upholstery (Fig. 18.37b).

Olivier Mourgue (1939–)

Olivier Mourgue, a French designer, studied at the *École des Arts Décoratifs* in Paris and

Figure 18.38b
Mourgue's Djinn duo armchair, with metal frame covered with foam and Helanca stretch nylon, manufactured by Airborne, designed in 1965.

Figure 18.39a
Nelson's Action Office with bright polished
aluminum base, oiled brown ash tambour and file bin,
laminated plastic top with soft vinyl edge. Herman
Miller, 1965.

Figure 18.39b
Nelson's Coconut chair with chromium-plated legs.
Herman Miller.

Figure 18.39c
Nelson's Swag-leg chair of molded reinforced plastic
shell on curved tubular steel legs, was designed in
1958. Herman Miller.

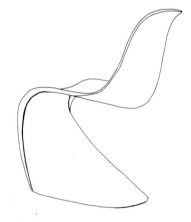

Figure 18.40a
Panton's stacking fiberglass and polyester chair in
various bright colors, designed in 1960. Herman Miller
AG.

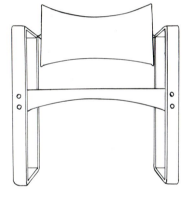

Figure 18.40b
Panton's modular seating group of painted plywood,
with three sizes of bent-plywood frames, two sizes
contoured seat units, and contoured swiveling back rest
was designed in 1967.

began designing furniture for the Airborne
Company in 1962. His designs are very supple
(Fig. 18.38a). He utilizes a bent, curved steel
tubing frame covered with molded foam-rubber padding zipped into a fitted cover of Helanca stretch nylon (Fig. 18.38b).

George Nelson (1908–   )

George Nelson not only designs furniture for
the Herman Miller Company, he has also
written many books on design and began the
periodical, *Architectural Forum,* with two col-
laborators in 1943. He was responsible for the
development of the storage wall and the *Action office* (Fig. 18.39a). He has also designed
many chairs, including the *Coconut* (Fig.
18.39b) and the *Swag-leg* chair (Fig. 18.39c).

Verner Panton (1927–   )

Verner Panton, a Danish designer living and
working in Switzerland, had designed chairs
in many styles and forms: metal cones, molded
fiberglass (Fig. 18.40a), plywood (Fig. 18.40b),
and chairs of sheet metal and wire (Fig. 18.40c).
He is a functionalist and experiments with the
many forms that interest him as well as with
modern and unconventional materials.

Edward Wormley (1907–   )

Edward Wormley was the designer for the
Dunbar Furniture Company from 1931 until
his retirement. He created many beautifully
made functional contemporary designs (Fig.
18.41a). His designs remained in the Dunbar

Figure 18.40c
Panton's sheet-metal and wire chair with upholstered pads was designed in 1962.

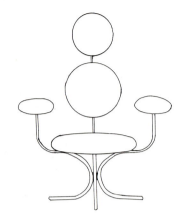

Figure 18.41b
Wormley's reclining rocker chaise longue with asymmetrical laminated ash frame, wood hinge and four adjustable positions, woven cane seat and back, manufactured by Dunbar.

Figure 18.42a
Zanuso's Baronet arm chair of laminated wood.

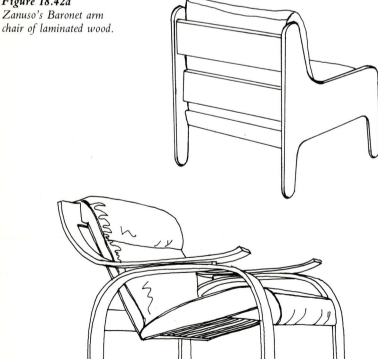

Figure 18.41a
Wormley's wood and leather chair manufactured by Dunbar.

Figure 18.41c
Wormley's cane-back chair with tilted seat suspended in laminated ash frame, manufactured by Dunbar.

catalog for many years owing to their timeless qualities (Fig. 18.41b). Like Klint, he was influenced by many things which he integrated into his furniture, such as the designs of Greene and Greene, Chinese and Scandinavian furniture, and Biedermeier designs (Fig. 18.41c).

Marco Zanuso (1916–)

Marco Zanuso, an architect, has received many gold medals for his furniture designs. He works in wood (Fig. 18.42a), plywood (Fig. 18.42b), and metal (Fig. 18.42c). He designs household appliances and accessories and is considered to be one of Italy's most creative designers.

Figure 18.42b
Zanuso's Wood-line chair, with molded laminated wood underframe, rigid seating element, loose leather cushions, manufactured by Arflex.

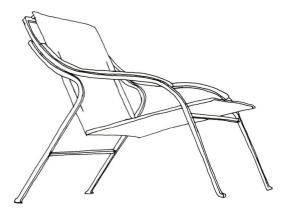

Figure 18.42c
Zanuso's Four-line chair, designed in 1964, has a metal frame, fabric or leather seat and back joined by hinges, soft metal springs, adjustable seat, manufactured by Arflex.

Glossary

Ferro-Concrete. Reinforced concrete.

Historicism. A movement based on past designs.

Knock-Offs. A copy of a particular design.

Repoussé (rĕ-pōō′-sā′). A raised pattern on metal formed by beating it from the reverse side.

Bibliography

AALTO, ALVAR. *Alvar Aalto.* New York: Whittenborn and Co., 1963.

ALOI, ROBERT. *L'Arredamento Moderno.* Milan, Italy: Ulrico Hoepli Editore, 1961.

ANDREWS, EDWARD DEMING. *The People Called Shakers.* New York: Dover Publications, Inc., 1963.

ANDREWS, EDWARD DEMING, and FAITH ANDREWS. *Religion in Wood.* Bloomington: Indiana University Press, 1966.

———. *Shaker Furniture.* New Haven, Conn.: Yale University Press, 1937.

Architecture and Furniture: Aalto. New York: Museum of Modern Art, 1936.

ARGAN, GUILIO CARLO. *Marcel Breuer.* Milan, Italy: Görlich editore, 1955.

ARONSON, JOSEPH. *The Book of Furniture and Decoration.* New York: Crown Publishers, Inc., 1952.

———. *The Encyclopedia of Furniture,* 3rd ed. New York: Crown Publishers, Inc., 1965.

ARTARIA, PAUL. *Carl Malmsten, Swedish Furniture.* Basel, Switzerland: Wept and Co., 1954.

ASLIN, ELIZABETH. *Nineteenth Century English Furniture.* New York: Thomas Yoseloff, 1962.

BALCHI, DAVID ARNOLD. *Elbert Hubbard, Genius of Roycroft.* New York: Frederick A. Stokes Co., 1940.

BARR, ALFRED H., JR., *De Stijl, Museum of Modern Art Bulletin.* Vol. 20 (Winter 1952–1953).

———. *Fantastic Art Dada Surrealism.* New York: The Museum of Modern Art, 1936.

BAYER, HERBERT, WALTER GROPIUS, and ISE GROPIUS. *Bauhaus, 1919–1928.* New York: Museum of Modern Art, 1938.

BLAKE, PETER. *Marcel Breuer: Architect and Designer.* New York: An Architectural Record Book published in collaboration with the Museum of Modern Art, 1949.

———. *Marcel Breuer: Sun and Shadow.* New York: Dodd, Mead and Co., 1956.

BØE, ALF. *From Gothic Revival to Functional Form.* Oslo, Denmark: Oslo University Press, 1957.

BOESIGER, WILLY, and HANS GIRSBERGER. *Le Corbusier, 1910–1960.* New York: George Wittenborn, Inc., 1960.

BOGER, LOUISE ADE. *The Complete Guide to Furniture Styles.* New York: Charles Scribner's Sons, 1959.

———. *Furniture Past and Present.* New York: Doubleday & Co., Inc., 1966.

BOK, EDWARD. *The Americanization of Edward Bok.* New York: Charles Scribner's Sons, 1923.

BUTLER, JOSEPH T. *American Antiques, 1800–1900.* New York: Odyssey Press, 1965.

CLEMMENSEN, TOVE. *Danish Furniture of the Eighteenth Century.* Copenhagen: Gyldendalske Boghandel Nordisk Forlage, 1948.

CLIFFORD, C. R. *Period Furnishings.* New York: Clifford and Lawton, Inc., 1927.

CRANE, WALTER. *William Morris to Whistler.* London: G. Bell and Son, Ltd., 1911.

DE WOLF, ELSIE. *The House in Good Taste.* New York: The Century Co., 1920.

DREXLER, ARTHUR. *Ludwig Mies Van Der Rohe.* New York: George Braziller, Inc., 1960.

DREXLER, ARTHUR, and GRETA DANIEL. *Introduction to 20th Century Design from the Collection of the Museum of Modern Art.* New York: Doubleday & Co., Inc., 1959.

Fantasy Furniture. New York: The Museum of Contemporary Crafts or the American Craftsmen's Council, 1966.

FARR, MICHAEL. *Design in British Industry.* Cambridge: At the University Press, 1955.

FERRIDAY, PETER (ed.). *Victorian Architecture.* New York: J. B. Lippincott Co., 1964.

FITCH, JAMES MARSTON. *American Building.* Boston: Houghton Mifflin Co., 1948.

FLEMMING, WILLIAM. *Arts and Ideas.* New York: Holt, Rinehart and Winston, 1963.

FRANKL, PAUL T. I. *Form and Reform.* New York: Harper & Row, Publishers, 1930.

GIEDION, SIGFRIED. *Space, Time, and Architecture,* 4th ed. Cambridge, Mass.: Harvard University Press, 1963.

GILLIOTT, MARY. *English Style in Interior Decoration.* New York: The Viking Press, Inc., 1967.

GIRARD, A. H., and W. D. LAURIE, JR. (eds.). *An Exhibition for Modern Living*. Detroit: The Detroit Institute of Arts, 1949.

GLOAG, JOHN. *The Chair, Its Origin, Design, and Social History*. New York: A. S. Barnes and Co., 1967.

———. *A Social History of Furniture Design from B.C. 1300 to A.D. 1960*. London: Cassell and Co., 1966.

———. *Time, Taste, and Furniture*. London: The Richards Press, 1949.

———. *Victorian Taste*. London: Adam and Charles Black, 1962.

GOLDWATER, ROBERT in collaboration with René d'Harnoncourt. *Modern Art in Your Life, The Museum of Modern Art Bulletin XVII*, 1949.

GOODFRIEND, ARTHUR. *What is America?* New York: Simon & Schuster, Inc., 1954.

HALD, ARTHUR, and SVEN ERIK SKAWONIUS. *Contemporary Swedish Design*. New York: Pellegrini and Cudaly Publishers, 1951.

ULF HÅRD AF SEGERSTAD. *Modern Scandinavian Furniture*. Totowa, New Jersey: The Bedminister Press, 1963.

———. *Scandinavian Design*. New York: Life Style Stuart, 1961.

HAUGLID, ROAR (ed.). *Native Art of Norway*. New York: Frederick A. Praeger, 1967.

HAYWARD, HELENA (ed.). *World Furniture*. New York: McGraw-Hill Book Co., 1965.

HENNALL, THOMAS. *British Craftsmen*. London: Adprint, Ltd., 1946.

HENNESSEY, WILLIAM J. *Modern Furnishings for the Home*. New York: Van Nostrand Reinhold Co., 1952.

HILBERSEIMER, LUDWIG. *Mies Van Der Rohe*. Chicago: Paul Theobald and Co., 1956.

HOLDT, ÅKE, and EVA BENEDICKS (eds.). *Design in Sweden Today*. Stockholm: The Swedish Institute for Cultural Relations, 1948.

HOLME, RATHBONE, and KATHLEEN M. FROST (eds.). *Decorative Art in Modern Interiors*. London: The Studio Publications, 1949.

———. *Decorative Art 1951–2*. London: The Studio Publications, 1952.

HOLME, RATHBONE, and S. B. WAINWRIGHT. *Decorative Art 1930*. London: The Studio Ltd., 1930.

HOWARTH, THOMAS. *Charles Rennie Mackintosh and the Modern Movement*. New York: Whittenborn Publications, Inc., 1953.

JAFFÉ, H. C. L. *De Stijl, 1917–1931*. London: Alec Tiranti Ltd., n.d.

JANSEN, H. W. *History of Art*. Englewood Cliffs, N.J.: Prentice-Hall, Inc., 1966.

JOEL, DAVID. *The Adventure of British Furniture*. London: Ernest Benn, Ltd., 1953.

JONES, CRANSTON. *Marcel Breuer Buildings and Projects 1921–1961*. New York: Frederick A. Praeger, 1962.

JOY, EDWARD T. *The Book of English Furniture*. New York: A. S. Barnes Co., 1964.

———. *English Furniture AD 43-1950*. New York: Arco Publishing Co., 1962.

KAHLE, KATHERINE MORRISON. *Modern French Decoration*. New York: G. P. Putnam's Son's, 1930.

KARLSEN, ARNE. *Contemporary Danish Design*. Copenhagen: The Danish Society of Arts and Crafts and Industrial Design, 1960.

——— and ANKER TIEDEMAN. *Made in Denmark*. New York: Van Nostrand Reinhold Co., 1960.

KAUFMANN, EDGAR, JR. *Prize Designs for Modern Furniture*. New York: Museum of Modern Art, 1950.

———. *What is Modern Design*. New York: The Museum of Modern Art, 1950.

———. *What is Modern Interior Design?* New York: The Museum of Modern Art, 1953.

KIMERLY, W. L. *How To Know Period Styles in Furniture*. Grand Rapids, Mich.: Periodical Publishing Co., 1912.

KOUWENHOVEN, JOHN A. *The Arts in Modern American Civilization*. New York: W. W. Norton & Co., Inc., 1948.

———. "The Background of Modern Design," *An Exhibition for Modern Living*. Detroit: The J. L. Hudson Co., 1949.

LAURIN, CARL, EMIL HANNOVER, and JENS THIIS. *Scandinavian Art*. New York: The American-Scandinavian Foundation, 1922.

LENNING, HENRY F. *Art Nouveau*. The Hague: Martinus Nijohff, 1951.

LICHTEN, FRANCES. *Decorative Art of Victoria's Era*. New York: Charles Scribner's Sons, 1950.

LINDBECK, JOHN R. *Design Textbook*. Bloomington, Ill.: McKnight and McKnight Publishing Co., 1963.

LYNES, RUSSELL. *The Domesticated Americans*. New York: Harper & Row, Publishers, 1963.

———. *A Surfeit of Honey*. New York: Harper & Row, Publishers, 1957.

———. *The Tastemakers*. New York: Harper & Row, Publishers, 1954.

McCLINTON, KATHERINE MORRISON. *Christian Church Art Through the Ages*. New York: Macmillan Publishing Co., Inc., 1962.

MADSEN, STEVEN TSCHUDI. *Art Noveau*. New York: McGraw-Hill Book Co., 1967.

———. *Sources of Art Noveau*. New York: George Wittenborn, Inc., 1955.

MANSON, GRANT CARPENTER. *Frank Lloyd Wright, to 1910*. New York: Van Nostrand Reinhold Co., 1958.

MELCHER, MARGUERITE FELLOWS. *The Shaker Adventure*. Princeton: The Princeton University Press, 1941.

MICHELSEN, PETER, and RASMUSSEN GOLGER. *Danish Peasant Culture*. Copenhagen: guide to the Danish National Museum, 1955.

MOODY, ELLA (ed.). *Decorative Art in Modern Interiors 1961–2*. New York: The Viking Press, Inc., 1961.

————. *Decorative Art in Modern Interiors 1967–68.* New York: The Viking Press, Inc., 1967.

MUMFORD, LEWIS. *Roots of Contemporary Architecture.* New York: Van Nostrand Reinhold Co., 1952.

NEAL, JULIA. *By Their Fruits.* Chapel Hill: The University of North Carolina Press, 1947.

NEWTON, ERIC. *The Meaning of Beauty.* Harmondsworth, Middlesex: Penguin Books, Ltd., 1962.

NORDHOFF, CHARLES. *The Communistic Societies of the United States.* New York: Harper & Row, Publishers, 1875.

NOYES, ELIOT F. *Organic Design in Home Furnishings.* New York: The Museum of Modern Art, 1941.

OTTO, CELIA JACKSON. *American Furniture of the Nineteenth Century.* New York: The Viking Press, Inc., 1967.

PEPIS, BETTY. *Betty Pepis' Guide to Interior Decoration.* New York: Van Nostrand Reinhold Co., 1957.

PETER, JOHN. *Masters of Modern Architecture.* New York: Bonanza Books, 1958.

PREVSNER, NICOLAUS. *Pioneers of Modern Design From William Morris to Walter Gropius.* New York: The Museum of Modern Art, 1949.

PREZ, MARIO. *An Illustrated History of Furnishings.* New York: George Braziller, 1964.

READ, HERBERT. *Art and Industry.* London: Faber and Faber Ltd., 1934.

REMLOV, ARNE (ed.). *Design in Scandinavia.* Oslo, Norway: Kirstes Boktrykkeri, 1954.

ROE, GORDON. *Victorian Furniture.* London: Phoenix House, Ltd., 1952.

ROGERS, MEYRIC R. *Italy at Work: Her Renaissance in Design Today.* Rome: The Compagniz Nazionale Artigiana, 1950.

RUSSELL, GORDON. *The Things We See: Furniture,* 2nd ed. Harmondsworth, Middlesex: Penguin Books, 1953.

SAARINEN, ALINE B. (ed.). *Saarinen on His Work.* New Haven: Yale University Press, 1962.

SAVAGE, GEORGE. *A Concise History of Interior Decoration.* New York: Grosset & Dunlap, Inc., 1966.

SCHEIDIG, WALTER. *Weimar Crafts of the Bauhaus.* New York: Van Nostrand Reinhold Co., 1966.

SELZ, PETER, and MILDRED CONSTANTINE (eds.). *Art Nouveau.* New York: Doubleday & Co., Inc., 1959.

SPEENBURGH, GERTRUDE. *The Arts of the Tiffanys.* Chicago: Lightner Publishing Corp., 1956.

SWEENY, JAMES JOHNSON and JOSEP SERT. *Antoni Gaudí.* New York: Frederick A. Praeger, 1960.

TEMKO, ALLEN. *Eero Saarinen.* New York: George Braziller, 1962.

TODD, DOROTHY, and RAYMOND MORTIMER. *The New Interior Decoration.* New York: Charles Scribner's Sons, 1929.

TRAPPES-LOMAX, MICHAEL. *Pugin, A Medieval Victorian.* London: Sheed and Ward, 1932.

VAN DOMMELEN, DAVID B. *Designing and Decorating Interiors.* New York: John Wiley & Sons, Inc., 1965.

VARNUM, WILLIAM H. *Creative Design in Furniture.* Peoria, Ill.: The Manual Arts Press, 1937.

WALKER, R. A. *The Best of Beardsley.* London: Spring Books, n.d.

WANSCHER, OLE. *The Art of Furniture.* New York: Van Nostrand Reinhold Co., 1966.

WEIL, BENJAMIN HENRY and VICTOR J. ANHORN, *Plastic Horizons.* Lancaster, Penn.: Jacques Catell Press, 1940.

WELLMAN, RITA. *Victoria Royal.* New York: Charles Scribner's Sons, 1939.

What Is Modern Industrial Design? Museum of Modern Art Bulletin, XIV, New York, Fall 1966.

WILSON, JOSÉ and ARTHUR LEAMAN. *Decoration U.S.A.* New York: Macmillan Publishing Co., Inc., 1965.

WINCHESTER, ALICE (ed.). *The Antiques Book.* New York: Bonanza Books, 1950.

WRIGHT, FRANK LLOYD. *Modern Architecture.* Princeton: Princeton University Press, 1931.

YARWOOD, DOREEN. *The English House.* London: B. T. Batsford, Ltd., 1956.

ZAHLE, ERIK (ed.). *A Treasury of Scandinavian Design.* New York: The Golden Press, 1961.

Historic Preservation*

Historic Preservation is a highly specialized field. The education requirements in programs in interior design provide a broad base for study in this area. The intent of this discussion is to provide an overview so that the interior designer's role in the Historic Preservation movement will be better understood.

Historic preservation is a comprehensive program of scientific research and study, protection, restoration, maintenance, and interpretation of sites, buildings, and objects significant in American history and culture. The preservation field has many facets. Many historians, architectural historians, architects, archeologists, landscape architects, museologists, and experienced craftsmen have been concerned with preservation for a long time. As a result, they have established organizations to coordinate their efforts and to develop principles and guidelines to assist them in their research. Many excellent publications are devoted to disseminating information on this subject (see the bibliography at the end of this chapter).

Although interior restoration has been an important aspect of historic preservation, until recently few interior designers have been involved. Now, however, interior designers can draw upon a wide variety of research resources and publications. These include specialized programs in colleges, short courses and seminars by preservation specialists; books and periodicals on the subject; membership in the National Trust and other related organizations; as well as contact with knowledgeable people who have been involved with historic preservation for many years. There are also many others who have had little or no formal training but who have a great store of knowledge.

Americans want and need a tie to their cultural past, and with many historical landmarks already destroyed, it is becoming even more essential that those remaining be saved. Preserved and restored, urban areas are revitalized, increasing property values and encouraging tourism. One byproduct of this endeavor is an increasing appreciation of the beauty of the craftsmanship of the past.

Historic preservation, in a rapidly evolving technological society, is also very important to emotional well-being. Before the middle of the nineteenth century, the continuity of the home and family was taken for granted. Now, with the environment changing at an accelerating rate, family disintegration and geographic and family change have become the mode. The toll on individual and family identity is manifested in painful emotional maladjustment. Tranquilizers are the most frequently prescribed drug, second only to aspirin in volume of consumption. The divorce rate is currently 50 per cent in the nation —and higher in metropolitan areas, where environmental change is more rapid. Preservation of historic sites can be beneficial to individuals and families in reducing the stress that results from too many changes. The number of life changes within a given time is linearly related to illness, and the greater the number of life changes which an individual experiences the more likely he is to have an accident or become sick. Through the saving of historic buildings, ties with the past can be maintained and the number of environmental changes facing each individual can be reduced.

Historical Background

Historical restoration and preservation were undertaken first in France, England, and Scandinavia.

France

In 1830, Louis Philippe of France recognized the need not only to halt the vandalism of great national monuments but also to repair the destruction that occurred during the French Revolution. He established the *Commission des Monuments Historiques,* which employed professionals, usually architects, to assist in the work. This was the first government involvement in preservation and restoration. The commission was unsuccessful at first, for most architects had little or no understanding of Gothic construction methods.

One who did was *Eugene Emmanuel Viollet-le-Duc* (1814–79), a young French architect who was enchanted by the Gothic Period, had a passion for historical research and archeology, and devoted his life to restoring cathedrals and to creating a doctrine of historical restoration. Believing architecture to be an expression of the history of a society, he studied it scientifically. He believed each building should be restored to its original appearance and structure. This belief, and the methods he

_____

* Most of the information in this chapter was furnished by Dinah Lazor, ASID, Vicksburg, Mississippi.

undertook to achieve his results, were not suited to Gothic buildings, many of which had been constructed over a period of many years and reflected many influences and styles. An example is the Cathedral of Nôtre-Dame, built between 1163 and 1235, which Viollet-le-Duc restored. He frequently took the liberty of removing all the additions and tried to return the building to its original construction date or removed the ornamentation of an early period to restore the building to a later period. His intellectual background and his experience, in a time when there were no architectural historians or builders to offer assistance, was unique. He understood the problems of Gothic buildings as no one else did, and his talents as a writer and draftsman made him famous, not only in France but in England as well. His influence was immense.

England

England has been involved in preservation since the Victorian Period. Much of the restoration during the Victorian Period was a threat to old architecture because it was undertaken by people who were educated but uninformed. John Ruskin, whose views on this subject influenced so many, believed the sheer age of a building was its most important aspect and so it must be built with materials that would age well. He said of an old building:

> Take proper care of your monuments, and you will not need to restore them. . . . Watch an old building with anxious care; guard it as best you may, and at *any* cost from every influence of dilapidation. Count its stones as you would jewels of a crown; set watches about it as if at the gates of a besieged city; bind it together with iron where it loosens; stay it with timber where it declines; do not care about the unsightliness of the aid; better a crutch than a lost limb . . . and let no dishonouring and false substitute deprive it of the funeral offices of memory.[1]

Ruskin was very opposed to the restoration method popular in the middle 1800s, in which the stone was tooled away to reach a new firm surface—a practice that distorted all the original ornamentation. He believed that restoration was "as impossible as to raise the dead, to restore anything that has ever been great or beautiful in architecture."[2]

In 1877, William Morris founded the Society for the Protection of Ancient Buildings, a group which evolved excellent repair techniques. He wrote in a letter to Count Zorzi concerning the restoration of St. Mark's in Venice:

> The single principle is . . . every external stone should be set back in its actual place: if any are added to strengthen the wall, the new stone, instead of being made to resemble the old ones, should be left blank of sculpture, and every one have the date of its insertion engraved upon it.[3]

It is obvious that both Ruskin and Morris were opposed to Viollet-le-Duc's methods. So was another Englishman, Philip Webb, a contemporary of Morris who was inspired by thirteenth-century Gothic designs. He repaired ancient structures without destroying their history, believing that conservation should be the object of repair. This would provide evidence that the building was valued and understood. The art of conservation, thus, became an essential part of English Victorian philosophy.

Sweden

In the 1890s, Sweden, under the direction of *Authur Hazelius,* developed the concept of the outdoor museum by bringing together objects and buildings to create the atmosphere of a certain period of its culture. This concept has spread to many countries.

United States

In the United States, preservation began under the aegis of individuals or private foundations. *Ann Pamelia Cunningham* began the first important organized effort toward preservation in 1853 by forming the Mount Vernon Ladies' Association Union to save the home of George Washington and women continued to play a prominent role in the preservation movement in the early years by restoring the homes of famous people. Williamsburg, the result of private endeavor, was the first open museum in the United States (1926). In 1890,

[1] John Ruskin, *The Seven Lamps of Architecture* (London: J. M. Dent & Sons Ltd, 1907), pp. 200–201.

[2] *Ibid,* p. 199.
[3] Letter from William Morris to Count Zorzi, Venice, Italy.

the American Institute of Architects became the first professional group to become involved in restoration. Since that time, many other organizations have joined in the effort to save our historic buildings.

In 1906 the Federal government became interested in the preservation movement and passed the Antiquities Act, which provided for the protection and scientific investigation of historic or prehistoric remains on Federal lands. In 1935 the Historic Sites Act was passed to encourage the preservation of historic or archaeologically significant properties. The National Register of Historic Places was initiated at this time, and certain sites were designated National Historic Landmarks. The Historic American Building Survey and the National Survey of Historic Sites and Buildings were also important programs designed to identify important historical areas. Beginning in 1929, historical districts were designated by the government and the first of these were the Vieux Carré in New Orleans and one in Charleston, South Carolina.

In the 1960s and 1970s, the Federal government took an increasingly active role in preservation. The Reservoir Salvage Act (1960) provided for the recovery and conservation of historical and archaeological data that would otherwise be lost as a result of dam construction. The National Historic Preservation Act (1966) established the concept of historic preservation as a national policy, provided incentives for preservation activities in the form of matching grants to states, and expanded the National Registery of Historic Places to include state and local historic sites. In 1971 a supplement to the 1966 Act directed Federal agencies to lead in the selection of important sites. Federally owned properties were evaluated as well; to preserve the cultural environment of the nation, these would be restored and maintained. Many of these programs are administered by the National Park Service, and records of surveys by the Historic American Engineering Record are available on request from the Library of Congress.

The efforts of private and professional organizations as well as those of local, state, and national governments have resulted in many forms of preservation. These include:

1. House museums
2. Outdoor or working museums
3. Historic districts, both residential and commercial

4. Adaptive use, residential or commercial
5. Display of elements or portions of a structure which could not be completely saved
6. Documentation of the existence of historic structures before demolition or change.

General Standards for Historic Preservation Projects[4]

The following general standards apply to all treatments undertaken on historic properties listed in the National Register:

1. Every reasonable effort shall be made to provide a compatible use for a property that requires minimal alteration of the building structure, or site and its environment, or to use a property for its originally intended purpose.
2. The distinguishing original qualities or character of a building, structure, or site and its environment shall not be destroyed. The removal or alteration of any historic material or distinctive architectural features should be avoided when possible.
3. All buildings, structures, and sites shall be recognized as products of their own time. Alterations which have no historical basis and which seek to create an earlier appearance shall be discouraged.
4. Changes which may have taken place in the course of time are evidence of the history and development of a building, structure, or site and its environment. These changes may have acquired significance in their own right and this significance shall be recognized and respected.
5. Distinctive stylistic features or examples of skilled craftsmanship which characterize a building, structure, or site, shall be treated with sensitivity.
6. Deteriorated architectural features shall be repaired rather than replaced, wherever possible. In the event replacement is necessary, the new material should match the material being replaced in composition, design, color, texture, and other visual qualities. Repair or replacement of missing architectural features should be based on accurate duplications of features, substan-

[4] Morton Brown and Gary Hume, *The Secretary of the Interior Standards for Historic Preservation Projects* (Washington, D.C.: U.S. Department of the Interior Heritage Conservation and Recreation Service Technical Preservation Services Division), 1979, p. 3.

tiated by historical, physical, or pictorial evidence rather than on conjectural designs or the availability of different architectural elements from other buildings or structures.

7. The surface cleaning of structures shall be undertaken with the gentlest means possible. Sandblasting and other cleaning methods that will damage the historic building materials shall not be undertaken.

8. Every reasonable effort shall be made to protect and preserve archeological resources affected by, or adjacent to, any acquisition, protection, stabilization, preservation, rehabilitation, restoration, or reconstruction project.

Glossary⁵

Acquisition. Is defined as the act or process of acquiring fee title or interest other than fee title of real property (including the acquisition of development rights or remainder interest).

Protection. Is defined as the act or process of applying measures designed to affect the physical condition of a property by defending or guarding it from deterioration, loss or attack, or to cover or shield the property from danger or injury. In the case of buildings and structures, such treatment is generally of a temporary nature and anticipates future historic preservation treatment; in the case of archeological sites, the protective measure may be temporary or permanent.

Stabilization. Is defined as the act or process of applying measures designed to reestablish a weather resistant enclosure and the structural stability of an unsafe or deteriorated property while maintaining the essential form as it exists at present.

Preservation. Is defined as the act or process of applying measures to sustain the existing form, integrity, and material of a building or structure, and the existing form and vegetative cover of a site. It may include initial stabilization work, where necessary, as well as ongoing maintenance of the historic building materials.

Rehabilitation. Is defined as the act or process of returning a property to a state of utility through repair or alteration which makes possible an efficient contemporary use while preserving those portions or features of the property which are significant to its historical, architectural, and cultural values.

Restoration. Is defined as the act or process of accurately recovering the form and details of a property and its setting as it appeared at a paticular period of time by means of the removal of later work or by the replacement of missing earlier work.

Reconstruction. Is defined as the act or process of reproducing by new construction the exact form and detail of a vanished building, structure, or object, or a part thereof, as it appeared at a specific period of time.

Bibliography

American Heritage Magazine Editors. *Historic Houses of America Open to the Public: An American Heritage Guide.* Beverley Da Costa, ed. New York: American Heritage Publishing Co., Inc., 1971.

BROWN, MORTON, and GARY HUME. *The Secretary of the Interior Standards for Historic Preservation Projects.* Washington: U.S. Dept. of the Interior Heritage Conservation and Recreation Service Technical Preservation Services Division, 1979.

BULLOCK, ORIN M., JR. *The Restoration Manual: An Illustrated Guide to the Preservation and Restoration of Old Buildings.* Written for the Committee on Historic Buildings of the American Institute of Architects. Norwalk, Conn.: Silvermine Publishers, Inc., 1966.

A Guide to State Programs. 1972 ed. Washington D.C.: National Trust for Historic Preservation, 1972.

Historic Preservation Tomorrow: Revised Principles and Guidelines for Historic Preservation in the United States, Second Workshop, Williamsburg, Virginia. Washington, D.C.: National Trust for Historic Preservation; and Williamsburg, Va.: Colonial Williamsburg, 1967.

HOSMER, CHARLES B., JR. *Presence of the Past: A History of the Preservation Movement in the United States Before Williamsburg.* New York: G. P. Putnam's Sons, 1965.

INSALL, DONALD W. *The Care of Old Buildings Today: A Practical Guide.* London: The Architectural Press, 1972.

JAKLE, HOHN A. *Past Landscapes: A Bibliography for Historic Preservationists Selected from the Literature of Historical Geography.* Monticello, Ill.: Council of Planning Librarians (Exchange Bibliography No. 651), 1974.

LANDAHL, WILLIAM L. *Perpetuation of Historical Heri-*

⁵ Ibid, p. 2.

tage for Park and Recreation Departments. Wheeling, W. Va.: American Institute of Park Executives, Inc. (Management Aids Bulletin No. 55), 1965.

McKee, Harley J., comp. *Recording Historic Buildings.* Historic American Buildings Survey. Washington, D.C.: U.S.: Government Printing Office, 1970.

Menges, Gary L. *Historic Preservation: A Bibliography.* Monticello, Ill.: Council of Planning Librarians (Exchange Bibliography No. 79), 1969.

Miner, Ralph W. *Conservation of Historic and Cultural Resources.* Chicago: American Society of Planning Officials, 1969.

Montague, Robert L., III, and Tony P. Wrenn. *Planning for Preservation.* Chicago: American Society of Planning Officials, 1964.

National Trust for Historic Preservation. *A Guide to Federal Programs: Programs and Activities Related to Historic Preservation.* 1974 ed. Washington, D.C.: National Trust for Historical Preservation, 1974.

National Trust for Historic Preservation and the Colonial Williamsburg Foundation. *Historic Preservation Today: Preservation and Restoration, Williamsburg, Virginia, September 8–11, 1963.* Charlottesville, Va.: University Press of Virginia, 1966.

Preservation Bookstore Catalogue. Washington, D.C.: National Trust for Historic Preservation, Spring, 1974.

Rath, Frederick L., Jr., and Merrilyn Rogers O'Connell, comps. *Guide to Historic Preservation, Historical Agencies, and Museum Practices: A Selective Bibliography.* Cooperstown, N.Y.: New York State Historical Association, 1970.

Rooney, William F. *Practical Guide to Home Restoration.* New York: N.Y.: Bantam/Hudson Idea Books, March 1980.

Ruskin, John. *The Seven Lamps of Architecture.* London: J. M. Dent & Sons Ltd. 1907.

———. (edited by J. G. Links) *The Stones of Venice.* New York: Hill & Wang, 1964.

Whiffen, Marcus. *American Architecture Since 1780: A Guide to the Styles.* Cambridge, Mass.: M.I.T. Press, 1969.

The Development of the Modern Interior Designer*

Background of Interior Design

Very early interiors were caves or primitive shelters, serving only as a protection against the elements. There was strength in numbers, yet the size of caves necessitated that family size be limited. When humans discovered that they could grow crops and store the harvest, cave dwellings were gradually replaced by more or less permanent man-made shelters.

Once the home was built and the land claimed, the family stayed even when the crops and domesticated animals failed to provide food for them. The family home became a sanctuary and not just a temporary refuge. It was at this point that the design of the interior became important to generation after generation who lived within the same family dwelling.

Cultural Determinants

The first culture studied is that of ancient Egypt. The Egyptians produced sufficient quantities of food for their own consumption. In addition, they typically managed to have a surplus for trade. The home changed from a simple shelter designed for protection from the elements to a place of comfort and then to a place of business and leisure. The Egyptians' skill in producing more than was required for the immediate needs of the family allowed them to erect structures of timeless value. The pyramids, examples of outstanding engineering achievements were designed to perpetuate the immortality of the pharoahs.

The ancient Greeks and Romans dominated architecture long after their civilization had vanished; until about 1750, many buildings were modeled after ancient Greek and Roman temples. Interiors were monumental, built to impress people but unrelated to human scale or need. Interior decoration was a branch of architecture, and if identified at all, was identified with architects.

Social and personal habits have also undergone vast changes. Except for brief periods in Greece and Rome, until the seventeenth century, small coteries held power and there were

* This chapter grew out of a graduate course at The Florida State University in which the students researched the work of architects, decorators, and interior designers of the past and today. The authors are indebted to these students for their inspiration and for their research. Some of the material in this chapter has been discussed in earlier chapters but is repeated here to provide an overview of the development of the interior designer of today.

no democratic governments as we have today. Thus, there was no reason for more than one or two chairs and the few available were an indication of special privileges.

About 1700, in France, people became interested in comfort, luxury, and more intimate forms of living. By 1730, the influence of women began to be felt for the first time. Madame de Pompadour, the king's mistress, dominated French taste and Madame du Barry and Marie Antoinette continued the feminine influence.

The Influence of Architects

William Kent (1685–1748), in England, was probably the first designer to integrate the interior with its furnishings. The splendor of his designs reflect the mood of England at that time. He was followed by *Robert Adam* (1728–92), who went further to unify the exterior with the interior and the furnishings. After the ruins of Pompeii and Herculeanum were discovered, Adam became concerned about the size of the human body and its relationship to furniture and interior space. This is apparent in his designs, particularly in the delicate ornamentation he used. Another Englishman, *Thomas Hope* (1770–1831), helped to acquaint the public with ancient Greek, Italian, Egyptian, and Turkish designs and his book, *Household Furniture and Interior Decoration* (1807) influenced residential interiors as well as museum layout.

Bricklayers and carpenters built early American homes, and the profession of architecture was almost unknown in the United States until about 1830. The first truly American architect was *Thomas Jefferson,* whose inspiration came from the current pattern books of classical architectural designs and a combination of French influence and Roman classicism. His design for Popular Forest in 1773 resulted in the first octagonal house in America. He was also interested in interior decoration and designed functional, mechanical furniture. Another American, *Samuel McIntire* (1757–1811), who was greatly influenced by Adam, designed many houses in Salem, Massachusetts, in which interior detailing was coordinated with furniture design. *Andrew Jackson Downing* (1815–52) had a desire to educate the American public to good design. He wanted the house to fit the owner, with the landscape, architecture, furniture, and accessories all well designed. He believed that the Grecian temples, with their columns

Figure 20.1
A. J. Downing illustrated many interiors in The Architecture of Country Houses *(1850).*

Figure 20.2a
The Beecher sisters' plan for a house with a center for heating and cooking.

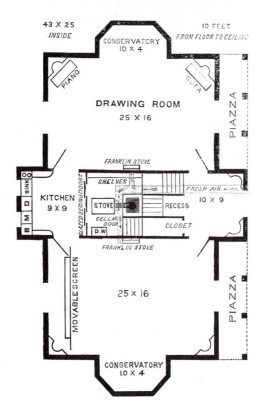

and porticos, that dotted the American landscape were nonfunctional. He wrote a number of books between 1841 and his death in an 1852 steamboat explosion. Many of his books had seven to nine printings. *Rural Houses, Cottage Residences, The Architecture of Country Houses,* and *Villas and Cottages* were the titles of some of his works. These books contained illustrations of some of his ideas for interiors (Fig. 20.1).

In 1869, *Catharine Beecher* and *Harriet Beecher Stowe* published *American Woman's Home,* in which they have advised women to have a house that was comfortable and convenient, with abundant natural light: "Sunshine is the best ornament of a house."[1] They showed examples of floor plans (Fig. 20.2a) and details of interiors (Fig. 20.2b).

A few creative and original architects who were interested in the home were responsible for many of the developments of contemporary architecture and interiors. *Louis Sullivan* believed that form follows function and his inventive buildings were noted for their expanses of glass, their steel frames, and their naturalistic ornamentation. Wright believed that form was function. His interest throughout his life was to design houses as shelters for people. Many of the things taken for granted today were Wright's innovations, such as wall-hung toilets, radiant heat, latex-foam cushions (first used in Kaufmann's Falling Water house), airconditioning, sliding-glass doors, and the open plan. He developed the house from the inside out and related it to its site through his use of design elements.

Around the same time that Wright was working, California architects pioneered in designing what came to be known as the California bungalow style. *The Greene brothers,* Charles (1868–1957) and Henry (1870–1954), designed both the interior and exterior of these houses in wood, with built-in furniture as well as free-standing furniture. Local materials were combined with the beautifully detailed wood.

Bernard Maybeck (1862–1957), another California architect, attempted to tailor the interior and exterior to the client. He like his interiors to be open and large and beautifully embellished. *R. M. Schindler* (1887–1953) designed beautifully proportioned interiors and

[1] Catharine Esther Beecher and Harriet Beecher Stowe, *The American Woman's Home* (New York: J. B. Ford & Co., 1869), p. 33.

The recess occupied by the sofa stands between these two closets. In case the room is used for sleeping, the double couch on page 30 might be substituted for the sofa, serving as a lounge by day, and two single beds by night. The curtain hanging above can be so fastened by rings on a strong semi-circular wire as to be let down while dressing and undressing, as is done in some of our steamboats.

exteriors, and his inventiveness paved the way for later developments. *Richard Neutra* (1892–1970) believed that the design of any environment was a human issue not a construction one. The environment should be of a scale suited to human needs. This he called *biorealism*. His aim was to design a house that was a profile of the client, not a monument.

Joseph Hoffman (1870–1969) advocated architecture that was functional and unified with the interior. His work was abstract and austere, with geometric ornamentation. Modern design was, to him, a way to shape and enrich life with the machine.

Walter Gropius (1883–1969) developed the concept of the interpenetration of space and the flow of one area into another. He also expressed Bauhaus concepts in a functional, practical manner. *Marcel Breuer* (1902–81) was another architect who was interested in the home. He designed the two-centered or *bi-nuclear* house to meet the needs of the family. He was also convinced of the advantages of the split-level house and helped to popularize it. *Mies van der Rohe* (1886–1969) was also interested in open planning and divided interior space with furniture arrangements, floor coverings and free standing dividers. His philosophy of "less is more" was expressed in his structures of "skin" (glass) and "bones" (the steel skeleton).

The Influence of English Reformers

In England, during the latter part of the Victorian Period, the design of the interior was greatly influenced by Victorian reformers, whose work was published in England, on the Continent, and in the United States. *William Morris* had a shop that specialized in all kinds of articles for the interior, including fabrics, carpets, furniture, stained glass, and accessories. Some of his patterns were so well designed that they are still produced today (Fig. 20.3). *C. F. A. Voysey* designed light, airy, simple interiors as well as furniture, wallpapers, and carpets. His designs were an inspiration to *Hugh Baillie Scott*, *Charles Rennie Mackintosh* (Scotland), and *Henri van de Velde* (Belgium). Many articles on the work of these men were published in the *Studio* (England) and in *House Beautiful*.

The Influence of Periodicals and Books

Charles Locke Eastlake, in his *Hints on Household Taste* (1864), blamed the consumer for not demanding well-designed furniture. He

Figure 20.3
The Pimpernel, a Morris-designed fabric, is again on the market. (Courtesy of A. Sanderson & Sons).

Curtains for an Every-day Window.
No. 48.

Clarence Cook, *The Decoration of Houses* (1897) by Edith Wharton and Ogden Codman, Jr., *The Bungalow Book* (1910) by Henry L. Wilson, and *The House in Good Taste* (1913), by Elsie de Wolfe. Magazines, such as *Ladies' Home Journal, Godey's Lady's Book, The Craftsman, House Beautiful, The Studio,* and *Good Housekeeping* all tried to inspire homeowners to make home furnishings more suitable or rooms more beautiful. Clarence Cook (Fig. 20.4), author of *The House Beautiful* (1876) wrote:

> There never was a time when so many books were produced on [architecture and decoration] and magazine articles and newspaper articles, to the end that on a matter that converns everybody, everybody may know what is the latest word. . . . We are set to thinking and theorizing about the dress and decoration of our rooms: how best to make them comfortable and handsome.[2]

Edith Wharton and Ogden Codman, Jr., wrote in *The Decoration of Houses* (1897) that a "reform in house decoration, if not necessary, is at least desirable."[3] Wharton and Codman claimed that their book was the first publication on home decoration as a branch of architecture.

In 1899, Joseph Twyman, a Chicago decorator, traced the art of decoration to the very earliest civilizations and Alice Neale, another Chicago decorator, wrote that decoration would "follow closely in the footsteps of architecture."[4] Louis Millet, a designer and a professor at the Chicago Art Institute, prophesied that America would lead all nations in design in the twentieth century.

Gustav Stickley, who published *The Craftsman* between 1901 and 1916, led and reflected American taste in home furnishings (Fig. 20.5), art, gardens, and sculpture. Stickley published articles on garden cities and city planning. He also published house plans.

Edward Bok (1863–1930), editor of the *Ladies' Home Journal* for thirty years, believed that the principles of design were important,

listed guidelines on all aspects of interiors, but with few illustrations of the furniture. Four editions of his book were published in England, and six in the United States. It was considered the "bible" of home design and this resulted in a demand for his furniture (of which there was none). Manufacturers put "Eastlake furniture" on the market, to meet that demand.

In the latter part of the nineteenth century and the early part of the twentieth, some of the numerous books published on design were *The American Cottage Builder* (1854) by John Bullock, *The House Beautiful* (1881) by

[2] Clarence Cook, *The House Beautiful* (New York: Charles Scribner's Sons, 1881), p. 19.
[3] Edith Wharton and Ogden Codman Jr., *The Decoration of Houses* (New York: Charles Scribner's Sons, 1897), p. xxi.
[4] George T. B. Davis, "The Future of House Decoration," *House Beautiful,* **5** (May 1899), pp. 261–65.

y

Figure 20.6
"Inside 100 Homes," from the Ladies' Home Journal *(November 1902).*

A dining-room, exceedingly attractive for its simplicity, in a house at Pasadena, California. The color scheme is pale green. The curtains are of linen taffeta and fishnet. From plans by Greene & Greene.

One of the best arrangements imaginable of windows with glass closets underneath in the living-room of an Army Surgeon in California. From plans by the Surgeon himself.

Awarded First Prize in the July Hand Box Contest.

Living-room of a suburban house in the West, showing a unique and effective way of treating a corner fireplace. The table was especially designed for this room. From plans by Myron Hunt.

A dining-room in a house at Clifton, Massachusetts. The large fire-place and china-closets are the feature of the room. Their even balance is particularly noticeable. From plans by Chapman & Frazer.

and he was responsible for some of the first design articles published by the magazine. He had two features that appeared monthly and created much interest: "Inside 100 Suburban Homes" (Fig. 20.6) and "Good and Bad Taste."

Bok also commissioned Will Bradley to design the Bradley House, the designs for which he published in eight installments in the *Ladies' Home Journal* in 1901. Bradley's rooms included such devices as the tenon and key, diamond-shaped window panes, and built-in furniture. Curved lines were apparent in the

ornamental detail of the interiors (Figs. 18.8a, 18.8b).

The Influence of Interior Decorators

A French architect, *James Gallier,* traveled to New York in 1832 and discovered that most people "built without having any regular plan" at all. It was not until the *Duveen* brothers, furniture and art dealers working between 1879 and 1939, began to decorate homes of many wealthy families that decoration became important. Tiffany established a business with "decorative art as a profession" in 1879 to

y

y

y

y

y

y

y

y

y

y

y

y

y

y

y

y

y

y

y

y

y

y

y

y

y

y

y

y

y

y

y

y

y

y

y

y

y

y

y

y

y

y

y

y

IN THIS HALL, SIMPLICITY, SUITABILITY AND PROPORTION ARE OBSERVED

make a "combination for interior decoration of all sorts." *Candace Wheeler,* who worked with Tiffany, wrote in *Outlook* that interior decoration was a good profession for women because they had natural good taste, and an "instinctive knowledge of textiles and intimate knowledge of the conveniences of domestic life." She prophesied that interior decoration would be recognized as a profession and that colleges would train students for this "dignified profession."[5]

Russell Lynes believes that interior decoration, as a separate profession, became inevitable when the apartment house was introduced because the exterior of the building no longer had anything to do with the interior. The architect's responsibility ended after he determined the interior distribution of space.[6] The first modern apartment house was built in New York City in 1870 and over the next twenty-three years, more than seven hundred apartment houses were built in that city alone.

Elsie de Wolfe was one of the first women to make the profession of interior decoration profitable. She wrote in 1913 that

> I know of no other more significant development than the awakening of men and women throughout the country to the desire to improve their homes. . . . It is a most startling and promising state of affairs.[7]

Whether de Wolfe really improved the interior is questionable, but she certainly influenced it. When she began her career, the field of interior decoration was a hobby reserved for the wealthy, but it has gradually changed over the years to a highly technical endeavor with cognitive, affective, and physi-

[5] Candace Wheeler, *Principles of Home Decoration* (New York: Doubleday, Page & Co., 1908), pp. 3–16.

[6] Russell Lynes, "What Did They Do Till the Decorator Came?" *House Beautiful,* **107** (October 1965), p. 250.

[7] Elsie de Wolfe, *The House in Good Taste* (New York: Appleton-Century-Crofts, 1913), p. 3.

cal aspects. De Wolfe challenged people to have beautiful, servicable things in the home, because she believed that their surroundings affected their attitude toward life. In her book, *The House in Good Taste* (1913), she tried to solve all the problems of the interior. Even though her book was directed toward the owners of big houses, there was much to be gained from it, and she even discussed such things as the placement of light sockets. She designed a hall which mirrored her belief in *"simplicity, suitability, and porportion"*[8] (Fig. 20.7).

The Interior Designer Today

Today's interior designer is required to do far more than merely decorate, as Elsie de Wolfe did, although in the public's mind the words *designer* and *decorator* are often interchangeable. The interior designer must have a broad background and be able to work with the architect and other specialists involved with interior space. The designer is concerned with the design of "all interior spaces within the human environment," according to the definition of an interior designer by the *Foundation for Interior Design Education Research,* the national accrediting body for schools offering programs designed to train professional interior designers. Another important body is *The American Society of Interior Designers (ASID)*, which was created by a merger of the American Institute of Interior Designers and the National Society of Interior Designers. To become a professional member of this organization, a prospective member must meet certain educational qualifications, must have worked for a certain number of years, and must pass the national examination developed by the *National Council for Interior Design Qualifications* (NCIDQ). *The National Home Fashions League* is composed of women who are in fields related to interior design (public relations representatives, writers in the interior design field, manufacturers' representatives, and so on), together with some interior designers who have passed the NCIDQ examination.

There are many today who meet the criteria for professional interior designers and the home is richer for their work with interior space. A few selected designers, by no means

[8] Ibid., p. 5.

the only qualified ones, will be discussed in the following section.

Selected Modern Interior Designers

Billy Baldwin

Billy Baldwin, employed by Ruby Ross Woods in 1935, gained much of his knowledge from her. Baldwin, now retired, was a flexible, innovative designer who believed that clients should participate in the design process and that their own personal treasures should be included. He wrote a monthly column for *House and Garden* for many years as well as two books *Billy Baldwin Decorates* (1972) and *Billy Baldwin Remembers* (1976). He designed homes for many famous clients, always avoiding fads. He was interested in creating elegant uncluttered interiors.

William Pahlmann

William Pahlmann attended Parsons School of Design and spent a year and a half in Paris on a Parsons' scholarship. After designing the home of Walter Hoving, a Lord & Taylor executive, he was employed to design model rooms for Lord & Taylor; these attracted international attention. During World War II, while stationed in the Pacific, he was influenced by Oriental/Polynesian furniture. His residential interiors include many antiques. He likes to mix periods and Oriental/Polynesian furniture. His book, *The Pahlmann Book of Interior Design* and his syndicated column, "A Matter of Taste," have kept his name before the public. Pahlmann has always been interested in upgrading the qualifications of the interior design profession.

Melanie Kahane

Melanie Kahane, the daughter of an architect, is known for her design of apartments. She is a leader in many other areas, however, and was retained by General Electric Central Air Conditioning to Design an "Interior of Distinction." In 1954 she included many imaginative features in "An Interior to Come in 1960." Features in use today were included as well as some that have yet to be invented. She designed the great New York mansion, the Gobe House, for Billy Rose in the 1960s. She also believed in teaching children about good design, and in her book, *There's a Decorator in Your Dollhouse,* suggested that they be encouraged to use a doll house as a laboratory.

Barbara D'Arcy

Barbara D'Arcy, as fashion coordinator for home furnishings and model rooms for Bloomingdale's, created a demand for good interior design. Her designs were published in her book, *Bloomingdale's Book of Home Decorating* (1973). She is aware of the mood to be created in the interior and believes it should be liveable. Her exciting designs combine the traditional with modern designs. Care and attention to detail are characteristic of her work. Since 1970, she has written numerous articles for national publications.

David Hicks

David Hicks, a British interior designer, works on many aspects of interior design, including carpets, fabrics, bed and bath linens, and tiles. He wants to elevate public taste, for he does not believe that taste depends upon money. His books, *David Hicks on Living with Taste* (1968), *David Hicks on Bathrooms* (1970), *David Hicks on Decoration with Fabrics* (1971), *David Hicks on Home Decoration* (1972) and *David Hicks' Book of Flower Arranging* (1976), have enabled many to view his work. He carefully interprets his clients' tastes and believes in simplicity in design (Plate 1a).

Emily Malino

Emily Malino, who received a degree in economics from Vassar and studied architecture at Columbia University, is one of the most influential designers today. She also has written a book, *Super Living Rooms* (1973) and writes a weekly column, "Design for People," in which she emphasizes that good design is not a matter of money. She believes in saving the best from the past while creating new designs for life today. She designs hospitals, colleges and universities, restaurants, and other commercial spaces as well as apartments and homes.

Angelo Donghia

Angelo Donghia graduated from the Parsons School of Design. He designs furniture, fabric, and wallcoverings, linens, and accessories as well as interiors. The ceilings and floors of his interiors are given as much importance as the walls. He wants people to feel comfortable in his spaces and believes in studying nature to understand how to combine colors. Usually his interiors have neutral backgrounds that allow people to become the important element. Simplicity is important to Donghia (Figs. 3.30, 3.44).

Glossary

American Society of Interior Designers. National professional interior design organization.

Bauhaus. German school which included a designer and craftsman in each discipline.

Biorealism. Richard Neutra's philosophy that the human environment should be scaled to human needs.

Foundation for Interior Design Education Research. The national accrediting body for professional interior design programs.

Interior Design Educators Council. An international organization composed of interior design educators.

National Council for Interior Design Qualifications. The testing body for professional interior designers.

National Home Fashions League. A national organization of women in interior design and related fields.

Bibliography

ANDREWS, WAYNE. *Architecture, Ambition, and Americans.* New York: Harper & Row, Publishers, 1955.

BEECHER, CATHERINE E., and HARRIET BEECHER STOWE. *The American Woman's Home.* New York: J. B. Ford and Co., 1869.

BEHRMAN, S. N. *Duveen.* New York: Random House, Inc., 1951.

BEMELMANS, LUDWIG. *To the One I Love Best.* New York: The Viking Press, Inc., 1955.

BETJEMAN, JOHN. "Baillie Scott and Beresford." *The Architectural Review* (May 1933), 206–207.

BETTS, EDWIN, ed. *Thomas Jefferson's Garden Book.* Philadelphia, Pa.: Independence Square, 1944.

BRODIE, RAWN M. *Thomas Jefferson, An Intimate History.* New York: W. W. Norton & Company, Inc., 1974.

CRIPE, HELEN. *Thomas Jefferson and Music.* Charlottesville, Va.: University of Virginia Press, 1974.

DE WOLFE, ELSIE. *After All.* New York: Harper & Row, Publishers, 1935.

————. *The House in Good Taste.* New York: Appleton-Century-Crofts, 1913.

DOWNING, ANDREW. J. *Architecture of Country Houses,* New York: Appleton-Century-Crofts, 1850.

DUVEEN, JAMES HENRY. *Art Treasures and Intrigue.* New York: Doubleday & Company, Inc., 1935.

————. *The Rise of the House of Duveen.* New York: Alfred A. Knopf, Inc., 1957.

————. *Secrets of an Art Dealer.* New York: E. P. Dutton & Co., Inc., 1938.

GERSON, NOEL B. *Harriet Beecher Stowe.* New York: Praeger Publishers, Inc., 1976.

HAMMETT, RALPH W. *Architecture in the United States: A Survey of Architectural Style Since 1776.* New York: John Wiley & Sons, Inc., 1976.

HEYER, PAUL. *Architects on Architecture.* New York: Walker and Co., 1966.

HITCHCOCK, HENRY RUSSELL, et al., *The Rise of an American Architecture.* New York: Praeger Publishers, Inc., 1970.

HOWELLS, JOHN. *Lost Examples of Colonial Architecture.* New York: Dover Publications, Inc., 1963.

JORDY, WILLIAM H. *American Buildings and Their Architects: Progressive and Academic Ideals at the Turn of the 20th Century.* Garden City, N.Y.: Doubleday & Company, Inc., 1972.

KIRKER, HAROLD. *California's Architectural Frontier: Style and Tradition in the 19th Century.* Santa Barbara and Salt Lake City: Peregrine Smith, Inc., 1973.

LOUDON, J. C. *Encyclopaedia of Cottage, Farm and Villa Architecture and Furniture.* London, 1853.

MCCOY, ESTHER. *Five California Architects.* New York: Van Nostrand Reinhold Company, 1960.

————. *Richard Neutra.* New York: George Braziller, Inc., 1960.

RICHARDS, J. M. ed. *Who's Who in American Architecture from 1400 to the Present.* New York: Holt, Rinehart and Winston, 1977.

RUGOFF, MILTON. *The Beechers.* New York: Harper & Row, Publishers, 1981.

SMITH, G. E., KIDDER. *A Pictoral History of Architecture in America.* New York: American Heritage Publishing Co., 1976.

SMITH, PAGE. *Daughters of the Promised Land.* Boston: Little, Brown and Company, 1970.

STICKLEY, GUSTAV. *The Craftsman.* 1901–15.

SWAN, MABEL M. *Samuel McIntire, Carver, and the Sandersons, Early Salem Cabinetmakers.* Salem, Mass.: The Essex Institute, 1943.

WRIGHT, FRANK LLOYD. *Modern Architecture.* Princeton, N.J.: Princeton University Press, 1931.

IMPLEMENTATION TECHNIQUES

FOUR

Drafting of the Environmental Interior Plan*

An interior cannot be designed without an architectural drawing. Drafting it requires certain basic equipment and techniques. This chapter is not designed to be a short course in architectural drafting; rather, it outlines some essential guidelines.

Basic Materials and Techniques

Cleanliness and Protection of Drawings

Work must be kept neat and clean. If it is not, certainly no one will think it valuable. The surface of the skin contains oils which board and papers will absorb, causing dirt to collect on its surface. To prevent this absorption, it is important always to work with a sheet of tracing paper under the arm and hand so that the skin does not touch the drawing surface. For drafting, a product such as Skum–X (ground-up art gum in a pouch or box) for cleaning, and a paper holder, will be helpful. The finished drawing should be reproduced and corrections should be noted on the reproduction and later transferred to the original drawing.

Tracing-Paper Drafting Method

The tracing-paper method of drafting eliminates erasing and saves time. The Preliminary plan is drawn on tracing paper, then second sheet of paper is placed over the drawing to refine it and make the necessary changes. Several sheets of tracing paper may be needed before a drawing is completed. This saves time since completed areas need not be redrawn.

Equipment

Drawing Boards

The drawing board should be at least thirty-six inches by forty-eight inches. A metal edge (attached to the left side for a right-handed person) parallel bars, on a drafting machine insures straight lines. The T–square is held with the left hand, and moved away from lines as they are drawn to prevent smearing.

Close-grain woods, such as gum, birch, white pine, and basswood provide a smooth drawing surface. Board covers insure uniform line quality as well as regular lines. On a coverless board, the pencil tends to follow the wood grain, which may result in an irregular

line. Dents, thumbtack holes, and scratches ruin the drawing surface.

T–Square

A thirty-six-inch T–square with a wooden head and blade and transparent beveled plastic edges allows the designer to see work slightly below the edge of the plastic blade. The bevel prevents ink from blotting. The T–square should be held firmly against the working edge of the drawing board to provide a straight edge for drawing horizontal lines. As the line is being drawn from left to right, the pencil should be rotated, which insures an even, consistent line. If the pencil is slightly slanted in the direction of the line, the same angle will be maintained the entire length of the line. Beginnings and ends of lines should be definite so that there is no need to go back over them.

Triangle

Horizontal lines are *always* made with a T–square and vertical lines are *always* made with a triangle. Triangles should be of heavy plastic so they will not chip or wear. Triangles are forty-five degrees or thirty-sixty degrees. They should be long enough so that continuous lines do not have to be spliced. A twelve- to eighteen-inch triangle is usually adequate.

The T–square should be held firmly and the triangle slid along the T–square with its vertical side facing left. The line should be drawn upward along the edge of the triangle away from the T–square, with the point of the pencil leaning in the direction of the line. Pencil rotation should be continued for all vertical and horizontal lines.

The Architect's Scale

The architect's scale enables the designer to think, plan, and design in a reduced size comfortable to work with. The scale comes in a flat or triangular shape of plastic or wood. Four to eight different scales are available on each scale, depending upon its shape. Each edge contains two scales, with the smaller of the two scales beginning on the left and reading to the right. The scale beginning on the right and reading to the left is twice as large as the one reading to the right. The divisions overlap, so care must be used in reading the scale. Usually the smaller scale has shorter division marks. Measurements should be accurately taken, with the edge of the scale kept parallel to the line being measured (Fig. 21.2).

* The illustrations and much of the material in this chapter were furnished by Peggy Carlson, A.S.I.D., Tallahassee, Fla.

Figure 21.1
*Use of the drawing board,
T–square, and triangle.
(Courtesy of Peggy
Carlson, ASID)*

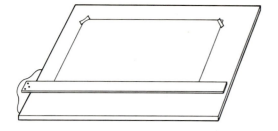

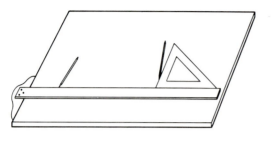

Irregular Curves

Irregular curves, used for curved lines, are made of plastic and comes in a variety of shapes. Often several curves are required for a complicated shape.

Protractor

A protractor is used to measure angles so that inclined lines can be drawn at specific angles; it produces angles at an increment of one degree.

Compass

Compasses are used to draw circles, arcs, and symbols with curved edges. Often compasses will have interchangeable tips for inking, cutting, graphite, and metal points. The instrument should be held vertically, with the lead or point extending no farther than the metal point about which it rotates. The compass should be pivoted in a clockwise direction with a smooth, swift stroke. Going around a circle more than once increases the width of the line; an abrupt stop makes the connecting point obvious. A soft lead sharpened to a forty-five-degree angle insures a dark, sharp line.

Drafting Tape

Drafting tape is superior to masking tape for securing drawings to the board. It is not as sticky and leaves no marks or residue on the board. However, the surface of the board must be dry, for dampness makes the tape stick to the surface.

Templates

Plastic, metal, or cardboard templates which have forms cut out of them are useful and save time. Templates are made in many varieties including geometric shapes, arcs, equipment-shapes, symbols, plant shapes, furniture shapes, plumbing, and so on. One-fourth and one-eighth-inch scale templates are most common. If a design feature is to be used frequently, a template can be constructed from cardboard or flexible plastic. Although templates facilitate drafting, they also cut down on drafting quality, but the time saved usually outweights the quality lost.

Underlays and Overlays

Underlays and overlays are a design aid, similar to templates. When details are repeated frequently throughout a drawing, they may be drawn on a sheet of paper, positioned under the tracing paper and traced onto the original. This is called an *underlay*. The *overlay* is a transparent sheet, usually of acetate or clear plastic, which is attached to the original drawing. Overlays can be used to clarify the work and may contain additional information which would crowd the original drawing, such as furniture arrangements, lighting overlays, or additional solutions to the design problem. Transfer sheets of press-on letters, landscape symbols, and so on, or lettering machines, such as Kroy-type, lend a professional

Figure 21.2
*a: a ¼-inch scale; b: a
½-inch scale; c: an
architect's rule. (Courtesy of
Peggy Carlson, ASID)*

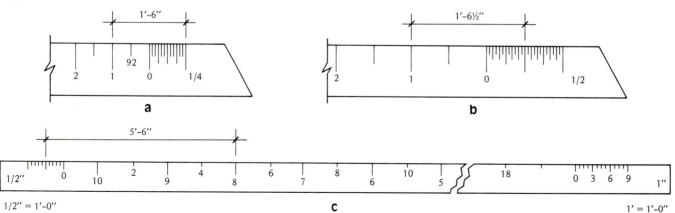

appearance to title blocks and notes on working drawings and notes. These are carefully positioned on the original.

Erasers

Graphite erasers, a necessity on any project, come in several types. One is the pouch (mentioned earlier) that is filled with powdered art gum eraser and acts as a dry cleaner. Sprinkled lightly over the paper, the gum attracts all loose graphite. White vinyl erasers and pink pearl erasers are also used. White vinyl erasers are soft and are used on delicate surfaces, while the pink pearl is used on harder surfaces. Colored erasers may leave a color residue on the paper if care is not exercised. Art gum erasers are used for cleaning the drawing surface. Special ink erasers such as glass fibers are available that will remove India ink. Some work best when moistened with saliva.

The kneaded eraser, which is soft blue or gray, picks up graphite by absorbing it and does not leave particles on the paper. It is pulled like taffy candy for cleaning. It can be shaped to a point to pick up tiny areas or pressed on dark lines to lighten them.

An erasing shield is a flat metal or plastic plate filled with cutouts of various sizes. It is useful in erasing small areas of a drawing while leaving the rest of the work untouched. The opening that best fits the area to be eradicated should be selected, the shield held firmly, and the area rubbed with an eraser. The shield should always be kept clean so it will not soil the drawing.

The softest eraser possible should be used to clean the drawing surface. Erasing leaves a residue. Because oils from the skin may smear the work, this residue should not be brushed off by hand but always with a draftsman's brush.

Pencils and Graphite

Pencils or graphite are used on most drawings. The graphite or lead comes in several degrees of hardness or softness, the amount of China clay in it determining the degree. The designer uses lead in the H or HB series, which is generally mild-range. Leads vary from 9H (hardest) to 6B (softest). Hard leads make lighter, thinner lines which are difficult to remove, but line quality can be controlled by choice of the lead number (Fig. 21.3a). A light, thin line would require 4H to 6H while a dark line requires a HB lead. Softer leads are easier to erase but are also more apt to smear.

Line Vocabulary

Border line
Center line
Construction line
Cutting plane line
Dimension line
Extension line
Guidelines
Hidden lines
Leader lines
Long break line
Object line
Poche'

Proper point

Improper points

Lead holders with sticks of graphite are commonly used and leads can be quickly changed.

Conventional pencils are also available. These can be sharpened with a draftsman's sharpener, a knife, or a hand-held sharpener. Pencil pointers are available for sharpening leads in lead holders. All types of pencils should be sharpened to a long conical point (Fig. 21.3b). The length of the point is easier to control when the lead is placed in a holder (Fig. 21.3c). Files and sandpaper pads are used to shape points. After the graphite is pointed, the loose graphite should be removed by sticking the lead in a block of styrofoam or wiping with a tissue or cloth.

Papers

Paper is an essential part of every architectural drawing. There are many kinds; the one best suited for the purpose should be selected. An inexpensive, light-weight paper, is used for sketching and quick overlays. Transparent papers are best for preliminary sketches and may be purchased in pads or in rolls. Sixteen-pound paper is used for preliminary drawings and a sixteen- to twenty-pound, 100 per cent rag vellum, which is extremely durable and will accept most media, is used for finished drawings. Clear polyester film is used for drawings that will be worked on or kept for an extended period.

Pens

The inking pen is used to outline areas or to finish drawings. Thin, thick, and uneven lines are possible with the pen. *Technical fountain*

Figure 21.4a
A floor plan indicating
dimensions, room numbers,
windows, and so on.
(Courtesy of Peggy
Carlson, ASID)

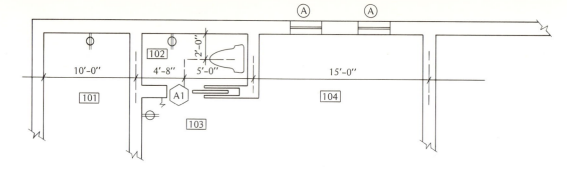

Figure 21.4b
Room numbers are indicated
on the plan. (Courtesy of
Peggy Carlson, ASID)

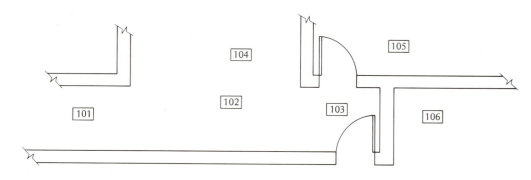

Figure 21.4c
A wall elevation
identification sample; north
should always be indicated
on the plans. (Courtesy of
Peggy Carlson, ASID)

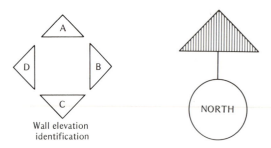

pens, which are made for drafting ink, are especially useful to draw even lines. They come in various point sizes from 00000 (finest) to 6 (widest). A wire inside regulates the ink flow in most pens. Because these instruments tend to clog, best results are obtained if the pen is emptied after each use and flushed with water. Wrapping the pen in a damp sponge helps to prevent it from drying out.

Inks

Most brands of drafting inks are satisfactory. Ink comes in nonwaterproof black (for washes), plastic black (for acetate), extra-dense or superblack, fine-line black, and waterproof black. Waterproof black is suitable for most purposes. Ink can be made to adhere to acetate by adding a few drops of liquid detergent. The ink bottle should be kept tightly closed when not in use. If it becomes too thick, a few drops of distilled water and ammonia will thin it to proper consistency.

The ink should be wiped from the pen point with a cloth while using and after each use to prevent the point from clogging.

Reproduction Methods

The _Ozalid_ process is the most popular reproduction process and makes it possible to re-produce drawings on bond paper, vellum, polyester, and mylar in blue line, brown line, black line, or sepia. Drawings can also be reduced by using a special machine.

These prints can be studied, corrections or changes can be made on them, and the alterations made on the original. In order that no change may be overlooked, each correction is marked through with a broad-tipped marker as each corresponding correction is made on the original drawing.

Architectural Drawings

At one time or another, architectural drawings of an interior or of an entire structure must be produced. Almost everyone has seen these drawings at some time, but most people fail to realize that every product—automobiles, packages, furniture—begins with a drawing. Designs are developed in a trial-and-error process on paper to prevent the waste of valuable time and money. Architectural drawings are detailed drawings that instruct the contractor and fabricator and provide information to the client. Plans indicate the exact location of walls, windows, special equipment, and furnishings. It is impossible to imagine designing an interior without drawings, elevations and sections.

Dimensioning

Dimensions must always be correct. The use of the architect's scale simplifies the conversion process by enabling the interior designer to think, plan, and design in a comfortable scale. If a building is not yet under construction, the dimensions are taken from the architectural drawings. Measurements from an existing building must *always* be verified, even if architectural drawings exist, because changes are frequently made during construction. If architectural drawings of an existing building are unavailable, measurements are taken, with a metal tape or folding carpenter's rule of inside walls, openings, and such architectural details as fireplaces, built-ins, stairs, and wall irregularities. Stair details, placement of electrical and phone outlets, direction of door swings, and types of doors and windows must be noted.

The architectural drawing is always dimensioned. Often exterior as well as interior dimensions are included. Interior dimensions include the length and width of the room proper, thickness of the walls, and all offsets (Fig. 21.4a). Doors are best dimensioned to the edges of the rough opening. The location of installed equipment is usually included on the floor plan. Electrical symbols are also included, but are not always dimensioned.

A symbol may be placed on the floor plan to indicate which wall is shown in elevation. Elevations may be indicated by using a wall orientation and room numbers (Figs. 21.4b, 21.4c). Notes explaining materials, construction details, ceiling heights, and other general points not made clear or shown on the drawing are used where necessary.

Elevations

Elevations are drawings in which the surface is shown and no depth is represented (Fig. 21.4d). A single elevation view is often not enough to describe a three-dimensional object, but when that view is combined with the floor plan, precise information about size and shape can be determined.

Table 21.1
Architectural Drawings (Fig. 21.1)

1. Block in outline of exterior and interior walls using T−square and triangle; lines should cross or meet at corners.
2. Dimension doors and windows.
3. Indicate fireplaces, stairs, and so on.
4. Draw door and window symbols and door swings.
5. Draw fixtures and built-in storage.

Title Blocks and Borders

Title blocks are usually placed in the lower right corner (Fig. 21.5a). Borders are placed one-half inch from the paper's edge on the top, bottom, and right side. The depth of the border on the left side may vary. If a folded binder is to be used, the left border should be at least one inch wide. The border line should be heavier and darker than other lines to provide a visible frame and to keep the viewers' eyes from wandering away from the drawing.

Title blocks may be placed along the entire bottom edge of the paper, in the bottom right-hand corner, or along the entire right-hand edge. Every drawing includes a title block containing pertinent information concerning the designer, the firm, and the draftsman, as well as the content of the drawing (Fig. 21.5b). The firm's logo might also be included. When scale is included in the title block, it indicates that all drawings on that sheet have been drawn to the same scale; otherwise, the scale is placed under the title of each item on the sheet. If several items are placed on one sheet, enough space should be provided around each for dimensions and notes. The spacing between items should be fairly consistent. If only one item is placed on a sheet, it should be centered. Lettering should be professional and properly spaced (Fig. 21.5c).

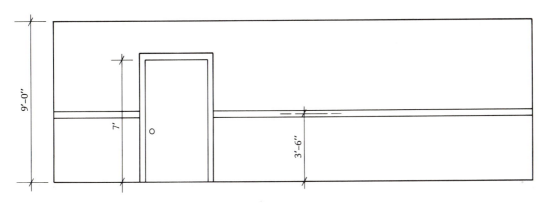

Figure 21.4d
An elevation. (*Courtesy of Peggy Carlson, ASID*)

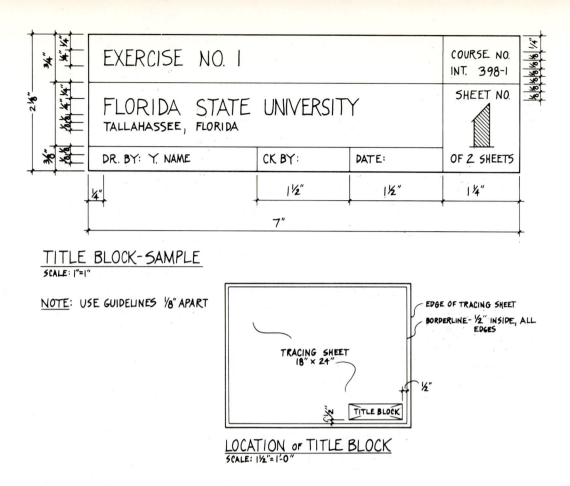

Figure 21.5a
A sample showing the title block and its location. (Courtesy of Peggy Carlson, ASID)

TITLE BLOCK-SAMPLE
SCALE: 1"=1"

NOTE: USE GUIDELINES 1/8" APART

LOCATION OF TITLE BLOCK
SCALE: 1½"= 1'-0"

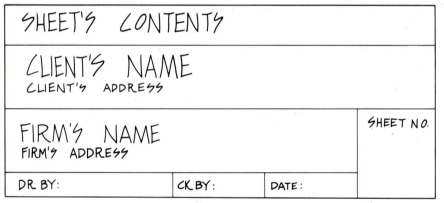

Figure 21.5b
A title block. (Courtesy of Peggy Carlson, ASID)

Figure 21.5c
Simple lettering, carefully spaced and slanted in one direction, is a requirement for a presentation. (Courtesy of Peggy Carlson, ASID)

ABCDEFGHIJKLMNOPQRSTUVWXYZ 1234567890
CONDENSED LETTERING STYLE

ABCDEFGHIJKLMNOPQRSTUVWXYZ 1234567890
EXTENDED LETTERING STYLE

ABCDEFGHIJKLMNOPQRSTUVWXYZ 1234567890
VARIATION LETTERING STYLE

ABCDEFGHIJKLMNOPQRSTUVWXYZ 1234567890

LHOPE
IMPROPER SPACING

LHOPE
PROPER SPACING

LE
CORRECT

LE
INCORRECT

This discussion has been very elementary, but it will give the reader some basic guidelines on developing architectural drawings. More detailed information may be found in the books listed in the bibliography.

Glossary

Architect's Scale. A flat or triangular ruler marked in various scales used to make quick measurements to scale.

Irregular Curve. An instrument with various curves for the drawing of true curves.

Graphite. Used to make pencil lead.

Ozalid Process. A reproduction process resulting in sepia, blue-line, black-line, and mylar prints.

Protractor. An instrument for measuring angles.

Technical Fountain Pen. A pen with interchangeable size points for technical drawing.

Template. A piece of plastic, cardboard, or metal with forms cut out.

Bibliography

FLYNN, JOHN E., and ARTHUR W. SEGIL. *Architectural Interior Systems: Lighting, Air Conditioning, Acoustics.* New York: Van Nostrand Reinhold Company, 1970.

HELPER, DONALD E., and PAUL I. WALLACH. *Architecture Drafting and Design.* 2nd ed. New York: McGraw-Hill Book, Company, 1971.

KICKLIGHTER, CLOIS E., *Architecture Residential Drawing and Design.* Sough Holland, Ill.: The Goodheart-Willcox Co., Inc., 1973.

MULLER, EDWARD J. *Architectural Drawing and Light Construction.* Englewood Cliffs, N.J.: Prentice-Hall, Inc., 1967.

RAMSEY, C. G., and H. R. SLEEPER. *Architectural Graphic Standards,* 7th ed. New York: John Wiley & Sons, 1980.

WYATT, WILLIAM. *General Architectural Drawing.* Peoria, Ill.: Charles A. Bennett Co., Inc., 1969.

These terms and abbreviations are defined here because they are commonly used in the interior design profession and while not included in the body of the book, are important.

Absolute Sale. A transaction without restrictions from buyer or seller.

Additional Markdown. An additional decrease over a sale price.

Additional Markup. A price increase over the original markup.

Add-ons. The purchase of additional merchandise before the previous charge has been paid in full.

Approval Sale. The designer has unlimited return privileges of articles on approval.

ASAP. As soon as possible (similar to rush).

As is. Irregular, damaged, soiled or worn merchandise which may not be returned or adjusted.

B.L. Bill of lading (may be termed B/L).

B.O.M. Beginning of the month.

Back Order. A portion of the order not shipped because it was out of stock.

Broken Case-Lot Selling. Selling of less than the standard unit lot usually to accommodate small firms.

C.A.F. The cost of goods plus the shipping costs, literally means cost and freight.

C.L. (carload) Freight Rates. Cost of shipping a full carload.

C.O.D. Collect on delivery which means the buyer must pay for the goods at the time of delivery.

C.O.M. Customer's own material means the use of a fabric which is not purchased from the furniture manufacturer. It is ordered by the customer and shipped by the fabric vendor to the furniture manufacturer.

C.W.O. Cash with order; same as pro forma, C.B.D. (cash before delivery), and C.I.A. (cash in advance).

Cash Discount. A percentage reduction on the total cost for paying cash. 2/10 net 30 for example means that the buyer gets a 2% discount for paying for the merchandise within ten days of the date on the invoice, but it must be paid in thirty days.

Caveat Emptor. Latin for "let the buyer beware."

Credit Agency. Maintains credit information about various businesses. The three most commonly used by interior designers are *Dun and Bradstreet, Lyon Furniture Mercantile Agency* (for furniture retailers, interior designers and so on), and the *Allied*

Board of Trade (interior designers, drapery, upholstery and allied decorative trades).

Ceiling Price. The highest price the law permits for a specific item.

Certification Mark. A mark which testifies to the quality, point of manufacturer, quality, and so on.

Claim. A statement of the amount of damage to goods, such as furniture, while being shipped or in the possession of the carrier.

Conditional Sale Contract. The title of the goods does not pass to the buyer until certain contractual obligations are fulfilled. Upon delivery, however, the responsibility for maintenance is the buyer's until after all payments are made. If they are not, the seller may repossess the item.

Consignee. The person to whom products are shipped and delivered.

Contract. A legal agreement in writing between buyer and seller.

Cost Code. A method of indicating the actual price of an item on the price ticket. Often a word, such as hypodermic may be used with none of the letters being repeated in the word, For example, H = 1, Y = 2, P = 3, O = 4, D = 5, E = 6, R = 7, M = 8, I = O, and C = O.

Delivered Price. A price that includes the delivery cost to the warehouse, freight terminal, or a place agreeable to both the buyer and seller.

Draft. A bill of exchange or a written order to transfer a specified sum of money.

F.O.B. Free on board. There are six F.O.B. terms of sale:

F.O.B. Origin, Freight Prepaid and Charged Back. The buyer bears the freight charges but the seller charges them to him after delivery (charging them to the invoiced amount), the buyer owns the items in transit and must file any damage claims.

F.O.B. Origin, Freight Collect. The buyer pays the freight charges when the items are received, owns the goods in transit with the title of the goods passing to the buyer when they leave the seller and must file damage claims, if any.

F.O.B. Origin, Freight Prepaid. The seller pays the freight costs, but the buyer owns the goods while being shipped and must file any damage claims.

F.O.B. Destination, Freight Prepaid. The seller pays the freight costs, owns the items while in transit and files any damage claims.

F.O.B. Destination, Freight Collect. The

buyer pays the freight cost, but the title does not pass to him while the items are being shipped and the seller must also file any damage claims.

F.O.B. Destination, Freight Collect and Allowed. The buyer pays the freight charges, but the seller deducts them from the invoiced amount, the seller keeps title to the items in transit and files any damage claims.

Fixed Assets. Office furniture, building, land, and so on—the things owned to carry on the business and not bought to be sold.

Fixed Costs. Operating expenses of a business that do not vary.

General Partner. An owner of a firm who is liable for the firm's debts, either alone or with others.

General Partnership. Two or more people who own a business.

Gross Margin of Profit. The difference between net sales and the total cost of the goods sold.

Jobber. A middleman who buys wholesale from manufacturers and sells to retailers.

Kickback. A method whereby the seller or buyer receives some portion of the original bill returned to him for the business. It is not an ethical method of doing business.

Pro-forma. Payment in advance, i.e., before performance; C.O.D.

Quantity Discount. A decrease in the cost of the merchandise based on the size of the order, i.e., 100 items per unit would cost less than fifty per unit.

Silent Partner. A member of a firm who is not known to the public, but nonetheless has a voice in the operation of the firm.

Trade Discount. A decrease in price of an item to members of a specific group, e.g., a special discount to interior designers.

Index